be a stand-out in the policy agenda arena. Unlike any other text, the nature of the policy agenda's creation alongside policymakers, academics, and community organizers together make the contribution of this book emblematic not only as a model of policy but also as method."

Terrell Winder, *author of* Shameless: The Making of Black Gay Identities in LA

"This book offers a rigorous, critical, timely, and useful tool to readers seeking to turn research into actionable outcomes with specific and concrete policy recommendations, which really is the strength of the volume, and why it makes an important contribution at this present moment in US history."

Jason Sexton, *Lecturer in Sociology, University of California, Los Angeles*

"*The Black Papers* are an essential guide to renewing the spirit of resistance, survival, and power-building that have brought us thus far on our way. It is the work of a new generation of Black thinkers, workers, and warriors."

Joy-Ann (Joy) Reid, *Host of* The Joy Reid Show

"The NAACP has always known resistance alone is not enough. In this moment, resistance must be reimagined—not just as opposition to injustice, but as the construction of justice itself. *The Black Papers* embody that shift. Across 26 chapters, it delivers legislative frameworks, budget blueprints, and organizing strategies that move us from protest to policy—and from resistance to liberation."

Derrick Johnson, *President and CEO, NAACP*

"Intersectionality is a lens through which you can see where power collides and interlocks. *The Black Papers* extends that lens to every dimension of Black life: democracy, education, health, justice, and economics. But the chapters don't just diagnose structural racism; they map comprehensive pathways to dismantle it. This volume shows what happens when scholars, organizers and policymakers refuse to accept single-axis solutions, and it is essential for anyone serious about liberation."

Dr. Kimberlé Crenshaw, *Executive Director, African American Policy Forum; Isidor and Seville Sulzbacher Professor of Law, Columbia; Distinguished Professor and Promise Institute Chair on Human Rights, UCLA*

"After George Floyd and Breonna Taylor were murdered, I said we're in a state of emergency. My book *State of Emergency* explained how we got here. *The Black Papers* map how we get free, 26 chapters of actionable policy across democracy, justice, health, education, and economic empowerment. This is the comprehensive roadmap for the transformation we're demanding."

Tamika D. Mallory, *Co-Founder, Until Freedom; Youngest Executive Director, National Action Network; Author,* State of Emergency *and* I Lived to Tell the Story

"In a political moment when Black communities need more than hashtags and hot takes, *The Black Papers* delivers what we've been missing: comprehensive policy frameworks rooted in our lived experiences and ready for implementation. From democracy to education to justice, this volume doesn't just diagnose our crises—it hands us the blueprints for building something better. This is the policy handbook the movement needs—and our people built it from the ground up."

Brittany Packnett Cunningham, *Activist, Educator, Host of* UNDISTRACTED

"2025 brought an insurmountable surge of attacks on LGBTQ people—from the tireless recycling of anti-LGBTQ and especially anti-trans legislation, to social media companies retreating from trust & safety to appease right-wing activists. As our movement pushes for visibility and accountability across the media landscape on the daily, we also need comprehensive policy infrastructure. *The Black Papers* provide exactly that—rigorous frameworks that don't compromise on what liberation requires. From voting rights to media justice to LGBTQ+ policy, this volume meets the moment."

Sarah Kate Ellis, *President of GLAAD*

"For 50 years, the National Coalition on Black Civic Participation has built intergenerational civic engagement infrastructure in Black communities. For 30 years, I've led that work. *The Black Papers* provides the policy infrastructure our civic power demands—comprehensive frameworks across voting rights, economic justice, health equity, education, and more. Black Women's Roundtable's priorities are centered throughout. This is a timely policy roadmap that meets the moment that calls for vision and transformational change."

Melanie L. Campbell, *President & CEO, National Coalition on Black Civic Participation; Convener, Black Women's Roundtable; Founder, NCBCP Thomas W. Dortch Jr. Institute, anchored at Clark Atlanta University*

"The Task Force's tagline is 'Be You'—but being yourself requires policy protection. *The Black Papers*, Volume I provides a blueprint to that protection across LGBTQ+ rights, reproductive justice, voting rights, healthcare, and economic security. The last 25 years of my career have proven to me that in addition to building resilience and agile organizing, we need comprehensive policy infrastructure that doesn't ask us to choose which identity to fight for."

Kierra Johnson, *President, task force, 2025 OUT 100 honoree, pansexual Black woman, Southern Queer Mom of Three*

"As a child of immigrants, a Black man, and a gay man, I know firsthand that intersectional organizing isn't optional—it's essential. *The Black Papers* offers the comprehensive policy framework we need to protect, expand, and sustain our communities. From voting rights to immigration to health justice to LGBTQ+ liberation, this volume centers the realities our movement lives every day. Proud to stand with this work."

Kenya Hutton, *MPH, President & CEO, Center for Black Equity*

"*The Black Papers* offers a timely contribution to the contemporary policy implications impacting the lives of Black Americans (and other Americans more broadly). As a collection of essays and policy proposals from leading and emerging scholars who are aiming to impact policymakers, the book will

The Black Papers

Presenting the most comprehensive Black policy agenda produced in a generation, offering concrete, actionable recommendations across every dimension of Black life in America, this book features contributions from over 100 leading scholars, policymakers, and community organizers to transform research into policy action.

Born from the State of the People movement, a national call to action rallying, restoring, and reimagining what's possible for Black communities, *The Black Papers: A Policy Agenda for Black Liberation in the 21st Century* stands in the lineage of the 1905 Niagara Movement, the 1972 Gary Political Convention, and decades of Black political organizing to address what previous efforts left incomplete: sustained infrastructure for collective liberation. Through 26 rigorously researched policy briefs, the volume covers economic justice, education reform, health equity, democratic governance, criminal justice transformation, environmental justice, reparations, and specialized policy domains. Each section provides specific federal, state, and local recommendations, translating complex policy analysis into accessible frameworks for action. *The Black Papers* deliver what policymakers, organizers, educators, and community members need most: evidence-based roadmaps for systemic change. Contributors include university professors and grassroots activists, former White House officials and community organizers, attorneys and artists—representing the breadth of Black genius and the depth of collective commitment to Black flourishing.

This volume will serve undergraduate and graduate courses in public policy, sociology, African American studies, urban planning, and education while remaining accessible to undergraduate students, advocacy professionals, and general readers. Developed alongside the State of the People Power Tour, which activated grassroots movements in 13 cities nationwide, the project integrates scholarship with community organizing. Companion digital resources at stateoftheppl.com provide multimedia content, data visualizations, and advocacy tools that extend the book's impact beyond the page.

David J. Johns is an education policy expert and advocate for Black people and Queer youth. Former Executive Director of the White House Initiative on Educational Excellence for African Americans, he now leads the National Black Justice Collective, a civil rights organization, advancing equity through research, advocacy, and intersectional leadership. He earned BA, MA, and PhD degrees from Columbia University.

Sociology Re-Wired

Edited by Jodi O'Brien,
Seattle University, and Marcus Hunter, University of California, Los Angeles

Sociology Re-Wired captures this combustible moment in American and global societies with new books that innovate and re-configure social and political issues. This hybrid series publishes timely, relevant, original research and textbooks that address significant social issues informed by critical race theory, Black feminism and Queer Studies traditions. Series books are written in a publicly accessible, multi-vocal style broadening the reach and impact of significant scholarly contributions beyond traditional academic audiences.

Some titles published in this series were published under an earlier series name and a different editorship.

Published:

Black Feminist Sociology: Perspectives and Praxis, edited by Zakiya Luna and Whitney Pirtle

Social Theory Re-Wired: New Connections to Classical and Contemporary Perspectives, Second Edition, by Wesley Longhofer and Daniel Winchester

Cresheim Farm: 400 Years of History at an American Farm by Antje Ulrike Mattheus

Social Statistics: Managing Data, Conducting Analyses, Presenting Results, Fifth Edition, by Thomas J. Linneman

Introduction to Media Sociology: All Media Are Social, Second Edition, by Andrew M. Lindner and Stephen R. Barnard

Black Feminist Sociology: Perspectives and Praxis, Second Edition, edited by Zakiya Luna, Whitney Pirtle, and Jasmine Kelekay

The Black Papers: A Policy Agenda for Black Liberation in the 21st Century, edited by David J. Johns

Latinx Feminist Thought: Ideas, Movements, and the Pursuit of Reproductive Justice, by Rocío R. García

For more information about this series, please visit
https://www.routledge.com/Sociology-Re-Wired/book-series/SOC

The Black Papers

A Policy Agenda for Black Liberation in the 21st Century

Edited by David J. Johns

Routledge
Taylor & Francis Group
NEW YORK AND LONDON

Designed cover image: Avahnii Lewis

First published 2027
by Routledge
605 Third Avenue, New York, NY 10158

and by Routledge
4 Park Square, Milton Park, Abingdon, Oxon, OX14 4RN

Routledge is an imprint of the Taylor & Francis Group, an informa business

ISBN: 978-1-041-27096-6 (hbk)
ISBN: 978-1-041-27090-4 (pbk)
ISBN: 978-1-003-75264-6 (ebk)

DOI: 10.4324/9781003752646

Typeset in Optima
by SPi Technologies India Pvt Ltd (Straive)

Contents

Acknowledgments

This work would not exist without the collective brilliance, dedication, and love of many hands and hearts.

My brother, Dr. Marcus Anthony Hunter, led the Reparations paper with the intellectual rigor and moral clarity this topic demands. At the LA stop of the Power Tour, Marcus spoke truth to power in ways that moved us all and reminded us why this work matters. His commitment to ensuring this book would be birthed—through late-night editing sessions, strategic guidance, and unwavering belief in the vision—made all the difference.

Corena Wiggins and Caitlin Radigan deserve special recognition for their tireless work supporting editing, author engagement, and production. They managed the logistics that transform vision into reality, kept authors on track, ensured quality and consistency across papers, and did the unglamorous but essential work that makes projects like this possible. Caitlin also led the critical paper on child welfare, bringing her expertise and heart to one of our community's most urgent issues.

Avahnii Lewis is a genius creative responsible for all of the design work in the Black Papers project at www.stateofheppl.com. We're thankful for your contributions to the project. Thank you. Her visual artistry transformed policy into accessible, beautiful, and culturally resonant materials that honor our community's aesthetic traditions while meeting the moment's urgency.

Victoria Kirby York (VKY) supported paper production and the Power Tour with the strategic brilliance and operational excellence that have become her signature. Her ability to seamlessly transition between high-level strategy and granular execution ensured that nothing fell through the cracks.

Thank you, **Emily Leugers**, for always showing up and handling business. Thank you for your research acumen, for your creative contributions, for liaising and bridging, thank you for leading with love.

To the **contributors** who poured their expertise, lived experience, and love into these pages—you are the heart of this project. Your willingness to write, rewrite, engage feedback, and trust this process is a testament to your commitment to our collective liberation.

To the **National Black Justice Collective team**—you held down the organization while I poured into this project. Your excellence makes everything possible.

To my heartstrings, **André** and **Baldwin**, thank you for enabling me to live a purpose-driven life and for your love for our people and defense of our democracy.

And to **Angela Rye**—for seeing what I couldn't see in myself, trusting me with this sacred work, and being my sister in struggle for over two decades. This book exists because you believed it could.

Contributors

LaTricea D. Adams, MAT, Ed.S. (she/her), is Founder, CEO, and President of Young, Gifted & Green, a national environmental justice organization. A former K-12 educator, she served on the White House Environmental Justice Advisory Council and has led national efforts addressing lead exposure, climate justice, and civil rights.

Roshana Agarrat is Program Director of the Children's Advocacy Center in Bartow, Florida. A compassionate leader in public service, she amplifies the voices of children, families, and underserved communities. Through strategic planning, grant management and collaborative programs, she bridges policy and people to create lasting impact and more resilient communities.

A. Prince Albert III, known as Prince The Culture Keeper™, is a human rights advocate, law and world culture professor, and multidisciplinary artist. Founder of The Culture Keepers Circle, he teaches Cultural Sustainability Law at Georgetown and uses music and film to celebrate, preserve, and reimagine Afro-Indigenous folk traditions.

Erica Baganza is Policy Manager at the Black Alliance for Just Immigration, leading state and local advocacy. Formerly with the United States House Foreign Affairs Committee and Suffolk County DA's Office, she brings expertise in foreign policy and criminal justice. Erica holds degrees from the University of New Haven and George Washington University.

Brea Baker (she/her) is a writer and activist whose acclaimed book *ROOTED* explores Black land ownership and reparations. With a BA in Political Science from Yale, Brea contributes to *ELLE* and *Refinery 29* and also serves on the boards of The Gathering for Justice, YWCA USA, and Black Farmers' Market NC. Black LGBTQIA+ Migrant Project (BLMP). Launched in 2017, the Black LGBTQIA+ Migrant Project (BLMP) builds the power of Black LGBTQIA+ migrants to advance the liberation of all Black people. BLMP is led by directly impacted members and staff, and it runs regional organizing networks across the United States. Its work includes base-building, political education, deportation defense, and direct services. BLMP envisions a world where no one is forced to give up their homeland.

Brianna Baker is a social justice educator and founder of Justice for Black Girls, a national nonprofit advancing liberation and safety for Black girls. A graduate of Spelman College and Teachers College, Columbia University, her work reimagines education to honor and empower Black girlhood.

Brittany Packnett Cunningham is an activist, educator, and writer working at the intersection of culture, justice, and policy. She founded the social impact agency Love & Power Works and hosts and executive produces the podcast UNDISTRACTED. A co-founder of Campaign Zero, she served on President Obama's Task Force on 21st Century Policing and the Ferguson Commission. She began her career as an elementary school teacher and is currently Vice President and Chief Strategy Officer at Children's Defence Fund.

Dara Baldwin is Principal of DMadrina, LLC, and an adjunct professor at Georgetown University. A global consultant, activist, and author of *To Be a Problem: A Black Woman's Survival in the Racist Disability Rights Movement*, she advances disability justice through policy, advocacy, and education.

Wes Bellamy is a nationally recognized educator, activist, former Vice-Mayor of Charlottesville, NC and award-winning author. He serves as Chair of the Political Science Department at Virginia State University, CEO of the Black College Invitational Championship (BCIC), and National Public Policy Chairman for the 100 Black Men of America.

Rose Berry is a Black, queer, migrant organizer, activist and social justice freedom fighter who has been doing racial, migrant, and gender justice work for over 20 years. Rose is one of the founders and Co-Executive Directors of Black LGBTQIA+ Migrant Project (BLMP). BLMP builds and centers the power of Black queer, trans, and non-binary migrants and first-generation people to ensure the liberation of all Black people through organizing, base-building, strategic communications, and long-term viability and sustainability.

Ashley N. Brevil, Ph.D., LCSW, is a doctoral candidate and licensed clinical social worker whose research examines Black perinatal mental health and health equity. Grounded in reproductive justice, her scholarship integrates research, advocacy, and practice to advance maternal well-being and center Black voices in shaping equitable care solutions.

LaTosha Brown is an award-winning visionary, activist, and Co-Founder of Black Voters Matter Fund. She leads the Southern Black Girls & Women's Consortium's $100 million initiative, transforming Black political power and philanthropy. Featured by *Glamour* and *Forbes*, she is a global voice on *MSNBC, CNN, PBS*, and *NPR*.

Ronald Claude is Policy Director at the Black Alliance for Just Immigration, leading federal and international advocacy. Formerly with Congresswoman Ayanna Pressley's office, he has shaped policy on transportation, immigration, and foreign affairs. A proud son of Haitian immigrants, Ronald holds a BA in International Relations from Boston College.

Christopher Coes is a nationally recognized transportation and land use expert with over 15 years advancing equitable infrastructure and sustainable development. Former Acting Under Secretary for Policy at USDOT, he also led Smart Growth America's land use initiatives and founded LOCUS, fostering billions in smart-growth investments and community revitalization nationwide.

Natalie Madeira Cofield is an award-winning entrepreneur and executive dedicated to small business development and innovation. With over twenty years of experience, she has partnered with Fortune 500 companies, governments, and nonprofits to expand access to capital and opportunity, advancing entrepreneurship, innovation, and equitable economic growth nationwide.

Brittney Cooper is Professor of Women's, Gender, and Sexuality Studies and Africana Studies at Rutgers University. She is a leading Black feminist scholar and author of *Eloquent Rage* and *Beyond Respectability*. She co-founded the Crunk Feminist Collective and directs Rutgers' Race and Gender Equity (RAGE) Lab.

Jonathan M. Cox is an engaged public scholar, researcher, and former educator with expertise at the intersection of race, social life, and educational equity. As a Vice President with the Congressional Black Caucus Foundation, he leads public policy and research strategies to eliminate disparities in Black communities.

Brittany Packnett Cunningham is an activist, educator, and writer working at the intersection of culture, justice, and policy. She founded the social impact agency Love & Power Works and hosts and executive produces the podcast UNDISTRACTED. A co-founder of Campaign Zero, she served on President Obama's Task Force on 21st Century Policing and the Ferguson Commission. She began her career as an elementary school teacher and is currently Vice President and Chief Strategy Officer at Children's Defence Fund.

Alphonso David is President & CEO of the Global Black Economic Forum and a leading civil rights attorney with over two decades of experience advancing equity. Former Chief Counsel to New York's Governor and Deputy Attorney General, his work combats discrimination and shapes national dialogue on economic and social justice.

Imani D. Edwards is a policy and government relations professional focused on advancing equity through strategic partnerships. After serving on Capitol Hill and with the Biden–Harris Administration at the United States and Urban Development, she now works at Taft Stettinius & Hollister LLP, building public–private collaborations and advancing cross-sector initiatives that expand opportunity for underserved communities.

Sharif El-Mekki is Founder/CEO of the Center for Black Educator Development and former Principal Ambassador Fellow at the United States Department of Education. A veteran teacher and principal, he founded The Fellowship: Black Male Educators for Social Justice and co-hosts the Freedom Friday podcast, amplifying educational and racial justice.

Linda Elam is a health policy and management expert with extensive government, philanthropic, academic, and private sector experience. As President of Elam Strategies, she advises clients on health equity, Medicaid and healthcare access. She holds degrees from Howard University, UC Berkeley, and Johns Hopkins University.

Jasmine Esquilin is a policy professional dedicated to community-driven support. She holds an MPA from Clark Atlanta University and a BFA from SUNY Brockport, merging arts and social science to advance change. Jasmine's work in policy analysis and community development prioritizes accessibility, collaboration, and people-centered decision-making.

Nadia French-Graham is a community leader and educator from Waterbury, Connecticut. She is a Co-Lead Community School Coordinator with Waterbury Bridge to Success, holds a BA in Criminal Justice, and is pursuing an MA in Education. Her experience includes legal work, youth mentorship, and a recent congressional internship with Congresswoman Jahana Hayes.

Marcia L. Fudge served as United States Secretary of Housing and Urban Development from 2021 to 2024, advancing affordable housing and fair housing policy. Previously, she represented Ohio's 11th District in Congress, chaired the Congressional Black Caucus, and championed housing, nutrition, and equity for working families.

Jessica Fulton is a respected economist, policy consultant, and media commentator. She advances policies to strengthen the socioeconomic status of Black communities, informed by federal, state, and local research and engagement experience. She formerly served in leadership at the Joint Center for Political and Economic Studies.

Christina Grant is the Executive Director of the Center for Education Policy Research at Harvard University. Throughout her career as an educator, administrator, and executive in some of America's largest school systems,

Dr. Grant has focused on data-driven leadership and strategic management to improve student outcomes and drive academic acceleration.

Nieta M. Greene is a disabled Puerto Rican Black gay, gender-nonconforming advocate dedicated to intersectional disability justice. As founder and CEO of Disability Community for Democracy, she champions civil rights, accessibility, and liberal democracy, emphasizing that marginalized people should never have to hide parts of their identity to belong or participate fully.

Nana Gyamfi is Executive Director of the Black Alliance for Just Immigration, advancing racial justice and migrant rights through advocacy, organizing, policy, research, and narrative building. A Movement attorney for over 30 years, she co-founded Justice Warriors 4 Black Lives. She holds degrees from Cornell University and UCLA School of Law.

Nancy Hanks is a nationally recognized education strategist and leadership coach with two decades of experience across schools, nonprofits, and government. A former teacher and principal, she now serves as a Senior Partner at The Management Center, supporting superintendents and senior federal officials in building equity-centered, high-performing systems.

Dreisen Heath is a reparations expert, movement strategist, and human rights advocate. She is the principal of Heath Strategies & Consulting and the founder and convener of the Why We Can't Wait Reparations Coalition. From 2018 to 2023, she led Human Rights Watch's racial justice and reparations work, including The Case for Reparations in Tulsa, Oklahoma. She co-authored landmark federal reparations legislation with then-Congresswoman Cori Bush in 2023 and has testified before Congress.

Marcus Anthony Hunter is the Scott Waugh Endowed Chair in the Social Sciences Division and Professor of Sociology and African American Studies at UCLA, where he served as the inaugural chair of the African American Studies Department. He is the author and editor of five books, including Radical Reparations: Healing the Soul of a Nation. He drafted and advised then-Congresswoman Barbara Lee's bill to establish the first United States Truth, Racial Healing, and Transformation Commission. He served two terms as president of the Association of Black Sociologists and serves on the board of the National Black Justice Collective.

Iheoma Iruka is a professor at the UNC Gillings School of Global Public Health and the founding director of the Equity Research Action Coalition. Her work centers on racial equity in early childhood systems. She leads national research and policy projects, serves on multiple federal advisory committees, and authored *We Are the Change We Seek*.

Cemeré James is the CEO of the Mary Elizabeth House, advancing racial equity across public systems. She previously held senior leadership roles at the Children's Defense Fund and the National Black Child Development

Institute. James holds advanced degrees from the University of Chicago and Northwestern University.

David J. Johns is an education policy expert and advocate for Black and LGBTQ+/SGL youth. Former Executive Director of the White House Initiative on Educational Excellence for African Americans, he now leads the National Black Justice Collective, advancing equity through research, advocacy, and intersectional leadership. He earned BA, MA, and PhD degrees from Columbia University.

Lee Johnson III is Founder and Principal of Early Quest Strategies and Senior Fellow for Early Childhood Education at the Southern Education Foundation. He leads the Southern Early Childhood Education Justice Network and chairs the Maternal Mental Health Leadership Alliance, advancing early learning, maternal mental health, and family well-being.

Quinton Johnson is an activist & certified firearm instructor. He is the founder of Armed and Educated Inc., a community safety organization. His work includes training communities & organizations on conflict management skills, firearm safety & responsibility, and youth mentoring.

Kayla Jones is an editor and digital designer for the State of the People Power Tour. Founder of KG Digital Creativity, she helps entrepreneurs build brands through creative brand strategy and intentional marketing. She holds degrees from East Carolina and North Carolina A&T State Universities.

Leilah Naila Jones is a Howard Senior majoring in Strategic, Legal, and Management Communications with a minor in Afro-American Studies. With professional roots as a youth educator in Seattle, she co-founded the Miami-based non-profit, Letters to the System, and leads advocacy for Black communities at Impact Strategies.

Stephanie J. Jones is president of the Nathaniel R. Jones Foundation and senior legal advisor to the NAACP. A former senior Obama administration official, she was a lead author of the House Select Committee's January 6 report and has held leadership roles in Congress, the Clinton Administration, the National Urban League, academia, and private law practice.

Ashley C. Kenneth is President and CEO of the Commonwealth Institute for Fiscal Analysis. A mother and descendant of Virginians once enslaved, she champions racial and economic justice. Her leadership has advanced progressive policies, including expanding healthcare access, raising the minimum wage, and strengthening Virginia's Earned Income Tax Credit.

Andraéa LaVant is a disability inclusion expert and founder of LaVant Consulting, Inc., helping brands "speak disability with confidence." Known as the Impact Producer of the Oscar-nominated *Crip Camp*, she advocates for intersectional disability justice and authentic representation of disabled people of color in media and culture.

Nicol Turner Lee is a leading technology policy expert, author of *Digitally Invisible: How the Internet is Creating the New Underclass*, podcaster, and founder of the AI Equity Lab. Her work advances equitable and inclusive technology, including AI systems, and she is a regularly sought-after writer and speaker before Congress, industry, and civil society organizations. She holds a MA and PhD in Sociology from Northwestern University.

Emily Leugers serves as the Special Projects Manager at the National Black Justice Collective. In the role, she drafts communication for the organization, including the monthly newsletter, supports the development of events, such as the Black Institute, OUT on the Hill, Equity Week and the Audre Lorde Wisdom and James Baldwin Legacy Awards and supports their year-round internship program.

Chris Lewis is President and CEO of Public Knowledge, where he leads national advocacy for digital equity and open internet policies. A former FCC Office of Legislative Affairs Deputy Director and two-term Alexandria City School Board member, he brings expertise from Capitol Hill, federal agencies, and local government to advance technology policy that serves the public interest. A Harvard graduate in Government, he continues civic advocacy in Alexandria, VA.

Bunny McKensie Mack (they/them) is Founder and CEO of MMG Earth and ECON CLUB. A trilingual writer, economist, and social impact leader from Chicago's South Side, Bunny advances racial, economic, and gender justice through research, financial strategy, and consulting. Their work appears in *Teen Vogue, NPR*, and *Fast Company*.

Ashley Bland Manlove is a Kansas City native and former Missouri State Representative who served six years representing Jackson County. A former intelligence analyst with the Missouri National Guard, she focused on civic engagement, urban education, and workforce development. She was the first openly LGBTQIA+ Chair of the Missouri Legislative Black Caucus.

Dee C. Marshall is an award-winning CEO, global DEI thought leader, and board chair of the National Association for Equity, Diversity & Inclusion. A Wall Street alumna and certified executive coach, she founded D&I Honors and advises top leaders, with features in Forbes, CNBC, Fortune, and the Financial Times.

Yaribel Mercedes is an adjunct assistant professor at Hunter College and an educational administrator in New York City. Her research examines race, racism, and systems of subjugation across educational contexts; the practices of critically race-conscious leaders, particularly Black educators; and (re)membering as a praxis and site for healing.

Joshua Miller is Director of Strategic Engagement at the Council for Global Equality and a longtime advocate in the Gun Violence Prevention Movement. Formerly with Everytown for Gun Safety, he builds bridges across communities and identities to advance inclusive gun safety reform. He holds a BA in Political Science.

Oluchi Omeoga is a Minnesota-born organizer, born from Igbo immigrants from Nigeria. Oluchi serves as the co-founder and co-executive director of the Black LGBTQIA+ Migrant Project (BLMP). Oluchi is also the co-founder and founding Core Team member of Black Visions.

Lauren Christine Mims is an Associate Professor at NYU Steinhardt and a former Assistant Director of the White House Initiative on Educational Excellence for African Americans. She studies the brilliance of Black children and their families to develop research, policies, and practices that ameliorate inequalities.

Preston D. Mitchum is a Black queer attorney, advocate, and founder of PDM Consulting, advancing the power of Black, LGBTQ+, and young people. With 15 years in law and policy, he has led national advocacy, taught at Georgetown and American University, earned major civil rights honors, and appears on *Bravo's Summer House: Martha's Vineyard.*

Susana Morris is an Associate Professor at Georgia Tech. She studies African American literature, contemporary Black women's writing, Hip-Hop feminism, and digital culture. She co-founded the Crunk Feminist Collective and co-edited *The Crunk Feminist Collection*.

Kelcey P. Morrow is a San Antonio-based public school educator and literacy advocate. A Baylor University graduate with a master's in Literacy Studies from Prairie View A&M University, she serves the Dallas community through education, nonprofit volunteering, and civic organizations, believing deeply in the liberating power of equitable, truthful education.

Regina Davis Moss, PhD, MPH, MCHES, is President and CEO of In Our Own Voice: National Black Women's Reproductive Justice Agenda. A leading public health and Reproductive Justice advocate, she brings over 20 years of national leadership, policy expertise, and media visibility, and authored Black Women's Reproductive Health and Sexuality.

Metzlal Ocbazghi is Research Manager at the Black Alliance for Just Immigration, leading policy research and data analysis. Through her work, she advances human rights for Black migrant and diaspora communities. A second-generation Eritrean American, she earned degrees in Economics and Political Science from Ohio State and International Affairs from George Washington University.

Oluchi Omeoga is a Minnesota-born organizer, born from Igbo immigrants from Nigeria. Oluchi serves as the co-founder and co-executive director of the Black LGBTQIA+ Migrant Project (BLMP). Oluchi is also the co-founder and founding Core Team member of Black Visions.

Latham Thomas is the founder of Mama Glow, a global maternal health and education brand, and a doula education platform that supports birth workers around the world. She also co-founded the Mama Glow Foundation, which advances reproductive justice through education, advocacy, and the arts. She has served as Visiting Assistant Professor of the Practice of Gender and Sexuality Studies at Brown University. Named to Oprah Winfrey's SuperSoul 100, she is the best-selling author of Mama Glow and Own Your Glow and a graduate of Columbia University.

Mark A. Thompson is a lifelong civil and human rights activist who has used ministry and radio broadcasting to build movements. He hosts Make It Plain, a political, human rights, and news podcast. He began broadcasting in 1988 at Radio One, and Make It Plain was the first talk show to sign on to XM Satellite Radio in 2001. He co-chaired the 1996 National Black Political Convention and has emceed the Million Man March. The NAACP honored him in 2013 for 25 years of journalism and civil rights leadership.

Vilissa Thompson, LMSW, is a licensed master social worker from Winnsboro, South Carolina, and the founder and CEO of Ramp Your Voice!, an organization that promotes self-advocacy and empowerment among disabled people. Her work centers Black disabled voices, challenges ableism and racism, and pushes for equity and justice in disability spaces and beyond. In 2024, she launched the Ramp Your Voice! Conference, a virtual gathering that centers disabled Black people who are not cisgender, heterosexual men. The second conference took place in June 2026.

Cyntasia Palmer is a social justice advocate with a background in research and community engagement. She holds a BA in Journalism with a minor in Justice from American University, where she served as a Community-Based Research Scholar. Her work centers on amplifying underserved voices, media transparency, and inclusive storytelling.

Lawrence "Larry" Parks is a policy and advocacy expert and former Senior Vice President at the Federal Home Loan Bank of San Francisco. He authored key provisions in the Dodd–Frank Act and created the $100 million Quality Jobs Fund to promote workforce development and inclusive economic growth.

James Peterson is a scholar, author, and cultural critic exploring race, politics, media, and Hip-Hop. A frequent media commentator, Peterson bridges academia and public discourse through his work, writings, and radio show Evening WURDs (on WURD in Philadelphia), advancing education, equity, and racial justice.

Melanye Price is an Endowed Professor of Political Science and Director of the Ruth J. Simmons Center for Race and Justice at Prairie View A&M University. She is a leading scholar of Black politics and public opinion and author of *The Race Whisperer: Barack Obama and the Political Uses of Race*.

Caitlin Radigan is the Statewide Policy Manager at California Youth Connection and Chair of the San Diego Juvenile Justice Commission. She leads youth-driven policy advocacy advancing foster youth rights and system accountability. A former nonprofit leader and co-author of *Life Changing Choices*, her work bridges grassroots organizing and policy reform, centering kinship and youth leadership.

Fred Redmond is Secretary-Treasurer of the AFL-CIO and the highest-ranking African American officer in its history. A lifelong labor leader and former USW Vice President, he champions workers' rights, racial equity, and economic justice, advancing inclusive solidarity, fair wages, workplace safety, and collective bargaining across industries.

Ebonie C. Riley is Senior Vice President of Policy and Strategic Partnerships at the National Action Network (NAN) and its highest-ranking woman. A leading federal policy advocate, she directs NAN's Washington bureau, advancing civil rights, voting rights, and economic justice by engaging Congress, the White House, and the courts.

Arian Simone is the CEO and Founding Partner of Fearless Fund, the first VC fund by and for women of color. A serial entrepreneur, philanthropist, investor, and author, she brings 17+ years of experience in PR, marketing, and women's entrepreneurship, backed by an MBA from Florida A&M and major entertainment industry partnerships.

Tim Simons is a corporate and government relations leader with 20 years' experience in regulated industries. Formerly Vice President at the Federal Home Loan Bank of San Francisco, he co-designed the $100 million Quality Jobs Fund and is known for legislative strategy, risk assessment, and grassroots advocacy expertise.

Courtney R. Snowden is a Washington, D.C.-based government relations strategist and founder of The Blueprint Strategy Group. A former D.C. Deputy Mayor, she has led national advocacy on education, economic opportunity, and LGBTQ equity, representing major nonprofits and corporations, and advancing workforce development, civil rights, and inclusive public policy.

DeShuna Elisa Spencer is a social impact executive and media founder advancing narrative change through storytelling and technology. She is the founder and CEO of Kweli TV, a Black-owned streaming platform for indie Black creators, and leads national programs supporting Black filmmakers, media equity, and cultural transformation.

The National Women's Law Center fights for gender justice—in the courts, in public policy, and in our society—working across the issues that are central to the lives of women and girls. For 50 years, we have been on the leading edge of every major legal and policy victory for women.

Shatema Threadcraft, Associate Professor of Women's and Gender Studies and Philosophy at Vanderbilt University, researches Black feminist political thought and the politics of embodiment. She is the author of *Intimate Justice: The Black Female Body and the Body Politic* (2016).

Nicole Tisdale is a national security expert and attorney who served as director at White House National Security Council and Congress' Homeland Security Committee. She crafted cybersecurity laws and founded Advocacy Blueprints, promoting civic engagement. Author of *Right to Petition*, she holds BA and JD degrees from the University of Mississippi.

Ivory A. Toldson is a Howard University professor and Editor-in-Chief of *The Journal of Negro Education*. Former Executive Director of the White House Initiative on HBCUs, he advances data-driven solutions to educational disparities and challenges myths about Black achievement through research, advocacy, and public scholarship.

Monique S. Toussaint is a public servant with over 15 years of experience. She served as Senior Advisor for the White House Initiative on Advancing Educational Equity, Excellence, and Economic Opportunity for Black Americans. Her expertise includes strategic planning, leadership development, coaching, and leading education initiatives that empower communities.

Alisa Valentin is a telecom and tech policy advocate focused on expanding digital access in historically marginalized communities. A former FCC and civil rights advisor, she continues to advance digital inclusion at a DC-based non-profit. She holds a PhD in Communications from Howard University.

Jeffery T. D. Wallace, Jr. is President & CEO of Leaders Up, driving equity-focused innovation across education, workforce, and economic systems. Recognized by Fast Company and Black Enterprise, he has generated over $1 billion in economic impact while shaping investments and policies to expand opportunity for Black and Brown talent.

Jada Capri Ward is a social justice advocate and performer from Prince George's County, Maryland. A St. Mary's College graduate, she serves as Community Outreach Manager at G.S. Proctor & Associates, chairs her NAACP Political Action Committee, co-hosts the Relentless Love Podcast, and is a professional actress, dancer, and singer.

Britt Weinstock is Principal and Chief Strategist at the Health Equity Strategies Group, LLC, with over 25 years of experience in health equity and public health policy. Dr. Weinstock brings extensive expertise across federal and state government, grassroots, academia, philanthropic and private sector initiatives focused on advancing health equity.

André White is a Project Manager in the State Office of Policy Planning and Innovation, leading Person-Centered Thinking initiatives for people with intellectual and developmental disabilities. With 18+ years of experience, he trains and mentors teams statewide and is a certified Person-Centered Thinking Mentor Trainer and Human Resources learning and development specialist.

Verneda Adele White is an antiracism strategist, speaker, and award-winning writer, and founder of BLACK PEOPLE ARE AMERICA'S HOT SAUCE®. She leads a cross-industry consulting firm and writes for major outlets. A 2024 ILEA Esprit finalist and Points of Light honoree, her acclaimed work advances racial equity.

Latham Thomas is the founder of Mama Glow, a global maternal health and education brand, and a doula education platform that supports birth workers around the world. She also co-founded the Mama Glow Foundation, which advances reproductive justice through education, advocacy, and the arts. She has served as Visiting Assistant Professor of the Practice of Gender and Sexuality Studies at Brown University. Named to Oprah Winfrey's SuperSoul 100, she is the best-selling author of Mama Glow and Own Your Glow and a graduate of Columbia University.

Corena D. Wiggins is an award-winning College Advisor with nearly 20 years of experience assisting students in navigating the college process. She is President for The Scholarship Plug, Inc., a political activist and commentator whose features include Roland S. Martin's Black Star Network, Tavis Smiley's KBLA radio, and the Broward Democrat's podcast.

Kirsten F. Wilder is Director of the Georgia Safety Coalition and State Organizer for REFORM Alliance. A Georgia-born policy strategist, she leads reentry and community-supervision reform efforts statewide. With degrees from Georgia State University, her work centers directly impacted communities while building coalitions for structural justice transformation.

Melanie Willingham-Jaggers (they/she) is the Executive Director of GLISTEN, leading national efforts to make K-12 schools safe and affirming for LGBTQ+ youth. Their work centers racial, gender, and disability justice in education. Previously at Cornell's Worker Institute, Melanie holds degrees from USF and CUNY and has taught applied theater.

Victoria Kirby York is the Director of Public Policy and Programs at the National Black Justice Collective, leading advocacy for Black LGBTQ+/SGL communities. A seasoned organizer, she has driven major national campaigns on healthcare, racial equity, LGBTQ+ rights, and voting access. Her leadership has earned multiple national recognitions.

Introduction to the Black Papers

A Love Letter to Our Community

David J. Johns

The Call

> Good morning, brother. I have a crazy idea. You can't say no. Are you listening?

Angela Rye knows me. She had me at "crazy idea." She also knows I would walk through fire for her. This conversation, one early morning before our 9 a.m. State of the People Tour planning call, would become the genesis of my career's most significant intellectual and activist undertaking. What began as Angela's "crazy idea" evolved into the Black Papers: a comprehensive policy agenda, a strategic blueprint, and, ultimately, a love letter to our community.

We discussed the 1972 Gary Political Convention, what they got right, and the gaps we could fill. We discussed their policy paper and how sad it was that we were still demanding many of their policy demands, including D.C. statehood. She spoke about the opportunity—the obligation—we had to connect the policy dots for our community in ways we are uniquely equipped to do. And then she said: "You're the only person I can trust to get the job done."

In hindsight, I am honored she recognized my unique positioning and skills to make this project happen. It is a beautiful reflection of our decades-long friendship forged in collaboration—beginning with IMPACT, where we cut our teeth on advocacy and organizing in the early 2000s; continuing through our years on Capitol Hill, where she led the Congressional Black Caucus (CBC) as Executive Director and I worked alongside her, including on the CBC Jobs Tour with Chairman Emanuel Cleaver; and evolving through our leadership within the State of the People movement. Angela and I are often described as "passionate" when people want to be polite about our shared

DOI: 10.4324/9781003752646-1

commitment to identifying promising and proven solutions to problems, developing strategic plans, and executing them relentlessly.

Why Now? Why This?

We stand at a crossroads. Again. As it seems we always have.

But before we chart where we are going, we must honor the foundation upon which we continue to build. **Bayard Rustin**—the architect of the 1963 March on Washington for Jobs and Freedom, the strategist who taught Dr. King about nonviolent resistance, the co-founder of the Congress of Racial Equality and the Southern Christian Leadership Conference—laid the groundwork for everything we do today. In just eight weeks, without cell phones, without email, without fax machines, without apps or algorithms, Rustin organized a march that brought 250,000 people to the National Mall and changed the course of American history.

Rustin understood what we know now: that civil rights without economic justice are incomplete. That organizing requires both brilliance and grit. That our liberation is bound up with the liberation of all oppressed people. And perhaps most importantly, for me personally, Rustin showed us what it means to live as an openly same-gender loving/gay Black man doing freedom work, refusing to hide even when forced to work in the shadows, and when his identity was weaponized to diminish his contributions.

As a queer Black leader standing in the tradition Rustin pioneered, I understand viscerally what he knew—that we cannot wait for the perfect conditions or universal acceptance to do this work. Rustin organized the 1963 March on Washington for Jobs and Freedom, knowing he was relegated to "deputy director" because of his sexuality. He mentored Dr. King while critics attacked their friendship. He built the movement infrastructure that made the Civil Rights Act and Voting Rights Act possible, even as he was erased from photos and written out of histories.

In 2013, President Barack Obama—whose election the March on Washington made possible—posthumously awarded Rustin the Presidential Medal of Freedom. Better late than never. But we do not have time to wait for posthumous recognition. As Rustin himself said in 1986, testifying for New York State's Gay Rights Bill: "Gay people are the new barometer for social change." He understood that justice delayed for some is justice denied for all.

I often think about Rustin and the March on Washington, which he built in record time and in the face of tremendous opposition. His legacy reminds me that being an architect of not just moments but of movements enables so many of us to continue doing things that directly result from his teaching and sacrifice. The National Black Justice Collective (NBJC) attributes its advocacy successes in the Black queer space directly to Rustin's legacy. This project—the Black Papers, the State of the People movement—is part of that lineage.

From the Niagara Movement in 1905, when W.E.B. Du Bois and 28 other Black intellectuals gathered near Niagara Falls to demand full political, civil, and social rights for African Americans, we have consistently charted our path forward. They declared: "We refuse to allow the impression to remain that the Negro-American assents to inferiority, is submissive under oppression and apologetic before insults." That mighty current of protest they unleashed became the foundation for the NAACP and generations of civil rights organizing.

In 1972, over 10,000 Black Americans descended on Gary, Indiana, for the National Black Political Convention. They came from every corner of the nation—Socialists, Black Panthers, Republicans, Democrats, Nationalists—diverse in ideology but unified in their determination to create a cohesive political strategy to advance Black civil rights. The Gary Declaration stated clearly: "The American system does not work for the masses of our people, and it cannot be made to work without radical fundamental change." They produced a 68-page National Black Agenda that included demands for a guaranteed minimum income, proportionate Black representation in Congress, and an end to the Vietnam War.

Years later, from 2000 to 2010, Tavis Smiley convened the State of the Black Union, gathering thousands annually to discuss the pressing challenges facing African Americans. Those conversations drew luminaries like Jesse Jackson, Maxine Waters, Louis Farrakhan, and future Senator Barack Obama, spawning the bestselling "Covenant with Black America" series. When Tavis ended the series after a decade, he acknowledged that Black issues were finally being addressed by more voices across media—a sign of progress, even as the work remained unfinished.

Since 1976, the National Urban League has published its annual State of Black America report, providing comprehensive analysis and data on racial inequality across economics, employment, education, health, housing, criminal justice, and civic participation. The 2025 report declared a "state of emergency" for democracy and civil rights, documenting systematic efforts to roll back decades of hard-won progress.

Since 1970, the Joint Center for Political and Economic Studies—America's Black think tank—has been at the forefront of rigorous policy research and analysis advancing Black political and economic power. Through groundbreaking research on the racial wealth gap, tax policy reform, economic mobility, and political participation, the Joint Center has provided the empirical foundation for evidence-based advocacy. Their Wealth Agenda and commitment to data-driven policy solutions have informed national conversations about economic justice and continue to shape the strategic direction of Black advancement efforts. The Joint Center's partnership and contribution to the Black Papers project exemplify their ongoing dedication to translating research into actionable policy that strengthens Black communities.

This is our lineage, our tradition. We are not inventing a new wheel—we are standing on the shoulders of giants and learning from their triumphs and shortcomings.

What Gary Got Wrong (And What We're Trying To Get Right)

The Gary Convention was powerful, necessary, and ultimately incomplete. Like many of our historic gatherings, the energy dissipated, the coalition fractured, and, within years, much of the momentum had stalled. By the 1974 convention in Little Rock, Arkansas, intellectual historian Harold Cruse observed that the gathering had become "a betrayal of the Black militant potential built up during the Sixties."

We studied Gary not just for inspiration but to understand why so many agendas faded. Why the fire dimmed. Why promises went unfulfilled.

The State of the People movement and the Black Papers (Papers) were designed with these lessons embedded in our DNA. This time, we are not letting it die on the table. We are building infrastructure, not just inspiration. We are creating tools for sustained organizing, not just moments of collective catharsis. We are ensuring that when this tour ends, the work continues—in our churches, community organizations, policy briefs to elected officials, and organizing.

Who We Are: The Original Influencers

As my mentor Sharon Lettman-Hicks reminds us: **Own Your Power**.

Sharon, who led NBJC before me, has dedicated her career to empowering Black people. Her mantra—"Own Your Power"—became not just NBJC's rallying cry but a north star for this entire project. The truth is, we have always possessed everything we needed to meet the critical needs of ourselves and our community.

We are the original influencers, the progenitors of cool, and the curators of culture. From jazz to hip-hop, from the Harlem Renaissance to Black Twitter, from the freedom songs of the Civil Rights Movement to the viral moments that shape global conversations, we have always set the tempo, defined the aesthetic, and pushed the boundaries of what is possible.

And yet, for too long, we have been told to wait our turn. To be patient. To trust the process. To believe that the democratic institutions we helped build would eventually work for us.

Nah!

This moment requires us to own our power—not in some distant future, but right now. We must remember that we built this country with our labor, defended it with our service, enriched it with our culture, and continually pushed it towards its stated ideals. We do not need permission to organize for our liberation. We do not need validation to center our own needs. We already have the power. The Black Papers are a tool to help us wield it more effectively.

The Breadth and Depth of the Black Papers

The Black Papers represent one of the most comprehensive policy agendas produced by and for Black America in a generation. Across these pages, over 100 contributors—scholars, activists, policymakers, practitioners, and community leaders—have poured their expertise, passion, and vision into more than 26 papers covering:

Economic Justice: From building an economy that works for us to the power of Black entrepreneurship, tax policy reform, and labor organizing, we chart a path to economic freedom and community wealth.

Education: From early childhood care to K-12 reform, higher education, Historically Black Colleges and Universities (HBCUs), and addressing the Black male enrollment crisis, we demand systems that nurture our brilliance rather than punish our Blackness.

Health and Wellness: We confront America's 12-year Black health equity gap, reproductive justice in post-Roe America, and the importance of centering Black bodies in healthcare policy.

Democracy and Governance: From D.C. statehood to voting rights, we reclaim democracy to ensure that the people and institutions we helped build actually serve us.

Public Safety and Justice: We reimagine safety through the lens of Ujima (collective responsibility), address gun violence, challenge mass incarceration, and demand citizenship rights from Dred Scott to deportation policing.

Infrastructure and Environment: From transportation justice to climate resilience, Black land stewardship, and environmental racism, we assert our right to thriving, sustainable communities.

Identity and Liberation: Papers on gender equity, disability justice, LGBTQ+ liberation, Black immigration, and Pan-African solidarity remind us that our freedom is indivisible and our community is beautifully diverse.

Reparations and Repair: These Papers grapple with the question of repair.

Specialized Justice: These Papers address housing as a human right to digital equity as a civil right, and Black military service to national security frameworks that center our needs.

Each Black Paper reflects not just academic rigor but lived experience. Not just policy prescription but practical wisdom. Not just diagnosis of problems but blueprints for solutions. This is scholarship in the service of liberation;

research grounded in community. This is the work—a compilation of love letters focused on our liberation with clear directives to get us all closer to freedom, and our country to its founding promises and potential.

The contributors span generations, geographies, and experiences: university professors and community organizers, former White House officials and grassroots activists, entrepreneurs and educators, artists and attorneys. Some are household names, and others are doing transformative work in communities that mainstream media ignores. Together, they represent the breadth of Black genius and the depth of our commitment to our own flourishing.

My "Yes" and My "Why"

Beyond Angela's call, beyond being "voluntold," I said yes because I am uniquely positioned to lead this work. I am one of the few Black professionals with leadership experience across—Capitol Hill, the White House, and a presidential campaign. I am a trained researcher with a PhD who understands policy development and implementation, having spent years as an elementary school and university educator and practitioner who collaborates deeply with the community. I bring my experience as a Black same-gender loving person navigating systems not designed for my survival, let alone my thriving. Every dimension of my identity and experience prepared me for this project.

But more than qualifications, I said yes because I believe in us. I believe in our capacity not just to survive but to flourish. We do not have to choose between our diverse identities and collective power. We can be fully ourselves—in all our complexity, beauty, and strength—while building the coalitions necessary for liberation. The students I taught in New York City Public Schools and universities in Washington, D.C. and throughout the country deserve a world where their brilliance is assumed, their safety is guaranteed, and their joy is protected. I believe that my ancestors who survived the Middle Passage, who survived enslavement, who survived Reconstruction's betrayal, who survived Jim Crow, who survived COINTELPRO—their wildest dreams for liberation are our inheritance to manifest.

This project means everything to me because it represents what we can do when we trust ourselves, resource our visions, and refuse to wait for permission to be free.

How to Use the Black Papers

These Black Papers are tools, not texts to sit on a shelf. They are meant to be used, debated, adapted, and deployed. Here is how:

For Individuals: Use these Papers to sharpen your awareness, deepen your understanding, and arm yourself with facts, data, and analysis. When your uncle says something uninformed at Thanksgiving, you will have receipts.

When you are navigating systems—healthcare, education, housing, criminal justice—you will have frameworks and language to advocate for yourself and your loved ones.

For Organizers and Activists: Let these Papers inform your campaigns, direct actions, and coalition-building. Use them to develop talking points, craft policy demands, and educate your base. They can help you connect the dots between seemingly disparate issues and build more intersectional movements.

For Faith Communities: Use these Papers in Bible studies, sermon series, and justice ministries. Let them ground your prophetic witness in spiritual truth and practical strategy. Your congregations are hungry for this kind of integration of faith and action.

For Nonprofits and Community-Based Organizations: Let these Papers guide your programming, advocacy, and funding priorities. Use them in your grant applications to demonstrate the evidence base for your work. Share them with your boards, staff, and volunteers.

For Educators: Integrate these Papers into your curricula, research, and pedagogy. They can serve as texts for undergraduate and graduate courses, frameworks for K-12 lesson planning, and models for engaged scholarship.

For Professionals: Whether you are a doctor, lawyer, social worker, architect, or engineer, these Papers can help you understand how your profession intersects with racial justice and what specific changes your field needs to make. Bring them into your professional associations and licensing boards.

For Elected Officials and Public Servants: These Papers are your roadmap. We are not asking you to figure it out—we are telling you what we need. Use them to craft legislation, inform budget priorities, shape regulations, and hold systems accountable. The people who elected you deserve leadership grounded in our needs, not consultant-driven assumptions.

For Everyone, Everywhere: Print them, share them, discuss them, argue with them, build on them, translate them into action in your corner of the world, tag us on social media when you use them@BlackPapers_SOTP & @StateOfThePPL, and tell us what is working and what needs revision. This is a living document of our collective liberation.

The Invitation

Our Black Papers are not a set of papers to be released and forgotten. Our Power Tour is not a conference that ends when people leave the building. State of the People is not a moment—it is a movement.

We invite you, beloved community, to join us in the long work of liberation. To organize on your block, in your building, your borough. To attend city council meetings with policy demands grounded in these analyses. To run for the school board with a clear vision for what Black children need. To start a business that fills the gap in your neighborhood. To have the hard conversations at your family reunion about what it means to hold institutions accountable. To vote, to volunteer, to vocalize our needs without apology.

The State of the People Power Tour shared these Black Papers with communities nationwide because we know the real work happens in the next 13 cities—yours—in the spaces between the tour stops, in the months and years after the cameras stop rolling.

We are not waiting for saviors. We are showing up for each other. We are not centering whiteness in Black advancement. We are putting on our own oxygen mask, and we are doing that communally.

Angela said I was the only person she could trust to complete the job. And I have. But now I am passing the baton to you. Because liberation is not a spectator sport. Freedom is not given—it is taken. Justice is not granted—it is won. And we win together, or we do not win at all.

As Sharon taught us: **Own your power**.

As Gary declared: "We will not be satisfied to take one jot or tittle less than our full manhood rights."

As the Niagara Movement proclaimed: "We refuse to allow the impression to remain that the Negro-American assents to inferiority."

As the National Urban League reminds us: "Freedom is never really won. You earn it and win it in every generation."

And as the State of the People affirms: **We will not center whiteness in Black advancement. We are putting ourselves first**.

This is our time. These are our Black Papers. This is our power.

Let us use it.

In love and continued pursuit of freedom,
Dr. David J. Johns, PhD.
Black Papers Editor-in-Chief

A Vision Beyond Pain: Reimagining America for All—Together in Solidarity

There is a lot of hurt in America today, and a natural trauma response is to pretend that the pain will go away. But avoidance has never healed our nation's wounds. The State of the People Black Papers (Papers) acknowledge the depth of that pain while refusing to be defined by it. Instead, we grapple with tough questions and describe a materially different future. In this future, every Black American and our active accomplices can be acknowledged and see themselves in the "We the People" enshrined in our Constitution.

For Black Communities: Owning Our Power

We stand at a critical juncture in our history. Democracy is fragile, and its promise remains unfulfilled for too many. The rights, protections, and opportunities that should be available to all continue to be denied to Black Americans through systems designed to maintain inequality. Recent policy rollbacks and executive actions directly threaten decades of progress in healthcare access, economic opportunity, voting rights, environmental justice, and much more.

As Angela Davis reminds us: "Freedom is a constant struggle" (Davis, 2016). The struggle continues because true liberation has not yet been achieved. These Black Papers are rooted in the understanding that Black liberation is not simply about removing chains; it is about building sustainable power that can transform systems and create new possibilities.

Within our current reality, we see unprecedented potential for transformation when we harness our collective power. These Black Papers speak directly to Black communities across America, and, at times, throughout the Diaspora, calling us to own our power not just on election day, but every day. We must build and sustain our own systems, strategies, and infrastructure to build wealth, strengthen our communities, and experience the joy that is our birthright on the journey toward freedom.

In Coalition with Active Accomplices: The Power of Solidarity

The vision of an America that lives beyond its principled potential cannot be realized in isolation. As Dr. Martin Luther King Jr. wrote in his final book, *Where Do We Go From Here: Chaos or Community?* "We are caught in an inescapable network of mutuality, tied in a single garment of destiny. Whatever affects one directly affects all indirectly." It's called shared fate. Dr. King's Poor People's Campaign recognized that true liberation requires coalition-building with all who are burdened by forces working to uphold white privilege, steal and hoard government resources to enrich wealthy oligarchs, and upend civil, political, and social customs—including the rule of law, due process, and respect for constitutional governance (King, 1968; Jackson, 2007).

Bayard Rustin, the brilliant strategist behind the March on Washington, understood this even as he wrote: "When an individual is protesting society's refusal to acknowledge his dignity as a human being, his very act of protest confers dignity on him." Today, we must confer that dignity on one another through intentional coalition-building that recognizes our shared humanity while honoring our distinct struggles (D'Emilio, 2003).

We extend our hands to poor and working-class white Americans who face economic neglect while being manipulated by fear and xenophobia; to other people of color who recognize the anti-democratic messaging in attacks on diversity, equity, and inclusion (DEI); to Lesbian, Gay, Bisexual, Transgender, Queer/Questioning (LGBTQ+) communities fighting for dignity; to people defending bodily autonomy; and to all who understand that Make America Great Again (MAGA) Republicans are attacking the very foundations of American democracy. Our struggles are interconnected, and our liberation must be collective. This understanding drives our approach to coalition-building—not as a strategy of convenience, but as a moral necessity.

The Black Panthers understood the importance of radically inclusive, Black-centered coalition building when they formed rainbow coalitions with diverse groups fighting similar battles. Fred Hampton, deputy chairman of the Illinois chapter of the Black Panthers, articulated this vision: "We're going to fight racism with solidarity. We're not going to fight capitalism with Black capitalism. We're going to fight capitalism with socialism." From the Mississippi Freedom Democratic Party to global solidarity movements across the Global South, history shows us that the most successful resistance movements unite across differences while maintaining cultural specificity and autonomy (Bloom & Martin, 2016; Spencer, 2016).

Youth Leadership: Teaching Democracy's Next Defenders

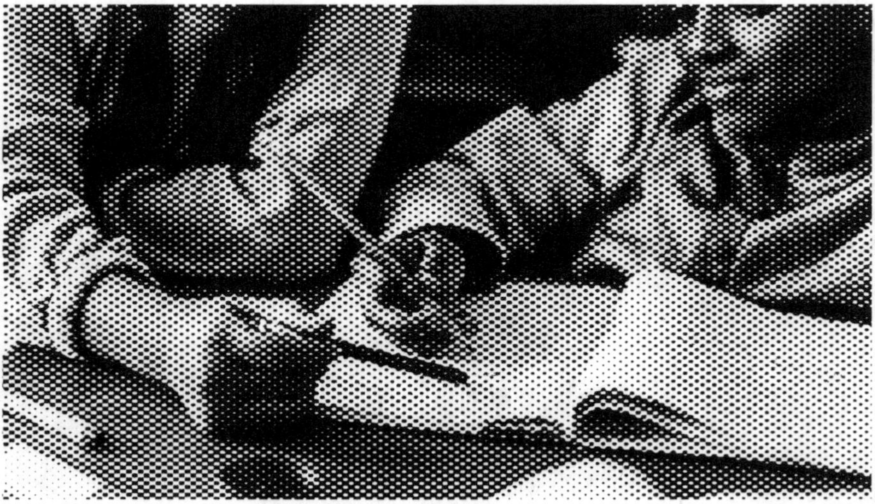

No successful movement for justice has ever triumphed without the leadership of young people. As bell hooks reminds us, democracies must be defended with each generation, and education is its midwife (hooks, 2010). Our children and youth are not merely beneficiaries of our struggle—they are essential leaders within it.

The truth of this was evident during the Civil Rights Movement, when Diane Nash, John Robert Lewis, and other student leaders brought new energy and tactics to the struggle. Today, we see this legacy carried forward by youth activists addressing climate justice, gun violence, and systemic racism. As John Lewis said in his final message: "Each generation must do its part to help build what we call the Beloved Community, a nation and world society at peace with itself" (Lewis, 2020).

Ella Baker, whose vision guided the Student Nonviolent Coordinating Committee (SNCC), articulated the transformative power of youth leadership when she said: "Strong people don't need strong leaders." Baker's model of group-centered leadership—where power is distributed rather than concentrated—remains our guiding principle in nurturing youth leadership today (Ransby, 2003; Payne, 2007).

From the Freedom Schools of the Civil Rights Movement to today's youth-led climate justice organizations, young people have consistently brought moral clarity, creative tactics, and uncompromising vision to social movements. These Black Papers supplement efforts to empower youth leadership through intentional mentorship, resource allocation, and genuine decision-making power in our collective work (Ginwright, 2015; Kelley, 2002).

The Power of Civic Engagement: Our Democratic Imperative

The State of the People Black Papers are not just academic exercises—they are tools for civic empowerment. When Black Americans remain engaged in democracy alongside our allies, we change the trajectory of this nation. From Reconstruction to the Civil Rights Movement to the present day, our participation has consistently expanded what is possible in America.

Fannie Lou Hamer's powerful testimony reminds us what is at stake in this engagement: "I'm sick and tired of being sick and tired." Her words speak to the exhaustion many feel in confronting systems designed to exclude us. Yet, as she demonstrated through her life's work, civic engagement is not optional when the alternative is continued oppression.

The policies described in these Black Papers impact our daily lives, determining whether we can afford healthcare, secure housing, build wealth, access quality education, breathe clean air, drink clean water, and protect our families from violence. These are not abstract concerns; they are realities shaping our lived experiences.

Historical Context: Building on a Legacy of Truth-Telling

These Black Papers draw inspiration from groundbreaking efforts that came before us:

In 1968, the National Advisory Commission on Civil Disorders—known as the Kerner Commission—released its landmark report following the civil unrest in 1967. Rather than blaming "riffraff" or outside agitators, the

Commission boldly named white racism as the fundamental cause: "White institutions created it, white institutions maintain it, and white society condones it." The report became a bestseller, forcing America to confront uncomfortable truths about its racial hierarchy (National Advisory Commission on Civil Disorders, 1968; Gillon, 2018).

Four years later, the 1972 National Black Political Convention in Gary, Indiana, gathered 8,000 Black leaders, politicians, and activists—the largest Black political gathering in American history. This historic convention sought to build a coalition across ideological differences to establish new political strategies for Black America in the post-Civil Rights era.

Since 1976, the National Urban League's annual State of Black America reports have provided essential benchmarks and analysis of racial equality across economics, employment, education, health, housing, criminal justice, and civic participation.

In 2006, Tavis Smiley launched "The Covenant" (formally titled *The Covenant with Black America*). The book, which was a collection of essays written by Black scholars, professionals, and practitioners, offered a national plan of action. The book was accompanied by a national tour (The Covenant Tour) in local churches across the country the same year. Smiley has since released updated versions of this work.

These Black Papers continue this tradition of truth-telling while moving beyond diagnosis to prescription and moving beyond naming what is wrong to envisioning what could be right.

Finding Strength and Joy in Community

Our vision for America's future is not rooted in isolation but in the power of community. Throughout our history, Black Americans have found resilience, innovation, and joy through collective action and mutual support. From mutual aid societies to civil rights organizations, faith communities to neighborhood associations, we have consistently demonstrated that our greatest strength lies in our connections to one another.

Audre Lorde reminds us that "Caring for myself is not self-indulgence, it is self-preservation, and that is an act of political warfare" (Lorde, 1988). This care extends beyond the individual to encompass community care—the networks of support that sustain us through difficult times and allow us to imagine and build new possibilities.

These Black Papers recognize that policy solutions must reinforce rather than undermine communal bonds. They highlight how targeted investments in Black communities—from healthcare centers to small businesses, educational institutions to transportation infrastructure—can strengthen the social fabric that sustains us through difficult times.

The policies we advocate for are designed to protect not just individual rights but collective wellbeing. They acknowledge that true freedom requires both personal autonomy and communal responsibility—the ability to care for ourselves while also caring for each other.

Resisting Divide-and-Conquer Tactics

For every member of our beautifully diverse community to get free, we must confront how power elites have historically pitted marginalized groups against one another to maintain their dominance. As Kimberlé Crenshaw notes in her groundbreaking work on critical race theory, "The problem with identity politics is not that it fails to transcend difference, as some critics charge, but rather the opposite—that it frequently conflates or ignores intragroup differences" (Crenshaw, 1991).

Understanding the dynamics of difference allows us to recognize when we are being manipulated into seeing other oppressed groups as enemies rather than potential co-conspirators. The current attacks on Blackness, critical race theory, LGBTQ+ and transgender rights, immigration, and voting-rights are not isolated phenomena—they represent coordinated attempts to divide communities that might otherwise find common cause against economic exploitation and political disenfranchisement.

Our Approach: Accessible Wisdom for Community Empowerment

The Black Papers translate complex policy realities into accessible language for our communities. They are written for those who feel righteous rage at systems that do not work for them by design—people who may lack the capacity, resources, or energy to engage with traditional policy discussions but whose lives are profoundly shaped by them.

As Paulo Freire wrote, "Education either functions as an instrument which is used to facilitate integration of the younger generation into the logic of the present system and bring about conformity, or it becomes the practice of freedom, the means by which men and women deal critically and creatively with reality and discover how to participate in the transformation of their world" (Freire, 1970). These Papers are tools for the practice of freedom—resources that empower communities to transform their reality (Love, 2019).

We reject the false choice between scholarly rigor and community accessibility. These Black Papers are both deeply researched and deliberately accessible, written at a level that honors the wisdom of our communities while providing the information needed to advocate effectively for meaningful and measurable change.

An Afrofuturistic Vision Rooted in Policy Reality

Our vision is Afrofuturistic, not just in its imagination but also in its practicality. It reflects a future where Black people are not only free and thriving but also leading innovation in every field of human endeavor, shaping the very structures that define our society, again. We envision a future where Black people are not merely included but are architects of systems that work for everyone. Our perspectives, experiences, and solutions are valued not as token additions but as essential components of a functioning democracy, and we are compensated equitably.

Octavia Butler, whose visionary fiction imagined new ways of being, wrote: "All that you touch, you change. All that you change, changes you." This reciprocal relationship between individual and collective transformation guides our work. As we change policies and systems, we are changed—expanded in our capacity to imagine and build something new (Butler, 2000; Imarisha & Brown, 2015).

The policy pillars articulated in these Black Papers—healthcare, economics, housing, justice reform, and combating anti-Blackness—form the foundation of this vision. They address the most pressing concerns identified by Black

Americans while pointing toward a future where these concerns have been transformed into strengths.

Economic Justice and Wealth-Building

Economic justice is a cornerstone of true liberation. In his final years, Dr. King observed, "What good is having the right to sit at a lunch counter if you cannot afford to buy a hamburger?" Today, this question remains painfully relevant as Black Americans continue to face staggering wealth disparities, employment discrimination, and barriers to entrepreneurship (Hamilton & Darity, 2017; Berry, 2021).

The Black Papers address these realities by outlining concrete strategies for building individual and collective wealth within Black communities while simultaneously confronting the structural barriers that reproduce inequality.

We draw inspiration from historical examples like Black Wall Street in Tulsa, Oklahoma—a thriving center of Black economic power before its state-sanctioned violent destruction in 1921—while recognizing that today's economic landscape requires new approaches.

These strategies include community-owned businesses, cooperative economic models, local investing initiatives, and policy reforms that address discrimination in lending, hiring, and contracting. By building economic power, we create the material foundation for other forms of freedom.

The Presentation of The Black Papers

Initial Black Papers were released electronically at each of the thirteen State of the People Power Tour stops, beginning April 26, 2025, in Atlanta, Georgia.

These Black Papers are designed to serve as:

1. A resource directory of trusted Black subject matter experts capable of speaking with authority on critical policy issues.
2. Transcripts documenting the lived experiences of Black Americans across the country.
3. A formal agenda that political leaders and policymakers can embrace and implement.
4. Educational tools for community organizations, schools, and advocacy groups.

Together, these Papers constitute a critique and a roadmap—an assessment of where we are and a blueprint for where we can go.

A Call to Collective Action

We call on all readers, Black Americans and active accomplices alike, to join us in building a multiracial coalition for democracy and justice. Together, we can:

1. **Organize locally** within our communities to build economic self-sufficiency, political power, and cultural vitality.
2. **Build solidarity networks** across race, class, and geography that address our shared struggles while respecting our distinct histories.
3. **Create power-sharing structures** that resource and amplify youth leadership, centering their vision and energy.
4. **Directly confront racist policies and institutions** through coordinated political action.
5. **Develop alternative institutions and systems** that model the democratic values we seek.
6. **Practice radical inclusion** that centers the most marginalized voices in our communities.
7. **Engage in ongoing political education** that connects personal struggles to systemic causes.
8. **Support mutual aid networks** that meet immediate needs while building long-term power.
9. **Protect voting rights and expand democratic participation** in every community.
10. **Connect local organizing to national policy change** through coordinated advocacy and action.

As Stacey Abrams reminds us: "Organizing is not just about knocking on doors; it's about transforming the way we see ourselves as citizens and neighbors." This transformation begins with each of us claiming our power—not just as voters or consumers, but as active participants in shaping our collective future (Abrams, 2020; Bailey & Ransby, 2022).

There is indeed a lot of hurt. But there is also tremendous power in our collective vision and action. These Black Papers are offered in the spirit of what Audre Lorde called "the transformation of silence into language and action"—a transformation that begins with naming our realities honestly and continues through building the world we know is possible.

As James Baldwin wrote: "Not everything that is faced can be changed, but nothing can be changed until it is faced." These Papers face our current realities with unflinching honesty while pointing toward the changes we know are possible when we act together (Baldwin, 1962; Glaude, 2020).

In love and continued struggle,

Dr. David J. Johns & The State of the People Black Papers Project Team

References

Abrams, S. (2020). *Our time is now: Power, purpose, and the fight for a fair America*. Henry Holt and Co.

Bailey, M., & Ransby, B. (Eds.). (2022). *Radical Black feminism and the fight for social justice*. Beacon Press.

Baldwin, J. (1962). *The fire next time*. Dial Press.

Berry, D. R. (2021). *The price for their pound of flesh: The value of the enslaved, from womb to grave, in the building of a nation*. Beacon Press.

Bloom, J., & Martin, W. E. (2016). *Black against empire: The history and politics of the Black Panther Party*. University of California Press.

Butler, O. E. (2000). *Parable of the sower*. Grand Central Publishing.

Crenshaw, K. (1991). Mapping the margins: Intersectionality, identity politics, and violence against women of color. *Stanford Law Review, 43*(6), 1241–1299.

D'Emilio, J. (2003). *Lost prophet: The life and times of Bayard Rustin*. Free Press.

Davis, A. Y. (2016). *Freedom is a constant struggle: Ferguson, Palestine, and the foundations of a movement*. Haymarket Books.

Freire, P. (1970). *Pedagogy of the oppressed*. Continuum.

Gillon, S. M. (2018). *Separate and unequal: The Kerner Commission and the unraveling of American Liberalism*. Basic Books.

Ginwright, S. (2015). *Hope and healing in urban education: How urban activists and teachers are reclaiming matters of the heart*. Routledge.

Glaude, E. S. (2020). *Begin again: James Baldwin's America and its urgent lessons for our own*. Crown.

Hamilton, D., & Darity, W. (2017). The political economy of education, financial literacy, and the racial wealth gap. *Federal Reserve Bank of St. Louis Review, 99*(1), 59–76.

hooks, b. (2010). *Teaching critical thinking: Practical wisdom*. Routledge.

Imarisha, W., & Brown, A. M. (Eds.). (2015). *Octavia's brood: Science fiction stories from social justice movements*. AK Press.

Jackson, T. F. (2007). *From civil rights to human rights: Martin Luther King, Jr., and the struggle for economic justice*. University of Pennsylvania Press.

Kelley, R. D. G. (2002). *Freedom dreams: The Black radical imagination*. Beacon Press.

King, M. L., Jr. (1968). *Where do we go from here: Chaos or community?* Harper & Row.

Lewis, J. (2020). Together, you can redeem the soul of our nation. *The New York Times*. https://www.nytimes.com/2020/07/30/opinion/john-lewis-civil-rights-america.html

Lorde, Audre. (1988). *A burst of light: Essays by Audre Lorde*. New York: Firebrand Books.

Love, B. L. (2019). *We want to do more than survive: Abolitionist teaching and the pursuit of educational freedom*. Beacon Press.

National Advisory Commission on Civil Disorders. (1968). *Report of the National Advisory Commission on civil disorders*. U.S. Government Printing Office.

Payne, C. M. (2007). *I've got the light of freedom: The organizing tradition and the Mississippi freedom struggle* (2nd ed.). University of California Press.

Ransby, B. (2003). *Ella Baker and the Black freedom movement: A radical democratic vision*. University of North Carolina Press.

Spencer, R. C. (2016). *The revolution has come: black power, gender, and the Black Panther Party in Oakland*. Duke University Press.

References

[illegible] (19[illegible]). [illegible] Henry Holt and Co.

[illegible] (19[illegible]). [illegible] Boston [illegible]

Baldwin, J. (19[illegible]). [illegible]

Bennett, R. (20[illegible]). [illegible]

Bloom, J., & Martin, W. E. (2016). [illegible] of California Press.

[illegible] Penguin [illegible]

[illegible] (199[illegible]). [illegible] politics, and [illegible]

D[illegible] (200[illegible]). [illegible]

[illegible] (20[illegible]). [illegible] Books.

[illegible] (19[illegible]). [illegible]

[illegible] of the [illegible]

[illegible] and [illegible]

[illegible] (20[illegible]). [illegible] our own [illegible]

Hamilton, [illegible] (19[illegible]). The [illegible]

[illegible] (2010). [illegible]

[illegible] (20[illegible]). [illegible] Press.

Jackson, [illegible] University of Pennsylvania Press.

[illegible] Beacon Press.

[illegible] (19[illegible]). [illegible] The New York Times.

[illegible] Books.

[illegible] (20[illegible]). [illegible]

[illegible] the National [illegible] Office.

[illegible] (2008). [illegible] University of California Press.

[illegible] (20[illegible]). [illegible] the Black [illegible] Press.

[illegible] (20[illegible]). [illegible] and the Black Panther Party [illegible] University Press.

Section I

Democracy and Governance

This section examines the continuous struggle to actualize American democracy through three interconnected dimensions of citizenship and political participation. The opening Black Paper, "Foundational People Power: Embracing the Challenge to Reclaim Democracy," establishes the theoretical framework for understanding citizens not merely as participants but as architects of democracy itself—co-creators responsible for building and defending democratic institutions against forces of erosion and exclusion. Drawing on Dr. Martin Luther King Jr.'s assertion that "human progress never rolls in on wheels of inevitability," this Black Paper challenges the assumption that democratic advancement occurs naturally, instead positioning deliberate citizen action as the essential catalyst for democratic renewal.

"Architects of Democracy: Reclaiming Voting Rights and Reimagining America" traces the ongoing battle for voting rights from Reconstruction through the present "Third Reconstruction," presenting a comprehensive Vision 2100 blueprint that addresses both immediate threats to ballot access and transformative structural reforms. This Black Paper explores the creation of a quasi-governmental Department of Democracy—an independent entity modeled on the Federal Reserve—designed to protect voting rights from partisan manipulation across administrations. It argues for universal civic duty voting, abolishing the Electoral College, and constitutional amendments to establish voting as an explicit right rather than an implied privilege.

Together, these Black Papers challenge readers to recognize that democracy is neither static nor guaranteed, but rather an ongoing construction project requiring continuous effort, structural redesign, and unwavering commitment to the principle that legitimate governance derives from the full and free participation of all citizens.

DOI: 10.4324/9781003752646-2

Chapter 1

Foundational People Power

Embracing the Challenge to Reclaim Democracy

James Peterson

Executive Summary

American democracy faces existential challenges that require urgent collective action. This Black Paper examines the historical context of democracy in America, particularly through the lens of Black Americans' experiences, and argues that democracy's survival depends on everyday citizens reclaiming their power. This Black Paper traces democracy from ancient Greece to present-day America, highlighting how Black Americans have been both systematically excluded from democratic processes and paradoxically among democracy's most steadfast defenders. From the Three-Fifths Compromise to modern voter suppression efforts, this Black Paper illustrates how democracy has been intentionally structured to limit participation while highlighting how grassroots movements have opened doors and expanded the meaning of democracy. This Black Paper concludes that democracy is not merely a system of government, but a daily practice requiring vigilance, commitment, and collective action at the community level. It calls for a renewed focus on "people power"—one that goes beyond elections and sees democracy as something we live out daily.

DOI: 10.4324/9781003752646-3

Introduction

American democracy is not a given. It does not run on autopilot or get managed by Artificial Intelligence (AI). It either thrives or dies based on the actions of everyday people. At its core, democracy is the collective agreement that our voices matter and that we each have a role in shaping the decisions that govern our lives. And yet, for far too many in our communities, the workings of democracy feel distant, complicated, and deliberately out of reach. This Black Paper (Paper) is for everyone who knows the system isn't broken—it is working exactly as designed. It is for those who feel the impact of political decisions without ever being a part of the conversations that make them. This is a resource, a roadmap, and a rallying cry for reclaiming the power that belongs to the people.

We live in a country shaped by policies that touch every part of our lives—how much we earn, how we are educated, whether we can afford to go to the doctor, and how safe we feel in our neighborhoods. These decisions are often made in rooms most of us never see, using language most of us never use. As a result, many of us are left out—not because we do not care, but because the systems were not built for us to understand or access easily. But the problem is not apathy—it's access. This disconnect has created a dangerous gap—between the people and the power, between everyday experiences and political outcomes, between what democracy promises and what it delivers.

This project is rooted in a simple but urgent belief—democracy only works when we do. Not just during election season, not just for those with degrees or titles, and not only when the issues are trending. Our democracy depends on everyday people staying informed, asking questions, showing up, and holding power to account. But to do that, we need tools that are honest, clear, and built for real life. We need to break down the language of politics and policy into something that speaks to people at their kitchen tables, in beauty salons, group chats, and community meetings, not just lecture halls or government hearings.

This Black Paper is just one in a series of plainspoken, truth-telling resources designed to bridge that gap. Together, these Black Papers break down complex policies and political dynamics in ways that speak to our lived experiences. They are rigorous enough to be trusted, and accessible enough to be useful. They speak not just to policy wonks and academics, but to parents juggling multiple jobs, elders watching their neighborhoods change, and young people trying to gain control over their futures. These are the people who already understand what is at stake. What they need—and what we hope to offer—are the tools to act.

This is not an academic exercise. It's a political intervention. It is a call to those who know the system isn't working, who feel the righteous rage that comes from being ignored or excluded. We see you. We hear you. And we believe that your voice, your story, and your power are essential to the future of our democracy.

Let this be a starting point for conversation, for connection, and, most importantly, for action. Because democracy isn't just something we inherit. Democracy is something we must build together, continually.

The History of the Word

The word "democracy" carries a weight that stretches back thousands of years. From its origins in ancient Greece to the present-day fight for equitable representation in towns, cities, and countries around the world, democracy is both an ideal and a work in progress. It is a word often spoken, but not always fully understood. It is praised as the best form of government while simultaneously being chipped away in subtle and blatant ways.

To fully appreciate the value of democracy and why it demands our attention and protection, we must explore its etymology, examine its global and American histories, and reflect on what it means to participate in democracy not just every four years but every single day.

The word *democracy* comes from the Greek words *demos*, meaning "people," and *Kratos*, meaning "power" or "rule." Translated, it means "rule by the people." The earliest-known democracy emerged in Athens around the 5th century BCE, where free male citizens could participate in decision-making through a direct vote. Like many systems that followed, this early democracy excluded large portions of the population, including enslaved people, women, and foreigners. From the start, democracy was a radical idea limited by the realities of who counted as "the people."

Three-Fifths of a Human Being

This early contradiction—democracy for some, exclusion for many—remains a feature of democratic systems today. Around the globe, many countries have adopted democratic principles while struggling to live up to them fully. In some nations, voting rights are regularly restricted; in others, the appearance of choice masks authoritarian control. Even in the United States—often celebrated as the world's oldest democracy—foundational documents and political structures were built to protect power, not distribute it evenly. This fact may be most evident in the Three-Fifths Compromise (Compromise).

The Three-Fifths Compromise is one of the most critical and painful moments in Black Americans' long and complex relationship with American democracy. It showed early on how the founding of the United States was full of contradictions—a country that claimed "all men are created equal," but still allowed slavery to exist (National Archives, 2022a).

In 1787, delegates from the 13 original states met at the Constitutional Convention in Philadelphia. They tried to fix the Articles of Confederation and create a stronger government. But a huge argument broke out, raising the question: Should enslaved people be counted in a state's population?

Southern states, where slavery was common, wanted enslaved people to be counted when deciding how many seats each state got in the United States House of Representatives. More people meant more political power. Northern states, where slavery was less common, thought this was unfair because enslaved people had no rights and could not vote (Library of Congress, 2022a).

The compromise they reached was shocking. They agreed that each enslaved person would count as three-fifths of a person when adding up a state's total population. In other words, for every five enslaved people, three would be counted toward political representation (National Constitution Center, 2023a).

The Three-Fifths Compromise gave southern states more political power in Congress than they would have had otherwise. It also helped protect slavery for many more decades. As a result of the compromise, states like Virginia and South Carolina gained more seats in the House of Representatives and more influence over national decisions (Gordon-Reed, 2021).

Even worse, the Compromise showed Black Americans early on that democracy in America did not yet include them. The very people who fought for freedom from Britain were willing to deny freedom to others to protect their power.

The Three-Fifths Compromise remained until after the Civil War. It was erased by the 13th and 14th Amendments to the Constitution, which ended the formal institution of slavery and gave citizenship rights to anyone born in the United States, including formerly enslaved people (National Archives, 2022a).

While the Compromise disappeared, the idea that Black Americans were somehow "less than" in American political life did not. Even after slavery ended, new laws and practices like Jim Crow, voter suppression, and segregation, which continued to deny Black people full participation in democracy, were enacted and enforced with zeal (Alexander, 2010).

The Three-Fifths Compromise reminds us that freedom and equality were not accessible to everyone. Black Americans have had to fight generation after generation to be meaningfully included in democracy's promises. Understanding this history helps us realize that the fight for true equality is not just a part of the past—it is still an active part of our lives today. The American democratic experiment may be at its most fragile point in our lifetime.

Why is the American democratic experiment so fragile today? Because the forces that have historically limited democracy are once again gaining strength. Economic inequality continues to grow, disinformation and misinformation spread rapidly through technology, and systematic efforts to restrict voting access to steal elections persist. Today's challenges may look different from those faced by our ancestors, but they pose equally significant threats to democratic participation and representation.

History has shown us that democratic backsliding often begins not with loud declarations but with small steps: changes to voting laws, redistricting, attacks on freedom of the press, or weakening judicial systems. When citizens stop participating—or are systematically discouraged from doing so—democracy begins to falter. The people's power only works when the people use it.

The Compromise enshrined the dehumanization of Black people into the very fabric of American democracy. It gave slaveholding states disproportionate power in Congress and presidential elections via the Electoral College, which remains in place today.

The Electoral College was designed to balance power between small and large states and preserve the political influence of slaveholding states. To this day, the Electoral College can result in presidents being elected without winning the popular vote—a contradiction to the idea that each person's vote counts equally. The United States is the only country in the world that uses the Electoral College system for presidential elections. The Electoral College comprises 538 electors, with a majority of 270 electoral votes required to elect the President. Each state has the same number of electors as it does members in its Congressional delegation: one for each member in the House of Representatives plus two Senators (National Archives and Records Administration, n.d.).

When Black American Men First Voted

During Reconstruction—the period after the Civil War—Black people were allowed to vote for the first time. However, gaining and keeping that right showed just how complicated America's democracy has always been for Black citizens.

The Reconstruction Era occurred between 1865 and 1877, right after the Civil War ended. The country needed to rebuild itself, especially the South, where most of the fighting happened. Even more important, the United States had to figure out how to treat the four million Black Americans who were no longer enslaved (National Archives, 2023).

At first, there was meaningful progress. The 13th Amendment ended slavery. The 14th Amendment made Black people citizens. And the 15th Amendment, ratified in 1870, said that no one could be stopped from voting because of their race, color, or because they had been enslaved (Library of Congress, 2022b).

Black men began voting in large numbers as soon as voting became legal. In fact, during Reconstruction, hundreds of thousands of Black men registered to vote, especially in the South (Foner, 2014). For the first time, Black voters helped elect state lawmakers, governors, and members of Congress. Black men also began to run for elected office.

In 1870, Hiram Revels of Mississippi became the first Black United States Senator. Later that year, Joseph Rainey of South Carolina became the first Black member of the United States House of Representatives (U.S. Senate Historical Office, 2023). Over 2,000 Black Americans held public office during Reconstruction at the local, state, and national levels (National Park Service, 2022).

Revels' election was an incredible achievement. For the first time in American history, democracy seemed to include everyone, finally.

This progress made many white Americans angry, especially in the United States South. They created groups like the Ku Klux Klan to use fear and violence to stop Black people from voting (Foner, 2014). They attacked Black voters, burned Black churches, and threatened anyone who tried to help Black citizens participate in elections.

Southern states also started passing laws called Black Codes and later Jim Crow laws, designed to make voting harder—if possible at all. They used tricks like poll taxes (charging people to vote), literacy tests (making people pass intentionally complex reading tests), and grandfather clauses (only letting people vote if their grandfathers had voted—a purposefully impossible barrier for most Black families to overcome) (Alexander, 2010).

By the end of Reconstruction in 1877, when federal troops were pulled out of the South, most Black Americans were once again pushed out of the voting booth. It would take nearly 100 more years—and the Civil Rights Movement—for fundamental voting rights to be protected again.

The fight for voting rights during Reconstruction taught us that democracy is not something you win once and keep forever. It has to be protected and strengthened over time. Black Americans' experiences show how fragile democracy can be and how hard people must work to make it real for everyone.

Today, when we vote, we honor the legacy of those brave Black citizens who first claimed their rightful place in American democracy during Reconstruction—we also restate our claim to full citizenship in the country that our ancestors built for free.

Democracy is Not Pure

Another persistent threat to democracy is gerrymandering, where politicians manipulate district boundaries to favor one political party or group over another. Rather than voters choosing their representatives, gerrymandering allows representatives to choose their voters. Gerrymandering undermines fair representation and reinforces political polarization, as districts are drawn to be "safe" for one party rather than competitive. Gerrymandering is not new; it dates back to the early 1800s and remains a powerful tool that skews political outcomes. It often affects communities of color and working-class neighborhoods most severely, diluting their voices and making it harder for their concerns to be reflected in policy.

Gerrymandering continues to be weaponized today. In the last decade, sophisticated mapping technology and data analytics have enabled more precise manipulation of district boundaries. When combined with restrictive voter ID laws, reduced early voting opportunities, and polling place closures in specific communities, these tactics create a modern system of exclusion that echoes historical patterns.

It is important to understand that the United States is not a *pure* democracy but a democratic republic. In a pure democracy, the people make all decisions directly through a majority vote. In a democratic republic, the people elect representatives who decide on their behalf. Ideally, a democratic republic balances efficiency with participation. In a functioning democratic republic, the people must be able to hold their representatives accountable. If elected officials do not truly represent their constituents' will, the system fails.

The distinction between a democracy and a democratic republic should remind us that democracy is more than just voting. It's about participation, deliberation, and the belief that government should reflect the will and well-being of the people. These themes drove the Civil Rights Movement's push to secure voting rights for all Americans regardless of race.

The Voting Rights Act

The Voting Rights Act of 1965 is one of the most important laws in American history. It helped Black Americans, men and women included, finally win the right to vote freely—a right they had fought for since the end of slavery. Even today, however, the story of voting rights shows how complex and ongoing the struggle for true democracy has been for Black citizens.

After the Civil War, the 15th Amendment said that no one could be denied the right to vote because of race (Library of Congress, 2022b). But for almost 100 years after that, especially in the South, Black Americans were still blocked from voting.

States continued to use unfair laws and practices like poll taxes, literacy tests, and grandfather clauses to stop Black citizens from voting. Many Black people were threatened, arrested, or even killed just for trying to register to vote (Foner, 2014). In places like Mississippi, only about 6% of eligible Black adults were registered to vote by 1965 (U.S. Department of Justice, 2022).

Black Americans never gave up. In the 1950s and 1960s, the Civil Rights Movement pushed hard for voting rights. Brave leaders like Bayard Rustin, Dr. Martin Luther King Jr., John Lewis, Fannie Lou Hamer, Anna Arnold Hedgeman, and many others organized marches and protests to build and harness power.

One of the most powerful moments came in March 1965, when peaceful marchers tried to walk from Selma to Montgomery, Alabama, to demand voting rights. On a day that became known as "Bloody Sunday," police attacked the marchers with clubs and tear gas at the end of the Edmund Pettis Bridge (National Archives, 2022b). Images of the violence shocked the nation and pushed President Lyndon B. Johnson and Congress to respond to the demands of the people and take action.

President Lyndon B. Johnson signed the Voting Rights Act (VRA) into law on August 6, 1965 (National Constitution Center, 2023b). The VRA did several important things:

- It banned literacy tests and other unfair barriers to voting.
- It allowed the federal government to send officials to places where voter discrimination was common to facilitate fair elections.
- It required certain states and counties with a history of discrimination to get permission (called "preclearance") before changing their voting laws to guard against gerrymandering and election theft (U.S. Department of Justice, 2022).

Following the VRA passage, the number of Black voters grew. In Mississippi alone, Black voter registration jumped from 6% to 59% by 1968 (Foner, 2014). For the first time in many places, Black Americans could vote without fear—and run for office, too.

Even though the Voting Rights Act made a huge difference, the fight for voting rights is far from over. In 2013, the United States Supreme Court decision in *Shelby County* v. *Holder* weakened a significant part of the VRA by striking down the preclearance requirement (Supreme Court of the United States, 2013). Since Shelby, several states have passed their own voting laws that some experts say make it harder for Black citizens and other minorities to vote (Brennan Center for Justice, 2023).

The Voting Rights Act was a significant step forward, but it also showed how fragile progress can be. Black Americans' long journey toward full citizenship reminds us that democracy is something people have to protect, not just once but every generation.

When we vote today, we honor the courage of the marchers from Selma, the leaders of the Civil Rights Movement, and every Black citizen who fought to make America's promises real for everyone. That historic fight should inspire us to work together to keep this democracy alive.

Democracies Die

American democracy has long been heralded as a global model, a beacon of hope, and a symbol of freedom. Yet, as Steven Levitsky and Daniel Ziblatt argue in *How Democracies Die*, democracy's demise cannot come through dramatic coups or revolutions but through more subtle, insidious means. They write—"But there is another way to break a democracy. It is less dramatic but equally destructive" (Levitsky & Ziblatt, 2018).

"Democracies may die at the hands not of generals, but of elected leaders—presidents or prime ministers who subvert the very process that brought them to power" (Levitsky & Ziblatt, 2018). This observation serves as a powerful lens through which to view America's ongoing democratic struggles, particularly when we consider the central role that Black Americans continue to play in protecting and advancing democratic ideals, even when the nation itself falls short.

Since the founding of the United States, Black Americans have been systematically excluded from the democratic process. From slavery to Jim Crow, and from voter suppression to mass incarceration, Black citizens have been targets of policies designed to limit our voices. Yet, paradoxically, it is often Black Americans who have fought hardest to realize the nation's democratic promises. Our struggles have been crucial not only for our rights but also for the preservation and expansion of democracy for all Americans.

Levitsky and Ziblatt emphasize that "democracies still die," but by different means. "Since the end of the Cold War, most democratic breakdowns have been caused not by generals and soldiers but by elected governments themselves" (Levitsky & Ziblatt, 2018). This is a crucial distinction. It suggests that democratic backsliding is often masked by legality and procedure, making it more challenging to identify and resist. When newspapers are "bought off or bullied into self-censorship" and citizens "continue to criticize the government but often find themselves facing tax or other legal troubles," democracy's erosion becomes, for many, "almost imperceptible" (Levitsky & Ziblatt, 2018).

For Black Americans, however, the erosion of democracy has rarely been imperceptible. It has been lived and hyper-visible, always palpable. Democratic erosion is embodied in discriminatory laws, violent repression, and economic disenfranchisement. From the moment Reconstruction-era gains were dismantled through violence and voter suppression, Black Americans understood that democracy could be hollowed out from within, even as official institutions remained standing.

This lived experience has often made Black Americans some of democracy's most vigilant defenders. During Reconstruction, newly freed Black citizens participated in political life with astonishing energy, only to face a brutal backlash that ushered in nearly a century of Jim Crow segregation. Despite these setbacks, Black Americans continued to push for a more inclusive democracy through grassroots organizing, legal challenges, and mass mobilizations, culminating in the Civil Rights Movement of the 1950s and 60s.

The fragility Levitsky and Ziblatt describe was evident in the backlash to Reconstruction, the establishment of Jim Crow laws, and the systemic efforts to disenfranchise Black voters. These were not instances of democracy being overthrown by generals; they were deliberate, "legal" subversions carried out by elected officials and rubber-stamped by compliant courts. The fact that "many government efforts to subvert democracy are 'legal,' in the sense that they are approved by the legislature or accepted by the courts" (Levitsky & Ziblatt, 2018) mirrors precisely the historical experiences of Black Americans.

The resilience of Black Americans in the face of these legal erosions is one of the most compelling aspects of American democratic history. Time and again, Black citizens have mobilized to expand and preserve democratic practices. From the National Association for the Advancement of Colored People (NAACP) legal battles in the early 20th century to the Freedom Summer of 1964, the Black struggle for civil rights has served as a defensive wall against the quiet death of democracy that Levitsky and Ziblatt warn about.

Levitsky and Ziblatt also note, "we know that extremist demagogues emerge from time to time in all societies, even in healthy democracies. The United States has had its share of them, including Henry Ford, Huey Long, Joseph McCarthy, and George Wallace" (Levitsky & Ziblatt, 2018). These figures rose to prominence by appealing to fear, prejudice, and resentment. Significantly, race has often been a central theme of American demagoguery. From Wallace's defense of segregation to McCarthy's attacks on civil rights activists, racism has been a potent tool for those seeking to undermine democratic norms.

Today, we see the continuation—and amplification—of that legacy. The twice-impeached and now convicted felon who once again looms over the Oval Office did not rise in a vacuum. His ascent follows a long arc of American demagogues who wield racial animus, cultural panic, and populist rhetoric to secure power. In the 1950s, McCarthyism thrived by casting civil rights as communist subversion. In the 1960s, George Wallace garnered national attention with vitriolic defenses of segregation. From the 1980s to the 2000s, dog-whistle politics became the preferred strategy, embedding racial resentment beneath the surface of right-wing political ideology. From 2016 to Present: the 47th president blows the dog whistle into a bullhorn with birtherism, Muslim bans, border walls, and white nationalist rhetoric, redefining the political norm. Each point on this timeline represents not just a moment in history, but an evolving strategy to consolidate power by scapegoating marginalized groups and sowing division. The 47th president is not an aberration; he is the most recent and perhaps most dangerous data point in a long-standing pattern.

Black Americans have had to confront and resist these demagogues not simply as political adversaries but as existential threats to our very lives and liberties. In doing so, we have acted as a conscience for the nation, challenging it to live up to its highest ideals. Our activism has constrained would-be authoritarians and reinforced the democratic norms that Levitsky and Ziblatt identify as essential.

"Once a would-be authoritarian makes it to power, democracies face a second critical test: Will the autocratic leader subvert democratic institutions or be constrained by them?" (Levitsky & Ziblatt, 2018). Institutions alone, they argue, are not enough. "Constitutions must be defended—by political parties and organized citizens, but also by democratic norms" (Levitsky & Ziblatt, 2018).

Black Americans have consistently stepped into the defender role. Organized citizens, from the Southern Christian Leadership Conference (SCLC) to Black Lives Matter, have insisted on defending constitutional rights and democratic institutions. The willingness to organize, protest, and demand accountability has often provided the critical mass needed to check the worst impulses of leaders who might otherwise erode democracy further.

Furthermore, Levitsky and Ziblatt stress that

> democracies work best—and survive longer—where unwritten democratic norms reinforce constitutions. Two basic norms have preserved America's checks and balances in ways we have come to take for granted—mutual toleration, or the understanding that competing parties accept one another as legitimate rivals, and forbearance, or the idea that politicians should exercise restraint in deploying their institutional prerogatives.
>
> (Levitsky & Ziblatt, 2018)

For much of American history, democratic norms were not extended to Black Americans. Competing parties did not regard Black citizens as legitimate participants in the political process. There was no mutual toleration; instead, there was violent suppression. Yet Black Americans have consistently modeled democratic norms in our activism. Civil rights leaders emphasize nonviolence, forge coalitions across political lines, and appeal to shared constitutional principles. In doing so, we reinforce democratic norms even when we are denied.

Levitsky and Ziblatt also observe that "the challenges facing American democracy run deeper. The weakening of our democratic norms is rooted in extreme partisan polarization that extends beyond policy differences into an existential conflict over race and culture" (Levitsky & Ziblatt, 2018).

This observation is especially significant. The "existential conflict over race and culture" that shapes American political life is not new; it is the latest chapter in a centuries-long struggle. From slavery to the present, race has been the principal focus upon which American democracy has turned—or failed to turn.

Black Americans have always understood this existential dimension of the struggle. Our fight for voting rights, fair representation, and equal protection under the law has never been just about "policy differences." It has always been about the core meaning of American democracy—who counts, who belongs, and who gets to participate.

In moments when democracy has faltered, it has often been Black Americans who have forced the nation to confront its failures. The Civil Rights Movement led to landmark legislation like the Civil Rights Act of 1964 and the Voting Rights Act of 1965—laws that secured rights for Black citizens and strengthened democratic protections for all Americans. More recently, the high turnout of Black voters in key elections has been crucial in safeguarding democratic processes.

Indeed, contemporary movements for racial justice continue to highlight how democracy remains incomplete. Efforts to restrict voting access disproportionately affect Black communities, echoing earlier eras of voter suppression. Yet the activism, legal challenges, and organizing led by Black Americans continue to counter these anti-democratic trends.

How Democracies Die offers a sobering analysis of how democratic erosion often happens quietly, legally, and in ways many citizens fail to recognize until it is too late. Black Americans have rarely had the luxury of such blindness. Our historical experience has made us some of the nation's most vigilant defenders of democracy. Our activism, sacrifice, and insistence on full citizenship have preserved and expanded the democratic project in ways that benefit everyone. As America faces new threats to its democratic norms, it is worth remembering that the nation's most consistent champions of democracy have often been those whom democracy was initially designed to exclude.

In this context, our charge and challenge are to practice democracy daily.

Practicing Democracy

What does it mean to practice democracy in everyday life? It means understanding that democracy doesn't only happen in Washington, D.C. or at the ballot box. It lives in our neighborhoods, schools, workplaces, and relationships. To embrace small "d" democracy means to take ownership of your role in shaping the world around you. Embracing democracy does not require a law degree or a seat in the city council. It requires care, commitment, and a willingness to act.

- **Work the polls**: Democracy doesn't happen without people showing up to run elections. Becoming a poll worker is a direct way to protect and support fair voting processes.
- **Join the Parent Teacher Association (PTA) & engage with school boards**: Schools are where civic values are learned—or lost. Parents, guardians, and concerned adults who engage with school leadership help shape the future of their children's education and their communities.
- **Be a crossing guard**: It may seem small, but being visible in your community and helping kids get to school safely is an act of care and civic engagement.
- **Volunteer at food banks and shelters**: Meeting your neighbors' basic needs is democracy in action. When people are fed, housed, and supported, they can meaningfully participate in civic life.

- **Reach out to your representatives**: Call, email, attend a town hall, and let your voice be heard. It doesn't matter if your words are polished or perfect—what matters is that your representatives know you're paying attention.
- **Join or support community organizations**: Local and national nonprofits, mutual aid networks, and community groups provide crucial support and advocacy. By joining these efforts, you help build the infrastructure of grassroots democracy.
- **Talk about it**: Democracy thrives on ***informed*** dialogue. Host discussion groups about local issues (in safe ways that account for recent pandemics), start a neighborhood newsletter, and curate digital media spaces focused on community concerns.
- **Attend public meetings**: City council sessions, school board meetings, and city commission hearings are where decisions affecting your community are made. Your presence matters, even if you don't speak. Consider running for elected office.

- **Support local, independent, and Black-owned journalism**: Local, independent, and Black-owned media outlets that cover local issues help keep communities informed and hold power accountable. Subscribe, donate, or share their work.
- **Vote in every election**—not just the presidential election, but local and state elections that often have a more direct impact on daily life. Research candidates and ballot measures beforehand. Given our history, Black folks must participate in every federal, state, and local election every single time.

Influential People in a Living, Breathing Process

Democracy is not a destination—it is a living process that must be nurtured by the people who believe in it. It requires vigilance, humility, and hope. It also requires us to confront hard truths: Our systems have often excluded the very people they claim to serve, access to power is uneven, and the future of democracy depends not on those who currently hold power but on those willing to challenge and reshape it.

We must move beyond the idea that democracy is simply a system of rules. It is a culture, a relationship, a promise we keep with one another that says—I see you. I hear you. Your voice matters. Our government should work for you, too! Embracing this sense of democracy generates political power among the people.

"Power to the people" is not just a slogan. It is a promise. A vision. A warning. It is the declaration that real power does not belong solely to presidents, parties, or corporations. It belongs to the people. To communities. To the collective will of those who organize, resist, build, and reimagine. And yet, in a country where inequality is deep-rooted, and democracy is too often treated as a spectator sport, "people power" can feel like a myth, a distant echo from the past. But history tells us otherwise. Over and over again, it has been the people—everyday people—who have moved this nation forward, often against the grain of injustice, exclusion, and systemic resistance.

So, what do we *really* mean when we say "people power"? What is the power that lives in the collective? And what does it mean to build a people-powered democracy today, especially for those whose very lives have been devalued and dismissed by the systems that claim to represent them?

At its core, people power is the ability of everyday people to effect change by working together. Alone, one voice may be ignored. Together, a chorus of voices becomes impossible to silence. This is more than a metaphor—it is a political reality. Whether in marches, mutual aid networks, voting drives, workplace walkouts, or grassroots campaigns, people power emerges when communities act in solidarity with one another, bound by shared values and a commitment to collective wellbeing.

People power is not about individual heroism or rhetorically gifted political leaders. It is about coordinated action, built on relationships, and organized by trust. When we say "power to the people," we are naming a force that has always existed, often beneath the surface, shaping history in ways that official textbooks rarely capture. We are calling on the possibility that when people are united around common goals—freedom, dignity, equity—they can confront and reshape even the most entrenched systems of power. The people's power can resist and overcome the tyranny of the most trusted misleaders.

This idea is not new. From abolitionist movements to labor unions, from the Civil Rights Movement to the Ferguson uprising, people power has always been democracy's most accurate pulse. If told honestly, the American story is one long struggle between hoarded power and the people's refusal to be controlled by it.

In Black communities, especially, people's power has never been theoretical. It has been a matter of survival. For those whose humanity has been systematically denied, organizing has always been more than a political strategy; it has been a spiritual, cultural, and deeply practical necessity.

Enslaved people resisted through escape, sabotage, and rebellion. Reconstruction-era Black citizens organized schools, churches, and governments despite the looming threat of white violence. The Montgomery Bus Boycott was not a one-day protest but a year-long demonstration of discipline and shared sacrifice. The Black Panther Party did not just monitor police; they fed children, educated communities, and built clinics. These are all manifestations of the people's power.

The tradition of defending ourselves and democracy has carried on throughout our time. When Hurricane Katrina hit New Orleans and government systems collapsed, it was Black residents and grassroots groups that rescued neighbors and shared supplies. When police murdered George Floyd, Breonna Taylor, Tony McDade and too many others, millions of people took to the streets—not for a single protest, but for a sustained uprising. These movements were not about one leader or one moment. They were about collective grief, collective memory, and collective demand that justice be real, not rhetorical.

"People power" lives and breathes in the rhythm of these movements—in the chants, the art, the organizing meetings, the mutual aid, the shared meals, and the unshakable belief that another world is possible.

Progressive people often say, "rest in power" on the occasion of a comrade's passing. This phrase is not just a substitute for "rest in peace"—it is a political and cultural intervention. It names the reality that for Black people in America, peace has often been denied in life. To rest "in peace" implies justice that rarely arrives. To rest "in power," however, is to acknowledge a life spent resisting, building, and holding on to dignity in the face of structural violence.

When we say "rest in power," we are not just mourning a life—we are lifting a legacy. We are refusing to let a person's impact be erased by silence or sanitized by platitudes. We are naming their struggle and contribution, whether they were known nationally or only within their neighborhood. The phrase echoes the ancestral recognition that many Black lives have been both lived and lost in the liberation struggle, and that death does not erase the power of that work.

In this way, "rest in power" is a form of people-powered memory. It resists erasure. It says: You mattered. You still matter. Your fight continues in us.

The charge and challenge before us now are how to move beyond slogans and build a people-powered democracy that works, not just in theory, but in everyday life. The process starts by reimagining what democracy looks like beyond the ballot box.

Democracy means investing in local leadership. The person organizing your neighborhood block cleanup has more influence on your daily life than most elected officials. The volunteer who helps new immigrants fill out paperwork is exercising "people power." The young person leading a teach-in about climate justice at their high school is practicing democracy.

Democracy means shifting resources toward mutual aid, housing justice, food sovereignty, and care work. A people-powered democracy does not wait for permission—it responds to community needs in real time, believing that we are accountable to each other, not just to systems.

Democracy also means cultivating political education. Many people know the system is not working, but they do not always have the language to describe why—or the tools to fix it. People power grows when we share knowledge, demystify the mechanics of governance, and learn how to disrupt, resist, and rebuild together.

A people-powered democracy insists on participatory structures that involve people in decision-making, not as tokens but as architects. These structures include participatory budgeting, community advisory boards, and democratic unions. These structures do not solve everything, but they shift power. And that is the point.

Finally, democracy means building movements that are intergenerational, intersectional, and rooted in love. Love is manifested in actions that ensure no one goes without shelter, food, education, safety, joy, or the right to self-actualization. It is the commitment to build structures that reflect our highest values, not our deepest fears.

We are in a pivotal moment. On one side is a growing wave of authoritarianism, disinformation, and political suppression. On the other hand, there is the rising tide of people who refuse to give up and are building the tools and networks we need to win—not just elections but freedom.

This is not easy work. It requires patience, creativity, and courage. The stakes are too high to settle for silence. The people have always had the power. The question is how we choose to use it.

Democracy is not the property of the powerful. It is the practice of the people. Let us speak it. Build it. Share it. Defend it. And let us ensure that when the next generation looks back, they will not wonder where we were or what we did in this urgent moment. They will know that we showed up. That we fought. That we kept the promise alive.

Power to the People. Now and Always.

Call To Action

The future of American democracy rests in our hands. Democracy has always been most vibrant and expansive when everyday citizens step forward to claim their rightful power. Now is the time for each of us to answer the call.

- **EDUCATE**: Commit to ongoing political education for yourself and your community. Host reading groups, attend workshops, or organize teach-ins about the democratic process and its challenges.
- **ORGANIZE**: Join or create local organizations focused on democratic participation. Build relationships with neighbors, coworkers, and community members to sustain long-term collective action.
- **PROTECT**: Become a defender of voting rights. Volunteer as a poll worker, support voter registration drives, and actively oppose voter suppression efforts in your community.

- **PARTICIPATE**: Engage in democracy beyond elections. Attend public meetings, submit comments on proposed legislation, join community advisory boards, and hold elected officials accountable.
- **REIMAGINE**: Dream beyond the limitations of our current systems. Envision and work toward a democracy that truly represents all people, especially those who have been historically marginalized.

The work of democracy does not begin or end with a single election, march, or movement. It is sustained through daily acts of courage, compassion, and conviction. When we say "power to the people," we must mean all the people—across race, class, gender, ability, sexuality, and citizenship status. True democracy leaves no one behind.

Join us in this collective endeavor. Share our Black Papers with your people. Discuss its insights in your community spaces. Use it as a starting point for deeper conversations about what democracy means to you and what you are willing to do to protect it. The time for passive citizenship is over. The time for transformative action is now.

References

Alexander, M. (2010). *The new Jim Crow: Mass incarceration in the age of colorblindness*. The New Press.

Brennan Center for Justice. (2023). Voting laws roundup 2023. *The Brennan Center for Justice*. https://www.brennancenter.org/

Foner, Eric. (2014). *Reconstruction: America's unfinished revolution, 1863–1877*. Harper & Row.

Gordon-Reed, A. (2021). America's original sin: Slavery and the legacy of white supremacy. *The Atlantic*.

Levitsky, S., & Ziblatt, D. (2018). *How democracies die*. Crown Publishing Group.

Library of Congress. (2022a). *A guide to the constitutional convention*. LOC.gov.

Library of Congress. (2022b). *The 15th amendment to the U.S. constitution*. LOC.gov.

National Archives. (2022a). *The 3/5 compromise and the constitution*. Archives.gov.

National Archives. (2022b). *Selma to Montgomery marches*. Archives.gov.

National Archives. (2023). *Reconstruction and its aftermath*. Archives.gov.

National Archives and Records Administration. (n.d.). *About the electors*. Retrieved from https://www.archives.gov/electoral-college/about

National Constitution Center. (2023a). *The three-fifths clause*. ConstitutionCenter.org.

National Constitution Center. (2023b). *The Voting Rights Act of 1965*. ConstitutionCenter.org.

National Park Service. (2022). *Black Americans in Congress during Reconstruction*. NPS.gov.

Supreme Court of the United States. (2013). *Shelby County* v. *Holder*, 570 U.S. 529.

U.S. Department of Justice. (2022). *The Voting Rights Act of 1965*. Justice.gov.

U.S. Senate Historical Office. (2023). *First African American senators*. Senate.gov.

Chapter 2

Architects of Democracy

Reclaiming Voting Rights and Reimagining America

LaTosha Brown[*]

Democracy Defined: *Throughout this Black Paper (Paper), we define democracy as a system of governance where power ultimately resides with the people, who exercise this power directly or through freely elected representatives chosen in elections with genuine, periodic, and universal suffrage. True democracy extends beyond procedural elements to encompass substantive rights and freedoms, including political equality, civil liberties, minority protections, and mechanisms for popular accountability. As envisioned in this Black Paper, a robust democracy must be representative, reflecting the full diversity of its citizenry in its governing bodies, and participatory, creating multiple meaningful pathways for civic engagement beyond periodic voting. Democracy is not merely a political system but a social compact that recognizes the inherent dignity and agency of every person in determining their collective future.*

Executive Summary

This Black Paper (Paper) examines the current crisis in voting rights within the framework of America's ongoing struggle for a more perfect democracy. As we acknowledge the 60th anniversary of the Voting Rights Act (VRA), we find ourselves in what Bishop William Barber calls the "Third Reconstruction"—a critical period requiring both defense of existing rights and visionary redesign of our democratic institutions. This Paper presents a comprehensive "Vision 2100" blueprint for democratic renewal, addressing urgent threats to voting access while proposing transformative solutions that include structural reforms, local engagement, community education, judicial reform, and a pathway to full representation for all Americans. By positioning citizens as architects of democracy rather than mere participants, this Paper calls for building a democratic system that genuinely reflects the will of all people.

* Supported by braintrust authors: Stephanie J. Jones, David J. Johns, and Corena D. Wiggins

DOI: 10.4324/9781003752646-4

Introduction: The Future Has A Past

While studying Dr. Martin Luther King's "Letter from Birmingham Jail," I was struck by his response to a white minister who suggested that segregation would naturally end given time. Dr. King wrote:

> We must come to see that human progress never rolls in on wheels of inevitability; it comes through the tireless efforts of men willing to be co-workers with God, and without this hard work, time itself becomes an ally of the forces of social stagnation.
>
> (King, 1963)

Dr. King's wisdom resonates powerfully today as we confront the task of becoming architects of democracy. The challenges facing voting rights weren't born in a vacuum—they are the latest chapter in a long struggle for a more perfect union. As we mark the 60th anniversary of the Voting Rights Act, we find ourselves at another critical juncture, facing sophisticated new threats that echo historical patterns of disenfranchisement. This is precisely when we must engage not simply as defenders of existing rights, but as designers and builders of a more inclusive democratic system.

The right to vote represents more than a procedural mechanism—it embodies our most sacred democratic principle: that the government derives its legitimacy from the consent of the governed. When this right is compromised, so too is the very foundation of our republic. True architects understand that foundations matter. Today, we are called to both shore up our democratic foundation and reimagine the structure built upon it.

The Historical Context of Voting Rights

Before examining the current crisis, we must understand the history of voting rights in America. The struggle for the ballot has been central to the American experience, particularly for communities of color. Following the Civil War, the First Reconstruction period established constitutional amendments protecting the citizenship and voting rights of formerly enslaved people. However, these protections were systematically dismantled by Jim Crow laws, poll taxes, literacy tests, and violent intimidation (Equal Justice Initiative, 2017).

The United States Commission on Civil Rights' 1965 report *Voting in Mississippi* documented the systematic discrimination that characterized this era. Black citizens attempting to register to vote faced nearly impossible barriers, including complex literacy tests and "understanding" clauses interpreted at white registrars' discretion (U.S. Commission on Civil Rights, 1965). White people employed violence to enforce voting barriers. The terror that enforced voting restrictions was brutal and effective. Between 1882 and 1968, more than 4,400 Black Americans were lynched, many for attempting to exercise their constitutional rights (Equal Justice Initiative, 2017).

The Second Reconstruction—the Civil Rights Movement—culminated in the Voting Rights Act of 1965, which prohibited discriminatory voting practices. Research has demonstrated the transformative impact of this legislation: counties with larger Black populations saw increased state funding transfers (Cascio & Washington, 2014), and Black political representation increased significantly in covered jurisdictions (Bernini et al., 2023).

The Current Crisis in Voting Rights

The assault on voting rights intensified dramatically in 2025. The Safeguard American Voter Eligibility (SAVE) Act, represents one of the most serious threats to voting access in decades. Requiring proof of citizenship to register, which disproportionately burdens naturalized citizens, low-income voters, and elderly Americans who may not have the required documents, and people who possess the required documents but whose names do not match the information on their documents.

The 47th presidential administration has implemented executive orders that further restrict voting access, including an order diverting federal resources away from voter outreach and education toward aggressive voter roll purges. Another order limits the Justice Department's ability to monitor local election procedures, effectively eliminating federal oversight of potentially discriminatory practices.

Perhaps most concerning is the current administration's zeal in implementing recommendations from Project 2025.[1] Project 2025, also known as the 2025 Presidential Transition Memo, is a plan to reshape the federal government and consolidate power in favor of right-wing policies and political ideology. Over 100 organizations contributed to this plan, led and published by the Heritage Foundation. Project 2025 priorities include centralizing election authority under partisan state officials, imposing restrictive voter ID requirements without adequate accessibility provisions, and limiting early voting options in urban areas. According to the Brennan Center for Justice, these combined efforts could disenfranchise millions of eligible voters, with communities of color bearing the heaviest burden.

This current assault on voting rights did not emerge suddenly. Between 2021 and 2022 alone, at least 18 states passed a total of 34 laws restricting access to voting (Brennan Center for Justice, 2022). The Supreme Court's 2013 *Shelby County v. Holder* decision gutted key VRA provisions, eliminating preclearance requirements that had previously restrained discriminatory practices. The impact was swift and severe: between 2012 and 2018, jurisdictions previously covered by the VRA's preclearance requirements closed 1,688 polling places (Leadership Conference Education Fund, 2019).

The most consequential blow came in 2026. On April 29 of that year, in *Louisiana v. Callais*, a 6–3 Supreme Court severely weakened Section 2 of the Voting Rights Act (the provision that bars voting practices that dilute the power of voters of color). The Court struck down a Louisiana congressional map that, after years of litigation, had finally produced a second majority-Black district and sent two Black Louisianians to Congress for the first time in the state's history. Writing for the majority, Justice Alito called that district an unconstitutional racial gerrymander and, in the same stroke, reworked the forty-year-old framework from *Thornburg v. Gingles* (1986) that had governed vote-dilution claims. A challenger must now show evidence supporting a "strong inference" that a state intentionally drew its districts to give minority voters less opportunity because of their race, while the Court instructed that historical discrimination and the present-day "effects of societal discrimination" be given far less weight (Brennan Center for Justice, 2026). In dissent, Justice Kagan warned that the ruling renders Section 2 "all but a dead letter." Justice Thomas, joined by Justice Gorsuch, went further still, arguing that Section 2 should not apply to redistricting at all (a signal of where this Court may be heading).

Let me be precise about what this decision did and did not do, because precision is itself a form of resistance. The Court did not erase the Voting Rights Act. The VRA still exists, and Section 2 still stands on the books. What the Court did was strip away the enforcement teeth (the practical standard that allowed everyday people to prove discrimination and win), leaving the right intact in name while gutting the remedy in fact. That distinction matters, because it tells us exactly what the work now is: we fight to restore the VRA's full force AND we build what comes next, at the same time. This is the heart of what I call "Block and Build." We block the immediate harm (the new wave of discriminatory maps and the gutting of our legal tools) while we build the durable democratic architecture this Black Paper lays out. Neither alone is sufficient. To only defend a weakened law is to manage our own decline. To only dream of a new system while the old protections fall is to surrender the ground our ancestors bled for. We must do both.

These attacks are not random or isolated incidents. They reflect a coherent strategy to maintain power by limiting who can participate in our democracy. The stark truth is that some political actors have calculated they cannot win in a truly representative system, so they have chosen to restrict access to the system rather than broaden their appeal. This calculus is fundamentally at odds with democratic principles and with the arc of American history, which—despite setbacks and resistance—has bent toward greater inclusion, not less.

Citizens as Architects: Reimagining Our Democracy

To protect our democracy, we must approach this struggle not merely as citizens defending existing rights, but also as architects and founders of a new democratic framework. A framework where all people are truly equal and free—not just in lofty rhetoric but in the practical mechanics of civic participation.

The original architects of the Constitution created a system with profound limitations and contradictions. They established a democratic republic that excluded most of its inhabitants from meaningful participation. Women, enslaved people, Native Americans, and those without property were denied the ballot and thus denied full citizenship. Even as we acknowledge their vision, we must transcend their limitations through deliberate, principled redesign.

Today, we are called to be the master builders of a more perfect union—one that fulfills the promise of democracy in ways the original framers could not imagine. True architects don't simply maintain existing structures—they envision and create spaces that better serve human needs as well as those of our planet. Our democracy requires the same visionary redesign to ensure that the government reflects the will of *all* the people.

Vision 2100: The Blueprint for Democratic Renewal

As architects of democracy, we must approach this moment in the Civil Rights movement with both a detailed blueprint and a grand vision. Just as those seeking to undermine democracy have created "Project 2025," we must pursue 2100 Voting Vision for the Future (Vision 2100)—a comprehensive, multigenerational blueprint for protecting and expanding voting rights for generations to come by the year 2100. 2100 sounds like a faraway date from a futuristic sci-fi movie, but the truth is that we are less than 75 years from the dawn of a new century.

The reality we must confront is that it is no longer appealing to Black voters to engage in a cycle of voting that repeatedly yields inadequate results.

The promise of democracy rings hollow when communities see their ballot power diminished through systematic barriers, observe elected officials fail to deliver meaningful change, or witness courts enact partisan political agendas. Vision 2100 must present new and innovative solutions that give people a greater sense of security in free and fair voting. It must describe solutions that translate electoral participation into tangible progress for communities historically left behind.

Unlike short-sighted power grabs, our vision stretches across generations, building democratic institutions that will endure. Vision 2100 represents our commitment to creating voting systems that are accessible, secure, and responsive to all Americans—particularly those communities whose voices have been historically marginalized. We must be far more innovative and exploratory in designing systems that achieve a fully representative government—one that truly reflects the diversity and needs of our entire population.

For several years, I have explored establishing a Department of Democracy—a quasi-governmental independent entity similar to the Federal Reserve to ensure elected officials cannot easily dismantle or ignore citizens' voting rights. Initially conceptualized as a cabinet-level department like Homeland Security, I now believe it should operate with greater independence from the executive branch to insulate it from partisan manipulation across changing administrations. This department would serve as a guardian of democratic participation, focused solely on maximizing citizen engagement in our democratic processes. It would have the authority to set minimum standards for ballot access, oversee redistricting to prevent partisan gerrymandering, and ensure that every eligible voter can exercise their constitutional right without equitable barriers—much as building codes ensure that structures are sound and accessible to all. Structural independence provides institutional protection for voting rights that transcends political cycles and ensures democratic processes remain responsive to all Americans, regardless of which party holds power.

Our 2100 Vision must also include these essential design elements:

1 **Structural Reforms**: We must implement automatic and same-day voter registration, ranked-choice voting, and universal voting, and also eliminate the Electoral College. These are systems that expand citizens' opportunities to participate rather than restrict them. In a true democracy, each citizen can vote for their elected leader; however, in the United States, voters cast a vote for presidential electors who then vote on behalf of individual citizens. In some states, members of the Electoral College are expected to vote in the same way that the majority of voters in their state voted. This expectation is not shared across states, however. Members of the Electoral College are elected by political parties or other groups in each state.

   Eliminating the Electoral College requires a constitutional amendment—approval from two-thirds of both houses of Congress and ratification by three-fourths of state legislatures—but this should not deter our pursuit of this essential reform. Our strategy must be multi-faceted: building broad public education about the Electoral College's anti-democratic impacts, advocating for the National Popular Vote Interstate Compact as an interim measure, and developing the deep cross-partisan coalition necessary for eventual constitutional change. Though the path is challenging, constitutional amendments have succeeded 27 times when the moral case was clear, and the public will was strong. These are not radical proposals; they are practical solutions already working in various jurisdictions, proving their effectiveness in creating more representative outcomes.

2 **Universal Civic Duty Voting**: As a cornerstone of our Vision 2100, we must advance toward universal civic duty voting. Universal voting is a transformative reform successfully practiced in over 20 democracies worldwide. While we support incremental reforms like automatic and same-day registration as critical stepping stones, universal voting represents our ultimate democratic destination. This approach treats voting as a civic responsibility similar to jury duty, making participation the default for eligible citizens while providing appropriate accommodations for those who cannot participate. Research shows this would dramatically increase representation across all demographic groups, reduce polarization, neutralize voter suppression tactics, and fundamentally alter campaign dynamics to focus on substantive issues rather than base mobilization. Implementation would be a gradual process—starting with local pilots and advancing to state and

federal adoption—and employing modest compliance incentives rather than punitive measures. The pioneering work of Miles Rapoport, who introduced this concept to me years ago and continues to lead national efforts through initiatives like "100% Democracy," offers a comprehensive roadmap for this transition (Rapoport, 2022). By establishing voting as both a right and a responsibility, we create a democracy where the breadth of participation matters as much as the freedom to participate. This process can ensure elected officials are responsive to the full spectrum of the American electorate rather than narrow partisan interests.

3 **Local Engagement**: We must secure representation on local election boards and among election officials, poll workers, and governing bodies in charge of elections. This democracy machinery operates in our counties and municipalities, and control of these processes determines whose votes count and whose are suppressed.
4 **Liberation Summer**: We need to create community circles, gatherings, and Saturday schools to talk about power, voting rights, and our vision for the future. Just as freedom schools educated citizens during the Civil Rights Movement in the 1950s and 1960s, these spaces for political education will build the collective consciousness needed for sustained activism.
5 **Judicial Reform**: Legal scholars suggest expanding the Supreme Court to force coalition politics instead of dominance by either party. Our judiciary must reflect our diverse population and protect fundamental rights rather than enabling their erosion. Additionally, it may be time for ethics standards to prevent Judges from legislating partisan political agendas.
6 **Full Representation**: Grant statehood to the District of Columbia, Puerto Rico, and the United States Virgin Islands to ensure all Americans have equal representation in our democracy. The denial of full political rights to millions of American citizens in these territories is a stain on our democratic credentials.
7 **Southern Strategy**: The United States South has historically been both the epicenter of voting rights struggles and a laboratory for democratic innovation. As I've previously argued, "As goes the South, so goes the nation" (Brown, 2020a, 2020b). Targeted investment in southern organizing, infrastructure, and leadership development will be essential to any national voting rights strategy, creating models that can be replicated nationwide. What followed bore this out, and in the South first. The decision triggered a wave of mid-decade redistricting across the region. Florida enacted new maps the same day the ruling came down. Within days, Tennessee drew and passed a map that erased its only majority-minority House district (the Memphis-based seat). South Carolina's governor ordered a special session to redraw its lines. And Alabama (whose maps a federal court had replaced under *Allen v. Milligan*, the 2023 ruling that ordered the state to draw two majority-Black districts) moved to undo that remedy: after the legislature passed a map removing the second Black-opportunity district and a

three-judge panel blocked it as intentionally discriminatory, the Supreme Court intervened in June 2026 to let the state use it anyway. The same Court that ordered Alabama to draw fair maps in 2023 cleared the path to dismantle them three years later. This is not abstract, and it is not behind us. It unfolded in the very states where this work is rooted, which is precisely why the South cannot be an afterthought in any serious democratic strategy. As goes the South, so goes the nation (Brennan Center for Justice, 2026).

8 **Economic Democracy**: Voting rights cannot be separated from economic justice. We must explore frameworks that connect political representation with economic opportunity, recognizing that political rights remain vulnerable to coercion and suppression without economic security.

Entering the Third Reconstruction

Bishop William Barber calls our current moment the "Third Reconstruction"—a time to reassess and execute a hard reset as we think about the next phase of our movement. Just as the First Reconstruction following the Civil War and the Second Reconstruction of the Civil Rights Movement transformed American democracy, this Third Reconstruction calls for us to be unyielding in our demand for full civic participation.

Barber's Third Reconstruction framework offers a powerful tool for understanding this period, characterized by "moral fusion politics"—coalition-building across lines of race, religion, and class that addresses interlocking injustices, including voting rights, poverty, healthcare, and environmental justice (Barber, 2016). The strength of this approach is that it connects voting rights to the broader struggle for human dignity and social justice. The recognition of this connection is important because these issues cannot be effectively addressed in isolation.

We must not allow those who govern to unilaterally dictate policies by disenfranchising millions of voters of color, young voters, and poor and working-class voters. We must treat voting rights as the central right that impacts how we make public policy to protect the democratic potential of the United States. Without equal access to the ballot, we cannot effectively address climate change, economic inequality, healthcare, education, or any other pressing issue.

The voting rights movement cannot be about protecting or preserving power for the two major parties. Instead, it must prioritize citizens' participation and the protection of voting rights. Our democratic systems need complete reformation—not to benefit political parties but to ensure the government truly represents the people.

Why This Moment Demands Action

Critics suggest that fighting for voting rights under an administration perceived as hostile to such efforts is futile. I fundamentally reject this perspective. The fight for voting rights cannot be conditional on favorable political winds. Rather, our commitment to democratic principles must be strongest during the most challenging times.

Dr. King understood that the ballot is not merely about political participation; it represents full citizenship and human dignity. "So long as I do not firmly and irrevocably possess the right to vote, I do not possess myself. I cannot make up my mind—it is made up for me." He further emphasized that it is "immoral to make decisions and not include or allow input by the people that the laws impact" (King, 1963).

History teaches that power is never voluntarily surrendered. Frederick Douglass reminded us that power concedes nothing without a demand. Those benefiting from the current system of restricted voting have little incentive to reform it. Change must come from mobilized citizens who understand that democracy is not a spectator sport but a participatory covenant requiring our active engagement.

Conclusion: Building a Democracy Worthy of Our Highest Ideals

The story of voting rights in America has never been a straight line toward progress. Each advance has faced backlash, and each victory has required vigilance to maintain the progress made. As architects of democracy, we understand that construction is never truly complete. Sound structures require maintenance, renovation, and sometimes fundamental redesign as needs evolve.

Voting rights form the essential foundation of a healthy democracy. Without them, all other rights become vulnerable to erosion. The current moment demands that we approach voting rights not just as advocates, but as visionary architects drawing up plans for a more perfect structure of governance. Governance that can withstand the storms of reactionary backlash while creating space for all citizens to participate fully.

The Third Reconstruction offers immense challenges **and** remarkable opportunities for democratic redesign. By organizing at every level and implementing innovative reforms like a Department of Democracy, we can build undisputed power. Vision 2100 must address sophisticated attacks on voting rights while laying the groundwork for future generations.

As architects of a renewed democratic system that fulfills the promise of equality and freedom, we have a profound responsibility. We must reimagine our democracy not as a finished product but as an evolving work in progress requiring our constant attention and skilled craftsmanship. The struggles of the past were not merely about accessing the existing system, but about transforming it into something more just and inclusive. Our task today is no different.

The future has a past. Let us honor and build on that past by designing and constructing a future worthy of those who struggled before us. Their dreams of full democracy remain our blueprint, but our hands must now lay brick upon brick. The tools and materials have been passed to us. Let us build with wisdom and vision, knowing that we are not merely maintaining history—we are creating new democratic architecture where all people can finally be equal and free.

Call to Action

The Vision 2100 Blueprint described in this Black Paper demands more than intellectual agreement. It requires committed action from citizens, organizations, and institutions across America. We call on readers to:

- **Organize Locally**:
  - Join or form voting rights coalitions in your community.
  - Run for positions on local election boards and commissions.
  - Monitor voter roll purges and polling place changes in your district.
  - Create neighborhood democracy teams to coordinate local actions.
- **Educate Constantly**:
  - Establish Liberation Summer schools in your community (leverage the Children's Defense Fund to support this critical work).
  - Host regular discussions on voting rights history and current challenges.
  - Develop curriculum connecting voting rights to other social justice issues.
  - Conduct "know your voting rights" workshops in underserved communities.
  - Partner with schools to enhance civic education programs.
- **Challenge Legally**:
  - Support litigation against discriminatory voting practices.
  - Document and report voting rights violations to civil rights organizations.
  - Volunteer as poll monitors and election observers.

- Advocate for greater transparency in election administration.
- Build relationships with voting rights legal advocacy groups.

- **Register and Mobilize Voters**:
  - Conduct community-based voter registration campaigns.
  - Develop robust "get-out-the-vote" strategies for historically marginalized communities.
  - Create transportation networks to polling locations.
  - Assist voters in navigating complex registration requirements.
  - Build year-round voter engagement beyond election cycles.

- **Reform Policy**:
  - Advocate for the structural reforms outlined in Vision 2100.
  - Draft model legislation for voting rights expansion.
  - Meet with elected officials to prioritize voting rights.
  - Testify at legislative hearings on election reform.
  - Create scorecards to track officials' voting rights records.

- **Build Cross-Movement Solidarity**:
  - Connect voting rights work with economic justice initiatives.
  - Form coalitions between housing, healthcare, and environmental movements.
  - Develop shared policy platforms across social justice organizations.
  - Host joint events highlighting intersectional approaches.
  - Create spaces for cross-movement strategy development.

- **Co-Create Democratic Futures**:
  - Organize community-led visioning sessions in neighborhoods and faith communities.
  - Host "Democracy Design Labs," bringing together diverse generational voices.
  - Document community visions through accessible media (videos, artwork, writing).
  - Implement small-scale participatory democracy experiments in local organizations.
  - Develop concrete proposals for voting systems that deliver tangible results.

This last call to action encourages people to move beyond defending existing democratic structures to actively envisioning and prototyping more responsive, representative systems. It recognizes that collective imagination is a crucial component of democratic evolution and provides concrete ways for communities to engage in this visioning process right now.

The time for half-measures and incremental thinking has passed. As Dr. King reminded us, "We are now faced with the fact that tomorrow is today. We are confronted with the fierce urgency of now" (King, 1963).

Let us answer the urgency of this call with courage, creativity, and unwavering commitment to becoming true architects of democracy.

Black Voters Matter: A Living Laboratory for Democratic Architecture

The work outlined in this Black Paper is not theoretical—it is already being practiced and refined by organizations across the country. Black Voters Matter (BVM) stands as a powerful example of the principles of Vision 2100 in action, demonstrating what becomes possible when communities are treated as architects of their own democratic futures rather than passive recipients of political mobilization.

Founded in 2016, Black Voters Matter embodies the core conviction that democracy requires attention not just on election day, but on the 364 days in between elections. This commitment to year-round organizing reflects this Black Paper's emphasis on sustained civic engagement rather than transactional electoral politics. BVM's five core beliefs align directly with the Vision 2100 framework: recognizing that Black voters matter everywhere, including in the rural counties and smaller cities often ignored by traditional political infrastructure; utilizing authentic messaging that speaks to community issues and affirms humanity; and investing in the leadership of Black women whose talent and commitment have proven essential to democratic progress.

The organization's approach exemplifies the Southern Strategy articulated in this Black Paper. Operating across more than 25 states with a particular focus on the South, BVM partners with grassroots activists already established in local communities, providing the financial support, training, and infrastructure needed to build sustainable power. Their iconic bus tours—carrying the message that change is possible to communities long overlooked—serve as mobile democracy centers, connecting voters to resources while building networks of local leadership.

Through the BVM Capacity Building Institute, the organization provides the kind of structural support that transforms isolated efforts into coordinated movements. This capacity-building work prepares local organizers, develops grassroots leaders, and creates the connective tissue between community-based organizations—precisely the kind of infrastructure needed to implement the Liberation Summer schools and local engagement strategies outlined in this Black Paper's call to action.

Black Voters Matter demonstrates that the architecture of democracy is not built through top-down mandates but through patient investment in local leadership, authentic community relationships, and a commitment to the long work of power-building. Their model proves that when communities are given resources, training, and genuine partnership, they become the most effective architects of their own democratic participation.

For those seeking to engage in the vital work of democratic renewal, Black Voters Matter offers pathways for partnership, support, and collaboration. Learn more about their work and how to get involved at blackvoters matterfund.org.

Notes

1 Project 2025 is a federal policy agenda and blueprint for a radical restructuring of the executive branch authored and published by current administration officials in partnership with The Heritage Foundation, a longstanding conservative think tank that opposes abortion and reproductive rights, LGBTQ rights, immigrants' rights, and racial equity. Project 2025's largest publication, *Mandate For Leadership*, is a 920-page manual for reorganizing the entire federal government agency by agency to serve a conservative agenda.

References

Barber, W. J. (2016). *The Third Reconstruction: Moral Mondays, Fusion Politics, and the Rise of a New Justice Movement*. Beacon Press.

Bernini, A., Facchini, G., Frattini, T., & Tabellini, M. (2023). *Coverage, Representation, and Mobilization: The Effect of the Voting Rights Act on Southern Politics*. Working Paper.

Brennan Center for Justice. (2022). *Voting Laws Roundup 2022*. https://www.brennancenter.org/our-work/research-reports/louisiana-v-callais

Brennan Center for Justice. (2026). *Louisiana v. Callais*. https://www.brennancenter.org/our-work/research-reports/louisiana-v-callais

Brown, L. (2020a). The Playboy Symposium: As Goes the South. *Playboy Magazine*. https://latoshabrown.com/news/the-playboy-symposium-as-goes-the-south/

Brown, L. (2020b, August 6). The Voting Rights Act Was Signed 55 Years Ago. Black Women Led the Movement Then, Too. *Elle*. https://www.elle.com/culture/career-politics/a33635576/voting-rights-act-voter-suppression/

Cascio, E. U., & Washington, E. (2014). Valuing the Vote: The Redistribution of Voting Rights and State Funds Following the Voting Rights Act of 1965. *The Quarterly Journal of Economics, 129*(1), 379–433.

Equal Justice Initiative. (2017). *Lynching in America: Confronting the Legacy of Racial Terror*. Equal Justice Initiative. https://eji.org/reports/lynching-in-america/?utm_source=google_cpc&utm_medium=ad_grant&utm_campaign=cbc_ggrant_racial_justice&gad_source=1&gad_campaignid=11133553173&gbraid=0AAAAAC9S6zfQ2M8LHhEdKsEI872NppTxm&gclid=CjwKCAjw0o3SBhBVEiwAh28-jc0ejTEGZRPKBY8kiVNQhRBcVBZrpKXcilIVPVPDZE5czJAum_cVdRoCd0EQAvD_BwE

King, M. L., Jr. (1963). Letter from Birmingham Jail. In J. M. Washington (Ed.), *A Testament of Hope: The Essential Writings and Speeches of Martin Luther King, Jr.* (pp. 289–302). HarperCollins.

Leadership Conference Education Fund. (2019). *Democracy Diverted: Polling Place Closures and the Right to Vote. Leadership Conference on Civil and Human Rights. https://civilrights.org/democracy-diverted/*

Rapoport, M. (2022). Miles Rapoport on How We Can Achieve Universal Voting [Interview]. *Democracy Paradox*. https://democracyparadox.com/2022/03/29/miles-rapoport-on-how-we-can-achieve-universal-voting/

U.S. Commission on Civil Rights. (1965). *Voting in Mississippi*. U.S. Commission on Civil Rights. https://www.usccr.gov/files/pubs/msdelta/ch3.htm

Section II

Economic Justice

This section examines the multifaceted struggle for Black economic liberation through four interconnected dimensions of economic empowerment: labor organizing, systemic economic transformation, tax equity, and entrepreneurial ownership. Together, these Black Papers articulate a comprehensive vision for dismantling the structural barriers that have sustained the racial wealth gap and building pathways toward genuine economic justice for Black Americans.

"Solidarity in Action: How Black Workers and Unions Are Building Economic Justice" challenges the narrative that economic security flows naturally from individual effort alone, instead positioning collective bargaining as essential resistance against racialized employer power and labor market discrimination. Drawing on the historical legacy from the Brotherhood of Sleeping Car Porters to contemporary organizing campaigns, this Black Paper demonstrates how unions serve as critical counterweights to exploitation in a stratified economy. When Black workers unionize, the data is unequivocal: they earn 20% more than their non-union counterparts, with 71% gaining employer-provided health insurance compared to just 47% without union representation. The racial wealth divide is cut in half in union households. This analysis argues that inclusive solidarity across racial lines represents not merely a moral imperative but a strategic necessity for building worker power capable of challenging concentrations of wealth and advancing democracy itself.

"Building an Economy That Works for Us: The Black Economic Vision" moves beyond critique to articulate an affirmative framework for economic transformation rooted in Black communities' lived experiences and aspirations. This Black Paper recognizes that the current economic system—characterized by extractive capitalism, predatory financial practices, and structural unemployment—was designed to concentrate wealth and power in ways that systematically exclude Black Americans. The Black Economic Vision challenges this paradigm by centering community ownership, cooperative economics, democratic workplaces, and local wealth building. It examines models ranging from community land trusts that prevent displacement to worker cooperatives that democratize production, demonstrating how

DOI: 10.4324/9781003752646-5

alternative economic structures can create resilience against exploitation while building collective prosperity. This vision extends beyond individual mobility to imagine fundamental reorganization of economic relationships toward equity, sustainability, and shared abundance.

"The Power of Ownership: How Black Entrepreneurship Builds Economic Freedom and Community Wealth" examines business ownership as a critical pathway for wealth accumulation and community empowerment in the face of persistent employment discrimination and wage gaps. While Black entrepreneurs face formidable barriers—receiving 50% less funding when approved for loans and less than 0.5% of venture capital despite comprising 13.7% of the population—research shows that Black business owners possess 12 times the wealth of non-business-owning Black Americans. This Black Paper traces entrepreneurship's role from Reconstruction-era mutual aid societies through contemporary social enterprises, demonstrating how ownership creates not only individual wealth but community anchors that generate local employment, circulate resources, and build collective economic resilience. If Black-owned employer businesses matched population share, an additional 757,000 businesses could emerge, creating 6.3 million jobs and generating $824 billion in revenue. The analysis presents entrepreneurship not as an escape from structural inequality but as one essential component of a comprehensive economic justice strategy, requiring supportive ecosystems including capital access, technical assistance, procurement reform, and succession planning to transform business ownership into sustained generational wealth.

Together, these Black Papers reject the false choice between individual advancement and collective transformation, instead demonstrating how labor organizing, systemic reform, equitable taxation, and business ownership must work in concert to achieve economic justice. They challenge readers to recognize that closing the racial wealth divide requires not incremental adjustments but fundamental restructuring of economic relationships—from how work is organized and compensated to how wealth is taxed and transferred, from who controls capital to who owns the means of production. This section articulates an expansive vision of economic justice that encompasses both immediate material needs and long-term wealth building, both workplace dignity and entrepreneurial autonomy, and both individual empowerment and collective liberation.

Chapter 3

Solidarity in Action

How Black Workers and Unions Are Building Economic Justice

*Fred Redmond**

Why Should You Care About Unions?

Think about your workplace. Do you have healthcare? Paid time off? A fair wage? Safety protections? If you do, chances are unions helped make that happen—even if you are not in one. For Black workers, unions have been game-changers. When Black workers join a union, they typically earn 13.2% more than non-union Black workers doing the same job (CEPR, 2025). That's money for buying a home, sending kids to college, or building savings. This Black Paper (Paper) explains why unions matter for Black workers and how inclusive solidarity—people of all backgrounds standing together—creates power that benefits everyone.

Terms to Know

Collective Bargaining: A process where workers negotiate as a group with employers over wages, benefits, and working conditions.

Union Advantage: The higher wages and better benefits that union workers receive compared to similar non-union workers.

Occupational Segregation: The concentration of workers of certain races/ethnicities or genders into specific jobs or industries, often those with lower pay and fewer benefits.

Inclusive Solidarity: When workers of all races/ethnicities, genders, and backgrounds stand together for mutual benefit rather than being divided.

Labor Market Discrimination: When employers treat workers differently based on race/ethnicity, gender, or other characteristics rather than their qualifications or job performance.

* Supported by braintrust authors: Ashley C. Kenneth and Kelcey P. Morrow

DOI: 10.4324/9781003752646-6

Executive Summary

This Black Paper (Paper) examines the critical relationship between Black workers and labor unions as pathways to economic justice and inclusive solidarity. It argues that unions serve as essential counterweights to discriminatory employment practices in a labor market historically shaped by racial hierarchy. The Paper demonstrates how collective bargaining helps reduce workplace discrimination, narrows racial wage gaps, and provides Black workers greater access to benefits and protections.

Historical analysis reveals Black Americans' dual struggle for civil rights and economic justice, from the Brotherhood of Sleeping Car Porters to the March on Washington for Jobs and Freedom. While acknowledging unions' mixed history with racial inclusion, this Paper highlights today's labor movement's commitment to inclusive solidarity as a moral and strategic necessity.

This Black Paper concludes that unions are critical for addressing economic inequality and strengthening democracy. By building worker power across racial lines, unions help create a more equitable economy that benefits all workers, with particularly significant advantages for Black workers. As America faces unprecedented inequality and threats to democratic institutions, inclusive solidarity through unions offers a powerful response to division and exploitation.

Introduction

Solidarity and collective bargaining are not just economic mechanisms or procedural tools. They are means of resistance against the arbitrary and racialized whims of employer power and how Black and marginalized workers assert agency in an economy structured by racial hierarchy and capital accumulation. In an unequal labor market shaped by historic and ongoing discrimination, unions serve as counterweight–a means to advance racial and economic justice.

Black workers have long understood that civil and economic rights are linked. Pursuing racial justice has always included demands for economic restructuring. The collective action of workers at the Pullman Company, many of whom were formerly enslaved men, reshaped an exploitative relationship and gave power to the workers, resulting in higher wages, better hours, and better working conditions. Unions themselves have a checkered history. In the early 20th century, many unions excluded Black workers, reinforcing racial hierarchy and leaving behind the full promise of worker solidarity. However, the unions of the early 20th century are not the unions of today. Today, unions provide a way to expand economic rights and reverse attacks on democracy. The call to action is to have unions meet the moment by being grounded in the promise of inclusive solidarity, employing workers, and advancing equality and inclusion.

As the United States faces unprecedented levels of inequality and the consolidation of wealth, the only solution for working people is inclusive solidarity through unions. An inclusive solidarity that encompasses all workers has the potential to build a strong and more just foundation of economic opportunity, and can structurally mitigate the politics of division that enable the hoarding of resources and wealth.

This Paper describes how labor market discrimination is a key mechanism to exploit and divide workers, and that unions and collective bargaining can mitigate the negative impacts of extractive capitalism while building a more just and inclusive economy.

Discrimination in the Labor Market as Design, Not Defect

Racial discrimination in employment is a feature, not a bug, of our extractive economic system. Consider the following:

- Hiring Discrimination: A substantial portion of Black workers (41%) report experiencing racial discrimination during the hiring process (Pew Research Center, 2023).
- Callback Gap: Controlled experiments consistently show that Black applicants are significantly less likely to receive a job callback than similarly qualified white applicants (Abel & Burger, 2023; Pager & Western, 2010).
- Occupational Segregation: Employment discrimination leads to occupational segregation, pushing Black workers into roles and industries with lower pay, fewer benefits, and fewer advancement opportunities (National Employment Law Project, 2024).

- Limited Mobility: The overrepresentation of Black workers in lower-paid positions restricts economic mobility and opportunities for long-term wealth building (National Fund for Workforce Solutions, 2022).
- Wage, Gender Gap: The impacts of employment discrimination are severe for Black women, who earn only 60 cents for every dollar earned by a white, non-Hispanic man (Center for American Progress, 2022).

Just as Black workers face discrimination in hiring, so too is discrimination apparent in unemployment statistics. Black workers are historically more likely to be unemployed than white workers. The Black unemployment rate rose to 7.5% in 2025, compared to 3.7% for white workers (DePillis, 2025). While this gap has narrowed since the Great Resignation, Black unemployment remains higher even when accounting for educational and skills differences.

Discrimination perpetuates racial subordination in the labor market. Its generational impacts can be profound, entrenching inequality in access to wages and benefits, and perpetuating generational wealth gaps. Discrimination also maintains an economic structure that benefits employers and the capital class while harming workers.

Racial stratification benefits employers through three reinforcing mechanisms. First, it allows employers to pay workers less, thus extracting more profit from those workers' labor. While the wage suppression is most explicit in the low wages paid to Black workers, having an exploited class of workers drives down all wages. Second, racial scapegoating breaks solidarity and divides the workforce to prevent collective action, shifting blame from corporate power and employers to vulnerable colleagues. Without solidarity, as unionization rates have declined, the wages of all workers are depressed. Finally, labor market discrimination creates precarity for workers of color, deepening employer control when there are no or few alternative employment options. These dynamics are not accidents but are instead core to a labor market designed to preserve the inequality of power between employers and workers, and which weaponizes race to do so.

What This Means For You

When employers can discriminate, everyone loses.

Wage discrimination represents a significant loss of wealth, preventing families from meeting basic needs and building future security.

- The wage gap results in an average annual loss of nearly $15,000 for women overall (National Partnership for Women & Families, 2025a, 2025b).
- Over a 40-year career, women overall lose an average of $400,000 to $694,000, though specific losses vary significantly by state (ranging to over $907,000) in Utah (NWLC, 2025a; American Association of University Women [AAUW], 2025).
- Black women stand to lose $1,019,200 over a 40-year career compared to white, non-Hispanic men (NWLC, 2025b; American Association of University Women [AAUW], 2025).
  - Latina women experience the highest lifetime loss at $1,282,800 (roughly 1.3 million) (NWLC, 2025b, 2025; American Association of University Women [AAUW], 2025).
- Eliminating this gap would reduce poverty for working women by more than 40%, providing additional money for rent, mortgage, and retirement savings (IWPR, 2025; NWLC, 2025b).

When specific communities of workers are underpaid, it causes pressure on overall wages and stunts national prosperity.

- Closing the gender gap could add approximately $4.3 trillion to the United States economy by increasing consumer spending and labor participation (based on a McKinsey Global Institute analysis updated in 2025). The potential increase in global GDP from closing the gap is estimated at up to 20%.
- Due to the persistent wage gap, women in the United States collectively lose nearly $2 trillion in wages every year (National Partnership for Women & Families, 2025a).
- Pay discrimination and workplace inequality incentivize skilled workers, primarily women, to leave the workforce or reduce hours. This results in lower overall economic productivity, reduced retention for businesses, and a decline in tax revenue.

These gaps persist across virtually all industries and occupations. These aren't just statistics—they represent people and families struggling to pay bills, build savings, afford rent, or buy homes. When one group of workers can be paid less, it puts downward pressure on everyone's wages.

The Impact of Unions

Unions break this pattern. Collective bargaining is the most powerful opposing force to employers' ability to discriminate and exploit employees. Through collective bargaining and negotiating a labor contract, unions can institutionalize equity at the job site by standardizing pay, enforcing fair hiring and firing rules, and ensuring equal access to benefits. The bargaining process promotes equity, transparency, and workplace democracy, benefiting all workers.

The Union Advantage in Real Numbers

When Black workers join unions, their lives change in measurable ways (Bucknor et al., 2016):

- Black workers represented by a union are paid on average 12.6 to 13.2% more in hourly wages than their nonunionized Black peers, which can amount to over $3.73 more per hour (CEPR, 2025; Economic Policy Institute [EPI], 2025).
- Unionized Black workers are 15.7% to 17.2% more likely to have employer-provided health insurance than non-unionized Black workers (CEPR, 2025).

- Union representation is associated with a 53.7% and 54.8% increase in access to employer-sponsored retirement plans (CEPR, 2025; EPI, 2025).

The racial wealth gap is cut in half in union households. For a typical Black worker, these differences mean thousands of extra dollars every year, plus security for their family's healthcare and retirement. This shows how unions do not just discuss equality—they create it through contracts that apply equally to everyone.

A large body of research demonstrates that unions shrink economic disparities between Black and white workers. Unions lead to a pay premium for all workers, called the "union advantage," but have the most significant impact on the wages of workers of color. Black and Hispanic workers receive a larger wage premium from union membership than their white counterparts, which serves as a critical mechanism for narrowing racial disparities (EPI, 2023). As of 2025, Black union members enjoy a 13.2% hourly wage premium relative to non-union peers, while Hispanic workers see a significantly higher wage advantage of approximately 17.6% (Center for Economic and Research Policy [CEPR], 2025; EPI, 2023). The wage advantage demonstrates two things: first, unions can be a powerful force in equalizing pay and ensuring employers cannot discriminate when determining wages; second, it's a result of Black workers' insistence on union membership and fighting for personal opportunities within their union. Black workers have exercised their rights within the structure to build more equality.

Unionized workers also have significantly better access to benefits than non-union workers (U.S. Bureau of Labor Statistics, 2019). As of 2025, 96% of unionized workers had access to medical care benefits compared to only 69% of non-unionized workers (AFL-CIO, 2025; BLS, 2025a, 2025b). This disparity is even more pronounced in participation rates, where union members are nearly 27 percentage points more likely to be enrolled in their employer-sponsored plans (Northwest Labor Press, 2025).

Beyond healthcare, union jobs are far more likely to provide defined-benefit pensions and paid leave, which are essential for long-term economic stability (BLS, 2025a). These benefits are significant for Black workers, who are frequently crowded into low-benefit roles due to occupational segregation (EPI, 2025). By providing guaranteed sick days and vacation, unions offer a critical safety net that improves job retention and overall financial security for marginalized workers (AFL-CIO, 2025).

Unions not only equalize wages but also powerfully impact wealth. Union workers have approximately twice the wealth of non-union workers, and the racial wealth gap is cut in half in union households. Unions are, therefore, a pathway to the middle class, allowing for the accumulation of wealth that can lead to intergenerational mobility.

Unions also make the workplace fairer. They protect workers from discriminatory firing and discrimination on the job overall. When workers can be fired "at will," there is little recourse for discriminatory firing. Workers covered by a collective bargaining agreement can challenge a dismissal and have access to redress. Contracts provide a mechanism whereby all workers are treated equally, getting equal pay raises, equal benefits and procedures to grieve workplace problems, including firing.

All of this points to the overwhelming evidence that highly unionized workplaces benefit Black workers. Union jobs have provided reliable pathways to the middle class. Regardless of the sector, good union jobs in steel plants, stockyards, and the industrial Midwest have led to Black families' financial stability. Public sector jobs have also offered a pathway to middle-class stability for Black families. Because civil rights protections are stronger in the public sector and unionization decreases pay disparities between Black and white workers, the public sector provides an essential pathway to upward mobility. In some states, like Georgia, the federal workforce is 43.8% Black (nearly four times higher than the national average for Black participation in the private sector). This high concentration in public service is a key factor in Black economic stability, as federal roles often provide more competitive wages and robust benefits compared to private-sector alternatives.

The current assault on public sector jobs intentionally targets economic pathways for Black Americans. And the elimination of public sector jobs will inflict outsized harm on Black workers. By eliminating these jobs, the 47th presidential administration is weakening the government's ability to serve the people and forcing these workers to seek private sector employment. The attacks on public sector jobs could lead to lower wages, since private sector non-union Black workers earn less than those in the public sector, and further exacerbate the racial wealth divide.

Perhaps the most important FEATURE of unions is their overall impact on *inequality*. Unions ensure workers benefit as companies prosper. When unionization is low, more benefits flow to the already wealthy, increasing inequality. Up to one-third of the growth of inequality since 1980 is due to the decrease in unions and the erosion of collective bargaining (EPI, 2021a; Western & Rosenfeld, 2011). This impact is comparable to the widening pay gap between college and high school graduates, as the loss of union "spillover effects" has depressed wages for both union and non-union workers alike (EPI, 2021a, 2021b).

When unions are powerful, they can increase wages across the board, impacting not only union jobs but also non-union ones. They reduce pay gaps between Black and white workers, between men and women, and between the wealthy and the working class. Unions provide workers with better access to health insurance and retirement plans, increasing equality across the lifespan of workers and their families.

Why does this matter? Because inequality constrains economic growth. When this happens, people cannot reach their full potential, demand is reduced, and our entire economy suffers.

Unions are not just part of the economic landscape. Unions are essential agents of democracy in the workplace and across the nation. Unions allow workers to articulate their preferences and exert their power in the workplace, gaining key concessions from capital. Unions are also essential to democratic governance. Unions focus the political power of workers and result in the advancement and defense of policies that benefit the broad interests of workers, their families, and their communities. In this moment of democratic backsliding, unions are an essential partner in revitalizing America's democracy.

Black Workers and the Labor Movement

There is a long and rich history of collective action and union organizing to achieve economic and civil rights, because one cannot be realized without the other. From A. Philip Randolph's organizing of the Pullman Porters into the Brotherhood of Sleeping Car Porters (BSCP) to the 1968 "I AM A MAN" strikes of Memphis sanitation workers who were organized and represented by the American Federation of State, County and Municipal Employees (AFSCME), even though the city of Memphis did not recognize their union, Black workers have led the charge to link racial justice with labor rights. Economic and civil rights have always been linked to Black American history through unions and solidarity.

The March on Washington for Jobs and Freedom, led by Bayard Rustin and Dr. Martin Luther King, Jr. in 1963, is a key moment in Civil Rights history. Speakers and attendees supported civil and voting rights bills, emphasizing equality and justice. The march represented a collaboration between civil rights groups, student organizations and unions allied to fight for fair wages and economic justice. Civil rights have always required economic rights, and unions are essential to operationalizing workers' power.

- Unions have not always been racially diverse, and the path of inclusion has not always been easy. Throughout the early 20th century, many unions did not welcome Black workers. In fact, labor unions were almost exclusively white. Some were actively hostile toward civil rights and integration. White workers who accepted exclusionary unionism in pursuit of relative gains sacrificed not only the economic advancement of other workers but also worker power more broadly. At the same time, anti-union individuals exploited fear among white elites of inter-racial solidarity inside labor unions and the idea of Black people organizing at all to pass anti-union laws in the 1940s and 1950s that weakened the ability of working people to stand together to improve their lives.

As civil rights progressed throughout the mid-20th century, so did unions and union rights. Unions adopted anti-discrimination goals and policies enforced in contracts through wage-setting practices. These policies have led to greater intra-firm and economy-wide equality. Today's labor movement affirmatively rejects the exclusion of the past and is actively centering inclusive solidarity as a moral and economic imperative. Those who focus only on past failings without accounting for the diversity and inclusion of today's labor movement are weaponizing that past to defeat solidarity today. We must acknowledge the failings while embracing the evolution of unions and the labor movement.

As long as labor is not in solidarity and can be divided into factions through divisive politics and the lure of relative status, capital will always have a way to hoard power. The relative gains that accrue to white workers when they do not stand in solidarity with Black workers result in them costing all workers. Short-term gains in relative status are never worth the long-term sacrifice of justice and values that promote equity.

A Path Forward: Removing Barriers to Organizing

Black people have always been leaders in organizing our communities and workplaces. Just as some labor unions in the early 20th century made racist choices to exclude Black workers, elite policymakers have put up barriers to organizing by Black workers and other workers. Dismantling these barriers will allow a full flourishing of the Black-led organizing happening today and help build a truer democratic society.

- Pass the Protecting the Right to Organize (PRO) Act to better protect working people who are organizing from threats and interference by their bosses and ensure everyone pays their fair share for union representation.
- Build pathways for Black workers, women of all races, and other historically excluded working people into building trades and labor unions through pre-apprenticeship programs and other initiatives. Protect incentives in the Inflation Reduction Act for pro-worker policies that build a stronger, more inclusive workforce.
- Stand up to the illegal attacks by the current presidential administration on the rights of working people—in the public and private sectors—to come

together in unions and collectively bargain over wages, benefits, and working conditions. Additionally, in states where it has been taken away, restore recognition of the rights of state and local public workers to come together in unions and collectively bargain.

- Strengthen and enforce workplace protections against discriminatory actions that are used to divide and weaken working people (see Building an Economy That Works for Us: The Black Economic Vision).

Conclusion: Building a Movement for the Future

This Black Paper has outlined how Black workers have been exploited by employers and the labor market, while highlighting how unions can push back and become a force for justice if they are inclusive. Our goal is to remove policy barriers to facilitate working people organizing together. Unions lead to higher wages, better working conditions, and safer workplaces, and they are working to build a stronger and more just foundation to ensure economic opportunity for all. We need a labor movement built on inclusive solidarity that promotes the long-term wellbeing of all workers. Racial justice and economic justice cannot exist without each other. We must come together as we confront new challenges in the current administration, from rolling back the right to collectively bargain to banning Diversity, Equity, and Inclusion. The labor movement is the most powerful force for working people in fighting for justice, and all workers must reap the benefits.

Call to Action

What You Can Do Today

Building worker power is not just for union organizers or policy experts—it's for everyone who believes in fairness.

Here are Concrete Steps You can Take

- Learn your rights: Visit the National Labor Relations Board (NLRB) to understand what protections you have.
- Learn about the labor policy in your state and locality, and advocate for strong worker protections.
- Connect with co-workers: Start conversations about your workplace concerns, and contact local unions to organize your workplace.
- Support union campaigns: When workers organize, show your solidarity.
- Vote for pro-worker candidates: Research elected officials' voting records on labor issues.
- Spread the word: Share this information with friends and family.

Remember, the strongest unions include everyone. When we stand together across differences of race, gender, and background, we build power that can transform workplaces and our entire economy. The choice is clear: continue with a system that divides workers and maintains inequality, or build inclusive solidarity that lifts everyone. The future of work—and our democracy—depends on which path we choose.

References

Abel, M., & Burger, R. (2023). *Employers discriminate against job applicants with Black-sounding names, study indicates*. Bowdoin College.

AFL-CIO. (2025). *Union facts: The value of collective voice*. https://aflcio.org/formaunion/collective-voice

American Association of University Women. (2025). *The not-so-simple truth: 2025 update*. https://www.aauw.org/app/uploads/2025/03/The_Simple_Truth_Gender_Pay_Gap_2025.pdf

Bucknor, C., Baker, D., Cashman, K., Mcinnis, T., Barber, A., & Ratliff, M. (2016). *CEPR Black workers, unions, and inequality acknowledgements*. Center for Economic and Policy Research. https://cepr.net/images/stories/reports/black-workers-unions-2016-08.pdf

Center for American Progress. (2022). *Occupational segregation in America*. https://www.americanprogress.org/article/occupational-segregation-in-america/

Center for Economic and Policy Research [CEPR]. (2025). *The union advantage for Black workers: Wages, benefits, and the path to economic justice*. https://cepr.net/publications/the-union-advantage-for-black-workers/

DePillis, L. (2025). Black unemployment is surging again. This time is different. *The New York Times*. https://www.nytimes.com/2025/10/12/business/economy/black-unemployment-federal-layoffs-diversity-initiatives.html
Economic Policy Institute. (2021a). *The enormous impact of eroded collective bargaining on wages*. https://www.epi.org/publication/eroded-collective-bargaining/
Economic Policy Institute. (2021b). *Racial representation in professional occupations: By the numbers*. https://www.epi.org/publication/racial-representation-prof-occ/
Economic Policy Institute. (2023). *New fact sheet shows that unions support a more equitable economy*. https://www.epi.org/press/new-fact-sheet-shows-that-unions-support-a-more-equitable-economy/
Economic Policy Institute. (2025). *Unions aren't just good for workers–they also benefit communities and democracy*. https://www.epi.org/publication/unions-arent-just-good-for-workers-they-also-benefit-communities-and-democracy/
Institute for Women's Policy Research. (2025). *IWPR's new national annual women's wage gap analysis shows second consecutive year of decline*. https://iwpr.org/iwprs-new-national-annual-womens-wage-gap-analysis-shows-second-consecutive-year-of-decline-2/
National Employment Law Project. (2024). *Occupational segregation of Black women workers in the U.S*. https://www.nelp.org/insights-research/occupational-segregation-of-black-women-workers-in-the-u-s/
National Fund for Workforce Solutions. (2022). *Racial bias in hiring practices widens the Black-white wealth disparity*. https://nationalfund.org/racial-bias-in-hiring-practices-widens-the-black-white-wealth-disparity/
National Partnership for Women & Families. (2025a). *America's women and the wage gap*. https://nationalpartnership.org/wp-content/uploads/2023/02/americas-women-and-the-wage-gap.pdf
National Partnership for Women & Families. (2025b). *The wage gap #IRL (in real life) for women of color*. https://nationalpartnership.org/wp-content/uploads/2023/02/quantifying-americas-gender-wage-gap.pdf
National Women's Law Center. (2025a). *The wage gap, state by state*. https://nwlc.org/resource/the-wage-gap-state-by-state/
National Women's Law Center. (2025b). *The lifetime wage gap by state for women overall*. https://nwlc.org/resource/the-lifetime-wage-gap-by-state-for-women-overall/
National Women's Law Center. (2025). *Latinas face a severe lifetime wage gap [Fact sheet]*. https://nwlc.org/wp-content/uploads/2025/03/EPD-FS-2025-Latina-3.18.25v3.pdf
Northwest Labor Press (2025). *Union members have superior benefits*. https://nwlaborpress.org/2025/10/union-members-have-superior-benefits/
Pager, D., & Western, B. (2010). Identifying discrimination at work: The use of field experiments. *The ANNALS of the American Academy of Political and Social Science, 628*(1), 106–121. https://pmc.ncbi.nlm.nih.gov/articles/PMC3807133/
Pew Research Center (2023). *For Labor Day, Black workers' views and experiences of work*. https://www.pewresearch.org/short-reads/2023/08/31/black-workers-views-and-experiences-in-the-us-labor-force-stand-out-in-key-ways/

U.S. Bureau of Labor Statistics. (2019). *Union workers more likely than nonunion workers to have healthcare benefits in 2019*. [News Release]. https://www.bls.gov/opub/ted/2019/union-workers-more-likely-than-nonunion-workers-to-have-healthcare-benefits-in-2019.htm

U.S. Bureau of Labor Statistics. (2025a). *Employee benefits in the United States news release*. https://www.bls.gov/news.release/archives/ebs2_09252025.htm

U.S. Bureau of Labor Statistics. (2025b). *Usual weekly earnings of wage and salary workers - Third Quarter 2025*. [News Release]. https://www.bls.gov/news.release/wkyeng.nr0.htm

Western, B., & Rosenfeld, J. (2011). Unions, norms, and the rise in U.S. wage inequality. *American Sociological Review, 76*(4), 513–537.

Chapter 4

Building an Economy That Works for Us

The Black Economic Vision

*Jessica Fulton, Jeffery T. D. Wallace Jr., Alphonso David, Lawrence "Larry" Parks, and Tim Simons**

Executive Summary

Our labor built this nation. Our ideas move culture. Our businesses keep neighborhoods alive. Our data trains the next generation of technology. We are not broken; we are not behind. **We are being blocked from maximizing our full economic potential**.

Despite being essential to America's economy, Black families face a wealth gap of 6-to-1, unemployment rates twice that of white Americans, and access to less than 2% of venture capital. These disparities didn't happen by accident—they are the direct result of policy choices that can and must be remade.

This Black Paper (Paper) is our blueprint for economic liberation. It connects our community's undeniable strengths to the specific policy changes that will remove structural barriers to Black economic success. We write with righteous rage—but also with vision.

* Supported by braintrust authors: Corena D. Wiggins and Nadia French-Graham

DOI: 10.4324/9781003752646-7

What We Demand

- **Learning**: Tuition-free community college, $5 billion in new Historically Black Colleges and Universities (HBCU) funding, expanded Pell Grants, universal broadband access;
- **Working**: $17/hour federal minimum wage, universal paid family leave, strengthened union protections, workplace anti-discrimination enforcement;
- **Lower Costs**: Eliminated sales taxes on essentials, expanded Supplemented National Assistance Program (SNAP) benefits and child care support, restored Affordable Connectivity Programs, and implemented progressive tax reform;
- **Starting Businesses**: $5 billion for Community Development Financial Institutions, equitable access to government contracts, business accelerators in Black communities;
- **Building Wealth**: Affordable homeownership through community land trusts, Baby Bonds for newborns, student debt relief, and reformed predatory banking practices.

The stakes are clear: When we unlock Black economic participation, we unleash growth and innovation that benefits everyone. This is not just about justice—it's about America reaching its full economic potential.

The time is now: Read this Paper. Share it. Demand these changes from your elected officials. Join the movement for an economy that works for all of us.

How to Use This Paper

This Black Paper is designed to be both a comprehensive policy document and a practical tool for advocacy. Here's how different readers can use it:

Community Organizers & Advocates: Each section includes specific policy demands you can present to local, state, and federal officials. Use the data and citations to support your advocacy campaigns.

Elected Officials & Policymakers: The demands in each section are actionable policies you can champion through legislation. Model language and funding levels are provided to facilitate implementation.

Educators & Students: This Paper connects historical context to current policy, making it an educational resource for understanding systemic economic barriers and solutions.

Business Leaders & Employers: The sections on work and entrepreneurship outline how you can advance equity within your organization and industry.

Individual Citizens: The Call-to-Action section provides concrete steps you can take today to support these policies and strengthen Black economic power.

The Economic Status of Black America Today

Despite decades of contribution to the American economy, Black people in the United States continue to face significant disparities. The wealth of a typical white family ($285,000) is nearly six times that of a typical Black family ($44,900) (Aladangady & Forde, 2021). Black unemployment consistently remains about twice the rate of white unemployment (Kyle K. Moore, 2025). Black-owned businesses receive less than 2% of venture capital funding annually. These disparities are not accidental—they are the documented result of deliberate policy choices, from redlining to discriminatory lending to underinvestment in Black communities. What was made by policy can be remade by policy.

The policies described in this Paper directly address the challenges facing Black households. Of the 17 most important problems polled by the Black Futures Lab Black Census, six were economic issues, four of which ranked in the top tier of concerns. These issues include low wages, schools that fail to prepare our children, a lack of affordable housing, and a lack of affordable healthcare (2023 Black Census Executive Summary, 2023). Black people are worried about the rising costs of living and low wages that are not enough to sustain themselves or their families. Black Census respondents strongly support policies outlined in this Black Paper that would make Black people more economically secure, including guaranteeing higher wages and increasing affordable housing, child care, and education.

Learning: Investing in Black Brilliance

Black learners are brilliant. Our young people create, question, build, and dream every day—even as they face barriers to success in the education system. Most Black students want to pursue post-secondary opportunities after graduating from high school. However, broken public policy leaves students facing high tuition, underfunding for the colleges that serve Black students, and outdated learning models. We must move from filtering out talent to fueling it—from seeing Black students as problems to solve to recognizing them as assets to invest in.

HBCUs produce 25% of all Black STEM (Science, Technology, Engineering & Mathematics) graduates despite receiving 30% less funding per student than predominantly white institutions (HBCUs Make America Strong: The Positive Economic Impact of Historically Black Colleges and Universities, 2022). Meanwhile, just four years after graduation, Black students owe twice as much debt for their education as white students (Scott-Clayton & Li, 2016). Educational apartheid is not just an education issue—it is an economic issue.

We Demand

- **Tuition-free Career Technical Education and Community College Programs** with clear pathways to good jobs (with family-sustaining wages and opportunities for advancement). These programs must include wraparound support services—counseling, tutoring, transportation assistance—that address the full needs of Black learners.
- **Investments in HBCUs**. HBCUs support Black leaders and communities. HBCUs account for 16% of bachelor's degrees earned by Black college

students while representing just 3% of the nation's colleges and universities (Anderson & Hatfield, 2024). Federal funding should increase by at least $5 billion annually—this specific amount addresses the documented funding gap between HBCUs and predominantly white institutions and would support infrastructure improvements, faculty recruitment, research capacity, and student support services. This investment recognizes that HBCUs are not charity cases but national assets that produce outsized returns in Black leadership, innovation, and community impact.

- **Expansion of Federal Pell Grants.** Pell grants support low-income students who might otherwise be unable to afford college. Pell grants should rise with the cost of college and be protected from inflation. Workforce Pell Grants for short-term programs passed as part of the reconciliation bill in July 2025 (H.R. 1/OBBBA). Maximum Pell Grant awards should increase to cover at least 80% of the average cost of attendance at public four-year institutions, up from the current 29%.

- **Access to broadband internet and the technical devices required for basic education.** Students need broadband and devices to learn and be competitive in the economy of the future. One in four Black teens reports being unable to do homework because they lack internet or a computer (Schaeffer, 2021). Policymakers must partner with the private sector to provide devices and home broadband for free or at low cost, treating them as essential utilities rather than luxuries—just as we once electrified rural America, we must now ensure digital equity for Black America.

- **Support paid internships, dual enrollment programs, and child care subsidies to support learners working or caring for a family.** Black students comprise nearly one in five low-income working learners (Carnavale & Smith, 2018). Over one in three Black students in community college also care for a child (Nalley & Finnie, 2025). Institutions receiving federal funding should be required to provide paid internships at minimum wage or higher, and on-campus child care centers should be expanded with federal support to serve student parents.

These investments could increase Black college completion rates, reduce student debt burden, and create a pipeline of Black STEM graduates over the next decade.

Improving Work: Fair Pay for Fair Labor

From hospital floors to construction sites, classrooms to cash registers—Black workers keep this country running. But we do not just show up to work. We show up with skills, leadership, and solutions. We are not asking to be saved. We are asking to be seen, supported, and paid fairly.

The Current Reality

Because of discrimination, occupational segregation, and other challenges, Black workers often do not reach their full potential in the workplace. On average, Black workers earn 76 cents for every dollar earned by white workers. While the Black–white wage divide has narrowed since 2019, it remains significant (Gould & deCourcy, 2024). The 47th presidential administration intends to make this worse by removing Diversity, Equity, and Inclusion (DEI) programs and eliminating workplace protections—actions that threaten decades of hard-won progress and will cost Black workers billions in lost wages ("The Trump Administration Has Made 36 Million Workers Newly Vulnerable to Discrimination and Harassment," 2025).

We Demand

- **Strengthen protections against workplace discrimination.** The 47th presidential administration began attacking workplace protections during its first month in office by eliminating worker protections and firing a Black member of the Equal Employment Opportunity Commission (EEOC). The EEOC is in charge of protecting workers and job applicants from discrimination based on race, color, religion, sex, and national origin. The EEOC's budget should be increased, and its enforcement capabilities should be expanded to include proactive audits of companies with documented discrimination patterns. State-level Fair Employment Practices Agencies (FEPAs) should receive additional federal support to investigate discrimination claims.

- **Implement Universal Paid Family and Medical Leave and Paid Sick Days.** Workers sometimes need time off to care for their loved ones, to welcome a new child, or to heal from an illness. However, over one in three Black workers cannot take time off without losing wages (Boyens et al., 2022). The FAMILY Act should be passed to provide workers with up to 12 weeks of paid leave using a progressive scale to ensure that lower-wage workers receive up to 85% of their wages, funded through a small payroll tax. All workers should receive at least 7 paid sick days annually.
- **Ensure access to good jobs (with family-sustaining wages and opportunities to advance, at a minimum)** through pre-apprenticeship programs, training programs, career technical education, and workforce development. Hard work in training programs should pay off with high-wage jobs with benefits, and not dead-end gigs with no advancement opportunities. Successful models like Project QUEST in San Antonio have shown sustained impact, with participants earning over $5,000 more annually than control groups and maintaining those gains over nine years (Roder & Elliott, 2019). This evidence-based program has demonstrated 90% completion rates, with participants entering careers in healthcare, technology, and skilled trades with living wages and advancement opportunities. Congress should allocate $2 billion annually to replicate and scale evidence-based workforce development models like Project QUEST in 100 cities with significant Black populations.

- **Strengthen protections to allow workers to unionize.** From sleeping car porters to domestic workers, Black workers have led the fight for workers' rights. Unions protect workers from discrimination, boost women's pay, and reduce pay gaps between Black and white workers (Josh Bivens et al., 2023). Unionized Black workers earn 10.8% more than non-unionized peers (Sachin, 2024). Congress should pass the Protecting the Right to Organize (PRO) Act to strengthen collective bargaining rights, ban captive audience meetings, establish meaningful penalties for union-busting, and protect workers' right to strike.
- **Prioritize Black workers and young adults** in public investments through the Workforce Innovation and Opportunity Act (WIOA) and infrastructure funding. President Joseph R. Biden sent funding to states to build infrastructure. State and local policymakers must ensure these investments benefit Black workers and business owners by implementing targeted hiring requirements (30% minimum for workers from underrepresented communities), local hire provisions within 50 miles of projects, and training partnerships with Black-led organizations. States should report quarterly on workforce diversity outcomes or risk losing federal funding.

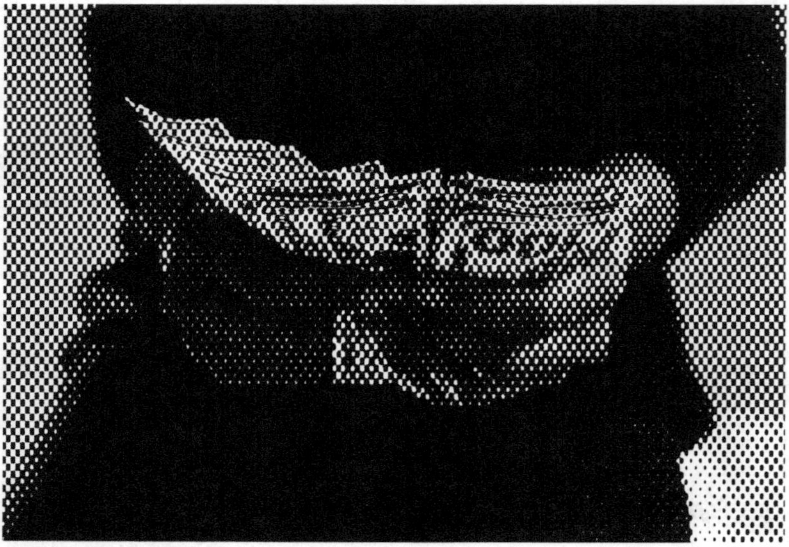

- **Increase the federal minimum wage.** Workers in 20 states can be paid as little as the federal minimum wage, which is just $7.25 per hour, a rate that has not increased since 2009 (*Minimum Wage Tracker*, n.d.). Black workers are overrepresented in minimum wage jobs, with nearly one in three (32%) of Black workers earning less than $17 per hour (Kaitlyn Henderson, 2024).

Policymakers must increase the federal minimum wage to at least $17 per hour—a level that reflects the actual cost of living and ensures full-time workers can afford necessities—and index it to inflation. Hence, wages keep pace with rising costs. This increase would directly benefit millions of Black workers and their families.

These workplace protections would reduce the Black–white wage divide, lift millions of Black workers out of poverty, and increase Black household income annually.

Lowering Costs: Making Life Affordable

Higher prices and inflation limit our buying power and prevent our households from buying what they need to thrive. In mid-2024, the United States Census Bureau found that 68% of Black households found price increases very or moderately stressful. In 2022, 65% of Black adults in the United States reported that high inflation prevented them from achieving their financial goals and aspirations (Fulton et al., 2023). While wages matter, affordability matters just as much. Black families should not have to choose between groceries and medicine, between rent and child care.

We Demand:

- **Lower prices on food and goods by decreasing sales taxes and increasing taxes on the wealthy**. Sales taxes rise as prices rise, which increases the cost of our everyday expenses. Decreasing or eliminating sales taxes on essential items like groceries, diapers, menstrual products, and over-the-counter medications helps lower-income and middle-class households afford to buy what they need (*What Happens When States Ditch Income Tax for Sales Tax?*, 2023). To compensate for the lost revenue, states can raise taxes on the wealthy and highest-income individuals through income and wealth taxes—ensuring that those with the most contribute their fair share to the public good.
- **Block Harmful Tariffs**. In 2025, the 47th President's tariffs, as predicted, increased costs and further slowed down the economy (Christopher Rugaber, 2025). Tariffs raise prices on the items American business owners buy from other countries. Business owners pass those costs along to everyday consumers. Congress should pass the Trade Review Act of 2025 to limit the president's ability to impose unilateral tariffs without Congressional approval (*Senators Cantwell & Grassley Introduce Bipartisan Bill to Reassert Congressional Trade Role | U.S. Senator Maria Cantwell of Washington*, n.d.).
- **Expand eligibility and benefits for support programs such as the Supplemental Nutrition Assistance Program (SNAP [food stamps]), the Low-Income Heat and Energy Assistance Program (LIHEAP), and Affordable Care Act subsidies, particularly in states with high Black populations**. SNAP benefits should be increased to reflect actual food costs, LIHEAP funding should double to address energy insecurity, and Affordable Care Act (ACA) subsidy eligibility should extend to families earning up to 600% of the federal poverty level in high-cost areas.

- **Lower costs for high-quality care.** The cost of child care, special needs care, and elder care is often too high for workers to pay. At the same time, the people who work to take care of children, older adults, and people with disabilities often earn too little. Black families in many states spend over 20% of their median income on child care for an infant, compared to the 7% benchmark the United States Department of Health and Human Services considers affordable. The federal government needs to support families by increasing wages for child care workers, while capping child care family costs through an expanded Child Care and Development Block Grant program.
- **Reduce the tax burden for people who can least afford to pay by increasing tax credits for low- and middle-income households.** Expand the Child Tax Credit to decrease poverty for Black children. The expansion previously lifted over 700,000 Black children out of poverty and provided monthly advance payments for parents (Burns et al., 2022). Expand the Earned Income Tax Credit for workers without children in their homes, and extend eligibility to workers up to age 65.

- **Institute affordable broadband access.** High-speed internet is necessary for workers, students, and those who need to make doctor's appointments online. Often, however, the internet is neither available nor affordable. In the Black Rural South, for example, 38% of Black residents do not have access to the internet in their homes (Harrison, 2021). In 2024, Congress allowed the Affordable Connectivity Program, which lowered the cost of home internet, to lose all its funding. Congress must restore and expand this program to ensure families have affordable access to high-speed internet. Additionally, infrastructure investments should prioritize broadband deployment in underserved Black communities, particularly in rural areas.
- **Protect Black users online.** Tech companies invade Black privacy and use Black content and data online to generate profit. Algorithms have been shown to discriminate against Black users in everything from housing to healthcare. We need strong data privacy laws and policies to ensure tech companies pay users for their data and content. The European Union's General Data Protection Regulation (GDPR) can be helpful in working to ensure that tech companies compensate users for their data and content, including by establishing data as property that users own and control. We also need robust civil rights audits of AI systems used in employment, housing, lending, and healthcare, with specific protections against facial

recognition and predictive technologies that have documented racial bias. Companies using these technologies should be required to prove they do not discriminate, rather than forcing victims to prove they were harmed.

These affordability measures can reduce household costs for Black families, lift millions of Black children out of poverty, and save Black households annually.

Starting Businesses: Fueling Black Entrepreneurship

We start businesses that solve problems, serve neighbors, and create jobs. And we do it with less money/capital, fewer connections, and more barriers than most. Black entrepreneurship is a growth engine that has been ignored, underfunded, and overregulated. But the will is there. The ideas are there. We need the capital and the contracts to match—not as charity, but as recognition of the economic power Black businesses represent.

The Current Reality

Black business owners support our communities and our economy. Black business owners own 3.5 million businesses and employ over 1.2 million workers (Facts About Small Business, 2024). However, Black businesses have trouble getting loans, affordable training, support, and contracts. The 47th presidential administration has also eliminated diversity targets for contracts, threatening to reverse decades of progress. Fewer than one in every three Black applicants receives full funding for their business as compared to 56% of white applicants (2024 Report on Employer Firms, 2024)—a disparity that cannot be explained by creditworthiness or business plans, only by discrimination.

We Demand

- **Establish business accelerators in our communities**. Provide federal funding to establish and support business accelerators that help schools, workforce investment hubs, and faith- and community-based networks support entrepreneurs in our communities. Programs like the Atlanta-based RICE Business Accelerator have shown 80% business survival rates after five years, compared to the national average of 50%—demonstrating that culturally competent support works. These accelerators should offer mentorship, access to capital, technical assistance, and connections to markets.

- **Preserve and strengthen the banks and institutions** supporting Black business owners. Traditionally, big banks and corporations offer very little support for Black business owners. Instead, Black entrepreneurs access funding through community banks, which the federal government has committed to supporting through law. The Financial CHOICE Act should be amended to strengthen Community Development Financial Institutions (CDFIs) and Minority Depository Institutions (MDIs) with at least $5 billion in additional annual funding. This investment recognizes that CDFIs and MDIs are not just lenders; they are ecosystem builders that understand the unique challenges Black businesses face.

- **Increase access to government contracts**. The federal government spends over $1 trillion annually to purchase private companies' products and services. The government awards 89% of its federal contracts and makes 94% of its federal payments to white-owned businesses (Diverse Business Government Contracting Opportunities Unequal, Untapped & Under Attack, 2025). Despite the 47th President's efforts to weaken support for Black business owners, policymakers must ensure that Black entrepreneurs have equitable access to public contracting opportunities and training through:
    - Setting and enforcing a goal of awarding 10% of federal contracts to Black-owned businesses, reflecting our proportion of the population;
    - Providing training and technical assistance to help Black businesses navigate the federal procurement process;
    - Breaking large contracts into smaller pieces that emerging businesses can bid on;
    - Requiring prime contractors to subcontract at least 15% of work to diverse suppliers;
    - Creating a transparent database tracking contract awards by race/ethnicity to ensure accountability.
- **Eliminate discriminatory lending practices**. Strengthen the Community Reinvestment Act to hold banks accountable for serving Black communities

and businesses, with specific lending targets and consequences for failure. Require lenders to collect and report small business lending data disaggregated by race/ethnicity to identify and address discrimination—making invisible bias visible. Establish an independent commission to investigate racial disparities in business lending with the power to levy significant fines and require corrective action plans.

While business ownership creates opportunity, we must also address the systemic barriers that prevent Black Americans from building and preserving wealth across generations.

These entrepreneurship policies would create new Black-owned businesses, generate billions in economic growth, create jobs, and increase the average revenue of Black-owned businesses.

Building Wealth: Creating Generational Economic Security

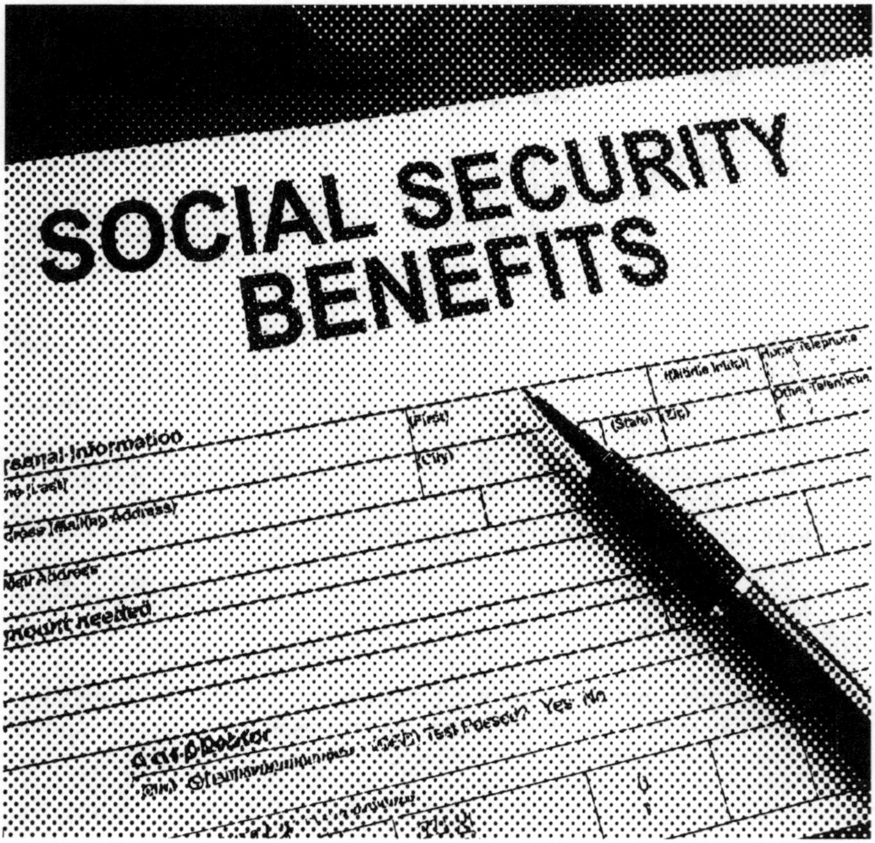

Black families save. We stretch every dollar. We support entire households. But we do so in a financial system built to extract, not reward. Our dreams are not too big—they are too often unfunded. Our work ethic is not lacking—our access to wealth-building tools has been systemically denied.

As stated earlier, the typical white family has $285,000 in wealth, compared to $44,900 for the average Black family. While Black wealth has increased in recent years, wealth divides persist despite Black gains in education and employment (Aladangady & Forde, 2021). Just 44% of Black adults own homes compared with 74% of whites, a gap wider than when redlining was legal (National Association of REALTORS Research Group, 2025). This wealth divide is not natural or inevitable—it is the predictable result of centuries of policy choices, from slavery to Jim Crow to redlining to discriminatory lending. Addressing this requires structural changes to how wealth is built and preserved in America, not individual behavior changes.

We Demand

- **Make Homeownership Affordable and Sustainable.** Models like community land trusts, deed-restricted homes, and limited equity housing cooperatives can ensure that housing stays affordable in our community and build wealth for Black homeowners (Shared Equity Housing | NeighborWorks America, n.d.). Programs like the Douglass Community Land Trust in Washington, D.C., have preserved affordability while allowing homeowners to build $100,000+ in equity within five years—proving that affordability and wealth-building are not contradictory goals. Congress should provide $5 billion annually to scale these models in 100 cities, with priority for communities experiencing rapid gentrification. Additionally, the federal government should provide down payment assistance for first-generation Black homebuyers.
- **Ensure a Secure Retirement.** Increase the Social Security payroll tax so high earners pay their fair share, then use that revenue to increase Social Security pension payments for retirees. Give tax incentives to employers to provide pension plans or establish automatic-enrollment retirement accounts for their employees (Teresa Ghilarducci, 2024). Less than half (44.9%) of all Black workers participate in a retirement plan (Banerjee, 2022)—this is not because Black workers do not want to save, but because they lack access to employer-sponsored plans. Federal policy should establish automatic IRAs for all workers whose employers do not provide retirement benefits.

- **Increase Shared Employee Ownership.** Business owners 55 and older own 2.9 million businesses in the U.S. and employ 321 million employees (Silver Tsunami | Small Business Closure Crisis, n.d.). Helping small business owners transition to shared employee ownership through Employee Stock Ownership Plans (ESOPs) as original owners can improve job security and increase wealth for Black workers (*What Is an ESOP and How Does It Work?*, n.d.). Congress should provide tax incentives and technical assistance for business succession planning that prioritizes employee ownership, particularly for businesses in Black communities. ESOPs have been shown to increase worker wealth by an average of $66,000 over 10 years while maintaining business continuity.
- **Address Student Loan Debt.** Thirty-six % of Black households have student loans, compared with 20% of white households (Cohn, 2024). Implementing targeted debt relief ($50,000 per borrower for those earning under $125,000) and interest rate caps (maximum 2% for all federal student loans) would free up capital for wealth-building activities like homeownership and entrepreneurship. Additionally, all borrowers who attended HBCUs should receive an additional $10,000 in debt relief, recognizing these institutions' underfunding. These policies would redirect billions from debt servicing to wealth building over the next decade.
- **Establish "Baby Bonds" for wealth creation.** Create federally-backed trust accounts for every newborn, with deposits of $1,000 at birth plus $2,000 annually for children in families with income below the national median. These accounts would grow tax-free until age 18 and could be used for wealth-building investments like education, homeownership, or business creation. Research shows Baby Bonds could reduce the racial wealth divide by 80% within one generation while costing approximately $80 billion annually—less than 10% of annual defense spending (Hamilton & Darity, 2019). This is an investment in America's future.

- **Reform predatory banking practices.** Black households are five times more likely than white households to be unbanked (2023 FDIC National Survey of Unbanked and Underbanked Households, 2023). Strengthen the Consumer Financial Protection Bureau's enforcement capabilities by increasing its budget and expanding its authority to impose significant penalties on predatory lenders. Require all banks receiving FDIC insurance to offer basic, fee-free checking accounts with no minimum balance requirements—a "banking public option" that ensures universal access. Incentivize the expansion of Community Development Credit Unions and postal banking services in underserved areas.

These wealth-building policies would increase median Black family wealth, close the homeownership divide, and ensure more Black workers have retirement savings.

Conclusion: Building an Economy That Works for All

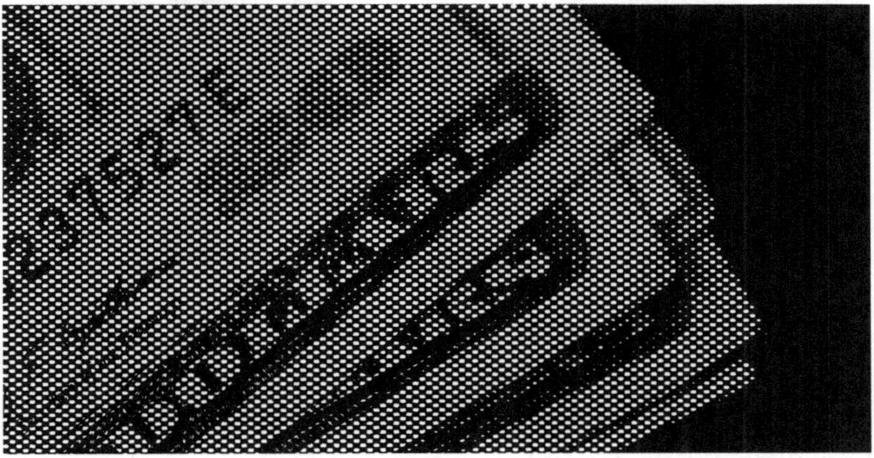

These demands are not just about justice for Black people in the United States—they represent a vision for an economy that works better for everyone. When we remove the barriers blocking Black economic participation and success, we unlock growth and innovation that benefits the nation. History proves this: every major expansion of economic rights—from Social Security to Medicare to the GI Bill—has strengthened America when implemented equitably, and weakened it when implemented discriminatorily.

More importantly, we would create an economy where everyone can participate fully and benefit equitably from their contributions. This work is about more than closing gaps—it's about unleashing potential. It's about recognizing that Black economic power is not a zero-sum threat but a multiplicative opportunity.

This is our economic vision: a nation where Black brilliance is celebrated **and** compensated. Where Black labor is not just extracted but rewarded, and where Black wealth is not only generated but sustained across generations. This vision is not just morally necessary—it is economically essential for America to reach its full potential.

Call to Action: What You Can Do Right Now

The policies in this Black Paper will only become reality through sustained, coordinated action. Here are specific steps you can take today, this week, and this year to advance Black economic power:

Immediate Actions (Today)

Share This Paper Widely

- Post this Black Paper on social media with the hashtag #BlackEconomicVision.
- Email it to your networks with a personal note about why it matters.
- Print copies for your church, community center, or workplace.
- Discuss it at your next family gathering or community meeting.

Educate Yourself and Others

- Read the full Paper carefully, paying attention to the data and policy recommendations.

- Host a discussion group to explore the implications for your community.
- Invite local economists, business owners, or policy experts to speak about these issues.
- Use the Paper as a curriculum in schools, churches, and community organizations.

Support Black Economic Power Directly

- Bank with Black-owned financial institutions or Community Development Financial Institutions (CDFIs).
- Shop at Black-owned businesses—make it a weekly practice, not just during Black History Month.
- Hire Black-owned contractors, consultants, and service providers.
- Invest in Black-owned businesses through crowdfunding platforms or community investment funds
- If you're an employer, recruit from HBCUs and Black professional networks.

Short-Term Actions (This Month)

Contact Your Elected Officials

Use this template to contact your representatives:

[SAMPLE EMAIL TEMPLATE]

Subject: Support Black Economic Empowerment Policies

Dear [Representative/Senator Name],

As your constituent, I am writing to urge you to support policies that address the racial wealth gap and promote Black economic empowerment. Specifically, I ask that you:

[Choose 3–5 specific demands from this paper to include, e.g.: —Support $5 billion in increased annual funding for HBCUs—Co-sponsor the PRO Act to strengthen workers' rights—Vote to increase the federal minimum wage to $17/hour—Expand the Child Tax Credit with full refundability—Restore and expand the Affordable Connectivity Program]

These policies are not only morally right—they are economically necessary for our nation's prosperity. Black Americans have contributed immeasurably to this country's wealth, and we deserve policies that enable us to build and sustain our own wealth.

I look forward to your response and will be watching your votes on these issues.

Sincerely, [Your Name] [Your Address] [Your Contact Information]

Find Your Representatives

- Federal: www.congress.gov/members.
- State: Search "[Your State] find my legislator."
- Local: Search "[Your City] city council members."

Join Organizations Fighting for Economic Justice

Consider joining and supporting:

- **Black-Led National Organizations**: National Black Justice Collective (NBJC), National Association for the Advancement of Colored People (NAACP), National Urban League, Color of Change, Black Futures Lab.
- **Labor Organizations**: Black Workers Center, Coalition of Black Trade Unionists.
- **Economic Justice Organizations**: PolicyLink, National Community Reinvestment Coalition.
- **Faith-Based Organizations**: Samuel DeWitt Proctor Conference, PICO National Network.
- **Local Organizations**: Search for Black chambers of commerce, business associations, and community development organizations in your area.

Mobilize Your Community

- Organize letter-writing campaigns to elected officials.
- Host town halls or candidate forums focused on Black economic issues.
- Create accountability scorecards tracking how local representatives vote on these issues.
- Develop relationships with local journalists to ensure Black economic issues get media coverage.
- Connect with local Black-owned businesses to understand their needs and barriers.

Medium-Term Actions (This Year)

Build Political Power

- Register to vote and ensure your friends and family are registered.
- Volunteer for candidates who support these policies—and hold them accountable once elected.
- Run for office yourself—school board, city council, state legislature.
- Attend city council, county commission, and school board meetings to advocate for these policies at the local level.

- Support ballot initiatives that advance economic justice in your state.
- Donate to political action committees focused on Black economic empowerment.

Create Economic Alternatives

- Start or join a buying club that pools resources to support Black businesses.
- Establish a community land trust in your neighborhood to preserve affordable housing.
- Create a mutual aid network to support Black families facing economic hardship.
- Form an investment club focused on Black-owned businesses.
- Launch a crowdfunding campaign for a Black entrepreneur in your community.
- Organize a community baby shower to provide supplies for Black families with newborns.

Demand Accountability

- Track government spending on programs that benefit Black communities.
- Monitor corporate diversity commitments and call out backsliding.
- Document discrimination in lending, employment, and contracting.
- File complaints with appropriate agencies when you experience or witness discrimination.
- Support class-action lawsuits challenging discriminatory practices.
- Use shareholder advocacy to pressure corporations on racial equity issues.

Build for the Long Term

- Mentor young Black people interested in business, policy, and activism.
- Create or support scholarship funds for Black students.
- Establish giving circles that pool resources for Black-led organizations.
- Develop succession plans for Black-owned businesses to keep them in Black hands.
- Build cross-generational knowledge about wealth building and advocacy.
- Create family traditions around economic education and activism.

Specific Actions by Role

If You're a Student

- Organize on your campus, and in your community around these issues.
- Demand that your institutions increase support for Black students.
- Choose coursework and research topics that explore these issues.

- Join Black student organizations and professional societies.
- Apply for internships with organizations working on economic justice.

If You're an Educator

- Integrate this Black Paper into your curriculum.
- Connect students with Black professionals and entrepreneurs.
- Advocate for increased funding for schools serving Black students.
- Support Black colleagues facing discrimination.
- Challenge bias in textbooks and teaching materials.

If You're a Business Owner/Executive

- Review your own practices: Are you providing fair wages, benefits, and advancement opportunities?
- Diversify your supplier base to include more Black-owned businesses.
- Implement transparent pay equity audits.
- Support unionization efforts or improve worker protections.
- Partner with CDFIs and Black business organizations.
- Offer paid internships to Black students.

If You're a Faith Leader

- Preach about economic justice as a moral imperative.
- Use your building to host community meetings and workshops.
- Connect congregants with resources for business development and financial literacy.
- Advocate for policies that lift the economically vulnerable.
- Create congregational investment funds that support Black businesses.

If You're a Healthcare Professional

- Advocate for addressing the social determinants of health, including economic security.
- Support expanded access to affordable healthcare.
- Provide education about how economic stress affects health outcomes.
- Connect patients with economic support services.

If You're in Media/Communications

- Cover Black economic issues regularly, not just during crisis or Black History Month.
- Interview Black economists, business owners, and policy experts.
- Challenge dominant narratives that blame Black people for structural problems.

- Investigate and expose discriminatory practices.
- Amplify the voices of Black advocates and organizations.

If You're a Policymaker

- Champion the policies outlined in this Black Paper.
- Ensure your office reflects the diversity of your constituency.
- Hold regular town halls in Black communities.
- Vote for budgets that invest in Black communities.
- Use your platform to educate others about racial economic disparities.

Track Your Impact

Personal Accountability Tracker

Create a Personal Accountability System

- Set monthly goals (e.g., "Contact 2 elected officials" or "Spend $200 at Black-owned businesses").
- Track your progress in a journal, spreadsheet, or app.
- Share your commitment with an accountability partner.
- Celebrate wins and learn from setbacks.
- Adjust your approach based on what is working.

Resources for Continued Learning

Research and Data

- Economic Policy Institute: www.epi.org.
- Joint Center for Political and Economic Studies: www.jointcenter.org.
- Brookings Institution: www.brookings.edu/topic/race-and-ethnicity.
- Federal Reserve Bank reports on racial wealth gaps.

Advocacy Tools

- Resistbot (text "RESIST" to 50409)—Easy way to contact Congress.
- 5 Calls (5calls.org)—Daily action items with scripts.
- Countable (countable.us)—Track legislation and contact representatives.
- GovTrack (govtrack.us)—Monitor bills and voting records.

Black-Owned Business Directories

- Official Black Wall Street App.
- The NAACP Buy Black Directory.
- Black Owned Market.
- WeBuyBlack.

Join the Movement

This Black Paper is part of the State of the People Black Paper Policy Project. Visit stateoftheppl.com to:

- Access papers and resources.
- Sign up for action alerts.
- Find local organizing opportunities.
- Connect with other advocates.
- Get policy updates and implementation progress.

A Final Word

Economic justice does not happen by accident. It happens because people like you decide enough is enough and commit to sustained action.

You do not have to do everything. But you must do something. Start where you are. Use what you have. Do what you can.

The future of Black economic power—and America's prosperity—depends on what we do next.

References

2024 Report on Employer Firms: Findings from the 2023 Small Business Credit Survey. (2024). *Small business credit survey*. Federal Reserve Banks. https://doi.org/10.55350/sbcs-20240307

Aladangady, A. & Forde, A. (2021). *Wealth inequality and the racial wealth gap*. https://www.federalreserve.gov/econres/notes/feds-notes/wealth-inequality-and-the-racial-wealth-gap-20211022.html

Anderson, M. & Hatfield, J. (2024). *A look at historically black colleges and universities in the U.S.* Pew Research Center. https://www.pewresearch.org/short-reads/2024/10/02/a-look-at-historically-black-colleges-and-universities-in-the-u-s/

Banerjee, S. (2022). *Race, retirement, and the savings gap*. T. Rowe Price Insights. https://www.troweprice.com/content/dam/ide/articles/pdfs/2022/q1/race-retirement-savings-gap.pdf

Bivens, J., McNicholas, C., Moore, K.K., & Poydock, M. (2023). *Unions promote racial equity*. Economic Policy Institute. https://www.epi.org/publication/unions-promote-racial-equity/

Black Census Executive Summary. (2023). *Black Futures Lab*. https://blackfutureslab.org/wp-content/uploads/2024/08/BCP-ExecutiveSummary0806.pdf

Boyens, C., Karpman, M., & Smalligan, J. (2022). *Access to paid leave is lowest among workers with the greatest needs*. Urban Institute. https://www.urban.org/research/publication/access-paid-leave-lowest-among-workers-greatest-needs

Brainerd, J. (2023). *What happens when states ditch income tax for sales tax?* National Conference of State Legislatures. https://www.ncsl.org/state-legislatures-news/details/what-happens-when-states-ditch-income-tax-for-sales-tax

Burns, K., Fox, L., & Wilson, D. (2022). *Expansions to child tax credit contributed to 46% decline in child poverty since 2020*. U.S. Census Bureau. https://www.census.gov/library/stories/2022/09/record-drop-in-child-poverty.html

Carnavale, A.P. & Smith, N. (2018). *Balancing work and learning: Implications for low-income students*. Georgetown University Center on Education and the Workforce. https://cew.georgetown.edu/cew-reports/learnandearn/

Center for American Progress. (2025). *The Trump administration has made 36 million workers newly vulnerable to discrimination and harassment*. Center for American Progress. https://www.americanprogress.org/article/the-trump-administration-has-made-36-million-workers-newly-vulnerable-to-discrimination-and-harassment/

Cohn, J. (2024). *As student debt amounts decreased during the payment pause, more Black borrowers took on loans*. Urban Institute. https://www.urban.org/urban-wire/student-debt-amounts-decreased-during-payment-pause-more-black-borrowers-took-loans

Dawson, S. (2023). *5 Black-led labor unions that have paved the way for Black workers' rights*. The Chicago Crusader. https://chicagocrusader.com/5-black-led-labor-unions-that-have-paved-the-way-for-black-workers-rights/

Diverse Business Government Contracting Opportunities Unequal, Untapped & Under Attack. (2025). *Global Black Economic Forum*. https://cdn.prod.website-files.com/6441a6dce24875806337a0b0/67ec970fb6a8681404b50363_Diverse%20Business%20Government%20Contracting%20Opportunities%20-FINAL%20(1).pdf

Facts About Small Business: Black-Ownership Statistics 2024. (2024). *Office of Advocacy*. https://advocacy.sba.gov/2024/02/01/facts-about-small-business-black-ownership-statistics-2024/

Federal Deposit Insurance Corporation. (2023). *2023 FDIC national survey of unbanked and underbanked households*. https://www.fdic.gov/household-survey

Fulton, J., Brenson, L., Donoso, J.C., & Vince, W. (2023). *Pessimism and hope: A survey of the financial status and aspirations of Black Americans*. Joint Center for Political and Economic Studies. https://jointcenter.org/wp-content/uploads/2023/10/Pessimism-and-Hope-A-Survey-of-the-Financial-Status-and-Aspirations-of-Black-Americans.pdf

Ghilarducci, T. (2024). *Taking a serious look at the retirement crisis in America: What can we do to expand defined benefit pension plans for workers?* [Testimony]. United States Senate Health Education Labor and Pensions Committee. https://www.help.senate.gov/imo/media/doc/f95f3998-ba66-d2ac-054a-e90e7080a705/Ghilarducci%20written%20testimony%20Taking%20a%20Serious%20Look%20at%20the%20Retirement%20Crisis%20in%20America.pdf

Gould, E. & deCourcy, K. (2024). *Fastest wage growth over the last four years among historically disadvantaged groups: Low-wage workers' wages surged after decades of slow growth*. Economic Policy Institute. https://www.epi.org/publication/swa-wages-2023/

Hamilton, D. & Darity, W. (2019). *Can 'baby bonds' help the U.S. close its staggering racial wealth gap?* (P. Solman, Interviewer). PSB NewsHour. https://www.pbs.org/newshour/show/can-baby-bonds-help-the-u-s-close-its-staggering-racial-wealth-gap

Harrison, D. (2021). *Affordability & availability: Expanding broadband in the Black rural south*. Joint Center for Political and Economic Studies. https://jointcenter.org/affordability-availability-expanding-broadband-in-the-black-rural-south/

Henderson, K. (2024). *The crisis of low wages*. Oxfam. https://oxfamilibrary.openrepository.com/bitstream/handle/10546/621608/rr-2024-crisis-of-low-wages-090724-en.pdf

Minimum Wage Tracker. (n.d.). Economic Policy Institute. Retrieved April 10, 2025, from https://www.epi.org/minimum-wage-tracker/

Moore, K. K. (2025). *2024 Q4 | State unemployment by race and ethnicity*. Economic Policy Institute. https://www.epi.org/indicators/state-unemployment-race-ethnicity/

Nalley, J. & Gabrielle Smith Finnie. (2025). *Black student parents' access to affordable child care support at community colleges*. Joint Center for Political and Economic Studies. https://jointcenter.org/black-student-parents-access-to-affordable-child-care-support-at-community-colleges/

National Association of REALTORS Research Group. (2025). *2025 Snapshot of race and home buying in America*. https://www.nar.realtor/sites/default/files/2025-03/2025-snapshot-of-race-and-home-buying-in-america-03-17-2025.pdf

National Center for Employee Ownership. (n.d.). *What is an ESOP and how does it work?* Retrieved April 12, 2025, from https://www.esop.org/index.php

Roder, A. & Elliott, M. (2019). *Nine year gains: Project QUEST's continuing impact*. The Economic Mobility Corporation. https://economicmobilitycorp.org/wp-content/uploads/2019/04/NineYearGains_web.pdf

Rugaber, C. (2025). *Trump tariffs likely to raise inflation slow us economic growth*. AP News. https://apnews.com/article/tariffs-inflation-economy-trump-powell-490417656971634592bbeb3b2ade3593

Sachin S. (2024). *4 Ways unions make our economy and democracy stronger*. Center for American Progress. https://www.americanprogress.org/article/4-ways-unions-make-our-economy-and-democracy-stronger/

Schaeffer, K. (2021). *What we know about online learning and the homework gap amid the pandemic*. Pew Research Center. https://www.pewresearch.org/short-reads/2021/10/01/what-we-know-about-online-learning-and-the-homework-gap-amid-the-pandemic/

Scott-Clayton, J. & Li, Jing. (2016). *Black-white disparity in student loan debt more than triples after graduation* (Evidence Speaks Reports). Brookings Institution. https://www.brookings.edu/wp-content/uploads/2016/10/es_20161020_scott-clayton_evidence_speaks.pdf

Shared Equity Housing | NeighborWorks America. (n.d.). Retrieved April 12, 2025, from https://www.neighborworks.org/Community/Shared-Equity-Housing

Silver Tsunami | Small Business Closure Crisis. (n.d.). *Project equity*. Retrieved April 10, 2025, from https://project-equity.org/impact/silver-tsunami/

U.S. Senator Maria Cantwell of Washington. (n.d.). *Senators Cantwell & Grassley introduce bipartisan bill to reassert congressional trade role*. Retrieved April 9, 2025, from https://www.cantwell.senate.gov/news/press-releases/senators-cantwell-and-grassley-introduce-bipartisan-bill-to-reassert-congressional-trade-role

United Negro College Fund. (2022). *HBCUs make America strong: The positive economic impact of historically Black colleges and universities*.https://uncf.org/programs/hbcu-impact

Chapter 5

The Power of Ownership

How Black Entrepreneurship Builds Economic Freedom and Community Wealth

*Natalie Madeira Cofield, Arian Simone, and Alphonso David**

Executive Summary

Black entrepreneurship has long stood as a cornerstone of economic resilience, civic empowerment, and generational progress in Black communities across America. From the rise of Black Wall Street in the early 20th century to the current wave of Black-owned businesses emerging in the post-pandemic economy, business ownership remains one of the most powerful tools for self-determination and collective advancement.

This Black Paper (Paper) examines the critical role of Black entrepreneurship in building economic freedom, closing the racial wealth divide, and strengthening democracy in America. Drawing on historical precedents and current data, we demonstrate how business ownership creates pathways to financial independence, community development, and political power for Black Americans. We outline persistent structural barriers—including capital access, contracting disparities, and information gaps—that limit Black business growth, and propose targeted policy solutions to overcome these obstacles. Our recommendations include expanding capital access, modernizing federal contracting, developing local business infrastructure, and integrating entrepreneurship education for sustained impact.

* Supported by braintrust authors: Corena D. Wiggins, Nadia French-Graham, and Verneda Adele White.

DOI: 10.4324/9781003752646-8

Introduction: The Promise and the Problem

Entrepreneurship has been an economic cornerstone of Black American identity and a powerful expression of freedom, self-determination, and resistance against oppression. Beyond providing livelihoods, Black businesses have served as community gathering spaces, funded civil rights initiatives, and created platforms to facilitate cultural expression and preservation when mainstream institutions were closed to Black Americans.

From the post-emancipation era to today, business ownership has served as a critical means of survival, autonomy, and progress. Immediately after emancipation, formerly enslaved Black people established thriving business districts across the South, often near Historically Black Colleges and Universities (HBCUs) and in self-sufficient enclaves where economic cooperation was essential. These HBCUs served as more than educational institutions—they were incubators for Black business development, providing formal business training, networking opportunities, and a ready customer base of students, faculty, and staff, which helped sustain these emerging enterprises. Schools like Howard University and Tuskegee Institute specifically incorporated business education in their curricula, directly nurturing generations of Black entrepreneurs. These businesses provided goods, services, jobs, and pride to communities excluded from mainstream markets.

One of the most potent examples of Black business success is the Greenwood District of Tulsa, Oklahoma—known as "Black Wall Street." By 1921, this thriving community boasted more than 300 Black-owned businesses, including banks, hotels, grocery stores, and theaters. Residents could shop, dine, receive healthcare, and enjoy entertainment without leaving their neighborhood. The district represented true economic independence and wealth creation within the Black community.

The success of Black Wall Street demonstrated what was possible when Black entrepreneurs had the freedom to build. However, this success was tragically cut short when white mobs destroyed the district in the 1921 Tulsa

Race Massacre—one of the worst acts of racial terrorism in American history. In just 24 hours, this prosperous community, among several thriving self-sufficient Black communities that met a similar fate, was reduced to ashes, with hundreds killed and thousands left homeless.

This pattern of success followed by resistance and suppression has recurred throughout history, from the redlining and urban renewal policies of the mid-20th century to the undercapitalization of Black businesses during the COVID-19 pandemic to the well-funded and coordinated attacks on institutions and individuals investing in Black-owned businesses.

Despite these obstacles, Black entrepreneurship has persisted as powerful economic liberation and community development vehicles. The resilience of Black entrepreneurs speaks to both the determination of Black business owners and the essential role these enterprises play in creating independent economic power that often fuels local economies and supports our national economy.

Despite erected obstacles, Black entrepreneurship has endured and evolved. Economic empowerment has been central to Black liberation throughout

American history. Early pioneers like Madam C.J. Walker, who built her hair-care empire in the early 1900s, established the precedent of using business success to fund social causes. Later, leaders of the Civil Rights Movement like A. Philip Randolph leveraged economic power through labor organizing to advocate for broader racial equity.

The Civil Rights Act of 1964 laid the foundation for further financial inclusion. Still, meaningful federal support for Black business owners did not materialize until the Office of Minority Business Enterprise was created in 1969. Now, the Minority Business Development Agency (MBDA), this federal agency remains the only one dedicated to the growth and competitiveness of minority-owned businesses, despite ongoing attempts to defund, delegitimize and neuter its work, function, and impact.

In the decades following the launch of the MBDA, efforts to expand Black participation in government contracting emerged. The Small Business Administration's 8(a) Business Development Program aimed to help socially and economically disadvantaged entrepreneurs compete for federal contracts. These efforts were essential, as federal government spending constitutes a significant market opportunity. Despite these agencies and their efforts, Black businesses still receive a disproportionately small share of federal contracting dollars, less than 2%, despite Black Americans comprising over 13% of the United States population (Joint Center, 2026; MBDA, 2022).

Black entrepreneurship is not merely an economic engine—it is fundamental to a healthy democracy. When Black Americans build businesses, they also create economic independence, which translates directly into political power. Financial self-determination enables democratic participation through increased civic engagement, campaign contributions, and the ability to withstand economic pressure when exercising political rights. Throughout American history, economically independent Black communities have been better positioned to advocate for justice, facilitate voter engagement, and fund legal challenges to discriminatory policies. Simply put, Black economic power is essential for ensuring that America's democratic institutions represent all citizens.

Why Entrepreneurship Matters

Owning a business provides more than financial security; it supports community stability, independence, and pride. Black-owned businesses hire from their communities, boost local economies, and reduce unemployment. Black businesses serve as role models and pathways to success for people, young and old. Moreover, Black businesses reinvest profits into local neighborhoods, fostering sustainable local economies where dollars circulate multiple times within the community before leaving. Economists call this the multiplier effect. It creates a more significant impact, uplifting entire communities.

According to the United States Census Bureau's Annual Business Survey, there are more than 200,000 Black-owned employer businesses in the United States, generating nearly $250 billion in annual receipts and employing more than 1.6 million workers, and paying out nearly $70 billion in salaries (United States Census Bureau, 2026; Black Executive Brief, 2026; United States Census Bureau, 2023, Journal of Blacks in Higher Education, 2026). These businesses are essential to the national economy and to the well-being of the communities they serve. Yet, these numbers only scratch the surface.

Black households represent roughly 13.6% of the United States population (U.S. Census Bureau, 2025). Black-owned businesses represent just 3.4% of all employer businesses in the country as of 2023 (Journal of Blacks in Higher Education, 2026) and just 2.2% of firms with paid employees (Perry & Stephens, 2025). If Black businesses employed and generated revenue at the same rate as all United States businesses, the economy would gain $9.1 billion in additional economic output annually (Brookings, 2026). These gaps are not about ambition or effort. It's about access to capital, contracts, and customers. This reality is further illustrated in the venture capital space, where more than $270 billion is allocated each year, and less than 1% (0.32%) is invested in startups with a Black founder or co-founder (Azevedo, 2026; Teare, 2026).

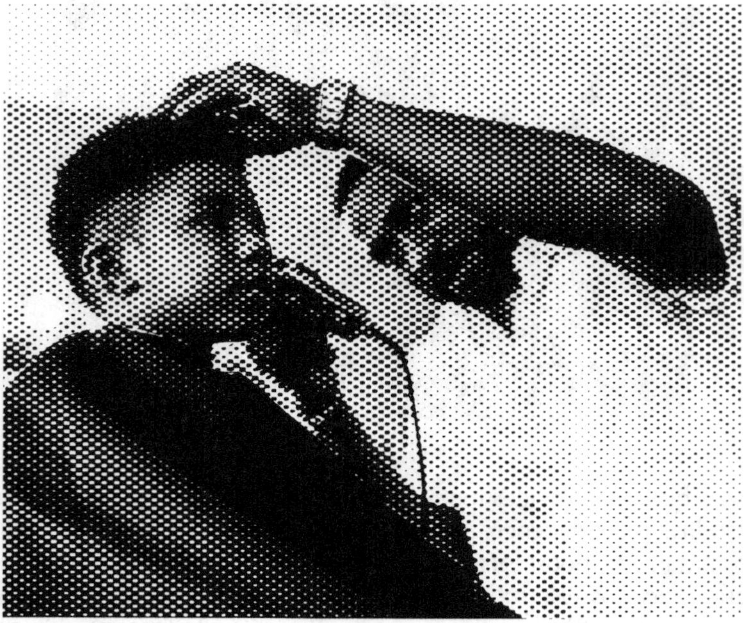

What does this mean in real terms? It means a Black entrepreneur might struggle to secure the business loan that's handed to their white counterpart without labor or effort. It means having to bootstrap a business with personal savings because traditional funding sources are unavailable. It means starting with less and working harder just to stay afloat.

Community Impact: Beyond Economics

Black-owned businesses do far more than create jobs and generate revenue. They transform entire communities. In the Black community, entrepreneurship is viewed as a gateway to financial independence, community reinvestment, and long-term wealth creation. Small businesses are personal ventures and tools for uplifting the broader Black community by creating jobs, supporting underserved areas, and reinvesting locally. For decades, entrepreneurship has been a cornerstone of progress, with small businesses acting as the engine to power upward mobility, job creation, and generational wealth in Black communities.

Black-owned businesses specifically play crucial roles in:

- **Closing the Wealth Divide**: Black-owned businesses circulate money within the community, helping to close the racial wealth divide. They create jobs locally, often hiring from within the community and reducing unemployment. The North Carolina Sustainable Business Council reports that Black business owners have, on average, 12 times the wealth of their Black peers who do not own businesses (North Carolina Sustainable Business Council, 2026). This statistic highlights the impact of entrepreneurship on wealth building within the Black community.
- **Innovation and Market Disruption**: Black founders often innovate to fill overlooked needs, especially in health, beauty, technology, and media sectors. Their businesses frequently challenge mainstream norms and drive inclusion in product development. McKinsey and Company's report, *The Black unicorn: Changing the game for inclusivity in retail*, highlights that nearly half (45%) of United States consumers believe companies should commit to supporting Black-owned brands, suppliers, and vendors (McKinsey & Company, 2022).
- **Generational Wealth**: Owning a business is closely tied to the desire to leave a legacy and provide assets for future generations. It also shifts the narrative by positioning Black founders as leaders, employers, and wealth-builders. Black Wealth is increasing, but so is the racial wealth divide. This shift emphasizes how business equity is a vital component of wealth accumulation for Black families, representing 21% of their wealth growth (Perry et al., 2024).
- **Community Reinvestment**: Many Black-owned businesses prioritize giving back, supporting schools, nonprofits, and youth programs in Black communities.
- **Health and Wellness**: Black-owned grocery stores and restaurants can provide healthier food options in neighborhoods traditionally lacking access to healthier options.
- **Cultural Preservation**: Black businesses serve as cultural anchors, preserving traditions and creating spaces for community gatherings. From bookstores highlighting Black authors to salons specializing in natural haircare, these Black spaces affirm cultural identity and pride while strengthening community.
- **Youth Development**: Young people living in areas with visible Black entrepreneurship can literally see paths to success in their daily lives, which can increase educational aspirations and decrease involvement in high-risk behaviors.

Ownership-driven economic empowerment enables people and communities to shape their futures, both economically and politically. Furthermore, small business ownership nurtures the next generation of entrepreneurs. Children raised in homes with business owners are three times more likely to start their own ventures later in life (Dunn and Holtz-Eakin, 2000). Each Black-owned business plants seeds for long-term community transformation.

This multidimensional impact illustrates why Black entrepreneurship must be viewed not merely as an economic strategy but also as a comprehensive approach to community development, political empowerment, and cultural sustainability. The ripple effects of successful Black-owned businesses extend far beyond their immediate financial contributions.

Black Entrepreneurship as a Mode of Wealth Creation and Transfer

Entrepreneurship is a powerful driver of wealth creation and one of the few avenues historically available to Black Americans to build financial security and pass assets through generations. Owning a business allows individuals to build equity, generate income, and create legacy assets that support future generations. In fact, business equity represents approximately 34% of non-financial assets for families that own businesses (U.S. Small Business Administration, 2021).

However, disparities often stunt the potential for wealth creation. The reality is, white families are far more likely to own businesses, and when they do, their businesses generate higher revenues and employ more people. According to the Small Business Administration (SBA), business equity makes up about one-third of non-financial assets for white non-Hispanic families but only one-eighth for Black or Hispanic families. In a report published by the Brookings Institute, Perry and Romer argue that business ownership is a major driver of wealth accumulation, calling for structural policies to better support Black founders (2019). Improving the success rate of Black founders is crucial for leveraging business ownership as a tool to reduce the racial wealth divide.

We are in the middle of what financial experts call the "Great Wealth Transfer"—an estimated $84 trillion moving from Baby Boomers to their children and grandchildren by 2045 (Cerulli Associates, 2022). This massive wealth movement makes business ownership and succession planning more important than ever. Yet, too few Black entrepreneurs can access the tools and guidance needed for effective succession planning. Without proper planning, the business assets that took decades to build can be lost instantly.

To ensure wealth created through Black entrepreneurship is preserved and transferred, we must invest in estate planning education, succession tools, and legal services. These education and wealth tools are critical for safeguarding individual legacies and narrowing the racial wealth divide.

Barriers Black Entrepreneurs Face

Despite undeniable drive and resilience, Black entrepreneurs face several persistent structural barriers:

- **Access to Capital**: Black-owned businesses are less likely to be approved for loans and often receive lower loan amounts and higher interest rates. According to the Federal Reserve, only 43% of Black-owned firms that applied for financing received all the funding they needed, compared to 68% of white-owned firms (Federal Reserve Banks, 2022).

  This capital gap manifests in daily business decisions that limit growth potential. For example, a Black restaurant owner might delay expanding to a second location despite customer demand, or a tech startup might struggle to hire critical talent during a crucial growth phase because of constrained capital. The compounding effect of delayed or diminished business decisions creates an ever-widening gap between similarly positioned Black and white businesses.

What does this look like in practice? It might mean a Black entrepreneur with a strong business plan and good credit score is still getting denied a loan or offered terms that make growth nearly impossible. It means relying on personal credit cards or family loans just to keep the lights on. Without adequate capital, even the most promising business ideas can wither.

- **Extreme Underfunding**: In of 2024, less than 1% of total venture capital went to Black founders, and less than 0.036% went to Black women founders (Global Economic Forum, 2024). This disparity was highlighted in the recent *Fearless Fund*[1] federal litigation, where they were challenged for essentially trying to reinvest in their community. Due to barriers in accessing capital, most Black women fund their startups through personal savings, which limits risk-taking and increases the wealth divide.

  Black women are also underrepresented in venture capital firms, both as founders and funders, which leads to pattern matching and a lack of warm introductions as reasons not to fund Black women. Project Diane continues to expose a systemic bias in startup funding and underscores the urgent need for equity in capital distribution, institutional change, and targeted investment, especially for Black women (Digitalundivided, 2020).
- **Federal Contracting Disparities**: Less than 2% of federal contracting dollars are awarded to Black-owned businesses, even though they make up more than 13% of the United States population (Joint Center, 2023). This disparity represents billions in lost opportunity. When the federal government spends approximately $600 billion annually on contracts, the gap between 2% and 13% equates to roughly $66 billion that could be flowing to Black-owned businesses and their communities each year.
- **Information and Mentorship Gaps**: Many Black entrepreneurs lack access to the professional networks, mentorship, and technical assistance that fuel growth and sustainability. Mentorship and knowledge sharing matter because business success often depends on "who you know" as much as "what you know." Without mentors who have successfully navigated similar challenges or networks that can open doors to opportunities, Black entrepreneurs must figure things out independently, often learning expensive lessons through trial and error.
- **Wealth and Credit Inequities**: Due to historic and ongoing economic inequality, Black entrepreneurs often start with less personal or family wealth to finance their businesses. Ongoing economic inequality leads to heavier reliance on personal credit and smaller margins for reinvestment or risk.

What Needs to Change: Policy Recommendations

To address the aforementioned inequities, we recommend bold, targeted, and transformative solutions implemented by policymakers at every level of government:

1. **Expand Access to Capital**: Support increased investment in community banks and lending programs that understand and serve diverse Black communities. Create more grant programs specifically for Black-owned businesses that do not require repayment.

   Establish a federally backed loan guarantee program specifically for Black-owned businesses, similar to SBA loans but with streamlined requirements and community-based administration. Direct 5% of Community Reinvestment Act (CRA) funding toward Black business development in historically disinvested neighborhoods.
2. **Modernize Federal Contracting Systems**: Ensure transparency, simplify application processes, and create accountability measures to increase the share of contracts awarded to Black-owned firms. Institute a technical assistance navigator program within each federal agency to help Black-owned businesses successfully navigate the contracting process, implement a public dashboard tracking progress toward procurement goals by agency, and create consequences for agencies that consistently fail to meet diversity contracting benchmarks.
3. **Fund Black Business Hubs and Incubators**: Invest in local infrastructure, including co-working spaces, accelerators, and technical assistance programs tailored to the unique challenges Black entrepreneurs face. Launch a national network of Black business development centers in partnership with HBCUs, providing shared resources, early-stage funding, and industry-specific mentorship programs in collaboration with successful Black entrepreneurs.
4. **Integrate Youth Entrepreneurship Education**: Introduce entrepreneurship and business literacy into Black communities' K-12 and higher education curricula. Develop age-appropriate entrepreneurship curriculum starting in elementary school, fund summer business incubator programs for high school students, and create pathways for youth entrepreneurs to access micro-grants for first ventures.
5. **Improve Data Collection and Reporting**: We need to track better who receives business funding and government contracts and make this information public, so we measure progress and hold institutions accountable in the process.
6. **Improve Data Sampling**: Research on the Black population benefits from using weighted sample sizes that more accurately reflect the population of Black people across America. Additionally, research would further benefit from standardized reporting requirements across all federal agencies and financial institutions on capital access by race, ethnicity, and geography,

and an annual "State of Black Business" congressional report with specific metrics for measuring progress.

Addressing Different Perspectives

Some critics argue that we don't need targeted support for Black businesses—that general economic policies and "race-neutral" approaches are sufficient. They might suggest that market forces alone should determine business success or that focusing on racial disparities creates division rather than unity. **These perspectives miss several important realities**:

First, our economy has never been race-neutral. From slavery to redlining to discriminatory lending practices that continue today, economic systems have been deliberately structured to exclude Black Americans from wealth-building opportunities. Targeted interventions are not about special treatment. Targeted interventions exist to repair intentional harm.

Second, the data show that general economic policies alone do not close racial gaps. After decades of "race-neutral" approaches, the disparities remain stubbornly wide. What works for the socially constructed majority does not necessarily work for communities facing unique historical barriers.

Third, strengthening Black businesses strengthens the entire economy. McKinsey & Company estimates that closing the racial wealth gap could add $1.5 trillion to the United States economy by 2028. Supporting Black entrepreneurship is not just about equity—it's about unleashing untapped economic potential that benefits everyone (Noel et al., 2017).

Conclusion: Entrepreneurship as Power and Resistance

Entrepreneurship has long been a mechanism of resistance and resilience in Black communities. It allows for autonomy, agency, and the power to challenge structural barriers by building parallel systems of economic empowerment. Throughout history, Black entrepreneurs have led the way in social and political movements—from supporting civil rights organizing to challenging segregation and exclusion by establishing independent enterprises.

As discussed in *A history of the Black dollar*, the creation of Black-owned financial institutions, like Capital Savings Bank (1888) in Washington, D.C., and Citizens Trust Bank (1921) in Atlanta, provided capital for Black entrepreneurs. These institutions were critical in founding Black businesses when access to mainstream credit and capital was denied. Jim Crow laws limited access to white-owned establishments, leading to the rise of Black economies. Necessity fueled innovation, leading Black entrepreneurs to build insurance companies, barbershops, grocery stores, beauty salons, and media outlets like *Ebony* and *Jet*. This era proved the resilience and creativity of Black business owners under oppression.

Increased awareness the racial wealth divide has inspired a new generation of Black entrepreneurs and consumers to continue a legacy of intentionally supporting Black-owned businesses locally and online. Black entrepreneurs are using their businesses as platforms to shift narratives, build community, and advocate for justice. Through ownership, we assert our right to define our value, shape our futures, and fully engage in American democracy.

Call to Action

The time for transformative change is now. We must move beyond acknowledging disparities to implementing solutions that create lasting economic opportunity and wealth for Black communities.

To policymakers: Prioritize legislation, procurement, and economic recovery strategies that center Black entrepreneurs. Make funding more accessible and reduce barriers that hinder business growth.

To investors and institutions: Commit to transparency, equity, and real investment in the growth of Black-owned businesses.

To the community: Buy Black, invest Black, and believe in Black excellence—not just in word, but in deed. Support can be as simple as choosing a Black-owned restaurant for dinner, sharing positive information about Black businesses on social media, or investing in a Black entrepreneur's crowdfunding campaign.

To everyday consumers: Your purchasing power matters. With Black purchasing power projected to reach $2.1 trillion by 2026 (Nielsen, 2025), your decisions carry immense weight. When you decide where to spend your money, you vote for the economy and society you want to see. Look for opportunities to support Black-owned businesses in your daily life—from your morning coffee to your weekend shopping.

To aspiring entrepreneurs: Your ideas matter. Your dreams are valid. You belong in the boardroom, the storefront, and the startup ecosystem. We need you.

Together, let's build an economy that truly works for all of us—one business, one job, and one dream at a time.

Notes

1 Fearless Fund is among the first venture capital firms built by Women of Color (WOC) for WOC. We invest in under-resourced entrepreneurs including women of color led businesses seeking pre-seed, seed level or series A financing. Our mission is to bridge the gap in venture capital funding for women of color founders building scalable, growth aggressive companies".

(https://www.fearless.fund/)

References

Azevedo, Mary Ann. (2026). *Crunchbase Data: Venture Dollars For Black Startup Founders Stay Scarce Despite AI Funding Boom*. Crunchbase News. https://news.crunchbase.com/diversity/black-startup-founder-venture-funding-data-q1-2026/

Black Executive Brief. (2026). Black-Owned Business Statistics (2026 Report). https://www.blackexecutivebrief.com/insights-black-business-statistics/

Brookings. (2026). *Black Business Parity Dashboard*. https://www.brookings.edu/articles/what-if-black-businesses-were-equitably-represented-in-every-metro-area-in-america/

Cerulli Associates. (2022). U.S. high-net-worth and ultra-high-net-worth markets 2022. *The great wealth transfer*. https://www.cerulli.com/knowledge-center/reports/271/us-high-net-worth-and-ultra-high-net-worth-markets-2022

Digitalundivided. (2020). *Project Diane 2020: The State of Black & Latinx women founders*. https://www.projectdiane.com/

Dunn, T., & Holtz-Eakin, D. (2000). Financial capital, human capital, and the transition to self employment. Evidence from Intergenerational links. *Journal of Labor Economics*, 18(2), 282–305.

Federal Reserve Banks. (2022). *2022 report on firms owned by people of color: Small business credit survey*. https://www.fedsmallbusiness.org/medialibrary/FedSmallBusiness/files/2022/2022-report-on-firms-owned-by-people-of-color

Global Economic Forum. (2024). *Fighting for economic freedom. Addressing the venture capital gap for Black women entrepreneurs*. https://www.essence.com/event/fighting-for-economic-freedom/

Joint Center for Political and Economic Studies. (2023). *Black business ownership and political participation metrics*. Washington, DC.

Joint Center for Political and Economic Studies. (2026). *OpEd: The Slow Strangulation of Black Business Opportunity*. https://jointcenter.org/op-ed-the-slow-strangulation-of-black-business-opportunity-2/

Journal of Blacks in Higher Education (2026). *Data Shows Significant Growth in Black Employers in the United States*. Brookings. https://jbhe.com/2026/04/data-shows-significant-growth-in-black-employers-in-the-united-states/

McKinsey & Company. (2022). *The Black unicorn: Changing the game for inclusivity in retail*. https://www.mckinsey.com/industries/retail/our-insights/the-black-unicorn-changing-the-game-for-inclusivity-in-retail

Minority Business Development Agency. (2022). *All minority owned firms fact sheet*. U.S. Department of Commerce. https://www.mbda.gov/sites/default/files/2022-06/All%20Minority%20Owned%20Firms%20Fact%20Sheet%20-%20FINAL%206.10.2022.pdf

Nielsen. (2025). *Connecting through culture with Black audiences*. https://www.nielsen.com/insights/2025/connecting-black-america/

Noel, N., Pinder, D., Duwain, P., Stewart, S., & Wright, J. (2017). *The economic impact of closing the racial wealth gap*. McKinsey & Co. https://www.mckinsey.com/~/media/mckinsey/industries/public%20and%20social%20sector/our%20insights/the%20economic%20impact%20of%20closing%20the%20racial%20wealth%20gap/the-economic-impact-of-closing-the-racial-wealth-gap-final.pdf

North Carolina Sustainable Business Council. (2026). *Black Businesses and the Generational Wealth Gap*. https://www.ncsbcouncil.org/generational-wealth-gap

Perry, A. M., & Romer, C. (2019). *To expand the economy, invest in Black businesses.* Brookings Institution. https://www.brookings.edu/articles/to-expand-the-economy-invest-in-black-businesses/

Perry, A. M., & Stephens, H. (2025). *Driving prosperity: How Black-owned businesses fueled recent economic growth.* Brookings Institution. https://www.brookings.edu/articles/driving-prosperity-how-black-owned-businesses-fueled-recent-economic-growth/

Perry, A. M., Stephens, Hanna, & Donoghoe, M. (2024). *Black wealth is increasing, but so is the racial wealth gap,* Brookings Institution. https://www.brookings.edu/articles/black-wealth-is-increasing-but-so-is-the-racial-wealth-gap/

Teare, G. (2026). *Global venture funding surged as startup deals and valuations set all-time records.* Crunchbase News. https://news.crunchbase.com/venture/funding-data-third-largest-year-2025/

U.S. Census Bureau. (2023, October 26). *Census Bureau releases new data on minority-owned, veteran-owned and women-owned businesses.* https://www.census.gov/newsroom/press-releases/2023/annual-business-survey-employer-business-characteristics.html

U.S. Census Bureau. (2025). *American Community Survey [Data set]. U.S. Department of Commerce.* https://www.census.gov/programs-surveys/acs/data.html

U.S. Census Bureau. (2026). *National Black History Month: February 2026.* https://www.census.gov/newsroom/facts-for-features/2026/black-history-month.html

U.S. Small Business Administration. (2021, August 17). *Small business facts: The importance of business ownership to wealth.* Office of Advocacy. https://advocacy.sba.gov/2021/08/17/small-business-facts-the-importance-of-business-ownership-to-wealth

Section III

Education

This section examines the full spectrum of educational experiences for Black learners, from the earliest moments of brain development through higher education, revealing how systemic anti-Blackness operates across every level of the American education system while documenting the liberatory alternatives Black communities have continuously created. Together, these Black Papers challenge deficit narratives and demand a fundamental redesign of educational institutions to serve Black excellence rather than perpetuate oppression.

"Start With Us: How Early Care and Education Shapes Democracy" establishes that democracy begins not at the voting booth but at the crib, arguing that investments in early childhood care reveal everything about the kind of society we are building. By age three, children's brains have formed over one million neural connections per second. Yet, Black families spend disproportionately more of their income on child care—often over 14% compared to other groups—while Black early educators earn among the lowest wages in the sector. This Black Paper repositions early care and education as essential democratic infrastructure rather than private family responsibility, demonstrating that every dollar invested in high-quality early learning returns up to $7 to society. Democracy built on care ensures Black children experience more than survival, creating space to dream, build confidence, and discover their place in the world. The analysis presents concrete policy recommendations, including, living wages for educators, culturally affirming programs that reflect Black families' lived experiences, and protection of proven programs like Head Start and Early Head Start.

"Beyond Protest, Toward Power: K-12 Education and Thriving Black Students in America" confronts the reality that American public education was never designed for Black success, documenting how systems from antebellum literacy laws through contemporary resegregation, punitive discipline, and curriculum erasure function as sophisticated racial control mechanisms. Over one-third of Black students attend schools with 90–100% non-white enrollment—segregation levels unseen since the 1960s. Black girls face suspension at six times the rate of white girls starting in preschool. Only 7% of teachers are Black, while 15% of students are. And with 6,870+ books banned in

DOI: 10.4324/9781003752646-9

2024–2025 targeting Black histories, this Black Paper argues we face a design crisis requiring movement beyond critique toward construction. Drawing on the legacy of clandestine literacy circles, Rosenwald Schools, Freedom Schools, and contemporary models like the Village of Wisdom, this analysis presents a dual strategy: transforming existing systems where possible while building an adjacent ecosystem of liberatory learning spaces that operate with clarity of purpose rooted in self-determination and collective responsibility.

"Higher Learning: The Black Learner in Higher Education—Pathways, Challenges, and Opportunities" traces how post-secondary credentials serve as gateways to economic prosperity while revealing the structural barriers that limit Black access and completion. Black students face systematic obstacles, including inadequate K-12 preparation stemming from under-resourced schools, financial barriers with higher debt burdens and lower family wealth to draw upon, campus climates marked by isolation, micro- and macroaggressions at predominantly white institutions, and policy threats masked as anti-DEI legislation that eliminates support programs. This Black Paper examines the full landscape of pathways from community colleges serving as crucial access points for nearly half of Black undergraduates to four-year institutions where persistence gaps reveal the cumulative impact of financial stress, lack of belonging, and inadequate support services. The analysis demonstrates that Black learner success requires not individual resilience alone but comprehensive institutional transformation addressing affordability, culturally responsive support, diverse faculty representation, and protection of programs proven to work.

"Institutional Contexts for Black Learners: The Role of HBCUs, Community Colleges, and Digital Education" explores how different institutional settings shape Black educational journeys and outcomes. While approximately 80% of Black students attend non-HBCU institutions, Historically Black Colleges and Universities produce outsized results—awarding 17% of bachelor's degrees to Black students from just 3% of colleges, generating 80% of Black judges, and producing 50% of Black doctors despite resource inequities stemming from historical underfunding. Community colleges serve as democracy's colleges, offering accessible entry points with open admissions and affordable tuition. Yet, Black students face completion challenges requiring guided pathways, comprehensive support addressing both academic and non-academic needs, and transfer agreements that honor credits earned. The digital transformation accelerated by COVID-19 reveals both promise and peril, as online education expands access while simultaneously exposing digital divides in connectivity, device access, technical literacy, and the absence of culturally responsive design that Black learners require for success in virtual spaces.

Together, these Black Papers refuse the premise that Black learners must adapt to educational systems designed for their failure, instead demanding wholesale transformation while documenting the rich tradition of Black educational innovation that has sustained communities from slavery through the present. They challenge readers to recognize that achieving educational justice requires more than access to existing institutions—it demands building from Black intellectual traditions, centering Black joy and brilliance rather than trauma, investing resources proportionate to historical debt owed, and creating learning environments where Black children and youth don't merely survive but thrive as their whole, authentic selves. This section articulates education as a site of both oppression and liberation, calling on Black communities to move beyond protest toward the power of creation.

Chapter 6

Start With Us

How Early Care and Education Shapes Democracy

David J. Johns, Lee Johnson III, Cemeré James, Iheoma Iruka, and Lauren Christine Mims[*]

Executive Summary

High-quality early care and education (ECE) during children's critical developmental window from prenatal to age five shapes their cognitive, social, emotional, and physical development for life. Despite scientific consensus on ECE's importance, Black families face inequitable access to quality care, including higher costs, limited availability in their communities, and environments where few books, teachers, or tangible resources reflect their culture or experiences. Meanwhile, the ECE workforce—predominantly Black and Brown women—remains severely underpaid despite performing crucial societal work. This Black Paper (Paper) analyzes these systemic inequities, presents key data, and provides actionable recommendations for policymakers, advocates, and communities to build a more just ECE system that prioritizes the needs of Black children, affirms their identities and experiences, and recognizes care work as essential democratic infrastructure.

* Supported by braintrust authors: Nadia French-Graham and Roshana Agarrat.

DOI: 10.4324/9781003752646-10

Introduction

Before children utter their first words, they mimic the nature of a sponge, absorbing the world around them. Children notice and respond when someone smiles at them. They feel the rhythm of music and learn from feeling safe in someone's arms. Across communities, adults witness the joy children show when they stack blocks—again and again—until they tumble.

A child's early years are critical for development. What we invest in during those years shows what kind of society we want to build. So, before we discuss policy, let us define early care and education and explain why it is so special for all children.

A Child's Experience: Why This Matters

Four-year-old Zion enters his Head Start classroom, running to his teacher excitedly. "Ms. Tanya! Look what I can do!" He carefully writes the first two letters of his name—something he's been practicing at home. Ms. Tanya, who has known Zion since he was two, kneels to his level and celebrates this milestone. "I see you, Zion! You've been working hard on writing your name."

Later, during story time, Zion points excitedly at a character in the book who has curly hair like his. "That boy looks like me!" he exclaims.

For Zion, this classroom is more than a place where his mother leaves him while she works as a nurse. It's where he builds confidence, sees himself in learning materials, forms relationships with caring adults who look like him, and develops the foundations for academic and social success. Research shows that positive early experiences like Zion's have lasting impacts. Children who feel seen, affirmed, and supported in their early years are more likely to develop healthy self-concepts, strong academic skills, and resilience that carries them through life's challenges (Iruka et al., 2021a). This is what quality, culturally affirming early care and education looks like. But for too many Black children, these experiences remain out of reach due to the systemic barriers their families face.

What Is Early Care and Education (ECE)?

Early care and education (ECE) encompasses all experiences and environments that support children's cognitive, social, emotional, and physical development before kindergarten. It includes formal spaces like child care centers, Head Start classrooms, and Pre-kindergarten (Pre-K) programs. ECE can also include care from extended family members, neighbors, and elders who nurture children when parents have to work. While most research and policy have focused on formal, regulated care settings like child care centers and preschools, many children grow and thrive in home and community-based care. Strong early development does not depend on a classroom—it begins with strong relationships, no matter the setting. It is not babysitting. It is relationship-focused brain-building.

When children experience care, try something new, and feel comfort when upset, they learn what it means to feel seen, loved, and safe. Early care and education must affirm each child's culture, identity, and spirit. By age three, a child's brain forms over one million new neural connections every second and grows to about 80% of its adult size, shaping how they think, feel, and connect with others (Cole, Trexberg, & Schaffner, 2023). To understand why this window of time matters so much, we have to look at what science tells us—learning begins at birth, and the preparation for learning starts well before birth.

Who This Black Paper Is For

This Black Paper speaks to multiple audiences who have the power to transform early care and education systems: policymakers who shape funding and regulations; institutional leaders in ECE programs, school districts, and philanthropic organizations; community advocates; and families themselves. Throughout this Paper, we provide actionable recommendations tailored to these groups, recognizing their distinct roles in building a more equitable ECE system. We particularly address decision-makers with resource allocation authority, as sustainable funding is essential to creating the systemic change Black children and families deserve.

The Science of Early Development

The first few years of life are more than just preparation for school. They provide a foundation for everything that follows well into adulthood. Decades of research confirm what Black families have long known: how a child is cared for in their earliest years—at home and in the community—shapes how they grow, learn, and lead. Understanding the science behind early development helps explain why investing in care and education during these early years is critical for a thriving democracy. The science is precise. Here are three things to know for sure:

Three Things To Know for Sure

1 **Learning begins in the womb and never stops**. Brain development begins before birth and continues rapidly in the first years of life. While 85% of the brain develops by age three, and 92% by age five, this growth depends

on the everyday experiences and interactions a child has with their parents and caregivers, with parents serving as their child's first and most important teachers (Center on the Developing Child, 2023).

2 **Prenatal to age three is the most critical window of human development**. This period lays the foundation for all future learning and development. The quality of a child's earliest experiences—especially those shaped by parents and caregivers—can have lifelong effects on how they think, relate to others, and handle emotions (National Scientific Council on the Developing Child, 2023).

3 **Strong brain development depends on safe, stable, nurturing relationships with engaged and supportive adults**. When parents and caregivers consistently respond to a child's needs, they help build strong brain architecture. Conversely, chronic stress from adverse childhood experiences—also called ACEs—such as exposure to violence, caregiver mental health challenges, or housing instability (not having a steady or safe place to live)—can disrupt healthy brain development (Johnson III, 2020; National Academies of Sciences, Engineering, and Medicine, 2019).

But knowing this, we must ask: Why do our public policies and democracy not reflect this knowledge? The answer has everything to do with how and for whom the United States care system was built.

ECE as Democratic Infrastructure

Why Early Childhood Is Where Democracy Begins

Democracy is about power. It is about whether people have the freedom and support to live with dignity and choice. Freedom, dignity, and choice can be seen in the simple things: whether a parent can go to work knowing their child is safe, whether a caregiver is paid enough to support their own family, and whether a 3-year-old, especially a Black child, gets to play, learn, and grow—or must wait for access to the kinds of opportunities and environments that help children thrive.

The truth is, democracy does not begin at the voting booth. It begins in the womb and is shaped in the crib—especially for Black children, whose earliest experiences and lives are too often shaped by systems that deny them the care, dignity, and opportunity they deserve (Sankineni, 2024).

May we remember: Democracy is built—or broken—in the places where children learn to trust the world: in classrooms, on back porches, in living rooms, and in circle time. Democracy is present in every diaper change, every story read aloud, every backyard adventure, and every soft "I believe in you."

When well-designed, culturally affirming, and grounded in relationships, ECE can nurture a child's sense of belonging, safety, and possibility. Science, policy, and funding have long focused more narrowly on formal, regulated spaces, leaving out the everyday ways families and communities foster development. What we invest in—and whom we exclude—tells us everything about the kind of society we are building (Sankineni, 2024).

The people who power this country—working parents, caregivers, and early childhood educators—must have access to voting, reliable information, and economic stability to participate in democracy fully. However, many of the people driving our economy are being left out. When families cannot make ends meet, and life feels overwhelming, it becomes difficult to attend a school board meeting, contact a lawmaker, or advocate for better laws.

That absence is not accidental, and it comes at a cost. When the people needing child care are too overburdened to speak up for it, their voices are not heard, and policies remain unchanged. Families are left without a seat at the table where decisions are made, even though they help sustain the economy and community.

Black families have always known what democracy should look like: care for all, respect for labor, and futures filled with possibility (Iruka, James, Reaves, & Forte, 2021b). What is suitable for Black children is ideal for all children and the nation. A strong democracy ensures everyone, especially those most impacted, can be heard, supported, and free.

Systemic Inequities in ECE

How the System Fails Black Families—By Design

The early care and education system is not working for most families, not by accident. Black families often face the longest waitlists, the fewest affordable options, the highest costs, and the poorest quality, creating significant barriers to care. Many live in 'child care deserts' where no licensed programs exist nearby (Jessen-Howard, Malik, & Falgout, 2020; Child Care Aware of America, 2023). Care may not be stable, culturally affirming, or safe even when available.

At the same time, Black early childhood educators—primarily women—are doing some of the most critical work in our society while earning some of the lowest wages (McLean et al., 2024). As of 2024, the median salary for early childhood educators is $13.07 per hour, with wages ranging from $10.60 in Louisiana to $18.23 in Washington, D.C. On average, Black early childhood educators earn about 78 cents less per hour than their white peers, even when they have the same level of education (McLean et al., 2024).

This unjust system is not new. It is built on a long history of denying Black people the full rights of citizenship while relying on their labor to support the economy (Aladangady & Forde, 2021). It reflects a belief that Black families should contribute to society without receiving the care, protection, or recognition they deserve. For generations, Black families have been expected to help sustain the economy while lacking the infrastructure and resources to care for their children.

The inequity does not stop there. Women working in child care—especially Black women—are still expected to help raise and support families across the country, yet are rarely seen for the actual value they bring, either socially or financially.

The roots of this system trace back to United States slavery, when Black women were forced to care for others' children while being denied the right to care for their own. An enduring legacy from that period is the "Mammy" stereotype. This harmful image began during slavery and continues to influence how society undervalues care work, particularly when it is done by Black women (Sykes & Ostendorf, 2022).

Current Data Reflecting Systemic Inequities

In addition to the historical systemic inequities discussed above, there is recent data that further highlights the need to invest in ECE.

- **Access and Affordability**: 60% of Black children under age six have all available parents in the workforce, making child care a necessity, not a luxury (Cole, Trexberg, & Schaffner, 2023).
- **Financial Burden**: Black families are more likely to spend over 14% of their income on child care, higher than any other racial group and well above the 7% threshold considered affordable by the Department of Health and Human Services (National Women's Law Center, 2024; U.S. Department of Health and Human Services, 2022). This burden is compounded by the persistent racial wealth divide that limits Black families' economic flexibility and financial security (Aladangady & Forde, 2021).
- **Child Care Deserts**: 57% of Black Americans live in areas classified as child care deserts. These are neighborhoods where there are more young children than there are licensed child care providers. Often, there are more than three children under age five for every available licensed child care slot (Child Care Aware of America, 2023).
- **Workforce Inequities**: The early childhood workforce is predominantly women (94%) and disproportionately women of color (40%). Despite the critical importance of their work, the median hourly wage for child care workers is $13.07, placing many below the poverty line (McLean et al., 2024).

- **Quality Gaps**: Even when ECE programs are available, they may not meet high-quality standards. Many programs do not have enough funding for materials that reflect children's cultures, safe and welcoming spaces, or well-trained and supported staff. This is often true in communities that have experienced long-term underinvestment, including many Black communities. Programs need stable and ongoing funding to provide strong early learning experiences that support children's growth and reflect their families' cultures, languages, and values (National Institute for Early Education Research, 2024).

Black families have long built robust networks of care and learning, often filling gaps left by an ECE system without enough investment. While resilience in the building of these networks is inspiring, it should not be necessary to survive an ECE system shaped by limited access, high costs, low pay, and uneven quality, especially for Black families. A just ECE system—within a democracy built on care—would match the brilliance of community-based care networks with real support, community-informed policy, and sustained public investment.

The Economic and Social Case for Investment

The science is precise—and so is the math. Every dollar invested in high-quality early learning returns up to $7–$13 to society in the long run. Research shows that these returns manifest through improved education outcomes, higher lifetime earnings, and reduced interaction with the criminal justice system (Heckman et al., 2010). Recent legislative sessions reflect an increase in bipartisan momentum to prioritize ECE as a critical economic and social issue, though comprehensive federal reform remains essential (Schneider & Grant, 2025). Importantly, the benefits of early childhood investments do not stop with the child. Longitudinal studies show intergenerational gains, including improved life outcomes for children who attended high-quality programs. These findings reinforce the potential of early education to strengthen families and disrupt the cycle of poverty (Heckman, 2019). In the meantime, high-quality ECE continues to show strong returns.

These returns manifest as:

- **Improved educational outcomes**: Higher graduation rates and reduced special education placement.
- **Better economic outcomes**: Higher lifetime earnings and reduced dependency on social services.
- **Stronger health outcomes**: Improved mental and physical health across the lifespan.
- **Improved long-term stability**: Children are more likely to grow into adults with stable relationships, steady employment, and active civic participation.

For Black children, specifically those who face disproportionate barriers to opportunity, high-quality ECE can be particularly transformative. Studies show that Black children who attended high-quality preschool programs experience more significant gains in school readiness and are more likely to achieve positive long-term outcomes than peers without such opportunities (National Institute for Early Education Research, 2024).

A Vision for Democracy Built on Care

Reimagining Care as a Public Good

Black children and families have a right to life, liberty, and the pursuit of happiness. Our democracy requires that we have the right to life. A democracy built on care can include:

- A society where child care costs do not deplete Black families' resources or force impossible choices between work and caregiving.
- A society where Black early childhood educators are equitably compensated and protected, with benefits like paid leave, healthcare, and job security that reflect the essential nature of their work.
- A society where every child, regardless of race, zip code, or family income, can access high-quality, culturally affirming early learning experiences.

Democracy built on care can ensure children experience more than survival and have space to freely dream, laugh, learn, build confidence, solve problems, and discover their place in the world.

If we want a just future, we must build it from the beginning, starting with a deep belief in Black children's joy, brilliance, and promise. At birth, a child cannot say, "Start with us!" but the adults who care for and teach them can.

Case Study: Community-Based Solutions

Black Family, Friend, and Neighbor Care

Black families have long relied on Family, Friend, and Neighbor (FFN) caregivers, including relatives, friends, and neighbors, to nurture and educate young children (National Black Child Development Institute [NBCDI], n.d.). FFN care is the most common form of non-parental child care in the United States particularly among infants and toddlers, and is also widely used among Black families (ACF, 2025; Gibbs & Peeks, 2026; Susman-Stillman & Banghart, 2008; Powell et al., 2023). Through its Reimagining Child Care initiative, NBCDI shows how communities can strengthen this culturally affirming expression of care. Launched in 2022, the initiative engaged 51 Black FFN providers and families across four communities in an Afrofuturist exploration of Black care grounded in participants' experiences (NBCDI, n.d.).

The initiative illustrates four principles:

- **Community expertise**: Black caregivers and families are recognized as experts whose lived experiences can inform research, advocacy, and policy (NBCDI, n.d.).

- **Cultural affirmation**: FFN care can foster belonging and affirm children's Black identities, family histories, values, and cultural traditions (NBCDI, n.d.).
- **Recognition of care work**: The initiative highlights Black FFN caregivers as an essential yet historically undervalued part of the child care system (NBCDI, n.d.; Powell et al., 2023).
- **Community-informed systems change**: Community experiences can inform policy and advocacy that better recognize and resource Black FFN care (NBCDI, n.d.).

Together, these principles show how community experience and expertise strengthen care systems for Black children and families (NBCDI, n.d.).

Policy Recommendations

Five Key Policy Areas

1 **Universal Affordability**: Commit to and fund ways to make child care free or affordable for every family (Smith et al., 2023). Specific approaches include:

   - Capping family child care expenses for low-income families.
   - Expanding Child Care and Development Block Grant funding.
   - Creating refundable child care tax credits.
   - Implementing sliding-scale subsidies that reach middle-income families.

2 **Living Wages for Early Educators**: Invest in ways to pay Early Childhood Educators a Living Wage (McLean et al., 2024). This requires:

- Establishing minimum compensation standards tied to qualifications.
- Creating wage scales comparable to K-12 education.
- Providing benefits, including health insurance and paid leave.
- Offering scholarship and loan forgiveness programs for professional development.
- Providing housing support to help early childhood educators live in the communities where they work.

3 **Expanded Community-Based Programs**: Fund more programs in Black communities—including those that reflect the culture, language, and lived experiences of the families they serve (Malik & Hagler, 2016). This means:

- Investing in facilities in underserved areas.
- Supporting networks of family child care providers.
- Funding programs with non-traditional hours.
- Creating incentives for culturally responsive programming.
- Developing career pathways for Black early childhood educators through apprenticeships and pipeline programs, like the San Francisco Black ECE Pipeline initiative.
- Launching child care programs in child care deserts, especially those led by community members. Start-up funds should prioritize Black-led providers who are often overlooked for funding, even though they care for children most in need.
- Providing direct grants to trusted local caregivers and educators to open centers or home-based programs that reflect the culture, values, and needs of their communities, not models imposed by outside organizations.
- Ensuring that federal investments reach areas with the fewest services, particularly Black communities that continue to be left out despite contributing through taxes.

4 **Black Family Leadership in Decision-Making**: Center Black families, parent leadership, and Early Childhood Educators in funding decisions. Implementation includes:

- Requiring parent and provider representation on policy boards.
- Creating community advisory councils with decision-making authority.
- Funding parent leadership development.
- Requiring tools that measure whether policies help reduce racial disparities, expand opportunity, and support economic stability, especially for Black families and providers—models like the Early Childhood Equity Strategic Plan Template and Black Child National Agenda show how this can be done in practice. (Blevins, Meek, & Iruka, 2021)

5 **Protection and Expansion of Effective Programs**: Protect and expand what's working, such as Head Start and Early Head Start, child care subsidies, and home visiting programs, and supportive policies like the Earned Income Tax Credit (EITC) and the Family and Medical Leave Act (FMLA) (Catherine, Alexander, Iruka, Meek, & Edwards, 2024; National Women's Law Center, 2024). This involves:

- Increasing Head Start and Early Head Start funding to serve all eligible children.
- Expanding eligibility for child care subsidies.
- Supporting evidence-based home visiting, including community-based home visiting programs.
- Strengthening quality rating and improvement systems.
- Preserving and expanding policies like EITC and FMLA that help families maintain income and caregiving time.
- Reducing administrative barriers to accessing these programs, so that help reaches those who need it most.

Community Action Framework

What You Can Do

You do not need to be a policymaker to help. You can care—and act.

- **Engage with Elected Officials**: Talk to your elected officials about ECE. Share your experiences, ask specific questions about their plans to support ECE in your community, and share the policy recommendations outlined in this Black Paper with them.

- **Support Early Educators**: Advocate for better wages and working conditions for ECE professionals. Recognize and respect their expertise and essential role in society.
- **Join Advocacy Efforts**: Connect with organizations focused on Black children's development and ECE justice, such as:
    - National Black Child Development Institute (NBCDI)
    - Black Child Development Institute (BCDI) local affiliates/villages
    - Black Maternal Health Caucus initiatives
    - Center for Racial Equity in Early Care and Education
    - Center for the Study of Black Children and Families
    - National Association for Family Child Care's Black Provider Network
    - LIFT (Low-Income Families Together) Early Learning Networks
    - Southern Education Foundation
    - The First 72+ Early Childhood Collaborative
    - Black Wildflowers Fund (blackwildflowers.org)
- **Vote for Pro-ECE Candidates**: Research candidates' positions on early childhood issues and prioritize ECE when casting your ballot.
- **Share Your Story**: Personal narratives are powerful advocacy tools. Share your experiences with child care—as a parent, provider, or community member—through social media, testimony at public hearings, or letters to the editor.

Promising Strategies and Innovative Models

Beyond policy recommendations, several promising strategies are already demonstrating success in addressing ECE inequities:

Shared Services Alliances

Shared Services Alliances bring together multiple child care providers to share business services, reduce overhead costs, and improve quality. In the Detroit Black Child Development Institute-led alliance, participating centers reduced administrative costs by 15–20%, redirecting those funds to teacher compensation and classroom materials (National Black Child Development Institute, 2013).

Dual-Generation Approaches

Programs like Educare, which combine high-quality ECE with family support services, show particular promise for Black families. Educare schools are public–private partnerships, with many also serving as Head Start programs. A unique feature of the model is its partnership with local evaluation teams to track progress and outcomes. Educare has significantly improved child development and family engagement in predominantly Black communities. Children who attend Educare often enter kindergarten with school readiness skills on par with their more advantaged peers (Start Early, 2023).

"Being Black Is Not a Risk Factor" Approach

The National Black Child Development Institute's "Being Black Is Not a Risk Factor" initiative reframes the narrative around Black children's development by highlighting strengths rather than deficits. In communities such as Milwaukee and Detroit that are implementing this framework, early childhood programs have shifted their assessment practices, cultural competency training, and family engagement strategies. These changes build upon Black children's cultural assets within learning environments (National Black Child Development Institute, 2013).

Community Schools as ECE Hubs

Integrating ECE into community schools creates comprehensive support systems for families. The Children's Aid Society community schools in Harlem and the South Bronx provide high-quality early childhood programs alongside health services, adult education, and family support—all in neighborhoods where Black families have historically lacked access to such integrated services (Children's Aid, 2024).

Union-Led Quality Improvements

In places where early educators have unionized, like Philadelphia and Seattle, they have secured better wages and funding for professional development and quality improvements. Often led by women of color, these unions have created pathways to higher credentials while advocating for compensation that reflects those increased qualifications (Gould & Blair, 2020).

Promoting Black Joy and Countering Bias Through Infant and Early Childhood Mental Health Consultation

The Center of Excellence for Infant & Early Childhood Mental Health Consultation's "Promoting Black Joy and Countering Bias Through Infant and Early Childhood Mental Health Consultation (IECMHC)" resource describes the importance of creating spaces for Black joy through four elements: Black Brilliance, Black Innovation, Black Agency, and Black Beauty. This resource lists promising practices to reimagine early learning environments that promote joy and safety for Black children and their families (Blevins et al., 2023).

The San Francisco Black ECE Career Development Pipeline Program

The San Francisco Black Early Childhood Educator (ECE) Career Development Pipeline is a local initiative designed to recruit, train, and support Black early childhood educators. The program offers paid apprenticeships, mentorship, and career coaching to help participants grow and remain in the long-term workforce. It also works to reduce barriers that often prevent Black educators from entering and advancing in ECE careers. This model shows how investing in Black educators strengthens the quality and diversity of the early learning system (Children's Council of San Francisco, 2023).

Anticipating Criticism

As with any call for significant systemic change, proposals to transform the ECE system face criticism. Here, we address common counter-arguments:

"Universal ECE Is Too Expensive"

Critics often cite cost as the primary barrier to universal access. However, this argument fails to consider both:

1 **The return on investment**: High-quality ECE returns $7–$13 for every dollar invested (Heckman, 2021), making it one of the most fiscally responsible investments the government can make.
2 **The cost of inaction**: Our economy's current fragmented system costs an estimated $57 billion annually in lost earnings, productivity, and revenue (ReadyNation, 2023).

"ECE Should Remain a Family Responsibility"

Some argue that child care is primarily a family responsibility. This position overlooks several realities:

1 **Economic necessity**: For most families, including 60% of Black families with young children, all available parents must work to maintain economic stability (Cole, Trexberg, & Schaffner, 2023).
2 **Societal benefit**: Quality ECE benefits not just individual families but society. Children who experience quality ECE are more likely to grow into adults with stable relationships, steady employment, and active civic participation.
3 **False binary**: Supporting out-of-home care does not diminish family care—it supports it. Early childhood educators partner with families by providing options to support their caregiving needs and circumstances.

"Universal Programs Will Reduce Quality and Choice"

Some suggest government involvement will lead to "one-size-fits-all" approaches that reduce quality and family choice. However:

1 **Existing models**: Successful universal systems like Boston and Washington, D.C., maintain diverse delivery models, including centers, family child care, and faith-based providers.
2 **Quality standards**: Public funding can be tied to quality standards while allowing diverse approaches, including culturally specific programming.
3 **Current reality**: The existing market-based system already severely restricts choice for many Black families who cannot afford quality options or live in child care deserts.

Conclusion

We face a clear choice: continue with a fragmented, inequitable system that fails too many children and families, particularly those who are Black, or build a democracy that truly values care as essential infrastructure.

The scientific evidence is irrefutable, the economic case compelling, and the moral imperative clear. When we invest in high-quality, accessible, and culturally responsive early care and education for all children, starting with those who are most marginalized, we build the foundation for a more equitable society.

Black children deserve to begin their lives in environments that nurture their full humanity, affirm their identities, and unlock their limitless potential. Black families deserve support systems that honor their strengths and address their needs. Black early childhood educators deserve compensation and respect that reflects the crucial importance of their work.

Democracy built on care begins with our youngest citizens. It is time we start with them.

Resources for Black Child Development

Organizations and Initiatives

Black Child Development Institute (BCDI) Affiliates https://www.nbcdi.org/strength-in-community-our-national-village-network/ Local chapters implement culturally relevant programs in communities across the country, with significant ECE initiatives in:

- Atlanta, GA
- Detroit, MI
- Denver, CO
- Charlotte, NC
- Sacramento, CA
- Washington, DC
- Milwaukee, WI

Black Maternal Health Caucus Early Childhood Initiatives https://blackmaternalhealthcaucus-underwood.house.gov/ Addresses the maternal–child continuum from birth through early childhood.

Center for the Study of Black Children and Families https://www.african.american.studies.research.centers.com Conducts research specifically focused on the developmental needs of Black children and effective family support practices.

Equity Research Action Coalition at the University of North Carolina at Chapel Hill (UNC) https://equity-coalition.fpg.unc.edu/ Focuses on research, program development, and advocacy, specifically on Black children from birth to age eight.

National Black Child Development Institute (NBCDI) https://www.nbcdi.org. Founded in 1970, NBCDI provides resources, programs, and leadership on issues affecting Black children and families, with local affiliates across the country. Their initiatives include:

- "Being Black Is Not a Risk Factor" publication series
- NBCDI Academy for Early Learning Leadership
- Family Engagement program
- Good for Me! Nutrition and Physical Activity Program
- Early Care and Education Policy Agenda
- Public Voices Fellowship in partnership with the OpEd Project

National Head Start Association's Black Directors Council https://www.nhsa.org/our-network/black-directors-council/ Focuses on expanding and strengthening Head Start's impact in Black communities.

Southern Education Foundation (SEF) https://southerneducation.org Founded in 1867, SEF advances equity and excellence in education for Black students, low-income students, and students of color across the South. SEF works to transform education systems from early childhood through college through research, policy, advocacy, and leadership development.

The Center for Racial Equity in Early Care and Education https://centerforracialequity.org Provides training, research, and policy advocacy focused on dismantling systemic racism in early childhood education systems.

References

Administration for Children and Families. (2025). *Where do family, friend, and neighbor child care providers turn for support? Findings from the Home-Based Child Care Practices and Experiences Study*. Office of Planning, Research, and Evaluation; U.S. Department of Health and Human Services. https://acf.gov/opre/report/where-do-family-friend-and-neighbor-child-care-providers-turn-support-findings-home

Aladangady, A., & Forde, A. (2021). *Wealth inequality and the racial wealth gap*. Board of Governors of the Federal Reserve System. https://www.federalreserve.gov/econres/notes/feds-notes/wealth-inequality-and-the-racial-wealth-gap-20211022.html

Blevins, D., with Gordon, L., Keyes, A., & Meek, S. (2023). *Promoting Black joy and countering bias through infant and early childhood mental health consultation*. Center of Excellence for Infant and Early Childhood Mental Health Consultation. https://www.iecmhc.org/documents/CenteringEquityResource_BlackJoy_508.pdf

Blevins, D., Meek, S., & Iruka, I. U. (2021). *Start with equity: Early childhood equity strategic plan template*. Children's Equity Project. https://childandfamilysuccess.asu.edu/cep/initiatives/equity-strategic-plan-template-advance-equity-early-care-education-systems

Catherine, E., Alexander, B., Iruka, I. U., Meek, S., & Edwards, M. C. (2024). *Review of policy effects on black families and children: Advancing the Black child national agenda*. FPG Child Development Institute.

Center on the Developing Child. (2023). *Brain architecture*. Harvard University. https://developingchild.harvard.edu/science/key-concepts/brain-architecture/

Child Care Aware of America. (2023). *Child care at a standstill: Price and landscape analysis 2023*. https://www.childcareaware.org/thechildcarestandstill/

Children's Aid. (2024). *Community schools: Early childhood integration model*. https://www.childrensaidnyc.org/programs/early-childhood

Children's Council of San Francisco. (2023). *How San Francisco is graduating more Black early educators—and why it matters*. https://www.childrenscouncil.org/how-san-francisco-is-graduating-more-black-early-educators-and-why-it-matters/

Cole, P., Trexberg, K., & Schaffner, M. (2023). *State of babies yearbook: 2023*. Zero to Three. https://stateofbabies.org/

Gibbs, H., & Peeks, C. (2026). *America's licensed child care deserts*. Center for American Progress. https://www.americanprogress.org/article/americas-licensed-child-care-deserts/

Gould, E., & Blair, H. (2020). *Who's paying now? The explicit and implicit costs of the current early care and education system*. Economic Policy Institute. https://www.epi.org/publication/whos-paying-now-costs-of-the-current-ece-system/

Heckman, J. J. (2019). *Early childhood education strengthens families and can break the cycle of poverty*. Perry Preschool: Intergenerational Effects. https://heckmanequation.org/resource/perry-intergenerational-effects-summary/

Heckman, J. J., Moon, S. E., Pinto, R., Savelyev, P. A., & Yavitz, A. (2010). The rate of return to the High Scope Perry Preschool Program. *Journal of Public Economics, 94*(1–2), 114–128. https://doi.org/10.1016/j.jpubeco.2009.11.001

Home Grown & Erikson Institute. (2022). *An evidence-based framework for high-quality home-based child care networks*. https://homegrownchildcare.org/wp-content/uploads/2022/08/HomeGrown-Erikson-BENCHMARKS-BRIEF-Final.pdf

Iruka, I. U., Curenton, S. M., Durden, T. R., & Gardner-Neblett, N. (2021a). *Don't look away: Embracing anti-bias classrooms*. Gryphon House. https://www.naeyc.org/resources/pubs/books/dont-look-away

Iruka, I. U., James, C., Reaves, C., & Forte, A. (2021b). *Black Child National Agenda: America must deliver on its promise*. Equity Research Action Coalition, Frank Porter Graham Child Development Institute, The University of North Carolina at Chapel Hill. https://fpg.unc.edu/publications/black-child-national-agenda-america-must-deliver-its-promise

Jessen-Howard, S., Malik, R., & Falgout, M. K. (2020). *Costly and unavailable: America lacks sufficient child care supply for infants and toddlers*. Center for American Progress. https://www.americanprogress.org/article/costly-unavailable-america-lacks-sufficient-child-care-supply-infants-toddlers/

Johnson III, L. (2020). *Emotional determinants of health: exploring prevalence and the impact of adverse childhood experiences on physical and mental health outcomes of Black adult men: results from the 2012 behavioral risk factor surveillance system*. Doctoral dissertation, University of Alabama Libraries. https://bit.ly/3EvmfvO

Katz, E. (2024). *Federal funding streams for child care and early childhood education*. National Conference of State Legislatures. https://www.ncsl.org/state-federal/federal-funding-streams-for-child-care-and-early-childhood-education

Malik, R., & Hagler, J. (2016). *Black families work more, earn less, and face difficult child care choices*. Center for American Progress. https://www.americanprogress.org/article/black-families-work-more-earn-less-and-face-difficult-child-care-choices/

McLean, C., Austin, L. J. E., Powell, A., Jaggi, S., Kim, Y., Knight, J., Muñoz, S., & Schlieber, M. (2024). *Early childhood workforce index 2024*. Center for the Study of Child Care Employment, University of California, Berkeley. https://cscce.berkeley.edu/workforce-index-2024/

National Academies of Sciences, Engineering, and Medicine. (2019). *Vibrant and healthy kids: Aligning science, practice, and policy to advance health equity*. The National Academies Press. https://doi.org/10.17226/25466

National Black Child Development Institute. (n.d.). *Reimagining child care*. Retrieved September 20, 2026, from https://www.nbcdi.org/ffn-care/

National Black Child Development Institute. (2013). *Being Black is not a risk factor: A strengths-based look at the state of the Black child*. https://youthrex.com/wp-content/uploads/2019/05/Being-Black-Is-Not-a-Risk-Factor_0.pdf

National Institute for Early Education Research. (2024). *The state of preschool 2023*. Rutgers University. https://nieer.org/yearbook/2023

National Scientific Council on the Developing Child. (2023). *Connecting the brain to the rest of the body: Early childhood development and lifelong health are deeply intertwined.* Center on the Developing Child at Harvard University. https://developingchild.harvard.edu/resources/connecting-the-brain-to-the-rest-of-the-body/

National Women's Law Center. (2024). *Women and families struggle with child care following the federal funding cliff.* https://nwlc.org/wp-content/uploads/2024.05/Pluse-4.0-Child-Care-Fact-Sheet-May-2024-2.pdf

Powell, A., Adejumo, T., Austin, L. J. E., & Copeman Petig, A. (2023). *Parent preferences in family, friend, neighbor, and nanny care.* Center for the Study of Child Care Employment, University of California, Berkeley. https://cscce.berkeley.edu/publications/report/parent-preferences-in-family-friend-neighbor-and-nanny-care/

ReadyNation. (2023). *$122 billion: The growing, annual cost of the infant-toddler child care crisis.* Council for a Strong America. https://www.strongnation.org/articles/2038-122-billion-the-growing-annual-cost-of-the-infant-toddler-child-care-crisis

Sankineni, S. R. (2024). *Policy research brief: Civil rights principles for early care and education.* Equity Research Action Coalition. https://equity-coalition.fpg.unc.edu/wp-content/uploads/ECE-Policy-Research-Brief.pdf

Schneider, A., & Grant, E. (2025). *Increased bipartisan focus on child care must lead to congressional action.* Center for American Progress. https://www.americanprogress.org/article/increased-bipartisan-focus-on-child-care-must-lead-to-congressional-action/

Smith, L. K., Walsh, B., Owens, V., Osborne, C., Mercado, K., & Rotolo, O. (2023). *Building bipartisan support for child care toolkit: 2023 update.* Bipartisan Policy Center. https://bipartisanpolicy.org/wp-content/uploads/2023/02/BPC-ECI-Bipartisan-Toolkit-2023-Update-Full-Report.pdf

Start Early. (2023). *Educare learning network: Outcomes for Black children and families.* https://www.startearly.org/what-we-do/early-learning-programs/networks/educare-learning-network/

Susman-Stillman, A., & Banghart, P. (2008). *Demographics of family, friend, and neighbor child care in the United States.* Child Care & Early Education Research Connections, National Center for Children in Poverty. https://www.nccp.org/publication/demographics-of-family-friend-and-neighbor-child-care-in-the-united-states/

Sykes, M., & Ostendorf, K. (Eds.). (2022). *Child care justice: Transforming the system of care for young children.* Teachers College Press. https://bookshop.org/p/books/child-care-justice-transforming-the-system-of-care-for-young-children-maurice-sykes/18395299?ean=9780807767580&next=t

U.S. Department of Health and Human Services, Office of Child Care. (2022). *Using maps to inform decisions about child care and early education.* https://acf.gov/sites/default/files/documents/opre/using_maps_inform_ccee_decisions_dec2022.pdf

Chapter 7

Beyond Protest, Toward Power

K-12 Education and Thriving Black Students in America

*David J. Johns, Sharif El-Mekki, Monique S. Toussaint, Lauren Christine Mims, Yaribel Mercedes, Brianna Baker, and Christina Grant**

Executive Summary

American public education was designed to fail Black children—and it's working precisely as intended. This Black Paper (Paper) examines how systems of educational oppression function, reclaims our legacy of educational innovation, and provides a blueprint for building liberatory learning spaces where Black children thrive.

The Opportunity

From slavery-era literacy bans to today's resegregated schools, the United States public education system operates as a sophisticated tool of racial control:

- **Over one-third of Black students** attend schools with 90–100% non-white enrollment—segregation levels unseen since the 1960s (Meckler, 2022; Frankenberg et al., 2019).
- **Black girls are suspended** at six times the rate of white girls, starting in preschool (Crenshaw et al., 2015).
- **Only 7% of teachers are Black (non-Hispanic)**, while 15% of students are Black; Black male teachers represent just 2% (NCES, 2020).
- **6,870+ books banned** in 2024–2025, targeting Black histories and experiences (PEN America, 2025).

High-stakes testing, special education overrepresentation, zero-tolerance discipline, and curriculum erasure combine to label, track, punish, and exclude Black children from equitable opportunities. Book bans and anti-Diversity, Equity and Inclusion (DEI) legislation intensify this assault on Black educational freedom.

* Supported by braintrust author: Kelcey P. Morrow.

DOI: 10.4324/9781003752646-11

Our Blueprint: Ancestral Intelligence and Proven Solutions

Black communities have always built powerful educational alternatives—from literacy circles during slavery to Freedom Schools and independent Black institutions. These spaces prove what is possible when education centers Black excellence:

- **Black students with one Black teacher by third grade** are 13% more likely to enroll in college; with two, 32% more likely (Gershenson et al., 2018).
- **Culturally responsive curriculum** significantly improves reading and math achievement (Gay, 2018).
- **Community-based programs** positively impact academic achievement, attendance, and behavior (Maier et al., 2017).

The Solution: A Dual Strategy

Transform existing systems where possible while building an affirming, self-sustaining educational ecosystem alongside them:

Six Actions for Liberation

1. **Identify a collective vision** through community gatherings in trusted Black spaces.
2. **Leverage resources** by coordinating funding, expertise, and networks across sectors.
3. **Make systems work for us** through political activation and school board engagement.
4. **Create Black educational spaces** in after-school and out-of-school programs, weekend academies, independent schools.
5. **Reclaim Black teaching traditions** by documenting elder wisdom and centering African-centered pedagogy.
6. **Build libraries of resistance** to combat book bans and preserve intellectual freedom.

We hope this Black Paper helps you understand how education systems were designed to harm Black children—and how we build the liberatory alternatives our babies deserve. Share it at churches, barbershops and beauty shops, community centers, and with school boards. Use it to start conversations, demand accountability, and create educational spaces rooted in Black-centered and affirming love, rigor, and self-determination.

Our children deserve better. Our democracy requires it.

Introduction

At the time of writing, civil rights offices are being dismantled, equity programs eliminated, and non-discrimination laws revoked—all to manufacture the myth of anti-white racism and reverse hard-won progress. Amidst a rising tide of anti-Diversity, Equity, and Inclusion efforts, erasure of Blackness in official histories, and attacks on educational institutions and centers of power within civil society, Black America finds itself in imminent material danger and facing substantive questions about how it will continue liberatory work.

While the work of confronting, combatting, and ultimately evolving institutions and their effects on our bodies, lives, and communities must continue, Black America finds itself where it has always been across history: blocked from seats of power and coincidentally placed into a position where we must simultaneously rely on the power of community, build a new civic sinew, and social fabric architected by liberatory designs. Reliance on white-centered institutions, even those we have counted as allies, will always expose us to various degrees of oppression, anti-Blackness, and stochastic (or state-sanctioned) violence.

We are not just in a policy crisis. What we see unfolding—whether in literacy gaps, the criminalization of Black children in schools, or the loss of Black educators from the profession—is not accidental. These are the predictable outcomes of a system built to destroy and murder our minds, bodies, and spirits (Love, 2019).

Black people have always stood in the gaps of creating figurative spaces that transform schools into educational sites for liberation. We must make this (re)turn. This return means moving beyond symbolic approaches and celebratory gestures toward structural and systemic changes that see, honor, and value our communities' humanity, dignity, literacies, histories, and ways of being.

Schools must become sites of refusal and resistance, committed to critical pedagogy and disrupting systems of dominance and subjugation. This adjacent educational ecosystem does not wait for permission or reform but operates with clarity of purpose and confidence in our own traditions. We are reclaiming Ancestral Intelligence—the real AI. Our vision is rooted in self-determination and collective responsibility, where our schools become not sites of harm but hubs of healing, intellectual rigor, cultural excellence, and civic preparation.

Our schools, as always, are a vital place to start.

Schools are the bedrock of democracy. Schools are more than buildings or bureaucracies. They are sacred spaces where we shape memory, identity, and destiny. When we design education systems rooted in Black collectivist teaching traditions, cultural memory, and liberatory practices, we create the conditions for flourishing far beyond the classroom. We create spaces of transgression, where education becomes a praxis of freedom, transforming people, communities, and the world (hooks, 1994).

So, while we push, we must also plant. While we challenge, we must also construct. We must destroy to build. As Kaba (2021) reminds us, we must call on our radical imaginations to dream anew, beyond the systems we are working to dismantle. The future of Black education depends on our willingness to invest in a dual strategy that transforms the existing system where possible, and builds an affirming, rigorous, self-sustaining ecosystem alongside it.

It is our charge to build educational futures that avoid the deadly mishaps of relying solely on a system that has failed millions, mis-educated, undereducated, underfunded, relegated to impoverishment, incarcerated, and given misery through anti-Black curricula, pedagogy, and frameworks. While we continue to push the broader system, we must constantly make and affirm an adjacent ecosystem that affirms rigorous instruction and citizenship, a positive racial identity, accurate history, community building, and self-determination.

Public schools must be spaces where students—our babies—can thrive. Schools must serve as bridges to spaces of critical love and learning, cultural knowledge, and critical consciousness.

Understanding this history is essential for moving beyond reform to reimagine and rebuild educational spaces designed for Black liberation and thriving. Yet we are not starting from scratch. Long before mainstream institutions failed us, our ancestors built our own models of educational excellence that can guide our work today.

A History of American Public Education: Systems Working as Designed

The American public education system was never designed to serve Black children equally or effectively. As civil rights lawyer Bryan Stevenson notes, systems work exactly as they are designed to work (Stevenson, 2014). Understanding the historical context of American public education reveals how these systems were deliberately structured to maintain racial hierarchies that benefit white Americans, particularly white males.

The Foundations of Inequality

Public education in America has always been a site where democracy is contested, as bell hooks describes in her work *Teaching to transgress* (hooks, 1994). Public schools served a dual purpose from their earliest days: providing basic education while reinforcing existing social orders and hierarchies. During the antebellum period, laws explicitly prohibited the education of enslaved Black people. These laws reflected a recognition that literacy is a pathway to freedom and resistance (Anderson, 1988).

After the Civil War, the Reconstruction era briefly saw the establishment of schools for formerly enslaved people, many led by Black educators and Northern missionaries. These schools emphasized classical education, citizenship preparation, and community leadership—establishing educational models that centered Black excellence. This period represented a brief flourishing of Black educational opportunity before being systematically dismantled during the Jim Crow era through violent intimidation, defunding, and the deliberate destruction of Black education infrastructure (Du Bois, 1935/1998). The legacy of this dismantling persists today: contemporary inequalities such as the persistent funding gaps between predominantly Black and white school districts averaging $23 billion annually (EdBuild, 2019), the digital divide leaves Black students with less access to technology and broadband, and curriculum erasure that continues to marginalize or distort Black history in classrooms across America all reflect historical patterns of educational disinvestment and control.

Segregation, Desegregation, and Resegregation

The 1896 *Plessy* v. *Ferguson* Supreme Court decision enshrined the "separate but equal" doctrine, legitimizing segregated schooling that was anything but equal. Black schools received significantly less funding, inferior facilities, and limited resources compared to white schools (Siddle Walker, 1996). Despite these barriers, many all-Black schools developed powerful educational traditions centered on rigor, cultural affirmation, and community responsibility—a testament to the resilience and ingenuity of Black educators and communities.

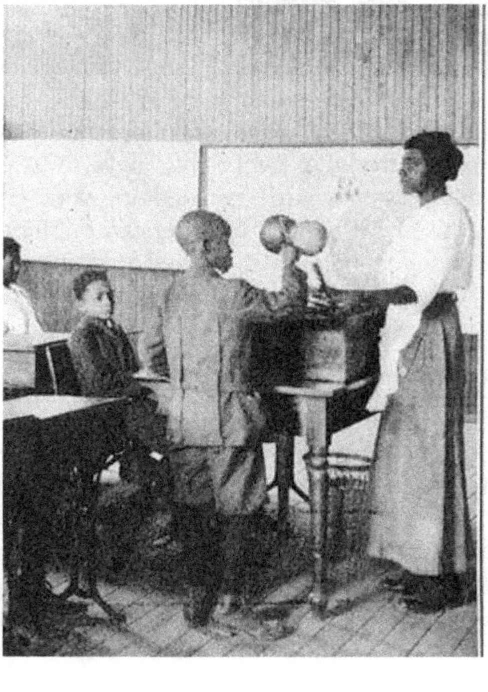

The landmark 1954 *Brown* v. *Board of Education* decision legally ended segregation and was implemented with unintended negative consequences for Black education. Integration often meant closing Black schools, firing Black educators (teachers and administrators), and subjecting Black students to hostile environments where their cultural knowledge was devalued (Tillman, 2004). While desegregation was a necessary legal victory, it resulted in the loss of educational spaces designed to nurture Black excellence. It also resulted in what Carol Anderson calls "white rage," the unleashing of anti-Black policy and law in society. Love (2023) writes, "White rage" is what has built America's institutions, working to cunningly craft laws, policies, covenants, and approaches that undercut democracy, halt Black advancement, and cage Black bodies while leaving white supremacy intact and often even stronger (Love, 2023).

In the decades following integration efforts, United States public schools have become increasingly resegregated through white flight, economic segregation, and housing discrimination (Frankenberg et al., 2019). By 2020, more than one-third of Black students attended schools where 90–100% of students were non-white—a level of segregation not seen since the 1960s (Meckler, 2022, Frankenberg et al., 2019). Today's "school choice" initiatives—specifically voucher programs and charter school expansion efforts—co-opt and weaponize the language of liberation while often reinforcing segregation patterns via racial and economic isolation (Hannah-Jones, 2017a). Research shows that voucher programs have diverted over $1 billion annually from public schools, with states like Florida, Arizona, and Wisconsin leading the way (National Center for Public Education, n.d.). Evidence affirms that these programs disproportionately benefit white and higher-income families while draining resources from public schools serving predominantly Black communities to subsidize private education. In some districts, voucher expansion has led to school closures in Black neighborhoods, reduced course offerings, and the layoff of experienced educators—deepening rather than addressing educational inequity (Hannah-Jones, 2017b).

KEY STATISTIC: By 2020, over 1/3 of Black students attended schools where 90–100% of students were non-white—segregation levels not seen since the 1960s.

Education Policy as a Racial Control Mechanism

Beginning in the 1980s and accelerating through the early 2000s, three interlocking policy regimes—standardized testing mandates, special education classification expansion, and increased adoption of zero-tolerance disciplinary policies—converged to create what amounts to a sophisticated system of racial control within schools. While presented as neutral, evidence-based reforms designed to improve educational outcomes have functioned to label, track, punish, and ultimately exclude Black children from equitable educational opportunities. Understanding how these mechanisms operate reveals the intentional design behind educational inequity.

The rise of high-stakes testing and accountability movements disproportionately penalizes schools serving Black students without addressing fundamental inequities in resources, teacher quality, and curriculum (Love, 2019). Rooted in eugenics and racist ideologies, standardization is carceral at its very root (Love, 2023). Far from neutral reforms, these policies function as sophisticated tools of racial control that have evolved from segregation to more subtle, but equally devastating forms of educational inequality.

KEY STATISTIC: Black children are overrepresented in remedial courses and special education and are twice as likely to be retained once during their K-12 schooling.

Black children are overrepresented in remedial courses and special education and are twice as likely to be retained once during their K-12 schooling (Theoharis, 2009). These systems often label Black children as deficient rather than recognizing the systemic failures that create an education debt (Ladson-Billings, 2006).

Meanwhile, zero-tolerance disciplinary policies have criminalized normal childhood behavior, particularly for Black children. Black students are suspended and expelled at rates far exceeding their white peers for the same behaviors, creating what has been termed the "school-to-prison pipeline" and, for some, the "school-to-sex trafficking pipeline" (Morris, 2016). The suspension rate of Black girls is six times higher than that of their White counterparts (Morris, 2016). These disciplinary disparities begin as early as preschool, where Black children face disproportionate scrutiny and punishment. Black students are constantly under duress, facing the violence of racism, anti-Blackness, and white supremacist delusion in schooling spaces that do not see, honor, or value their ways of knowing and being.

KEY STATISTIC: Black girls are suspended at six times the rate of white girls—disparities that begin as early as preschool.

Each major educational reform movement—from No Child Left Behind to Race to the Top to the current accountability frameworks—has claimed to address educational disparities while leaving fundamental structures intact. These reform movements maintain structures that produce racial inequities in education. Reform policies tend to focus on individual achievement while ignoring the structural conditions that maintain educational inequality (Ladson-Billings, 2006). The focus on individual outcomes serves to obscure systemic failures, allowing policymakers to blame students, families, and communities rather than confronting the accumulated effects of historical and ongoing disinvestment.

As Ladson-Billings (2006) argues, the "achievement gap" might better be understood as an "education debt" accumulated over generations of systematic disinvestment in Black education. This framing demands not just incremental improvements but a comprehensive accounting and a reparative approach to educational justice.

The history of American public education reveals that these systems were not broken but instead designed to reproduce and cement hierarchies rooted in the lies of meritocracy and the so-called "American Dream." For Black folks, we remain in the nexus of this nightmare—freedom dreaming of a better world for ourselves and our children while being stuck in an educational nightmare. Public schools remain contested spaces where the promise of democracy confronts the reality of structural racism.

Understanding this history of systemic failure makes it clear why Black communities have consistently built their own educational alternatives. These alternatives represent not just resistance to oppression, but affirmative visions of what education can be.

Ancestral Intelligence (AI) & Blackprints: Liberation Schools to Intellectual Maroons

The "adjacent ecosystem" we propose does not emerge from thin air—it builds upon a rich historical tradition of Black-created educational alternatives that have consistently provided what mainstream institutions could not. These spaces have served as both refusal and resistance to oppression and affirmative visions of education rooted in Black intellectual traditions, cultural excellence, and joy deeply connected to our justice orientations. This type of ecosystem requires remembering. A way of being and knowing that calls us to understand who and whose we are. Going back. Sankofa. A shift in our minds, bodies, and spirits. A (re)turn to our African diasporic memory, to the soul and wisdom of our people (Dillard, 2021).

Across history, in the face of injustice and oppression, Black communities have built our own models of education (Givens, 2021). These Black-built ways of learning have their roots in survival and sovereignty. From the bastions of learning STEM and STEAM, literacy, the arts, and African history and culture, to the clandestine learning circles of our enslaved ancestors, to the Rosenwald Schools, Freedom Schools of the Civil Rights Movement, Independent Black Schools during the Black Power Movements and beyond, Black education has functioned as both a locus of resistance and a vehicle for possibility.

"Black educational traditions were never simply about academic content—they have always been about liberation, empowerment, and the development of the whole child." As Dr. Asa Hilliard powerfully reminds us, we will never encounter children in any group who are not geniuses. There is no mystery in how to teach them. The first thing we do is treat them like human beings, and the second thing we do is love them. This foundational truth anchors our work: Black children are not the problem—they are brilliant, capable, and deserving of educational environments designed for their flourishing.

The educational revolution in the mid-20th century transformed teachers into freedom fighters, curriculum into counternarratives, and schools into sites of political awakening. It was far from a spontaneous moment. It was the product of a long lineage of Black educational community-determination. This revolution includes Marcus Foster's urban education leadership, the Black Panther Party's Liberation Schools, the Nation of Islam's Clara Muhammad Schools, and independent Black institutions such as Nidhamu Sasa and the Institute of Positive Education (IPE) from the 1960s through the 1980s. These institutions represent a rich legacy of Black educational innovation that continues to inform and invigorate our work today.

These schools were staffed by servant leaders and activist educators who turned their organizing energy toward the classroom. They were teachers, curriculum designers, political educators, dreamkeepers, and community developers. The adults who made these learning environments possible for multiple generations of Black children saw themselves as the trusted servants of providing an affirming, intellectually rigorous, future-building education to the children of our communities. They were the vanguards for Black youth's intellectual, cultural, spiritual, and emotional development.

This tradition lives on in places like the Children's Defense Fund Freedom Schools, organizations like Reconstruction founded by Kaya Henderson, and the ethos of schools like Sankofa Academy Charter School, Ile Omede, and the Jubilee School. These are Black institutions that center literacy, excellence, and the fulsome development of Black children, whose brilliance is so often overlooked or criminalized.

Contemporary Examples of Black Educational Excellence

Today, we see this legacy continued in innovative educational models across the country:

- **The Village of Wisdom** in Durham, NC, which partners with families to protect the genius of Black children through culturally affirming education.
- **The Freedom School Network** serves over 12,000 children nationwide through culturally relevant summer and after-school programming.
- **The Center for Black Educator Development** recruits, trains, and retains Black teachers through high school and college apprenticeship programs, professional learning for veteran educators, and advocacy.
- **Black Teacher Collaborative** is working to cultivate culturally affirming learning environments across the nation.
- **Gye Nyame School** in Chicago centers African cultural principles in comprehensive education.
- **Little Sun People** is a community child care center founded in 1980 by Mama Fela in Bedford-Stuyvesant.

To understand the power of these Black-made institutions, we must also recognize the intellectual frameworks that undergird them. These schools were not simply alternatives to failing mainstream institutions. They represented a fundamentally different philosophy of education, one rooted in African diasporic traditions of knowledge-making, collective responsibility, and liberation. Uhuru Hotep's (2008) concept of the intellectual maroon is a useful tool to do this work. The intellectual maroon is the thinker or teacher who breaks away from the dominant, Eurocentric paradigms that hold captive the Black imagination and instead constructs liberatory spaces that foster freedom of thought and action. Intellectual maroons are heirs to the Maroon communities of the past; they are self-emancipated, strategic, and sovereign.

At these Black-made institutions, Black educators understand the transformational power of schools as centers of liberation. Far from neutral sites of academic instruction, these spaces provide opportunities for constructing new futures premised on justice and self-determination. Here, educators are positioned to create an ecosystem where Black children are equipped with a positive racial identity, purpose, and self-sufficiency.

These institutions and the transformational work they have pioneered are not just historical artifacts. They are living blueprints. Their lessons archive our survival and our refusal to succumb to death-dealing institutions. They safeguard our joy, histories, and ancestral wisdom.

From Deficit to Abundance: Reframing Educational Challenges for Black Students

For too long, the narrative around Black student achievement has been dominated by a deficit perspective, focusing on what Black children lack rather than the rich cultural, intellectual, and social assets they possess. The challenges Black students face are real, and these challenges reflect failures of systems, not deficiencies in our children.

Moving Beyond Crisis Framing

While recognizing the urgency of our current educational moment, we must be precise about what makes this a distinct "design crisis" rather than simply the continuation of historical patterns. What distinguishes our present reality is the intensification and coordination of attacks on multiple fronts: the systematic dismantling of hard-won policy gains in educational equity; the explicit targeting of culturally responsive curriculum through anti-Critical Race Theory (CRT) legislation; anti-Black sentiment and policy, and unprecedented assaults on the professional autonomy of educators committed to teaching truthful and inclusive histories.

While acknowledging the urgency of educational inequality, we must resist framing Black education solely through the lens of crisis, which can inadvertently reinforce deficit-based approaches. Instead, drawing on Dr. Lauren Mims' (2021) framework of Black flourishing and brilliance, we must center asset-based approaches that recognize and nurture the inherent brilliance, resilience, and potential of Black children.

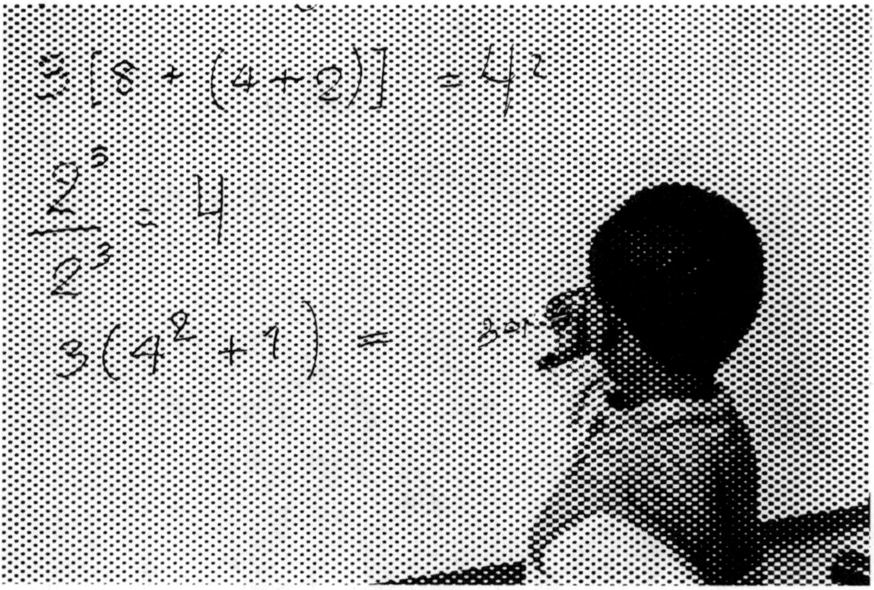

Mims' research demonstrates that academic outcomes improve alongside social-emotional wellbeing when educational environments focus on supporting Black students' thriving, not just surviving. This approach recognizes that Black children are not problems to be fixed but brilliant minds to be cultivated.

Student Voices on Thriving

When asked what thriving looks like in education, Black students consistently express desires that align with fundamental human needs:

- "Being able to bring my whole self to school without hiding parts of who I am."
- "Having teachers who believe I can excel and push me to reach my potential."
- "Learning about my history and seeing people who look like me in the curriculum."
- "Having space to ask questions and explore ideas without being judged."
- "Connecting what I learn to real issues in my community."

Our babies remind us that Black students don't simply want to survive school. Black students want to thrive within educational environments that affirm their identities and nurture their dreams.

Black Girls Theorizing Their Own Liberation

Additionally, Black students deserve to thrive within educational environments that affirm their intersectional identities and permit them to produce knowledge from spaces rooted in safety and care. This lesson is echoed powerfully in the reflections of young leaders from the Justice for Black Girls (JBG) Ambassadors Program:

- "I realized I deserved classrooms where I could come as I was and be recognized as brilliant and that I could hold my teachers and administrators accountable."
- "It opened my eyes to how crucial healing is in school. I realized that if I'm going to dedicate my life to uplifting Black girls, then I need to take my own healing seriously. I learned that it's okay to heal and I'm not selfish for doing so."
- "Being Afro-Latina, I struggled with affirming the various parts of my identity. But through JBG, I learned that Black girls are multifaceted beings. We can be brilliant and unapologetic at once."
- "The JBG program gave me a space where I feel like I can be my true self, unapologetically and beautifully."
- "This was the biggest breath of fresh air in a suffocating world."

These student reflections do not simply echo the theory of thriving—they embody it. They are theorizing about thriving. Our students deserve educational spaces that move beyond deficit approaches and toward the co-construction of liberatory environments that see, value, and affirm the genius within Black people. JBG Ambassadors are creating safe spaces that allow them to think, critique, be curious, and radically love themselves and others.

Centering Student Voice: Lessons from Federal Leadership

The imperative to center student voice was underscored throughout education summits hosted by the White House Initiative on Educational Excellence for African Americans' (AfAmEducation—hereafter AfAmEd summits) during the Obama administration. These summits—held across the country, including in Atlanta, Jackson, Oakland, Los Angeles, and Philadelphia—brought together students, families, educators, and community leaders to address the holistic development of African American children and youth. AfAmEd summits highlighted successful models of amplifying student perspectives on what they needed to thrive, not just survive.

The one non-negotiable rule that informed these spaces was that the only experts who held space on the stage or on the mic were STUDENTS, of all ages. Caring and concerned adults were invited to listen, not to respond in real time with all of the work they felt was designed to address the priorities, needs, and invitations made by the students we engaged, but to respond in love by working ***with*** young people to build and advance political agendas anchored and animated by ***their*** dreams and desires.

The Initiative, established by Executive Order in 2012, recognized that improving outcomes for Black students required listening to Black communities, creating partnerships across sectors, and maintaining an unwavering focus on equity and excellence. Additional programming created by the Initiative upheld the precedent set by the summits where youth voice was essential at Presidential Advisory Commission meetings, including one at the White House where Vice President Kamala Harris was on the agenda, another on Capitol Hill where speakers included prominent leaders such as Representative Jasmine Crockett, as well as the Power Up series, AfAmWomenLead, STEAM summit, #BlackMenTeach events, listening sessions, and other key programs. The intentional inclusion of youth speakers at Initiative events created a domino effect as programming was shared with the Interagency Working Group, modeling for other agencies the importance of youth presence in the federal landscape.

Additionally, the Initiative regularly highlighted youth in its Connector Newsletter with a distribution list of over 300,000 subscribers, and created a youth engagement team that specifically ensured that there was programming for youth, by youth. This team planned youth panels virtually and across the country as well as identified youth speakers to supplement subject matter experts tapped as a resource for policy and community engagement work and events.

While much of this federal infrastructure has since been dismantled, the model of centering student voice and community wisdom remains vital for the work ahead. Two of the authors of this Black Paper, Dr. David J. Johns and Dr. Lauren C. Mims, led this groundbreaking work on behalf of the Obama administration. A third author, Dr. Monique S. Toussaint, supported and sustained programming that centered student voice for the next two Administrations until the Initiative was eliminated in January 2026.

Today's Educational Crisis: So Widespread, It's Invisible

The unending crisis Black students face has persisted across time. It is a pervasive and normalized problem that risks becoming invisible, made easily digestible through clinical expert language, distanced through policy prescriptions, and buried beneath statistical noise. The plain fact, however, is that the vast majority of Black children are not being educated adequately, and many are being outright abandoned. Too often, we are left with celebrating their ability to survive the systems that claim to serve them, but were never designed for their success.

The result of the current crisis is that even those institutions specifically designed by us and for us are flashing warning signs. Black men are the canaries in this socially constructed coal mine.

> Recent reporting found that the number of Black men attending four-year colleges has plummeted across the board. And nowhere is this deficit more pronounced than at historically Black colleges and universities, or HBCUs. Black men account for 26% of the students at HBCUs, down from an already low 38% in 1976, according to the American Institute for Boys and Men. There are now about as many non-Black students attending HBCUs as there are Black men.
>
> (American Institute for Boys and Men [AIBM], 2024)

This backsliding accompanies the systematic dismantling of equity-focused programs. Already, hundreds of millions in federal grants intended for teacher development and diversifying the teaching workforce have been cut, with millions more threatened for any school system pursuing Diversity, Equity, and Inclusion (DEI).

This moment exposes what Kofi Addae and Uhuru Hotep call comfortable captivity: a psychological state where we accept a degree of access to majority systems—a grant here, a DEI position there—as sufficient progress. Comfortable captivity is the illusion of inclusion, which numbs us to the truth that these systems were never designed to love, affirm, or support our babies—or us.

Worse still, we internalize their logic.

Our children deserve more than survival. Our children matter. The responsibility of mattering has always been the moral imperative of Black folx—since the formation of the human caste—to serve those racialized as white, who continue to benefit from the preservation and poison of white supremacy (Love, 2019). They deserve brilliance, belonging, and the full power of an education that sees them not as problems to be overcome but as people to be formed and freed.

Proven Strategies for Black Student Success

Research consistently identifies several key components that support Black student achievement and wellbeing:

1 **Culturally Responsive Pedagogy**: Gloria Ladson-Billings' (1995) foundational work shows that academic engagement and achievement increase significantly when teachers connect academic content to students' cultural frameworks and lived experiences. This approach does not water down content—it makes learning more accessible and meaningful. In her 1995 work, Ladson-Billings named it culturally relevant pedagogy, a framework that has since evolved within the field of education. It is essential to recognize that this foundational approach is grounded in advancing students' literacies, numeracies, cultural competence, and sociopolitical consciousness. This work prepares students to be active citizens of the world, with the ability to critically analyze both the word and the world (Freire, 2017).
2 **Critically Conscious and Responsive Leadership**: School leadership is a fundamental determinant of student success. Critically conscious leaders with a justice-oriented disposition are essential to cultivating equitable learning environments. Genao and Mercedes (2021) posit that race-conscious and responsive educational leadership is necessary to rectify anti-Black racism. Conscious and responsive leadership demands anti-racist solidarity by centering race and developing a deep understanding of racism, power, and privilege.
3 **Affirming Racial Identity Development**: Research by Rowley and colleagues (2014) demonstrates that when Black students develop a positive racial identity, they show greater academic persistence, higher self-esteem, and better mental health outcomes. Educational environments that affirm Black identity rather than requiring its suppression support both academic and psychological development.
4 **High Expectations Combined with High Support**: Lisa Delpit's (1995) research highlights that Black students thrive when teachers maintain rigorous academic standards while providing the scaffolding and support needed to meet those standards, balancing warmth and demand. The combination of challenge and support creates optimal conditions for growth.

5 **Community-Based Learning**: Programs that connect classroom learning to community contexts and real-world problem-solving show particular promise for engaging Black students (Baldridge et al., 2017). These approaches recognize students as knowledge creators and world changers, not just knowledge consumers.
6 **Relationship-Centered Learning**: Strong, affirming relationships with teachers who believe in students' potential are consistently linked to better outcomes for Black students (Ferguson, 2003). These relationships buffer against the negative (or adverse) effects of racism and stereotype threat.

Data on What Works

The evidence for these approaches is compelling:

> **KEY STATISTIC**: Black students with one Black teacher by 3rd grade are 13% more likely to enroll in college; with two Black teachers, 32% more likely.

- Black students who have at least one Black teacher by third grade are 13% more likely to enroll in college, while those with two Black teachers are 32% more likely (Gershenson et al., 2018). Black boys appear particularly impacted by Black teachers—they can be up to 39% less likely to drop out of high school and 29% more likely to enroll in college with a single Black teacher in early grades.
- Schools that implement culturally responsive curriculum significantly improve reading and math achievement among Black students (Dee & Penner, 2017).
- Out-of-school time programs grounded in positive youth development frameworks significantly positively affect Black youth's academic achievement, attendance, and behavioral outcomes (Baldridge et al., 2017).
- Early literacy interventions that build on Black communities' oral traditions and linguistic strengths show particularly strong results for young Black learners (Charity Hudley & Mallinson, 2017).

These approaches don't just work—they transform. They demonstrate that remarkable growth is possible when educational environments are designed around Black children's strengths, needs, and dreams rather than requiring them to adapt to environments not designed for them.

Reclaiming Our Legacy: Black Educators Past, Present, and Future

Black educators have been pivotal in advancing Black communities throughout history. From the secret teaching of literacy during slavery to developing pedagogical innovations that center Black students' experiences, Black teachers and educational leaders have consistently served as intellectual guides and community anchors. Maintaining this legacy requires addressing the current shortage of Black educators and creating pathways toward a teaching force that reflects the diversity of America's students.

A Rich and Resilient History

Before desegregation, Black teachers and principals formed the backbone of many Black communities. These educators were often the most educated members of their communities and served multiple roles as academic instructors, character developers, political organizers, and cultural custodians. In her groundbreaking work, Vanessa Siddle Walker (2001) documented how Black educators in segregated schools created nurturing educational environments characterized by high expectations, cultural affirmation, and deep community connections.

Black educational leaders like Anna Julia Cooper, Mary McLeod Bethune, Septima Clark, Marva Collins, and Booker T. Washington developed innovative approaches to education that addressed both academic excellence and the social realities of racism. Their work demonstrates that Black educational traditions have always been about more than subject matter—they have been about liberation, economic community-sufficiency, and full participation in a democratic society.

The Impact of Desegregation on Black Educators

The *Brown* v. *Board of Education* decisions, while legally necessary, had devastating consequences for Black educators. As schools integrated, tens of thousands of Black teachers and principals lost their jobs as white school boards and superintendents chose not to hire them for newly integrated schools (Tillman, 2004). Between 1954 and 1965, approximately 38,000 Black teachers and administrators in the South lost their positions (Ethridge, 1979). This massive displacement represented not just individual job losses but the dismantling of an educational infrastructure that nurtured generations of Black students.

The loss of these educators and infrastructure meant that Black students increasingly found themselves in educational environments without caring and concerned adults who shared their cultural background, understood their lived experiences, or weaved their history and culture into the classroom. It also meant the marginalization of pedagogical approaches specifically developed to support Black student success.

Current Challenges and Promising Approaches

> **KEY STATISTIC**: Only 7% of teachers are Black, while 15% of students are Black. Black male teachers represent just 2% of all teachers.

Between 6 and 9% of America's teaching force is Black depending on the survey and year, while Black students make up approximately 15% of the public school population. Black male teachers represent less than 2% of all teachers. For every 112 students, there is only one Black teacher (African American Teaching Fellows, 2025). This underrepresentation matters deeply, as research consistently shows that same-race teachers can have significant positive effects on Black students' academic outcomes, disciplinary experiences, and long-term educational attainment (Gershenson et al., 2018).

The question of who leads our adjacent ecosystem is critical. While research demonstrates the positive impact of Black educators on Black students, we must acknowledge that not all Black educators inherently bring liberatory practices into their classrooms. Many have been formed within the same Eurocentric educational paradigms they now seek to transform. What matters most is not simply demographic representation, but a commitment to culturally responsive pedagogy, anti-racist practice, and a deep understanding of Black educational traditions. Stated plainly: all skinfolk aren't kinfolk. Operate accordingly.

Our education ecosystem requires both the recruitment of more Black educators who love Black people and the development of all educators, of diverse backgrounds and lived experiences, who can embody the principles of liberatory teaching. This work requires creating pathways for educators from various backgrounds to learn Black educational traditions, while simultaneously prioritizing the recruitment, support, and leadership development of Black educators who bring critical lived experience to their work.

This underrepresentation stems from:

Barriers to Entry: Standardized testing requirements for teacher certification disproportionately exclude Black candidates, despite limited evidence that these tests predict teaching effectiveness (Petchauer, 2012).

Hostile Work Environments: Black teachers often report experiencing racial microaggressions, having their authority questioned, and being pigeonholed into disciplinary or "diversity" roles rather than being recognized for their pedagogical expertise (Bristol, 2018).

Limited Career Advancement: Black educators are underrepresented in leadership positions, with fewer opportunities for advancement into administrative roles (Williams & Loeb, 2012).

Economic Disincentives: As college-educated professionals, Black graduates have increasingly chosen higher-paying fields as teacher salaries have stagnated relative to other professions (Ingersoll & May, 2011).

Despite these challenges, innovative programs are creating pathways to increase and sustain Black educator representation:

Grow Your Own Programs: Initiatives identifying and supporting community members, paraprofessionals, and high school students interested in becoming educators show particular promise for recruiting educators committed to serving their communities (Gist et al., 2019). The Center for Black Educator Development's Teaching Academy exemplifies this approach by providing year-round support for Black students interested in teaching careers.

Alternative Certification Pathways: Programs that provide job-embedded training while reducing financial barriers to certification have recruited more diverse candidates (Carver-Thomas, 2018).

HBCU Teacher Preparation: Historically Black Colleges and Universities (HBCUs) continue to produce a disproportionate share of Black teachers. Strengthening these programs and creating direct pathways from HBCUs to high-need schools can significantly increase Black teacher representation (Gasman & Nguyen, 2014).

Targeted Retention Strategies: Programs that provide mentoring, affinity groups, and leadership development designed explicitly for Black teachers show promise for improving retention rates (Griffin & Tackie, 2016). The African American Teaching Fellows Program is an exemplary model that provides Black preservice and in-service teachers with financial, professional, and social support starting in college and continuing through Black teachers' early years in the classroom.

Policy Reforms: Addressing discriminatory practices in hiring, evaluation, and promotion, as well as reforming certification requirements can remove structural barriers to Black teacher success (Cook, 2015).

Numerical representation is not our goal; instead, we seek to create and sustain conditions where Black educators can teach authentically, bringing their full cultural knowledge and pedagogical expertise to their work without being forced to assimilate to white normative practices or engage in anti-Black praxis.

Black Teaching Traditions, Techniques, and Building the Ecosystem We Need

The dual strategy we propose—transforming existing systems while building adjacent ones—requires deliberate navigation of predictable tensions. These approaches are not separate tracks but interlocking gears in a broader machinery of educational possibility. When we work within systems to create pockets of liberation, we demonstrate what is possible and create breathing room for more radical reimagining and possibilities. Simultaneously, the independent spaces we build should pressure mainstream institutions to change in ways that center Blackness, Black students, and our communities' rich cultural legacy, serving as both critique and exemplar.

This relationship means that success in one arena can facilitate progress in another. A teacher incorporating culturally responsive pedagogy in a traditional school benefits their immediate students and contributes to a growing body of practice that can inform adjacent ecosystems. Similarly, the innovation and success of independent Black educational spaces can provide compelling evidence for broader system change.

The key is approaching this work with both tactical flexibility and strategic clarity. We move between these approaches based on context, opportunity, and need—sometimes pushing for reform from within, sometimes building anew always with the ultimate goal of creating educational environments where Black children thrive. This work requires us to embrace both the pragmatism of incremental change and the vision of transformative possibility. As we engage in this important work, we benefit from acknowledging the contradictions, embracing the fumbling, and continuing in the pursuit of co-constructing dream spaces with our young people and their communities. We can do all things.

Dr. Martin Luther King Jr. poignantly shared with Harry Belafonte, "I fear I am integrating my people into a burning house" (Belafonte & Shnayerson, 2011). We can no longer sustain the fires of the master's house. We must let it burn—and allow the ashes to fertilize the soil for new ground. The way forward must not come from tweaking a broken structure's architecture alone. We will need to build our own at the same time.

Fortunately, a trail has been blazed by our forebearers. Indeed, we are heirs to a vast and powerful lineage of Black teaching traditions, ways of knowing, methods of instruction, and philosophical commitments that have been passed down with love, purpose, and rigor.

These traditions reject the deficit narratives often imposed on Black children and our communities and instead locate genius in the same community, in our culture, and in the spiritual and intellectual capacities of our people. These traditions are rooted in African epistemologies, ways of knowing, pedagogies, and ways of teaching. They prioritize understanding, communal accountability, repetition as mastery, and education as character development.

We can leverage our traditions to reimagine what schools and formal learning spaces can be and should become. Schools are not merely places of academic preparation but also centers of cultural transmission, political development, and personal transformation. To span the divide between where schools are currently and where they must be to become what is described here requires designing a parallel ecosystem, a full-spectrum infrastructure that nurtures the whole child and engages the entire community.

Core Elements of Black Educational Ecosystems

- **Critical Love and Racial Care**: Environments that see and honor young people's ways of being and the complexities of their humanity.
- **Culturally Affirming Curriculum**: Materials that center Black histories, scientific contributions, literary traditions, and cultural knowledge.
- **Community Governance**: Decision-making structures that include families (those recognized by schools and school districts and beyond), community elders, and local stakeholders.
- **Intergenerational Learning**: Models that connect youth with elders through mentorship, storytelling, and cultural transmission.
- **Holistic Assessment**: Approaches to measuring growth that capture intellectual, social, emotional, and cultural development.
- **Restorative Practices**: Discipline approaches that heal harm while maintaining community bonds.
- **Ethical Development**: Attention to character formation and values-based learning.

Parallel ecosystems can form through several approaches, efforts, and strategies. One example is micro schools and extended-day/year programs that better align with the rhythms and needs of Black families, rather than dominant models built for the economic efficiencies of a bygone era. When centering the ecosystem on a whole-child approach to support Black student success include access to rigorous coursework, especially science, technology, engineering, mathematics and the arts. These systems should also employ and provide fair disciplinary practices, mental health services, restorative healing-centered approaches, and strong family and community engagement.

Emphasize literacy, numeracy, and tools for self-sufficiency including: Black history, vocational skills, financial and digital literacy, and cultural rites of passage rituals. These strategies require culturally competent educators and curricula centered on learner sovereignty. Curriculum must be coupled with a civic education that prepares students for life as engaged citizens, community builders, and stewards of our shared future. Ultimately, the goal is schooling experiences that enable students to dream, experience joy, and cultivate their curiosity. Skills that prepare them to thrive as both individuals and contribute to the greater wellbeing of their community is a schooling experience designed for the future. As we work to build the education ecosystem we need and deserve, we benefit from asking the following question: ***How are we creating spaces where students leave with more questions than answers?***

To support an empowering education ecosystem, educators and youth workers must have strong academic knowledge ***and*** the ability to connect with students meaningfully. They must also have the cultural fluency to understand the complexities of our young people's lives and build within them a positive racial identity to which they can hold tight despite the historical forces that blow against it ever harder every day.

Schools that empower Black children also expand the aperture of who can be an educator within the community by drawing on the wisdom and knowledge of neighborhood elders, parents, artists, and organizers to create powerful family and community partnerships that extend schooling and its impact far beyond the schoolhouse walls. These partnerships, along with Black community-based organizations, weave together the existing strengths of a school community into a living ecosystem that affirms cultural identity, reinforces academic excellence, and builds the civic and emotional infrastructure our children need to thrive.

Call To Action: Building That Which Cannot Be Dismantled

The work described in this Black Paper is not idealism. It is realism informed by our history. It is what our ancestors built under far more hostile conditions—from hush harbors (Dillard, 2021), Black literary societies (McHenry, 2002) and so-called "pit schools" during slavery, to Rosenwald and Freedom Schools across the 20th century.

Some of our communities are still building the education ecosystem our babies and our democracy deserve today, in small pockets, in after-school and out-of-school programs, in church and mosque basements, and in digital spaces. What is needed now is coordination, investment, and a shared vision.

We must stop asking permission to do what we already know works and scale up what is ours.

We can build something that cannot be undermined by shifting sands in the political wind or stripped away by policy reversals. We can create a community-determined educational foundation powerfully rooted in history, sustained by our own communities, and accountable to a real vision of liberation.

The blueprint outlined in this Black Paper is only as powerful as our collective will to implement it. Building a liberatory educational ecosystem for Black children requires all of us—educators, families, community leaders, policymakers, and students themselves—to take meaningful and measurable action.

The recommendations below operate on two complementary tracks—pushing for transformation within existing systems while simultaneously building autonomous spaces outside them. These parallel efforts strengthen each other: our work within systems creates openings and resources for independent initiatives, while our independent spaces generate innovative practices that can influence mainstream education.

Recommendations

Support a Collective Vision

Student success is reliant on all responsible parties playing a role. Find ways to engage students, families, teachers, administrators, businesses, and community partners and outline how each can support Black excellence. This may involve hosting town halls at churches, mosques, barber and beauty shops, community centers, and other trusted safe spaces in Black communities. Provide a space for continual conversation and evaluation of progress. Create a timeline and redefine the action plan to implement the shared vision as much as necessary to get the desired results.

Specific Actions

- Host quarterly community visioning sessions with diverse stakeholders.
- Create a "Black Student Success Coalition" with representatives from various sectors.
- Develop and distribute a "Community Educational Asset Map," identifying resources.
- Establish metrics for measuring progress toward shared goals.

Leverage Resources

Collaborating to share funds, expertise, and networks will be the lifeline for many schools, districts, organizations, and institutions working to impact K-12 public education positively. Identify alliances, partnerships, and opportunities to connect where possible. Many stakeholders serve the same audiences and stretch their resources when a system of support might be the most effective. Federal-funded programs like Promise Neighborhoods, Choice Neighborhoods, Full-Service Community Schools, etc., all provide examples of ways to coordinate resources to support communities. These initiatives allow partnerships between businesses, institutions of higher education, districts, and/or schools to provide necessary services to students, families, and communities. With the limitation of federal funds now and in the near future, leaders should rally together to identify ways to sustain the work and join efforts to replicate what has been effective.

Specific Actions

- Create a shared digital platform for connecting resource needs with available supports.
- Establish a regular convening of investors focused on Black educational excellence.
- Develop cooperative purchasing agreements among Black-led educational organizations.
- Map existing federal and foundation funding opportunities and coordinate applications.

Make the Systems Work for Us

For some of us, making the system work for us means political activation. Call your local, state, and federal representatives and demand that they fund programs that support Black student success. Some of these programs fund teacher training, access to mental health services, afterschool programs, college preparation programs, and other vital interventions that support Black student academic success. This work may involve serving on school boards or becoming a district, state, and/or national leader. Find the best way that you can show up to be the change our students need.

Finally, we can all contribute to the work described throughout this Black Paper by being mentors, educators, and volunteers. With schools, districts, and organizations having limited resources to support students outside of classrooms, community members can and should give back. Find what works for you and commit to it.

Specific Actions

- Create a "Black Education Advocacy Toolkit" with templates for contacting officials.
- Establish a pipeline program for developing Black educational leaders.
- Form "Education Watch" committees to advocate for resources and monitor local school board decisions especially those around curricula, school safety, school leadership, and other critical needs of Black students.
- Develop a volunteer database connecting skilled community members with schools.

Create and Support Black Educational Spaces

Establish and sustain independent Black educational institutions, from after-school and out-of-school programs to weekend academies to full-time schools. Support them with your time, talent, and treasures. These spaces can implement the proven strategies that center Black excellence, cultural affirmation, and academic rigor without compromise. As a result, they can serve as both direct service providers for our children and as laboratories of innovation that can influence broader educational systems.

Specific Actions

- Create a network of community-based "Liberation Learning Labs" for after-school programming.
- Develop a "Black Education Startup Fund" to support new educational initiatives.
- Establish shared facilities agreements to maximize the use of community spaces.
- Create a mentorship program connecting established programs with emerging ones.

Reclaim and Advance Black Teaching Traditions and Techniques

Document, study, and implement the rich pedagogical traditions developed by Black educators who love Black people across generations. This work includes mentoring new educators in these methods, creating curriculum that draws on these approaches, and establishing teacher education programs that center on Black educational philosophy. The work of groups like the Center for Black Educator Development provides templates for revitalizing these traditions for contemporary contexts.

Specific Actions

- Create an oral history project documenting the wisdom of veteran Black educators.
- Develop an "African-Centered Pedagogy Certificate" program for teachers.
- Establish a curriculum repository of teaching materials grounded in Black traditions.
- Host an annual "Black Education Traditions Conference" for sharing practices.

Build Libraries of Resistance

The current wave of book banning represents a direct assault on educational freedom and the right to historical truth. Fascist regimes throughout history have targeted books and knowledge as the first step in broader campaigns of oppression, understanding that controlling what people can learn is essential to controlling what they can imagine and achieve. These modern bans—targeting works that feature Black, LGBTQ+, and other marginalized experiences—follow this dangerous pattern and demand our organized resistance.

In the 2024–2025 school year, 6,870 book bans were documented in school districts across America, with a disproportionate focus on works addressing racial justice, Black history, and LGBTQ+ experiences. These bans are not merely about individual books but represent coordinated attempts to erase the histories, experiences, and voices of marginalized communities from educational spaces (PEN America, 2025).

We must respond to authoritarian tactics by building libraries of resistance in our homes, community centers, faith spaces, and independent educational spaces. The National Black Justice Collective (NBJC) and the African American Policy Forum's (AAPF) Freedom to Learn initiative provide resources for combating these bans and ensuring Black children maintain access to their intellectual heritage. Similarly, GLISTEN Rainbow Library project connects schools and community organizations to affirming books representing the full diversity of the human experience.

Supporting critical media literacy spaces, where knowledge is shared and community is cultivated, is vital. Consider the Teach the Babies Podcast, Higher Heights Live Brunch Sundays, Undistracted Podcast and Native Land Podcast as resources. As times evolve, the media will be essential to moving us forward in this digital world.

Building liberatory libraries is not just about providing books. It is about creating sanctuaries of knowledge where young people can encounter the full breadth of human experience and develop critical thinking and media literacy skills. By collecting banned books and making them available in community spaces, we continue the tradition of Black educational resistance that dates back to our ancestors, who taught reading in secret during slavery.

Specific Actions

- Create "Freedom Libraries" in community spaces with books that have been banned.
- Organize read-alongs featuring banned authors and texts.
- Develop a "Banned Books Mobile Library" to reach underserved communities.
- Partner with independent bookstores to donate banned books to schools and families.
- Host intergenerational discussions about the historical context of book banning.

Leadership Spotlight

Artist and cultural steward Solange Knowles demonstrates what resistance looks like in practice through the Saint Heron Community Library—a free, honor-based digital archive and physical lending library dedicated to rare, out-of-print, and first-edition works by Black and Brown authors, poets, and artists. Launched in September 2025, Saint Heron Library represents more than a book collection; it is a cultural infrastructure that ensures Black intellectual and creative contributions remain accessible rather than relegated to obscurity. With over 2,150 titles and growing, borrowers can request works and keep them for 45 days—a model built on trust and community that directly counters the scarcity and control inherent in book-banning campaigns. This vision of democratized access, where anyone with curiosity can engage with Octavia Butler, Audre Lorde, and countless other voices, shows us what is possible when we refuse to let our culture be priced out or locked away.

We must respond to authoritarian tactics by building libraries of resistance in our homes, community centers, faith spaces, churches, masjids, and independent educational spaces.

Conclusion

Ultimately, our collective goal is to empower everyone to do something. We all have everything to lose and nothing to gain by allowing our students not to have the educational experiences they need and deserve. Our ancestors demonstrated the power of unity and how we continue to support each other to move forward. This time is no different. We have what it takes to be strong, innovative, and successful. We owe it to our students to ensure they are safe, supported, and engaged.

It is in our DNA—embedded in the very fabric of our being, passed down through generations who survived and thrived against all odds.

This is a time to listen—and to make the (re)turn to what has always been ours. The wisdom, rhythm, and spirit that live in our bones, stories, and breath. Our children deserve better; our democracy requires it too!

Let's Teach The Babies. All of them!

References

African American Teaching Fellows. (2025.). *Who we are*. https://www.aatf.org/who-we-are

American Institute for Boys and Men. (2024). *HBCUs at a crossroads: Addressing the decline in Black male enrollment*. https://aibm.org/research/hbcus-at-a-crossroads-addressing-the-decline-in-black-male-enrollment/

Anderson, J. D. (1988). *The education of Blacks in the South, 1860-1935*. University of North Carolina Press.

Baldridge, B. J., Hill, M. L., & Davis, J. E. (2017). New possibilities: (Re)engaging Black male youth within community-based educational spaces. *Race Ethnicity and Education*, *20*(3), 348–365.

Belafonte, H., & Shnayerson, M. (2011). *My song: A memoir of art, race, and defiance*. Alfred A. Knopf.

Bristol, T. J. (2018). To be alone or in a group: An exploration into how the school-based experiences differ for Black male teachers across one urban school district. *Urban Education*, *53*(3), 334–354.

Carver-Thomas, D. (2018). *Diversifying the teaching profession: How to recruit and retain teachers of color*. Learning Policy Institute.

Charity Hudley, A. H., & Mallinson, C. (2017). "It's worth our time": A model of culturally and linguistically supportive professional development for K-12 STEM educators. *Cultural Studies of Science Education*, *12*(3), 637–660.

Cook, D. A. (2015). Shifting the center in teacher education: An introduction to the special issue on critical race theory and teacher education. *The Urban Review, 47*(2), 233–236.

Crenshaw, K. W., Ocen, P., & Nanda, J. (2015). *Black girls matter: Pushed out, overpoliced, and underprotected*. Center for Intersectionality and Social Policy Studies, Columbia Law School & African American Policy Forum. https://www.law.columbia.edu/news/archive/girls-color-face-disproportionately-harsh-discipline-school

Dee, T. S., & Penner, E. K. (2017). The causal effects of cultural relevance: Evidence from an ethnic studies curriculum. *American Educational Research Journal, 54*(1), 127–166.

Delpit, L. (1995). *Other people's children: Cultural conflict in the classroom*. The New Press.

Dillard, C. B. (2021). *The spirit of our work: Black woman teachers (re)member*. Beacon.

Du Bois, W. E. B. (1935/1998). *Black reconstruction in America*. Free Press.

EdBuild. (2019). *23 Billion Report*. https://democrats-edworkforce.house.gov/imo/media/doc/edbuild_23_billion_report.pdf

Ethridge, S. B. (1979). Impact of the 1954 *Brown* vs. *Topeka Board of Education* decision on Black educators. *The Negro Educational Review, 30*(4), 217–232.

Ferguson, R. F. (2003). Teachers' perceptions and expectations and the Black–White test score gap. *Urban Education, 38*(4), 460–507.

Frankenberg, E., Ee, J., Ayscue, J.B., & Orfield, G. (2019). *Harming our common future: America's segregated schools 65 years after Brown v. Board of Education*. Civil Rights Project/Proyecto Derechos Civiles. https://cecr.psu.edu/assets/uploads/documents/Brown-65-050919v4-final.pdf

Freire, P. (2017). *Pedagogy of the Oppressed*. Penguin. (Original work published in 1968).

Gasman, M., & Nguyen, T. H. (2014). Historically Black Colleges and Universities (HBCUs): Leading our nation's effort to improve the science, technology, engineering, and mathematics (STEM) pipeline. *Texas Education Review, 2*(1), 75–89.

Gay, G. (2018). *Culturally responsive teaching: Theory, research, and practice* (3rd ed.). Teachers College Press.

Genao, S., & Mercedes, Y. (2021). All we need is one mic: A call for anti-racist solidarity to deconstruct anti-Black racism in educational leadership. *Journal of School Leadership, 31*(1–2), 127–141. https://doi.org/10.1177/1052684621993046

Gershenson, S., Hart, C. M. D., Hyman, J., Lindsay, C., & Papageorge, N. W. (2018). *The long-run impacts of same-race teachers*. National Bureau of Economic Research Working Paper No. 25254. https://www.nber.org/system/files/working_papers/w25254/w25254.pdf

Gist, C. D., Bianco, M., & Lynn, M. (2019). Examining grow your own programs across the teacher development continuum: Mining research on teachers of color and nontraditional educator pipelines. *Journal of Teacher Education, 70*(1), 13–25.

Givens, J. R. (2021). *Fugitive pedagogy: Carter G. Woodson and the art of Black Teaching*. Harvard University Press.

Griffin, A., & Tackie, H. (2016). *Through our eyes: Perspectives from Black teachers*. The Education Trust.

Hannah-Jones, N. (2017a). Have we lost sight of the promise of public schools? *The New York Times Magazine*.

Hannah-Jones, N. (2017b). The resegregation of Jefferson County: What one Alabama town's attempt to secede from its school district tells us about the fragile progress of racial integration in America. *The New York Times Magazine*.

hooks, b. (1994). *Teaching to transgress: Education as the practice of freedom*. Routledge.

Hotep, U. (2008). Intellectual maroons: Architects of African sovereignty. *The Journal of Pan African Studies, 2*(5), 3–19.

Ingersoll, R., & May, H. (2011). *Recruitment, retention, and the minority teacher shortage*. Consortium for Policy Research in Education, University of Pennsylvania and Center for Educational Research in the Interest of Underserved Students, University of California, Santa Cruz.

Kaba, M. (2021). *We do this till we free us: Abolitionist organizing and transforming justice*. Haymarket.

Ladson-Billings, G. (1995). Toward a theory of culturally relevant pedagogy. *American Educational Research Journal, 32*(3), 465–491.

Ladson-Billings, G. (2006). From the achievement gap to the education debt: Understanding achievement in U.S. schools. *Educational Researcher, 35*(7), 3–12.

Love, B. L. (2019). *We want to do more than survive: Abolitionist teaching and the pursuit of educational freedom*. Beacon Press.

Love, B. L. (2023). *Punished for dreaming: How school reform harms Black children and how we heal*. St. Martin's Press.

Maier, A., Daniel, J., Oakes, J., & Lam, L. (2017). *Community schools as an effective school improvement strategy: A review of the evidence*. Learning Policy Institute. https://learningpolicyinstitute.org/product/community-schools-effective-school-improvement-brief

McHenry, E. (2002). *Forgotten readers: Recovering the lost history of African American literary societies*. Duke University Press.

Meckler, L. (2022). School segregation is getting worse, even as the nation grows more diverse. *The Washington Post*.

Mims, L. C. (2021). Theorizing joy and thriving for Black elementary-age children. *Journal of Black Psychology, 47*(7), 475–506.

Morris, M. W. (2016). *Pushout: The criminalization of Black girls in schools*. The New Press.

National Center for Education Statistics [NCES]. (2020). *Race and ethnicity of public school teachers and their students* (Data Point NCES 2020-103). U.S. Department of Education. https://nces.ed.gov/pubs2020/2020103/index.asp

National Coalition for Public Education. (n.d.). *Facts about*. National Coalition for Public Education. https://www.ncpecoalition.org/facts

PEN America. (2025). *Banned in the USA: The normalization of book banning (Inex of School Book Bans 2024-2025)* https://pen.org/report/the-normalization-of-book-banning/

Petchauer, E. (2012). Teacher licensure exams and Black teacher candidates: Toward new theory and promising practice. *The Journal of Negro Education, 81*(3), 252–267.

Rowley, S. J., Sellers, R. M., Chavous, T. M., & Smith, M. A. (2014). The relationship between racial identity and self-esteem in African American college and high school students. *Journal of Personality and Social Psychology, 74*(3), 715–724.

Siddle Walker, V. (1996). *Their highest potential: An African American school community in the segregated South*. University of North Carolina Press.

Siddle Walker, V. (2001). African American teaching in the South: 1940–1960. *American Educational Research Journal, 38*(4), 751–779.
Stevenson, B. (2014). *Just mercy: A story of justice and redemption*. Spiegel & Grau.
Theoharis, G. (2009). *The school leaders our children deserve: Seven keys to equity, social justice, and school reform*. Teachers College Press.
Tillman, L. C. (2004). (Un)intended consequences? The impact of the Brown v. Board of Education decision on the employment status of Black educators. *Education and Urban Society, 36*(3), 280–303.
Williams, P. L., & Loeb, S. (2012). Race and the principal pipeline: The prevalence of minority principals in light of a largely white teacher workforce. *Working Paper*.

Chapter 8

Higher Learning

The Black Learner in Higher Education—Pathways, Challenges, and Opportunities (Higher Learning Black Paper Part I)

*David J. Johns, Ivory A. Toldson, Nancy Hanks, Melanie Willingham-Jaggers, James Peterson, Yaribel Mercedes, Leilah Naila Jones, and Corena D. Wiggins**

Introduction

Higher education in the United States has long been a key route to economic success, social mobility, and civic participation. Systemic barriers and notable accomplishments have shaped this journey for Black Americans. Postsecondary education—through degrees, certificates, and credentials—has been critical in determining life outcomes, often acting as a gateway to economic success and career advancement.

Post-secondary credentials translate to concrete benefits: higher lifetime earnings (with bachelor's degree holders earning approximately $1 million more over their lifetimes than high school graduates), greater job security (college graduates experienced half the unemployment rate during economic downturns), access to employer-provided health insurance and retirement benefits, and increased homeownership rates (Federal Reserve Bank of New York, 2024; Bureau of Labor Statistics, 2023).

* Supported by braintrust author: Nadia French-Graham.

DOI: 10.4324/9781003752646-12

Post-secondary credentials have proven transformative for Black Americans, serving as tools for individual advancement and community uplift. Black adults experience a 67% increase in median lifetime earnings, which grow from $1.36 million with a high school diploma to $2.27 million with a bachelor's degree (Carnevale et al., 2021). Educational attainment is also linked to lower incarceration rates, better health outcomes, and higher civic participation among Black Americans (Chetty et al., 2020). However, access to these credentials has been uneven across racial lines throughout United States history, leading to disparities that still shape contemporary society.

This Black Paper (Paper) examines these disparities and the experiences of Black learners in American higher education through several key themes: access and enrollment, persistence and completion, educational environments across different institutional types, and policy landscapes that affect Black student success. While Black students attend a diverse array of institutions—with approximately 80% enrolled in non-Historically Black Colleges and Universities (HBCUs) settings (National Center for Education Statistics, 2022; BestColleges, 2025; National Public Radio, 2022)—they face shared challenges and distinct opportunities across these varied contexts.

Historical Context: The Evolution of Black Access to Higher Education

Early Barriers and Breakthroughs

American higher education originated with institutions primarily designed for wealthy white men. Harvard College, established in 1636, set the foundation for early American higher education; institutions focused on educating clergy and cultivating a civic leadership class (Thelin, 2019). For nearly two centuries, higher education remained mainly inaccessible to women, Black Americans, and those without financial means.

Before the Civil War, higher education was virtually inaccessible to Black Americans, and those who did receive formal education typically studied in informal settings or abroad. Following the Civil War and emancipation, the first HBCU emerged to educate formerly enslaved people and their descendants. The earliest HBCUs included Cheyney University of Pennsylvania (1837), Lincoln University (1854), and Wilberforce University (1856), all established before the Civil War. However, most HBCUs were founded after the Civil War with support from northern religious organizations, philanthropists, and, later, federal land-grant funding through the Second Morrill Act of 1890 (Anderson, 1988).

HBCUs were crucial in creating an educated Black middle class and professional community during the late 19th and early 20th centuries. They produced the majority of Black doctors, lawyers, teachers, and other professionals at a time when predominantly white institutions largely excluded Black students (Allen et al., 2007). Many continue this tradition.

The landscape of American higher education began to shift with the passage of the Morrill Land-Grant Acts of 1862 and 1890. The first Morrill Act established public land-grant institutions focused on agriculture, science, and engineering. The second Morrill Act specifically required states to establish or designate land-grant institutions for Black students in states where segregation prohibited their admission to the existing land-grant institutions (Gasman & Tudico, 2008).

The Civil Rights Era and Expanded Access

The Civil Rights Movement of the 1950s and 1960s marked a watershed moment for higher education access for Black students. *Brown* v. *Board of Education* (1954) struck down segregation in public education, though its implementation in higher education was slow and uneven. The Civil Rights Act of 1964, notably Title VI, prohibited discrimination in federally funded programs. Later, Title IX of the Education Amendments of 1972 prohibited sex-based discrimination in education.[1]

The Higher Education Act of 1965 established federal financial aid programs that made college more affordable for millions of Americans. These programs, including Pell Grants (originally called Basic Educational Opportunity Grants), were vital for Black students and others from low-income backgrounds interested in post-secondary education (St. John et al., 2013). This era also saw the growth of community colleges, which opened additional pathways to higher education for Black students.

The Black Learner Experience

Access and Enrollment: Barriers and Pathways

Today, American higher education includes a wide range of institutions serving nearly 20 million students, about 2.1 million (10.5%) of whom identify as Black or African American (National Center for Education Statistics, 2023). While HBCUs remain essential to Black higher education, approximately 80% of Black college students attend non-HBCUs. These students are distributed across community colleges, regional public universities, elite research institutions, small liberal arts colleges, and for-profit institutions.

Black students face several significant barriers to college enrollment:

1 **Financial barriers and debt**: The financial aid system itself perpetuates inequities through its structure. Need-based financial aid relies on a universal calculator, typically based on family income, to determine the expected family contribution. However, this approach obscures racialized generational wealth extraction and hoarding, and in doing so, contributes to the perpetuation of generational debt for Black families. As a result, Black students carry disproportionate student loan debt, with higher average debt loads ($52,000 for Black bachelor's degree holders compared to $28,000 for white graduates) and default rates three times higher than their white counterparts (Federal Reserve Bank of New York, 2022). Black women in particular bear the heaviest burden, owing 22% more in student debt than white women on average and facing greater barriers to repayment due to gender pay gaps compounded by racial discrimination in the labor market (American Association of University Women, 2021).
2 Furthermore, those who attended HBCUs owed 130% more than their original loan balance a decade after entering repayment, compared to non-HBCU borrowers, who owed 67% (Inside Higher Ed., 2024). This pattern of excessive loan accumulation and repayment barriers is not incidental but rooted in structural racial inequality and discrimination that extends from higher education financing into labor markets (Houle & Addo, 2022).

The current merit-based scholarship system often rewards students from well-resourced schools, in turn placing Black students from underfunded schools at a greater disadvantage.

3 **K-12 preparation gaps and teacher demographics**: Inequities in K-12 education funding, advanced course offerings, and college counseling resources create uneven preparation for higher education among Black students.

   Schools serving predominantly Black communities are more likely to have less experienced teachers, fewer advanced course offerings, and lower per-pupil expenditures (Education Trust, 2023a). These disparities have profound implications for college readiness and success. With approximately 79% of the K-12 teaching force consisting of white teachers and 76% being female (National Center for Education Statistics, 2022), many predominantly Black schools lack educators who share students' cultural backgrounds or understand their lived experiences. This representation gap often results in lower expectations for Black students, fewer recommendations for advanced courses and special programs, and less culturally responsive teaching practices. Research shows that Black students with at least one Black teacher by third grade are 13% more likely to enroll in college. Yet, many Black students, particularly in suburban and rural districts, may never be taught by a Black educator throughout their K-12 experience (Gershenson et al., 2021). This underrepresentation affects everything from disciplinary practices to identifying gifted students to college counseling quality, creating cumulative disadvantages that directly impact higher education access and persistence.

4 **Information barriers**: Many Black students, particularly first-generation college students, face challenges in navigating the complex processes of the college search, application process, financial aid, and enrollment. Higher education's "hidden curricula" can create significant barriers even for academically qualified students (Jack, 2019). Research by Hoxby and Avery (2013) revealed that over 50% of high-achieving, low-income students—many of whom are Black—do not apply to any selective colleges despite having academic credentials that would make them competitive applicants. This "undermatch" phenomenon affects tens of thousands of qualified Black students annually who have the grades and test scores for college admission but lack the informational resources, guidance, and structural support to navigate complex application and financial aid systems (Dynarski et al., 2022). Hoxby and Turner (2013) found that when provided with targeted application assistance and fee waivers, qualified Black students' applications to selective institutions increased by 31%, suggesting that information barriers—not academic preparation—are the primary obstacle. These barriers include understanding complex financial

aid forms, navigating institutional bureaucracies, meeting deadlines, securing effective recommendation letters, and crafting compelling personal statements—skills that are rarely taught explicitly but are essential for college access (Castleman & Page, 2020).

5 **Gender disparities and changing demographics**: Black student enrollment patterns show significant gender differences, with women outnumbering men at most institutions. According to a 2025 New York Times report, Black men account for only 26% of students at HBCUs, down from 38% in 1976. At Howard University, one of the nation's most prestigious HBCUs, only 19% of students are Black men (McGrady, 2025). Institutional acceptance rates cannot explain this disparity, as most colleges and universities accept Black men and women at similar rates when controlling for academic qualifications. A more comprehensive analysis by DiPrete and Buchmann (2013) found that the gap emerges earlier in the pipeline. Black men are less likely to complete college applications, less likely to meet minimum eligibility requirements due to K-12 disciplinary disparities and tracking practices, and more likely to choose employment over higher education due to immediate financial pressures. When applications are submitted with comparable qualifications, acceptance rates show minimal gender differences, indicating that the primary challenge is getting Black men into the applicant pool.

   This demographic shift requires an intersectional analysis that moves beyond traditional assumptions about family structure and economic impact. Rather than viewing this trend through the outdated lens of male-headed households (reminiscent of the problematic Moynihan Report), we should consider how these patterns reflect and potentially reshape wealth generation, family formation, and economic mobility in Black communities.

   Several factors contribute to these disparities: K-12 disciplinary practices that disproportionately impact Black boys, economic pressures that push young men into the workforce earlier, and differences in social support for educational achievement. Research by the Education Trust (2023b) suggests that Black girls and women face significant gender-based barriers yet demonstrate remarkable educational resilience, often navigating both racial and gender discrimination while pursuing higher education.

   The increasing educational attainment of Black girls and women has facilitated economic independence and leadership in households and communities. This shift challenges us to reimagine success metrics beyond traditional family structures and recognize how college-educated Black women create new pathways for wealth building and community development.

This demographic shift affects educational institutions and reshapes Black communities and economic structures. As Black women increasingly attain higher levels of education than Black men, we are witnessing evolving patterns of wealth generation and family formation. College-educated Black women are creating new pathways for community development through entrepreneurship (with Black women representing the fastest-growing group of entrepreneurs in America), leadership in nonprofit and community organizations, and intergenerational wealth building despite challenges like the gender pay gap and student loan debt burdens. Rather than viewing these trends solely as a problem to be fixed, a more nuanced perspective, informed by Black womanist feminist teachings, recognizes how educated Black women are transforming economic and family structures, often serving as both primary earners and caregivers while establishing alternative models of success and community support beyond traditional family formations.

Several promising approaches have emerged to address these barriers:

1 **College promise programs**: State and local "college promise" programs that provide free or significantly reduced tuition have shown promising results in increasing Black student enrollment. Tennessee's pioneering Promise Program has increased enrollment among Black students by 40% since its implementation, and has served as a model for similar initiatives in more than 20 states (Carruthers & Fox, 2023).
2 **Comprehensive college advising**: Intensive advising programs that provide personalized guidance through the college selection, application, and financial aid processes have demonstrated significant impacts on enrollment rates for Black students. Programs like the College Advising Corps, which places recent college graduates as advisers in underserved high schools, have increased college enrollment rates by up to 30% in participating schools (College Advising Corps, 2022).
3 **Early college high schools**: Programs that allow students to earn college credits while in high school have been particularly effective for Black students. These programs reduce the time and cost required to earn a degree while providing structured support for the transition to college-level work (Bernstein et al., 2020).

Persistence and Completion: Supporting Black Student Success

Successfully enrolling is only the first step. Ensuring Black students persist through graduation presents significant challenges. On average, Black students who attend HBCUs have a 6-year graduation rate of about 32%, compared to a 46% graduation rate for Black students at all school types (BestColleges, 2025).

1 **Financial pressures**: Financial constraints often force Black students to work long hours while attending college, reducing the time available for studying and campus engagement. Emergency financial needs, sometimes as small as a few hundred dollars, can derail educational progress (Goldrick-Rab, 2016).
2 **Sense of belonging across intersecting identities**: The feeling that a student belongs on campus represents a critical factor in student success, and is consistently identified as one of the strongest predictors of persistence and wellbeing (Strayhorn, 2012). For Black students, particularly at predominantly white institutions, experiences with systemic, structural, institutional and interpersonal racism, anti-Blackness, racial aggressions, tokenization, and isolation can undermine academic performance and psychological wellbeing. Mental health support is also critical, especially considering data from the COVID-19 pandemic showing **49% of surveyed HBCU**

students met the clinical cutoff for depression and 39% for anxiety (Wang and Goodman, 2024).

This challenge becomes more complex when considering intersecting identities. Black students who also identify as lesbian, gay, bisexual, transgender, queer or questioning+/same-gender loving (LGBTQ+/SGL), have disabilities, come from low-income backgrounds, or are first-generation college students may experience compounded barriers to belonging. Research by Means and McGuire (2023) found that Black students with multiple marginalized identities often engage in additional "identity work" to navigate campus environments—shifting how they present themselves across different campus spaces to minimize discrimination.

For example, Black LGBTQ+/SGL students often navigate both racial prejudice from the broader campus and potential homophobia or transphobia within some Black campus spaces. Similarly, Black students with disabilities may face both racial bias and ableism when seeking accommodations or support services. These intersectional challenges require comprehensive approaches to fostering belonging that address the full complexity of student identities, rather than focusing on race alone.

Institutions that successfully foster belonging across intersecting identities typically incorporate multiple strategies—diverse faculty and staff representation, identity-conscious mentoring programs, inclusive curriculum and teaching practices, and student organizations that affirm students' full identities.

3 **Academic preparation gaps**: Inequities in PreK-12 education can leave some Black students less academically prepared for college-level work, particularly in mathematics and sciences. Without appropriate support, these preparation gaps can widen over time (Chen, 2016).

4 **Socioeconomic factors and competing responsibilities**: Black students frequently navigate complex socioeconomic realities that shape their educational experiences. Nearly 40% of Black college students are over 25, and 65% are financially independent (Lumina Foundation, 2023). These statistics reflect broader socioeconomic patterns rather than simply individual choices.

Structural factors, including wealth gaps, housing segregation, and labor market discrimination, create conditions where Black students often bear significant financial and family responsibilities while pursuing higher education. These class-based pressures interact with racial inequities in ways that create distinct challenges. While economic pressures affect many students across racial groups, research by Goldrick-Rab and Kelchen (2022) found that Black students are more likely to support extended family members, including parents and siblings, rather than only focusing on individual or nuclear family needs.

Additionally, gender expectations within and beyond the family often shape how these responsibilities are distributed. Black women students, in particular, report higher rates of caregiving responsibilities than their male counterparts, creating additional time constraints alongside academic and work obligations. These patterns reflect broader social structures rather than cultural preferences or individual choices.

Effective institutional responses include emergency aid programs, campus child care, flexible course scheduling, and family-inclusive campus programming that acknowledges students' roles and responsibilities.

The good news is that several evidence-based approaches have demonstrated effectiveness in supporting Black student persistence and completion:

1 **Structured pathways**: Clear, well-defined academic pathways with proactive advising have significantly benefited Black student completion rates.

For example, the Guided Pathways model has increased graduation rates for Black students by 11 percentage points at Georgia State University's Perimeter College (Jenkins et al., 2022).

2 **Comprehensive support services**: Integrated academic, financial, and personal support services have demonstrated impressive results in supporting Black student success. The City University of New York, Accelerated Study in Associate Programs (CUNY ASAP), which provides comprehensive support, including financial assistance, structured scheduling, and intensive advising, has nearly doubled participants' three-year graduation rates (Strumbos et al., 2020).
3 **Faculty diversity and development**: Institutions with more diverse faculty tend to have better outcomes for Black students. Additionally, faculty development programs focused on culturally responsive teaching practices have positively impacted student engagement and achievement (Hagedorn et al., 2017).
4 **Learning communities**: Structured learning communities that create cohorts of students taking multiple courses together have demonstrated positive effects on persistence and completion for Black students. These communities create built-in peer support networks and deeper faculty connections (Tinto, 2012).

The Digital Divide and Online Education

The rapid expansion of online and hybrid education has created new opportunities and challenges for Black learners. While online education offers increased flexibility and access, Black students face several barriers to equitable participation:

- Digital divide: Black households are less likely to have reliable high-speed internet access and adequate computing devices. Approximately 32% of Black households lack reliable broadband access compared to 17% of white households (Pew Research Center, 2023). This digital divide directly impacts students' access to higher education opportunities, particularly as institutions increase their online and hybrid offerings. The challenge extends across institutional types, including community colleges, Predominantly White Institutions (PWIs), and other educational settings where many Black students pursue their education.
- Digital literacy gaps: Effective online learning requires digital literacy skills that are unevenly distributed. First-generation college students and older students may face particular challenges in navigating complex learning management systems and digital tools (Czerniewicz, 2018).

Several approaches have shown promise in creating more equitable online learning experiences:

- **Hybrid models**: Programs that blend online and in-person components have generally shown better outcomes for Black students than fully online programs. These models maintain some of the flexibility benefits of online learning while preserving in-person support and community (Jaggars & Xu, 2016).
- **Technology access programs**: Institutional programs that provide students with laptops, hotspots, and technical support have helped address digital divide issues. Some institutions have expanded campus Wi-Fi to parking lots and nearby community spaces to increase access options (Galanek & Brooks, 2020).
- **Culturally responsive online pedagogy**: Online courses with culturally responsive pedagogy incorporate diverse perspectives, create opportunities for students to connect content to their lived experiences, and use inclusive assessment approaches (Woodley et al., 2017).

Note: For a more detailed analysis of Historically Black Colleges and Universities and Digital Opportunities' unique role in serving Black students, please refer to the companion Black Paper on Institutional Contexts for Black learners.

Call to Action: Supporting Black Learners

The evidence is clear: Post-secondary education remains a critical pathway to economic opportunity, social mobility, and civic engagement for Black Americans. Supporting Black student success across all institutional contexts requires coordinated action from people, organizations, policymakers, and educational institutions.

For Individuals

- **Financial support**: Consider donating to post-secondary institutions and colleges, as well as donating scholarship funds to support Black students. Even small recurring donations can make a significant difference, especially when directed to student emergency funds, scholarships, or other direct student support. The stark contrast in institutional endowments illustrates the critical importance of financial support: Harvard University's endowment exceeds $50 billion, providing a financial buffer that allows the institution to withstand political pressures and funding threats from hostile administrations (Tarrant Gulla et al., 2025). By comparison, even the wealthiest HBCUs have endowments that are a fraction of those at elite predominantly white institutions. Howard University, with the largest HBCU endowment, just surpassed $1 billion. This financial vulnerability is particularly concerning given that HBCUs are explicitly targeted by recent administrative actions threatening federal funding streams. Unlike well-endowed institutions, which can weather financial storms through investment returns, most HBCUs rely heavily on tuition revenue, annual giving, and federal support, making them especially vulnerable to political retaliation. Individual and institutional donors can help build financial resilience through unrestricted gifts and targeted endowment contributions that provide sustainable support regardless of shifting political winds.

- **Mentorship and expertise**: Volunteer as a mentor, guest lecturer, or advisory board member. Your professional knowledge and networks can provide valuable resources for students navigating academic and career pathways. Programs like Howard University's "Burning of the Fears" initiative for young men demonstrate how creating supportive spaces for Black male students can help address isolation and concerns about failure (McGrady, 2025).
- **Advocacy and voter engagement**: Contact elected representatives to express support for equitable funding and policies that strengthen educational pathways for Black students. Research candidates' positions on higher education funding and policies, and support those committed to educational equity.

For Communities and Organizations

- **Business partnerships**: Create internship programs, apprenticeships, and workforce development pathways targeting Black students.
- **Community-based support systems**: Coordinate support services like child care, transportation assistance, or food pantries that address barriers facing many Black college students.

- **College promise programs**: Work with philanthropic, corporate, and creative partners to establish or expand programs that guarantee college affordability for residents.

For Educational Institutions

- **Culturally responsive practices**: Develop and implement culturally responsive teaching practices, curricula, and support services that recognize and build upon Black students' cultural knowledge and experiences.
- **Faculty and staff diversity**: Invest in recruiting, supporting, retaining, and promoting diverse faculty and staff who can serve as mentors and role models for Black students.

- **Transparent pathways**: Create clear, structured academic pathways with integrated support services and proactive advising to help Black students navigate complex higher education systems.
- **Data-informed interventions**: Use disaggregated data to identify and address equity gaps in access, persistence, completion, and post-graduate outcomes.

Organizations Supporting Black Students in Higher Education

Several organizations are working to address barriers to access and success for Black students in higher education. These organizations offer resources, mentorship, scholarships, and advocacy that can make a critical difference in educational outcomes:

- **United Negro College Fund (UNCF)**: Provides scholarships and internships for students at HBCUs and has awarded more than $5 billion in financial assistance to students at HBCUs since its founding in 1944. www.uncf.org
- **Thurgood Marshall College Fund (TMCF)**: Supports nearly 300,000 students at 47 publicly-supported HBCUs through scholarships, capacity building, research initiatives, and strategic partnerships. www.tmcf.org
- **National Association for Equal Opportunity in Higher Education (NAFEO)**: Advocates for policies supporting HBCUs and PBIs (Predominantly Black Institutions) at the federal and state levels. www.nafeo.org
- **100 Black Men of America**: Provides mentoring, educational support, and leadership development for Black youth with chapters nationwide. www.100blackmen.org
- **Black Male Collegians**: Focuses specifically on supporting the enrollment, retention, and graduation of Black men in higher education through mentorship, professional development, and advocacy. www.blackmalecollegians.org
- **The Education Trust**: Advocates for high academic achievement for all students, specifically focusing on closing opportunity gaps for students of color and those from low-income backgrounds. www.edtrust.org
- **College Advising Corps**: Places recent college graduates as advisers in underserved high schools to increase the number of low-income, first-generation, and underrepresented students entering and completing higher education. www.advisingcorps.org
- **Jack Kent Cooke Foundation**: Provides scholarships to exceptionally promising students with financial need, with specific programs for community college transfer students. www.jkcf.org
- **The Steve Fund**: The only national organization focused on supporting the mental health and emotional well-being of young people of color, with specific programs for college students. www.stevefund.org

Conclusion

Higher education in the United States has evolved from an exclusive system serving primarily wealthy white men to a more accessible system with diverse pathways to credentials and degrees. Throughout this evolution, various institutional types have played crucial roles in expanding opportunity, particularly for Black Americans and other historically marginalized groups. The evidence demonstrates that post-secondary credentials remain powerful determinants of economic opportunity, civic engagement, and social mobility.

Today's policy landscape presents both challenges and opportunities. Recent Supreme Court decisions limiting race-conscious admissions threaten to undermine diversity efforts, while ongoing debates about Title IX protections have created uncertainty about the scope of sex discrimination prohibitions. The significant barriers Black students face—from information gaps and financial constraints to digital divides—demand coordinated responses across all institutional types serving Black learners. The political weaponization of federal agencies to limit programs supporting Black students creates additional hurdles for achieving educational equity.

At the same time, unprecedented philanthropic interest in institutions serving Black students, growing recognition of the value of community colleges, and continued advocacy for educational equity create openings for transformative change. The resilience of these institutions in the face of historical and ongoing challenges underscores their fundamental importance in American higher education.

Supporting Black student success is not merely charity but an investment in economic prosperity, racial justice, and democratic vitality. By combining individual actions, community partnerships, and policy reforms, we can ensure vital institutions continue serving as engines of opportunity for future generations. For Black Americans, strengthening these pathways to higher education represents a critical step toward addressing historical inequities and creating a more just society.

Call to Action: Five Steps for Supporting Black Learners

The time for action is now. Here are five concrete steps that stakeholders can take to support Black learners in higher education.

For Individuals

- **Become a mentor**: Connect with local colleges or national organizations like the National Mentoring Partnership to guide Black students navigating higher education. Mentorship from professionals who understand both academic and career pathways can make a critical difference, especially for first-generation college students.
- **Support scholarship funds**: Make targeted donations to scholarship funds dedicated to Black students, such as the UNCF or institutional scholarships at HBCUs and community colleges. Even small monthly contributions add up and can help address financial barriers that often derail Black students' educational journeys.
- **Advocate for policy change**: Contact your local, state, and federal representatives to advocate for equitable funding for institutions serving large numbers of Black students.

  Specifically mention support for:

  - Increased federal funding for HBCUs and community colleges.
  - Expanded Pell Grant eligibility and award amounts.
  - Student loan forgiveness programs.
  - Support for male-focused initiatives to address the gender enrollment gap.

For Educators and Educational Leaders

- **Implement evidence-based practices**: Adopt and scale programs with proven success in supporting Black student persistence and completion, such as:

  - Guided pathways with proactive advising.
  - Comprehensive support services addressing academic and non-academic needs.
  - Early alert systems that identify and address challenges before they derail student progress.
  - Learning communities that foster peer support and faculty connections.

- **Diversify faculty and staff**: Set concrete goals and timelines for increasing the representation of Black faculty and staff across all institutional levels. Create supportive pathways for advancement and establish mentoring programs for early-career Black academics.

- **Create culturally responsive environments**: Evaluate curriculum, teaching practices, and campus policies through an equity lens. Incorporate diverse perspectives and culturally responsive pedagogy across disciplines, not just in specialized courses or programs.

For Business and Community Leaders

- **Develop meaningful partnerships**: Create substantive, long-term partnerships with institutions serving Black students that go beyond one-off donations. Consider:
  - Paid internship programs with clear pathways to employment.
  - Equipment donations and facility upgrades for technical programs.
  - Executive mentoring, professional development, and employment opportunities.
  - Research collaborations addressing community needs.
- **Support basic needs initiatives**: Partner with educational institutions to address the basic needs that often derail Black students' educational progress, such as:
  - Emergency housing assistance.
  - Food security programs.
  - Transportation solutions.
  - Child care access and subsidies.
- **Invest in dual pathways**: Support programs that allow students to earn while they learn, such as:
  - Apprenticeship programs combining classroom instruction with paid work experience.
  - Employer tuition assistance with flexible scheduling.
  - Career advancement pathways that recognize incremental credential completion.

For Policymakers

- **Increase institutional funding**: Address historic funding disparities through:
  - Formula-based financing that accounts for student needs, not just outcomes.
  - Infrastructure investments for schools successfully serving significant concentrations of Black students.
  - Matching programs incentivizing private philanthropy.

- **Strengthen transfer pathways**: Implement policies that facilitate seamless transfer between institutions, such as:
  - Statewide articulation agreements with guaranteed credit transfer.
  - Dual admission programs between community colleges and four-year institutions.
  - Financial aid policies that support transfer students.
- **Support data-informed interventions**: Fund comprehensive data systems that allow for:
  - Tracking student outcomes across institutions and into the workforce.
  - Identifying equity gaps at key transition points.
  - Evaluating the effectiveness of support programs.
  - Sharing best practices across institutions.

For Students and Families

- **Start early**: Begin college planning in middle school by:
  - Taking rigorous courses that prepare you for college-level work.
  - Exploring career interests through research and job shadowing.
  - Saving for education through 529 plans or other vehicles.
  - Building relationships with mentors who can guide your educational journey.
- **Maximize opportunities**: Take advantage of programs (school-based and within community-based educational spaces) designed to support your success:
  - Participate in dual enrollment or early college programs while in high school.
  - Apply for scholarships and financial aid, even if you think you might not qualify.
  - Seek out research opportunities, internships, and other high-impact experiences.
  - Establish regular meetings with academic advisors who can help navigate institutional requirements and connect you with resources.
  - Utilize campus mental health services and wellness programs, recognizing that addressing psychological wellbeing is essential for academic success.
  - Join or form study groups that provide both academic support and community connection.
- **Use your voice**: Advocate for yourself and future students:
  - Document and report discriminatory practices or policies.
  - Participate in student government and institutional committees.

- Share your experiences and success strategies with younger students.
- Hold institutions accountable for their Diversity, Equity, and Inclusion (DEI) commitments.

By taking these concrete steps, we can collectively create a more equitable higher education system that empowers Black learners to achieve their full potential. The future of our nation depends on developing all our talent, and supporting Black student success in higher education is essential to building a more just, prosperous, and democratic society.

Notes

1 It is worth noting the irony that these same civil rights laws, originally designed to expand educational access and opportunity for marginalized populations, are now being weaponized to dismantle race-conscious programs. The 2023 Supreme Court decision in *Students for Fair Admissions* v. *Harvard* used Title VI as the basis for ending race-conscious admissions, illustrating how civil rights legislation can be reinterpreted to reverse progress toward educational equity.

Bibliography

Allen, W. R., Jewell, J. O., Griffin, K. A., & Wolf, D. S. (2007). Historically Black colleges and universities: Honoring the past, engaging the present, touching the future. *The Journal of Negro Education, 76(3)*, 263–280.

American Association of University Women. (2021). *Deeper in debt: women and student loans*. aauw.org

American Council on Education. (2023). *Campus climate survey: Post-SFFA Decision*. https://www.acenet.edu/Research-Insights/Pages/Campus-Climate-Post-SFFA.aspx

American Council on Education. (2023). *Campus climate survey: Post-SFFA Decision*. https://www.acenet.edu/Research-Insights/Pages/Campus-Climate-Post-SFFA.aspx

American Council on Education. (2024). *Analysis of federal directives on higher education diversity programs*. https://www.acenet.edu/Documents/Analysis-Federal-Directives-Higher-Education-Diversity-2024.pdf

Anderson, J. D. (1988). *The education of Blacks in the South, 1860–1935*. University of North Carolina Press.

Anderson, M. (2023). HBCU enrollment trends: Challenges and opportunities. *Journal of Higher Education, 94(2)*, 233–256.

Bernstein, L., Edmunds, J., & Fesler, L. (2020). *Closing the gap: The effect of a targeted, tuition-free promise on college choices of high-achieving, low-income students*. NBER Working Paper, 27690.

BestColleges. (2025, February 18). *HBCU facts and statistics*. https://www.bestcolleges.com/research/hbcu-facts/

Brint, S., & Karabel, J. (2017). *The diverted dream: Community colleges and the promise of educational opportunity in America, 1900–1985 (Revised edition)*. Routledge.

Brown v. *Board of Education*, 347 U.S. 483 (1954).

Bureau of Labor Statistics. (2023). *Earnings and unemployment rates by educational attainment*. U.S. Department of Labor. https://www.bls.gov/emp/chart-unemployment-earnings-education.htm

Carnevale, A. P., Cheah, B., & Van Der Werf, M. (2021). *The college payoff: More education doesn't always mean more billions*. Georgetown University Center on Education and the Workforce. georgetown.edu

Carruthers, C. K., & Fox, W. F. (2023). Tennessee promise: College enrollment and completion effects. *Education Finance and Policy, 18(1)*, 55–78.

Castleman, B. L., & Page, L. C. (2020). *Summer melt: Supporting low-income students through the transition to college*. Harvard Education Press.

Century Foundation. (2021). *Recommendations for providing community colleges with the resources they need*. https://tcf.org/content/report/recommendations-providing-community-colleges-resources-need/

Chen, X. (2016). *Remedial coursetaking at U.S. Public 2- and 4-year institutions: Scope, experiences, and outcomes*. National Center for Education Statistics.

Chetty, R., Hendren, N., Jones, M. R., & Porter, S. R. (2020). Race and economic opportunity in the United States: An Intergenerational Perspective. *The Quarterly Journal of Economics, 135(2)*, 711–783.

College Advising Corps. (2022). *Annual Impact Report*. https://advisingcorps.org/our-impact/

Community College Research Center. (2023). *Community College FAQs*. https://ccrc.tc.columbia.edu/Community-College-FAQs.html

Czerniewicz, L. (2018). Inequality as higher education goes online. In N. Bonderup Dohn, S. Cranmer, J.-A. Sime, M. de Laat, & T. Ryberg (Eds.), *Networked Learning* (pp. 95–106). Springer.

DiPrete, T. A., & Buchmann, C. (2013). *The rise of women: The growing gender gap in education and what it means for American schools*. Russell Sage Foundation. https://www.russellsage.org/sites/default/files/riseofwomen_brief_04082013_web.pdf

Douglas-Gabriel, D. (2021). Maryland enacts $577 million HBCU settlement. *The Washington Post*. https://www.washingtonpost.com/education/2021/03/24/maryland-hbcu-lawsuit-settlement/

Dynarski, S., Libassi, C. J., Michelmore, K., & Owen, S. (2022). Closing the gap: The effect of reducing complexity and uncertainty in college pricing on the choices of low-income students. *American Economic Review, 112(6)*, 1721–1756.

Education Trust. (2022). *How Black women experience student debt*. https://edtrust.org/rti/how-black-women-experience-student-debt/

Education Trust. (2023a). *Funding gaps: An analysis of school funding equity across the U.S. and within each state*. https://edtrust.org/resource/funding-gaps-2023/

Education Trust. (2023b). *The state of Black women in higher education: Persistence against multiple barriers*. https://edtrust.org/resource/black-women-in-higher-education-2023/

Executive Order 13950. (2020). Combating race and sex stereotyping. *Federal Register*, 85(188).https://www.federalregister.gov/documents/2020/09/28/2020-21534/combating-race-and-sex-stereotyping

Executive Order 13985. (2021). Advancing racial equity and support for underserved communities through the federal government. *Federal Register*, 86(7). https://www.federalregister.gov/documents/2021/01/25/2021-01753/advancing-racial-equity-and-support-for-underserved-communities-through-the-federal-government

Federal Reserve Bank of New York. (2022). *Student Loan Data and Demographics*. https://www.newyorkfed.org/microeconomics/topics/student-debt

Federal Reserve Bank of New York. (2024). *The labor market for recent college graduates*. https://www.newyorkfed.org/research/college-labor-market/college-labor-market_compare-earnings.html

Galanek, J. D., & Brooks, D. C. (2020). *EDUCAUSE QuickPoll results: Fall readiness for teaching and learning*. EDUCAUSE Research Notes.

Gasman, M. (2021). The state of research on historically Black Colleges and Universities. *Journal for Multicultural Education, 15(1)*, 19–37.

Gasman, M., & Tudico, C. L. (Eds.). (2008). *Historically Black colleges and universities: triumphs, troubles, and taboos*. Palgrave Macmillan.

Georgia State University. (2023). *Student Success Programs Annual Report*. Georgia State University.

Gershenson, S., Hansen, M., & Lindsay, C. A. (2021). *Teacher diversity and student success: Why racial representation matters in the classroom*. Cambridge University Press.

Goldrick-Rab, S. (2016). *Paying the price: College costs, financial aid, and the betrayal of the American dream*. University of Chicago Press.

Goldrick-Rab, S., & Kelchen, R. (2022). *Beyond financial aid: Understanding the complex needs of today's college students*. Harvard Education Press.

Government Accountability Office. (2017). *Higher education: Students need more information to help reduce challenges in transferring college credits (GAO-17–574)*. U.S. Government Printing Office.

Government Accountability Office. (2018). *Historically Black colleges and universities: Action needed to improve participation in education's HBCU capital financing program (GAO-18-455)*. U.S. Government Printing Office.

Hagedorn, L. S., Chi, W., Cepeda, R. M., & McLain, M. (2017). An investigation of critical mass: The role of Latino representation in the success of urban community college students. *Research in Higher Education, 48(1)*, 73–91.

Harper, S. R., & Hurtado, S. (2007). Nine themes in campus racial climates and implications for institutional transformation. *New Directions for Student Services, 2007(120)*, 7–24.

Harris, A. (2021). The Transformation of the HBCU in an Age of Racial Awakening. *The Atlantic*. https://www.theatlantic.com/magazine/archive/2021/11/howard-university-black-politics/620174/

HBCU Transfer Alliance. (2023). *Annual Impact Report: Creating pathways to success*. https://www.hbcutransferalliance.org/impact

Houle, J.N., & Addo, F.R. (2022). A dream defaulted: the student loan crisis among Black students. Howard Education Press.

Hoxby, C., & Avery, C. (2013). The missing "one-offs": The hidden supply of high-achieving, low-income students. *Brookings Papers on Economic Activity, 2013(1)*, 1–65.

Jack, A. A. (2019). *The privileged poor: How elite colleges are failing disadvantaged students*. Harvard University Press.

Jaggars, S. S., & Xu, D. (2016). How do online course design features influence student performance? *Computers & Education, 95*, 270–284.

Jenkins, D., Lahr, H., Fink, J., & Ganga, E. (2022). *How guided pathways reforms can improve support for adult students: Lessons from three Tennessee community colleges*. Community College Research Center, Teachers College, Columbia University.

Liptak, A. (2023). Supreme Court strikes down affirmative action programs at Harvard and UNC. *The New York Times*. https://www.nytimes.com/2023/06/29/us/politics/supreme-court-affirmative-action-harvard-unc.html

Lumina Foundation. (2023). *A stronger nation: Learning beyond high school builds American talent*. https://www.luminafoundation.org/stronger-nation/report/

Lundy-Wagner, V., Vultaggio, J., & Gasman, M. (2014). Preparing underrepresented students of color for doctoral success: The Role of Undergraduate Institutions. *International Journal of Doctoral Studies, 9*, 73–90.

McGrady, C. (2025). At Black colleges, a stubborn gender enrollment gap keeps growing. *The New York Times*. https://www.nytimes.com/2025/03/30/us/black-men.html

Means, B., & Neisler, J. (2021). Teaching and learning in the time of COVID: The student perspective. *Online Learning, 25(1)*, 8–27.

Means, D. R., & McGuire, K. M. (2023). Black student identity management within and beyond higher education: The role of identity work in collegiate and post-collegiate experiences. *Journal of Diversity in Higher Education, 16(1)*, 78–90.

Mobley, S. D., & Johnson, J. M. (2023). "We were here": LGBTQ+ Experiences and visibility at historically Black colleges and universities. *Journal of Diversity in Higher Education, 16(2)*, 191–202.

National Center for Education Statistics. (2022). *Fast facts: Historically Black colleges and universities (667)*. https://nces.ed.gov/fastfacts/display.asp?id=667

National Center for Education Statistics. (2023). *The Condition of education 2023: Undergraduate enrollment*. https://nces.ed.gov/programs/coe/indicator/cha

National Public Radio. (2022, August 15). *After the rise of BLM, Black students and their families are heading back to HBCUs*. https://www.npr.org/2022/08/15/1117437412/hbcu-black-students-applications-enrollments-increase

National Science Foundation. (2023). *Women, minorities, and persons with disabilities in science and engineering*. https://ncses.nsf.gov/pubs/nsf23315/

North Carolina A&T State University. (2023). *College of Engineering: Creating pathways to success*. North Carolina A&T State University Press.

Pew Research Center. (2023). *Internet/Broadband Fact Sheet*. https://www.pewresearch.org/internet/fact-sheet/internet-broadband/

Posse Foundation. (2023). *Annual Outcomes Report*. https://www.possefoundation.org/about-posse/our-impact

Spelman College. (2023). *STEM at Spelman: A decade of growth and innovation*. Spelman College Press.

St. John, E. P., Daun-Barnett, N., & Moronski-Chapman, K. M. (2013). *Public policy and higher education: reframing strategies for preparation, access, and college success*. Routledge.

Steele, C. M. (2010). *Whistling Vivaldi: how stereotypes affect us and what we can do*. W. W. Norton & Company.

Strayhorn, T. L. (2012). *College students' sense of belonging: A key to educational success for all students*. Routledge.

Strumbos, D., Linderman, D., & Hicks, C. C. (2020). Postsecondary pathways out of poverty: City University of New York accelerated study in associate programs and the case for national policy. *RSF: The Russell Sage Foundation Journal of the Social Sciences, 6(3)*, 271–292.

Thelin, J. R. (2019). *A history of American higher education* (3rd ed.). Johns Hopkins University Press.

Tinto, V. (2012). *Completing college: Rethinking institutional action*. University of Chicago Press.
U.S. Department of Education. (2018). *Dear colleague letter on race-conscious admissions*. https://www2.ed.gov/about/offices/list/ocr/letters/colleague-201807-title-vi.pdf
U.S. Department of Education. (2023). Notice of proposed rulemaking: Nondiscrimination on the basis of sex in education programs or activities receiving federal financial assistance: Sex-related criteria in athletics. *Federal Register, 88(82)*, 26527–26569.
UMBC. (2023). *Meyerhoff Scholars Program outcomes and impact*. University of Maryland, Baltimore County.
UNCF. (2022). *HBCUs make America strong: The positive economic impact of historically Black colleges and universities*. https://uncf.org/programs/hbcu-impact
Urban Institute. (2023). *Higher education and economic mobility for Black Americans*. https://www.urban.org/research/publication/higher-education-economic-mobility-black-americans
Williams, K. L., & Davis, B. L. (2019). *Public and private investments and divestments in historically Black colleges and universities*. American Council on Education.
Woodley, X., Hernandez, C., Parra, J., & Negash, B. (2017). Celebrating difference: Best practices in culturally responsive teaching online. *TechTrends*, *61*, 470–478.
Xavier University of Louisiana. (2022). *Pre-Med program: Four decades of excellence*. Xavier University Press.

Chapter 9

Institutional Contexts for Black Learners

The Role of HBCUs, Community Colleges, and Digital Education (Higher Learning Black Paper Part II)

*David J. Johns, Ivory A. Toldson, Wes Bellamy, Nancy Hanks, Melanie Willingham-Jaggers, James Peterson, Yaribel Mercedes, and Corena D. Wiggins**

Introduction

This Black Paper (Paper) is a companion to "Higher Learning: The Black Learner in Higher Education—Pathways, Challenges, and Opportunities," which examines the broader landscape of Black student experiences in American higher education. While the first Black Paper explores themes of access, persistence, and policy impacts across the higher education spectrum, this second Paper analyzes the specific institutional contexts shaping Black learners' educational journeys.

Understanding where and how Black students learn is critical to developing effective strategies for supporting their success. Though approximately 90% of Black college students attend non-HBCU institutions, Historically Black Colleges and Universities (HBCUs) continue to play an outsized role in producing Black graduates and leaders (McKinsey & Company, 2021; NCES, n.d.). Community colleges serve as crucial access points for nearly half of all Black undergraduates. At the same time, predominantly white institutions (PWIs) present both significant challenges and innovative models for supporting Black student achievement.

Additionally, as higher education increasingly moves into digital spaces, understanding the unique barriers and opportunities that online education and tools like Artificial Intelligence presents for Black learners becomes essential. The digital divide—in access, literacy, and support—represents both a significant challenge and a potential avenue for expanding educational opportunity.

* Supported by braintrust author: Nadia French-Graham

DOI: 10.4324/9781003752646-13

This Black Paper examines these institutional contexts through an equity-focused lens, identifying persistent barriers and promising practices that can inform policy and practice across the higher education landscape. By understanding the distinctive roles of different institutional types and learning modalities, we can develop more targeted and effective approaches to supporting Black student success.

Where We Learn: HBCUs & Digital Education

Historically Black Colleges and Universities (HBCUs)

While serving approximately 10% of Black college students, HBCUs play a distinctive and vital role in American higher education. These 107 accredited institutions produce approximately 20% of all African American college graduates despite representing just 3% of all higher education institutions (United Negro College Fund [UNCF], 2024).

HBCUs have demonstrated remarkable effectiveness in several key areas:

1 **Social Mobility**: HBCUs excel at moving students from low-income backgrounds to economic security. HBCUs propel more than twice as many of their graduates into the middle class as predominantly white institutions (United Negro College Fund, 2024). Quantitatively, HBCUs demonstrate a mean **economic mobility rate of 34.3%** (the percentage of students moving from the bottom 40% to the top 60% of national income distribution), which is more than double the average of all other U.S. colleges (Hammond et al., 2021).
2 **Science, Technology, Engineering, and Mathematics (STEM)**[1] **education and gender equity**: HBCUs demonstrate remarkable efficiency in producing Black STEM graduates despite their limited resources. These institutions produce 25% of African American graduates with bachelor's degrees in

STEM fields despite representing only 3% of higher education institutions (National Science Foundation, 2023).

When analyzed through an intersectional lens, this achievement becomes even more significant. Given the gender distribution at HBCUs—where women now constitute approximately 70% of the student population—these institutions are playing a crucial role in addressing both racial/ethnic and gender gaps in STEM fields. HBCUs are graduating more Black women with STEM degrees than many predominantly white institutions, representing a significant contribution to diversifying these fields.

This success reflects intentional strategies at many HBCUs—culturally responsive teaching in STEM courses, early research opportunities, comprehensive academic support programs, and visible women faculty role models in STEM disciplines. Spelman College, a historically Black women's college, has become a national leader in producing Black women who earn doctorates in STEM fields, demonstrating how institutions can effectively address both racial and gender underrepresentation simultaneously.

Rather than viewing the gender distribution at HBCUs as solely a challenge, we benefit by recognizing and celebrating their effectiveness in preparing Black women for success in fields where they have been historically unwelcome, unsupported, and thus underrepresented. This success provides models for other institutions and industries seeking to address the persistent underrepresentation of both women and people of color in STEM fields.

3 **Graduate Education Preparation**: HBCUs produce a disproportionate share of Black doctoral recipients. Recent data from the National Science Foundation (2023) shows that among Black STEM doctorate recipients between 2018 and 2022, approximately 30% earned their bachelor's degrees at HBCUs. However, these institutions enroll only about 9% of all Black undergraduates. This overrepresentation in the STEM doctorate pipeline highlights HBCUs' exceptional effectiveness in preparing students for advanced study. Key to this success are federally funded programs like the Ronald E. McNair Post-Baccalaureate Achievement Program, which prepares first-generation, low-income, and underrepresented minority undergraduates for doctoral studies through research opportunities, mentorship, and graduate school preparation. HBCUs have been particularly successful in leveraging these programs—Hampton University's McNair Scholars Program, for example, has achieved a 90% graduate school acceptance rate for its participants over the past five years. Other undergraduate research initiatives, like the MARC U-STAR (Maximizing Access to Research Careers Undergraduate Student Training in Academic Research) program, have similarly demonstrated success in facilitating successful pathways to graduate education for Black students at both HBCUs and predominantly white institutions.

It is worth noting that the 47th presidential administration has significantly impacted the Ronald E. McNair Post-Baccalaureate Achievement Program through repeated budget proposals requesting its elimination and substantial funding delays and cancellations, that created considerable instability for institutions and students. The 47th presidential administration's annual budget requests frequently advocates for the complete removal of all Federal TRIO programs, based on the assertion that college access was no longer a primary obstacle for students of limited means (The Institute for College Access & Success, 2025; UnidosUS, 2025). In one instance, the Department of Education (DOE) under the 47th presidential administration withheld congressionally-approved McNair grant funds for months (Inside Higher Ed, 2025a; Trinitonian, 2025) and eventually canceled approximately 18 program grants entirely (Pappas, 2025), citing issues with Diversity, Equity, and Inclusion (DEI) initiatives and ongoing legal challenges as justifications (Inside Higher Ed, 2025b). Advocacy efforts by the Council for Opportunity in Education (COE) and program participants led to the eventual release of most funds, but the actions caused widespread anxiety and disrupted research and travel opportunities for scholars (Council for Opportunity in Education, n.d.; Truman State University, 2025).

4 **Supportive environments and expansion**: Research consistently shows that Black students at HBCUs report more positive overall campus experiences, stronger faculty relationships, and a greater sense of racial belonging than Black students at predominantly white institutions (Strayhorn, 2012). The

majority-Black environment can reduce race-related stressors and provide valuable cultural affirmation.

Support can vary significantly based on Sexual Orientation, Gender Identity and Expression (SOGIE). Black lesbian, gay, bisexual, transgender, queer or questioning+/same-gender loving (LGBTQ+/SGL) students at HBCUs report complex experiences that resist reductionist characterization. While these students generally experience less racism than at predominantly white institutions, many HBCUs have historically maintained more conservative approaches to SOGIE diversity.

Recent research by Mobley and Johnson (2023) found significant variations among HBCUs in LGBTQ+/SGL inclusion. Some institutions have established comprehensive resource centers, inclusive policies, and active student organizations, while others maintain more traditional approaches shaped by historical ties to conservative religious denominations. Howard University, Spelman College, and Morehouse College have developed notable LGBTQ+/SGL initiatives, though implementation and student experiences vary across campuses and administrators.

Transgender and gender-expansive students face particular challenges related to housing policies, facilities access, and administrative recognition at many HBCUs. While progress has occurred at some institutions, transgender and gender-expansive students often report navigating complex institutional environments where policies may not fully support their identities.

HBCUs that successfully support students across SOGIE diversity typically engage in comprehensive approaches, including: explicit non-discrimination policies, dedicated professional staff, faculty development around culturally competent and inclusive teaching, student peer education programs, and visible administrative support. These practices demonstrate that institutions can simultaneously affirm both racial and SOGIE identities while maintaining their distinct cultural and historical missions.

Despite these impressive outcomes, **HBCUs face significant challenges that threaten their sustainability and impact**:

1 **Historic and ongoing underfunding**: HBCUs have historically received less public funding and accumulated smaller endowments than predominantly white institutions. Highlighting this historic state-level inequality, a joint analysis by the United States Department of Education and the United States Department of Agriculture (2023) revealed that between 1987 and 2020, 16 states underfunded their 1890 Black land-grant institutions by between \$12.6 billion and \$12.8 billion when compared to their land-grant counterparts. This chronic resource deficit impacts campus development. In June 2018 the Government Accountability Office (GAO) issued a report detailing HBCU infrastructure needs. Almost all of the HBCUS that responded to the

GAO survey reported that 46% of their building space needed to be repaired or replaced (Thurgood Marshall College Fund, 2024). The public HBCUs that GAO surveyed reported, on average, $67 million in deferred maintenance of infrastructure needs. In 2021, the Thurgood Marshall College Fund surveyed these same institutions and found an average of $81 million in deferred maintenance expenses (Thurgood Marshall College Fund, 2024). The survey was repeated in 2024 and the total increased to $96 million (a nearly 20% increase from 2021 and more than a 40% increase from 2018) (Thurgood Marshall College Fund, 2024).

2 **Gender enrollment gap**: As noted previously, HBCUs are experiencing a growing gender disparity in enrollment. Black men account for only 26% of students at HBCUs, down from 38% in 1976 (McGrady, 2025). This gap reflects broader societal issues, including higher incarceration rates for Black men, K-12 disciplinary disparities, and socio-economic pressures that push Black young men into the workforce prematurely.
3 **Cultural competency for diverse student populations**: While HBCUs have always welcomed students from all backgrounds, they serve increasingly diverse student populations today. As federal requirements for accommodations have expanded and cultural awareness has grown, HBCUs are working to create welcoming environments for students across intersecting identities, including non-Black students, international students, and students with disabilities. Many HBCUs have made significant strides in establishing resource centers and support services to ensure all students can thrive.
4 **Talent management and compensation gaps**: Attracting and retaining faculty and staff is complicated by significant salary disparities at HBCUs. HBCU employees experience profound salary disparities, earning **$10,000 to $18,000 less** on average than their peers at non-HBCUs (National Educational Association, 2021). These challenges can be exacerbated by leadership instablity. HBCU presidential tenure averages approximately 4 to 4.22 years, which falls short of the national average of 5.9 years, years for all college executives (American Council of Education, 2023; Johnson, 2026). Together, these compensation and leadership deficits point to manufactured structural and institutional challenges deserving attention.

Despite these challenges, many HBCUs have demonstrated remarkable innovation and resilience. **Exemplary HBCU success stories include**:

1 **Xavier University of Louisiana's Pre-Medical Program**: Xavier consistently ranks first among all United States colleges and universities in the number of Black graduates who complete medical school. The university's success stems

from comprehensive academic support, structured curriculum pathways, early intervention systems, and a culture of high expectations. In 2021, Xavier sent 77 graduates to medical schools nationwide, representing 25% of all Black students entering medical school that year (Xavier University of Louisiana, 2022).

2 **Spelman College's STEM Programs**: Spelman has emerged as a leader in producing Black women in STEM fields. The college's comprehensive approach includes research opportunities in the first year, strong mentorship programs, and partnerships with industry and research institutions. Between 2011 and 2021, Spelman increased its number of STEM majors by 43%, becoming the top producer of Black women who complete doctoral degrees in STEM fields (Spelman College, 2022).
3 **North Carolina A&T State University's Engineering Program**: North Carolina A&T graduates more Black engineers than any other university in the country. The university's College of Engineering has developed robust academic support systems, industry partnerships, and research opportunities that prepare students for success in a field where Black professionals remain significantly underrepresented.
4 **Claflin University's Biotechnology and Bioinformatics Programs**: Located in South Carolina, Claflin has built a strong reputation for its programs in biotechnology and bioinformatics, fields that are critical to the future of medicine, agriculture, and environmental science. Claflin's intentional focus on undergraduate research, internships, and graduate school placement has led to a 75% graduate/professional school placement rate for STEM students within six months of graduation (Claflin University, 2023).
5 **Dillard University's Film and Digital Media Program**: Dillard, a smaller HBCU in New Orleans, has emerged as a national leader in preparing Black creatives for success in film, media production, and storytelling. Through partnerships with Hollywood studios, intensive hands-on training, and a curriculum rooted in cultural authenticity, Dillard is helping diversify an industry where Black voices are still critically underrepresented.
6 **Fayetteville State University's Cybersecurity Program**: Fayetteville State has developed one of the leading cybersecurity programs among minority-serving institutions. As a designated National Center of Academic Excellence in Cyber Defense by the NSA and Department of Homeland Security, Fayetteville is preparing Black students for high-demand careers in cybersecurity, information assurance, and national security, in industries where diversity is desperately needed.

Community Colleges: Critical Access Points for Black Learners

Community colleges serve more than 10.2 million students annually—about 40% of all undergraduate students in the United States (American Association of Community Colleges, 2023). For Black students, community colleges often serve as crucial pathways to higher education. Approximately 39% of Black undergraduates attend community colleges (American Association of Community Colleges, 2023).

Community colleges play several critical roles for Black students:

1 **Affordable access**: With an average annual tuition of approximately $3,800—compared to over $10,000 at public four-year institutions—community colleges provide a financially accessible entry point to higher education, especially for Black students from low-income backgrounds (American Association of Community Colleges, 2023).
2 **Geographic proximity**: Community colleges are often located in or near Black communities, making them physically accessible to students with transportation limitations or family responsibilities that require them to be close to home.
3 **Flexible scheduling**: Most community colleges offer evening, weekend, online and otherwise individualized courses that accommodate work and family responsibilities.

4 **Multiple educational pathways**: Community colleges providing multiple routes to economic mobility offer career-focused credentials for direct workforce entry and transfer pathways to four-year institutions.

The historical significance of community colleges for Black students' access should not be overlooked. Following the Civil Rights Movement, community colleges became crucial entry points to higher education for Black students who had previously been excluded from many four-year institutions. In 1965, Black students were 5% of college enrollments in community colleges; this increased to 10% by 1975 (Ravich, 1976).

Community colleges also became sites of community empowerment in predominantly Black areas. Institutions like Malcolm X College in Chicago, Medgar Evers College in Brooklyn, and Atlanta Metropolitan State College were established in direct response to community activism demanding accessible higher education in Black neighborhoods. These institutions often developed curricula addressing community needs and celebrating Black culture and history.

Despite their importance as access points, community colleges face several challenges in supporting Black student success:

1 **Low completion rates**: Approximately 21% of Black community college students graduate within three years. Only 16% of all community college students successfully transfer to a four-year institution and complete a bachelor's degree within six years (Community College Research Center, 2023).
2 **Funding disparities**: Community colleges serving predominantly Black populations have historically received less funding than those in predominantly white areas. A 2021 study found that community colleges where Black and Hispanic students made up at least 40% of enrollment received an average of $1,025 **less** per student in state and local appropriations than colleges with predominantly white student bodies.
3 **Limited support services**: Despite serving students with significant academic and non-academic needs, many community colleges lack adequate resources to provide comprehensive support services like academic advising, tutoring, mental health counseling, and emergency financial assistance.
4 **Transfer challenges**: Transferring from community colleges to four-year institutions remains complex and inefficient, causing many students to lose an average of 43% of credits in the transition (Government Accountability Office, 2017). This structural barrier, combined with advising gaps, disproportionately impacts Black students, who achieve a six-year bachelor's degree transfer completion of 9% compared to the national average of

16% (Community College Research Center, 2025). Credit loss occurs for multiple reasons. Some four-year institutions refuse to accept credits from courses they deem not equivalent to their own, particularly in subjects like mathematics and sciences. Others cap the total number of transferable credits. And still others will only accept credits as electives rather than as fulfilling major requirements, effectively forcing students to retake similar courses.

For Black community college students, who are more likely to attend part-time and take longer to accumulate credits due to work and family responsibilities, these transfer policies can be especially devastating. Each non-transferable credit represents wasted time, money, and effort. The Government Accountability Office (GAO) report found that transfer students lose, on average, 43% of their credits when moving between institutions, which translates to approximately 13 credits or about a semester of full-time enrollment—essentially erasing the cost savings and time advantages that community colleges are intended to provide. This credit loss contributes significantly to extended time-to-degree, increased debt, and higher dropout rates among transfer students.

Several promising approaches have emerged to address these barriers:

1 **College promise programs**: State and local "college promise" programs providing free or significantly reduced tuition have shown promising results in increasing Black student enrollment. Tennessee's pioneering Promise Program has increased enrollment among first-time, full-time

first-year students at the state's community colleges by at least 40% since implementation, while also showing positive results in attendance among Black and Hispanic students. The program has served as a model for similar initiatives in more than 20 states (Carruthers & Fox, 2020). This demonstrates what is possible when we invest directly in creating access to higher education opportunities. When the financial burden is lifted, our young scholars also rise to the occasion.

2 **Comprehensive college advising**: Intensive advising programs that provide personalized guidance through the college selection, application, and financial aid processes have demonstrated significant impacts on enrollment rates for Black students. Programs like the College Advising Corps, which places recent college graduates as peer-mentors in underserved high schools, have increased college enrollment rates by 3 to 5 percentage points. Furthermore, students who directly engage with these advisers are 30% more likely to apply to college compared to non-advised peers (College Advising Corps, 2022). We should not underestimate the power of relationship-building and mentorship. When our young people see people who look like them, who also believe in them, it changes the trajectory of what they think is possible.

3 **Early college in high school**: Programs like Advanced Placement (AP), Dual Enrollment, International Baccalaureate (IB), and the Advanced International Certificate of Education (AICE), which allow students to earn college credits while still in high school, have been particularly effective for Black students. These programs reduce the time and cost required to earn a degree while providing structured support for the transition to college-level work. When we give students a head start in college spaces, it creates a sense of belonging, making students feel prepared and confident to enter college and complete their degrees.

4 **Intentional partnerships**: Beyond the classroom, partnerships with trusted community groups are key to building sustainable college pipelines. Organizations rooted in the community can help connect students with scholarships, internships, mentorships, and consistent one-on-one support that traditional school systems can struggle to offer. When we engage our religious communities and institutions, fraternities and sororities, nonprofits, and civic groups, to name a few—when we move as a collective, we can multiply the significance of an impact these partnerships can have.

5 **Mentorship initiatives like 100 Black Men, Collegiate 100, and Call Me MISTER**: Targeted mentoring programs are playing a transformational role in boosting Black student enrollment, retention, and success. 100 Black Men of America and their Collegiate 100 chapters provide Black male students with positive role models, professional development, academic support, and a brotherhood that reinforces the expectation of excellence. Similarly, initiatives like the Call Me MISTER program are working to increase the number of Black male teachers—not just to diversify the workforce, but to show

young Black boys Black men who demonstrate daily examples of leadership, brilliance, and care. These mentorship models work because they affirm our young people's identities while pushing them to reach higher and become the best versions of themselves.

6 **Centering student voice and agency**: It is not enough to build programs **for** Black students—we have to build them **with** Black students. We must listen to their lived experiences, trust their insights, and allow them to lead in shaping what real access and success look like; this must be at the core of every strategy we push forward. When our young people are empowered to lead, they don't just "survive" college—they thrive in the real world.

Predominantly White Institutions and Small Liberal Arts Colleges

While HBCUs and community colleges play vital roles in higher education, the majority of Black students (approximately 90%) attend predominantly white institutions (PWIs). These institutions, which include elite private universities and regional public universities, present both unique challenges and opportunities for Black students.

Black students at PWIs often encounter challenges, including campus climate issues, gaps in faculty and staff representation, cultural disconnects in curriculum and teaching practices, and psychological burdens, such as stereotype threat and imposter syndrome (Harper & Hurtado, 2007; Steele, 2010). Small liberal arts colleges, in particular, may present additional challenges related to demographic isolation and limited specialized support services for Black students.

Despite these challenges, several PWIs have developed exemplary programs for supporting Black student success:

1 **The Meyerhoff Scholars Program at UMBC**: The University of Maryland, Baltimore County (UMBC), under the leadership of Dr. Freeman Hrabowski, president emerita, has developed one of the nation's most successful models for supporting Black achievement in STEM fields. The Meyerhoff Scholars Program provides comprehensive financial, academic, and social support to high-achieving students from underrepresented groups. The program has produced more than 1400 graduates, including more than 300 who have earned PhDs or MD/PhDs, making UMBC the top predominantly white institution in the country for producing Black bachelor's degree recipients who go on to earn STEM PhD's (UMBC, 2023).

   Key elements of the program include summer bridge experiences, cohort-based learning communities, research opportunities beginning in the first year, and intensive mentoring. The program's success demonstrates that with appropriate support and a culturally responsive approach, PWIs can achieve exceptional outcomes for Black students, particularly in fields where they have been historically underrepresented.
2 **Georgia State University's Proactive Advising System**: Georgia State has dramatically improved graduation rates for Black students through a data-informed advising system that identifies and addresses potential academic problems before they derail student progress. The university's Graduation and Progression Success (GPS) system uses predictive analytics to identify more than 800 risk factors and prompt immediate intervention from advisors. Since implementing this system, Georgia State has reduced achievement gaps based on race, ethnicity, and income (Georgia State University, 2023).
3 **Posse Foundation partnerships at liberal arts colleges**: Numerous liberal arts colleges partner with the Posse Foundation to recruit, support, and graduate cohorts of students from diverse backgrounds. Posse Scholars receive full-tuition scholarships and participate in pre-collegiate training and ongoing campus support programs. Partner institutions, highly ranked liberal arts colleges including Bucknell University and Hamilton College, have significantly increased Black student enrollment success and retention metrics through this cohort pipeline program (Posse Foundation, 2024).

The Digital Landscape: Barriers and Opportunities for Black Learners

The digital transformation of higher education has accelerated dramatically in recent years, with the COVID-19 pandemic catalyzing widespread adoption of online and hybrid learning models. For Black learners, this shift presents both significant challenges and potential opportunities that warrant careful analysis.

Digital Divides: Beyond Access

While online education offers increased flexibility and potential access, Black students face multifaceted digital divides that create barriers to equitable participation:

1 **Infrastructure and device access**: Black households face systemic digital infrastructure disdvantages rendering them less likely to have reliable high-speed internet access or dedicated computing devices. Approximately 29% of Black adults lack home broadband access compared to 20% of white households (Pew Research Center, 2021). This structural inequality is geographically concentrated, as 82% of HBCUs are located in designated broadband deserts, with limited reliable high-speed internet access in the communities (McKinsey & Company, 2021).

   Data found that during the pandemic, nearly 35% of underrepresented college students having to complete assignments on smartphones rather than computers due to device limitations. This smartphone practice is associated with lower performance on assessments and higher course withdrawal rates (McKinsey & Company, 2021).

2 **Digital literacy gaps**: Effective online learning requires a complex set of digital literacy skills that are unevenly distributed. First-generation college students and older students may face particular challenges navigating complex learning management systems and digital tools (Czerniewicz, 2018).

Researchers have identified specific digital literacy gaps that disproportionately impact Black students, including trouble with advanced features of learning management systems, collaborative digital tools, and academic database navigation—skills rarely explicitly taught but often assumed by instructors.

3 **Learning environment constraints**: Environmental factors impact learning environments. National data highlights that a quiet environment and adequate space to organize study materials are the two most important physical factors required for effective learning (EDUCASE, 2020). Conversely, a lack of access to dedicated, quiet, organized working spaces presents persistent challenges disproportionately impacting non-traditional, minoritized, and low-income college students (Community College Research Center, 2022).
4 **Online learning design barriers**: Most online courses have not been designed with the needs of Black students in mind. Research demonstrates that the absence of culturally responsive instructional content, minimal opportunities for community building, and inadequate mechanisms for addressing microaggressions creates significant barriers to engagement and retention for Black students in digital learning environments (Heitner & Jennings, 2016; Woodley et al., 2017).

HBCUs and Digital Innovation, despite facing resource constraints, many HBCUs have demonstrated remarkable innovation in digital education:

1 **HBCU Digital Network Initiative**: To leverage stronger institutional economies of scale, the United Negro College Fund, in consortium with a network of HBCUs established the HBCUv, a digital network, to share resources, faculty development support, course offerings, and support community across institutions. This collaborative platform supports student success through shared resource (and course) delivery while pooling technological resources and faculty development tools to optimize investments and opportunities across partner institutions (United Negro College Fund, 2024). This platform has increased course availability for students and created economies of scale for digital infrastructure investment (UNCF Digital Learning Infrastructure Report, 2022).
2 **Mobile-first design approaches**: Recognizing that many students access content via smartphones, tools like the student-designed Front Porch Portal integrate critical academic deadlines and benchmarks, financial alerts, and campus resources into a mobile tool designed to increase student engagement and retention at HBCUS (Gasman, 2026).

3 **Culturally responsive online pedagogy**: To support Black students, HBCUs and other post-secondary institutions are increasingly incorporating asset-based digital tools. Rather than using traditional delivery methods, culturally responsive online instructional tools rely on community building, inclusive course content, and alternative assessment strategies that recognize and build upon the unique cultural capital that Black students bring with them (Heitner & Jennings, 2016; Woodley et al., 2017).

Community College Virtual Pathways

Community colleges have also been at the forefront of developing accessible online pathways that serve Black students:

1 **Hybrid support models**: Programs that blend online coursework with in-person community support services have generally shown better outcomes for Black students than fully online, asynchronous programs. These models maintain some flexibility benefits of online learning while preserving in-person support and community. Longitudinal programs show that while fully online data exacerbated achievement gaps for students from minority groups, hybrid and blended models improved course completion rates (Jaggars & Xu, 2016; Xu & Jaggars, 2014).

2 **Technology access programs**: HBCUs and other institutions of higher education providing students with laptops, hotspots, and technical support have helped narrow the digital divide. Some institutions have expanded campus Wi-Fi to parking lots and nearby community spaces to increase access options. Long-term data demonstrated that loaning students equipment and providing them with technical support reduces barriers to engagement and success.

3 **Virtual student support services**: Research affirms that offering virtual support, including virtual advising, tutoring, telehealth, and counseling services, significantly increased utilization rates and engagement (Carroll et al., 2024) These digital supports remove trasnportation and scheduling/timing barriers, providing important flexibility for students dealing with life (Carroll et al., 2024).

Promising practices across institutional types—Several evidence-based approaches have demonstrated success in creating more equitable digital learning experiences across institutional contexts:

1 **Inclusive course design**: Universal Design for Learning (UDL) principles, when applied to online courses, have shown particular benefits for Black students. These include providing content in multiple formats, offering flexible assessment options, and incorporating diverse perspectives and examples throughout course materials.
2 **Community-building approaches**: Online courses that intentionally foster community through structured collaborative activities, identity-affirming

spaces, and regular synchronous interaction show higher engagement and completion rates among Black students (HBCUs Foster a Virtual Sense of Belonging, 2023; Heitner & Jennings, 2016). Some institutions have implemented digital affinity spaces where Black students can connect around shared identities and experiences while pursuing their academic work.

3 **Digital mentorship programs**: Peer and near-peer digital mentorship models, where more experienced students provide guidance and support to newer students navigating online learning, have shown promise in several institutional contexts. These programs address both technical challenges and the sense of isolation that can accompany online learning (Webb et al., 2022).
4 **Faculty digital equity training**: Professional development programs explicitly focused on digital equity issues have improved outcomes for minoritized students. These programs typically address unconscious bias in online teaching, multicultural competence, culturally responsive digital pedagogy, and strategies for creating inclusive online communities. Instructors shift away from fixed-mindset deficit frameworks toward asset-based approaches to teaching and learning. Equipping educators with these critical competencies enables identity-affirming communities that can support the academic engagement and retention of Black learners (Heitner & Jennings, 2016).

The digital transformation of higher education presents both challenges and opportunities for advancing educational equity for Black learners. By addressing infrastructure barriers, investing in culturally responsive approaches to online teaching and learning, and leveraging technology to expand access to high-quality educational experiences, institutions can harness digital innovation to serve Black students across the educational landscape better.

Institutional Contexts and the Future of Black Student Success

As our examination of institutional contexts reveals, higher education in the United States continues to evolve from its exclusive origins toward a more accessible ecosystem with diverse pathways to certifications, credentials, and degrees. Throughout this evolution, different institutional types have played complementary roles in expanding opportunities for Black Americans.

HBCUs, despite representing just 3% of higher education institutions, continue to produce a disproportionate share of Black graduates. Their demonstrated effectiveness in fostering social mobility, preparing students for graduate education, and creating supportive campus environments offers valuable lessons for institutions of all types seeking to serve Black students better. At the same time, the historic and ongoing underfunding of these institutions threatens their sustainability and impact, requiring intentional policy intervention and philanthropic investment.

Community colleges serve as critical access points for Black learners, particularly those from low-income backgrounds or with work and family responsibilities. The affordability, geographic proximity, and flexible scheduling of these institutions make them essential components of the higher education ecosystem. However, low completion rates and transfer challenges highlight the need for structural reforms and increased support services to ensure that access translates to success. PWIs, where the majority of Black students pursue their post-secondary certifications, credentials, and degrees, present both significant challenges and innovative models for supporting Black achievement. Exemplary programs like UMBC's Meyerhoff Scholars

Program demonstrate that with appropriate support and culturally responsive approaches, any institution can effectively serve Black students.

The digital transformation of higher education adds another dimension to this institutional landscape. As learning increasingly moves online, addressing digital divides in access, literacy, and support becomes essential for equitable educational opportunity. The innovative approaches developed by various institutional types offer promising directions for harnessing technology to serve Black learners better.

Today's policy landscape presents both challenges and opportunities in higher education that span across institutional contexts. Recent Supreme Court decisions limiting race-conscious admissions threaten to undermine diversity efforts, while ongoing debates about Title IX protections have created uncertainty about the scope of sex discrimination prohibitions. The political weaponization of federal agencies to limit programs supporting Black students creates additional hurdles for achieving educational equity.

At the same time, unprecedented philanthropic interest, growing recognition of the importance of institutional diversity, and continued advocacy for educational equity create openings for transformative change. The resilience demonstrated by HBCUs, community colleges, and model programs at PWIs in the face of historical and ongoing challenges underscores the fundamental importance of institutional diversity in American higher education.

Connecting back to the themes of access, persistence, and policy explored in the Higher Learning Black Paper, we see how institutional contexts shape and are shaped by these broader dynamics. Challenges to access manifest differently across institutional types, requiring tailored approaches to recruitment, admissions, and financial support. Persistence barriers vary by institutional context, necessitating context-specific strategies for student support. Policy impacts ripple through the institutional landscape in complex ways, often with unintended consequences for different types of institutions and the students they serve.

Supporting Black student success across this diverse institutional landscape is not charity, but an investment in economic prosperity, racial justice, and democratic vitality. By combining individual actions, community partnerships, and policy reforms tailored to specific institutional contexts, we can ensure that all institutions better serve as engines of opportunity for Black learners. For Black Americans, strengthening these diverse pathways to higher education represents a critical step in addressing historical inequities and creating a more just society.

Call to Action: Support Black Learners

The evidence is clear: Post-secondary education remains a critical pathway to economic opportunity, social mobility, and civic engagement for Black Americans. Supporting Black student success across all institutional contexts requires coordinated action from individuals, organizations, policymakers, and educational institutions.

For Individuals

- **Financial support**: Consider donating to post-secondary institutions, colleges, and scholarship funds supporting Black students. Small recurring donations can make a significant difference, mainly when directed to student emergency funds, scholarships, or other direct student support. The stark contrast in institutional endowments illustrates the critical importance of financial support: Harvard University's endowment exceeds $53 billion, providing a financial buffer that allows the institution to withstand political pressures and funding threats from the 47th presidential administration. By comparison, even the wealthiest HBCUs have endowments that are a fraction of those at elite predominantly white institutions. Howard University, at a billion, is the largest HBCU endowment, but still only a small fraction of Harvard's reported resources. This financial vulnerability is particularly concerning given that HBCUs are explicitly targeted by recent administrative actions threatening federal funding. Unlike well-endowed institutions that can weather financial storms through investment returns, most HBCUs rely heavily on tuition revenue, annual giving, and federal support, making them especially vulnerable to political retaliation. Individual and institutional donors can help build financial resilience through both unrestricted gifts and targeted endowment contributions, providing sustainable support regardless of shifting political winds.

- **Mentorship and expertise**: Volunteer as a mentor, guest lecturer, or advisory board member. Your professional knowledge and networks can provide valuable resources for students navigating academic and career pathways. Programs like Howard University's "Burning of the Fears" initiative for young men demonstrate how creating supportive spaces for Black male students can help address isolation and concerns about failure. The university also supports initiatives explicitly targeted at women, such as the Brown Girls Lead (BGL) Academy, founded by Howard alumna and former Trustee Stefanie Brown James. This national leadership development program engaged Black collegiate women through intensive training focused on personal empowerment, professional enrichment, and public engagement, connecting students with professional Black women mentors in the D.C. area. Stefanie Brown James, also known for her work as CEO of Vestige Strategies, LLC and Co-Founder of The Collective PAC, created BGL to build a robust pipeline of future Black women leaders.
- **Advocacy and voter engagement**: Hold elected leaders accountable for demonstrating support for equitable funding of institutions, programs, and policies that strengthen educational pathways for Black students. Research candidates' positions on higher education funding and policies, and support those committed to educational equity.

For Communities and Organizations

- **Business partnerships**: Create, strengthen, and sustain internship programs, apprenticeships, employment pipelines and scholarships targeting Black students.

- **Community-based support systems**: Implement support services like child care, transportation assistance, or food pantries that address barriers facing many Black college students.

For Educational Institutions

- **Culturally responsive practices**: Develop and implement culturally responsive and radically inclusive teaching practices, curricula, and support services that recognize and build upon Black students' cultural knowledge and experiences.
- **Faculty and staff diversity**: Invest in recruiting, supporting, retaining, and promoting diverse faculty and staff who can serve as mentors and possibility models for diverse Black students.
- **Transparent pathways**: Create clear, structured academic pathways with integrated support services and proactive advising to help Black students navigate the often-complex systems of higher education.
- **Data-informed interventions**: Use disaggregated data to identify and address equity gaps in access, persistence, completion, and post-graduate outcomes for Black students.

Organizations Supporting Black Students in Higher Education

Several organizations are working to address barriers to access and success for Black students in higher education. These organizations offer resources, mentorship, scholarships, and advocacy that can make a critical difference in educational outcomes:

- **United Negro College Fund (UNCF)**: Provides scholarships and internships for students at HBCUs and has awarded more than $5 billion in financial assistance to students at HBCUs since its founding in 1944. www.uncf.org
- **Thurgood Marshall College Fund (TMCF)**: Supports nearly 300,000 students at 47 publicly-supported HBCUs through scholarships, capacity building, research initiatives, and strategic partnerships. www.tmcf.org
- **National Association for Equal Opportunity in Higher Education (NAFEO)**: Advocates for policies supporting HBCUs and PBIs (Predominantly Black Institutions) at the federal and state levels. www.nafeo.org
- **100 Black Men of America**: Provides mentoring, educational support, and leadership development for Black youth with chapters nationwide. www.100blackmen.org
- **Black Male Collegians**: Focuses specifically on supporting the enrollment, retention, and graduation of Black men in higher education through mentorship, professional development, and advocacy. www.blackmalecollegians.org
- **The Education Trust**: Advocates for high academic achievement for all students, specifically focusing on closing opportunity gaps for students of color and those from low-income backgrounds. www.edtrust.org
- **College Advising Corps**: Places recent college graduates as advisers in underserved high schools to increase the number of low-income, first-generation, and underrepresented students entering and completing higher education. www.advisingcorps.org
- **Jack Kent Cooke Foundation**: Provides scholarships to exceptionally promising students with financial need, with specific programs for community college transfer students. www.jkcf.org
- **The Steve Fund**: The only national organization focused on supporting the mental health and emotional wellbeing of young people of color, with specific programs for college students. www.stevefund.org

Conclusion

Higher education in the United States has evolved from an exclusive system serving primarily wealthy white men to a more accessible system with diverse pathways to certificates, credentials, and degrees. Throughout this evolution, HBCUs and community colleges have played crucial roles in expanding opportunity, particularly for Black Americans and other historically marginalized groups. The evidence demonstrates that post-secondary credentials remain powerful determinants of economic opportunity, civic engagement, and social mobility.

Today's policy landscape presents both challenges and opportunities. Recent Supreme Court decisions limiting race-conscious admissions threaten to undermine diversity efforts, while ongoing debates about Title IX protections have created uncertainty about the scope of sex discrimination prohibitions. The widening gender enrollment gap at HBCUs, with Black men representing a declining share of students, demands urgent attention and targeted interventions. The political weaponization of federal agencies to limit programs supporting Black students creates additional hurdles for achieving educational equity.

At the same time, unprecedented philanthropic interest in HBCUs, growing recognition of the value of community colleges, and continued advocacy for educational equity create openings for transformative change. The resilience of HBCUs and community colleges in the face of historical and ongoing challenges underscores their fundamental importance in American higher education.

Supporting Black student success is an investment in economic prosperity, racial justice, and democratic vitality. By combining individual actions, community partnerships, and policy reforms, we can ensure vital institutions continue serving as engines of opportunity for future generations. For Black Americans, strengthening these pathways to higher education is a critical step in addressing historical inequities and creating a more just society.

Five Steps for Supporting Black Learners

The time for action is now. Here are five concrete steps that **YOU** can take to support Black learners in higher education:

For Individuals

- **Become a mentor**: Connect with local colleges or national organizations like the National Mentoring Partnership to guide Black students navigating higher education. Mentorship from professionals who understand both academic and career pathways can make a critical difference, especially for first-generation college students.
- **Support scholarship funds**: Make targeted donations to scholarship funds dedicated to Black students, such as the UNCF or institutional scholarships at HBCUs and community colleges. Even small monthly contributions add up and can help address financial barriers that often derail Black students' educational journeys.
- **Advocate for policy change**: Contact your local, state, and federal representatives to advocate for equitable funding for institutions serving large numbers of Black students.

  Specifically mention support for:

  - Increased federal funding for HBCUs and community colleges.
  - Expanded Pell Grant eligibility and award amounts.
  - Student loan forgiveness programs.
  - Support for male-focused initiatives to address the gender enrollment gap.

For Educators and Educational Leaders

- **Implement evidence-based practices**: Adopt and scale programs with proven success in supporting Black student persistence and completion, such as:
    - Guided pathways with proactive advising.
    - Comprehensive support services addressing academic and non-academic needs.
    - Early alert systems that identify and address challenges before they derail student progress.
    - Learning communities that foster peer support and faculty connections.

- **Diversify faculty and staff**: Set concrete goals and timelines for increasing the representation of Black faculty and staff across all institutional levels. Create supportive pathways for advancement and establish mentoring programs for early-career Black academics.
- **Create culturally responsive environments**: Evaluate curriculum, teaching practices, and campus policies through an equity lens. Incorporate diverse perspectives and culturally responsive pedagogy across disciplines, not just in specialized courses or programs.

For Business and Community Leaders

- **Develop meaningful partnerships**: Create substantive, long-term partnerships with institutions serving Black students that go beyond one-off donations. Consider:
  - Paid internship programs with clear pathways to employment.
  - Equipment donations and facility upgrades for technical programs.
  - Executive mentoring, professional development, and employment opportunities.
  - Research collaborations that address community needs.
- **Support basic needs initiatives**: Partner with educational institutions to address the basic needs that often derail Black students' educational progress, such as:
  - Emergency housing assistance.
  - Food security programs.
  - Transportation solutions.
  - Child care access and subsidies.
- **Invest in dual pathways**: Support programs that allow students to earn while they learn, such as:
  - Apprenticeship programs combining classroom instruction with paid work experience.
  - Employer tuition assistance with flexible scheduling.
  - Career advancement pathways that recognize incremental credential completion.

For Policymakers

- **Increase institutional funding**: Address historic funding disparities through:
    - Formula-based funding that accounts for student needs, not just outcomes.
    - Infrastructure investments for schools successfully serving significant concentrations of Black students.
    - Matching programs incentivizing private philanthropy.

- **Strengthen transfer pathways**: Implement policies that facilitate seamless transfer between institutions, such as:
    - Statewide articulation agreements with guaranteed credit transfer.
    - Dual admission programs between community colleges and four-year institutions.
    - Financial aid policies that support transfer students.
- **Support data-informed interventions**: Fund comprehensive data systems that allow for:
    - Tracking student outcomes across institutions and into the workforce.
    - Identifying equity gaps at key transition points.
    - Evaluating the effectiveness of support programs.
    - Sharing best practices across institutions.

For Students and Families

- **Start early**: Begin college planning in middle school by:
    - Taking rigorous courses that prepare you for college-level work.
    - Exploring career interests through research and job shadowing.
    - Saving for education through 529 plans or other vehicles.
    - Building relationships with mentors who can guide your educational journey.
- **Maximize opportunities**: Take advantage of programs (school-based and within community-based educational spaces) designed to support your success:
    - Participate in dual enrollment or early college programs while in high school.
    - Apply for scholarships and financial aid, even if you think you might not qualify.
    - Seek out research opportunities, internships, and other high-impact experiences.
    - Establish regular meetings with academic advisors who can help navigate institutional requirements and connect you with resources.
    - Utilize campus mental health services and wellness programs, recognizing that addressing psychological wellbeing is essential for academic success.
    - Join or form study groups that provide both academic support and community connection.

- **Use your voice**: Advocate for yourself and future students:
  - Document and report discriminatory practices or policies.
  - Participate in student government and institutional committees.
  - Share your experiences and success strategies with younger students.
  - Hold institutions accountable for their diversity, equity, and inclusion (DEI) commitments.

By taking these concrete steps, we can collectively create a more equitable higher education system that empowers Black learners to achieve their full potential. The future of our nation depends on developing all our talent, and supporting Black student success in higher education is essential to building a more just, prosperous, and democratic society.

Notes

1 While STEM traditionally stands for Science, Technology, Engineering, and Mathematics, it's important to note the growing recognition of STEAM education, which intentionally incorporates the Arts. The "A" in STEAM isn't simply about painting or music—it reflects the integration of creativity, design thinking, and critical innovation into scientific and technical work. In practice, STEAM education equips students to approach problems with both analytical rigor and creative vision: building solutions that are not only functional but also accessible, user-centered, and thoughtfully designed. This approach mirrors the kind of interdisciplinary thinking that has always been central to Black intellectual traditions—refusing false binaries between art and science, between technical skill and cultural expression. As we discuss STEM achievement throughout this Black Paper, we recognize that true innovation has always required the integration of logic and creativity, and that the most transformative work happens when we refuse to separate them.

References

American Association of Community Colleges. (2023). Fast facts 2023. nche.edu

Carruthers, C. K., & Fox, W. F. (2020). Free college? Assessing enrollment responses to the Tennessee Promise program. *Economics of Education Review*, 79, Article 102029.

Claflin University. (2023). Excellence in STEM: Institutional effectiveness and student career pathways outcomes report. https://www.claflin.edu

College Advising Corps. (2022). Bridging the gap: 2022 impact report. https://collegeadvisingcorps.org

Council for opportunity in education. (n.d.). *Take action now*. https://coenet.org/take-action-now/

Czerniewicz, L. (2018). Inequality as higher education goes online. In J. Case & J. Huisman (Eds.), *Researching higher education: International perspectives on theory, policy and practice* (pp. 89–105). Routledge.

Georgia State University. (2023). Approaching student success with predictive analytics. https://success.gsu.edu/approach/

Harper, S. R., & Hurtado, S. (2007). Nine themes in campus racial climates and implications for institutional transformation. *New Directions for Student Services*, 2007(120), 7–24.

Inside Higher Ed. (2025a). *Trump administration delays millions for TRIO programs*. https://www.insidehighered.com/news/government/student-aid-policy/2025/09/12/trump-administration-withholds-millions-trio-programs

Inside Higher Ed. (2025b). *Advocates worry about McNair Scholars program*. https://www.insidehighered.com/news/government/student-aid-policy/2025/09/19/advocates-worry-about-mcnair-scholars-program

McGrady, C. (2025). At Black colleges, a stubborn gender enrollment gap keeps growing. *The New York Times*. https://www.nytimes.com/2025/03/30/us/black-men.html

McKinsey & Company. (2021). *How HBCUs can accelerate Black economic mobility*. https://www.mckinsey.com/industries/education/our-insights/how-hbcus-can-accelerate-black-economic-mobility

Mobley, S. D., & Johnson, J. M. (2023). Title of the specific journal article or book chapter. *Title of the Journal*, Volume(Issue), page range. doi.org

National Center for Education Statistics. (n.d.) *Data on HBCU enrollment and institutions*. U.S. Department of Education. https://nces.ed.gov

National Science Foundation. (2023). *Science and engineering indicators*. National Center for Science and Engineering Statistics.

Pappas, C. (2025). *Pappas meets with UNH McNair Scholars as Trump administration cuts program*. United States House of Representatives. https://pappas.house.gov/media/press-releases/pappas-meets-with-unh-mcnair-scholars-as-trump-administration-cuts-program

Posse Foundation. (2024). 906 students win Posse scholarships totaling $187 million from partner colleges. possefoundation.org

Spelman College. (2022). 2021–2022 institutional fact book. *Spelman College Office of Institutional Research*. https://www.spelman.edu/_1_Docs-and-Files/about/institutional-research/2021-22-fact-book-final.pdf

Steele, C. M. (2010). *Whistling Vivaldi: How stereotypes affect us and what we can do*. W. W. Norton & Company. https://www.npr.org/2010/04/12/125859207/whistling-vivaldi-and-beating-stereotypes

Strayhorn, T. L. (2012). *College students' sense of belonging: A key to educational success for all students*. Routledge.

The Institute for College Access & Success. (2025). *Severe cuts to TRIO and GEAR UP programs hamper efforts to offer fair college access and success—and a more equitable society*. https://ticas.org/college-completion/trio-gear-up-proposed-cuts-blog-may-2025/

Trinitonian. (2025). *McNair programs in jeopardy after Trump administration delays funding*. https://trinitonian.com/2025/10/03/mcnair-programs-in-jeopardy-after-trump-administration-delays-funding/

Truman State University. (2025). *McNair program keeps its funding after a brief scare*. https://tmn.truman.edu/blog/news/campus/mcnair-program-keeps-its-funding-after-a-brief-scare/

UnidosUS. (2025). *Are TRIO Programs relics of the past? Latino students say no*. https://unidosus.org/progress-report/are-trio-programs-relics-of-the-past-latino-students-say-no/

United Negro College Fund. (2024). The numbers don't lie: HBCUs are changing the college landscape. uncf.org

Xavier University of Louisiana. (2022). *Title of the specific report, press release, or webpage used*. URL.

Section IV

Health and Well-Being

This section examines the interconnected crises threatening Black health and bodily autonomy across the lifespan, from prenatal care through end-of-life outcomes, revealing how systems ostensibly designed for health and protection instead function as mechanisms of control, surveillance, and premature death. Together, these Black Papers document not merely disparities in health outcomes but deliberate policy choices that sacrifice Black life while illuminating community-led resistance and the pathways toward health justice rooted in self-determination.

"Five Years Lost: Confronting America's Black Health Equity Crisis" opens with the stark reality that Black Americans live an average of Five years less than white Americans—a gap exceeded only by American Indian/Alaska Native populations—costing the nation $1.24 trillion annually in premature deaths, high medical costs, and lost productivity. This Black Paper dismantles the myth that health disparities stem from genetics or personal choices, instead documenting how structural racism embedded in healthcare access, environmental conditions, economic inequities, and social determinants creates systematic barriers to wellness. Black women face maternal mortality rates three to four times higher than white women, regardless of education or income, while Black babies die before their first birthday at more than twice the rate of white infants. With United States healthy life expectancy rankings projected to plummet from 80th globally in 2022 to 108th by 2050—and worse for Black Americans specifically—this analysis argues that addressing racial health inequities represents both a moral imperative and economic necessity, presenting evidence-based policy interventions spanning healthcare reform, environmental justice, economic security, and social support systems.

"Reproductive Justice at the Crossroads: Black Communities Navigating Care Deserts in Post-Roe America" examines how the Supreme Court's *Dobbs* decision weaponized existing healthcare apartheid, creating overlapping deserts where 3.7 million women of reproductive age live in counties without abortion access, and with no or low access to maternity care. For Black birthing people, this crisis manifests through compounded barriers: 60% of Black women ages 18–49 live in states with abortion bans or restrictions; maternal

DOI: 10.4324/9781003752646-14

mortality rates in banned states run 62% higher than states with access; and Black maternal mortality in these restrictive states reaches 60.9 deaths per 100,000 live births. Drawing on Sister Song Collective's 1994 reproductive justice framework—the human right to maintain bodily autonomy, have children, not have children, and parent in safe communities—this Black Paper documents how Black communities navigate intensifying threats through mutual aid networks, doula programs including models like Mama Glow, digital literacy initiatives, and community health worker programs. The analysis spotlights unique challenges facing transgender and gender-expansive people who experience multiplicative oppression through both anti-Black racism and transmisogynior. At the same time, Project 2025's surveillance proposals threaten to criminalize pregnancy outcomes, particularly for Black women already facing disproportionate policing.

"Protecting Black Mothers: Ending Disparities in Maternal Health" provides a deep examination of the maternal mortality crisis where Black women die from pregnancy-related causes at rates 3.5 times higher than white women—a disparity that persists across all income and education levels and actually widened as overall maternal mortality declined for other groups between 2022 and 2023. This Black Paper traces how historical medical exploitation from J. Marion Sims's experiments on enslaved women through forced sterilization campaigns created enduring mistrust. At the same time, contemporary manifestations of medical exploitation include implicit bias in pain assessment, delayed or denied emergency care, provider shortages in Black communities, and abortion restrictions that increased Texas' maternal mortality by 56% in the first year of implementation. The analysis documents how these factors compound for Black transgender and non-binary birthing people who face erasure from maternal health data and discrimination in accessing gender-affirming perinatal care. Proven interventions, including community-based doula programs reducing maternal mortality up to 30%, Medicaid expansion in states showing measurable improvements, implicit bias training demonstrating effectiveness when properly implemented, and enhanced data collection disaggregated by race and gender identity, offer pathways forward, yet require sustained funding and political will to achieve scale.

Together, these Black Papers refuse to accept premature death, reproductive coercion, obstetric violence, and forced family separation as inevitable features of Black existence, instead demanding recognition that health crises facing Black communities result from deliberate policy choices that can be unmade through equally deliberate commitments to justice. They challenge readers to understand health equity not as a charitable concern but as a prerequisite for functional democracy, economic prosperity, and collective thriving. From womb to tomb, from individual bodies to family structures, systemic anti-Blackness operates through ostensibly neutral institutions of medicine, public health, and child protection—making transformation of these systems essential to Black liberation. This chapter articulates health justice as encompassing bodily autonomy, family integrity, community self-determination, and the fundamental right to live full lives untruncated by preventable suffering, calling for investments proportionate to centuries of harm and creation of new systems designed from inception to honor Black life rather than extract from it.

Chapter 10

Five Years Lost

Confronting America's Black Health Equity Crisis

Britt Weinstock, Linda Elam, and David J. Johns

Executive Summary

Today, health inequities and disparities result in Black people dying roughly five years before white Americans (72.8 years vs. 77.5 years). In addition to the human health toll, health inequities cost the nation $1.24 trillion annually. Recent policy changes and proposals threaten to worsen these inequities and disparities by cutting Medicaid, which will affect over 13 million Black Americans; reducing Medicare reimbursements and spending, which will harm up to 5.5 million Black people; eliminating Diversity, Equity and Inclusion (DEI) programs; ending racial and ethnic health data collection and reporting; and drastically scaling back the capacity and funding for health equity research and related efforts at the National Institutes of Health (NIH) and the Offices of Minority Health (OMH), and other agencies and offices within the United States Department of Health and Human Services (DHHS).

This Black Paper (Paper) examines these challenges and their impacts on current and future health equity advancement, highlights successful equity initiatives, and provides actionable recommendations for people and organizations committed to eliminating health disparities and advancing health equity. Without coordinated and strategic interventions now, decades of progress stand to be reversed, and existing health inequities and disparities will be exacerbated, resulting in devastating human and economic consequences to the nation.

Key Terms

- **Health disparities** refer to preventable differences in health outcomes (e.g., higher diabetes rates among Blacks compared to whites).
- **Health inequities** focus on the historical and current laws, policies, and programs that are often rooted in racism and other forms of discrimination, which create these health disparities in the first place. These societal barriers prevent certain groups of people from accessing the resources they need to lead their healthiest lives (Dawes, 2020).

DOI: 10.4324/9781003752646-15

Introduction

The 47th President's 2025 executive orders and Presidential Actions, which were quickly implemented with little to no oversight or permission, have—and will likely continue to have—significant, negative impacts on healthcare access and health equity policies. Given the persistent and pervasive health and healthcare challenges facing Black people today, the 47th President's changes are expected to impact Black communities most severely. This Black Paper examines the implications of these sweeping policy and program changes and proposals, while acknowledging the ongoing national conversation about the urgent need for health equity and how to achieve it.

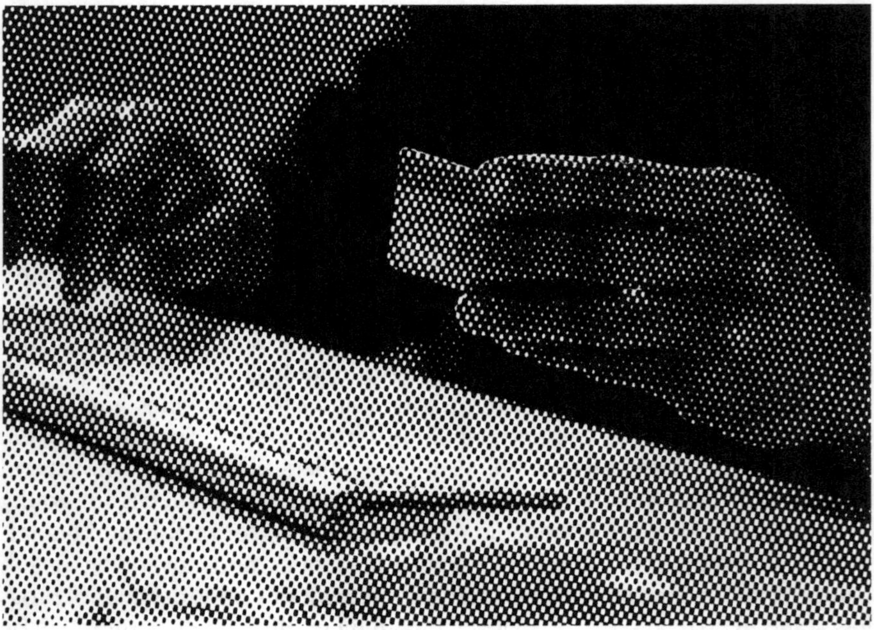

The State of Black Health and Wellness

The health and wellness of Black people and communities in the United States present complex challenges that deserve thoughtful attention and swift action. Data consistently show that overall, across the healthcare system and throughout their lifespan, Black people have less access to affordable, high-quality healthcare services and treatments, live in poorer states of health, and experience worse health outcomes, including dying prematurely from preventable causes, when compared to White people and sometimes other groups (CDC, 2023a).

Key Facts about Black Health:

- Black people live an average of five years less than white people (National Academy of Medicine, 2024).
- Black women are *three to four times more likely* to die from pregnancy-related causes than white women, regardless of their income or education levels (American Journal of Public Health, 2023).
- Black babies are *more than twice as likely* to die before their first birthday compared to white babies (March of Dimes, 2024).
- Black people with mental health illnesses are 1.5 times *less likely* than whites to receive mental health services (National Institute of Mental Health, 2023).

If current trends continue, the United States will drop from 80th globally in healthy life expectancy in 2022 to 108th by 2050—a dramatic decline in just over 25 years (Institute for Health Metrics and Evaluation, 2024). These projections are even worse for women in the United States, whose ranking is expected to fall from 19th (in 1990) to 74th by 2050. For men in the United States, the ranking will likely drop from 35th to 65th during that same timeframe. These drops in healthy life expectancy will likely be even worse for Black people and American Indian/Alaska Native people who already experience the lowest life expectancies in the United States.

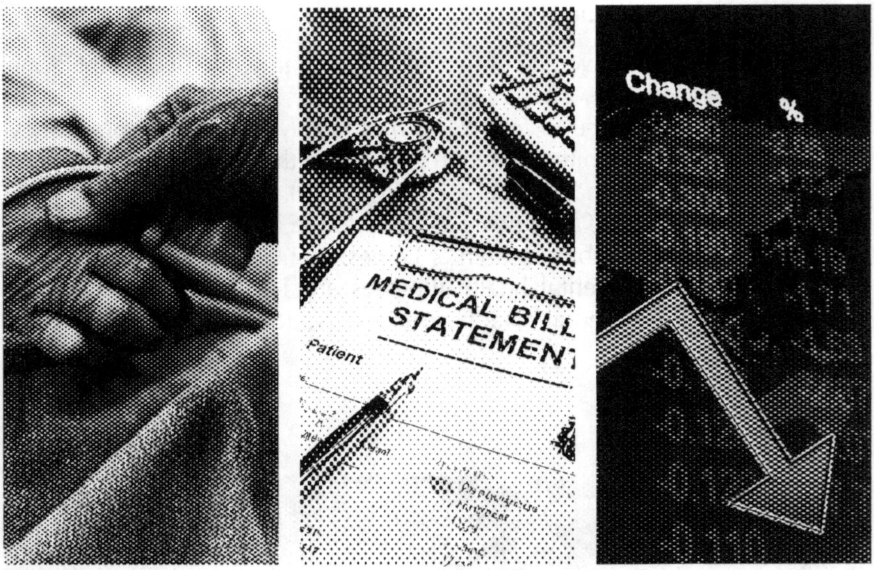

Health Disparities and Inequities Cost Lives and Money

Racial health disparities and inequities carry hefty human health and economic tolls. According to the Joint Economic Committee of the United States Congress (2023), these health disparities cost the United States economy an estimated $1.24 trillion annually through:

- Premature deaths.
- Excessive medical costs.
- Lost economic productivity.

Furthermore, mental health inequities cost the United States economy an estimated $477.5 billion every year. If nothing is done to address this now, that cost could rise to over $14 trillion by 2040. These economic impacts affect all Americans through increased healthcare costs, reduced workforce productivity, and increased strain on public resources. Addressing these grave disparities and inequities benefits the entire United States economy (Brookings Institution, 2024).

Key Takeaways

- Addressing health inequities and disparities creates economic benefits for ***all*** Americans.
- Eliminating health disparities and advancing health equity will not only save millions of lives, a disproportionate number of which are Black people, but also strengthen the overall economy.

Understanding Various Perspectives on Health Disparities

Multiple perspectives exist on why health disparities persist and how to address them, including:

Medical Perspective: Early research suggested inherent biological differences were the major drivers of health disparities between population groups. While it is true that certain population groups may be genetically predisposed to certain conditions (such as the rare kidney disease in Asian Americans and sickle cell anemia in African Americans), most health experts today recognize political, social, economic and environmental factors as more significant determinants (American Medical Association, 2024; Dawes, 2020).

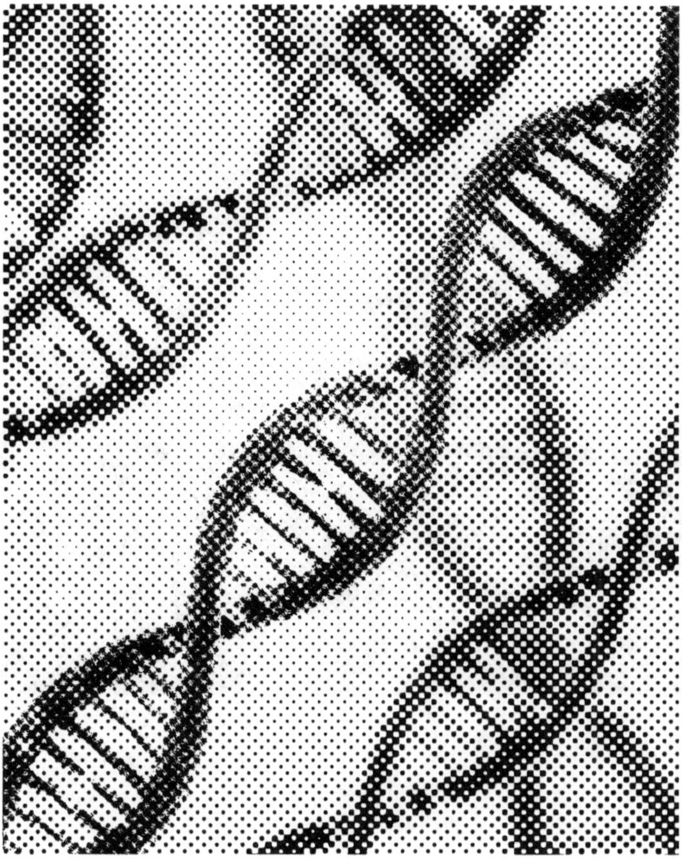

Personal Responsibility Perspective: While individual choices about diet, exercise, lifestyle and healthcare utilization have a direct impact on everyone's health outcomes, they alone do not account for the persistent and pervasive racial and ethnic health disparities and inequities observed today. In fact, recent research shows that these individual health choices are not only constrained but often shaped by political and social determinants of health (Robert Wood Johnson Foundation, 2023).

Economic Perspective: This perspective posits that economic inequalities primarily drive health disparities. While it is true that economic measures, such as income, job status, education, and wealth attainment affect healthcare and health outcomes, an extensive body of literature has demonstrated that racial inequalities and inequities that exist throughout the whole of society often override economic factors and have a disproportionate and negative impact on the healthcare and health outcomes of Black people and communities. Moreover, access to many of these economic determinants is impacted by structural and systemic racism and discrimination.

Social Determinants Perspective: This view holds that health is shaped by living, working, and social conditions, and the inequities and inequalities that exist therein. Neighborhood safety, access to healthcare, food access, protection from environmental hazards, education quality, and job opportunities significantly influence health outcomes regardless of an individual's health decisions (World Health Organization, 2023). Therefore, addressing all forms of social inequalities and inequities will have a direct impact on reducing health disparities and advancing health equity.

Structural Perspective: This approach examines how systemic and structural racism and discrimination have given rise to laws, policies, and practices that create and sustain different opportunities for different groups of people, leading to pervasive and persistent inequities and disparities, including those in healthcare and health outcomes. While rarely explicitly expressed, laws, policies and programs often are shaped by racial bias, historical and ongoing injustices, and skewed power dynamics that ensure that only certain population groups benefit while other population groups needlessly suffer. Because health is shaped by many different social, economic, and environmental factors, every policy has health equity consequences. This perspective then focuses on how and why laws and policies, both historical and enacted more recently, have affected—and continue to affect—health outcomes today (American Public Health Association, 2024). Furthermore, this perspective supports the idea that addressing widespread injustices from the past will play a significant role in eliminating health disparities and advancing health equity today.

Key Takeaways

- Various perspectives have been offered to identify the root causes of health disparities. However, current research has debunked some of them, affirming that health disparities are driven more by political determinants, including discriminatory laws, policies, practices, and social factors (such as where one lives and works) than by personal health decisions.
- There is an extensive body of evidence highlighting the negative impact that political and social determinants, systemic and structural racism, and discrimination have had—and continue to have—on the healthcare and health outcomes of Black people and communities.
- Comprehensive solutions to address health disparities must focus on the political and social determinants of health and the factors that arise from them in order to advance health equity meaningfully. Genetics and biology play a part, but current research shows they play a minor role compared to the impact and influence of social determinants.

A Closer Look at Health Disparities and Health Inequities

It is impossible to discuss Black health and wellness without focusing on the differences and relationship between health disparities and health inequities. While Black people experience higher rates of chronic and acute conditions, lack of insurance, poor healthcare quality, and worse health outcomes compared to whites, these disparities are not mainly due to genetics, personal choices, or biological reasons. They are primarily driven by a range of inequities in access to and quality of healthcare and other social, economic, educational, and geographic inequities that shape everyone's lives and life opportunities (National Academies of Sciences, Engineering, and Medicine, 2023).

Advancing Health Equity: Not Why, But How?

The negative health impacts of disparities and inequities on Black people and communities are well-documented, widespread, and persistent. So, too, are the significant economic costs to the United States healthcare system and nation as a whole. It therefore benefits us as a nation to eliminate health inequities and to level the health and wellness playing field for everyone. The question is not "why?" but "how?"

We know that inequities lead to disparities. Therefore, to eliminate health disparities, we must first address existing discriminatory laws, policies, and programs blocking health equity advancement. We also must prevent new health inequities and disparities (Commonwealth Fund, 2023). While these goals are ambitious, efforts must begin with acknowledging that racism does not just exist in society (for instance, as interpersonal racism or prejudice); it is built into our social fabric. While rarely stated openly, laws, policies, and programs are often shaped by historical injustices and power imbalances that benefit specific groups while harming others. Further, many reinforce each other, creating formidable barriers to health equity advancement.

All forms of racism, from systemic to unconscious to overt, are serious public health problems with profoundly negative impacts on the health and wellbeing of Black people and other people of color (American Public Health Association, 2023).

We need more significant action to "right the wrongs" and reshape discriminatory laws, policies, and programs that cause health inequities and disparities. Additionally, because health is shaped by many social, economic, and environmental factors, we must remember that every policy has a potential health equity impact. Ensuring that health impacts are considered across all laws, policies, and programs is essential to meaningfully advance health equity (Prevention Institute, 2023).

How Policies Affect Health: The Example of Redlining

Many policies, on their face, may not seem related to health but directly impact the health and wellness of people and communities. Examples of such policies that had particular detrimental effects on Black people include education policies (such as school segregation and the underfunding of public schools in Black neighborhoods) and environmental protection policies (such as the extreme lack of enforcement of the Clean Air Act in Black and other communities of color). They also can be found in economic policies (such as the initial widespread exclusion of Black people from the benefits in the New Deal and post-World War II economic benefits particularly Social Security and the GI Bill), criminal justice policies (such as "three-strikes" laws, crack cocaine sentencing and "zero-tolerance" policing practices), and employment policies (such as the persistent and unaddressed structural racism that led to few job offers, lower wages and salaries, and fewer protections for Black workers in comparison to white workers).

In housing policy, "redlining" is a classic example of what some might classify as a "non-health" policy with significant, long-lasting health impacts. Redlining, which started in the 1930s, is a discriminatory practice where the federal government and banks label Black neighborhoods "high-risk" and outline them in red on maps. The high-risk label meant residents in these neighborhoods and those looking to conduct business in these neighborhoods were often denied loans, insurance, and investment opportunities, regardless of their income level (Rothstein, 2017).

This systematic, systemic, and structural disinvestment in redlined communities proved to have long-lasting negative health impacts. In fact, today, numerous studies confirm that historic redlining has led to significant disparities and inequities in present-day incidence and prevalence of many major health conditions. For example, residents living in formerly redlined neighborhoods today have disproportionately higher rates (both in prevalence and in death) of heart disease, hypertension, diabetes, asthma, and other respiratory diseases (e.g., COPD); chronic and acute mental health conditions and illnesses; and infectious diseases.

How does Housing Policy affect Black Health and Wellness?

1 **Poor Housing Quality**: Owners and landlords in Black neighborhoods could not get financing to improve homes and properties, which led to exposure to lead paint, mold, pests, and other hazards that increased rates of stress, asthma, lead poisoning, and injuries (Urban Institute, 2023a).
2 **Environmental Hazards**: Highways, landfills, and industrial zones are often placed next to or in Black neighborhoods. Exposure to toxins, water and air pollution, and noise increases cancer rates, asthma, stress, and heart disease (Environmental Protection Agency, 2023).
3 **Lack of Community Resources**: Redlining caused underinvestment in Black neighborhoods, leading to fewer parks, unsafe streets, higher crime rates, economic instability, and less access to healthy food options and safe places to exercise. These factors contributed to higher obesity rates, stress, heart disease, diabetes, and shorter life spans (American Journal of Public Health, 2023).
4 **Limited Healthcare Access**: Fewer hospitals, pharmacies, and health clinics exist in Black neighborhoods, leaving fewer places for Black people to get healthcare and fill prescriptions, contributing to worse health outcomes (Health Affairs, 2023).

5 **Economic Impacts**: Redlining severely limited home and business ownership for Black people, which worsened economic inequities that sustained and created health disparities, leaving Black people and communities with worse health outcomes, less access to quality healthcare, and a higher risk of early death (Federal Reserve Bank, 2024).

Health equity cannot be retrofitted onto policies after the fact; it must be built in from the very beginning. As history and current research conveys, overlapping systems of disadvantage compound and often determine who gets sick, who receives care (and of what quality), and who is left behind entirely. Governments that sidestep this reality are not neutral, but rather complicit in reproducing and reinforcing conditions that generated historical injustice and created conditions for multigenerational harm to Black people and other people of color. The goal, therefore, cannot simply be to fix what is broken; it is to prevent the harm in the first place.

Selected Approaches to Health Equity Advancement

Before the administration of the 47th President began systematically dismantling decades of hard-won progress, there were several concrete, evidence-based approaches quietly and effectively doing what equity-centered policy is supposed to do: reach the people most harmed by documented structural and systemic neglect and disadvantage and work to right wrongs. What follows is a record of what was working well and what has currently been underfunded, downgraded, and/or lost altogether:

Community Health Worker Programs: In Philadelphia and Chicago, community health worker initiatives have reduced Black maternal mortality by up to 40% by providing culturally competent care and addressing vital social needs (American Journal of Preventive Medicine, 2023).

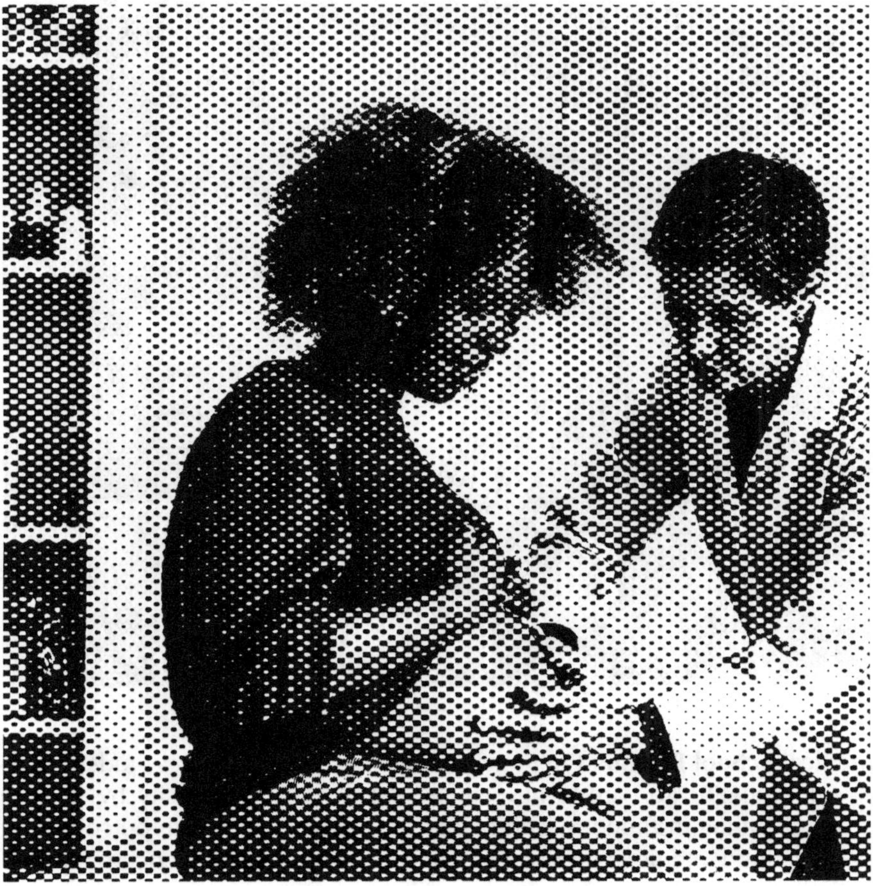

Food Access Initiatives: Programs bringing grocery stores and farmers markets to previously underserved neighborhoods have shown 25–30% improvements in diet-related conditions like diabetes, overweight and obesity, and hypertension among residents (Health Affairs, 2024).

Medical School Pipeline Programs: Programs supporting Black students pursuing healthcare careers have increased workforce diversity by 35% in participating institutions, improving care quality and health outcomes for racial and ethnic minority patients (Association of American Medical Colleges, 2023).

Hospital–Community Partnerships: When hospitals partner with community organizations to address social determinants of health, they have achieved 22% reductions in emergency department visits and 18% fewer hospitalizations while improving chronic disease management at the same time (National Academy for State Health Policy, 2024).

These approaches succeed by addressing both immediate healthcare needs and the underlying social factors that create and sustain health disparities and inequities.

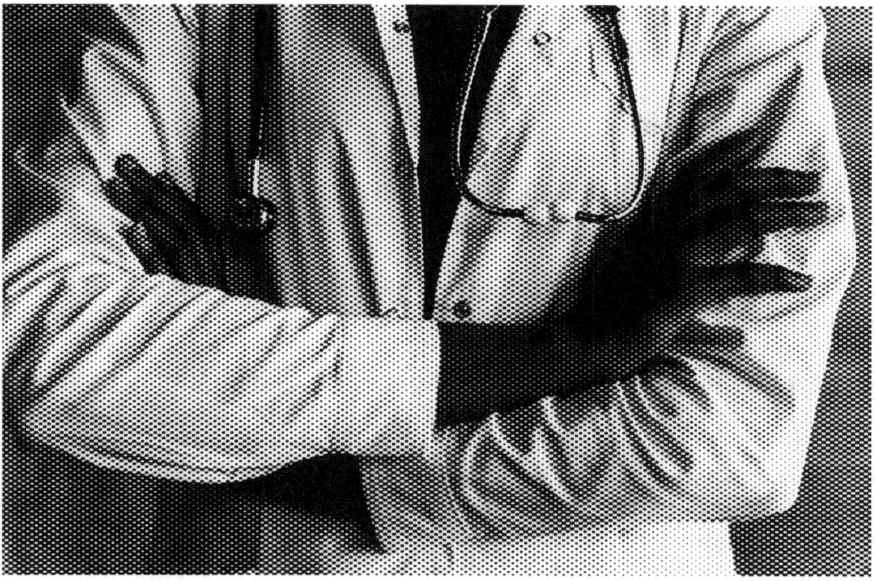

Key Takeaways

- Evidence-based health equity interventions produce measurable results.
- Successful approaches address healthcare access and needs and the underlying social factors affecting healthcare and health outcomes.
- Meaningful community engagement is a critical component of effective health equity programs.

Black Health Equity Under the Current Administration: What's Happening and What's at Stake?

The 47th presidential administration has quickly implemented policy and program changes affecting healthcare and health equity, claiming these changes will save billions of dollars every year through increased efficiency and reduced bureaucracy (Department of Health and Human Services, 2025). Critics question the amount of ultimate savings and further argue that if these policies worsen existing health disparities and inequities, they could ultimately cost the nation more in healthcare expenses and present a loss in productivity (Urban Institute, 2025).

During its first term, the 45th presidential administration's policies were criticized for undermining efforts to advance health equity. Critics pointed to deep cuts in public health funding and attempts to roll back the Affordable Care Act (Commonwealth Fund, 2024). Supporters of the administration, however, claimed that its deregulation efforts were intended to make healthcare more affordable and accessible through market-based approaches (Heritage Foundation, 2024).

Since the start of its second term, the 47th presidential administration's approach to issues around equity, disparities, and equality has sparked debate and immense outrage. While conservative-leaning voices argue that focusing on economic growth and job creation will ultimately benefit all Americans, including Black people (American Enterprise Institute, 2025), many experts have expressed concern that the 47th presidential administration's policy changes will actually worsen inequities (Joint Center for Political and Economic Studies, 2025). In fact, numerous politically neutral experts have publicly stated that the current administration's policy changes and policy/program proposals will contribute significantly to worsening racial inequities, economic inequities, and equitable access to healthcare. Further, they assert that these policies heavily favor wealthier people and corporations, expanding the divide between the nation's "haves" and "have-nots."

Consider the swift actions undertaken by the Department of Government Efficiency (DOGE), in 2025, which resulted in more than 280,000 job losses. While DOGE proponents argued these cuts streamline government operations, critics have deep concern over the impact on people and their families who lost jobs and their employer-sponsored health insurance (Congressional Budget Office, 2025), while also noting the small relative percentage of government spending addressed by these cuts.

Specific Policy Discussions

Changes to Medicaid

The 47th presidential administration directed a significant restructuring of Medicaid, including historically deep funding cuts, arguing that these changes give states more flexibility and reduce federal spending on Medicaid (Center for Medicaid and Medicare Services, 2025). Critics project that these changes could reduce healthcare coverage for more than 13 million Black people or 20% of the total Medicaid population, including pregnant women, seniors, and those with disabilities. This also includes children covered by Medicaid, a disproportionate number of whom (67%) are Black or other racial and ethnic minorities (Kaiser Family Foundation, 2025). Without Medicaid coverage, our nation's most vulnerable residents are at greater risk of experiencing worse health outcomes and premature death.

These radical changes will affect access to necessary healthcare and treatments, including mental health and substance abuse services for millions of not only medically and financially vulnerable Black people, but all people. The effects have already started to unfold, with healthcare facilities serving largely Medicaid populations downsizing the services they offer and struggling to remain operational. This has and will continue to limit healthcare access in underserved areas.

Proposed Medicare Reforms

About 5.5 million Black people rely on Medicare for healthcare services. While the 47th President has stated he will not cut Medicare benefits, his administration has supported budget proposals to reduce Medicare spending growth (Office of Management and Budget, 2025).

Policy analysts have differing views on the potential impact of these proposals. While some supporters claim that targeted Medicare reforms could improve efficiency without harming patient care, many others are concerned that reducing payments to Medicare providers could lead to fewer doctors accepting Medicare, decreasing access to healthcare for many Medicare beneficiaries. Additionally, analysts have also warned that cutting Medicare program spending on prescription drugs, which the 47th President has discussed supporting, will increase out-of-pocket spending for Medicare beneficiaries. Those with fewer financial resources would be at greater risk of having to decide whether to pay for food, rent, or their medications.

Attacks on DEI Programs

One of the 47th President's first actions was to sign executive orders and Presidential Actions reviewing and, in some cases, revoking Diversity, Equity, and Inclusion (DEI) programs, initiatives, and actions across the federal government, including those receiving federal funding. Those who do not understand the history, purpose, and impacts of DEI programs claim they have become inefficient and are not achieving their intended goals (Manhattan Institute, 2025). However, there is an impressive breadth and depth of evidence to the contrary. In fact, DEI programs have been crucial for addressing multiple levels of historical discrimination and creating more equitable systems in the United States. Countless studies have found that DEI programs, initiatives, and actions have served to the benefit of not only Black people and other people of color, but also women, people with disabilities, military veterans, families and active-duty service members, working parents, and caregivers, just to name a few (NAACP, 2025).

In healthcare specifically, DEI programs and initiatives have had positive impacts on the following:

- Diversifying the health workforce, which research shows improves patient outcomes (Health Affairs, 2023) and, in some cases, literally saves lives.
- Correcting biased algorithms that directly affected medical decision-making and negatively affected healthcare quality and health outcomes for Black people (Journal of the American Medical Association, 2023).
- Strengthening cultural competence in healthcare delivery which improved health outcomes (American Medical Association, 2024).

Rather than eliminate these valuable and effective programs and initiatives, efforts should be made to replicate and expand evidence-based DEI programs and practices that demonstrably improve health outcomes and advance health equity.

Harmful Changes to Health Data Collection and Reporting

Calling it an administrative and paperwork burden, the 47th presidential administration has proposed changes to how race and ethnicity data are collected and reported, including in healthcare settings (Department of Health and Human Services, 2025). This proposed change will likely allow existing health inequities and disparities to go unchecked and unaddressed. Additionally, it would make identifying and addressing new health inequities and disparities extremely difficult. Connecting accurate, inclusive, and disaggregated racial and ethnic data is critical to effective population health monitoring and resource allocation (American Public Health Association, 2025).

Data collection and reporting are essential for:

- Monitoring existing health inequities and disparities.
- Identifying and working to thwart new health inequities and disparities.
- Developing targeted solutions.
- Conducting vital research on the health needs of all Americans.
- Evaluating the effectiveness of targeted interventions.

The collection and reporting of health data by race and ethnicity is essential to health equity advancement and to improving health and wellness for all people and communities throughout the country.

Critical Funding Cuts That Threaten Health Equity Progress

The 47th presidential administration has significantly scaled back the capacity of key federal entities throughout DHHS, which have provided $500 million annually and have also been the backbone of health equity research efforts for decades. In particular, the current administration has taken aim at DHHS Offices of Minority Health, the National Institutes of Health, particularly the National Institute for Minority Health and Health Disparities (NIMHD), the National Institute on Nursing Research (NINR), and the National Institute of Allergy and Infectious Diseases (NIAID). Together, these offices and institutes supported:

- Studies on health and other conditions disproportionately affecting Black people and communities.
- The professional development of diverse healthcare researchers and emboldening community partnerships.
- The establishment of excellence at minority-serving institutions.

The elimination of these funding streams has created an immediate crisis. Most organizations previously receiving NIH support exhausted their funding by mid-2025, with no replacement sources identified. This gap is especially devastating as many philanthropic entities across foundation, nonprofit, and corporate sectors have simultaneously retreated from publicly supporting equity-focused initiatives in the current political climate (Daniels, 2026).

The Research Centers in Minority Institutions (RCMI) Program exemplifies this crisis. Established in 1985 and recently eliminated by the 47th President, this program provided essential infrastructure funding to Historically Black Colleges and Universities (HBCUs) like Howard University College of Medicine, Meharry Medical College, and the Morehouse School of Medicine. Without alternative funding, these institutions will lose critical research capacity that took decades to build, forcing program closures and staff reductions within months (National Minority Quality Forum, 2025).

Key Takeaways

- $500 million in annual health equity research funding has been eliminated.
- Many organizations with a successful history of health equity advancement exhausted their funding by mid-2025.
- Philanthropic sources are not adequately filling the health equity funding gap.
- Historic institutions serving Black communities and producing Black clinicians and researchers face imminent program closures.

Economic Benefits of Health Equity

Beyond the moral imperative, eliminating racial and ethnic health disparities and inequities creates substantial economic benefits to the nation. They include the following:

- **Healthcare Savings**: $135 billion annually in reduced direct medical costs (W.K. Kellogg Foundation, 2023).
- **Productivity Gains**: $42 billion yearly reduction in lost productivity (Economic Policy Institute, 2024).
- **Economic Growth**: $1 trillion increased economic output over a decade as people live longer, healthier, and more productive lives (McKinsey Global Institute, 2023).
- **Job Creation**: Approximately 230,000 new healthcare and related jobs (American Hospital Association, 2024).
- **Reduced Government Spending**: Significant decreases in disability benefits and safety net program costs (Urban Institute, 2023b).

These economic benefits would accrue to all Americans through lower health-care costs, increased productivity, and reduced pressure on public resources.

Key Takeaways

- Health equity is both a moral and an economic imperative.
- Economic benefits of health equity initiatives far outweigh their costs.
- All Americans benefit financially from reduced health disparities and inequities.

The "One Big Beautiful Bill Act": A Devastating Blow to Black Health Equity

Signed into law on July 4, 2025, the "One Big Beautiful Bill Act" (OBBBA) represents the most significant cut to social safety net programs in United States history. For Black communities already facing a 5-year life expectancy gap compared to white Americans (National Academy of Medicine, 2024), the bill's provisions threaten to reverse decades of health equity progress and exacerbate existing disparities.

Unprecedented Health Coverage Losses

The Congressional Budget Office (CBO) projects catastrophic impacts on health insurance coverage. The CBO estimates that 10.9 million people will lose health coverage by 2034 as a direct result of the OBBBA's provisions (Congressional Budget Office, 2025a). When combined with the expiration of enhanced Affordable Care Act (ACA) premium tax credits and other policy changes not included in the bill itself, total coverage losses could reach approximately 16 million people (Kaiser Family Foundation, 2025).

According to the Kaiser Family Foundation (2025), Black Americans represent approximately 20% of Medicaid enrollees, even though they make up only 14% of the United States population. The bill's Medicaid cuts will therefore hit Black communities disproportionately hard.

Medicaid: The Primary Target

The OBBBA cuts more than $900 billion from Medicaid over the next decade—the largest reduction in the program's history (Center on Budget and Policy Priorities, 2025). The bill's most damaging provisions include:

Work Requirements: The legislation imposes new monthly "community engagement" requirements for non-disabled adults to maintain Medicaid coverage. Effective January 1, 2027, enrollees ages 19–64 must engage in 80 hours per month of employment, education, work programs, or community service to maintain eligibility (Association of State and Territorial Health Officials, 2025). The CBO (2025a) estimates that 5.3 million people will lose Medicaid and become uninsured in 2034 as a result of failing to meet work requirements.

Work requirements disproportionately affect Black workers who are more likely to work in part-time, gig, or informal sectors. The legislation provides mandatory exemptions for parents and caretakers with children ages 13 and under, people who are "medically frail," and people who are pregnant or postpartum. However, historical evidence shows that exemptions often fail to protect eligible individuals (Center on Budget and Policy Priorities, 2025).

Increased Administrative Burden: The law requires states to conduct eligibility redeterminations twice a year (Association of State and Territorial Health Officials, 2025). This change historically leads to eligible people losing coverage due to paperwork errors and administrative confusion.

New Cost-Sharing Requirements: Effective October 1, 2028, states are required to impose cost-sharing of up to $35 per service on expansion to adults with incomes between 100% and 138% of the federal poverty line (Association of State and Territorial Health Officials, 2025). Working people earning more than $16,000 per year will face new out-of-pocket costs for medical care.

Affordable Care Act (ACA) Marketplace Changes

The bill makes significant changes to ACA marketplaces that compound coverage losses. The CBO (2025a) estimates that approximately 3 million people will lose marketplace coverage due to the bill's provisions, including:

- Eliminating income-based repayment caps that protected low-income enrollees from having to repay their premium tax credits if their income estimates were incorrect.
- Terminating continuous special enrollment periods for people with incomes below 150% of the federal poverty line.
- Shortening enrollment windows and eliminating automatic re-enrollment.
- Removing coverage options for certain lawfully present noncitizens with incomes below 100% of the federal poverty line (American Medical Association, 2025).

SNAP (Food Assistance) Cuts

The bill cuts $186 billion from the Supplemental Nutrition Assistance Program (SNAP) and expands work requirements (Center on Budget and Policy Priorities, 2025). According to the NAACP Legal Defense Fund (2025), approximately 25% of Black households in the United States receive SNAP benefits, meaning these cuts will disproportionately affect Black families already experiencing higher rates of food insecurity.

Direct Health Consequences

The human cost of these coverage losses extends beyond statistics. When people lose health insurance coverage, they lose access to preventive and primary care, care for life-threatening conditions, and treatments for chronic conditions (Center on Budget and Policy Priorities, 2025). A person with diabetes who loses health coverage, loses the ability to properly manage their condition, which can lead to complications, disability, and premature death.

For Black Americans who already experience disproportionately high rates of chronic conditions like diabetes and hypertension, as well as higher maternal mortality rates and infant mortality rates (Center on Budget and Policy Priorities, 2025), the loss of Medicaid coverage threatens to worsen already severe health disparities.

For too many of us, the loss of health insurance coverage can accelerate death. And, for most of us, loss of health insurance puts us at increased economic risk, up to and including bankruptcy.

Economic Burden Distribution

The CBO's distributional analysis reveals the regressive nature of the OBBBA. The CBO (2025b) found that the incomes for the highest 10% of earners would rise by an average of 2.7% by 2034, while the incomes of the lowest 10% would fall by 3.1%, primarily due to cuts to programs such as Medicaid and food assistance. Due to enduring racial wealth gaps and income disparities, Black households are less likely to benefit from tax deductions tied to homeownership, high earnings, or capital income—meaning they gain nothing from the tax cuts while suffering the full impact of program cuts.

Healthcare System Infrastructure

Beyond individual coverage losses, the OBBBA threatens the healthcare infrastructure serving Black communities. The loss of Medicaid revenues puts rural hospitals and safety-net facilities at risk of closure (Center for American Progress, 2025). The Center for American Progress (2025) estimates that the bill will generate billions of dollars in uncompensated care costs for providers, with hospitals, nursing homes, and community health centers left to absorb more of the cost of treating the uninsured.

Key Takeaways

- The OBBBA will result in approximately 11 million Americans losing health coverage by 2034 due to the bill's provisions, with total losses potentially reaching 16 million when combined with other policy changes (CBO, 2025a; Kaiser Family Foundation, 2025).
- More than $900 billion in Medicaid cuts will disproportionately impact Black Americans, who represent 20% of Medicaid enrollees (Center on Budget and Policy Priorities, 2025; Kaiser Family Foundation, 2025).
- Work requirements, increased administrative burdens, and new cost-sharing requirements create multiple pathways to coverage loss.
- SNAP cuts will worsen food insecurity in Black communities, where 25% rely on food assistance (NAACP Legal Defense Fund, 2025).
- The bill's tax cuts primarily benefit wealthy Americans while forcing costs onto low- and middle-income families, with the top 10% seeing income increases of 2.7% while the bottom 10% see income decreases of 3.1% (CBO, 2025b).
- The healthcare infrastructure serving Black communities faces potential collapse as Medicaid funding disappears.
- The combined impact threatens to reverse decades of health equity progress and widen the already devastating five-year life expectancy gap.

Without immediate and coordinated intervention, the "One Big Beautiful Bill Act" stands to devastate Black health outcomes for generations to come, transforming a health equity crisis into a full-scale catastrophe.

Call to Action: What You Can Do

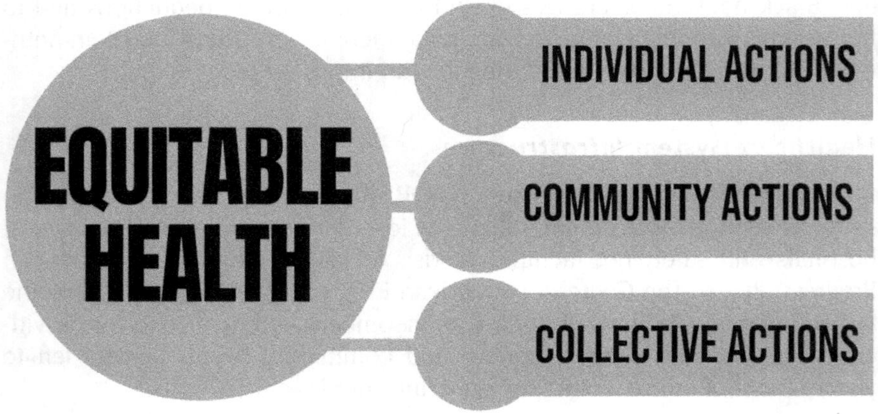

Individual Actions

- **Vote**: Vote in every election. And, consdier how your vote contributes to the advancement of health equity.
- **Get Informed**: Learn about health equity policy changes like the "One Big Beautiful Bill Act" (OBBBA) from *credible* sources.
- **Share Knowledge**: In your networks, distribute fact-based information about health disparities and inequities, and their impacts on the health and healthcare of Black people and communities.
- **Contact Elected Officials**: Express support for health equity programs regardless of their or your political affiliation.

Community Actions

- **Support Local Organizations**: Join or donate to groups addressing specific health needs and health equity advancement in your area.
- **Participate in Research**: Consider joining health studies, such as health survey research and clinical trials, especially those focused on conditions affecting the health and healthcare of Black people and communities.
- **Engage Locally**: Attend community meetings about healthcare, housing, education, and environmental issues.

Collective Actions

- **Build Coalitions**: Work across racial, ethnic, and economic lines to advocate for inclusive health policies that advance health equity.
- **Prioritize Prevention**: Focus on preventive care while advocating for resources to make healthy choices possible for everyone.

Key Takeaways

- Everyone has a role to play in advancing health equity.
- Actions at the individual, community, and policy levels are all necessary.
- Building diverse coalitions strengthens advocacy effectiveness because there is power in numbers.

Conclusion

The state of Black health in America presents both urgent challenges and actionable opportunities. Without thoughtful and coordinated action, the widespread inequities in society that shape and give rise to unjust, unfair, and discriminatory laws, policies and programs that touch healthcare and every other system (e.g., education and environmental systems) will persist. All of these systems ultimately impact all Americans' health and wellbeing.

While significant disparities and inequities persist and recent policy changes, and proposals threaten to worsen them while creating new ones altogether, we must advance evidence-based approaches to improve health outcomes and move toward a more equitable system. Federal, state, and local policy choices will significantly impact these efforts. While there may be disagreement about specific approaches, the goal of better health for all Americans should transcend political divisions. We can and should reimagine a reformed healthcare system that effectively serves everyone by rooting out the determinants of health inequities and disparities and focusing on evidence-based solutions.

Health equity is not just a Black issue. Health equity is an American issue. Removing unfair, unjust, and discriminatory barriers to good health for Black people and communities creates a healthier society for everyone, reduces healthcare costs, increases productivity, and strengthens our nation.

Key Takeaways

- Health equity benefits all Americans, not just specific people or communities.
- Evidence-based solutions exist and have proven successful.
- Action is needed ***now*** to prevent the reversal of decades of progress and the opportunity for new health inequities and disparities to rise.

References

American Enterprise Institute. (2025). *Economic growth and its effects on minority communities*. Washington, DC: AEI Press.

American Hospital Association. (2024). *The economic impact of health equity initiatives*. Chicago, IL: AHA.

American Journal of Preventive Medicine. (2023). Community health worker interventions and maternal health outcomes. 45(3), 112–129.

American Journal of Public Health. (2023). Racial disparities in maternal health: A systemic review. 113(4), 348–361.

American Medical Association. (2024). *Position statement on health equity and racial disparities*. Chicago, IL: AMA.

American Medical Association. (2025). *4 "Big, Beautiful Bill" changes that will reshape care in 2026*. https://www.ama-assn.org/health-care-advocacy/federal-advocacy/4-big-beautiful-bill-changes-will-reshape-care-2026

American Public Health Association. (2023). *Racism as a public health crisis*. Washington, DC: APHA Press.

American Public Health Association. (2024). *Structural racism and health inequities*. Washington, DC: APHA Press.

American Public Health Association. (2025). *The importance of race and ethnicity data in health systems*. Washington, DC: APHA Press.

Association of American Medical Colleges. (2023). *Diversity in medicine: Facts and figures 2023*. Washington, DC: AAMC.

Association of State and Territorial Health Officials. (2025). *One Big Beautiful Bill law summary*. https://www.astho.org/advocacy/federal-government-affairs/leg-alerts/2025/one-big-beautiful-bill-law-summary/

Brookings Institution. (2024). *The economic case for health equity*. Washington, DC: Brookings.

Center for American Progress. (2025). *New CBO estimates confirm a massive rise in uncompensated care costs under one big beautiful bill act*. https://www.americanprogress.org/article/new-cbo-estimates-confirm-massive-rise-in-uncompensated-care-costs-under-one-big-beautiful-bill-act/

Center for Medicaid and Medicare Services. (2025). *Medicaid modernization proposal*. Washington, DC: Department of Health and Human Services.

Center on Budget and Policy Priorities. (2025). *By the numbers: Harmful Republican megabill will take health coverage away from millions of people and raise families' costs*. https://www.cbpp.org/research/health/by-the-numbers-harmful-republican-megabill-will-take-health-coverage-away-from

Centers for Disease Control and Prevention. (2023a). *Health disparities and inequalities report—United States, 2023*. Washington, DC: CDC.

Centers for Disease Control and Prevention. (2023b). *Health disparities and inequalities report—United States, 2023*. Atlanta, GA: CDC.

Commonwealth Fund. (2023). *Strategies for advancing health equity in state policy*. New York, NY: Commonwealth Fund.

Commonwealth Fund. (2024). *Health policy under the first Trump administration: An assessment*. New York, NY: Commonwealth Fund.

Congressional Budget Office. (2025). *Economic and employment effects of federal workforce reduction*. Washington, DC: CBO.

Congressional Budget Office. (2025a). *Estimated effects on the number of uninsured people in 2034 resulting from policies incorporated within CBO's baseline projections and H.R. 1, the one big beautiful bill act.* https://www.cbo.gov/publication/61463

Congressional Budget Office. (2025b). *How H.R. 1, the one big beautiful bill act, would affect the distribution of resources available to households.*

Daniels, A. (2026). Retreating from race. The Chronicle of Philanthropy. https://www.philanthropy.com/news/retreating-from-race/

Dawes, D. E. (2020). *The political determinants of health.* Baltimore, MD: Johns Hopkins University Press.

Department of Health and Human Services. (2025). *Regulatory reform initiative: Annual report.* Washington, DC: HHS.

Economic Policy Institute. (2024). *The productivity cost of health disparities.* Washington, DC: EPI.

Environmental Protection Agency. (2023). *Environmental justice and health outcomes.* Washington, DC: EPA.

Federal Reserve Bank. (2024). *Long-term economic effects of housing discrimination.* Washington, DC: Federal Reserve.

Health Affairs. (2023). Healthcare facility distribution and health outcomes. 42(6), 789–802.

Health Affairs. (2024). Reducing food deserts and health outcomes: A five-year analysis. 43(2), 245–261.

Heritage Foundation. (2024). *Market-based approaches to healthcare access.* Washington, DC: Heritage Foundation.

Institute for Health Metrics and Evaluation. (2024). *Global burden of disease study: United States projections to 2050.* Seattle, WA: IHME.

Joint Center for Political and Economic Studies. (2025). *Analysis of federal policies affecting Black communities.* Washington, DC: Joint Center.

Joint Economic Committee of the U.S. Congress (2023). *2023 Economic Report of the President.* Washington, DC: Government Printing Office.

Journal of the American Medical Association. (2023). *Racial bias in clinical algorithms: Sources and solutions.* 329(10), 902–910.

Kaiser Family Foundation. (2025). *Potential impacts of Medicaid restructuring on coverage and access.* San Francisco, CA: KFF.

Manhattan Institute. (2025). *Evaluating the effectiveness of federal DEI programs.* New York, NY: Manhattan Institute.

March of Dimes. (2024). *Infant mortality disparities in the United States.* White Plains, NY: March of Dimes.

McKinsey Global Institute. (2023). *The economic potential of closing the racial health gap.* New York, NY: McKinsey & Company.

NAACP. (2025). *The continuing need for equity-focused programs in federal agencies.* Baltimore, MD: NAACP.

NAACP Legal Defense Fund. (2025). *President Trump's 'one big beautiful bill act,' explained.* https://www.naacpldf.org/case-issue/trumps-one-big-beautiful-bill-act-explained/

National Academies of Sciences, Engineering, and Medicine. (2023). *Social and structural determinants of health equity and health disparities.* Washington, DC: National Academies Press.

National Academy for State Health Policy. (2024). *Hospital–community partnerships to address social determinants of health*. Washington, DC: NASHP.
National Academy of Medicine. (2024). *The state of health disparities in the United States*. Washington, DC: National Academies Press.
National Institute of Mental Health. (2023). *Mental health disparities by race and ethnicity*. Bethesda, MD: NIMH.
National Minority Quality Forum. (2025). *Assessment of changes to federal minority health initiatives*. Washington, DC: NMQF.
Office of Management and Budget. (2025). *Budget of the United States Government, Fiscal Year 2026*. Washington, DC: U.S. Government Printing Office.
Prevention Institute. (2023). *Health in all policies: A guide for state and local governments*. Oakland, CA: Prevention Institute.
Robert Wood Johnson Foundation. (2023). *Beyond personal choice: Social determinants and health behaviors*. Princeton, NJ: RWJF.
Rothstein, R. (2017). *The color of law: A forgotten history of how our government segregated America*. New York: Liveright Publishing.
Urban Institute. (2023a). *Long-term health impacts of redlining and housing segregation*. Washington, DC: Urban Institute.
Urban Institute. (2023b). *The economic benefits of preventing chronic disease through equity initiatives*. Washington, DC: Urban Institute.
Urban Institute. (2025). *Projected impacts of federal health policy changes on health disparities*. Washington, DC: Urban Institute.
W.K. Kellogg Foundation. (2023). *The business case for racial equity*. Battle Creek, MI: W.K. Kellogg Foundation.
World Health Organization. (2023). *Social determinants of health: Key concepts*. Geneva: WHO.

Chapter 11

Reproductive Justice at the Crossroads

Black Communities Navigating Care Deserts in Post-Roe America

*The National Women's Law Center**

A Note on Language

Throughout this Black Paper (Paper), we acknowledge that terms such as "maternal," "women's health," and "mothers" are frequently used in healthcare settings, policy development, implementation, and research literature. We recognize that this gendered language can be alienating, excluding transgender men, nonbinary, and gender-expansive people who have the capacity for pregnancy. We use these terms when citing existing research, policy documents, or healthcare systems that employ this language. Where possible, we use inclusive terms such as "birthing people," "pregnant people," and "reproductive health" to honor the full spectrum of people who experience pregnancy and birth. Our commitment to reproductive justice includes advocating for gender-inclusive language in all aspects of reproductive healthcare.

Executive Summary

This Black Paper examines the intersection of reproductive justice and health equity crises disproportionately affecting Black communities across America. The devastating impact of the Supreme Court's decision in *Dobbs v. Jackson Women's Health Organization* decision[1] worsens existing inequities in reproductive healthcare access, creating overlapping "deserts" where essential services are limited or unavailable. Black communities are especially at risk for compounding challenges, facing systemic barriers to abortion care, prenatal care, and other essential healthcare services vital to reproductive autonomy and wellbeing. Additionally, transgender and gender-expansive people face unique challenges in accessing culturally/clinically competent and affirming reproductive care. Using the framework established by Sister Song Collective in 1994, Reproductive Justice is the human right to maintain personal bodily autonomy, have children, not have children, and parent the children we have in safe and sustainable communities. This Black Paper outlines critical policy

* Supported by braintrust authors: David J. Johns, Latham Thomas, Nadia French-Graham, Preston D. Mitchum, Regina Davis Moss, and Ashley Bland Manlove.

DOI: 10.4324/9781003752646-16

interventions, community-based solutions, and a call to action that centers the experiences of all birthing people.

Introduction: The Crisis of Overlapping Care Deserts

In post-*Roe* America, access to reproductive healthcare has become a geographic lottery where race, income, and zip code determine fundamental rights. For Black birthing people, this crisis manifests as overlapping "care deserts"—vast regions that lack both abortion access and basic maternity services and are further compounded by digital divides and food insecurity. About 3.7 million women of reproductive age in the United States live in counties without access to abortion and with no or limited access to maternity care (National Women's Law Center [NWLC], 2025a). These overlapping "maternity care deserts" and "abortion deserts" have devastating consequences, particularly for Black women, who are already three times more likely to die from pregnancy-related causes than white women (March of Dimes, 2024). The Supreme Court's *Dobbs* decision did not create these inequities; rather, it weaponized existing healthcare apartheid by transforming structural neglect into active harm.

Using Sister Song Collective's 1994 framework, reproductive justice encompasses the human right to maintain bodily autonomy, to have children, to not have children, and to be parents in safe communities. This Paper examines how Black communities navigate intensifying threats to these rights, spotlights the unique challenges facing transgender and gender-expansive people, and presents both community-led solutions and policy interventions that center those most impacted by reproductive oppression.

The State of Reproductive Healthcare Access: Multiple Forms of Deprivation

Medicaid and Insurance Barriers

Insurance-related barriers, particularly those stemming from Medicaid restrictions, significantly hinder access to reproductive healthcare. The Hyde Amendment, enacted in 1976, prohibits using federal funds for abortion services under Medicaid, except in cases of rape, incest, or when the pregnant person's life is at risk. This restriction disproportionately affects Black people, who are more likely to be insured through Medicaid. As a result, many are forced to pay out-of-pocket for fertility treatments and abortion services, which can be financially burdensome or prohibitive. While some states have opted to use their own funds to cover abortion services beyond the federal limitations, coverage remains inconsistent across the country, leading to a patchwork of access that disproportionately affects low-income people and people of color. These financial barriers, compounded by additional costs such as travel and child care, create significant obstacles for those seeking abortion care, particularly in states with restrictive policies or limited provider availability. Addressing these insurance and funding disparities is crucial to ensuring equitable access to reproductive healthcare for all people, regardless of income or geographic location. Regarding the point about geography, it's worth noting that many Southern states rejected federal Medicaid expansion dollars for decades, causing rural medical facilities and hospitals to operate with minimal staffing, if they were able to remain open.

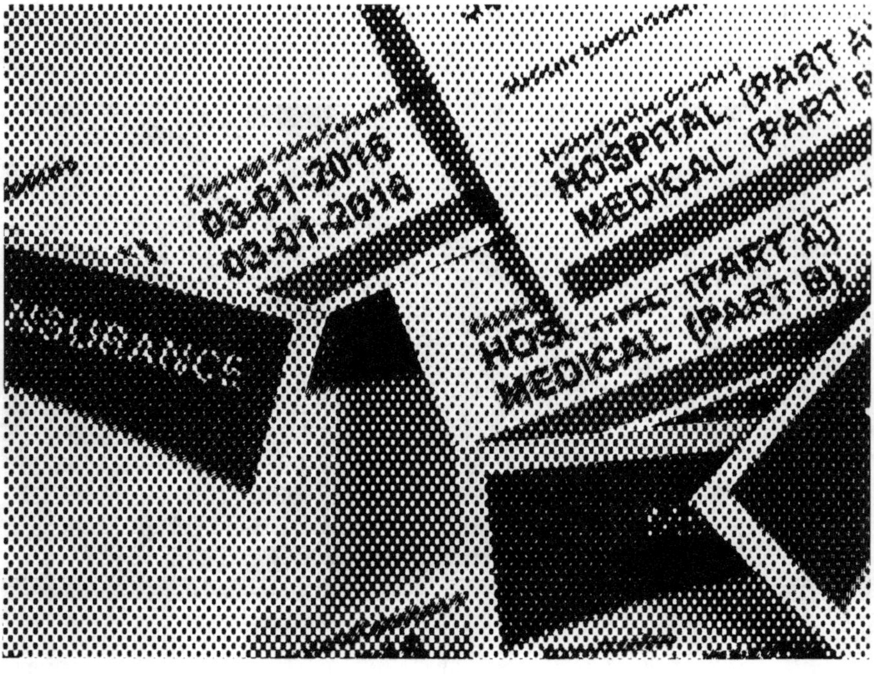

Abortion Care Deserts

Before *Roe* v. *Wade* was overturned, conservative states like Missouri filed unconstitutional legislation in the state house and senate to trigger a rehearing of *Roe* v. *Wade* in the State and Federal Courts. Legislation such as Missouri House Bill 126, passed in 2019, included a trigger provision for the impending Supreme Court decision and no exceptions for rape and incest. Since the Supreme Court overturned *Roe v. Wade* in June 2022, 14 states have implemented total abortion bans with minimal exceptions, which includes many others that have severely restricted access (Guttmacher Institute, 2025).

Despite these restrictions, the Guttmacher Institute (2025) reports 1,038,100 clinician-provided abortions in states without total bans in 2024—a slight increase from 2023. However, this statistic masks the immense barriers many must overcome to access care, with drastic regional disparities.

Abortion bans affect people far beyond the states where they are in place. In 2024, approximately 155,000 people traveled across state lines for abortion care, accounting for 15% of all abortions in states without total bans (Guttmacher Institute, 2025). For Black women and other birthing persons of color—who already face economic and transportation barriers—these long distances make abortion care nearly impossible to reach.

Pregnancy and Maternity Care Deserts

The crisis extends beyond abortion access. Many regions with restricted abortion access also lack adequate pregnancy and maternity care.

The scope of America's reproductive healthcare crisis is staggering. Over 35% of United States counties qualify as maternity care deserts—regions without hospitals, birth centers, or obstetric providers—affecting 2.3 million women of reproductive age (March of Dimes, 2024). These maternal care voids overlap catastrophically with abortion-restricted states: 1.7 million women now live in counties offering neither abortion access nor basic prenatal care, while 3.7 million face limited or nonexistent options for both services (National Women's Law Center, 2025a). This geographic lottery of care creates a reproductive healthcare apartheid, where ZIP codes determine fundamental rights.

The overlap between abortion bans and maternity care deserts is particularly devastating. About 1.7 million women of reproductive age live in counties with no maternity care and no access to abortion (NWLC, 2025a). This means they face a double burden: they may have to continue a pregnancy while also lacking basic prenatal and childbirth services.

Compounding Deprivations

The reproductive healthcare crisis extends beyond medical access, intersecting with other forms of structural inequality that intensify barriers for Black communities:

Historical Exploitation and Mistrust: The legacy of medical exploitation, such as non-consensual experiments on enslaved Black women and forced sterilizations, has fostered deep-seated mistrust in the healthcare system among Black communities. This contributes to hesitancy in seeking reproductive healthcare, potentially delaying critical interventions and exacerbating health disparities.

Housing Discrimination and Environmental Hazards: Discriminatory housing policies, such as redlining, have historically confined Black communities to areas with substandard housing and limited access to quality healthcare facilities. These neighborhoods often face environmental hazards, such as exposure to air and water pollutants or hazardous waste, which can adversely affect reproductive health outcomes.

Healthcare System Bias and Discrimination: Systemic biases within the healthcare system result in Black women receiving lower-quality care compared to their white counterparts. Implicit biases and discriminatory practices can lead to misdiagnoses, delayed treatments, and inadequate pain management during pregnancy and childbirth.

Employment Disparities and Economic Insecurity: Black women are disproportionately represented in low-wage, unstable jobs that often lack maternity leave, health benefits, and flexible schedules. This economic insecurity can deter people from seeking timely reproductive healthcare and exacerbate stress-related health issues.

Inadequate Transportation Infrastructure: Many Black communities lack reliable public transportation, making it challenging to access distant healthcare facilities, especially in maternity care deserts. This transportation barrier can lead to missed prenatal appointments and delayed emergency care, increasing the risk of adverse maternal and infant health outcomes.

Lack of Comprehensive Sex Education and Culturally Competent Information: The absence of comprehensive sex education in many schools, coupled with a lack of culturally competent reproductive health information from providers, leaves Black people of all ages without essential knowledge about their reproductive health. This information gap can lead to unintended pregnancies and delayed prenatal care, further contributing to health disparities.

Digital Exclusion: In an era of telehealth expansion—with 14% of abortions provided via online-only clinics in 2024—the lack of broadband access becomes a healthcare barrier. Communities without reliable internet cannot access virtual consultations, medication abortion services, or even research their options (National Women's Law Center, 2025a).

Nutritional Insecurity: Food deserts compound pregnancy risks, as inadequate nutrition increases complications requiring specialized care—precisely the care unavailable in maternity deserts.

These conditions create a vicious cycle where those most likely to need advanced obstetric support are least able to access it. These overlapping deprivations don't merely add barriers—they multiply them, creating compound disadvantages that fall heaviest on Black communities already navigating systemic healthcare discrimination.

Intersectional Complexity: In 2025, systemic inequalities in healthcare access persist, with Black women and LGBTQ+/SGL people experiencing higher rates of uninsurance compared to white and Asian women and straight people. Since 2023, approximately 9.8% to 10% of Black women remain uninsured, compared to roughly 6% to 7% for their white and Asian counterparts (Kaiser Family Foundation, 2025a; Kaiser Family Foundation, 2025b; Centers for Disease Control, 2025). Within the LGBTQ+ community, transgender and gender-expansive adults face even more severe gaps, with uninsurance rates reaching up to 23.5%, significantly exceeding rates for cisgender and straight people.

Even when people have health coverage, financial barriers often get in the way of necessary medical management.

- Out-of-Pocket Barriers: High deductibles and copayments can deter managing chronic conditions that can complicate pregnancy. For those with employer-sponsored plans, average out-of-pocket costs for maternity care and childbirth can create severe financial burdens.
- Preventive Care Deterrence: Cost-sharing requirements frequently prevent people from seeking early preventative care and timely reproductive services. This is particularly critical as unmanaged chronic conditions like hypertension, diabetes, and asthma can increase the risk of adverse birth outcomes and maternal complications.
- Systemic Compounding Risks: Financial hurdles have been compounded by recent federal and state-level policy shifts that have reduced health equity funding and restricted Medicaid coverage, further isolating marginalized communities from essential care.

Spotlight: The Disproportionate Impact on Black Communities

The reproductive healthcare crisis in the United States disproportionately affects Black communities, with intensified challenges arising from the intersection of systemic racism, historical oppression, and overlapping identities. Black women, transgender, and gender-expansive people often navigate a complex web of barriers shaped by race, sexual orientation, gender identity and expression, and socioeconomic status. These intersecting factors exacerbate disparities in access to reproductive care, leading to heightened risks and adverse health outcomes.

Anti-abortion policies, combined with failures in the healthcare and economic systems, have particularly devastating impacts on Black, Indigenous, and Latino communities and people with low incomes (Guttmacher Institute, 2023). These communities experience systematic denials of quality healthcare necessary to support reproductive autonomy.

Historical context is crucial to understanding today's disparities. Policies that restrict reproductive freedom build on a legacy of reproductive oppression targeting Black women, from forced breeding during slavery to coerced sterilization programs in the 20th century. Today's abortion bans and lack of maternal healthcare access continue this pattern of controlling Black women's reproductive lives.

The maternal mortality crisis among Black women cannot be separated from the abortion access crisis. When abortion is unavailable and maternity care is insufficient, Black women bear the heaviest burden. The persistent legacy of discrimination, unequal resource distribution, and inequitable access to care drives the stark maternal mortality disparities between Black women and white women (NWLC, 2025a). This disparity worsens in regions with abortion bans and maternity care deserts.

Transgender and Gender-Expansive Birthing People: Unique Challenges and Barriers

The reproductive health crisis is particularly severe and acute for transgender and gender-expansive (TGE) people who have the capacity for pregnancy. Their experiences are often overlooked in discussions about maternal health, reinforcing their invisibility in healthcare systems designed around cisgender experiences.

TGE people face unique barriers when seeking reproductive healthcare. They often encounter discrimination, misgendering, and a lack of understanding from healthcare providers who have limited training in gender-affirming care (PMC, 2022). Medical spaces remain heavily gendered, with services like prenatal care, labor and delivery, and postpartum support commonly labeled as "maternal" or "women's" health services, which can alienate TGE-birthing people.

Research indicates that TGE people seeking reproductive healthcare frequently experience hostility and incompetence from providers, leading to delayed or avoided care (Center for American Progress, 2020). Many healthcare facilities lack inclusive intake forms, gender-neutral bathrooms, and staff trained in gender-affirming communication, creating environments where TGE people feel unwelcome or unsafe, and sometimes questioning if they even want to return to the healthcare setting.

The compounding effects of these barriers are particularly severe for Black TGE people and other TGE people of color, who must navigate both racial discrimination and transphobia in healthcare settings. These intersecting oppressions create additional layers of marginalization and reduced access to quality care.

While statistics reveal the scope of this crisis, they cannot capture the human cost of policy failures. The following stories from Black birthing people across the South illuminate how overlapping care deserts translate into life-threatening situations, impossible choices, and profound injustices that no data point can fully convey. Behind these statistics lie humans forced to navigate impossible choices and life-threatening situations. The data cannot capture the fear of driving hours while in labor, the anguish of being denied care during a miscarriage, or the exhaustion of advocating for basic dignity while pregnant. The following accounts from Black birthing people across the South transform numbers into names, statistics into stories, revealing how policy failures become personal tragedies.

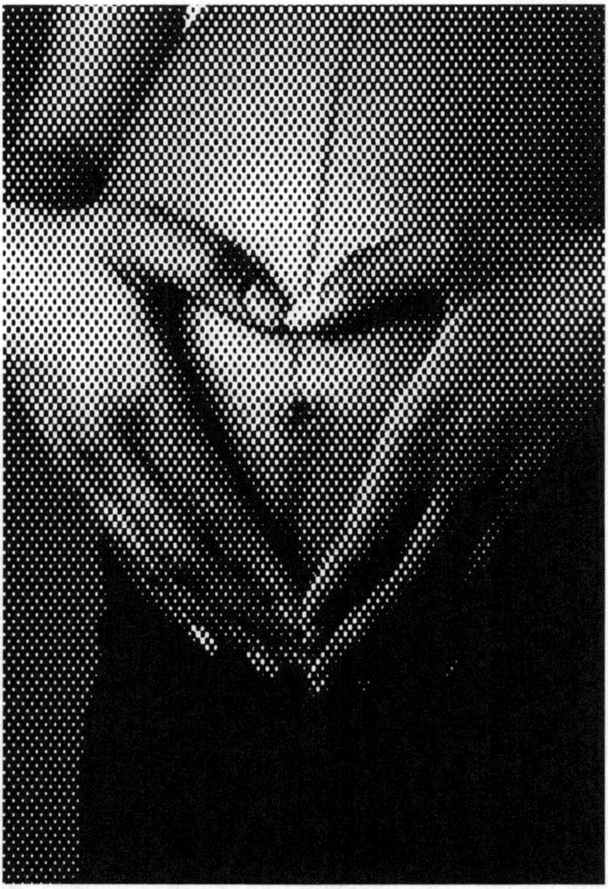

Personal Stories: The Human Cost of Policy Failure

Tamika's Story—Georgia: Tamika, a 32-year-old mother of two living in rural Georgia, discovered she was pregnant with her third child shortly after losing her job. Georgia's six-week abortion ban meant she could not access abortion care in her state by the time she confirmed her pregnancy. The nearest abortion provider was in North Carolina, more than five hours away.

"I couldn't take time off from job interviews, couldn't afford the gas, hotel, and procedure costs," Tamika explains. "And then I learned there was no OB-GYN in my county for prenatal care either. I had to drive 50 miles each way for every appointment, which meant arranging child care and spending money I didn't have on gas. I developed complications that could have been caught earlier if I had regular access to care."

Tamika gave birth to a healthy child but faced postpartum depression without adequate mental health support in her community. "I love my baby, but the system abandoned us at every turn," she says.

Her story reflects the reality documented by researchers who found that in Georgia, one of the most dangerous states in which to give birth, decades of disinvestment in rural Black communities have led to the closure of 41 labor and delivery units across the state since 1994 (Capital B News, 2023).

Marcus and Ayana's Story—Louisiana: After the local hospital closed its obstetrics unit, Marcus and Ayana lived in a Louisiana parish with no maternity care services. When Ayana experienced complications at 30 weeks of pregnancy, they drove over an hour to reach emergency care.

"We hit traffic, and by the time we reached the hospital, Ayana was in critical condition," Marcus recalls. "The doctors told us that if we had gotten there just 20 minutes later, we might have lost both Ayana and our baby. No one should have to drive that far for emergency care."

Their story illustrates how the shortage of healthcare providers in many communities creates life-threatening situations, particularly for Black families who already face bias in medical settings, as exemplified by Kaitlyn Joshua's case in Baton Rouge, Louisiana. In 2023, she nearly died from a life-threatening miscarriage after being denied timely care due that state's abortion ban (The Century Foundation, 2025).

Amber's Story—Mississippi: Amber, a 25-year-old from Mississippi, lives in one of the state's numerous maternity care deserts. When she became pregnant, the closest prenatal care provider was nearly an hour away.

"For my first pregnancy, I missed several appointments because my car broke down, and there's no public transportation," Amber shares. "I was high-risk due to high blood pressure, but I couldn't get the monitoring I needed. My baby came six weeks early, and we both spent weeks in the hospital."

Her experience mirrors the findings of a Mississippi Today investigation that documented how residents in maternity care deserts often face life-threatening delays in care, with some women giving birth in ambulances or grocery store parking lots while trying to reach distant hospitals (Mississippi Today, 2023).

Alex's Story—Texas: Alex, a 28-year-old transgender man who became pregnant, faced multiple layers of barriers to care in Texas. "When I called to make my first prenatal appointment, the receptionist was confused by my request. When I explained I was a transgender man who was pregnant, she put me on hold for ten minutes before telling me they 'don't handle cases like mine.'"

Alex eventually found a provider two counties away who was willing to provide gender-affirming prenatal care. "Every appointment meant a three-hour round-trip drive and a full day off work. My partner couldn't always come with me because we couldn't both miss work that often. Even with this provider, who tried to be supportive, I constantly had to educate the office staff about appropriate language and care. It was exhausting to advocate for myself while dealing with all the normal stress of pregnancy."

Like many TGE people seeking reproductive healthcare, Alex's experience demonstrates how systemic barriers and discrimination create additional burdens during an already vulnerable time (Birthing Advocacy Doula Trainings, 2025).

The Rising Threat: Project 2025's Anti-Reproductive Health Agenda

The challenges faced by Black communities seeking reproductive healthcare have intensified under policy agendas that explicitly target both abortion access and transgender rights. We should all be aware of how the 47th presidential administration is implementing recommendations from Project 2025, a policy blueprint that includes numerous attacks on reproductive rights. While the 47th President distanced himself from Project 2025[2] during his campaign, he appointed several of its authors to cabinet positions and implemented dozens of its recommendations (NWLC, 2025b). Project 2025's dual assault on reproductive and trans healthcare creates compounded harm for Black transgender and gender-expansive people, who face the intersection of racial discrimination, transphobia, and restricted reproductive autonomy. These interconnected policies weaponize both reproductive control and gender policing, echoing historical patterns of state violence against Black bodies while introducing new forms of surveillance and criminalization that particularly endanger Black trans and gender-expansive birthing people.

Project 2025 proposes several strategies to restrict and ultimately eliminate access to mifepristone; a medication used in the most common abortion regimen in the United States. The plan suggests revoking Food and Drug Administration (FDA) approval of the drug and reinstating medically unnecessary restrictions that would end telehealth provision of medication abortion (Guttmacher Institute, 2024).

Project 2025 also urges using the Comstock Act, a law from 1873, to criminalize mailing abortion medication (NWLC, 2025c). If enforced as proposed, this could effectively create a nationwide ban on all abortions since almost everything used in abortion procedures, from medical equipment to pain medications, is sent through the mail.

The surveillance and data collection proposals in Project 2025 are particularly concerning for Black communities. Project 2025 proposes a federal mandate for state reporting on abortion data, including details about patients' state of residence and reasons for seeking care (NWLC, 2025c). As states expand efforts to surveil and criminalize pregnancy outcomes, this personal medical data poses serious risks—especially for Black women, people of color, and immigrant communities already facing disproportionate criminalization.

Within his first week in office in 2025, the 47th President took direct aim at reproductive healthcare access through executive orders that dismantled the Interagency Task Force on Reproductive Healthcare Access and halted federal agency efforts to protect patient and provider privacy and security (NWLC, 2025d). These actions signal that the threats to reproductive autonomy outlined in Project 2025 are not theoretical but are actively being implemented.

Implementation and Impact: Project 2025's Reproductive Justice Assault

The 47th presidential administration's swift implementation of Project 2025's recommendations reveals a coordinated attack on reproductive autonomy that has moved from blueprint to reality. Within his first week in office, the 47th President:

- Dismantled the Interagency Task Force on Reproductive Healthcare Access through an executive order.
- Halted federal agency efforts to protect patient and provider privacy.
- Appointed multiple Project 2025 authors to key cabinet positions.
- Initiated reviews of FDA approval for mifepristone.

These actions demonstrate that Project 2025's threats are not theoretical but actively reshaping the reproductive healthcare landscape. The administration's early focus on surveillance infrastructure and data collection mechanisms particularly endangers Black communities, who already face disproportionate criminalization of pregnancy outcomes. By simultaneously targeting abortion access, contraception availability, and gender-affirming care, these policies create a web of restrictions that multiply barriers for those already navigating systemic healthcare inequities.

While institutional healthcare systems continue to fail Black birthing people, communities are not waiting for policy solutions. Across the country, Black-led initiatives are creating alternative support systems, reclaiming ancestral birthing wisdom, and building networks of care that center those most marginalized by the medical establishment. These community responses offer both immediate relief and blueprints for systemic transformation.

The Power of Doulas: Transforming Birth Experiences for Black Families

Amid these challenges, doulas have emerged as crucial advocates and support for Black birthing people, offering a pathway to reclaiming the ancestral wisdom of communal birth support while navigating modern healthcare systems. Doulas provide physical, emotional, and informational support before, during, and after birth, serving as a protective buffer between birthing people and a medical system that has historically mistreated Black bodies.

What Doulas Provide: More Than Birth Support

Doulas offer continuous care that modern hospital systems often cannot provide. As Latham Thomas, founder of Mama Glow, explains: "The work of the doula is to handhold, to be a constant presence of support, to be emotional support, educational support, an advocate, a person who's gonna support your partner if you have one present. And be sort of this birth village conduit, like a person who helps to protect the birth village" (Thomas, 2025).

Research consistently demonstrates the positive impacts of doula support, particularly for Black birthing people:

- Black women who receive doula support are 50% less likely to experience preterm birth and 30% less likely to have a low birth weight baby (National Health Law Program, 2024).
- Studies show that continuous doula support reduces the likelihood of cesarean births by 39% and increases the chance of a spontaneous vaginal birth by 15% (Association of Health Care Journalists, 2024).
- Doula support has been linked to increased breastfeeding initiation and duration, which has long-term health benefits for both parent and child (PMC, 2013).

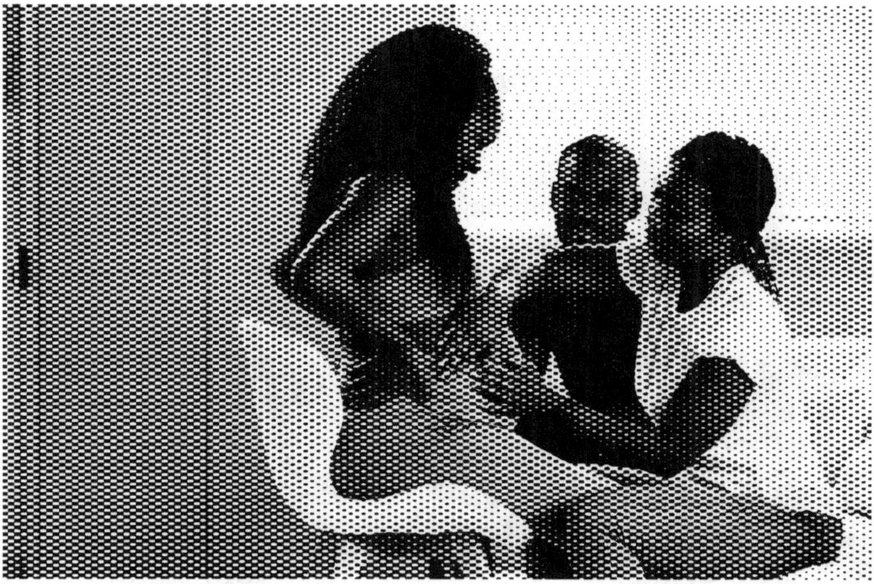

The Full Spectrum of Care: Beyond Traditional Birth Support

Modern doula services have expanded beyond traditional birth support to include:

1 **Full-Spectrum Doulas**: Non-medically trained community care workers who offer support to people during the full spectrum of pregnancy—from preconception, to birth, to abortion, to miscarriage, to adoption, to postpartum (Birthing Advocacy Doula Trainings, 2025; Cleveland Clinic, 2024; National Partnership for Women & Families, 2023; Payne & Al-Modhefer, 2024).
2 **Community-Based Doulas**: Provide culturally congruent care that addresses social determinants of health, such as food insecurity, housing, and transportation (PubMed, 2024).
3 **Postpartum Doulas**: Offer support during the critical weeks and months after birth, providing practical assistance and emotional support, and helping new parents adjust to their new roles.
4 **Gender Doulas**: Provide specialized support for transgender and gender-expansive people throughout pregnancy, birth, and postpartum, with particular attention to gender-affirming care (Birthing Advocacy Doula Trainings, 2025).

5 **End of Life Doulas**: Doulas work with individuals and their families who are experiencing serious illness, nearing the end of life, or who are physically well and ready to explore what living and dying consciously means for them (Maryland Doula Collective, 2025).

As demonstrated by organizations like Mama Glow, which has trained over 3,000 doulas globally, community-based doula initiatives led by Black women are making significant strides in addressing the maternal health crisis (MadameNoire, 2025). These initiatives transform how care is delivered by centering the needs of those most impacted by healthcare disparities.

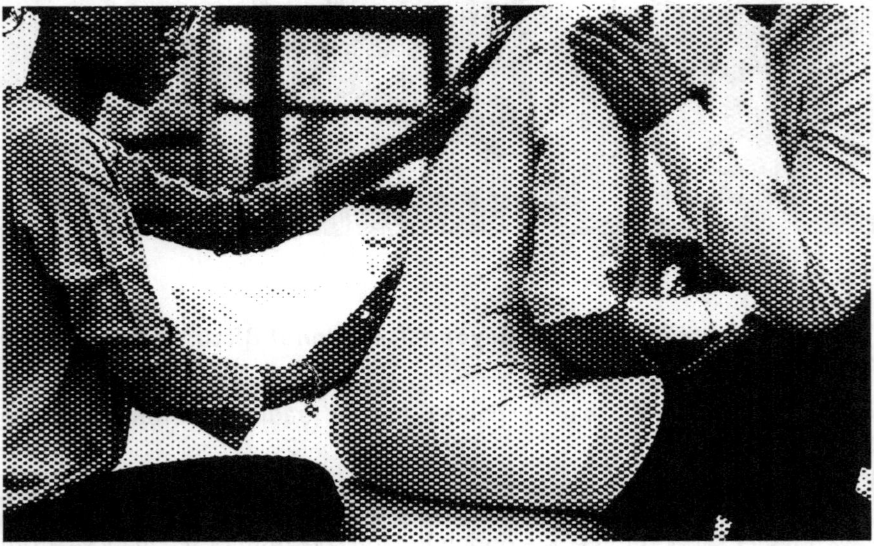

Birth as a Sacred Experience

A key aspect of doula work, particularly for Black doulas working with Black clients, is the reclamation of birth as a sacred, transcendent experience rather than merely a medical event to survive. Thomas notes: "It is not enough to survive. It is a journey that allows somebody to unfold into this new version of themselves that they get to meet on the other side" (Thomas, 2025).

This perspective honors African ancestral traditions of communal birth support. It recognizes birth as a rite of passage—when birthing, people can connect with ancestral wisdom and undergo a powerful transformation. By creating space for this spiritual dimension of birth, doulas help counter the dehumanizing experiences many Black birthing people encounter in medical settings.

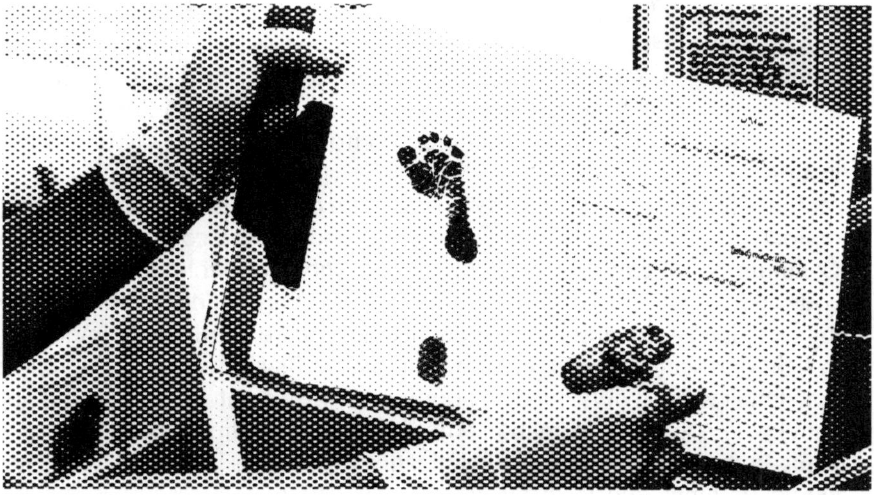

Community Responses and Resilience

Despite these daunting challenges, Black communities across America are demonstrating remarkable resilience and developing innovative responses to the reproductive healthcare crisis:

1 **Mutual Aid Networks**: Community-based funds are helping women travel across state lines for abortion care and covering costs that insurance will not, such as transportation, child care, and lodging. For example, networks of volunteers in Georgia, Mississippi, and other southern states help coordinate rides and accommodations for those needing to travel for care (Capital B News, 2023).
2 **Doula Programs**: Black-led doula initiatives provide critical support during pregnancy, childbirth, and postpartum periods in regions with limited obstetric care. A standout example is Mama Glow, founded by Latham Thomas in Brooklyn, which has trained over 3,000 doulas globally. Through the Mama Glow Foundation, they provide pro-bono doula services to Black, Indigenous, and People of Color (BIPOC) families in need across six major United States cities and serve as the largest provider of free doula support in New York City's underserved neighborhoods through the Citywide Doula Initiative (MadameNoire, 2025). Their recent expansion into "The Soft Space" in Williamsburg provides a physical location for wellness, education, and community building around maternal health (Mother Mag, 2024). Additionally, consider the Uzazi Doula Center in Kansas City, Missouri.

3 **Digital Literacy Programs**: Organizations are working to bridge the digital divide by providing internet access and training to help people navigate online healthcare resources and telehealth options. Bridging this digital divide has become increasingly important, as 14% of abortions in 2024 were provided via online-only clinics, up from 10% in 2023 (Guttmacher Institute, 2025).
4 **Mobile Clinics**: Some healthcare providers are creating mobile units to bring reproductive healthcare services directly to underserved communities.
5 **Community Education**: Grassroots organizations are conducting "know-your-rights" workshops to help community members understand the changing legal landscape around reproductive healthcare, particularly important in light of research showing that over a third of Black women (33%) report that if they wanted or needed an abortion in the near future, they would not know where to find information (The Century Foundation, 2025).
6 **Trans-Inclusive Resources**: Organizations like the Birthing Advocacy Doula Trainings and Birth for Every Body are creating resources specifically for transgender and gender-expansive birthing people, including doula training programs, provider directories, and support groups (Birthing Advocacy Doula Trainings, 2025; Birth for Every Body, 2023).

These community-based solutions provide critical support, but cannot substitute for comprehensive policy reform. They represent adaptations to a broken system rather than long-term solutions to structural inequities.

Successful Models and Positive Outcomes: What Works

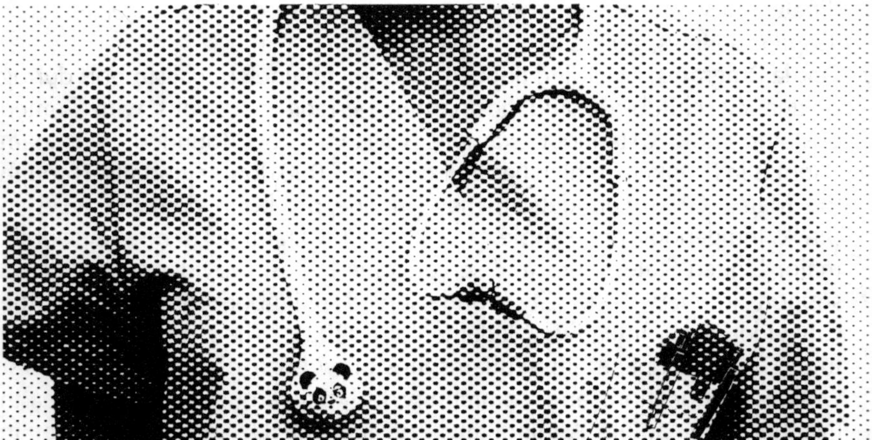

Providing comprehensive maternity care for at least one year postpartum improves reproductive health outcomes, particularly among Black birthing people who face disproportionately high risks. Research indicates more than half of pregnancy-related deaths occur between one week and one year after childbirth (CDC, 2024), underscoring the necessity for extended care during this vulnerable period. Extending Medicaid coverage to 12 months postpartum has been associated with increased healthcare utilization and improved maternal outcomes (Gordon, Sommers, & Wilson, 2022). Moreover, initiatives like the Centers for Medicare & Medicaid Services' Transforming Maternal Health (TMaH) model aim to support a whole-person approach to pregnancy, childbirth, and postpartum care, addressing physical, mental health, and social needs (CMS, 2023).

Despite overwhelming challenges, some promising models demonstrate significant improvements in reproductive health outcomes for Black birthing people. These successful approaches provide evidence-based pathways for expanding access to high-quality, culturally competent care.

Birth Centers and Midwifery Models

Birth centers integrating midwifery care have shown remarkable success in improving outcomes for Black birthing people. These centers provide comprehensive, personalized care that respects the autonomy and cultural needs of birthing people:

- A review of 32 studies found that birth centers result in fewer medical interventions, lower cesarean rates, and improved patient satisfaction compared to hospital births (Commonwealth Fund, 2021).
- Birth centers can reduce costs by more than $1,000 per birth while maintaining excellent safety records (Commonwealth Fund, 2021).

Community-Based Doula Programs

Community-based doula programs that train people from within the communities they serve have demonstrated robust results:

- The JJ Way, created by midwife Jennie Joseph, has successfully reduced rates of preterm birth and low birth weight through culturally competent, accessible care teams that reflect the diversity of their patients (Center for American Progress, 2022).
- Mama Glow's work in Brooklyn has shown that when doulas from the community provide continuous support throughout pregnancy, labor, and postpartum, both physical and emotional outcomes improve dramatically (Thomas, 2025).
- Participants in community-based doula programs report feeling more empowered, informed, and respected during their birth experiences (National Partnership for Women & Families, 2023)

Comprehensive Prenatal Care Models

Innovative prenatal care models that address both medical and social needs have shown significant promise:

- North Carolina's Pregnancy Medical Home (PMH) program, which refers at-risk patients to pregnancy care managers and develops individualized plans to prevent poor birth outcomes, has seen declines in elective deliveries and improved maternal health metrics (Center for American Progress, 2022).
- Group prenatal care programs have demonstrated reduced rates of preterm birth, NICU admissions, and emergency department use during pregnancy, as well as increased breastfeeding rates (Commonwealth Fund, 2021).

The common thread connecting these successful models is their recognition that reproductive healthcare must be holistic, addressing medical needs and social determinants of health. These approaches center on the lived experiences of birthing people, particularly those from marginalized communities, and recognize the importance of community-based, culturally congruent care.

Creating Communities of Care: Beyond Individual Support

A key insight from successful reproductive justice initiatives is the importance of building robust communities of care rather than focusing solely on individual interventions. As Latham Thomas emphasizes, "We are designed to birth in community. This is part of our ancestral blueprint" (Thomas, 2025).

Communities of care recognize that numerous interconnected factors and relationships shape reproductive health. These communities bring together various supporters—partners, family members, friends, healthcare providers, doulas, and community organizations—to create a support network that sustains birthing people throughout their reproductive journeys.

Elements of Effective Communities of Care

1. **Reciprocal Support Systems**: Communities of care involve mutual aid where resources, knowledge, and support flow in multiple directions rather than from provider to recipient. This approach honors the wisdom and contributions of all community members.
2. **Intergenerational Knowledge Transfer**: Effective care communities facilitate the sharing of wisdom across generations, allowing ancestral practices and contemporary knowledge to inform reproductive health support.
3. **Inclusive Design**: Communities of care must be intentionally designed to include marginalized groups, including LGBTQ+ people, people with disabilities, and those from diverse cultural backgrounds.
4. **Holistic Approaches**: Rather than separating physical, emotional, and spiritual aspects of reproductive health, care communities recognize their interconnection and provide support that addresses the whole person.

Building Stronger Communities of Care

To strengthen communities of care around reproductive health, we must:

- Invest in community-based organizations led by Black and other marginalized communities.
- Create physical spaces, like Mama Glow's "The Soft Space," where people can gather, learn, and support one another.
- Integrate traditional wisdom with contemporary medical knowledge.
- Ensure reproductive health policies and programs explicitly include transgender and gender-expansive people.
- Develop healthcare workforce pipelines that increase diversity among providers and birth workers.

By fostering robust communities of care, we can create more resilient systems that support reproductive autonomy and wellbeing even in the face of policy restrictions and healthcare gaps.

Community resilience, while remarkable, cannot substitute for systemic change. The innovative models and mutual aid networks described above point toward comprehensive policy solutions that must be implemented at every level of government. Drawing from these community-led successes, this Black paper presents policy recommendations to transform temporary fixes into permanent infrastructure for reproductive justice.

Policy Recommendations: A Comprehensive Approach to Reproductive Justice

Addressing the complex crisis of reproductive healthcare access for Black communities requires action at multiple levels:

Federal Level:

1. Restore and strengthen reproductive rights through federal legislation that protects abortion and contraceptive access nationwide (NWLC, 2025c). Federal action must also address threats to health coverage, including Medicaid work reporting requirements under H.R.1, which risk stripping coverage from millions of low-income people. Healthy pregnancies begin with healthy people; loss of coverage undermines health before and during pregnancy and increases the risk of delayed or inadequate care. Restoring federal investments in public health programs is essential to supporting maternal health and reproductive justice.
2. Increase funding for maternal healthcare in underserved communities.
3. Expand Medicaid coverage for postpartum care[3] from 60 days to at least 12 months in all states.
4. Provide incentives for healthcare providers to practice in maternity care deserts (March of Dimes, 2024).
5. Enforce existing protections for emergency abortion care under the Emergency Medical Treatment and Labor Act (EMTALA) (NWLC, 2025d).
6. Implement policies that explicitly recognize and address the needs of transgender and gender-expansive birthing people (PMC, 2022).
7. Enact policies that safeguard and expand voting access—recognizing its impact on reproductive healthcare access (IOOV, 2023).
8. Implement federal policies for universal basic income pilots and establish paid family leave programs (IOOV, 2023).
9. Enforce national standards to address environmental hazards in predominantly Black communities (IOOV, 2023).
10. Invest in telemedicine infrastructure in underserved communities.
11. Protect entities that provide reproductive healthcare, including contraceptive care, particularly those serving Medicaid enrollees and underserved populations (KFF, 2024).
12. Oppose and reverse policies that impose onerous work reporting requirements for Medicaid eligibility, which result in coverage loss and poorer health outcomes for people who may become pregnant.
13. Restore funding cuts to public health programs and research that support reproductive health and maternal health outcomes.
14. Ensure birth control access is protected and expanded, including coverage protections for those who lose Medicaid eligibility.

State Level:

1 Repeal abortion bans and restrictions (Guttmacher Institute, 2023).
2 Create incentives for obstetric providers to practice in rural and underserved areas.
3 Expand Medicaid coverage for reproductive healthcare services and protect entities that provide reproductive care, ensuring uninterrupted access to comprehensive, evidence-based services across states.
4 Fund community-based maternal health initiatives led by Black women.
5 Implement bias training requirements for healthcare providers.
6 Ensure state Medicaid programs cover doula services at equitable reimbursement rates (National Health Law Program, 2024).
7 Mandate inclusive, medically accurate, and culturally responsive sexuality education in public schools. (IOOV, 2023).
8 Invest in telemedicine infrastructure in underserved communities.

Local Level:

1 Create transportation assistance programs to help people reach distant healthcare providers (NWLC, 2025a).
2 Develop community health worker programs focused on reproductive health.
3 Support local abortion and birth doula training programs.
4 Invest in telemedicine infrastructure in underserved communities.
5 Establish local reproductive health education programs.
6 Implement community-based perinatal support programs that address social determinants of health (PubMed, 2024).
7 Provide local grants and support for Black-owned businesses and community development projects (IOOV, 2023).

Healthcare Systems:

1 Implement standardized protocols to address racial bias in maternal care.
2 Create integrated care models that address reproductive health, mental health, and social needs.
3 Expand telehealth options while addressing digital divides (Guttmacher Institute, 2025).
4 Collect and report data on reproductive health outcomes by race.
5 Increase diversity in the healthcare workforce.
6 Ensure all healthcare facilities provide gender-affirming care for transgender and gender-expansive patients (Center for American Progress, 2020).

7 Implement no-cost or nominal cost-sharing structures for reproductive health services to encourage healthcare engagement and use, particularly for preventative care and chronic condition management.

Policy recommendations alone, however comprehensive, remain merely words on paper without organized power to implement them. The reproductive justice crisis demands more than technical solutions. It requires a mass movement that connects reproductive rights to broader struggles for racial, economic, and gender justice. This movement must be led by those most impacted: Black women, transgender and gender-expansive people, and others whose bodily autonomy remains under constant threat.

Call to Action: Building a Movement for Reproductive Justice

The crisis of reproductive healthcare access demands more than individual solutions or incremental policy changes. It requires a broad-based movement grounded in reproductive justice principles that connect reproductive rights to broader social, economic, and racial justice.

We call on policymakers, healthcare providers, community leaders, and advocates to:

- **Center Black Voices**: Ensure that Black women, transgender, and gender-expansive people lead in developing solutions to the reproductive healthcare crisis affecting their communities.
- **Build Coalitions**: Connect reproductive justice work with movements addressing other forms of oppression, including housing insecurity, food insecurity, and environmental justice.
- **Shift Resources**: Direct funding to Black-led organizations working on reproductive health and justice in underserved communities.
- **Challenge Narrative**: Counter harmful narratives about Black women's reproduction with perspectives that honor bodily autonomy and recognize structural barriers to healthcare.
- **Demand Accountability**: Hold elected officials and healthcare institutions accountable for addressing racial disparities in reproductive healthcare access and outcomes.
- **Create Inclusive Frameworks**: Ensure that reproductive justice frameworks explicitly include transgender and gender-expansive people, recognizing their unique needs and experiences.
- **Educate Your Community on Civic Responsibility**: Ensure that your community knows how their vote drives these resolutions, and how direct democracy can override stagnant legislative bodies.

The State of the People Project represents an opportunity to build this movement by connecting communities facing similar challenges nationwide and developing shared strategies for change.

Conclusion: Toward a Future of Reproductive Justice

The reproductive justice emergency facing Black communities demands immediate action. As abortion bans proliferate and maternity care vanishes from entire regions, Black birthing people—particularly those who are transgender, gender-expansive, or economically marginalized—face an unprecedented assault on their fundamental human rights. This crisis requires more than incremental reforms; it demands a transformative reimagining of reproductive healthcare rooted in racial and gender justice.

Yet, within this crisis lies the possibility for transformative change. By connecting the struggle for reproductive healthcare access to broader movements for racial and economic justice, we can build momentum for policies and practices that truly support the reproductive autonomy and wellbeing of Black communities.

The path forward requires not just defending against further restriction, but advancing a proactive vision of reproductive justice where all people, regardless of race, gender identity, or economic status, have the resources, support, and freedom to make decisions about their bodies, families, and futures. By working together across movements and communities, we can create a future where reproductive justice is realized for all.

Notes

1 On June 24, 2022, the United States Supreme Court overturned *Roe* v. *Wade*—the 1973 landmark case that resulted in the legalization of abortion. The court's decision returned regulation of abortion back to individual states.

2 "A federal policy agenda and blueprint for a radical restructuring of the executive branch authored and published by former 47th presidential administration officials in partnership with The Heritage Foundation, a longstanding conservative think tank that opposes abortion and reproductive rights, LGBTQ rights, immigrants' rights, and racial equity. Project 2025's largest publication, *Mandate For Leadership*, is a 900-page manual for reorganizing the entire federal government agency by agency to serve a conservative agenda (American Civil Liberties Union [ACLU], 2025)."

3 Former Vice President Kamala Harris led the Biden–Harris administration's efforts on maternal health—resulting in 47 states plus the District of Columbia (D.C.) expanding postpartum Medicaid coverage from 60 days to 12 months.

References

American Civil Liberties Union (ACLU) (2025). *Project 2025 Explained*. https://www.aclu.org/project-2025-explained

Association of Health Care Journalists. (2024). *Could doulas improve maternal health outcomes in the U.S.?* https://healthjournalism.org/blog/2024/11/could-doulas-improve-maternal-health-outcomes-in-the-u-s/

Birth for Every Body. (2023). *About gender*. http://www.birthforeverybody.org/what-we-do

Birthing Advocacy Doula Trainings. (2025). *Our favorite queer and trans-centered resources for families and birth workers*. https://www.badoulatrainings.org/blog/our-favorite-queer-and-trans-centered-resources-for-families-and-birth-workers

Capital B News. (2023). *The maternity care deserts of Georgia's Black Belt.* https://capitalbnews.org/dangerous-deliveries-maternal-care-deserts/

Center for American Progress. (2020). *Community-based doulas and midwives.* https://www.americanprogress.org/article/community-based-doulas-midwives/

Center for American Progress. (2022). *Eliminating racial disparities in maternal and infant mortality.* https://www.americanprogress.org/article/eliminating-racial-disparities-maternal-infant-mortality

Centers for Disease Control and Prevention. (2024). *Pregnancy-related deaths: Data from Maternal Mortality Review Committees in 38 States, 2020.* U.S. Department of Health & Human Services. Retrieved May 12, 2025, from https://www.cdc.gov/maternal-mortality/php/data-research/index.html

Centers for Disease Control and Prevention. (2025). *U.S. uninsured rate drops by 15% since 2020.* https://www.cdc.gov/nchs/pressroom/releases/20250624.html

Centers for Medicare & Medicaid Services. (2023). *HHS to improve maternal health outcomes with new CMS care model that expands access to services, other proven maternal health approaches.* https://www.cms.gov/newsroom/press-releases/hhs-improve-maternal-health-outcomes-new-cms-care-model-expands-access-services-other-proven?utm_source=chatgpt.com

Cleveland Clinic. (2024). *Doula.* https://my.clevelandclinic.org/health/articles/23075-doula

Commonwealth Fund. (2021). *Community-based models to improve maternal health outcomes and promote health equity.* https://www.commonwealthfund.org/publications/issue-briefs/2021/mar/community-models-improve-maternal-outcomes-equity

Gordon, S. H., Sommers, B. D., & Wilson, I. B. (2022). Current evidence to guide practice, policy, and research: extending Medicaid postpartum coverage. *Journal of Obstetric, Gynecologic & Neonatal Nursing, 51*(1), 3–9.

Guttmacher Institute. (2023). *Inequity in US abortion rights and access: The end of Roe is deepening existing divides.* https://www.guttmacher.org/2023/01/inequity-us-abortion-rights-and-access-end-roe-deepening-existing-divides

Guttmacher Institute. (2024). *How Project 2025 seeks to obliterate sexual and reproductive health and rights.* https://www.guttmacher.org/fact-sheet/how-project-2025-seeks-obliterate-srhr

Guttmacher Institute. (2025). *Guttmacher Institute releases full-year us abortion data for2024.*https://www.guttmacher.org/news-release/2025/guttmacher-institute-releases-full-year-us-abortion-data-2024

In Our Own Voice: National Black Women's Reproductive Justice Agenda. (2023). *Black Reproductive Justice Policy Agenda.* https://blackrj.org/wp-content/uploads/2023/06/RJPolicyAgenda2023.pdf

Kaiser Family Foundation. (2025a). *Health coverage by race and ethnicity, 2010-2023.* https://www.kff.org/racial-equity-and-health-policy/health-coverage-by-race-and-ethnicity/

Kaiser Family Foundation. (2025b). *Key data on health and health care by race and ethnicity.* https://www.kff.org/racial-equity-and-health-policy/key-data-on-health-and-health-care-by-race-and-ethnicity/

KFF. (2024). *State variations in the role of the reproductive health safety net for contraceptive care among Medicaid enrollees*. https://www.kff.org/womens-health-policy/state-variations-in-the-role-of-the-reproductive-health-safety-net-for-contraceptive-care-among-medicaid-enrollees/

MadameNoire. (2025). *Mompreneurs: Revolutionizing maternal health care with Latham Thomas*. https://madamenoire.com/1428919/mompreneurs-revolutionizing-maternal-health-care-with-latham-thomas/

March of Dimes. (2024). *Nowhere to Go: Maternity care deserts across the US*. https://www.marchofdimes.org/maternity-care-deserts-report

Maryland Doula Collective. (2025). *What is a death doula?* https://www.marylanddoulacollecitve.org/about

Mississippi Today. (2023). *Mississippi's maternity care desert: A look inside*. https://mississippitoday.org/2022/11/03/mississippi-maternity-care-desert/

Mother Mag. (2024). *Latham Thomas on the soft space*. https://www.mothermag.com/latham-thomas-opens-the-soft-space/

National Health Law Program. (2024). *Doula care improves health outcomes, reduces racial disparities, and cuts cost*. https://healthlaw.org/doula-care-improves-health-outcomes-reduces-racial-disparities-and-cuts-cost/

National Partnership for Women & Families. (2023). *New analysis: Community initiatives are key to ending the Black maternal health crisis*. https://nationalpartnership.org/news_post/new-analysis-community-initiatives-are-key-to-ending-the-black-maternal-health-crisis/

National Women's Law Center. (2025a). *When women are deserted: The prevalence and intersection of abortion care deserts, pregnancy care deserts, broadband internet deserts, and food deserts in the United States*. https://nwlc.org/resource/when-women-are-deserted-the-prevalence-and-intersection-of-abortion-care-deserts-pregnancy-care-deserts-broadband-internet-deserts-and-food-deserts-in--the-united-states/

National Women's Law Center. (2025b). *Stranger than science fiction: The Trump administration's quiet enforcement of Project 2025's dystopian anti-abortion agenda*. https://nwlc.org/stranger-than-science-fiction-the-trump-administrations-quiet-enforcement-of-project-2025s-dystopian-anti-abortion-agenda/

National Women's Law Center. (2025c). *Understanding Project 2025's radical anti-abortion policies*. https://nwlc.org/understanding-project-2025s-radical-anti-abortion-policies/

National Women's Law Center. (2025d). *The Trump administration's first actions in 2025 targeting patients, providers, and reproductive health care access*. https://nwlc.org/resource/the-trump-administrations-first-actions-in-2025-targeting-patients-providers-and-reproductive-health-care-access/

Payne, J.D., & Al-Modhefer, A.K. (2024). The role of doulas and community birth workers in abortion care in the United States: A narrative review. *Current Opinions in Obstetrics and Gynecology, 36*(3), 162–167. https://www.sciencedirect.com/science/article/pii/S0010782424001549

PMC. (2013). *Impact of doulas on healthy birth outcomes*. https://pmc.ncbi.nlm.nih.gov/articles/PMC3647727/

PMC. (2022). *Reconceiving reproductive health systems: Caring for trans, nonbinary, and gender-expansive people during pregnancy and childbirth*. https://pmc.ncbi.nlm.nih.gov/articles/PMC9679586/

PubMed. (2024). *Beyond birth work: Addressing social determinants of health with community perinatal support doulas*. https://pubmed.ncbi.nlm.nih.gov/38600831/

The Century Foundation. (2025). *Why access to abortion care matters for black maternal health*. https://tcf.org/content/report/why-access-to-abortion-care-matters-for-black-maternal-health/

Thomas, L. (2025). Interview by D.J. Johns [Audio recording]. *Teach The Babies Podcast*. Retrieved from transcript.

Chapter 12

Protecting Black Mothers

Ending Disparities in Maternal Health

*Ashley N. Brevil**

Executive Summary

Black women[1] in the United States are three to four times more likely to die from pregnancy-related causes than white women (Safarzadeh, 2025). Since 2022, the persistent and widening disparity has been exacerbated by increasingly restrictive abortion bans that contribute to an increase in mortality rates for Black women (50.3 per 100,000) even as mortality rates for other racial and ethnic groups decrease (Hoyert, 2025). These preventable deaths reflect deep structural inequities across healthcare, research, and policy systems.

This Black Paper (Paper) presents a comprehensive analysis of maternal health disparities through a reproductive justice lens, examining not only clinical outcomes but also the intersecting impacts of abortion restrictions, transgender exclusion, and systemic racism. It centers Black women's voices and leadership while acknowledging the experiences of all Black birthing people, including transgender men and gender-expansive people who face compounded discrimination in the pursuit of maternal healthcare.

Too often, solutions do not center the lived experiences, cultural knowledge, or leadership of Black women. Achieving true maternal health equity requires shifting from a model of comparison and intervention to one of transformation and self-determination.

Key Findings and Priorities:

- **Policy**: Pass and fund Black maternal health legislation while building accountability mechanisms, expanding postpartum Medicaid coverage, and institutionalizing equity across federal and state systems.
- **Practice**: Collect and report disaggregated data that reflects diversity within Black communities, and fund participatory, community-driven studies that elevate lived experiences as valid evidence.

* Supported by braintrust authors: Jada Capri Ward, Nadia French-Graham, and Victoria Kirby York.

DOI: 10.4324/9781003752646-17

- **Community**: Invest in peer support networks, mutual aid funds, and culturally rooted maternal health educational and medical programs led by Black women and local organizations.
- **Science**: Center the diverse experiences of Black women, intersex and gender-expansive people, and transgender men in implementation science efforts to ensure groundbreaking outcomes.

Introduction

From the abuses of enslaved women used in gynecological experiments to forced sterilization, Black women have endured systemic harm at the hands of healthcare institutions (Roberts, 2014). This history is the foundation for the maternal health crisis that currently plagues the United States healthcare system—a foundation defined by high rates of maternal mortality and morbidity, 80% of which are preventable (Simmons, 2023), and unrelenting comorbidities such as eclampsia, postpartum depression, anxiety, and diabetes (McKinsey Health Institute, 2025).

The Centers for Disease Control and Prevention (CDC) defines a pregnancy-related death as a death that occurs during pregnancy or within one year of a pregnancy-related complication. Complications include events either initiated or aggravated by pregnancy (Centers for Disease Control and Prevention, 2024). Today's maternal health crisis is not new. The crisis is the continuation of an unbroken line of racial inequities in care. This ongoing cycle of harm requires more than incremental reform. It requires sweeping changes through a reproductive justice lens that reinforces Black women's right to safely give birth and parent their children in safe and healthy environments (Roberts, 2015; Ross & Solinger, 2017).

Background

Global studies of maternal mortality describe the majority (60%) of maternal, newborn, and child deaths as preventable, citing disabilities and illnesses that burden low- and middle-income countries as the cause (Galaa et al., 2016; Peterson et al., 2019). The United States, in this case, is an outlier because of its wealthy status coupled with poor maternal health outcomes. Other high-income countries comparable to the United States experienced a decrease in maternal mortality from 1990 to 2015, whereas the United States saw more than a doubling of maternal mortality between 2000 and 2014 (MacDorman et al., 2016). Within this broader crisis, Black women face especially stark disparities. For instance, Black women in their early twenties in the United States have maternal mortality rates similar to those of White women in their mid-thirties or older. Even more staggering and hard to reconcile is that during enslavement, Black mothers and their infants were more likely to survive childbirth than those who are currently living in a post-slavery era (Norwood et al., 2022).

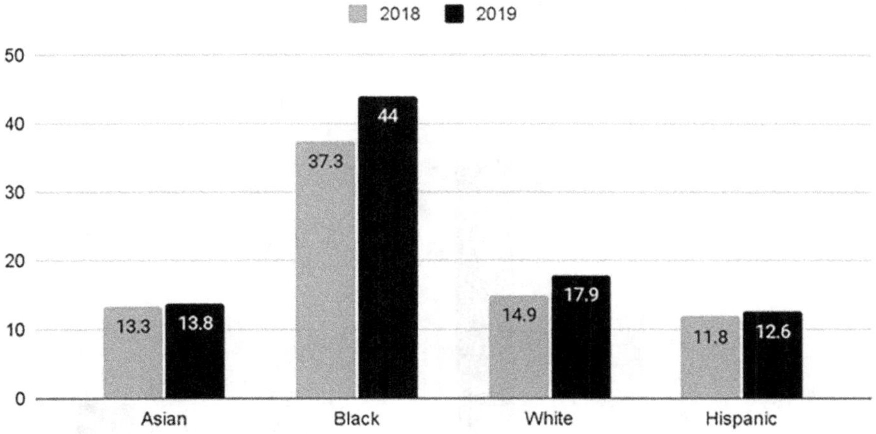

Figure 12.1 Maternal mortality per 100,000 births by race and ethnicity, 2018–2019.

Source: Hoyert (2024).

Note: Persons of Hispanic origin may be of any race but are categorized as Hispanic for this analysis; other groups are non-Hispanic. Other races are not included due to small sample sizes. Maternal deaths are defined as deaths that occur while pregnant or within 42 days of being pregnant.

Between 2018 and 2023, maternal mortality in the United States fluctuated sharply, reflecting the impact of the COVID-19 pandemic and the persistent racial inequities. Across racial groups, rates peaked in 2021—reaching 69.9 deaths per 100,000 live births among Black women, 26.6 among white women, 28.0 among Hispanic women, and 16.8 among Asian women—before declining somewhat in 2022 and 2023 (Figure 12.1).

The most recent data from 2023 reveals an even more troubling picture: Maternal mortality rates have significantly declined for White (14.5), Hispanic (12.4), and Asian women (10.7). The same is not true for Black women. The rate for Black women remained at 50.3 deaths per 100,000 live births—more than 3.5 times the rate for White women (Centers for Disease Control and Prevention, 2024) (Figure 12.2). This widening disparity demonstrates that the systemic barriers facing Black birthing people are not only persistent but also intensifying, even as overall maternal health outcomes improve for other groups (Hoyert, 2025). In 2025 alone, maternal health conditions could result in the loss of 350,000 healthy life years for Black women. The McKinsey Health Institute (2025) projects that Black maternal mortality could nearly double to 94 deaths per 100,000 by 2040 if current trends continue.

Women residing in states with abortion bans, such as Louisiana and Texas, are twice as likely to experience a pregnancy-related death compared to women in states where abortion remains legal and accessible (Gender Equity Policy Institute, 2025). Following the 2022 Supreme Court ruling that overturned the

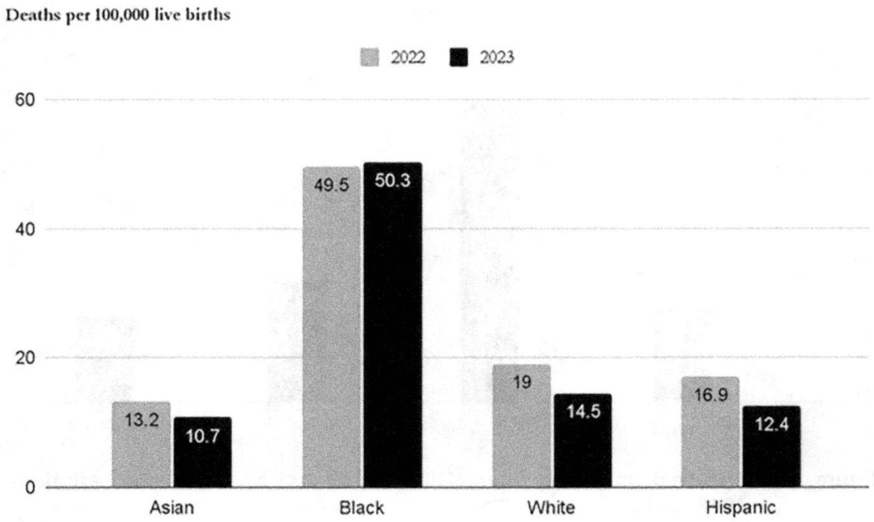

Figure 12.2 Maternal mortality rate, by race and Hispanic origin: United States, 2022 and 2023.

Source: National Center for Health Statistics, National Vital Statistics System, mortality data file.

Note: Race groups are single-race. People of Hispanic origin may be of any race.

constitutional right to abortion, access to abortion care remained available in 24 states. In those states, maternal mortality decreased by 21%, dropping from 17.7 maternal deaths per 100,000 live births in 2022 to 13.9 per 100,000 in 2023. Conversely, in the 13 states that implemented abortion bans at 6 weeks of gestation or earlier, maternal mortality increased by 5%, rising from 23.9 maternal deaths per 100,000 in 2019 to 25.1 maternal deaths per 100,000 in 2023. Consequently, the likelihood of maternal death in states with abortion bans was almost twice that of states where abortion remained legal (Mahase, 2025).

The tragic outcomes that many Black women face during pregnancy are only part of the story (McKinsey Health Institute, 2025). Maternal morbidity is an equally concerning and preventable condition that affects Black women at twice the rate of White women (Leonard et al., 2019). For every maternal death, approximately 100 other women experience near-fatal complications associated with severe maternal morbidity (SMM) (Canty, 2022). SMM includes conditions that may result in long-term or life-threatening consequences to a woman's health, including cardiovascular complications, organ failure, and severe hemorrhage. In 2025 alone, maternal health conditions were projected to account for the loss of approximately 350,000 healthy life years among Black women (McKinsey Health Institute, 2025). The prevalence of chronic conditions leading to severe maternal morbidity has continued to increase over time (Metcalfe et al., 2018).

Problem Statement

Despite scientific and medical advances, Black women continue to die at three to four times the rate of white women from preventable pregnancy-related causes (Safarzadeh, 2025). While this is not a new phenomenon, a clear gap exists between the problem and policy responses. This Paper aims to address the alarming and persistent racial disparities in maternal mortality and morbidity in the United States by examining the structural, systemic, and policy-level factors that disproportionately endanger the lives of Black women during pregnancy and childbirth. The goal is to identify actionable solutions that inform more equitable and adequate maternal health policies.

Maternal Mortality

When discussing women's health within the context of health disparities, a more comprehensive and nuanced approach is required. The intersection of race and gender has been studied extensively by Black feminist scholars, including Patricia Hill Collins (2022), bell hooks (1981), Audre Lorde (1983), Toni Morrison, Alice Walker, Kimberlé Crenshaw (1989, 1991), and others who articulated a self-defined, collective voice and standpoint on Black womanhood (Collins, 1996; Hull, 2016). On average, women have a life expectancy of 81.1 years. A closer examination reveals that this average life expectancy does not apply uniformly across racial groups. Black women have a life expectancy that is approximately three years shorter than white women (Smalley et al., 2020).

Black women also experience health disparities that are unique to their gender, such as reproductive health (Smalley et al., 2020). In 2013, maternal mortality rose from 7.2 deaths per 100,000 live births to 18 deaths per 100,000 live births. Black women experienced a maternal mortality rate of 42.4 deaths per 100,000 live births, compared to 13.0 deaths per 100,000 live births for White women. The maternal mortality rates of Black women are comparable to those of women in countries where significant proportions of the population live in poverty (Smalley et al., 2020).

Having established the historical context and current scope of the crisis, including the recent exacerbation caused by abortion restrictions, we now examine the specific health conditions and social factors driving maternal mortality and morbidity among Black women.

Key Drivers of Maternal Mortality and Morbidity

Researchers and clinicians often view health through the lens of hospitals and medical doctors. Over time, the perspective shifted to include the conditions that influence health outcomes (Brevil, 2025) and the social determinants of health (SDOH). The United States Department of Health and Human Services (2023) identified the social determinants of health as one of the priority areas of Healthy People 2030. The Office defines the social determinants of health as "the conditions in the environments where people live, learn, work, play, worship, and age that affect a wide range of health, functioning, and quality-of-life outcomes and risks" (World Health Organization, Commission on Social Determinants of Health, 2008). When referencing the social determinants of health, scholars often highlight factors that emphasize the unequal distribution of power, income, goods, and services at both global and national levels.

Healthy People 2030 groups the social determinants of health into five domains (Figure 12.3): economic stability; education access and quality; healthcare access and quality; neighborhood and built environment; and social and community context. These drivers often intersect in complex and multifaceted ways, amplifying the vulnerabilities of Black women, particularly those in underserved and low-resource settings. Recognizing how these factors interact is crucial for designing effective policies that address the root causes of maternal mortality (Hassan et al., 2024).

Scholars highlight the role that socioeconomic factors, including poverty, education, and income, play in determining maternal mortality outcomes. Research notes that women from low-income backgrounds often experience higher rates of maternal mortality due to limited access to quality healthcare services, proper nutrition, and adequate living conditions (Majebi et al., 2024). Financial limitations may cause women to delay or forgo seeking prenatal care or accessing emergency obstetric services that are essential for preventing pregnancy-related complications. Majebi et al. (2024) note that women living in poverty have an increased likelihood of giving birth at home or in facilities that are understaffed and lack appropriate training, increasing the risk of maternal death. This staffing shortage is particularly acute in rural and underserved areas, where there are limited numbers of midwives and obstetricians available to treat life-threatening conditions such as preeclampsia or postpartum hemorrhage (Hassan et al., 2024). When communities are subjected to chronic systemic racism and inequitable structures, interventions addressing adverse social determinants of health become significantly more challenging.

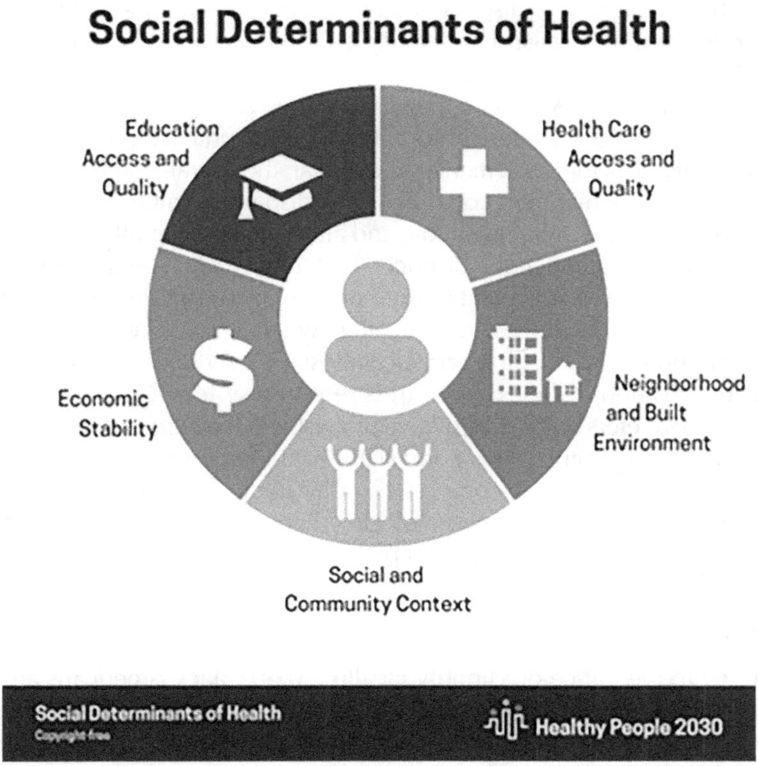

Figure 12.3 Social determinants of health framework United States Department of Health and Human Services, Office of Disease Prevention and Health Promotion. (n.d.). *Healthy People 2030: Social determinants of health*. Retrieved October 26, 2025, from https://health.gov/healthypeople/objectives-and-data/social-determinants-health

Current Disparities

Cardiovascular Disease (CVD)

Cardiovascular disease (CVD) is one of the leading causes of adverse maternal outcomes worldwide (Bhatla et al., 2003). Black women experience higher cardiovascular morbidity and mortality during pregnancy in comparison to white women (Njoroge & Parikh, 2020). As a result, CVD and pregnancy are deeply interconnected. Nearly 80 million people across the United States are affected by cardiovascular disease, a condition that affects the heart and blood vessels (Smalley et al., 2020). Of these conditions, the most common forms are hypertension, coronary heart disease, and stroke. Black Americans are disproportionately affected by CVD in comparison to other racial/ethnic groups. This disparity includes a higher likelihood of experiencing cardiovascular disease risk factors, as well as increased mortality and morbidity (Smalley et al., 2020).

Additionally, Black American men and women are less likely to receive disease management and treatment for CVD. Studies indicate that the heart disease mortality rates for Black men are more than the overall diabetes and stroke mortality rates in white men combined. This disparity can be traced in part to differences in stroke care, prevention, and allostatic load (Smalley et al., 2020).

Allostatic load, a concept introduced by McEwen and Stellar (1993), refers to the cumulative physiological burden of chronic racism and discrimination across the lifespan. Studies indicate that when environmental challenges exceed an individual's coping capacity, allostatic overload ensues, leading to repeated activation of the extreme stress response system (Guidi et al., 2020). Allostatic load refers to the cumulative physiological effects of everyday experiences, including both ordinary and significant life events. Studies also show that allostatic load may encompass the physiological effects of destructive behaviors, including poor sleep and circadian disruption, lack of exercise, alcohol consumption, smoking, and poor diet (Guidi et al., 2020).

Diabetes

According to the Office of Minority Health (2024), Black Americans are 60% more likely than non-Hispanic white adults to be diagnosed with diabetes and twice as likely to die from it. More specifically, the death rate for diabetes is 96% and 140% higher for Black men and women, respectively, compared to non-Hispanic white Americans (Smalley et al., 2020). In the context of pregnancy, a study conducted by Bornstein et al. (2020) noted an increase in diabetes prevalence among Black women. Similarly, Black women diagnosed with gestational diabetes during pregnancy have the highest risk of developing diabetes postpartum (Njoroge & Parikh, 2020). Historically, research examining racial and gender disparities in diabetes has focused on higher HbA1c levels, reduced access to healthy foods, lower health literacy, financial and cultural barriers to medication adherence, limited access to timely and adequate medical care and diagnosis, and lower levels of physician support and engagement with patient portals and other empowerment tools (Smalley et al., 2020).

While cardiovascular disease and diabetes are critical clinical factors, the maternal health crisis has been dramatically worsened by recent policy changes restricting reproductive healthcare access.

Abortion Restrictions and Maternal Mortality

The overturning of *Roe* v. *Wade* in June 2022 created a new and urgent dimension of the Black maternal health crisis. As of 2025, 14 states have implemented near-total abortion bans, with Black women disproportionately concentrated in these restrictive states (Kaiser Family Foundation, 2024). Some 60% of Black women ages 18–49 live in states with abortion bans or gestational restrictions, compared to 53% of white women (Kaiser Family Foundation, 2024).

The maternal health impacts of these restrictions are already measurable and devastating. Research by the Gender Equity Policy Institute (2025) found that maternal mortality rates in states with abortion bans are 62% higher than in states with abortion access. In Texas, which implemented a strict abortion ban, maternal mortality rose 56% in the first full year of the ban, with an increase of 95% among white women (Gender Equity Policy Institute, 2025). By 2023, the mortality rate in Texas was 155% higher than that in California. As illustrated in Figure 12.4, geographic patterns of maternal morbidity reveal a striking overlap between states with the highest maternal death rates and states with restrictive abortion bans.

While this Paper focuses primarily on the experiences of Black cisgender women—who represent the majority of those affected by maternal health disparities—it is crucial to acknowledge the experiences that Black trans men, gender-expansive people, and gender-expansive individuals experience within the gestational healthcare system. These individuals face compounded forms of oppression in healthcare settings.

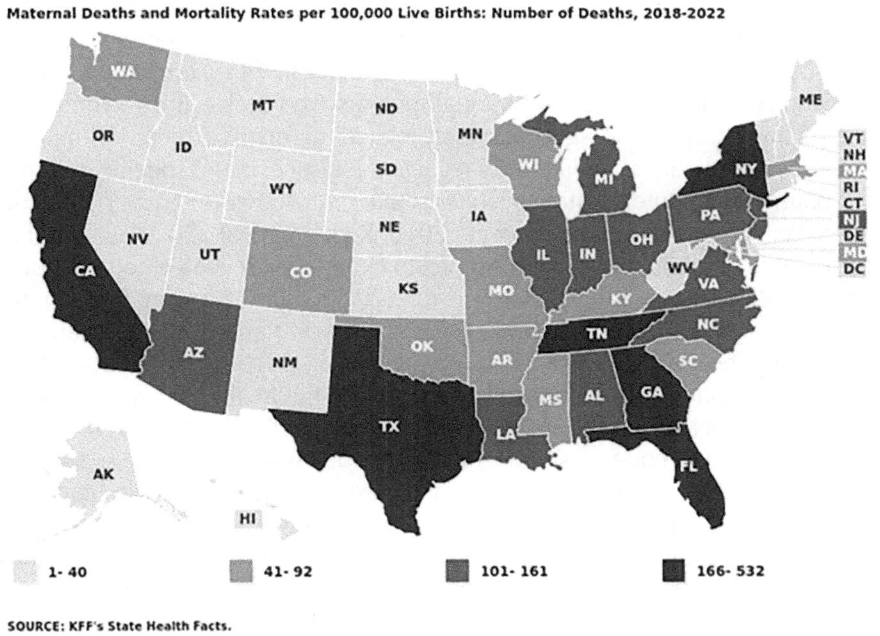

Figure 12.4 Maternal deaths and mortality rates per 100,000 live births: number of deaths, 2018–2022.

Intersectional Discrimination

Black lesbian, bisexual, queer, and same-gender loving (SGL) women; intersex and gender-expansive people; and transgender men face additional hurdles before, during, and after gestational healthcare. Many healthcare environments still function based on heteronormative assumptions, impacting all Black individuals seeking maternal care, and are also influenced by transphobia that dominates healthcare systems built solely around cisgender women (MacKinnon et al., 2021). Research based on the Multiple Minority Stress Model highlights that these forms of oppression are multiplicative rather than additive, leading to unique 'gender situated vulnerabilities' that elevate the risk of adverse outcomes (McConnell et al., 2018). Healthcare providers' use of incorrect terminology and pronouns intensifies gender-related psychological distress during pregnancy. In one study, 35% of transgender people who gave birth reported postpartum depression, with discriminatory language identified as a key contributing factor (MacKinnon et al., 2021). Additionally this discriminatory language leads to added stress related to birth certificates that lack both parents' names; intake forms that include only "mother" and "father" rather than gender-neutral language; interactions with healthcare staff who assume patients have male partners or express surprise or discomfort upon learning of same-sex relationships; and, in some cases, outright discrimination or judgmental attitudes from providers (Hudak, 2023; Isaac et al., 2025; Wojnar & Katzenmeyer, 2014).

Assumptions that SGL women do not require certain reproductive health screenings (Pharr et al., 2019); a lack of understanding of conception methods used by lesbian couples (e.g., donor insemination, In Vitro Fertilization [IVF]); inadequate support for non-gestational mothers who seek full involvement in pregnancy care, including challenges related to medical decision-making authority; and limited knowledge of legal and logistical issues specific to same-sex parents constitute additional stressors that many other pregnant people do not have to manage (LaVaccare et al., 2018; Richburg et al., 2022). Due to the increased likelihood for bisexual women to experience sexual, emotional, psychological violence, and stalking (Coston, 2021), Black bisexual women are more likely to need screenings for intimate partner violence, sexual health risk, and mental health than their peers (Bermea et al., 2018; Corey et al., 2023). Each of these factors has a significant impact on the health and well-being of the pregnant person and the fetus. The fundamental challenge is that bisexuality occupies a unique position—often invisible within healthcare systems designed around binary assumptions about sexuality. Unlike other lesbian, gay, transgender, queer (LGBTQ+) identities, bisexuality can be erased entirely based on a person's current partnership, leading to profound health disparities that often go unrecognized and unaddressed (Smith & George, 2021).

The cumulative stress of navigating these barriers can affect mental health during an already vulnerable time, potentially impacting pregnancy outcomes and postpartum wellbeing. The challenges cited underscore the need for more inclusive and affirming maternal healthcare practices, as well as targeted education for providers.

Black intersex people endure additional hardships that many healthcare providers and institutions are not prepared to address due to limited provider understanding and training (Atayan et al., 2024). Many healthcare providers have limited knowledge about intersex variations and how they may affect pregnancy, fertility, or maternal health. Intersex people may have undergone childhood surgeries or hormone treatments that affect reproductive anatomy or function (Dalke et al., 2020), which providers may not know how to interpret to ensure competent care and decision-making (Katta & Davoody, 2025). Pregnant intersex people often face inappropriate medical curiosity from providers or staff who view intersex bodies as "educational opportunities" rather than patients deserving of respectful care. Some intersex people have atypical reproductive anatomy that may affect pregnancy, delivery planning, or postpartum care, while others may have prior or ongoing hormone treatments that require adjustment during pregnancy.

Past genital surgeries may affect delivery options or create scar tissue concerns. Because many of these surgeries occurred during infancy, patients may be ill-equipped to know what to advocate for, or which questions to ask regarding a safe and healthy delivery (Sundin, 2020). Unfortunately, there are no standardized protocols or clinical guidelines for managing pregnancy in people with various intersex conditions due to limited evidence-based research about outcomes and best practices for intersex maternal or gestational care. Fragmented care creates difficulties in coordination between specialists (endocrinologists, geneticists, and OB-GYNs) who have different aspects of intersex health. The fundamental issue is that maternal healthcare systems are designed around very narrow assumptions about bodies and reproduction, leaving intersex people to navigate a system that often does not acknowledge their existence or needs. Improving care requires provider education, trauma-informed approaches, and intersex-inclusive policies and practices (Bane et al., 2024).

Black transgender and gender-expansive people face systemic exclusion from the beginning of their pregnancy journeys because gestational healthcare is saturated with terms such as "mother," "woman," "women's health," and "she," which can be deeply dysphoric for transgender men and gender-expansive people (Moseson et al., 2020). These experiences include being repeatedly referred to with incorrect pronouns by providers and staff and being required to sign documentation that fails to offer language or options that accurately represent their identities, thereby forcing them into binary gender categories. A study conducted by Burgart et al. (2022) found that half of the medical residents (49.4%) reported either formal didactics in transgender medicine or personal experience caring for a transgender patient, and only 14.5% of respondents had any surgical training. As a result, more than half of respondents felt there were barriers to training in their program, and

14% reported a perceived atmosphere of bias or discrimination toward the transgender patient population. There are often testosterone considerations for transgender men or gender-expansive people who have been on testosterone and its implications on fertility and pregnancy (Kinnear & Moravek, 2023). Transgender pregnant people who have had chest surgery may face complications or impossibility with infant feeding and lactation following chest masculinization surgery (top surgery) or binding. Healthcare providers must be knowledgeable about lactation and infant feeding regardless of the chosen feeding method (MacDonald et al., 2016).

During conception and pregnancy, healthcare providers may advise transgender men to stop gender-affirming testosterone therapy to support implantation and fetal development (Light et al., 2014). This typically leads to the return of feminizing physical traits, such as redistributed body fat, muscle changes, and the resumption of menstrual cycles, which may increase feelings of bodily incongruence and gender dysphoria. The cessation of hormone therapy, combined with the physical and hormonal shifts of pregnancy, can heighten feelings of alienation from one's body and may directly conflict with the individual's gender identity and expression (Coward et al., 2026). The cumulative burden of discrimination and marginalization can significantly affect mental health, increasing the risk of anxiety and depression. These barriers result in delayed or avoided prenatal care, substandard monitoring and support, increased risk of complications, and healthcare experiences that cause lasting psychological harm for transgender people (MacLean, 2021). Improving healthcare for transgender and gender-expansive people requires gender-neutral language and inclusive terminology (e.g. "pregnant person," "parent"), provider training on transgender health and trauma-informed care, inclusive intake forms and documentation systems, policy changes to ensure non-discrimination, research on transgender pregnancy outcomes, community-based support networks, and insurance reform to eliminate gender marker-based denials. Because gestational healthcare systems were built exclusively around cisgender women's experiences, transgender and gender-expansive pregnant people navigate systems that range from unwelcoming to actively hostile. Creating truly inclusive maternal and gestational healthcare requires a fundamental reimagining of how these services are structured and delivered.

Black surrogates for same-gender loving/gay men may carry heightened risk, but sometimes the clinical systems do not fully address their unique status (i.e., pregnancy for another). Evidence indicates elevated rates of certain pregnancy complications, including hypertensive disorders and postpartum hemorrhage, compared to non-gestational carrier pregnancies (Matsuzaki et al., 2024). These risks exist within the broader context of persistent racial disparities in maternal and gestational healthcare. This underscores the need for tailored pre and postnatal care and monitoring that accounts for both surrogacy and racialized risk. Clinical guidelines emphasize that gestational carrier arrangements involve complex medical, psychological, and legal considerations that require coordinated and individualized care (Practice

Committee of the American Society for Reproductive Medicine, 2022). Additionally, the maternal and gestational care teams should incorporate clear communication protocols that include surrogates, intended parents (including gay fathers), and ensure clarity about roles, expectations, and support. When the intended parents are same-gender loving/gay men, additional social and relational dynamics may emerge, including how the surrogate's role is constructed and interpreted within broader social contexts. Surrogates may experience complex emotional responses, including grief or attachment, even in planned arrangements and require comprehensive psychosocial support before, during, and after pregnancy (Yau et al., 2021).

Recommendations for improved care of Black surrogates include screening surrogates thoroughly for baseline physical and mental health, and ensuring robust informed-consent processes that include discussion of risks (including higher risk of hypertensive disorders, postpartum hemorrhage) and emotional and relational implications. Develop care pathways for surrogates that include regular prenatal visits with awareness of their dual role (carrying for intended parents). Ensure communication between surrogate, intended parents, and healthcare team is clear about expectations (who attends ultrasounds, who receives information, how decisions are made). Ensure the surrogate has support for post-partum period: physical recovery and mental health (screen for depression, anxiety, grief). For arrangements involving same-gender loving/gay male intended parents, provide inclusive materials and training for healthcare staff around surrogacy, non-traditional parent families, and nuances of fatherhood (e.g., two dads), and ensure the intended parents are incorporated into prenatal education and birth planning in ways that respect the surrogate's role and also affirm the intended parents.

Polyendocrine metabolic ovarian syndrome (PMOS)

Historically, polyendocrine metabolic ovarian syndrome (PMOS) has been seen as a reproductive endocrine disorder marked by irregular menstrual periods, hyperandrogenism, and the appearance of polycystic ovaries (Joham et al., 2022). It affects between 8 – 13% of women worldwide and is a leading cause of anovulatory infertility (Obeagu et al., 2021, Liu et al., 2021). The term "polycystic ovary syndrome" (PCOS)—used before PMOS—has been increasingly questioned because it does not fully capture the disorder's complexity. Many women diagnosed with PCOS lack ovarian cysts, making the name misleading (Parker & Hitch, 2025). We now understand that it is a multisystem disorder involving endocrine, metabolic, inflammatory, and reproductive pathways, not just the ovaries (Bafghi et al., 2024). The name focused on reproductive symptoms while underplaying metabolic issues like insulin resistance, obesity, dyslipidemia, type 2 diabetes, and cardiovascular risks (Beier et al., 2006). In 2026, a global multidisciplinary team proposed renaming PCOS to Polyendocrine Metabolic Ovarian Syndrome to better represent its multisystemic endocrine and metabolic characteristics. In this Paper, the condition will be called PMOS to reflect this updated terminology (Teede et al., 2026; Tewari et al., 2026).

PMOS is associated with a two- to three-fold increased risk of gestational diabetes compared to women without PMOS, necessitating glucose testing, dietary modifications, possible insulin therapy, and more frequent monitoring throughout pregnancy (Wang et al., 2025). Preeclampsia has a significantly elevated risk for people with PMOS, which requires close blood pressure monitoring and may necessitate early delivery (Jiang et al., 2024). Patients with PMOS experience higher rates of miscarriage, particularly in the first trimester, leading to increased anxiety, a need for closer early monitoring, and, in some cases, progesterone supplementation (Mayrhofer et al., 2020). Preterm birth carries an increased risk of delivery before 37 weeks for people with PMOS (Robinson & Yeung, 2021). Additionally, those with PMOS may also experience higher rates of high blood pressure during pregnancy (Amiri et al., 2020). Consequently, patients require enhanced surveillance, including more frequent appointments than typical pregnancies, additional testing (e.g., ultrasounds, glucose monitoring, and blood pressure checks) (Bahri Khomami et al., 2022), and consultations with maternal-fetal medicine specialists or endocrinologists. These demands may result in increased time off work, child care challenges, and unexpected expenses.

Unfortunately, not all providers are equally knowledgeable about PMOS in pregnancy, and its symptoms are often minimized or mistakenly attributed solely to typical pregnancy changes (Chemerinski et al., 2020). The medical field lacks standardized protocols for PMOS, leading to a variety of care approaches that vary among providers and may require coordination among multiple specialists. Patients lack even more information about the condition and its impact on pregnancy. Not all providers provide comprehensive information about PMOS-related pregnancy risks. Most pregnancy education materials do not address PMOS considerations, and there are few support groups specifically for pregnant individuals with PMOS. Conflicting recommendations from providers or online sources often leave patients uncertain about what to expect during their pregnancies.

Postpartum challenges include breastfeeding difficulties such as varied milk production due to hormonal imbalances, insulin resistance impacting lactation, and additional lactation support (Farah et al., 2021); postpartum depression due to pre-existing PMOS-related mental health issues, hormonal fluctuations, and stress from complicated pregnancy; metabolic concerns such as a higher risk of developing type 2 diabetes after gestational diabetes, continued insulin resistance, and the need for ongoing metabolic monitoring; more difficulty losing pregnancy weight due to PMOS metabolic effects; and PMOS symptoms may worsen postpartum. Long-term health monitoring postpartum should include diabetes screening, such as glucose tolerance testing, monitoring for increased cardiovascular risk, and improved transitions between pregnancy care to ongoing PMOS management often poorly coordinated.

Better maternal healthcare for people with PMOS requires:

- **Pre-conception counseling**: Preparing for pregnancy with PMOS-informed guidance.
- **Coordinated care teams**: Integration between OB-GYNs, endocrinologists, and nutritionists.
- **Evidence-based protocols**: Standardized approaches to PMOS pregnancy management.
- **Enhanced monitoring**: Appropriate surveillance without over-medicalization.
- **Mental health support**: Screening and resources for anxiety and depression.
- **Lactation support**: Specialists familiar with PMOS-related breastfeeding challenges.
- **Postpartum continuity**: Seamless transition to ongoing PMOS management.
- **Patient education**: Clear, comprehensive information about risks and management.
- **Weight-neutral care**: Focus on metabolic health rather than weight alone.

PMOS transforms pregnancy from a typically routine experience into one requiring specialized knowledge, increased surveillance, and management of multiple potential complications. The challenge lies in ensuring that heightened monitoring occurs without inducing unnecessary medicalization or anxiety, while still addressing genuinely elevated risks. Many individuals with PMOS have healthy pregnancies with appropriate care, yet the healthcare system must be better equipped to deliver that care consistently and compassionately.

Preeclampsia and Eclampsia

Preeclampsia is a hypertensive disorder of pregnancy with signs of end-organ dysfunction (for example, high blood pressure with proteinuria or other features) after 20 weeks of gestation. Eclampsia is defined as the onset of seizures in a patient with preeclampsia (or sometimes without the classic signs) and is a medical emergency. McKinsey Health Initiative (2025) notes that Black women are about 60% more likely to develop preeclampsia than white women. Maternal deaths from preeclampsia/eclampsia are much higher in Black women than in white women. For example, an analysis of 2016–2017 data found Black women were five times more likely than white women to die from preeclampsia/eclampsia.

Among delivery hospitalizations for preeclampsia/eclampsia (2004–2019, U.S. National Inpatient Sample), Black, Hispanic and Asian or Pacific Islander women all had higher in-hospital mortality and cardiovascular complication odds compared with white women—even when accounting for income. In fact, "high-income Black women had higher odds of many cardiovascular complications compared with low-income white women" (Zahid et al., 2022). Disparities in prenatal care access, delays in recognition or treatment of complications, and differential treatment in clinical settings have been flagged. Across all income levels, Black women had worse outcomes in the study of delivery hospitalizations for preeclampsia/eclampsia. This suggests that socioeconomic advantage alone is not sufficient to close the gap in these outcomes (Zahid, 2022). Black and Hispanic individuals also experience worse outcomes from these disorders, including higher maternal mortality rates and increased cardiovascular complications. These disparities persist across income levels and are influenced by a mixture of medical risk factors (e.g., hypertension, obesity), as well as social/structural factors (racism, stress, access to quality care.

A study at the University of Pittsburgh (August 2024) found that among 18,050 insured adults diagnosed with preeclampsia, non-Hispanic Black and Hispanic individuals were less likely than white individuals to have a postpartum primary care/cardiology visit within one year after delivery. The study suggested interventions such as virtual visits, remote blood pressure monitoring, and extended Medicaid coverage postpartum could reduce disparities. A systematic review of interventions to address perinatal outcome disparities by ethnicity (36 studies globally, including the United States) found that clinical-management interventions (e.g., increased fetal surveillance, screening for preeclampsia) showed promise. More work is needed on postpartum follow-up for women who had preeclampsia (since long-term cardiovascular risk is elevated) and on how to ensure equitable follow-up by race/ethnicity. Additional focus is needed on implementation: e.g., improving uptake of proven interventions (low-dose aspirin, antihypertensive management with IV, magnesium sulfate for seizure prophylaxis, rapid blood pressure control, biomarker use) among high-risk racial groups, embedding protocols to mitigate delays/escalation differences (Table 12.1).

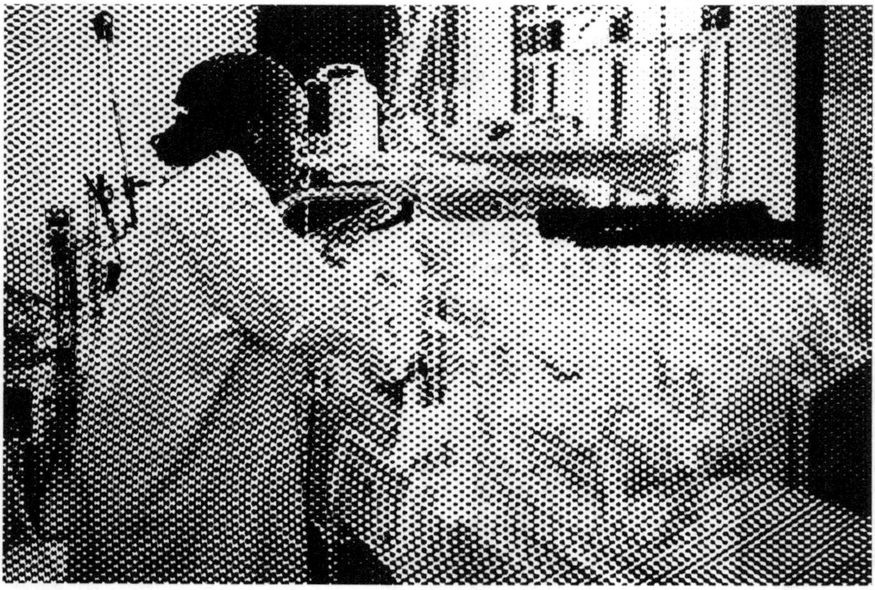

Table 12.1 Maternal Mortality Rates by State, 2018–2022 (Highest to Lowest)

State	*Rate*	*State*	*Rate*
Tennessee	41.1	Kansas	22.8
Mississippi	**39.1**	New York	22.4
Alabama	**38.6**	Maryland	21.3
Arkansas	**38.3**	Nevada	20.4
Louisiana	**37.3**	**Idaho**	**20**
Kentucky	**34.6**	Iowa	19.5
Virginia	32.7	Michigan	19.1
South Carolina	32.3	Illinois	18.1
Georgia	32.1	Washington	18
Indiana	30.9	Pennsylvania	17.5
Arizona	30	Oregon	16.6
Oklahoma	**29.6**	Massachusetts	16.4
Texas	**28.2**	Colorado	16
New Mexico	28	Connecticut	15.6
North Carolina	26.7	Utah	15.5
New Jersey	26	Wisconsin	13.2
Nebraska	25.1	Minnesota	12.3
Ohio	24.5	California	10.5
Florida	24.1	Missouri	23.8
West Virginia	**23.9**		

Source: Kaiser Family Foundation (2024). Maternal deaths and mortality rates per 100,000 live births (2018–2022). State Health Facts. https://www.kff.org/state-health-policy-data/state-indicator/maternal-deaths-and-mortality-rates-per-100000-live-births/

Notes:

[1] Data for the following states were suppressed due to small sample sizes or privacy limitations: Alaska, Delaware, District of Columbia, Hawaii, Maine, Montana, New Hampshire, North Dakota, Rhode Island, South Dakota, Vermont, and Wyoming.

[2] Bolded text indicates states designated as 'illegal' for abortion access. According to the Center for Reproductive Rights (2025), these states fall into categories with the most restrictive abortion laws.

For Black women, the consequences are especially severe. In states with abortion bans, Black maternal mortality reached 60.9 deaths per 100,000 live births—significantly higher than the rates for white (18.2) and Hispanic (18.2) women in the same states (Gender Equity Policy Institute, 2025). Black mothers living in abortion-banned states were 3.3 times as likely to die as white mothers in those states.

Abortion restrictions create harm through multiple pathways. Physicians in restrictive states report delaying or denying emergency obstetric interventions out of fear of prosecution, even when patients face life-threatening complications (Sabbath et al., 2024). Obstetricians and gynecologists are leaving states with abortion bans, resulting in the closure of labor and delivery wards and worsening existing maternity care deserts, which already disproportionately affect Black communities in rural and underserved areas (March of Dimes, 2024).

Abortion restrictions intersect with additional barriers faced by Black pregnant people. The Hyde Amendment has long prohibited federal Medicaid funds from covering abortion except in cases of rape, incest, or threats to life—a restriction that disproportionately affects Black women, who are more likely to rely on Medicaid for healthcare coverage (Jiang et al., 2025; Kim et al., 2025). State-level abortion bans compound this existing inequity, eliminating even private-pay abortion access in large swaths of the country.

Empirical evidence is clear: abortion restrictions are not pro-life policies—they are measures that demonstrably increase maternal mortality, with Black women disproportionately affected. Protecting Black maternal health requires safeguarding access to the full spectrum of reproductive healthcare, including abortion services.

Significance

In 2023, Olympic gold medalist Tori Bowie was found dead at home while eight months pregnant (Irving et al., 2023). Her autopsy revealed that she died from childbirth-related complications, including respiratory distress and eclampsia. Similarly, Sha-Asia Washington, a 26-year-old woman from Brooklyn, died during labor in 2020 due to complications from an epidural and cardiac arrest (Mugeni, 2022; Nash, 2021). In 2020, Dr. Chaniece Wallace, a pediatric chief resident in Indiana, died days after delivering her daughter due to complications related to pre-eclampsia (Givens, 2021; Mutcherson, 2022).

In Georgia in 2025, Adriana Smith—a 30-year-old Black nurse—was declared brain dead at 9 weeks pregnant. Her story highlights the extreme intersection of maternal health disparities, abortion restrictions, and reproductive justice. Her body remained on life support for months to sustain the pregnancy, despite her medical declaration of death. The decision was driven by the state's restrictive abortion law, H.B. 481, rather than the wishes of Adriana's family (Lewis et al., 2026; Associated Press, 2025). This scenario illustrates how maternal health policy failures extend beyond access—they infringe on control over the bodies of pregnant people, particularly Black women, diminish autonomy, and jeopardize maternal outcomes, dignity, and personhood. The experiences of these women reflect a broader pattern of Black women dying from preventable pregnancy-related causes. The disparities persist even when controlling for social determinants such as income and education level.

Inequitable outcomes in maternal health are pervasive. Failure to address this disparity continues to burden marginalized communities already burdened by racism, classism, sexism, ableism, and other systems of oppression (Julian et al., 2021) with poor health outcomes disproportionately. These issues are significant statistically and morally (Eichelberger et al., 2016). An overwhelming number of statistics show racial disparities within the healthcare system. These statistics are not indicative of broken Black women; they are indicative of a broken system (Eichelberger et al., 2016). Accepting that Black women do worse than white women across research studies should be challenged. This view conveys the message that racial disparities are too complex to be addressed effectively. The urgency behind addressing this need lies in the simple fact that Black mothers and babies are dying.

These stories—from Tori Bowie, Sha-Asia Washington, Dr. Chaniece Wallace, and Adriana Smith—illustrate not only the clinical crisis but also its deeply personal, human cost. Significant gaps remain in understanding and responding to Black maternal mortality, limiting the ability to design effective interventions.

Gaps in Research and Data

Efforts to promote health equity ensure every individual has a fair and just opportunity to achieve optimal health. Yet, persistent disparities continue to undermine this goal, revealing structural and systemic inequities that disproportionately affect Black communities. Much of the existing research on health equity has been built on frameworks that center on white, majority populations, measuring progress primarily by comparing marginalized groups to these benchmarks. This approach overlooks the lived experiences, aspirations, and self-defined goals of Black Americans. To achieve genuine health equity, the field must shift from comparison-based models to frameworks that center Black voices, values, and knowledge.

Additionally, current maternal health surveillance systems fail to capture the full scope of the crisis. Data collection often lacks sufficient disaggregation by race, ethnicity, geographic location, sexual orientation, gender identity and expression, and other intersecting identities. This limitation constrains the ability to understand and address the specific needs of Black women across varied contexts and lived experiences.

Recommendations

Achieving equitable maternal health outcomes requires coordinated action across policy, practice, research, and community systems. The following recommendations outline key steps to advance Black maternal health and ensure that the lives, voices, and leadership of Black women are centered in all aspects of maternal health equity work.

Immediate Actions

Policy

- Strengthen accountability mechanisms for hospitals, health systems, and insurers to ensure compliance with anti-bias, equity, and quality standards in maternal care.
- Oppose state-level abortion bans and gestational restrictions that demonstrably increase maternal mortality, particularly for Black women.
- Support state-level 'Momnibus' legislation that advances maternal health equity at the state level, particularly in states with high Black maternal mortality rates.
- Support codification of abortion rights at the federal level.
- Counter the exodus of OB-GYNs from abortion-restrictive states through federal programs supporting maternity care access.
- Invest in freestanding birth centers and community-based maternal health facilities.

Practice

- Recognize doulas and midwives as essential members of the maternity care team.
- Provide hospitals and birthing centers with training and frameworks for collaborative, culturally competent care models.

Community

- Invest in peer support and culturally grounded maternal health programs that offer immediate connection and advocacy for Black mothers.
- Fund community-based maternal health organizations that provide education, advocacy, and culturally affirming care.
- Elevate partnerships between healthcare institutions and community organizations to rebuild trust and expand access to care.

Short-term Policy Changes (1–2 Years, State and Federal):

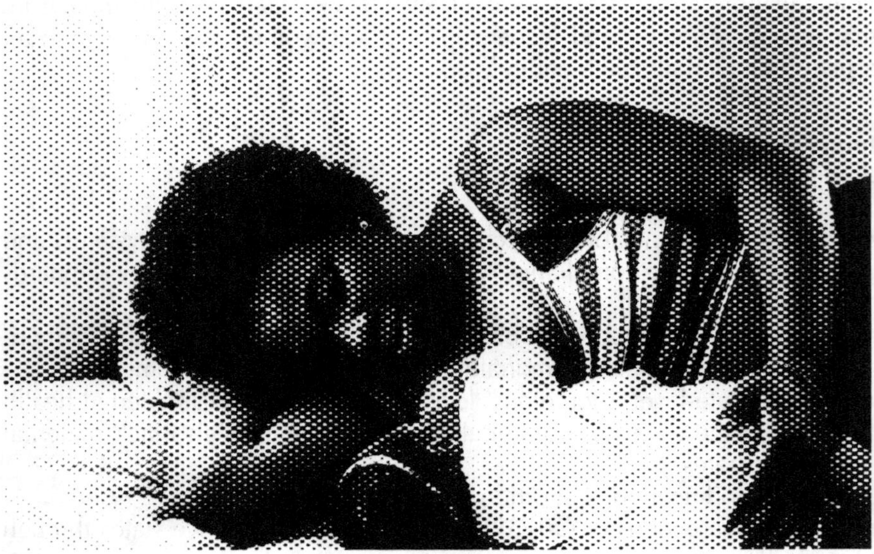

Policy

- Urge Congress to reintroduce and pass the Black Maternal Health Momnibus Act, building on the $200 million in Momnibus funding secured through appropriations since 2023.
- Ensure reimbursement for doula and midwifery services through Medicaid and private insurance to expand access and affordability.
- Ensure full funding ($1 billion+) for the 13-bill package addressing social determinants, workforce diversification, community-based organizations, data collection, and maternal mental health.
- Ensure emergency medical exceptions in any abortion regulations protect the health and life of pregnant people.
- Ensure that all states adopt the American Rescue Plan option, which extends Medicaid postpartum coverage from 60 days to 12 months.
- Make 12-month postpartum coverage mandatory, not optional, to eliminate state-by-state variation.
- Expand coverage to include doula services, mental healthcare, and preventive services during the extended postpartum period.
- Provide targeted funding and incentives for obstetric care in underserved areas, particularly in Southern states and rural communities where Black women are concentrated.

Research

- Fund community-based participatory research that centers Black women's lived experiences to identify factors shaping maternal health outcomes.
- Use research findings to inform predictive and preventive policy strategies, rather than solely documenting disparities.

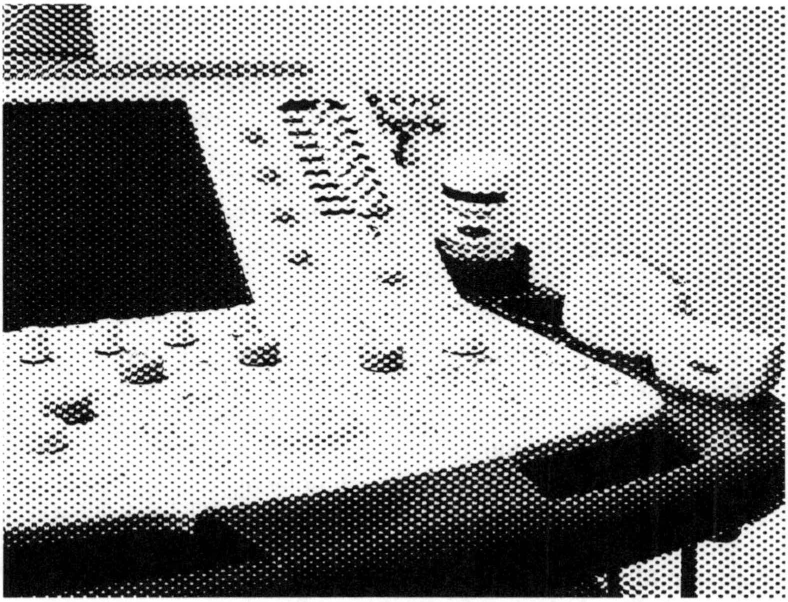

Long-term Systemic Transformation (3–5+ years)

Policy

- Pass and sustain Black maternal health legislation at the federal, state, and local levels, ensuring ongoing funding and enforcement.
- Institutionalize maternal health equity by embedding equity metrics in federal and state performance measures, diversifying the perinatal workforce, and creating permanent funding streams for maternal health equity initiatives.
- Repeal the Hyde Amendment to eliminate Medicaid-based barriers to abortion access.

Community & Practice

- Develop a sustainable, interdisciplinary maternal health infrastructure that integrates community-based care, midwifery, and mental health support services.
- Normalize culturally grounded, holistic maternity care models as the national standard for maternal health.

Community Call to Action

While federal and state legislation remains essential for advancing maternal health equity, progress often moves too slowly to address the urgent needs of Black women and families. History demonstrates that our communities have always organized, cared for one another, and innovated despite systemic neglect. As we continue pressuring policymakers for accountability, we must draw on the strength of our networks to protect, nurture, and uplift one another. The following community-driven actions offer practical, culturally rooted strategies that strengthen our collective power, ensuring that we are already creating the conditions for our liberation and wellness while we wait for systemic change.

- Support local doulas, midwives, and birth workers through cooperative networks, resource sharing, and community birthing funds to build and strengthen community health networks.
- Existing Organizations to Engage Immediately:
  - **Mama Glow Foundation**—Founded by Latham Thomas, the Mama Glow Foundation advances reproductive justice and birth equity through doula training, public education, and policy advocacy.
  - **Black Mamas Matter Alliance**—Founded Black Maternal Health Week, provides national advocacy and community organizing resources.
  - **BirthFUND**—Launched by Serena Williams and Elaine Welteroth, provides funding for doula and midwife care.
  - **National Black Doulas Association**—Offers certification pathways and support for Black doulas nationwide.
  - **Sista Midwife Productions**—Maintains a national directory connecting Black families with culturally grounded doulas and midwives.
  - **Black Maternal Health Center of Excellence (Los Angeles)**—Provides free and low-cost services, training, and hospital-based midwifery care.
  - **Ancient Song Doula Services**—Provides community-based doula care grounded in traditional practices.
  - **Jamaa Birth Village (Missouri)**—Community birth center and doula collective.
  - **Chicago South Side Birth Center**—Black woman-owned freestanding birth center.
- Create Community Resource Networks.
- Establish local maternal health resource hubs that provide:
  - Free pregnancy tests and prenatal vitamins.
  - Transportation assistance to prenatal appointments.

- Meal preparation and delivery for postpartum families.
- Child care support during medical appointments.
- Emergency funds for maternal health emergencies.
- Translation and interpretation services.
- Navigation assistance through Medicaid enrollment and healthcare systems.
- Example Models:
  - Mutual aid pregnancy funds (inspired by abortion fund model).
  - Church-based maternal health ministries.
  - Historically Black Colleges and Universities (HBCU) student-led doula collectives.
  - Workplace maternal health support groups.
  - Online networks connecting Black birthing people for peer support.

- Establish mutual aid funds to support prenatal and postpartum care, covering essential services such as transportation, child care, and nutrition for expectant mothers and their families.
- Develop safe birthing and postpartum hubs in churches, community centers, and grassroots organizations where women can access trusted, culturally grounded care.
- Document and teach traditional birthing wisdom from elders, midwives, and healers within the community.

  - Specific Actions:

    - Organize 'Grandmother Circles' where elders share birth stories and traditional postpartum practices.
    - Create digital archives of Black midwife oral histories.
    - Develop culturally specific childbirth education curricula.
    - Host community workshops on recognizing pregnancy warning signs.
    - Produce social media content educating about implicit bias in healthcare.
    - Create 'Know Your Rights' guides for hospital birth advocacy.

  - Resources to Develop:

    - Printable birth plan templates centered on Black birthing experiences.
    - Video series featuring Black doulas explaining the childbirth process.
    - Podcast featuring Black maternal health providers and survivors.
    - Instagram/TikTok content series on postpartum care in Black tradition.
    - Quarterly community newsletter on maternal health equity.

- Develop Black-led research collaboratives that partner with churches, HBCUs, and Predominantly White Institutions (PWI) serving Black students, and local clinics to collect data grounded in lived experience.
  - Community data initiatives:
    - Partner with HBCUs to conduct community-based participatory research.
    - Create community maternal health surveillance systems that track outcomes.
    - Develop surveys assessing Black women's experiences with maternal healthcare.
    - Organize 'listening sessions' to document barriers to care.
    - Collaborate with local health departments to disaggregate maternal health data by race.
    - Establish partnerships with academic researchers committed to community co-leadership.
  - Organizations supporting community research:
    - Black Mamas Matter Alliance Research Working Group.
    - Community-Campus Partnerships for Health.
    - Patient-Centered Outcomes Research Institute (PCORI), an organization which funds community-led research.
- Mobilize faith leaders and congregations to educate members about maternal health inequities and advocate for care access.
- Mobilize for policy change while building community infrastructure, simultaneously pressure systems to change:
  - Form local Black Maternal Health Task Forces to monitor hospital practices.
  - Conduct 'report card' assessments of hospitals' maternal health equity efforts.
  - Organize testimony at state legislatures during maternal health hearings.
  - Create relationships with sympathetic legislators who will champion bills.

- Submit public comments on Medicaid policies and healthcare regulations.
- Coordinate letter-writing campaigns to hospital administrators demanding change.
- Document experiences of discrimination and bias to submit to patient advocacy organizations.
- Partner with local journalism outlets to investigate maternal health disparities.

- Support and participate in national days of action:
  - Black Maternal Health Week (April 11–17, annually).
  - National Black Doula Day (April 11, annually).
  - Black Maternal Health National Day of Rest (April 17, annually).

Vision: What Maternal Health Equity Looks Like

- Black maternal mortality rate equal to or better than that of other racial groups.
- Every Black birthing person has access to:
  - A doula or midwife of their choosing.
  - Culturally competent, gender-affirming care.
  - Comprehensive reproductive healthcare, including abortion services.
  - 12 months of postpartum coverage.
- Community-based maternal health hubs in every county with significant Black populations.
- Black women and birthing people lead all maternal health initiatives, research, and policy development.
- Zero preventable maternal deaths.

Conclusion

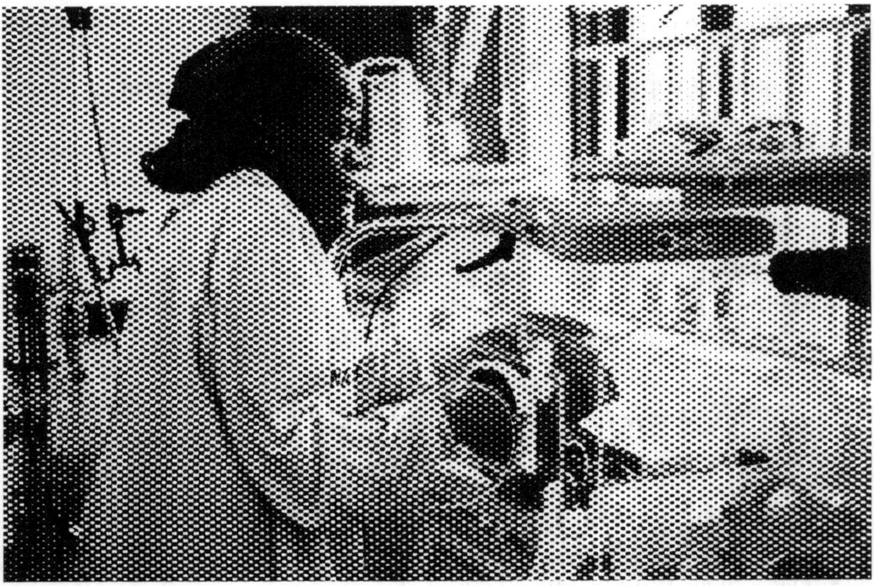

Achieving maternal health equity for Black women requires more than reform; it demands transformation. The question before us is not whether we have the knowledge or resources to solve this crisis. We do. The question is whether we have the collective will to redistribute power, resources, and decision-making authority to Black communities who have always known how to care for our own. This Paper serves as both a documentation of the crisis and a blueprint for liberation. The time for incremental change has passed. Black mothers and babies are dying now. We must act now. The solutions are neither distant nor abstract; they exist within our communities, within the leadership of Black women, and in the collective wisdom of women passed down through generations. While policy work continues, we cannot wait for the system to rescue us. We have the power to build, heal, teach, and organize from within. We keep us safe.

Glossary of Terms

Cardiovascular Disease (CVD) A group of disorders of the heart and blood vessels, including hypertension, coronary heart disease, and stroke. CVD is a leading cause of pregnancy-related deaths in the United States and disproportionately affects Black women.

Doula A trained professional who provides continuous physical, emotional, and informational support to a person before, during, and shortly after childbirth to help achieve the healthiest, most satisfying experience possible.

Health Equity The attainment of the highest level of health for all people, requiring focused efforts to address avoidable inequalities and eliminate disparities.

Hypertension Persistently high blood pressure that can damage the heart, kidneys, and other organs. Chronic hypertension and hypertensive disorders during pregnancy (e.g., preeclampsia, eclampsia) are major causes of maternal morbidity and mortality.

Implicit Bias Unconscious attitudes or stereotypes that affect understanding, actions, and decisions in healthcare delivery.

Intersectionality An analytic framework that examines how multiple forms of social stratification (e.g., race, gender, class) intersect to create unique experiences of oppression or privilege. (Crenshaw, 1989, 1991)

Maternal Health Equity Ensuring that all birthing people have fair and just access to quality maternal care and outcomes, regardless of race, income, or geography.

Maternal Morbidity Physical or mental conditions caused or aggravated by pregnancy or childbirth that negatively impact a woman's health but do not result in death.

Maternal Mortality The death of a woman during pregnancy or within 42 days of the termination of pregnancy, from any cause related to or aggravated by the pregnancy or its management, excluding accidental or incidental causes.

Pregnancy-Related Death Death of a woman while pregnant or within one year of pregnancy termination, regardless of the cause, if the death is pregnancy-related or aggravated by pregnancy.

Reproductive Justice A framework that links reproductive rights with social justice, asserting that every person has the right to have a child, not have a child, and parent children in safe and sustainable communities (SisterSong, 1994).

Severe Maternal Morbidity (SMM) Unexpected outcomes of labor and delivery that result in significant short- or long-term consequences to a woman's health (CDC, 2024).

Social Determinants of Health (SDOH) The conditions in which people are born, live, learn, work, and age that affect health outcomes, such as housing, education, transportation, and access to care.

Stroke A medical emergency that occurs when the blood supply to part of the brain is interrupted or reduced, preventing brain tissue from receiving oxygen. Stroke risk increases during pregnancy and postpartum, particularly among women with hypertension or preeclampsia.

Structural Factors The totality of ways in which societies foster racial discrimination through mutually reinforcing systems such as housing, education, employment, and healthcare.

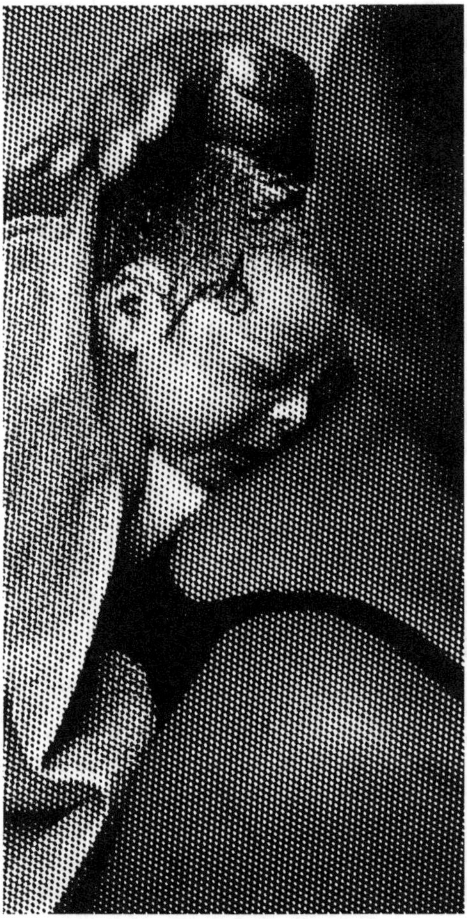

Appendix

Organization	*Contact Info*	*Notes/Additional Info*
Mama Glow Foundation	Address: 379 W. Broadway, 2nd Fl., New York, NY 10012. (Mama Glow Foundation) Email: info@mamaglowfoundation.org	Focus: reproductive justice, birth equity.
Black Mamas Matter Alliance	Address: P.O. Box 571894, Atlanta, GA 30357. (Black Mamas Matter Alliance) General email: info@blackmamasmatter.org (Black Mamas Matter Alliance)	National advocacy and network for Black maternal health.
birthFUND	Website: https://www.thebirthfund.com/ (The Birth Fund)	Founded by Serena Williams & Elaine Welteroth; funding for doula/midwife care.
National Black Doulas Association	Address: 4775 Jimmy Carter Blvd, #300, Norcross, GA 30093. (Black Doulas) Email: hello@blackdoulas.org (Black Doulas)	Certification path, directory of Black doulas.
Sista Midwife Productions	Contact form via website: "Consultation" page. (SMP Primary Site) Email for training inquiries: Training@SistaMidwife.com	Maintains a directory of Black families & doulas/midwives, training agency.
Black Maternal Health Center of Excellence	Address: 1731 E 120th St, Los Angeles, CA 90059. Phone: (323) 563-9320. (Black Maternal Health Center)	Based at Charles Drew University; free/low-cost services, hospital-based midwifery care.
Ancient Song Doula Services	Address: 521 Halsey Street, Brooklyn, NY 11233. Phone: (347) 778-3490. Email: info@ancientsongdoulaservices.com. (Ancient Song Doula Services)	Community-based doula care grounded in traditional practices for low-income Black & Latinx families.
Jamaa Birth Village	Address: 40 N Florissant Rd., Ferguson, MO 63135. Phone: 1-833-4-MIDWIFE. Email: info@jamaabirthvillage.org. (Jamaa Birth Village)	Community birth center and doula collective – St. Louis region.
Chicago South Side Birth Center	Address: 8301 S South Shore Dr., Chicago, IL 60617. Email: hr@chicagosouthsidebirthcenter.org. (Idealist)	Black woman–owned freestanding birth center (opening planned).

Inclusive Language for Pregnant People

Here's a breakdown of **inclusive terms** and when/how to use them. These explicitly include cisgender women, transgender men, intersex, and nonbinary people:

Term	*When to Use*	*Notes*
Pregnant people	Most common inclusive term in public health, research, and clinical writing	Broad and neutral; widely used by WHO, CDC, and medical journals. Example: "Access to care for pregnant people should be equitable."
People who are pregnant	Common in clinical/academic contexts	Similar to "pregnant people," sometimes preferred in formal or descriptive text.
People capable of pregnancy	Used when referring to reproductive capacity (not current pregnancy)	Helpful when discussing rights, contraception, or abortion care (e.g., "Policies must support people capable of pregnancy").
People who can become pregnant	Common in health policy and research	Emphasizes capability, not gender. Used by organizations like the Guttmacher Institute and the American Medical Association (AMA).

Gender-specific But Inclusive Phrasing

Sometimes you may want to **acknowledge all groups explicitly**:

> This guideline applies to women, transgender men, nonbinary, and intersex people who are pregnant. This wording is precise and affirming when space allows (for example, in research inclusion criteria, public statements, or community materials).

When Gendered Terms ('Women') Are Still Appropriate

- When the discussion is **about gender-specific social experiences**, such as sexism or maternal identity, and the population studied **only includes cis women**.
- In these cases, clarity matters: specify the scope (e.g., "In this study of cisgender women…").
- You can also blend inclusive and gendered language thoughtfully:

All pregnant people—including women, transgender men, and nonbinary people—deserve respectful care during childbirth.

Recommended by Major Health Organizations

- **American College of Obstetricians and Gynecologists (ACOG)**: encourages terms like *"pregnant individuals"* or *"pregnant people"* to be inclusive of all who may experience pregnancy.
- **The World Health Organization (WHO)** and United Nations Population Fund (**UNFPA**): increasingly use *"pregnant people"* in global guidelines to include transgender and nonbinary populations.
- **Centers for Disease Control and Prevention (CDC)**: uses *"pregnant people"* in many current communications, especially about vaccines and prenatal health.
- **American Medical Association (AMA)**: supports gender-inclusive terminology in clinical care and research documentation.

Examples of inclusive phrasing in use

- "All **pregnant people** should have access to evidence-based prenatal care."
- "This program serves **women, transgender men, and nonbinary people** who are pregnant or postpartum."
- "Healthcare systems must ensure safe environments for **people capable of pregnancy**, regardless of gender identity."

1 **General healthcare communication**

   a **Before**: "All pregnant women should receive prenatal vitamins and regular check-ups."
   b **After (inclusive)**: "All pregnant people should receive prenatal vitamins and regular check-ups."
   c **Why**: Neutral, simple, covers anyone pregnant.

2 **Public health guidance/vaccine campaigns**

   a **Before**: "Mothers-to-be are encouraged to get the flu vaccine."
   b **After (inclusive)**: "Pregnant people are encouraged to get the flu vaccine.
   c **Alternative, if highlighting gender identities**: "Pregnant women, transgender men, and nonbinary people are encouraged to get the flu vaccine."
   d **Why**: Avoids the assumption that all who are pregnant identify as mothers.

3 **Research or study eligibility**

   a **Before**: "This study enrolled women aged 18–40 who were pregnant."
   b **After (inclusive)**: "This study enrolled people aged 18–40 who were pregnant, including cisgender women, transgender men, and nonbinary people."
   c **Why**: Clarifies who is included while remaining accurate.

4 **Forms/surveys**

   a **Before**: "Mother's age: ______", "Mother's occupation: ______"
   b **After (inclusive)**: "Pregnant person's age: ______", "Pregnant person's occupation: ______"
   c **Alternative if space allows**: "Pregnant person (woman, transgender man, nonbinary, or intersex): ______"**Why**: Allows self-identification and avoids misgendering.

5 **Educational/patient materials**

   a **Before**: "As a mother, you should monitor your blood pressure daily."
   b **After (inclusive)**: "If you are pregnant, monitor your blood pressure daily."
   c **Alternative**: "Pregnant people should monitor their blood pressure daily, regardless of gender identity."
   d **Why**: Focuses on pregnancy health, not gendered roles.

6 **Policy documents or institutional guidance**

   a **Before**: "Maternity leave policies should support women during pregnancy and postpartum."
   b **After (inclusive)**: "Parental leave policies should support all people during pregnancy and postpartum, including women, transgender men, and nonbinary parents."
   c **Why**: Acknowledges diverse gender identities while maintaining clarity about the experience.

Key principles for inclusive language:

1 Prefer neutral terms like *pregnant people, people who are pregnant*, or *people capable of pregnancy*.
2 Explicitly name gender identities when context requires clarity.
3 Avoid assuming pregnancy equals motherhood or womanhood.
4 Use perinatal, prenatal, or pregnancy-related instead of maternal when discussing health systems or research outcomes.

Inclusive Language Cheat Sheet: Pregnancy & Parenthood

Common Phrase/Term	*Inclusive Alternative*	*Notes/Why*
Pregnant women	Pregnant people/People who are pregnant	Covers cis women, trans men, nonbinary, and intersex.
Expectant mother/ Mother-to-be	Pregnant person/ Pregnant individual	Avoids assuming gender identity or motherhood role.
Maternal health	Perinatal health/ Pregnancy-related health	Focuses on the health experience, not a gendered label.
Maternity leave	Parental leave/Pregnancy leave	Inclusive of trans men, nonbinary, and adoptive parents.
Mother's age/Mother's occupation	Pregnant person's age/ Pregnant person's occupation	Neutral and avoids misgendering.
Women giving birth	People giving birth/ Individuals giving birth	Recognizes non-cisgender parents.
Postpartum depression in mothers	Postpartum depression/ Post-birth depression	Inclusive of all genders experiencing postpartum changes.
Women who can get pregnant	People capable of pregnancy/People who can become pregnant	Useful for reproductive health policies or contraception discussions.
Prenatal care for women	Prenatal care for pregnant people	Broadens scope beyond cisgender women.
Breastfeeding/Nursing mothers	Chestfeeding or nursing parents	Optional term if discussing feeding, inclusive of trans men and nonbinary parents.

Tips for using this cheat sheet

1. **Default to neutral terms** like "pregnant people" unless gender specificity is necessary.
2. **Name identities** explicitly when space allows, e.g., "women, transgender men, and nonbinary people who are pregnant."
3. **Review forms and educational materials** to replace gendered terms (mother/father) with neutral options (parent/guardian/pregnant person).
4. **Adjust medical terms**:

   a. "maternal morbidity" → "perinatal morbidity"
   b. "maternal care" → "pregnancy care"

5. **Context matters**: if discussing social experiences (like sexism in pregnancy), naming cis women may be accurate, but clarify the scope.

Notes

1 This Black Paper primarily uses the term 'Black women' to reflect both the language used in much of the existing research and the reality that the majority of people experiencing pregnancy-related mortality and morbidity identify as women. When we use 'Black women', we honor the specific gendered experiences of Black women while recognizing that not all people who give birth identify as women. Where appropriate, we use 'Black birthing people' or 'Black mothers and birthing people' to intentionally acknowledge the identities of all people who can become pregnant. This linguistic choice reflects our commitment to reproductive justice—the right of all people to bodily autonomy, to have children or not have children, to raise children in safe and healthy environments, and to make decisions about their bodies and families without coercion or barrier (Ross & Solinger, 2017).

References

Amiri, M., Ramezani Tehrani, F., Behboudi-Gandevani, S., Bidhendi-Yarandi, R., & Carmina, E. (2020). Risk of hypertension in women with polycystic ovary syndrome: a systematic review, meta-analysis and meta-regression. *Reproductive Biology and Endocrinology, 18*(1), 23. https://doi.org/10.1186/s12958-020-00576-1

Associated Press. (2025). Hospital tells family brain-dead Georgia woman must carry fetus due to abortion ban. *National Public Radio*. Retrieved October26, 2025, from https://www.npr.org/2025/05/16/nx-s1-5400266/georgia-brain-dead-fetus-abortion-ban-hospital

Atayan, A. B., Huerne, K., Palmour, N., & Joly, Y. (2024). Towards equity & inclusion: a critical examination of genetic Counselling Education on Intersex Healthcare. *BMC Medical Education*, 24(1), 942. https://doi.org/10.1186/s12909-024-05898-x

Bafghi, Z. R., Ahmadi, A., Mirzaee, F., & Ghazanfarpour, M. (2024). The effect of mindfulness-based art therapy (MBAT) on the body image of women with polycystic ovary syndrome (PCOS): a randomized controlled trial. *BMC Psychiatry*, 24(1), 611.

Bahri Khomami, M., Teede, H. J., Joham, A. E., Moran, L. J., Piltonen, T. T., & Boyle, J. A. (2022). Clinical management of pregnancy in women with polycystic ovary syndrome: An expert opinion. *Clinical Endocrinology*, 97(2), 227–236.

Bane, S. S., Obedin-Maliver, J., Ragosta, S., Hastings, J., Lunn, M. R., Flentje, A., Capriotti, M. R., Lubensky, M. E., Tordoff, D. M., & Moseson, H. (2024). Pathways to parenthood among transgender men and gender diverse people assigned female or intersex at birth in the United States: analysis of a Cross-Sectional 2019 Survey. *AJOG Global Reports*, 4(3), 100381. https://doi.org/10.1016/j.xagr.2024.100381

Beier, K. M., Wille, R., & Wessel, J. (2006). Denial of pregnancy as a reproductive dysfunction: a proposal for international classification systems. *Journal of Psychosomatic Research*, 61(5), 723–730.

Bermea, A. M., van Eeden-Moorefield, B., & Khaw, L. (2018). A systematic review of research on intimate partner violence among bisexual women. *Journal of Bisexuality*, 18(4), 399–424.

Bhatla, N., Lal, S., Behera, G., Kriplani, A., Mittal, S., Agarwal, N., & Talwar, K. K. (2003). Cardiac disease in pregnancy. *International Journal of Gynecology & Obstetrics, 82*(2), 153–159. https://doi.org/10.1016/S0020-7292(03)00159-0

Bornstein, E., Eliner, Y., Chervenak, F. A., & Grünebaum, A. (2020). Racial disparity in pregnancy risks and complications in the United States: Temporal changes during 2007–2018. *Journal of Clinical Medicine, 9*(5), 1414. https://doi.org/10.3390/jcm9051414

Brevil, A. N. (2025). A model for interdisciplinary collaboration in oncology. *Health & Social Work, 50*(3), 229–239. https://doi.org/10.1093/hsw/hlaf021

Burgart, J. M., Walters, R. W., & Shanahan, M. (2022). Transgender education experiences among obstetrics and gynecology residents: a national survey. *Transgender Health, 7*(1), 30–35. https://doi.org/10.1089/trgh.2020.0018

Canty, L. (2022). The lived experience of severe maternal morbidity among Black women. *Nursing Inquiry, 29*(1), e12466.

Center for Reproductive Rights. (2025). *After Roe fell: Abortion laws by state. Center for Reproductive Rights*. Retrieved October26, 2025, from https://reproductiverights.org/maps/abortion-laws-by-state/

Centers for Disease Control and Prevention. (2024). *Preventing pregnancy-related deaths*. U.S. Department of Health and Human Services. Retrieved October26, 2025, from https://www.cdc.gov/maternal-mortality/preventing-pregnancy-related-deaths/index.html

Chemerinski, A., Cooney, L., Shah, D., Butts, S., Gibson-Helm, M., & Dokras, A. (2020). Knowledge of PCOS in physicians-in-training: identifying gaps and educational opportunities. *Gynecological Endocrinology, 36*(10), 854–859.

Collins, P. H. (1996). What's in a name? *The Black Scholar, 26*(1), 9–17. https://doi.org/10.1080/00064246.1996.11430765

Collins, P. H. (2022). *Black feminist thought: Knowledge, consciousness, and the politics of empowerment*. Routledge.

Corey, J., Duggan, M., & Travers, Á. (2023). Risk and protective factors for intimate partner violence against bisexual victims: a systematic scoping review. *Trauma, Violence, & Abuse, 24*(4), 2130–2142. https://doi.org/10.1177/15248380221084749

Coston, B. M. (2021). Power and inequality: Intimate partner violence against bisexual and non-monosexual women in the United States. *Journal of Interpersonal Violence, 36*(1–2), 381–405.

Coward, C. O., Swaminathan, K., Hahn-Holbrook, J., & Howell, J. L. (2026). Understanding risk and resiliency in transmasculine pregnancy: An application and biopsychosocial extension of the Gender Minority Stress Theory. *International Journal of Transgender Health*, 1–23. https://doi.org/10.1080/26895269.2026.2656939

Crenshaw, K. (1989). *Demarginalizing the intersection of race and sex*. University of Chicago Legal Forum. Retrieved October26, 2025, from http://chicagounbound.uchicago.edu/uclf/vol1989/iss1/8

Crenshaw, K. (1991). Mapping the margins: Intersectionality, identity politics, and violence against women of color. *Stanford Law Review, 43*(6), 1241–1299.

Dalke, K. B., Baratz, A. B., & Greenberg, J. A. (2020). Chapter 14: Protecting children with intersex traits: legal, ethical, and human rights considerations. In M. J. Legato (Ed.), *The plasticity of sex* (pp. 207–224). Academic Press. https://doi.org/10.1016/B978-0-12-815968-2.00010-4

Eichelberger, K. Y., Doll, K., Ekpo, G. E., & Zerden, M. L. (2016). Black lives matter: Claiming a space for evidence-based outrage in obstetrics and gynecology. *American Journal of Public Health, 106*(10), 1771–1772. https://doi.org/10.2105/ajph.2016.303313

Farah, E., Barger, M. K., Klima, C., Rossman, B., & Hershberger, P. (2021). Impaired lactation: review of delayed lactogenesis and insufficient lactation. *Journal of Midwifery & Women's Health*, *66*(5), 631–640. https://doi.org/10.1111/jmwh.13274

Galaa, S., Umar, H., & Dandeebo, G. (2016). Reducing maternal mortality through community participation: The Gbanko example. *UDS International Journal of Development*, *1*, 86–102.

Gender Equity Policy Institute. (2025). *Maternal mortality in the United States after abortion bans: Mothers living in abortion ban states at significantly higher risk of death during pregnancy and childbirth*. https://doi.org/10.5281/zenodo.14713213

Givens, R. (2021). One of us. *New England Journal of Medicine*, *384*(6), e18. https://doi.org/10.1056/NEJMpv2100228

Guidi, J., Lucente, M., Sonino, N., & Fava, G. A. (2020). Allostatic load and its impact on health: A systematic review. *Psychotherapy and Psychosomatics*, *90*(1), 11–27.

Hassan, S., Okoye, N., Adindu, K., & Agbo, P. (2024). Health workers' perception on the key drivers of maternal mortality. *IOSR Journal of Dental and Medical Sciences*, *23*, 33–40. https://doi.org/10.9790/0853-2310053340

hooks, b. (1981). *Ain't I a woman: Black women and feminism*. South End Press.

Hoyert, D. L. (2024). *Health E-stat: Maternal mortality rates in the United States, 2022*. National Center for Health Statistics.

Hoyert, D. L. (2025). *Maternal mortality rates in the United States, 2023*. National Center for Health Statistics.

Hudak, N. (2023). "Who's the Mom?": Heterosexism in patient-provider interactions of queer pregnant couples. *Health Communication*, *38*(1), 114–123.

Hull, A. (Gloria T.). (2016). *But some of us are brave: Black women's studies* (2nd ed.). The Feminist Press at CUNY.

Irving, S., French, T. O., Johnson, K. D., & Isaac, A. R. (2023). *Tori Bowie: Don't ever stop saying her name*. Obstetric Medicine.

Isaac, S. M., Dawes, M., Howell, E. R., & Oladipo, A. F. (2025). Gender-inclusive language in public-facing labor and delivery web pages in the New York tristate area: cross-sectional study. *JMIR Human Factors*, *12*, e53057. https://doi.org/10.2196/53057

Jiang, R., Yao, Y., Wang, T., Li, B., Jiang, P., Wang, F., & Qu, F. (2024). Preeclampsia in pregnant women with polycystic ovary syndrome: risk factor analysis based on a retrospective cohort study. *Ginekologia Polska*, *95*(5), 365–372. https://doi.org/10.5603/gpl.92311

Jiang, J. W., et al. (2025). *State-level variation in and barriers to Medicaid abortion coverage*. Health Affairs.

Joham, A. E., Norman, R. J., Stener-Victorin, E., Legro, R. S., Franks, S., Moran, L. J., Boyle, J., & Teede, H. J. (2022). Polycystic ovary syndrome. *Lancet Diabetes Endocrinol*, *10*(9), 668–680. https://doi.org/10.1016/s2213-8587(22)00163-2

Julian, Z., Mengesha, B., McLemore, M. R., & Steinauer, J. (2021). Community-engaged curriculum development in sexual and reproductive health equity: Structures and self. *Obstetrics & Gynecology*, *137*(4), 723–727. https://doi.org/10.1097/aog.0000000000004324

Kaiser Family Foundation. (2024). *What are the implications of the Dobbs ruling for racial disparities?* Retrieved October31, 2025, from https://www.kff.org/womens-health-policy/issue-brief/what-are-the-implications-of-the-dobbs-ruling-for-racial-disparities/

Katta, S., & Davoody, N. (2025). Exploring health care professionals' perspectives on education, awareness, and preferences for digital educational resources to support transgender, nonbinary, and intersex care: Interview study. *JMIR Medical Education, 11*, e67993. https://doi.org/10.2196/67993

Kim, T., et al. (2025). Abortion rate increased and birth rate decreased after introduction of Medicaid abortion coverage in Illinois. *Health Affairs, 44*(2), 224–233.

Kinnear, H. M., & Moravek, M. B. (2023). Reproductive capacity after gender-affirming testosterone therapy. *Human Reproduction, 38*(10), 1872–1880. https://doi.org/10.1093/humrep/dead158

LaVaccare, S., Diamant, A. L., Friedman, J., Singh, K. T., Baker, J. A., Rodriguez, T. A., Cohen, S. R., Dary, F. Y., & Pregler, J. (2018). Healthcare experiences of underrepresented lesbian and bisexual women: a focus group qualitative study. *Health Equity, 2*(1), heq.2017.0041. https://doi.org/10.1089/heq.2017.0041

Leonard, S. A., Main, E. K., Scott, K. A., Profit, J., & Carmichael, S. L. (2019). Racial and ethnic disparities in severe maternal morbidity prevalence and trends. *Annals of Epidemiology, 33*, 30–36. https://doi.org/10.1016/j.annepidem.2019.02.007

Lewis, A., Quinn, G., & Mutcherson, K. (2026). Ethical controversies in the Adriana Smith case in Georgia: brain death/death by neurologic criteria in pregnancy. *The American Journal of Bioethics, 26*(1), 13–26.

Light, A. D., Obedin-Maliver, J., Sevelius, J. M., & Kerns, J. L. (2014). Transgender men who experienced pregnancy after female-to-male gender transitioning. *Obstetrics & Gynecology, 124*(6), 1120–1127.

Liu, X., Wang, L., Zuo, X., Li, C., & Teng, Y. (2021). Women with PCOS with a history of early pregnancy loss show a higher risk of gestational diabetes mellitus. *International Journal of General Medicine, 14*, 6409–6416. https://doi.org/10.2147/IJGM.S334666

Lorde, A. (1983). *The master's tools will never dismantle the master's house* (pp. 1670–1673). Routledge.

MacDonald, T., Noel-Weiss, J., West, D., Walks, M., Biener, M., Kibbe, A., & Myler, E. (2016). Transmasculine individuals' experiences with lactation, chestfeeding, and gender identity: a qualitative study. *BMC Pregnancy Childbirth, 16*, 106. https://doi.org/10.1186/s12884-016-0907-y

MacDorman, M. F., Declercq, E., Cabral, H., & Morton, C. (2016). Is the United States' maternal mortality rate increasing? *Obstetrics and Gynecology*, 128(3), 447–455.

MacKinnon, K. R., Lefkowitz, A., Lorello, G. R., Schrewe, B., Soklaridis, S. & Kuper, A. (2021). Recognizing and renaming in obstetrics: How do we take better care with language? *Obstetric Medicine*, 14(4), 201–203.

MacLean, L. R.-D. (2021). Preconception, pregnancy, birthing, and lactation needs of transgender men. *Nursing for Women's Health*, 25(2), 129–138. https://doi.org/10.1016/j.nwh.2021.01.006

Mahase, E. (2025). Abortion in US: Women in ban states are twice as likely to die during pregnancy or childbirth, report warns. *BMJ: British Medical Journal* (Online), 389. https://doi.org/10.1136/bmj.r879

Majebi, N. L., Adelodun, M. O., & Chinyere, E. (2024). Maternal mortality and healthcare disparities: Addressing systemic inequities in underserved communities. *International Journal of Engineering Inventions, 13*(9), 375–385.

March of Dimes. (2024). *Nowhere to Go: Maternity Care Deserts Report 2024*. Retrieved October26, 2025, from https://www.marchofdimes.org/peristats/reports/united-states/maternity-care-deserts

Matsuzaki, S., Masjedi, A. D., Matsuzaki, S., Anderson, Z. S., Erickson, K. V., Mandelbaum, R. S., Ouzounian, J. G., Paulson, R. J., & Matsuo, K. (2024). Obstetric characteristics and outcomes of gestational carrier pregnancies: a systematic review and meta-analysis. *JAMA Network Open, 7*(7), e2422634. https://doi.org/10.1001/jamanetworkopen.2024.22634

Mayrhofer, D., Hager, M., Walch, K., Ghobrial, S., Rogenhofer, N., Marculescu, R., Seemann, R., & Ott, J. (2020). The prevalence and impact of polycystic ovary syndrome in recurrent miscarriage: a retrospective cohort study and meta-analysis. *Journal of Clinical Medicine, 9*(9), 2700.

McConnell, E. A., Janulis, P., Phillips, G., Truong, R., & Birkett, M. (2018). Multiple minority stress and LGBT community resilience among sexual minority men. *Psychology of Sexual Orientation and Gender Diversity, 5*(1), 1–12. https://doi.org/10.1037/sgd0000265

McEwen, B. S., & Stellar, E. (1993). Stress and the Individual: Mechanisms Leading to Disease. *Archives of Internal Medicine, 153*(18), 2093–2101.

McKinsey Health Institute. (2025). *Closing the Black maternal health gap: Healthier lives, stronger economies*. Retrieved November1, 2025, from https://www.mckinsey.com/institute-for-economic-mobility/our-insights/closing-the-black-maternal-health-gap-healthier-lives-stronger-economies

Metcalfe, A., Wick, J., & Ronksley, P. (2018). Racial disparities in comorbidity and severe maternal morbidity/mortality in the United States: An analysis of temporal trends. *Acta Obstetricia et Gynecologica Scandinavica, 97*(1), 89–96. https://doi.org/10.1111/aogs.13245

Moseson, H., Zazanis, N., Goldberg, E., Fix, L., Durden, M., Stoeffler, A., Hastings, J., Cudlitz, L., Lesser-Lee, B., Letcher, L., Reyes, A., & Obedin-Maliver, J. (2020). The imperative for transgender and gender nonbinary inclusion: beyond women's health. *Obstetrics & Gynecology, 135*(5), 1059–1068. https://doi.org/10.1097/aog.0000000000003816

Mugeni, D. W. (2022). *An imbalanced scale: A dissection of the racial disparities in the US medical system* (Bachelor's thesis, Purchase College, State University of New York). SUNY Open Access Repository. http://hdl.handle.net/20.500.12648/12189

Mutcherson, K. (2022). On health disparities and motherless children. *In Beyond Death* (Vol. 29).

Nash, J. C. (2021). Birth geographies: race, reproductive justice, and the politics of the hospital. *Harvard Journal of Law & Gender, 44*(2), 299–328.

Njoroge, J. N., & Parikh, N. I. (2020). Understanding health disparities in cardiovascular diseases in pregnancy among Black women: prevalence, preventive care, and peripartum support networks. *Current Cardiovascular Risk Reports, 14*(7), 8. https://doi.org/10.1007/s12170-020-00641-9

Norwood, C., Jacquez, F., Carr, T., Murawsky, S., Beck, K., & Tuttle, A. (2022). Reproductive justice, public Black feminism in practice: A reflection on community-based participatory research in Cincinnati. *Societies, 12*(1), 17. https://doi.org/10.3390/soc12010017

Obeagu, E. I., Njar, V. E., & Obeagu, G. U. (2023). Infertility: Prevalence and consequences. *International Journal of Current Research in Chemistry and Pharmaceutical Sciences, 10*(7), 43–50.

Office of Minority Health. (2024). *Diabetes and African Americans*. U.S. Department of Health and Human Services. Retrieved October27, 2025, from https://minorityhealth.hhs.gov/diabetes-and-african-americans

Parker, J., & Hitch, V. (2025). New challenges and perspectives in polycystic ovary syndrome. *Journal of Clinical Medicine, 14*(24), 8867.

Peterson, E. E., Davis, N., Goodman, D., Cox, S., Syverson, C., Seed, K., Shapiro-Mendoza, C., Callaghan, W. M., & Barfield, W. (2019). Racial/ethnic disparities in pregnancy-related deaths — United States, 2007–2016. *MMWR*, 68(35). Retrieved October26, 2025, from https://www.cdc.gov/mmwr/volumes/68/wr/mm6835a3.htm

Pharr, J. R., Kachen, A., & Cross, C. (2019). Health disparities among sexual gender minority women in the United States: a population-based study. *Journal of Community Health, 44*(4), 721–728. https://doi.org/10.1007/s10900-019-00631-y

Practice Committee of the American Society for Reproductive Medicine. (2022). Recommendations for practices using gestational carriers: a committee opinion. *Fertility and Sterility, 118*(1), 65–74.

Richburg, C. E., Jackson Levin, N., & Moravek, M. B. (2022). Laboring to conceive: reducing barriers to fertility care for same-sex mothers pursuing parenthood. *Women, 2*(1), 44–55.

Roberts, D. (2014). *Killing the Black body: Race, reproduction, and the meaning of liberty*. Vintage.

Roberts, D. (2015). Reproductive justice, not just rights. *Dissent*, 62(4), 79–82. https://doi.org/10.1353/dss.2015.0073

Robinson, S. L., & Yeung, E. H. (2021). Polycystic ovary syndrome and preterm birth—what's going on? *Fertility and Sterility, 115*(2), 326–327. https://doi.org/10.1016/j.fertnstert.2020.09.169

Ross, L. J., & Solinger, R. (2017). *Reproductive justice: An introduction*. University of California Press.

Sabbath, E. L., et al. (2024). U.S. obstetrician-gynecologists' perceived impacts of post–Dobbs v. Jackson state abortion bans. *JAMA Netw Open, 7*(1), e2352109. https://doi.org/10.1001/jamanetworkopen.2023.52109

Safarzadeh, A. (2025). Dismantling inequities to end the Black maternal mortality crisis in the United States. *International Journal for Equity in Health, 24*(1), 114. https://doi.org/10.1186/s12939-025-02488-1

Simmons, R. S. (2023). Maternal health and American cultural values: Beyond the social determinants. In B. A. Anderson & L. R. Roberts (Eds.), *Global maternal and child health: Medical, anthropological, and public health perspectives*. Springer. https://doi.org/10.1007/978-3-031-23969-4

SisterSong Women of Color Reproductive Justice Collective. (1994). *Reproductive justice*. Retrieved May15, 2025, from https://www.sistersong.net/reproductive-justice

Smalley, K. B., Warren, J. C., & Fernandez, M. I. (2020). *Health equity: A solutions-focused approach*. Springer Publishing Company.

Smith, C. P., & George, D. R. (2021). Bisexual women's invisibility in health care. *AMA Journal of Ethics, 23*(7), E563–E568. https://doi.org/10.1001/amajethics.2021.563

Sundin, L. (2020). Imposing identity: why states should restrict infant intersex surgery. *SMU Law Review, 73*(3), 637.

Teede, H. J., Khomami, M. B., Morman, R., Laven, J. S., Joham, A. E., Costello, M. F., Patil, M., Rees, D. A., Berry, L., & Cree, M. G. (2026). Polyendocrine metabolic ovarian syndrome, the new name for polycystic ovary syndrome: a multistep global consensus process. *The Lancet, 407*(10545), 2329–2339.

Tewari, S., Khalua, R. K., & Parida, S. (2026). Redefining polycystic ovary syndrome (PCOS) as Polyendocrine Metabolic Ovarian Syndrome (PMOS): implications for diagnosis, pathophysiology and clinical management. *International Journal of Gynaecology Sciences, 8*(1), 17–25.

U.S. Department of Health and Human Services. (2023). Healthy people 2030. https://health.gov/our-work/healthy-people-2030

Wang, J., Cui, C., Hou, F., Wu, Z., Peng, Y., & Jin, H. (2025). Metabolic profiling and early prediction models for gestational diabetes mellitus in PCOS and non-PCOS pregnant women. *European Journal of Medical Research, 30*(1), 245. https://doi.org/10.1186/s40001-025-02526-2

Wojnar, D. M., & Katzenmeyer, A. (2014). Experiences of preconception, pregnancy, and new motherhood for lesbian nonbiological mothers. *Journal of Obstetric, Gynecologic & Neonatal Nursing, 43*(1), 50–60.

World Health Organization, Commission on Social Determinants of Health. (2008). Closing the gap in a generation: Health equity through action on the social determinants of health.

Yau, A., Friedlander, R. L., Petrini, A., Holt, M. C., White, D. E., II, Shin, J., Kalantry, S., & Spandorfer, S. (2021). Medical and mental health implications of gestational surrogacy. *American Journal of Obstetrics & Gynecology, 225*(3), 264–269. https://doi.org/10.1016/j.ajog.2021.04.213

Zahid, S., Tanveer Ud Din, M., Minhas, A. S., Rai, D., Kaur, G., Carfagnini, C., Khan, M. Z., Ullah, W., Van Spall, H. G. C., Hays, A. G. & Michos, E. D. (2022). Racial and Socioeconomic Disparities in Cardiovascular Outcomes of Preeclampsia Hospitalizations in the United States 2004-2019. *JACC. Advances, 1*(3), 100062.

Section V

Identity and Liberation

This section examines how intersecting identities shape the Black freedom struggle, revealing that liberation cannot be achieved through single-axis analysis but requires understanding how race intersects with gender, disability, immigration status, and sexuality to create unique experiences of oppression and resistance. Together, these Papers demonstrate that Black liberation demands centering those at the greatest margins—that the most comprehensive freedom comes when we organize around the needs of Black people in our beautiful diversity–Black women, Black immigrants, and Black Lesbian, Gay, Bisexual, Transgender, Queer/Questioning/ and Same-Gender Loving (LGBTQ+/SGL) people, whose leadership has always been essential to collective transformation.

"Gender Equity: A Black Paper" grounds its analysis in Black feminist thought, tracing from the Combahee River Collective's 1974 articulation of "interlocking oppressions" through Patricia Hill Collins's naming the power of Intersectionality Theory and situating it within the "matrix of domination," to Kimberlé Crenshaw's masterful demonstration of Intersectionality in explaining how Black women experience discrimination that cannot be understood by examining race or gender in isolation. Black women earn 64 cents for every dollar earned by white men, face maternal mortality rates 3.5 times higher than white women, and comprise two-thirds of Black college graduates. At the same time, their male counterparts' enrollment continues to decline, and they experience both hypersexualization and invisibility across professional contexts. This Black Paper documents how misogynoir—the unique combination of racism and sexism targeting Black women—operates through workplace discrimination, reproductive injustice, economic exploitation, and violence, while Black LGBTQ+/same-gender loving women face compounded marginalization. The analysis presents gender justice not as separate from but as essential to Black liberation, arguing that economic security, reproductive autonomy, freedom from violence, and political power for Black women benefit entire communities. Policy recommendations span pay equity enforcement, universal child care, comprehensive reproductive healthcare, criminal justice reform addressing gendered violence, and

DOI: 10.4324/9781003752646-18

leadership development programs ensuring Black women's full participation in decision-making.

"Disability Justice and Equity in the Black Community: An Intersectional Approach" documents how Black people with disabilities face what scholars call multiplicative oppression—experiencing both anti-Black racism and ableism that compound rather than simply add together. One in four Black adults lives with a disability. Yet, Black people with disabilities remain largely invisible in both disability rights movements that center white experiences and racial justice movements that assume able-bodied subjects. This Black Paper traces how the Disability Justice framework emerged in 2005 from disabled queers of color in San Francisco—Patty Berne, Mia Mingus, Stacey Milbern, and others—specifically because mainstream disability rights organizing failed to center those experiencing intersectional oppression. Black people with disabilities face higher rates of poverty, unemployment, police violence (with one-third to one-half of people killed by police being disabled), disproportionate incarceration, and systematic exclusion from services designed without cultural competence. Leaders like Leroy F. Moore Jr., Talila "TL" Lewis, Vilissa Thompson (who created #DisabilityTooWhite), and Aaron Rose Philip, who became the first wheelchair-using model to walk a major luxury brand's runway, demonstrate how centering Black disabled leadership transforms both disability and racial justice organizing. The 47th presidential administration's dismantling of DEIA initiatives threatens to erase gains while activists build cross-movement solidarity.

"Black Immigration Policies, Black Lives: A Call To Action" disrupts the myth that immigration policy affects only non-Black communities, documenting how Black immigrants comprise 10% of the Black population in the United States—4.6 million people from Africa, the Caribbean, and Latin America who face targeting based on both race and immigration status. While Black immigrants are less likely to be undocumented than other immigrant groups, they face deportation at disproportionate rates: 20% of those facing deportation are Black, despite undocumented Black migrants comprising only 5.6% of the undocumented population. This disparity stems from how over-policing in Black communities means Black immigrants are more likely to encounter criminal legal systems that trigger deportation, with Black drivers searched or arrested during traffic stops at 8.6% compared to 4.0% for Hispanic drivers and 3.1% for white drivers. This Black Paper examines how historical exclusion from the Chinese Exclusion Acts through the 1924 Johnson-Reed Act to the 47th presidential administration's "Muslim ban" affecting African nations reveals continuity of racist immigration policy, while current attacks, including refugee admission cuts, travel bans, mass detention, and family separation, inflict particular harm on Black migrant communities. For Black LGBTQ+/SGL asylum seekers fleeing persecution based on sexuality or gender identity in countries with colonial-era criminalization laws, policies create "no refuge from hate" as African leaders fuel anti-LGBTQ+

sentiment while Western politicians expand xenophobic legislation. The analysis emphasizes that Black migrants and Black Americans share experiences of anti-Blackness, teaching in the same schools, working in the same hospitals, and worshiping in the same churches, meaning immigration policies targeting Black migrants inevitably impact broader Black communities.

Together, these Black Papers demonstrate that identity is not additive but multiplicative: that Black women don't experience racism plus sexism but a unique form of oppression requiring specific analysis and response; that Black people with disabilities do not face racism plus ableism but interconnected systems demanding disability justice frameworks; that Black immigrants don't encounter racism plus xenophobia but anti-Blackness manifested through immigration enforcement; and that Black LGBTQ+/SGL people don't experience racism plus homophobia but interlocking oppressions requiring movement strategies that refuse single-issue organizing. They challenge readers to recognize that the most marginalized hold the most liberatory vision, that centering Black women, Black people with disabilities, Black immigrants, and Black LGBTQ+/SGL people in analysis and organizing doesn't dilute but strengthens movements for collective freedom. This section articulates identity as a site of both oppression and resistance, calling for frameworks that honor complexity, build coalitions across difference, and recognize that none of us are free unless and until all of us are free, all power to Fannie Lou Hamer.

Chapter 13

Gender Equity

A Black Paper

*Brittney Cooper, Shatema Threadcraft, Susana Morris, and Melanye Price**

Executive Summary

This Black Paper (Paper) examines the intersecting systems of white supremacy, capitalism, and patriarchy which negatively impact Black communities across gender lines. While Black communities have historically worked together to combat white supremacy, addressing gender equity within our communities is essential for creating specific, targeted solutions that benefit all Black people. This Paper offers a framework for understanding these interconnected systems of oppression. It provides concrete policy recommendations to advance gender equity for Black women, Black men, and Black LGBTQ+/SGL (Lesbian, Gay, Bisexual, Transgender, Queer, and Same-Gender Loving) communities.

Key Findings Include:

- Black women face unique challenges, including restricted reproductive rights, maternal health crises, disproportionate intimate partner violence, educational debt burdens, workplace discrimination, and housing insecurity.
- Black men contend with criminalization, economic marginalization, health disparities, and harmful masculine stereotypes that limit their full humanity.
- Black LGBTQ+/SGL communities experience heightened violence, discrimination, and erasure both within and outside Black communities.
- Intergenerational approaches to gender equity that center Black feminist principles offer promising paths forward.

This Paper concludes with actionable recommendations for community organizations, policymakers, and individuals committed to gender equity in Black liberation work. We strengthen rather than divide our collective struggle

* Supported by braintrust authors: David J. Johns, Jada Capri Ward, and Ashley Bland Manlove.

DOI: 10.4324/9781003752646-19

for freedom by addressing these intersecting oppressions with clarity and specificity.

Key Terms:

Intersectionality: Professor Kimberlé Crenshaw (1989) employed the term "intersectionality" in her pioneering essay "Demarginalizing the Intersections" to name the particular oppression Black women face because they are impacted at the same time by white supremacy, patriarchy, and capitalism, a core concept within Critical Race Theory. The negative impact of these systems often intersects to harm Black women in multiple ways. The theoretical underpinning of this concept was significantly established and expanded upon by sociologist Patricia Hill Collins. Collins is recognized as a foundational scholar and an archivist of Black feminist thought, known for elaborating the "matrix of domination" framework. Her extensive sociological work provides a comprehensive structure for understanding how various forms of oppression are interconnected and mutually reinforcing.

Patriarchy: The system that normalizes male domination over women and children as the proper order of society.

Biological sex: Based on one's reproductive organs, human beings fall into categories of female, male, or intersex. Intersex is a term that refers to folks with ambiguous reproductive organs or who have a combination of male and female reproductive organs.

Gender: The story we tell about our masculine, feminine, or gender-expansive preferences. Typically, we believe that one's reproductive organs determine one's gender preferences, but several decades of scholarship, particularly since the 1950s, have made clear that this idea is inaccurate. Gender is a matter of one's choice and preference, and it does not always match the biological sex one is determined to have at birth.

Transgender: This refers to people whose gender identity does not match their sex assigned at birth (AFAB—assigned female at birth, or AMAB—assigned male at birth). The proper term for reference is trans people or transgender people. It is not appropriate to refer to trans people as "transgenders" or a single trans person as "a transgender."

Cisgender: This refers to people whose gender identity matches the sex assigned at birth. These people tend to be dominant, and to be cisgender is to exist in a privileged category.

Same-Gender Loving: A term used by members of the Black community to express an alternative sexual orientation without relying on terms and symbols of Anglo/European descent.

For more information about these and related terms, download the National Black Justice Collective's Terminology Guide at https://nbjc.org/nbjc-resources_/.

Overview

For too long, Black communities have been told that talking about gender is a divisive subject. Since our emancipation from slavery, we have had to work together across lines of gender to survive the violent and continued assaults of white supremacy. Along with white supremacy, other systems that contribute to life complications for Black folks include capitalism and patriarchy. Capitalism stems from the focus on putting the almighty dollar over the needs of everyday people. Patriarchy is a system that prioritizes the needs of men over women and says that men should have more power, wealth, and access to leadership opportunities simply because they are men.

The focus of this Paper is to think about the way these three systems—white supremacy, capitalism, and patriarchy intersect to create negative impacts for Black women, Black men, Queer Black People, and trans and gender ender expansive Black people. Before going further, it is important to say that there is a theory that circulates in America that Black people are more homophobic and transphobic than in other communities. Recent data from the National Black Justice Collective (NBJC) shows that the plurality of Black people desire for the community to do more to support the Black LGBTQ+ and same-gender loving community (NBJC, 2025). Our voting behavior alone indicates that we do not seek to use formal political power structures to discriminate. In fact, we have consistently voted for federal and state leaders who support marriage equality, healthcare access, and employment protections.

Discussing gender within the broader context of the Black freedom struggle does not create division—it brings clarity and precision, which are powerful tools in the fight against oppressive systems.

The State of Black Women

Since the 2010s, Black women have experienced an expansion of positive representations in the media. They have also seen historic opportunities in leadership and education. In 2020, Kamala Harris became the first Black woman elected to a high federal office as the nation's first woman, Black, South Asian Vice President. In 2022, Ketanji Brown-Jackson became the first Black woman to serve as an Associate Justice on the United States Supreme Court. In 2023, Dr. Claudine Gay became the first Black and first woman president of Harvard University, the nation's oldest college. The 2020s have also seen a marked increase in Black educational opportunity, with Black women and men attending college, more than doubling since the 1990s.

These high-profile social gains have been met with severe backlash in the form of attacks on Diversity, Equity, and Inclusion (DEI) initiatives. Black women have also been disproportionately harmed by the *Dobbs* v. *Jackson* Supreme Court Decision that ended *Roe* v. *Wade* and dramatically reduced abortion access for Black women. According to the Centers for Disease Control and Prevention (CDC), Black women are three times more likely to die during pregnancy or in the year after pregnancy than their white counterparts. Black girls are disproportionately policed in schools, expelled at a rate of six to one compared to their white female counterparts, and are subjected to harsh discipline and culturally biased school dress codes.

Here are FOUR issues that matter for Black women's social wellbeing.

Reproductive Justice

Reproductive Justice Framework

Reproductive Justice is a framework created by Black women activists in the 1990s. In our community, conversations about pro-life versus pro-choice politics simply do not capture the complicated decisions that shape how we create families. Reproductive Justice says that each person has the right:

- To have children.
- Not to have children.
- To parent the children they have in a safe and healthy environment.

Black women's access to reproductive justice has been severely restricted by the 2022 *Dobbs* v. *Jackson* decision, which outlawed the right to abortion at the federal level, returning the authority of regulating abortion back to individual states. After 49 years, the landmark 1973 Supreme Court case *Roe* v. *Wade*, which established a person's constitutional right to decide whether to end or continue a pregnancy, was overturned, marking the first time in history that the Supreme Court has taken away a fundamental right. Since the *Dobbs* decision, more than a dozen states have either completely banned abortion with no exceptions for rape, incest, and medical emergencies—or regulated abortion with minimal exceptions and allow, at minimum, terminations as early as 6 weeks—when women typically do not even know they are pregnant.

Nonetheless, abortion is a common and highly safe medical procedure that many Black birthing people access over the course of their lives. One of the key markers of enslavement for Black women was a lack of choice regarding reproduction. When we do not have control over our own bodies, it is a loss of freedom comparable to slavery.

The history of reproductive control extends far beyond recent legal battles. Throughout the 20th century, Black women experienced forced sterilization through state-sponsored eugenics programs (Roberts, 1997). Even today, Black women report experiencing pressure from medical providers to use long-acting contraceptives or undergo sterilization procedures at higher rates than white women (Dehlendorf et al., 2018). This historical and ongoing control of Black women's reproductive decisions represents a continuation of state violence against Black bodies.

HIV Prevention

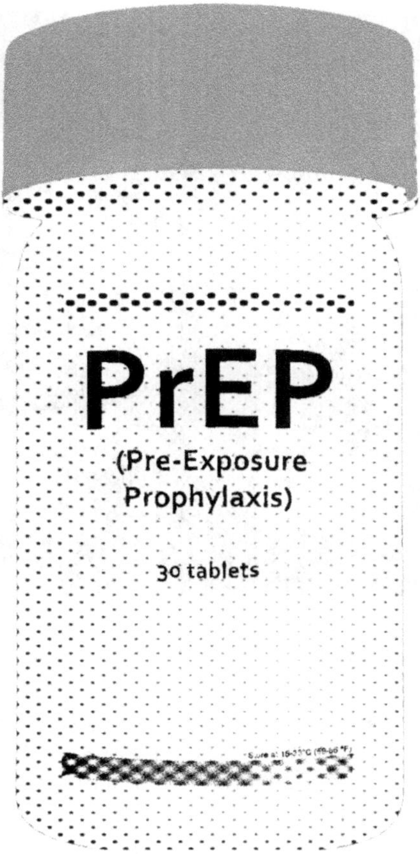

Black women represent 60% of all new HIV diagnoses among women. Today, HIV is no longer an automatically terminal disease. It can be managed with medication, and contracting it is preventable through access to "pre-exposure prophylaxis" (or PrEP) drugs. Yet, Black women's access to these medicines is low. Because of medical bias, many healthcare providers do not tell Black women about these options, their benefits and risks (Hull et al., 2021).

Research indicates that healthcare providers are less likely to discuss PrEP with Black women than with other demographic groups, even when risk factors are present (Calabrese et al., 2019). This disparity in care reflects broader patterns of medical racism and sexism that devalue Black women's health needs. Community-based interventions led by Black women have proven most effective in increasing awareness and access to HIV prevention tools (Auerbach et al., 2015).

Maternal Health

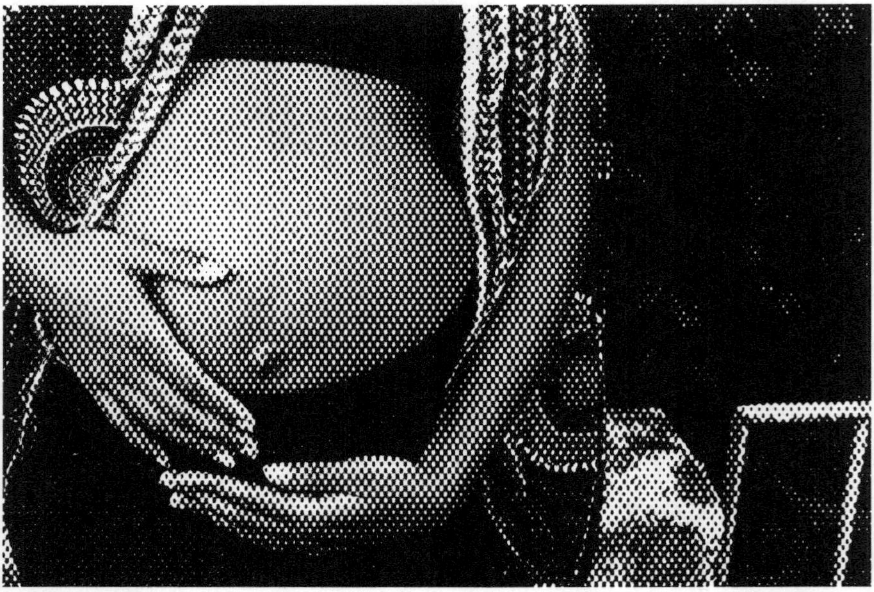

Black women are three times more likely to die during pregnancy or in the year after pregnancy than their white counterparts. Black maternal mortality, too, is a reproductive justice issue because a lack of access to quality healthcare and safe environments makes it dangerous for Black women to have children. Giving birth is more dangerous for Black women than being a police officer, a member of the United States military, or a construction worker (Bougher, 2024). Money alone cannot fix this problem. Middle-class Black women still have substantially worse birth outcomes than poor white women (Kennedy-Moulton et al., 2022).

The maternal health crisis facing Black women stems from multiple structural factors, including medical racism. Studies show that medical professionals are less likely to believe Black women's reports of pain or discomfort, leading to delayed or inadequate treatment (Hoffman et al., 2016). Additionally, chronic stress from experiencing racism throughout one's lifetime contributes to poorer health outcomes for pregnant Black women (Geronimus et al., 2010). The weathering hypothesis, developed by public health scholar Arline Geronimus, explains how racism-induced stress accelerates cellular aging and contributes to higher rates of pregnancy complications among Black women.

Community-based models such as doula and midwifery care have demonstrated significant improvements in birth outcomes for Black women. One study found that Black birthing people who received care from Black midwives experienced 50% fewer preterm births and C-sections compared to those receiving standard medical care (Hardeman et al., 2020). Despite these promising results, insurance coverage for these services remains limited, creating financial barriers for many Black families.

Intimate Partner Violence

Some 40% of Black women will experience intimate partner violence in their lifetime. The national average is 33% (Lindsey, 2022). Moreover, Black trans women experience exponentially higher rates of violence. In 2023, 50% of all transgender victims of murder in the country were Black women (Human

Rights Campaign, 2023). In the vast majority of cases, Black women (trans and cis) are being killed by Black cisgender men, whom they know.

This violence exists within a broader context of historical trauma and contemporary structural inequalities. During slavery, Black women's bodies were considered property, and violence against them was normalized. This historical legacy continues to impact how society views and responds to violence against Black women today. Police responses to domestic violence calls involving Black women are often inadequate or even harmful, with officers sometimes viewing Black women as "strong" enough to endure abuse or as the aggressors rather than victims (Richie, 2012).

Black women face additional barriers when seeking support for intimate partner violence. Fear of reinforcing negative stereotypes about Black men and concerns about subjecting Black men to a racist criminal justice system can prevent Black women from reporting abuse (Potter, 2008). Our community would benefit from learning to talk about and unlearn this guilt. Additionally, domestic violence shelters and services often lack cultural competency to address the specific needs of Black women, particularly those from low-income communities (Few, 2005).

Addressing intimate partner violence in Black communities requires community-based approaches that do not rely solely on punitive criminal justice responses. Transformative ethical models that hold abusers accountable while working toward healing and prevention have shown promise (Dixon & Kaba, 2020). These approaches recognize the complex intersections of race, gender, and economic marginalization that shape experiences of violence in Black communities.

Educational Equity and Economic Justice

Though Black women have gained extensive ground in obtaining higher education, it has also led to a generationally crushing load of debt. According to the Student Borrower Protection Center, "Black women have the highest average student loan balances." When Black women graduate, they make a lower median income than white women, white men, and Black men with the same degrees (Student Borrower Protection Center, 2022). High educational attainment does not ameliorate the race–gender wealth gap that shapes Black women's lives. Black women have 90% less wealth than white men (National Women's Law Center, 2022).

The economic challenges facing Black women extend beyond student debt and income disparities. Occupational segregation pushes Black women into lower-paying sectors with fewer benefits and protections. Black women are overrepresented in service industry jobs, domestic work, and care work—sectors that have historically been excluded from labor protections (Holder et al., 2021). Black women often face a perennial crisis of housing insecurity and, in many states, are evicted at twice the rate of their white counterparts (Higgins, 2020). During economic downturns, including the COVID-19 pandemic, Black women experienced higher rates of job loss and financial instability than other demographic groups (Gould & Wilson, 2020).

Workplace discrimination further compounds these economic challenges. Black women report higher rates of workplace harassment, discrimination in hiring and promotion, and hostile work environments (Frye, 2019). A 2021 study found that Black women were 3.8 times more likely than white women to report experiencing racial discrimination at work and 2.3 times more likely to have been passed over for promotion due to their race and gender (Lean In & McKinsey & Company, 2021).

Policy solutions must address both the educational debt crisis and structural workplace discrimination. Targeted student loan forgiveness, increased funding for HBCUs, workplace protections specific to addressing intersectional discrimination, access to quality and affordable housing, and universal child care would all help address the economic injustices facing Black women. Black girls deserve educational equity, too, and an end to the school-to-prison pipeline policies that lead to the over-policing and "pushout" of Black girls in schools (Couvson, 2015).

The State of Black Men

While the challenges facing Black women have received increased attention in recent years, Black men continue to face unique obstacles created by the intersections of racism, economic marginalization, and harmful gender expectations. Understanding these challenges is essential for creating comprehensive approaches to gender equity in Black communities.

Criminalization and Mass Incarceration

Black men are disproportionately targeted by the criminal justice system at every stage, from policing to sentencing to parole. One in 3 Black men born in 2001 can expect to be incarcerated in their lifetime, compared to one in 17 white men (The Sentencing Project, 2021). This mass criminalization has devastating effects on Black men, their families, and communities.

The school-to-prison pipeline begins early, with Black boys being three times more likely to be suspended or expelled than white boys for the same behaviors (U.S. Department of Education, 2019). Once in the criminal justice system, Black men receive sentences that are 19.1% longer than those of white men convicted of the same crimes (U.S. Sentencing Commission, 2017).

Beyond incarceration itself, having a criminal record creates nearly insurmountable barriers to employment, housing, education, and civic participation. The collateral consequences of involvement with the criminal justice system follow Black men for decades, limiting their economic opportunities and constraining their full participation in society.

Economic Marginalization

Historical and contemporary discrimination in employment, housing, and lending has created significant economic barriers for Black men. The unemployment rate for Black men has consistently been approximately twice that of white men, even when comparing individuals with similar educational backgrounds (Bureau of Labor Statistics, 2023).

Black men earn approximately 71 cents for every dollar earned by white men, and this wage divide persists across education levels (Economic Policy Institute, 2022). Even Black men with college degrees earn less than white men with the same credentials. This economic marginalization is compounded by occupational segregation that concentrates Black men in industries more vulnerable to economic downturns and automation.

Asset building is also more difficult for Black men due to discrimination in banking and lending. Studies show that Black men are more likely to be denied loans or offered higher interest rates than white men with similar financial profiles (Bhutta et al., 2021). These disparities in lending contribute to the racial wealth gap, with Black families holding only about 13% of the wealth of white families (Federal Reserve, 2023).

Health Disparities and Healthcare Discrimination

Black men face significant health disparities compared to other demographic groups. Life expectancy for Black men is 4.5 years shorter than for white men (CDC, 2022). Black men have higher rates of heart disease, diabetes, and prostate cancer, and are more likely to die from these conditions than white men (Office of Minority Health, 2022).

These health disparities stem from multiple factors, including limited access to quality healthcare, discrimination within medical settings, and the physical toll of experiencing racism throughout one's lifetime. Research shows that medical providers are less likely to prescribe pain medication to Black patients and are more likely to underestimate their pain levels (Hoffman et al., 2016). Many Black men report avoiding seeking medical care due to prior negative experiences with healthcare providers or fears of being disrespected (Hammond et al., 2010).

The psychological impact of navigating racism and meeting restrictive masculine expectations also contributes to health disparities. Black men experience higher rates of stress-related health conditions but are less likely to receive appropriate mental health support (Watkins & Jefferson, 2013). The stigma around mental health in many communities, combined with limited culturally competent mental health services, creates additional barriers to wellness for Black men.

Constraints of Harmful Masculine Stereotypes

Black men navigate a complex web of harmful stereotypes that constrain their full humanity. Media representations often portray Black men as threatening, hypersexual, or emotionally limited, reinforcing racist tropes that date back to slavery and Jim Crow (Jackson, 2006). These stereotypes influence how Black men are perceived in educational settings, workplaces, and public spaces, contributing to discrimination and social isolation.

The pressure to perform a narrow version of masculinity—one that emphasizes toughness, emotional stoicism, and financial success—can take a significant psychological toll. Black men who do not conform to traditional masculine expectations may face rejection from peers and family members. Simultaneously, attempting to meet these expectations in the face of structural racism and economic marginalization creates significant stress.

Research shows that adhering to restrictive masculine norms is associated with higher rates of depression, substance abuse, and risk-taking behaviors among Black men (Hammond et al., 2010). However, Black men who can develop more flexible gender identities and coping strategies show greater psychological resilience and life satisfaction (Griffith et al., 2012).

The State of Black LGBTQ+/SGL Communities

Black LGBTQ+/SGL communities face unique challenges at the intersections of racism, homophobia, transphobia, and economic marginalization. Addressing these challenges is essential for comprehensive gender justice within Black communities.

Violence and Safety Concerns

Black LGBTQ+/SGL people, particularly Black transgender women, face disproportionate rates of violence. Between 2013 and 2022, over 200 transgender people were murdered in the United States, with Black transgender women making up the majority of victims (Human Rights Campaign, 2023). This violence occurs within a broader context of racism, transphobia, and economic marginalization that limits safety and access to resources.

Police violence and harassment present additional safety concerns for Black LGBTQ+/SGL communities. Studies show that Black LGBTQ+/SGL people are more likely to experience police profiling, harassment, and excessive force compared to their white counterparts (National Center for Transgender Equality, 2016). These negative interactions with law enforcement make many Black LGBTQ+/SGL people reluctant to report crimes or seek assistance when they experience violence.

Community-based safety initiatives led by Black LGBTQ+/SGL people have emerged in response to these challenges. Organizations like the Marsha P. Johnson Institute and the Solutions Not Punishment Collaborative (SNaPCo) work to address violence against Black transgender women through community education, economic empowerment programs, and alternatives to police intervention (Bailey, 2020).

NBJC's Stolen Lives Initiative mourns the Black trans siblings lost due to violence. While covering the circumstances of their death, these statements also aim to remember who they were in life, sharing their jobs, ambitions, plans, and interests. It is essential to ensure trans people are more than just statistics in the ongoing epidemic of violence and are given their full humanity in both life and death.

Healthcare Access and Disparities

Black LGBTQ+/SGL people face significant barriers to accessing affirming healthcare. These barriers include discrimination from healthcare providers, lack of insurance coverage, and limited availability of culturally competent care. Black transgender and gender-expansive people report particularly high rates of mistreatment in healthcare settings, including being refused care, experiencing verbal harassment, or having to educate providers about their healthcare needs (James et al., 2016).

HIV continues to impact Black same-gender loving, gay, and bisexual men disproportionately. Despite representing less than 1% of the United States population, Black gay and bisexual men account for more than 26% of new HIV diagnoses (CDC, 2021). Structural factors—including limited access to PrEP, inadequate sexual health education, and stigma—contribute to these disparities.

Mental health is another significant concern for Black LGBTQ+/SGL communities. Navigating multiple marginalized identities can create significant minority stress, leading to higher rates of depression, anxiety, and suicidal ideation (Everett et al., 2021). Despite these needs, culturally competent mental health services remain limited in many areas.

Economic Security and Housing Stability

Economic discrimination affects Black LGBTQ+/SGL communities through multiple channels. Workplace discrimination, family rejection, and educational barriers can limit economic opportunities and contribute to higher rates of poverty and housing instability. One study found that 38% of Black transgender respondents reported living in poverty, compared to 24% of the general Black population (James et al., 2016).

Housing discrimination particularly impacts Black transgender and gender non-conforming people, who report high rates of homelessness and housing instability. When seeking shelter services, many face discrimination and harassment that make these spaces unsafe or inaccessible (James et al., 2016).

The lack of comprehensive non-discrimination protections in many states leaves Black LGBTQ+/SGL people vulnerable to being fired from jobs, denied housing, or refused service based on their sexual orientation or gender identity. This legal vulnerability compounds existing racial discrimination and creates significant barriers to economic security.

Community Resilience and Cultural Leadership

Despite these challenges, Black LGBTQ+/SGL communities have demonstrated remarkable resilience and leadership. Throughout history, Black LGBTQ+/SGL activists like Bayard Rustin, Marsha P. Johnson, and Audre Lorde have significantly contributed to civil rights, LGBTQ+ liberation, and feminist movements (Moore, 2018). Today, Black LGBTQ+/SGL organizers continue to lead intersectional justice movements addressing racism, homophobia, transphobia, and economic inequality.

Black queer and transgender cultural production—including literature, film, music, and visual art—has created spaces for authentic representation and community building. Artists and creators like Janelle Monáe, Lil Nas X, Janet Mock, and T.S. Madison have increased visibility for Black LGBTQ+ experiences while challenging restrictive gender norms (Bailey, 2019).

Black-led LGBTQ+/SGL organizations provide essential services and community support across the country. Groups like the Audre Lorde Project, THRIVE SS, Brave Space Alliance, the National Black Justice Collective, and the Black AIDS Institute offer healthcare resources, economic empowerment programs, and community-building opportunities specifically designed to address the needs of Black LGBTQ+/SGL communities (Bailey & Odumosu, 2020).

Building Gender Justice in Black Communities: A Path Forward

Creating gender justice within Black communities requires addressing the complex intersections of racism, sexism, homophobia, transphobia, and economic marginalization. The following recommendations offer concrete steps for community organizations, policymakers, and individuals committed to this work.

Center Black Feminist Leadership and Frameworks

Black feminist thought provides essential frameworks for understanding and addressing intersecting oppressions. Organizations and movements should:

- Prioritize leadership from Black women, particularly those most marginalized by class, sexuality, gender identity, and ability.
- Apply intersectional analysis to policy development and program design.
- Support Black feminist scholarship and incorporate these insights into community organizing strategies.
- Fund Black women-led organizations doing gender justice work.

The work of scholars and activists like Patricia Hill Collins, Angela Davis, bell hooks, and Kimberlé Crenshaw offers vital guidance for building movements that address multiple forms of oppression simultaneously (Collins, 2000). By centering these frameworks, we can develop more comprehensive approaches to gender justice.

Address Economic Inequities Through Structural Change

Economic justice is inseparable from gender justice for Black communities. Recommendations include:

- Support student loan forgiveness policies that would particularly benefit Black women, who hold the highest average student debt.
- Advocate for living wage policies and stronger workplace protections in industries where Black women and LGBTQ+/SGL people are concentrated.
- Invest in Black-owned businesses, particularly those led by Black women and LGBTQ+/SGL people.
- Expand access to affordable, quality child care to support working parents.
- Implement fair housing policies that address discrimination based on race, gender identity, and sexual orientation.

Research shows that economic policies targeting the intersections of race and gender have the potential to reduce poverty and increase opportunity in Black communities significantly (Holder et al., 2021). Universal basic income, baby bonds, and targeted loan forgiveness represent promising approaches to addressing the wealth gap faced by Black communities across gender lines.

Transform Health Systems to Eliminate Disparities

Addressing health disparities requires expanding access to care and transforming healthcare delivery. Recommendations include:

- Expand Medicaid in all states to increase healthcare access for low-income Black communities.
- Invest in community-based healthcare models like Black-led doula programs, which have demonstrated success in improving maternal health outcomes.
- Require anti-racism and gender-affirming care training for all healthcare providers.
- Increase funding for HIV prevention and treatment programs that specifically address the needs of Black women and gay/bisexual men.
- Expand insurance coverage for gender-affirming care for transgender and gender-expansive people.
- Support Black-led mental health initiatives that address trauma from racism, sexism, and anti-LGBTQ+/SGL bias.

Community-controlled health initiatives have shown promise in reducing disparities and building trust between Black communities and healthcare systems (Bailey & Krueger, 2018). By combining policy advocacy with community-based approaches, we can create healthcare systems that truly serve all Black people.

Confront Gender-Based Violence Through Community-Based Solutions

Addressing violence requires approaches that center survivors' needs while recognizing the complex impacts of criminalization on Black communities. Recommendations include:

- Fund Black-led organizations providing culturally specific services for survivors of intimate partner violence.
- Support transformative justice approaches that hold harm-doers accountable without relying on incarceration.
- Develop violence prevention programs that address harmful gender norms and promote healthy relationships.
- Create emergency housing options that are accessible and affirming for all genders and sexualities.
- Expand economic resources for survivors to reduce financial barriers to leaving abusive situations.

Research shows that community-based approaches to violence prevention and intervention are more effective than punitive criminal justice responses, particularly in communities that have experienced over-policing and mass incarceration (John Jay Advisory Group, 2020). By investing in these alternatives, we can address violence while avoiding the harms of the criminal legal system.

Foster Intergenerational Dialogue and Healing

Creating gender justice requires addressing historical traumas while building new visions for the future. Recommendations include:

- Create spaces for dialogue across generations about gender, sexuality, and Black liberation.
- Support youth leadership development programs that center gender justice.
- Document and preserve the wisdom of elder Black feminist and LGBTQ+/SGL activists.
- Develop healing justice practices that address intergenerational trauma related to gender and racial violence.
- Support Black families in having healthy conversations about gender and sexuality.

Intergenerational approaches recognize that gender justice work must both honor historical struggles and adapt to contemporary challenges. By bridging these perspectives, we can build more resilient movements for change.

Call to Action

Gender equality is not peripheral to Black liberation—it is essential. When we address the specific ways that racism, sexism, homophobia, transphobia, and economic exploitation impact different members of our communities, we build more effective strategies for collective freedom. As Audre Lorde (1984) reminds us, "I am not free while any woman is unfree, even when her shackles are very different from my own."

We call on:

- **Community organizations** to center gender justice in their work by applying intersectional frameworks, addressing gender-based violence, and creating affirming spaces for all gender identities and sexualities.
- **Policymakers** to implement comprehensive approaches to economic, health, and criminal justice reform that address the specific needs of Black women, men, and LGBTQ+/SGL people.

- **Religious institutions** should engage in theological reflection and community dialogue about gender equity and support affirming approaches to all community members.
- **Educational institutions** should teach intersectional frameworks and eliminate disciplinary practices that disproportionately impact Black students across gender lines.
- **Individuals** should examine their own gender biases, support Black-led gender equity organizations, practice gender equity in their relationships, and support policymakers who work towards these goals.

By taking up this work together—with clarity, specificity, and courage—we strengthen rather than divide our communities. Gender justice is Black justice.

References

Auerbach, J. D., Kinsky, S., Brown, G., & Charles, V. (2015). Knowledge, attitudes, and likelihood of pre-exposure prophylaxis (PrEP) use among US Women at risk of acquiring HIV. *AIDS Patient Care and STDs, 29*(2), 102–110.

Bailey, M. (2019). Black queer cultural production: A state of the field. *The Oxford Handbook of Queer of Color Critique*.173–189, Oxford University Press.

Bailey, M. (2020). *Misogynoir transformed: Black women's digital resistance*. New York University Press.

Bailey, M., & Krueger, P. (2018). Structural racism, anti-blackness, and health disparities: Exploring the associations. *Journal of Health Politics, Policy and Law, 43*(6), 915–942.

Bailey, M., & Odumosu, T. (2020). How digital activism can transform black queer lives. *Signs: Journal of Women in Culture and Society, 45*(4), 903–930.

Bhutta, N., Chang, A. C., Dettling, L. J., & Hsu, J. W. (2021). Disparities in wealth by race and ethnicity in the 2019 survey of consumer finances. *FEDS Notes*. Washington: Board of Governors of the Federal Reserve System.

Bougher, H. (2024). *Being pregnant in America is growing more dangerous. Shouldn't it be voluntary?* Indiana Capital Chronicle. https://indianacapitalchronicle.com/2024/01/31/being-pregnant-in-america-is-growing-more-dangerous-shouldnt-it-be-voluntary/

Bureau of Labor Statistics. (2023). *Labor force characteristics by race and ethnicity, 2022*. U.S. Department of Labor.

Calabrese, S. K., Willie, T. C., Galvao, R. W., Tekeste, M., Dovidio, J. F., Safon, C. B., ... Kershaw, T. S. (2019). Current US guidelines for prescribing HIV pre-exposure prophylaxis (PrEP) disqualify many women who are at risk and motivated to use PrEP. *Journal of Acquired Immune Deficiency Syndromes, 81*(4), 395.

Centers for Disease Control and Prevention (CDC). (2021). *HIV and African American gay and bisexual men*. U.S. Department of Health and Human Services.

Centers for Disease Control and Prevention (CDC). (2022). *Life expectancy at birth, by race and sex: United States*. National Center for Health Statistics.

Collins, P. H. (2000). *Black feminist thought: Knowledge, consciousness, and the politics of empowerment*. Routledge.

Couvson, Monique (2015). *Pushout: The criminalization of black girls in schools*. The New Press.
Crenshaw, K. (1989). Demarginalizing the intersection of race and sex: A Black feminist critique of Antidiscrimination doctrine, feminist theory and antiracist politics. *University of Chicago Legal Forum, 1989*(1), 139–167.
Dehlendorf, C., Park, S. Y., Emeremni, C. A., Comer, D., Vincett, K., & Borrero, S. (2018). Racial/ethnic disparities in contraceptive use: Variation by age and women's reproductive experiences. *American Journal of Obstetrics and Gynecology, 214*(4), 526–e1.
Dixon, E., & Kaba, M. (Eds.). (2020). *Beyond survival: Strategies and stories from the transformative justice movement*. AK Press.
Economic Policy Institute. (2022). *State of working America: Wages 2021*. https://www.epi.org/publication/swa-wages-2021/
Everett, B. G., Steele, S. M., Matthews, A. K., & Hughes, T. L. (2021). Intersectionality, minority stress, and mental health among gay, lesbian, and bisexual people of color. *Cultural Diversity and Ethnic Minority Psychology, 27(3)*, 353–361.
Federal Reserve. (2023). *Disparities in wealth by race and ethnicity in the 2019 survey of consumer finances*. Board of Governors of the Federal Reserve System.
Few, A. L. (2005). The voices of Black and white rural battered women in domestic violence shelters. *Family Relations, 54(4)*, 488–500.
Frye, J. (2019). *Racism and sexism combine to shortchange working black women*. Center for American Progress.
Geronimus, A. T., Hicken, M. T., Pearson, J. A., Seashols, S. J., Brown, K. L., & Cruz, T. D. (2010). Do US Black women experience stress-related accelerated biological aging? *Human Nature, 21(1)*, 19–38.
Gould, E., & Wilson, V. (2020). *Black workers face two of the most lethal preexisting conditions for coronavirus—Racism and economic inequality*. Economic Policy Institute.
Griffith, D. M., Gunter, K., & Watkins, D. C. (2012). Measuring masculinity in research on men of color: Findings and future directions. *American Journal of Public Health, 102*(S2), S187–S194.
Hammond, W. P., Matthews, D., Mohottige, D., Agyemang, A., & Corbie-Smith, G. (2010). Masculinity, medical mistrust, and preventive health services delays among community-dwelling African-American men. *Journal of General Internal Medicine, 25*(12), 1300–1308.
Hardeman, R. R., Karbeah, J., Kozhimannil, K. B. (2020). Applying a critical race lens to relationship-centered care in pregnancy and childbirth: An antidote to structural racism. *Birth, 47*, 3–7. https://doi.org/10.1111/birt.12462
Higgins, A. (2020). An eviction crisis is coming, experts warn. Black women will bear the brunt. *The Washington Post*. https://www.washingtonpost.com/gender-identity/an-eviction-apocalypse-is-coming-experts-warn-black-women-will-bear-the-brunt/
Hoffman, K. M., Trawalter, S., Axt, J. R., & Oliver, M. N. (2016). Racial bias in pain assessment and treatment recommendations, and false beliefs about biological differences between Blacks and whites. *Proceedings of the National Academy of Sciences, 113(16)*, 4296–4301.
Holder, A. B., Jones, J., & Masterson, T. (2021). The early impact of COVID-19 on job losses among Black women in the United States. *Feminist Economics, 27(1–2)*, 103–116.

Hull, S., Kelley, S., Clarke, J. L., Estrace, C., Aronowitz, A., Perkins, A., Leader, A., & Linton, S. (2021). Providers PrEP: Identifying primary health care providers' biases as barriers to provision of equitable PrEP services. *Journal of Acquired Immune Deficiency Syndromes (JAIDS), 86(1)*, 9–17.

Human Rights Campaign. (2023). *Fatal violence against the transgender and gender-expansive community in 2023*. https://www.hrc.org/resources/fatal-violence-against-the-transgender-and-gender-expansive-community-in-2023

Jackson, R. L., II. (2006). *Scripting the Black masculine body: Identity, discourse, and racial politics in popular media*. SUNY Press.

James, S. E., Herman, J. L., Rankin, S., Keisling, M., Mottet, L., & Anafi, M. (2016). The report of the 2015 U.S. Transgender Survey. National Center for Transgender Equality. https://www.icpsr.umich.edu/web/RCMD/studies/37229/versions/V1

John Jay College Research Advisory Group on Preventing and Reducing Community Violence. (2020). *Reducing violence without police: A review of research evidence*. Research Advisory Group on Preventing and Reducing Community Violence, John Jay College of Criminal Justice. https://johnjayrec.nyc/2020/11/09/av2020/

Kennedy-Moulton, K., Miller, S., Persson, P., Rossin-Slater, M., Wherry, L. R., & Aldana, G. (2022). Maternal and infant health inequality: New evidence from linked administrative data (Working Paper No. 30693). National Bureau of Economic Research. https://www.nber.org/papers/w30693

Lean In, & McKinsey & Company. (2021). *Women in the Workplace 2021*. https://rockthestreetwallstreet.com/inspiring-change-highlighting-mckinsey-leanin-orgs-decade-of-data-on-womens-workplace-representation/?gclid=CjwKCAjwl97RBhBWEiwAa9rbXQ2_Lig_hVk7wN8DOAuha0gCHkAaplSaQ91-LtGz2xtR2pjN17COthoCQ2gQAvD_BwE

Lindsey, Treva. (2022). *America Goddam: Violence, Black women, and the struggle for justice*. University of California.

Lorde, Audre. (1984). *Sister outsider: Essays and speeches*. Crossing Press.

Moore, Darnell. (2018). *No ashes in the fire: Coming of age: Black and free in America*. Bold Type Books.

National Black Justice Coalition. (2025). *Black Facts Research Study*. https://nbjc.org/blackfacts

National Center for Transgender Equality. (2016). *2015 U.S. Transgender Survey: Black respondents report*. https://transequality.org/sites/default/files/docs/usts/USTS-Black-Respondents-Report.pdf

National Women's Law Center. (2022). (*2022*). *Advancing gender and racial equity by taxing wealth*. https://nwlc.org/resource/advancing-gender-and-racial-equity-by-taxing-wealth/

Office of Minority Health. (2022). *Black/African American health*. U.S. Department of Health and Human Services. https://minorityhealth.hhs.gov/blackafrican-american-health

Potter, Hillary. (2008) *Battle cries: Black women and intimate partner abuse*. New York University Press.

Richie, Beth. (2012). *Arrested justice: Black women, violence, and America's Prison Nation*. New York University Press.

Roberts, Dorothy. (1997). *Killing the black body: Race, reproduction, and the meaning of liberty*. Pantheon.

Student Borrower Protection Center. (2022). *Title of report or policy brief.* https://protectborrowers.org

The Sentencing Project. (2021). *Trends in U.S. corrections*. https://www.sentencingproject.org/reports/mass-incarceration-trends/

U.S. Department of Education. (2019). Civil Rights Data Collection (CRDC) data snapshot: School discipline.

U.S. Sentencing Commission. (2017). *2017 demographic differences in federal sentencing*. https://www.ussc.gov/research/research-reports/2017-demographic-differences-federal-sentencing

Watkins, D. C., & Jefferson, S. O. (2013). Recommendations for the use of online social support for African American men. *Psychological Services, 10*(3), 323–332. https://pmc.ncbi.nlm.nih.gov/articles/PMC3950888/

Chapter 14

Disability Justice and Equity in the Black Community

An Intersectional Approach

David J. Johns, Andraéa LaVant, Dara Baldwin, Vilissa Thompson, André White, and Nieta M. Greene

Executive Summary

This Black Paper (Paper) examines the state of disability justice and equity in the Black community in the United States, highlighting key data, policy changes, and the intersectional nature of race and disability. Black Americans with disabilities face compounded marginalization through the overlapping systems of racism and ableism, creating unique challenges that require targeted solutions. This Paper analyzes prevalence data, educational outcomes, and policy impacts and presents an intersectional framework for understanding disability justice in the Black community. It concludes with actionable recommendations and a call to center Black disabled voices in advocacy efforts.

Note on terminology: Throughout this Paper, we use "special/accessible education" rather than "special education" to reflect the disability community's evolving language preferences. This shift emphasizes that education for disabled students should focus on accessibility and inclusion rather than segregation or othering. While "special education" remains the commonly used legal and institutional term, "accessible education" better aligns with disability justice principles.

Introduction

Disability is a natural part of human diversity that affects all communities, but its impacts are not experienced equally. For Black Americans, disability intersects with race in ways that compound marginalization, creating unique barriers to healthcare, education, employment, and social inclusion. Disability rights, like all rights movements, are based on centering the white body and experience. The Disability Rights Movement often ignores how ableism and structural racism intersect. Ableism is discrimination in favor of the non-disabled and prejudice against people with disabilities. It assigns value to bodies and minds based on what constitutes normalcy, productivity, fitness, etc. It is also deeply rooted in anti-Blackness, eugenics, and capitalism, among other

DOI: 10.4324/9781003752646-20

factors. The willful disregard has left many Black Americans with disabilities underserved by both disability rights and racial justice movements.

This Paper examines the current state of disability justice and equity in the Black community through an intersectional lens—a framework that acknowledges how multiple forms of discrimination overlap and interact. Kimberlé Crenshaw, a legal scholar, popularized the term "intersectionality" in her 1989 paper "Demarginalizing the Intersection of Race and Sex," while sociologist Patricia Hill Collins developed the concept with her framework of the "matrix of domination" in her 1990 book *Black Feminist Thought*. Together, their work has been instrumental in understanding how different aspects of identity interact to create unique experiences of oppression.

Crenshaw's work specifically examined how the legal system failed to recognize the unique discrimination faced by Black women, treating race and gender as separate categories. Meanwhile, Collins enriched our understanding by exploring how various systems of oppression are interlinked and organized within a matrix of domination. This theoretical foundation is essential for understanding the experiences of Black people with disabilities, who face the combined effects of racism and ableism, along with potentially other forms of marginalization.

As scholars in this field have noted, both Crenshaw and Collins built upon a longer history of Black feminist thought and activism. Their work provides vital tools for analyzing how disability, race, gender, class, and other aspects of identity combine to shape the experiences of Black Americans with disabilities and the unique barriers they face.

The reporting and discussion of people with disabilities is consistently a review of those living in the community. What many do not understand or recognize is the premise of the laws that protect the millions of disabled people in this country. The prominent laws—the Americans with Disabilities Act of 1990 (ADA), the Individuals with Disabilities Education Act of 1975 (IDEA), and the Rehabilitation Act of 1973—are meant to protect people with disabilities. The data used to develop and inform the implementation of programs provided for in these bills excludes people with disabilities who live in institutions. Black disabled bodies are institutionalized at higher rates and are rarely discussed—and often ignored—in the broader Disability Rights Movement.

This Paper aims to provide a comprehensive overview of the prevalence of disability in the Black community, analyze key policy changes affecting Black disabled Americans, examine educational outcomes for Black students with disabilities, assess the impact of the current administration's policies, and highlight promising practices and resources for advancing disability justice for Black Americans. By centering the experiences and leadership of Black disabled people, this Paper aims to contribute to a more equitable and inclusive future.

Prevalence of Disability in the Black Community

Overall Prevalence and Trends

Systemic disparities impact health outcomes and baseline disability rates. Approximately 13.7% of working-age Black people reported living with at least one functional disability, representing a higher statistical prevalence than the 11.2% documented among white people and 11.3% of Hispanic or Latino people. (Disability Statistic User Guide, 2024). This disparity reflects long-standing inequities in healthcare access, environmental hazards, economic opportunities, and other social determinants of health.

Black Americans not only have higher overall disability rates but also show elevated prevalence across specific disability types. In particular, Black Americans report the highest prevalence of any disability and each disability type measured in national surveys (Centers for Disease Control and Prevention [CDC], 2015). These disparities point to deeper systemic issues that combine racism and ableism in ways that disproportionately affect Black Americans.

Types of Disabilities

The disability community is diverse in range, complexity, and nuance. Disabilities can be apparent (visible), non-apparent (invisible), and include chronic illness. Disability can be acquired by birth, accident, illness, or age. Among Black Americans, higher rates of disability due to chronic conditions are particularly notable. Black adults aged 40 and up experience significantly higher rates of disability due to arthritis, diabetes, and hypertension than non-Hispanic white adults. For example, disability-related hypertension is about three times as common among non-Hispanic Black adults (3.5%) compared to non-Hispanic white adults (1.2%). According to the National Institute of Health's Lung and Blood Institute (NHLBI), Black people also have the highest rates of asthma of any United States racial or ethnic group and are 42% more likely to have asthma than white people.

In a national health study, a significantly higher percentage of non-Hispanic African Americans (14.8%) than non-Hispanic whites (10.2%) had severe disability, with Latino Americans at 8.1%. These statistics highlight how systemic health inequities contribute to disability disparities.

Intersectionality and Black Parents with Disabilities

Among parents with disabilities in the United States, approximately 15.5% are non-Hispanic Black, according to American Community Survey data from 2016 to 2020. Black parents with disabilities face unique challenges at the intersection of racism, ableism, and often economic disadvantage.

According to the National Research Center for Parents with Disabilities, "Disability Data Dashboard," Black disabled parents comprise 9.2% of the population. The percentage of Black parents with disabilities who live below the poverty line is 16.3%.

These statistics paint a clear picture: disability is a significant aspect of the Black experience in America, and understanding these prevalence patterns is crucial for developing effective policies and support systems.

Policy Changes Impacting Black Americans with Disabilities

Historical Policy Context

The Disability Rights Movement in the United States achieved significant legal victories with the Rehabilitation Act of 1973 and the Americans with Disabilities Act (ADA) of 1990. However, these landmark policies were not designed with the specific needs of Black disabled Americans in mind. The Civil Rights Movement was the framework and foundation for the Disability Rights Movement. Still, the concentration on white leadership (and proximity) led movement leaders to develop separately despite their overlapping constituencies and similar goals of equality and inclusion. In the Disability Rights Movement, there was little to no intersectional work done, which created either a void in or harmful policy outcomes for Black Americans with disabilities.

When reflecting on the intersection of disability rights and civil rights movements, a compelling image from the 1990s comes to mind: a disability rights activist at a rally with a sign attached to his wheelchair reading, "I can't even get to the back of the bus." This captures how the Disability Rights Movement built on the civil rights model and operated in tension with it. This tension continues to shape policy today.

Key Policy Developments

Several policy developments have significantly impacted Black Americans with disabilities:

1 **Individuals with Disabilities Education Act (IDEA)**: While IDEA guarantees a free, appropriate public education to all students with disabilities, implementation has been uneven, with Black students often facing disproportionate identification for specific disability categories and more restrictive placements.
2 **Affordable Care Act (ACA)**: The ACA, also known as "Obamacare," expanded healthcare access for many Americans with disabilities, including Black Americans who previously faced significant barriers to coverage. Attempts to repeal or weaken the ACA have threatened these gains.
3 **Medicaid Expansion**: States that expanded Medicaid under the ACA provided critical support for Black Americans with disabilities, who are more likely to rely on Medicaid for healthcare and long-term services and support.
4 **Employment Policies**: Despite protective legislation, employment discrimination against people with disabilities persists, with Black disabled workers facing compounded barriers to economic opportunity.
5 **Transition Policy**: States are mandated to set aside 15% of their Vocational Rehabilitation funding for the transition of youth with disabilities. Providing pathways to keep them in the community, but Black disabled youth have been left out of these services.
6 **Financial Security**: Federal law, known as the Achieving a Better Life Experience (ABLE) Act of 2014, allows people with disabilities to open tax-free savings accounts and ease some of their financial strains, allowing these funds to cover disability-related expenses. Most of the public outreach and education for such programs ignore the Black disabled community, and therefore, many of these accounts are not used by the community.

Recent Policy Shifts

Recent policy changes have had mixed impacts on Black Americans with disabilities.

Under the 47th presidential administration, policies targeting federal programs that many Black Americans with disabilities rely on have created new barriers. In January 2025, the administration called for terminating "all discriminatory programs," including Diversity, Equity, Inclusion (DEI), and accessibility policies and programs. This approach threatens to undo decades of progress (American Civil Liberties Union, 2025).

Rollbacks to programs supporting people with disabilities extend beyond new policies, including direct actions at specific agencies. For example, the firing of two Democratic commissioners from the Equal Employment Opportunity Commission (EEOC) left the commission without a quorum, preventing it from approving certain cases or issuing new guidance, when disability claims filed with the EEOC increased by 9% from 2023 to 2024.

Changes to Social Security verification procedures have created new challenges, particularly for older Americans and those with disabilities. As Kathleen Romig, Director of Social Security and Disability Policy at the Center on Budget and Policy Priorities, explains, "It's going to impact anyone who struggles with the online verification system that SSA[1] has … which often does include older people and people with disabilities."

In a process to restructure the Department of Health and Human Services (DHHS), its current secretary dismantled the Administration on Community Living (ACL), which was created through the Workforce Innovation and Opportunity Act of 2014 (WIOA). It was a section of the department with the task of reviewing programs, organizations, and the implementation of services for people with disabilities and older adults. The number of ACL staff being fired is unknown, and this work is supposed to be given to other areas within DHHS. It is not yet known how many people with disabilities will be harmed. Still, as historical data has shown with disruptions of services to people with disabilities, those who are Black in this community will always be harmed at a higher rate.

The Erosion of Disability Data: Impact on Black Americans with Disabilities

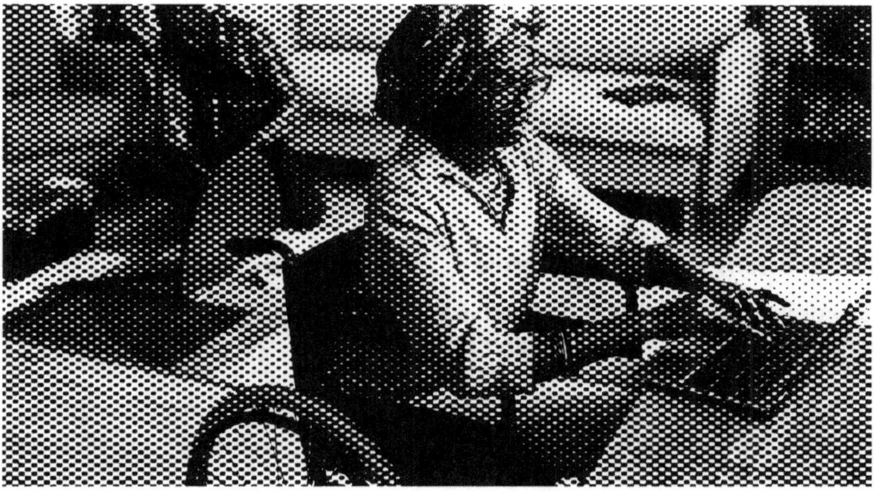

Historical Context of Disability Data Collection

The journey toward comprehensive disability data collection has been arduous and fragmented. Following the Rehabilitation Act of 1973, initial efforts to gather disability data were limited in scope and rarely disaggregated by race, gender, or other demographic factors. Only after decades of advocacy did federal agencies begin capturing more inclusive disability statistics reflecting intersectional experiences.

The Americans with Disabilities Act (ADA) of 1990 created momentum for improved data collection. Still, meaningful progress was not made until the early 2000s in gathering disability data that could be analyzed by race. The establishment of the Administration for Community Living (ACL) in 2012 represented a significant advancement, centralizing disability research and data collection across the lifespan.

Current Dismantling of Data Infrastructure

Recent administrative actions have severely undermined this progress. The dismantling of the ACL represents more than an organizational restructuring—it threatens the infrastructure necessary for understanding the specific experiences of Black Americans with disabilities.

Resources have also been stripped from the Office of Disability Employment Policy (ODEP) and the Bureau of Labor Statistics (BLS). These agencies have been instrumental in tracking employment outcomes for people with disabilities by race and ethnicity. These cuts have resulted in:

- Elimination of specialized research initiatives focused on intersectional disability experiences.
- Reduced sample sizes in national surveys, making racial and ethnic subgroup analysis statistically unreliable.
- Discontinuation of longitudinal studies tracking outcomes for Black Americans with disabilities over time.
- Fewer resources for community-based participatory research led by Black disabled researchers.

Implications for Black Americans with Disabilities

The destruction of disability data infrastructure has particularly severe implications for Black Americans with disabilities:

1 **Invisibility in Policy Development**: Without disaggregated data, the specific needs of Black disabled Americans remain invisible in policy development. As the saying goes in advocacy circles, "If you're not counted, you don't count."

2 **Funding Disparities**: Evidence-based funding decisions depend on reliable data. The erosion of intersectional disability data makes it nearly impossible to demonstrate disparities in program access and outcomes, perpetuating inequitable resource allocation.
3 **Barrier to Legal Remedies**: Civil rights enforcement often relies on statistical evidence of disparate impact. Without robust data collection, proving systemic discrimination against Black Americans with disabilities becomes significantly more challenging.
4 **Missed Opportunities for Targeted Interventions**: Effective interventions require understanding specific needs. The loss of intersectional data hampers the development of culturally responsive approaches for Black disabled communities.
5 **Challenges to Community Organizing**: Data has historically been a powerful tool for community organizing and self-advocacy. Its absence undermines efforts to build coalitions and create change.

Resistance and Alternative Data Sources

Despite these systematic challenges, Black disability communities are developing alternative approaches to data collection and knowledge creation:

- Community-based participatory research projects led by Black disabled researchers.
- Qualitative story-collecting initiatives that document lived experiences.
- Collaborative data-sharing networks between disability organizations and racial justice groups.
- Independent research initiatives by Historically Black Colleges and Universities (HBCUs) focused on disability issues.

The National Black Disability Coalition has launched the "Count Us In" initiative, creating a community-driven database that captures the experiences of Black Americans with disabilities across multiple domains. Similarly, the Digital Disability Justice Project is developing open-source tools for communities to gather data outside formal government structures.

Recommendations for Restoring Disability Data Infrastructure

To address the dismantling of disability data infrastructure, we recommend:

1 Restoring and expanding funding for the Administration for Community Living and the Office of Disability Employment Policy.
2 Mandating intersectional data collection across all federal disability programs.

3 Investing in community-based participatory research led by Black disabled researchers.
4 Developing data sovereignty approaches that give Black disabled communities control over their own information.
5 Creating independent oversight mechanisms to monitor the quality and inclusivity of government disability data.

The fight for comprehensive, intersectional disability data is fundamentally a fight for recognition, resources, and rights. Without a robust data infrastructure, the unique challenges faced by Black Americans with disabilities remain obscured, hampering efforts to create meaningful change.

These policy shifts highlight the need for an intersectional approach that addresses the unique needs of Black Americans with disabilities in policy development and implementation.

Black Students with Disabilities: Educational Outcomes and Challenges

Identification and Classification Patterns

Black students are disproportionately identified for specific disability categories within the educational system. According to the National Center for Education Statistics (2018), in the 2015–2016 school year, the percentage of students served under the Individuals with Disabilities Education Act (IDEA) was highest for American Indian/Alaska Native students (17%), followed by Black students (16%), compared to 14% for white students. This higher identification rate raises questions about potential biases in the evaluation process (Skiba et al., 2016).

The picture is complex. While Black students nationally received special education services at higher rates (12% compared to 8.5% for white students in 2016), research by Morgan et al. (2017) suggests that when factors other than race are considered, Black students, even in the South, may be under-identified for special education services relative to their needs. This apparent contradiction highlights the need for a nuanced analysis (Fish, 2019).

The United States Department of Education (2019) reports that the percentage of students receiving services for specific learning disabilities was higher for Black students (37%) compared to many other racial/ethnic groups. Black students also had the highest rate of receiving services for intellectual disabilities (9%). These patterns reflect a complex interplay of factors, including potential biases in evaluation, socioeconomic impacts, and varying access levels to early intervention (Annamma et al., 2018).

Educational Outcomes and Disparities

Black students with disabilities face significant educational disparities:

According to the United States Government Accountability Office (2020), Black students are nearly twice as likely to be suspended without educational services as white students and 3.8 times as likely to receive one or more out-of-school suspensions. This disciplinary disparity further limits access to quality education for Black students with disabilities (Losen et al., 2022).

Research by Ramey (2018) indicates that school segregation continues to shape educational experiences. In schools where more than 90% of students are minorities, Black students are approximately nine percentage points less likely to be identified as disabled than similar Black students in schools with fewer than 10% minorities. This suggests that Black students in predominantly minority schools may be underserved by special/accessible education (Harper, 2021).

Suspension rates are particularly troubling for students with disabilities overall, who are twice as likely as their peers without disabilities to receive at least one out-of-school suspension (12% versus 5%) according to the United States Department of Education Office for Civil Rights (2021a). These suspensions are associated with an increased risk of dropout, grade retention, and juvenile justice involvement. For Black students with disabilities, who face higher suspension rates due to both racial and disability-based discrimination, these risks are compounded (U.S. Department of Education Office for Civil Rights, 2021b; U.S. Government Accountability Office, 2018).

The National Disability Rights Network (2023) notes that transitioning youth with disabilities out of high school and into competitive integrated employment is part of the transition process, which is federally mandated and done through vocational rehabilitation services. In this practice, Black people with disabilities face significantly lower employment rates compared to their non-disabled and white counterparts, which demonstrates how sheltered workshops, which are used to facilitate this transition, have failed the Black disabled community in obtaining gainful and long-term employment (Moore et al., 2020).

According to the Society for Research in Child Development (2016), the practice of corporal punishment remains legal in many states in this country. Children with disabilities are more than 50% more likely to be punished than their peers who do not have disabilities. In the case of Black children, they are at least 51% more likely to be corporally punished than white children. We as a nation continue to use punitive systems that disproportionately impact Black bodies across multiple systems (Camacho & Krezmien, 2020).

Promising Approaches in Education

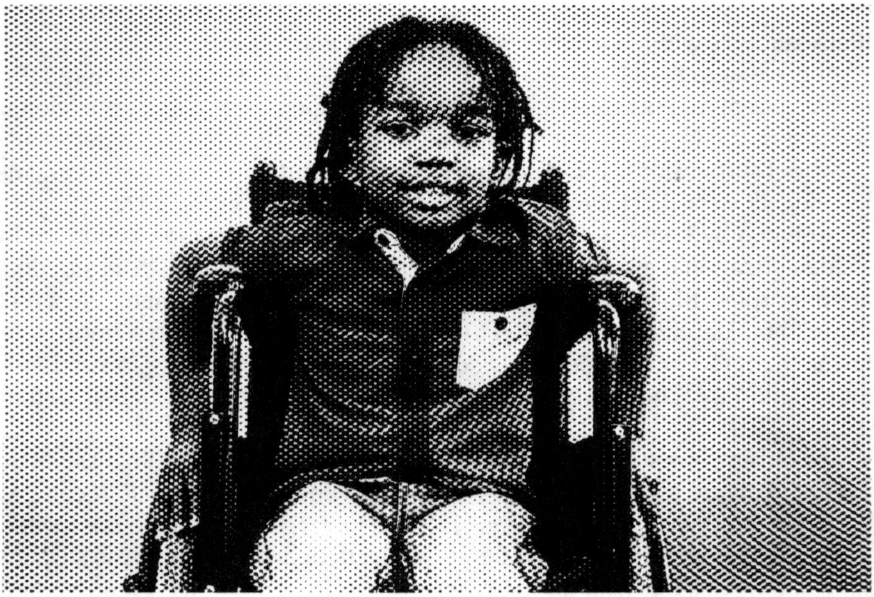

Despite these challenges, several approaches show promise:

- **Culturally Responsive Special/Accessible Education**: Training educators to recognize cultural differences and avoid misinterpreting them as disabilities or behavioral issues (Ford & Russo, 2016).

- **Early Intervention**: Ensuring Black children have equitable access to early screening and intervention services to address developmental needs before they enter school (Morgan et al., 2020).
- **Inclusive Education Models**: Promoting inclusive classroom environments that benefit all students while reducing stigma (Connor & Ferri, 2018).
- **Restorative Practices**: Implementing alternatives to punitive discipline that keep students with disabilities in school and learning (Gregory et al., 2021).
- **Competitive Integrated Employment**: A universal strategy offering the same level of benefits, salary, support, and opportunities to all employees with comparable experience, skills and education, whether or not they have disabilities (Taylor et al., 2022).
- **Alternatives to Corporal Punishment**: Practice positive reinforcements and recognize positive behaviors (Society for Research in Child Development, 2016).

Addressing educational disparities for Black students with disabilities requires a comprehensive approach that acknowledges an intersectional framework for all of the marginalizations these students experience, and it must work to dismantle each of them with a clear concentration on their race (Annamma et al., 2019; Erevelles & Minear, 2010).

The 47th Presidential Administration's Impact on Black Americans with Disabilities

Policy Changes During the First Term (2017–2021)

The 47th presidential administration implemented several policies that affected Black Americans with disabilities.

> Despite promising "No one has done more for people with disabilities than me," the 47th presidential administration's policies threatened the health, education, and economic security of people with disabilities and their families while simultaneously pursuing tax cuts that primarily benefited the wealthy and corporations.

Key first-term policies included:

1. **Attempts to Repeal the Affordable Care Act (ACA)**: These efforts threatened healthcare access for many Black Americans with disabilities who gained coverage through the ACA, which would be harmful for many, especially in the area of mental health services.
2. **Medicaid Work Requirements**: Several states received waivers to implement work requirements for Medicaid recipients, creating barriers for Black Americans with disabilities who rely on Medicaid for healthcare and support services.

3 **Changes to Disability Benefits**: The administration proposed changes to Social Security Disability Insurance (SSDI) and Supplemental Security Income (SSI), which would have made it harder for people with disabilities to qualify for and maintain benefits.
4 **Education Policy Rollbacks**: The administration rescinded guidance on school discipline that was designed to address racial disparities in suspensions and expulsions, which disproportionately affect Black students with disabilities.

Current Administration Policies (2025)

Since returning to the office in January 2025, the administration has taken several actions affecting Black Americans with disabilities:

> The administration's executive orders targeting Diversity, Equity, Inclusion, and Accessibility (DEIA) initiatives represent "a deliberate attempt to undo progress" and "create new barriers to opportunity" (ACLU, 2025). These orders have particularly affected Black Americans with disabilities, who benefit from intersectional approaches to inclusion.

In late January, after the tragic plane and helicopter crash in D.C., the 47th President made searing and derogatory comments about the Federal Aviation Administration (FAA) DEI program that included the hiring of people with disabilities. He read information from the hiring website about the lack of people with severe intellectual disabilities being hired for government work. The 47th President touted the fact that this had been removed at his direction. He then went on to express disdain of the fact that people with disabilities had the competency and could be air traffic controllers. He proclaimed, "They can be air traffic controllers. I don't think so" (Rev, 2025).

The Administration laid off hundreds of workers and downsized the Office of Civil Rights (OCR) in the Department of Education. At the time, there were 12,000 complaints, about 6,000 of them regarding students with disabilities being mistreated or denied services while in school (ProPublica, 2025).

The second term has been bolder and more aggressive in targeting immigrants, which affects those members of our society who live at the intersection of being a person with a disability and having an immigration status. How they are treated and the experience can be the root of an onset of disability, in particular, a mental health diagnosis. Unidentified, plain-clothed persons have taken people from the streets, brutally placed them in custody and detention centers here as well as deported them to centers in other countries.

Threats to cut Social Security, Medicare, and particularly Medicaid, which the republicans (also known as the Grand Old Party [GOP]) have long sought to eliminate or privatize, would disproportionately affect millions of disabled people who rely on the programs to survive (KFF, 2024; The Nation, 2021). As one disability studies expert noted, potential cuts to Medicaid would be "catastrophic" as "for many people, Medicaid is literally their lifeline."

The administration has also taken "direct actions at specific agencies," including firing EEOC commissioners and overseeing staffing cuts that disproportionately affect disabled federal employees. The federal government has traditionally maintained a strong reputation for actively recruiting, hiring, and providing reasonable accommodations for people with disabilities. People with identified disabilities comprise approximately 10.4% of the total federal sector workforce, providing a higher relative rate of disability representation and employment stability compared to the civilian workforce (The Conversation, 2025; U.S. Equal Employment Opportunity Commission, n.d.).

Public statements from administration officials have further stigmatized disability. The current Secretary of the Department of Health and Human Services (DHHS) is using ableist theories, practices, and rhetoric to dehumanize this community. He is falsely linking vaccines to conditions such as autism which advocates say "medicalizes disabilities, treating them as impairments that need to be fixed" rather than embracing a "social model" that emphasizes societal barriers. In his first press conference, which was about the United States Centers for Disease Control and Prevention (CDC) report on autism, he took the opportunity to falsely debunk the findings, stating that it is an ailment that is "preventable" and "part of a chronic disease epidemic that destroys children and families".

The Secretary then went on to spout hateful and harmful rhetoric about how those with autism will never be a fully functional part of our society. He said, "These are kids who will never pay taxes. They'll never hold a job. They'll never play baseball." He went on to discuss this community in even more hateful ways. All of this is in line with the plan of this administration to erase people with disabilities from our society.

Potential Future Impacts

The administration's policy direction suggests several concerns for Black Americans with disabilities:

1 **Reduced Healthcare Access**: Ongoing efforts to dismantle the ACA and restructure Medicaid threaten essential healthcare services, which will also contribute to the institutionalization and deny many the ability to stay or get out and live in the community. It will also reduce much-needed mental healthcare services.
2 **Employment Barriers**: Rolling back DEIA initiatives may reduce employment opportunities for Black Americans with disabilities, who already face significant hiring discrimination.

3. **Educational Inequities**: Changes to education policies may exacerbate existing disparities for Black students with disabilities.
4. **Research Funding Cuts**: Reductions in research funding related to disability, particularly research examining racial disparities, limit our understanding of effective interventions.

Resistance strategies include litigation, grassroots organizing, coalition-building, and continued advocacy for policies that center and are led by Black Americans with disabilities.

Intersectional Framework for Disability Justice

Understanding Intersectionality in Disability Justice

Disability Justice as a concept and activist practice was developed in 2005 by the Disability Justice Collective, a group that included disabled queers of color in the San Francisco Bay Area—Patty Berne, Mia Mingus, and Stacey Milbern—along with other activists. This framework explicitly centers on the experiences of multiply-marginalized disabled people (World Institute of Disability, 2022).

The Disability Justice framework emerged because the Disability Rights Movement and Disability Studies do not intentionally centralize the needs and experiences of folks experiencing intersectional oppression, such as disabled people of color, immigrants with disabilities, queer people with disabilities, and trans and gender non-conforming people with disabilities.

Key Principles of Disability Justice

Key principles of Disability Justice include a commitment to intersectional frameworks, relying on the leadership of those most impacted, adhering to an anti-capitalist political stance, dedication to cross-movement organization and cross-disability solidarity, recognizing each person's inherent worth outside capitalist relationships, working toward sustainability, meeting collective needs, and commitment to accessibility.

These principles provide a roadmap for more inclusive and effective advocacy that addresses the unique needs of Black Americans with disabilities.

Promising Strategies and Resources

Effective Approaches to Disability Justice for Black Americans

Several approaches have shown promise in advancing disability justice for Black Americans:

1 **Centering Black Disabled Leadership**: Prioritizing the leadership and expertise of Black disabled people in policy development and advocacy efforts.
2 **Cross-Movement Solidarity**: Building alliances between disability rights organizations, racial justice groups, and other social justice movements.
3 **Community-Based Support Systems**: Developing support networks within Black communities that address the specific needs of disabled members.

4 **Culturally Responsive Services**: Ensuring that disability services and supports are culturally appropriate and accessible to Black Americans.
5 **Intersectional Policy Advocacy**: Advocating for policies that specifically address the overlapping impacts of racism and ableism.

Organizations and Resources

The following organizations and resources provide support and advocacy for Black Americans with disabilities:

1 **Sins Invalid**: A disability justice performance project that centers disabled artists of color and LGBTQ+ disabled artists.
2 **The Disability Justice Collective**: A group focused on developing and promoting disability justice principles and practices.
3. **Ramp Your Voice!** Founded by Vilissa Thompson, this organization promotes disability rights and advocacy from an intersectional perspective.
4 **Black Disabled Creatives**: An initiative established to help bridge the divide for Black creatives with disabilities.

Funding for disability rights work is increasing, but intersectional support still lags. As Disability Inclusion Fund's Brown-Booker noted: "The disability justice movement intersects with so many other social justice movements, and I think there is a great opportunity for cross-movement funding" (Philanthropy News Digest, 2024). This highlights the need for more significant investment in organizations led by Black disabled people.

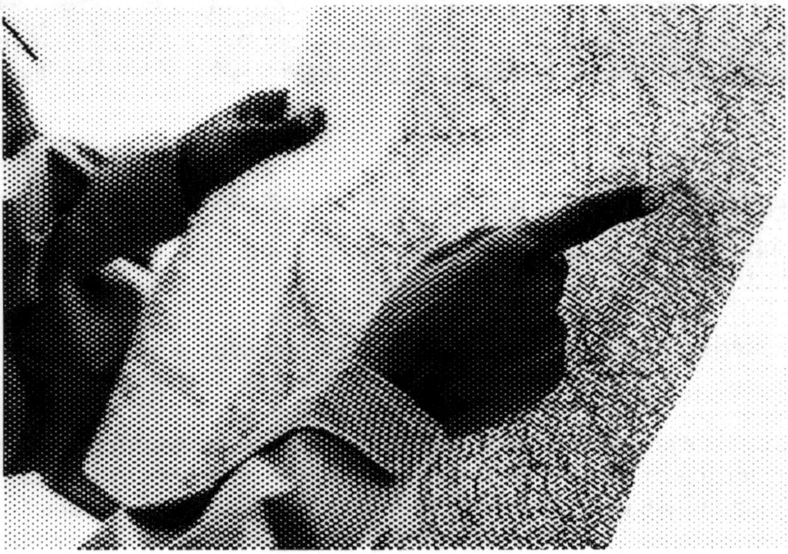

Case Study: Black Disabled Leadership in Action

The Story of Cynthia Jones

Note: This case study is a composite based on real experiences using a fictional name to protect privacy.

Cynthia Jones, a Black woman with multiple sclerosis living in Chicago, founded the Community Access Project after experiencing difficulties accessing public transportation and healthcare services in her predominantly Black neighborhood. Despite having the legal right to accessible services under the ADA, Cynthia found that implementation was lacking in communities of color.

Working with a coalition of local disability advocates and racial justice organizations, Cynthia conducted an audit of accessibility in her community, documenting disparities in ADA compliance between predominantly white and predominantly Black neighborhoods. This data-driven approach led to meetings with city officials and transportation authorities.

Through persistent advocacy, the Community Access Project secured commitments for improved accessible transportation routes, ADA training for healthcare providers, and a community advisory board to monitor implementation. Cynthia's leadership demonstrates how centering Black-disabled experiences can lead to concrete improvements in policy and practice.

This case illustrates several key principles of disability justice in action: leadership by those most affected, cross-movement solidarity, community-based approaches, and addressing the specific impacts of racism and ableism in Black communities.

Call to Action

Priority Areas for Policy Change

- **Healthcare Access**: Expand Medicaid coverage and strengthen the ACA to ensure Black Americans with disabilities have access to needed healthcare and long-term services and support.
- **Educational Equity**: Reform special/accessible education identification and discipline practices to address racial disparities and ensure Black students with disabilities receive appropriate support.

- **Economic Opportunity**: Strengthen enforcement of employment non-discrimination laws and develop targeted initiatives to increase employment of Black Americans with disabilities.
- **Housing Access**: Expand affordable, accessible housing options in Black communities and enforce fair housing laws to prevent discrimination.
- **Criminal Justice Reform**: Address the overrepresentation of Black Americans with disabilities in the criminal justice system through diversion programs and improved accessibility in courts and correctional facilities.
- **Transportation**: Provide various modes of safe, affordable, and accessible transportation such as bicycles, mass transit, and public transportation systems. Create safe and universally designed sidewalks and pathways of travel in cities and rural areas of our country.
- **Deinstitutionalization**: Prioritize the increase of Long Term Services and Supports (LTSS) and other healthcare and personal services needed for those with disabilities to leave institutions and live in the community.

Individual and Community Actions

- **Center Black Disabled Voices**: Ensure Black disabled people have leadership roles in disability rights and racial justice organizations.
- **Build Cross-Movement Solidarity**: Form coalitions between disability rights groups, racial justice organizations, and other social justice movements.
- **Support Black Disabled-Led Organizations**: Provide financial and other resources to organizations led by Black disabled people.
- **Educate and Advocate**: Learn about the intersections of race and disability and advocate for policies that address both forms of oppression.
- **Create Accessible Spaces**: Ensure community spaces and events are fully accessible to people with all types of disabilities.

Developing Options to Change Our System Of Support

Do You Know That You Have the Power to Make a Difference?

Person-Centered Thinking

We all can remember a time when something happened that compelled us to make a difference—this is what creates change. A person-centered approach for people with disabilities provides the necessary tools to support people effectively. This happens in communities where everyone has a voice and feels heard.

People without disabilities often benefit from the accommodations created to serve persons with disabilities. Though we all want to live in a world with equal access, this reality remains far from reach, especially for Black people with disabilities. Each of us must decide what we can personally do to improve our communities for every member of our beautifully diverse community.

Start with yourself: Are you willing to support the empowerment of people with disabilities? If so, be thoughtful in your actions toward this community. Ask yourself: "Am I being a good example of support?" Making change a priority creates opportunities to make a difference for yourself and others—your decision to change may help someone you have never met.

When looking at person-centered approaches, consider three levels of change:

1 **Personal change** (Level 1): Changes you make on your own that improve people's lives. These small changes grow larger over time and encourage others to join in.
2 **Organizational change** (Level 2): Changes at the community level happen when enough individuals adopt positive habits. The way we treat each other directly affects how others treat us.
3 **Systems change** (Level 3): Large-scale changes transforming policies and institutions. These happen when we act on what can be changed now, while being honest about what takes more time.

As we grow together, spotlight moments when you become the change by shifting how you respond to and support others. Remember the golden rule: treat others better than you would want to be treated. Through this collective approach, we all move closer to freedom.

Conclusion

Disability justice for Black Americans requires an intersectional approach that addresses the unique impacts of racism and ableism. By centering the leadership and experiences of Black people with disabilities, we can develop more effective policies and practices that promote true inclusion and equity.

The challenges are significant, but so is the resilience and leadership of the Black disability community. Through coalition-building, policy advocacy, and community support, we can work toward a future where Black Americans with disabilities can fully participate in all aspects of society.

As we move forward, it is essential to remember that disability justice is fundamentally linked to all other forms of social justice. As advocates note, "All struggles for rights and justice are inextricably intertwined," making it essential to center "the connection between racial justice and disability justice" to continue pushing for equitable access and rights in both movements.

By embracing an intersectional approach to disability justice, we honor the full humanity and dignity of Black Americans with disabilities and work toward a more just and inclusive society for all.

Resources for Further Learning and Support

Organizations

- Sins Invalid: http://www.sinsinvalid.org
- Ramp Your Voice!: http://www.rampyourvoice.com
- National Association of the Deaf Black Deaf Advocates: http://www.nbda.org/
- Autistic Women & Nonbinary Network: http://www.awnnetwork.org
- New Disabled South: https://www.newdisabledsouth.org
- Detroit Disability Power: https://www.detroitdisabilitypower.org
- Transgender Law Center: https://transgenderlawcenter.org
- The Learning Community for Person Centered Practices: http://www.tlcpcp.com
- Disability Community for Democracy, Inc.: https://www.disabilitycommunityfordemocracy.org/
- Divas With Disabilities: https://divaswithdisabilities.org/

Educational Resources

- Disability Visibility Project: http://www.disabilityvisibilityproject.com
- Disability Justice Toolkit by Showing Up for Racial Justice: http://www.surj.org
- "All the Weight of Our Dreams: On Living Racialized Autism," Edited by Lydia X. Z. Brown, E. Ashkenazy, and Morénike Giwa Onaiwu
- "Care Work: Dreaming Disability Justice" By Leah Lakshmi Piepzna-Samarasinha
- "Disability Visibility: First-Person Stories from the Twenty-First Century," Edited by Alice Wong
- What It's Like To Be Black and Disabled in America—The Atlantic—by Shalene Gupta. Sept. 21, 2021. "You Have to Scream Out"—Being Black and disabled is a constant struggle
- PBS—American Masters—Renegades—Explore the lives of diverse, lesser-known historical figures with disabilities. https://www.pbs.org/wnet/americanmasters/shorts/renegades/

Legal and Advocacy Resources

- Disability Rights Education and Defense Fund: http://www.dredf.org
- Center for Public Representation: http://www.centerforpublicrep.org
- NAACP Legal Defense Fund Disability Rights Resources: http://www.naacpldf.org/disability-rights
- National Disability Rights Network: http://www.ndrn.org

Mental Health Support

1 Black Emotional and Mental Health Collective (BEAM): http://www.beam.community
2 Therapy for Black Girls: http://www.therapyforblackgirls.com
3 Black Mental Health Alliance: https://blackmentalhealth.com/
4 Depressed While Black: http://www.depressedwhileblack.com
5 No More Martyrs: https://www.nomoremartyrs.org/our-mission

Note

1 The acronym SSA stands for Social Security Administration.

References

American Civil Liberties Union. (2025). *Trump's executive orders rolling back DEI and accessibility efforts, explained.* https://www.aclu.org/news/racial-justice/trumps-executive-orders-rolling-back-dei-and-accessibility-efforts-explained

Annamma, S. A., Connor, D., & Ferri, B. (2018). Disability critical race theory: Exploring the intersectional lineage, emergence, and potential futures of DisCrit in education. *Review of Research in Education, 42(1)*, 46–71.

Annamma, S. A., Jackson, D. D., & Morrison, D. (2019). Conceptualizing color-evasiveness: using dis/ability critical race theory to expand a color-blind racial ideology in education and society. *Race, Ethnicity and Education, 22(2)*, 147–162.

Camacho, K. A., & Krezmien, M. P. (2020). A statewide analysis of school discipline policies and practices: Implications for improving racial and disability disproportionality. *Journal of Special Education Leadership, 33(2)*, 70–84.

Centers for Disease Control and Prevention. (2015). Prevalence of disability and disability type among adults—United States, 2013. *Morbidity and Mortality Weekly Report, 64(29)*, 777–783.

Connor, D. J., & Ferri, B. A. (2018). The boundaries of inclusion: The development of inclusive education in the United States. In S. L. Gabel & S. Danforth (Eds.), *Handbook of inclusive education for educators, administrators, and planners* (pp. 111–132). Routledge.

Disability Rights Education and Defense Fund. (2020). *ADA implementation disparities by race and neighborhood*. DREDF Research Series.

Disability Statistics User Guide. (2024). *Demographic profiles of disability among working-age adults in the United States*. Cornell University. https://www.disabilitystatistics.org/

Erevelles, N., & Minear, A. (2010). Unspeakable offenses: Untangling race and disability in discourses of intersectionality. *Journal of Literary & Cultural Disability Studies, 4(2)*, 127–145.

Fish, R. E. (2019). Standing out and sorting in: Exploring the role of racial composition in racial disparities in special education. *American Educational Research Journal, 56(6)*, 2573–2608.

Ford, D. Y., & Russo, C. J. (2016). Historical and legal overview of special education overrepresentation: Access and equity denied. *Multiple Voices for Ethnically Diverse Exceptional Learners, 16(1)*, 50–57.

Gregory, A., Ward-Seidel, A. R., & Carter, K. V. (2021). Twelve indicators of restorative practices implementation: A framework for educational leaders. *Journal of Educational and Psychological Consultation, 31(2)*, 147–179.

Harper, S. R. (2021). Race-conscious educational policies versus color-blind approaches: Implications for Black students with disabilities. *Educational Researcher, 50(3)*, 161–173.

KFF. (2024). *Working-age adults with disabilities living in the community*. https://www.kff.org/medicaid/working-age-adults-with-disabilities-living-in-the-community/

Leppert, R., & Schaeffer, K. (2023). *8 facts about Americans with disabilities*. Pew Research Center. https://www.pewresearch.org/short-reads/2023/07/24/8-facts-about-americans-with-disabilities/

Losen, D. J., Martinez, T. E., & Shin, G. H. (2022). *Disabling Punishment: The need for remedies to the disparate loss of instruction experienced by Black students with disabilities*. The Civil Rights Project, UCLA.

Moore, E. J., Schelling, A., Verma, K., Trainor, A. A., & Moon, N. W. (2020). Barriers and facilitators to employment for individuals with disabilities: A Social Model Perspective. *Journal of Vocational Rehabilitation, 52(1)*, 89–97.

Morgan, P. L., Farkas, G., Cook, M., Strassfeld, N. M., Hillemeier, M. M., Pun, W. H., & Schussler, D. L. (2017). Are Black children disproportionately overrepresented in special education? *A Best-Evidence Synthesis. Exceptional Children, 83(2)*, 181–198.

Morgan, P. L., Farkas, G., Hillemeier, M. M., & Maczuga, S. (2020). Are minority children disproportionately represented in early intervention and early childhood special education? *Educational Researcher, 49(6)*, 405–418.

National Center for Education Statistics. (2018). *Status and trends in the education of racial and ethnic groups*. U.S. Department of Education.

National Disability Rights Network. (2023). *Transition to competitive integrated employment: Progress and challenges for youth with disabilities*. NDRN.

Philanthropy News Digest. (2024). *Focus on Disability Rights Growing, but Intersectional Support Lags*. https://philanthropynewsdigest.org/news/focus-on-disability-rights-growing-but-intersectional-support-lags

ProPublica. (2025). *Mass layoffs in the Department of Education erode its Office of Civil Rights Division*. https://www.propublica.org/article/education-department-civil-rights-division-eroded-by-massive-layoffs

Ramey, D. M. (2018). The social structure of criminalized and medicalized school discipline. *Sociology of Education, 91(3)*, 247–269.

Rev. (2025, January 30). *Trump speaks on DC plane crash*. https://www.rev.com/transcripts/trump-speaks-on-d-c-plane-crash

Skiba, R. J., Artiles, A. J., Kozleski, E. B., Losen, D. J., & Harry, E. G. (2016). Risks and consequences of oversimplifying educational inequities: A response to Morgan et al. (2015). *Educational Researcher, 45(3)*, 221–225.

Society for Research in Child Development. (2016). *Social policy brief: Corporal punishment in US Public schools*. https://www.srcd.org/sites/default/files/resources/SPR%20Brief_30-1_2016.pdf

Taylor, J. P., Whittenburg, H. N., Thoma, C. A., Gokita, T., & Pickover, G. S. (2022). Toward competitive integrated employment: A systematic review of interventions for youth and adults with disabilities. *Career Development and Transition for Exceptional Individuals, 45(2)*, 94–107.

The Conversation. (2025). *Cutting Medicaid and federal programs are among 4 key Trump administration policy changes that could make life harder for disabled people*. https://theconversation.com/cutting-medicaid-and-federal-programs-are-among-4-key-trump-administration-policy-changes-that-could-make-life-harder-for-disabled-people-244458

The Nation. (2021). *Donald Trump's next diversity target: People with disabilities*. thenation.com.

U.S. Department of Education. (2019). *41st annual report to Congress on the implementation of the Individuals with Disabilities Education Act*. Office of Special Education and Rehabilitative Services.

U.S. Department of Education Office for Civil Rights. (2021a). *Civil Rights data collection: An overview of exclusionary discipline practices in public schools*. U.S. Department of Education.

U.S. Department of Education Office for Civil Rights. (2021b). *2020-21 Civil Rights Data Collection: Student discipline and school climate in K-12 public schools*. https://www.ed.gov/media/document/crdc-discipline-school-climate-reportpdf-21409.pdf

U.S. Equal Employment Opportunity Commission. (n.d.). *The EEO status of workers with disabilities in the federal sector*. https://www.eeoc.gov/federal-sector/reports/eeo-status-workers-disabilities-federal-sector

U.S. Government Accountability Office. (2018). *K-12 education: Discipline disparities for Black students, boys, and students with disabilities* (Report No. GAO-18-258). https://www.gao.gov/products/gao-18-258

U.S. Government Accountability Office. (2020). *K-12 education: Discipline disparities for Black students, boys, and students with disabilities (GAO-18-258)*. U.S. Government Accountability Office.

World Institute on Disability. (2022). *Why multiply marginalized people with disabilities should be prioritized before, during and after disasters and emergencies*. https://wid.org/why-multiply-marginalized-people-with-disabilities-should-be-prioritized-before-during-and-after-disasters-and-emergencies/

Chapter 15

Black Immigration Policies, Black Lives

A Call to Action

*Nana Gyamfi, Rose Berry, and Oluchi Omeoga**

Executive Summary

This Black Paper (Paper) examines the critical intersection of immigration policy and racial justice through the lens of Black migrant experiences in the United States. At a time when immigration policies are being weaponized against communities, Black migrants face compounded challenges through the dual forces of anti-immigrant sentiment and anti-Black racism.

* Supported by braintrust authors: David J. Johns, Ronald Claude, Metzlal Ocbazghi, Erica Baganza, and Nadia French-Graham.

DOI: 10.4324/9781003752646-21

Key Findings Include:

1. The persistent framing of immigration as primarily a non-Black Latinx issue obscures the unique challenges faced by the 5.6 million Black immigrants in the United States (Pew Research Center, 2026).
2. Black migrants face disproportionate targeting by immigration enforcement, with higher rates of detention, deportation, bond amounts, and use of solitary confinement compared to non-Black immigrants.
3. Current administration policies specifically target protections for Black migrants through the dismantling of Temporary Protected Status (TPS), affecting over 500,000 people, primarily from Haiti.[1] There are five other majority-Black countries whose TPS designation is under threat, including South Sudan, Cameroon, Ethiopia, Somalia, and Sudan. Additionally, the administration has targeted the CHNV humanitarian parole program, affecting over 200,000 people from Haiti.[2] In immigration jargon, CHNV refers to humanitarian parole for nationals of Cuba, Haiti, Nicaragua, and Venezuela.
4. Black Lesbian, Gay, Bisexual, Queer, and Questioning (LGBTQ+) asylum seekers face particular dangers as African and Caribbean nations and Western countries implement increasingly hostile policies.
5. Immigration enforcement functions as an extension of the criminal legal system, with both systems disproportionately targeting Black communities.

This Black Paper outlines concrete policy recommendations while highlighting the essential role of Black-led organizations in protection, advocacy, and community-building efforts. It concludes with specific calls to action for people, communities, and policymakers, emphasizing that immigration policy must be understood as racial justice policy.

Introduction

The criminalization of Black migrants represents one of the most urgent, yet overlooked civil rights crises in America today. As immigration becomes increasingly weaponized through policy, Black migrants face a double burden—targeted by both anti-immigrant legislation and deeply embedded anti-Black racism that permeates American institutions. This Paper examines the challenges facing the 5.6 million Black immigrants in the United States, the communities they are a part of and contribute to, and the intersecting oppressions that shape their experiences.

As policies and rhetoric dehumanize migrants, Black immigrants—from Haiti, Central and Latin America, various African nations, and throughout the Caribbean—bear the heaviest burden through higher detention rates, longer incarcerations, higher bonds, and accelerated deportations. For every statistic, there are countless human stories: families separated, asylum seekers returned to danger, communities living in perpetual fear, and the quiet violence of exclusion from healthcare, education, and economic opportunity.

This Paper aims to disrupt the persistent framing of immigration as solely a Latinx issue, center the experiences of Black migrants, and outline actionable recommendations for policy change, community organizing, and coalition building. By understanding that immigration policy is racial justice policy, we reveal how the struggle for migrant rights is **inseparable** from the broader movement for Black liberation.

Shared Struggle, Shared Community: Black Migrants And Black Americans

The artificial division between Black migrants and Black Americans obscures a fundamental truth: we experience Blackness together in all aspects of American life. This concept is also referred to as shared fate. In classrooms, workplaces, places of worship, and neighborhoods across America, Black migrants and Black Americans share the burdens and joys of navigating a society still defined by its racial hierarchies. We sit beside each other in college seminars, collaborate as colleagues, serve as caretakers in healthcare settings, and build families and communities ***together***.

This shared experience of Blackness means that anti-immigrant policies targeting Black migrants inevitably harm the broader Black community. When a Haitian father is deported, the impact goes beyond his immediate family. A church that loses a deacon, the small business that loses a loyal customer, the neighborhood that loses a mentor. The criminalization of migration amplifies the already pervasive criminalization of Blackness, creating overlapping systems of surveillance and control that cannot be neatly separated. Black migrants face discrimination not merely as immigrants, but specifically as "Black immigrants." The same stereotypes, biases, and systemic barriers that target Black Americans extend to Black immigrants, compounded by language barriers, cultural differences, and precarious legal status. Meanwhile, within some immigrant communities, Black migrants often face additional marginalization based on their sexual orientation, gender identity and expression, creating multiple layers of exclusion.

The reality is that Black migrants and Black Americans are bound together not only by shared heritage but also by shared daily experiences. They teach in the same schools, care for patients in the same hospitals, worship in the same churches, and organize in the same communities. Current immigration policies that target Black migrants will inevitably ripple through these interconnected networks, affecting Black American communities that are already struggling against systemic racism. When Black immigrant nurses are deported from a community hospital, Black American patients lose culturally competent care. When Black immigrant business owners are forced to close their shops, Black American neighborhoods lose vital economic anchors. For Black communities, immigration is not a separate issue but an integral part of the struggle for racial justice. The same systems that oppress U.S.-born Black people—policing, incarceration, economic marginalization—also target Black immigrants.

By understanding immigration policy as racial justice policy, we recognize that the liberation of Black migrants and Black Americans is inextricably linked. We cannot achieve racial justice while allowing immigration policy to function as a tool of racial oppression, nor can we create humane immigration policies without addressing the anti-Blackness embedded within the system.

Policies That Dehumanize: The Threat To Black Migrant Communities

Criminalizing Migrants: Cops & Cages

The 47th presidential administration's immigration agenda is driven by three core strategies: to "kick us out," "lock us up," and "keep us out." Black migrants, who are disproportionately targeted, over-policed, and subjected to harsh treatment in detention facilities, face heightened risks.

Kick Us Out

This strategy criminalizes migrants by stripping away the legal protections that enable their lawful presence in the United States, fast-tracking deportations to bypass the right to seek asylum, and creating pathways for the removal and detention of migrants outside United States borders.

The dismantling of Temporary Protected Status (TPS) and the CHNV humanitarian parole program makes it clear that the 47th presidential administration is targeting the few remaining protections available to Black migrants. In March 2025, the administration revoked legal status for 532,000 people from Cuba, Haiti, Nicaragua, and Venezuela who had entered legally through the CHNV humanitarian parole program, including 213,000 Haitians (Montanaro, 2025). In February 2025, Haiti's TPS designation was shortened from February 2026 to August 2025, affecting approximately 500,000 Haitians (USCIS, 2025).

Across the country, Black immigrant communities are living in fear and uncertainty as their legal status hangs in the balance. Instead of upholding its obligations to provide refuge, the administration is slashing programs and shutting down pathways to safety, deliberately abandoning those most in need of humanitarian protection.

The 47th presidential administration is setting an alarming precedent through its expanded use of expedited removals and detaining migrants abroad. The case of Kilmar Abrego Garcia exemplifies this dangerous overreach. Garcia is a Maryland resident who was illegally deported to El Salvador on March 15, 2025. Despite the administration acknowledging this deportation was an error, and despite a Supreme Court order demanding his return to the United States, the administration has refused to comply. By June 2025, Garcia returned to the United States but remained under ICE custody and away from his community and his family. The administration made several attempts to remove him to a series of African countries, but this was blocked by an injunction from a Maryland federal judge. In December 2025, a federal Maryland judge ordered ICE to release Garcia while his legal challenge against his deportation proceeded (The Associated Press, 2025). Defying the highest court in the land reveals how this administration's mass deportation plan is state-sponsored kidnappings, where the government can disappear people across borders. Deportation without due process should be especially alarming for Black migrants, as the administration is aggressively stripping away existing protections while ramping up enforcement operations. Black migrants are already over-policed and are now at greater risk of being deported and detained in foreign countries.

In addition, the United States has increased the use of third-country deportation. In May 2025, the 47th presidential administration attempted to deport eight people to South Sudan, despite a federal judge's order requiring prior notice and an opportunity for the individuals to contest removal. January 2026, the United States government expanded and actively utilized third-country transfer and removal agreements with over 30 countries to deport non-citizens to nations other than their country of origin. These include forced transfers under Asylum Cooperative Agreements (ACAs) and direct third-country deportation flights. Over half of these agreements are with African and Caribbean, Black-majority countries (Human Rights First, 2026). Some of these countries include Nigeria, Ghana, Djibouti, Rwanda, Benin, Eswatini, and Libya. By using these tactics, such as imposing tariffs, enforcing visa descriptions, and threatening to add nations to the travel ban list, this administration has relied on economic and political coercion to pressure governments into compliance with its immigration agenda.

Alligator Alcatraz

The nightmare of offshore detention has come home with the opening of the South Florida Detention Facility ominously dubbed "Alligator Alcatraz" (Bailey et al., 2025). Florida Attorney General James Uthmeier coined the name to evoke the extreme isolation and cruel conditions of the now-closed federal prison, explicitly leveraging the Everglades' dangerous wildlife—alligators, pythons, and venomous snakes—as what officials call a "security feature." As one state official put it: "If somebody were to get out, there's nowhere to run, nowhere to hide, only the alligators and pythons are waiting" (NPR, 2025).

The facility exemplifies the 47th presidential administration's commitment to mass detention infrastructure. The United States Senate budget reconciliation bill allocated $45 billion for immigration detention centers—a 265% increase to ICE's annual detention budget. "Alligator Alcatraz" was constructed in just eight days without environmental review or meaningful local oversight, authorized under emergency powers granted by a 2023 executive order from Florida's Governor Ron DeSantis (American Civil Liberties Union, 2025). The facility had the capacity to house approximately 3,000 detainees and was built at a cost exceeding $360 million, with annual operating costs projected at $450 million (Bailey et al., 2025).

Reports from the facility describe conditions that amount to torture. In December 2025, Amnesty International released a damning report documenting cruel, inhuman, and degrading treatment at "Alligator Alcatraz," with findings revealing human rights violations that, in some cases, amount to torture. Detainees were held in makeshift tents and cages, exposed to extreme heat approaching 100 degrees, swarming mosquitoes, and unsanitary conditions. Detainees reported minimal and sometimes contaminated food, bug infestations, overflowing toilets, and lack of medical care—conditions so severe that they led detainees to stage hunger strikes (American Civil Liberties Union, 2025).

The use of prolonged solitary confinement at nearby Krome detention center and the use of outdoor punitive confinement units—known as "the box"—at "Alligator Alcatraz" have been documented by human rights organizations. Amnesty International considers that detention conditions at both facilities amount to cruel, inhuman, and degrading treatment, with the use of prolonged solitary confinement and "the box" amounting to torture or other ill-treatment (Amnesty International, 2025). State lawmakers who attempted to inspect the facility were repeatedly denied access, raising serious questions about transparency and accountability (Almanzar, 2025).

"Alligator Alcatraz" represents a dangerous blueprint for immigration enforcement: a state–federal partnership that bypasses normal oversight mechanisms, operates outside established detention standards, and deliberately inflicts suffering on detained individuals. The facility set a precedent for states to construct their own detention infrastructure, exponentially expanding the reach of mass deportation machinery while creating spaces where migrants can effectively disappear from legal tracking systems. For Black migrants—who already face higher rates of detention and harsher treatment in custody—facilities like "Alligator Alcatraz" represent the next evolution of racialized state violence.

On June 25, 2026, the South Florida detention center was closed, but the harm remains.

Lock Us Up

This strategy is achieved through increased enforcement efforts and expanding the capacity of the United States detention system, both achieved through the deliberate reversal of due process rights. The expansion of immigration enforcement bleeds into the same criminal legal system that disproportionately criminalizes and kills Black Americans.

Just as the United States has the largest prison population in the world, it also operates the most extensive immigration detention system. Both systems are marked by racial disparities that disproportionately impact Black people. The parallels are no coincidence. Black immigrants, like all Black people in the United States, are disproportionately targeted by the criminal industrial complex and are overrepresented in arrests, detentions, and deportations. More than 76% of Black immigrants are deported due to contact with law enforcement, compared to 54% overall (Morgan-Trostle & Zheng, 2016). As immigration detention expands, so too do the dangers for Black immigrants, who already face deeply unequal treatment in United States Immigration and Customs Enforcement (ICE) custody. Black migrants are more likely to face solitary confinement, higher bond amounts, and physical or emotional abuse.

The forced detention of Haitian refugees at Guantanamo Bay and in offshore camps during the 1990s laid the groundwork for today's immigration detention system. Now, the United States is pushing to expand offshore detention once again in El Salvador, reviving a troubling legacy of denying due process to migrants. Even more disturbing is the current administration's interest in deporting United States citizens, a move that poses a serious threat, given how Black people are disproportionately criminalized in this country.

The current administration has escalated militarized policing in cities with large Black American and Black immigrant populations, using violent ICE raids, deploying the National Guard, and threatening the use of militarized law enforcement agencies to suppress dissent. These efforts are a part of a broader strategy to intertwine immigration enforcement with local policing, federal agencies, and the military. Since January 2025, 287G agreements have more than quadrupled. There are now more than 2,500 active agreements nationwide (United States Immigration and Customs Enforcement, 2026). This means more local cops than ever before can act on behalf of ICE to arrest and detain suspected immigrants with little to no cause. Federal takeovers began in Los Angeles in June 2025 (during the weekend of the State of the People Power Tour Los Angeles and Altadena convening), expanded to Washington, D.C., and have since spread to cities like Chicago, Portland, Memphis, and Minneapolis, with others under threat.

Keep Us Out

The 47th presidential administration is building an immigration system with no re-entry path and no meaningful way for Black migrants to seek refuge in the United States From the outset of the second term, his administration has aggressively worked to slash refugee admissions and shut the door on those fleeing violence and persecution.

The administration is deliberately keeping Black migrants out by targeting majority-Black countries through expanded travel bans and dismantling the refugee admissions program. For many Black migrants, refugee resettlement was one of the last viable legal pathways to safety in the United States. Now, even that option is going away. Countries across Africa and the Caribbean will soon be disproportionately affected by visa restrictions, slow processing, and arbitrary denials.

Active Threats to Black Migrant Communities

In December 2025, the 47th presidential administration announced expanded travel restrictions to an additional 20 countries, bringing the total number of affected nations to approximately 36, with the majority being African countries (Johnson, 2025). The December 2025 expansion added Burkina Faso, Mali, Niger, South Sudan, and Syria to the full travel ban list, while placing 15 additional countries under partial restrictions, including Angola, Benin, Ivory Coast, Dominica, Gabon, Gambia, Malawi, Mauritania, Nigeria, Senegal, Tanzania, Zambia, and Zimbabwe (Johnson, 2025). Combined with earlier restrictions from June 2025, the 47th President's travel bans now cover roughly 60% of African countries (Pitts, 2025).

The scope of these restrictions is staggering. If all proposed countries are added to future bans, an additional 36 countries, it will reduce the number of specified green card applicants from sub-Sarahan Africa by more than 83%. The administration justifies these measures by citing inadequate vetting procedures, high visa overstay rates, and countries' refusal to accept deported nationals. However, the pattern is unmistakable: Africa has been the hardest-hit by the 47th presidential administration's expanded travel ban (Mutsaka, 2025), with 24 of 36 countries identified for future restrictions located in sub-Saharan Africa.

These bans have devastating implications for Black immigrant communities. For citizens of these countries living in the United States who are not naturalized, the travel ban will likely freeze them in place, as many will be fearful that they might not be permitted re-entry if they leave the United States temporarily (Al Jazeera, 2025). Families are being permanently separated, educational opportunities are being denied, and economic partnerships are being severed. The restrictions apply to both tourist and immigrant visas, effectively cutting off pathways to family reunification, educational advancement, and economic opportunity for millions of Black people.

The current administration persists in wielding immigration policy as a cudgel against Black-majority nations, further entrenching systems of global anti-Black racism.

Healthcare, Reproductive Rights, and Mental Health

"After my family was deported, I became the sole provider at age 19. The stress triggered panic attacks, but I was afraid to seek help. Our community health collective created a healing space where I didn't have to choose between my mental health and my safety."— Sophia J., Brooklyn, New York.

We know that our liberation cannot fully be actualized while we are unable to freely discuss our mental health and receive holistic, quality, affordable healthcare. We are labeled as overdramatic and emotional when we dare to show signs of weakness and assert that we are still human. We are denied the ability to be seen as complex beings, capable of embodying strength and weakness simultaneously. Consequently, we search for spaces and relationships that allow us to be. We need restorative moments to allow our bodies to break from hypervigilance. Moments where safety is unthought of. We all deserve moments where we are held tightly by our communities and lifted, when necessary (Black Alliance for Just Immigration, 2023).

The denial of reproductive rights for Black migrants is a global issue, and the United States Supreme Court's reversal of *Roe* v. *Wade* threatens progress worldwide. Race/ethnicity plays a critical role in the intersection of migration policy and reproductive rights. Racist, anti-immigrant leaders have long attacked reproductive rights to advance their power agendas, using rhetoric associated with "anchor babies" and fetal personhood attempts to stoke white fragility and enforce white nationalism. Legal abortion bans tend to increase exposure to unsafe alternatives, which will disproportionately affect Black and Indigenous women and birthing people, as well as intersecting vulnerable populations such as those with limited means, undocumented migrants, people with disabilities, and victims of sexual violence.

LGBTQ+ Rights and Asylum

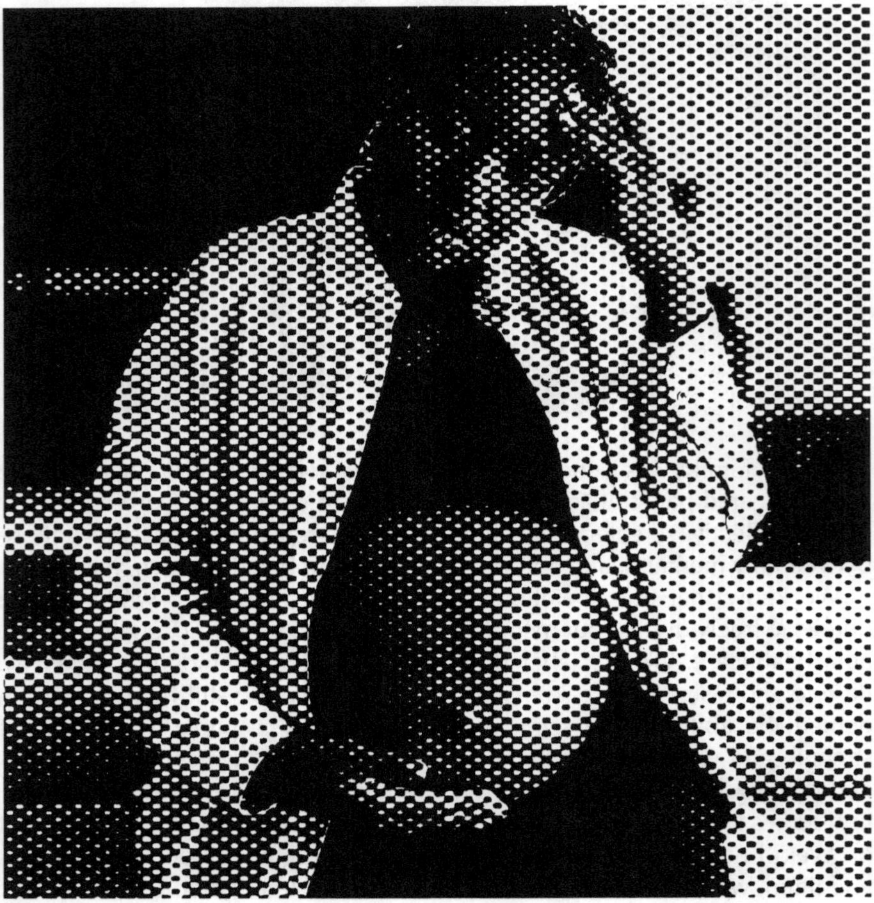

Policies that dehumanize transgender, queer, and gender-expansive communities not only undermine the spirit of human rights and international asylum law but also pose a grave danger to the Black, Lesbian, Gay, Bisexual, Transgender, Queer/Questioning and Same-Gender Loving (Black LGBTQ+/SGL) immigrant community in particular.

Finding refuge from hate is nearly impossible for Black LGBTQ+/SGL asylum seekers. As African leaders fuel anti-LGBTQ+ sentiment and stiffen anti-homosexuality legislation on the continent, Western politicians are utilizing xenophobic rhetoric and expanding anti-immigrant legislation (American Bar Association, 2025).

New policies introduced by the 47th presidential administration make it unsafe for queer, transgender, and gender-expansive people to exist. For example, requiring federal agencies to use only the term "sex," and not "gender," in official documents seeks to erase gender identity as a distinct concept.

In this hostile political climate, community spaces that respect and affirm gender identities are essential lifelines. In organizations like the Black LGBTQIA+ Migrant Project (BLMP) Black LGBTQ+/SGL migrants can find safety, community, and support. BAJI's and BLMP annual *Queer Home and Away* celebrations reflects these efforts, offering queer Black migrants a space to gather without fear of persecution

At The Crossroads: Black LGBTQIA+ Migrant Experiences

"We honor the unfathomable journeys our ancestors endured to get here, including surviving the anti-gay exclusion clauses in immigration law, which weren't repealed until 1990."—Black LGBTQIA+ Migrant Project (2025)

The experiences of Black LGBTQIA+/SGL migrants represent one of the most under-researched and overlooked dimensions of the immigration crisis. As BLMP powerfully documents in their groundbreaking report, *Shifting the Narrative; Changing the World: Black LGBTQIA+ Migrants Defining Our Own Experiences*, there exists a profound scarcity of information about communities at the intersections of race, immigration status, gender identity, and sexuality (Black LGBTQIA+ Migrant Project, 2025). This data gap is not incidental. It reflects the systematic erasure of Black LGBTQIA+ migrants from policy discussions, research priorities, and even within broader immigrant rights movements.

The BLMP report, based on a comprehensive survey with 323 respondents, Black migrants and first-generation people, reveals a community facing compounded violence, economic exploitation, healthcare barriers, and social isolation that far exceeds what either Black migrants or LGBTQIA+ people face separately. Their research provides critical quantitative evidence of experiences that have long been invisible, while centering the voices, visions, and wisdom of Black LGBTQIA+ migrants themselves.

A Legacy of Exclusion

Black LGBTQIA+ migrants carry the weight of multiple historical exclusions. Until 1990, United States immigration law contained explicit anti-gay exclusion clauses that prohibited LGBTQIA+ individuals from entering the country (Black LGBTQIA+ Migrant Project, 2025). This legal discrimination created a legacy of fear, invisibility, and vulnerability that continues to shape Black LGBTQIA+ migrant experiences today. Even as these explicit bans have been removed, Black LGBTQIA+ migrants face a hostile immigration system that fails to recognize the unique dangers they face—both in their countries of origin and throughout their migration journeys.

Currently, more than 30 African countries criminalize homosexuality (Black LGBTQIA+ Migrant Project, 2025). In Nigeria, LGBTQIA+ people face a 14-year prison sentence, while in Uganda, they may be executed. Across the Caribbean, anti-LGBTQIA+ legislation and social persecution force many to flee. Yet when Black LGBTQIA+ migrants seek refuge in the United States, they encounter an immigration system that neither understands nor adequately protects them. Of the BLMP survey respondents who were not born in the United States, 36% reported difficulty in the immigration process because they were ineligible for permanent residency or citizenship, the cost was too high, they did not understand the process, or they did not feel comfortable going to an immigration office (Black LGBTQIA+ Migrant Project, 2025).

The Violence Continuum: From Homeland to Border to Detention

Black LGBTQIA+ migrants experience violence at every stage of their journey. The BLMP report found that over 85% of survey respondents reported experiencing discrimination, with the most prominent source being gender and/or sexuality (77%), followed by race or ethnicity (52%), and immigration status (20%) (Black LGBTQIA+ Migrant Project, 2025). One respondent powerfully articulated the multiple points of vulnerability: attempts to escape violence in their homeland were met with violence along the migration route and continued violence upon arrival in the United States.

The statistics for Black transgender women and transfeminine migrants are particularly alarming. A staggering 70% of survey respondents who identified as trans, Black, and migrant reported experiencing violence (Black LGBTQIA+ Migrant Project, 2025). This represents an 8.2% increase from the already elevated violence rates experienced by all transgender people, which the National Crime Victimization Survey documented at 86.2 victimizations per 1,000 persons compared to 21.7 per 1,000 for cisgender people.

At the border, 57% of Black LGBTQIA+ migrant survey respondents reported firsthand encounters with law enforcement, with several subjected to body searches (Black LGBTQIA+ Migrant Project, 2025). These encounters reflect the intersection of anti-Black policing practices and anti-immigrant enforcement. Black people are more likely to be stopped and far more likely to be searched after being stopped by police compared to white people. This pattern extends to immigration enforcement and makes Black LGBTQIA+ migrants particularly vulnerable to detention, deportation, and violence.

Inside detention facilities, the violence intensifies. Trans women are more likely to be trafficked for commercial sexual exploitation, to be violently and sexually assaulted during migration to the United States, and to experience violence inside detention facilities (Black LGBTQIA+ Migrant Project, 2025). The lack of protocols for safely housing LGBTQIA+ detainees, combined with the broader violence endemic to immigration detention, creates conditions where Black LGBTQIA+ migrants face torture and abuse with little recourse or protection.

Economic Oppression and Survival

The economic realities facing Black LGBTQIA+ migrants reflect extreme exploitation and precarity. According to the BLMP report, 14% of survey respondents stated they do not have a job, while 37% work between two and three jobs in order to afford their cost of living (Black LGBTQIA+ Migrant Project, 2025). This economic desperation reflects how multiple forms of discrimination—based on race, immigration status, gender identity, and sexuality—compound to limit employment opportunities and suppress wages.

When Black LGBTQIA+ migrants do find employment, they face significant wage disparities. Women of African origin earn 10.1% less than U.S.-born non-Hispanic white women, while women of Caribbean origin earn 8.4% less. Haitian women earn 18.6% less (Black LGBTQIA+ Migrant Project, 2025). These disparities reflect the intersection of racial, gender, and nativity-based discrimination that Black LGBTQIA+ migrants navigate daily. According to Pew Research Center data cited in the BLMP report, one in five Black migrants lives below the poverty line; this group also has the highest unemployment rates amongst all migrant groups (Black LGBTQIA+ Migrant Project, 2025).

The economic vulnerability of Black LGBTQIA+ migrants is further compounded by the reality that many cannot access public benefits, face discrimination in housing markets, and must navigate employment without being able to be fully open about their identities. The result is a community working multiple jobs, living below the poverty line, and facing constant economic insecurity—all while contributing significantly to the United States economy through their labor.

The Healthcare Crisis: Disability, Illness, and Barriers to Care

The healthcare challenges facing Black LGBTQIA+ migrants represent a profound crisis. Nearly 24% of BLMP survey respondents reported they do not have insurance, while almost 35% reported having little to no access to healthcare (Black LGBTQIA+ Migrant Project, 2025). These gaps in coverage and access have devastating consequences for a community facing high rates of chronic illness and disability.

The BLMP report revealed striking disparities in disability rates: 47% of transgender respondents have a disability, compared to 31% of non-transgender respondents (Black LGBTQIA+ Migrant Project, 2025). Additionally, 33% of respondents who had more than one job and made less than $50,000 per year have a disability, highlighting how economic exploitation and health vulnerabilities are interconnected. Survey respondents named specific conditions, including bipolar disorder, major depression, anxiety, chronic pain, autism, post-traumatic stress disorder, physical muscle spasms, limited mobility, and attention-deficit/hyperactivity disorder.

For Black transgender women and transfeminine migrants, the healthcare crisis is particularly acute: 50% reported not having health insurance, while 80% reported having a chronic physical and/or mental illness (Black LGBTQIA+ Migrant Project, 2025). One first-generation, gender non-conforming Black lesbian and Muslim from the Ivory Coast shared: "Insurance is too expensive, moving states every year makes it impossible to find affordable, preferably Black or person of color (POC) woman providers" (Black LGBTQIA+ Migrant Project, 2025). Another first-generation woman from Nigeria stated: "It's difficult to receive physical therapy for my scoliosis because of the lack of facilities that accept Medicaid" (Black LGBTQIA+ Migrant Project, 2025).

These barriers to care are not merely inconveniences. They result in life-threatening gaps in a healthcare system that fails to recognize Black LGBTQIA+ migrants as deserving of care. The lack of access to gender-affirming healthcare, culturally competent mental health services, and basic preventative care contributes to the elevated rates of chronic illness and disability in this community. When combined with the trauma of migration, persecution, and ongoing discrimination, these healthcare barriers create a public health emergency that demands immediate attention.

Social Isolation and the Hunger for Community

Beyond the violence, economic exploitation, and healthcare barriers, Black LGBTQIA+ migrants face profound social isolation. The BLMP report found that 35.6% of survey respondents expressed a need for more acceptance, safe spaces, and community (Black LGBTQIA+ Migrant Project, 2025). This need reflects the multiple forms of exclusion Black LGBTQIA+ migrants experience—from broader society, from some immigrant communities that harbor anti-LGBTQIA+ sentiment, and even from some LGBTQIA+ spaces that fail to address anti-Black racism and the specific needs of migrants.

For Black transgender women and transfeminine migrants, the isolation is particularly severe. Of this population, 80% reported only sometimes having access to friends, 50% named a need for more community and safe spaces, 45% have limited or no access to legal services, and 20% reported having no access to friends at all (Black LGBTQIA+ Migrant Project, 2025). These statistics paint a picture of a community struggling not only with material deprivation but also with the profound pain of isolation in a society that marginalizes them on multiple fronts.

The isolation that Black LGBTQIA+ migrants experience compounds all other challenges they face. Without strong social networks, they are more vulnerable to exploitation by employers, landlords, and others. Without community support, they struggle to navigate complex immigration and healthcare systems. Without safe spaces to be fully themselves, they bear the psychological burden of constant vigilance and code-switching. As one survey respondent shared, the need is not just for services but for spaces of authentic belonging—spaces where one's Blackness, queerness, transness, and migration experience are not competing identities but integrated aspects of self that can be celebrated and supported.

Visionary Dreams: The Future Black LGBTQIA+ Migrants Deserve

Despite—and perhaps because of—the profound hardships documented in the BLMP report, Black LGBTQIA+ migrants hold visionary dreams for transformation. When survey respondents were asked about their vision for change in the United States and the world, they articulated expansive, imaginative, and prophetic dreams rooted in abolitionist and transformative justice frameworks:

> Abolition of prisons as the solution for immigration, poverty, tragedy and difficult mental health experiences; different ways we organize our system to welcome and support migrants; for white people to be moved out of all positions of power, Black and Indigenous led governance systems.
>
> (Black LGBTQIA+ Migrant Project, 2025)

> No more prisons, no more detention. Stop killing Black people. Housing and healthcare access for all.
>
> (Black LGBTQIA+ Migrant Project, 2025)

> Justice, reparations, centering the health and well-being of children and their families, COVID-related job support, universal healthcare, land back to Native Americans, decolonization of education, abolish police/ICE, remove dictators, end voting suppression.
>
> (Black LGBTQIA+ Migrant Project, 2025)

> Everything must change. The entire system needs to be dismantled: white supremacy, capitalism, patriarchy. Reparations to the Black and Indigenous populations. Free healthcare and education for all. Abolish the prison system. Abolish ICE. Defund the police. Ensure community engagement with funding for programs based on decolonization and equity work. Stop teaching revisionist history in public schools. Stop the veneration of the racist 'founding fathers' and the like by removing statues and names of public places. Dismantle the systems that allow the one percent to flourish, stop allowing corporations to play into the Zero Sum Game.
>
> (Black LGBTQIA+ Migrant Project, 2025)

These visions are not naïve wishes but sophisticated analyses of interconnected systems of oppression and clear articulations of the structural changes necessary for Black LGBTQIA+ migrants to not merely survive but thrive. They understand that piecemeal reforms will not address the root causes of their oppression. They demand the abolition of prisons and immigration detention, the dismantling of white supremacy and capitalism, reparations for historical harms, universal healthcare and housing, decolonized education, and Black and Indigenous governance. Their visions connect immigration justice to the broader struggle for Black liberation, Indigenous sovereignty, economic justice, and the transformation of all systems that perpetuate violence and inequality.

As BLMP states,

> Our task is to shape these dreams into areas for targeted policy advocacy, and to organize our people around concrete demands for substantive change. We know it will not come overnight. We are close on the heels of the work of our ancestors, fighting to carry on their legacies and 'avenge the suffering of our ancestors, to earn the respect of future generations, and be willing to be transformed in the service of the work.'
>
> (Black LGBTQIA+ Migrant Project, 2025)

The Path Forward: Centering Black LGBTQIA+ Migrant Leadership

BLMP's research represents more than documentation—it is an act of resistance against erasure and a foundation for targeted advocacy. By making visible what has been deliberately obscured, by quantifying experiences that have been dismissed as anecdotal, and by centering the voices and visions of Black LGBTQIA+ migrants themselves, BLMP has created a blueprint for how movements must evolve to serve those at the intersections of multiple marginalized identities.

Organizations like BLMP, BAJI, UndocuBlack Network, the National Black Justice Collective (NBJC), and others, are creating intentional spaces where Black LGBTQIA+ migrants can find safety, community, and support.

The path forward requires that we are inclusive of Black LGBTQIA+ migrant leadership in all immigration advocacy work. It requires that we collect disaggregated data that captures the intersections of race, immigration status, gender identity, and sexuality. It requires that we resource Black-led LGBTQIA+ migrant organizations not as afterthoughts in funding portfolios but as critical leaders in the immigration justice movement. It requires that we move beyond solidarity statements to genuine solidarity actions—showing up for Black LGBTQIA+ migrants' needs, demands, and visions with the same urgency we bring to other dimensions of social justice work.

Most importantly, it requires that we recognize immigration policy as fundamentally a racial justice issue and an LGBTQIA+ rights issue. Black LGBTQIA+ migrants cannot wait for broader movements to get around to their needs. Their liberation cannot be perpetually deferred. As the BLMP report demonstrates, Black LGBTQIA+ migrants face urgent, life-threatening challenges right now—70% experiencing violence, 80% of trans women and femmes living with chronic illness, 37% working multiple jobs just to survive, 35% with little to no healthcare access, and 20% with no access to friends at all.

The data demands action. The voices demand amplification. The visions demand implementation. Black LGBTQIA+ migrants deserve nothing less than a world without prisons and detention centers, a world with universal healthcare and housing, a world where Black and Indigenous governance replaces white supremacist power structures, and a world where migration is recognized as a human right rather than criminalized as a threat. Until we acquire such a world, we must fight with everything we have to protect, support, and celebrate Black LGBTQIA+ migrants in all their resilience, resistance, and brilliance.

Education and Youth Empowerment

The precarious position of Black migrant students in American educational institutions has reached crisis levels under the 47th presidential administration. Sharing resources with Black undocumented youth within university systems, which are often already inaccessible to Black people, is essential. These resources include healthcare information, housing support, legal services, food assistance, and mutual aid networks.

The 47th presidential administration's aggressive immigration enforcement has targeted international students. Black migrant students are having their visas arbitrarily revoked, being detained by ICE, and facing deportation threats despite maintaining valid student status. Most alarming is how quickly universities have capitulated to this administration's threats to withdraw federal funding. Rather than protecting their migrant student populations, many institutions have chosen to withhold guidance, legal support, and even basic information, leaving Black migrant students particularly vulnerable given their intersecting marginalized identities.

When a Kenyan doctoral student is unexpectedly detained during what should have been a routine check-in, their academic department often remains silent. When Haitian students face sudden visa revocations based on spurious national security claims, university administrators frequently offer platitudes rather than concrete assistance. This institutional abandonment intensifies the sense of isolation that many Black migrant students already experience on predominantly white campuses.

Our three pillars for empowering youth include centering youth voices, creating intentional spaces for healing and support (thriving), and building youth leadership to foster the next generation of organizers and community leaders. By establishing autonomous spaces for Black migrant youth within educational institutions, we can counter the chilling effect of current policies and ensure Black migrant students not only survive but thrive—even in hostile political environments.

Disrupting the Myth: Immigration as a Black Issue

The persistent framing of immigration as primarily a Latinx issue obscures the reality for Black immigrants, who face unique challenges:

- **Racial Profiling**: Black immigrants are more likely to be stopped, questioned about their status, and detained based on racial profiling.
- **Higher Bonds and Longer Detention**: Studies show Black immigrants receive bonds averaging 54% higher than those for non-Black immigrants with similar circumstances (Human Rights Watch, 2022).
- **Language Barriers**: Services for Black immigrants who speak languages other than Spanish are often limited or nonexistent.
- **Media Invisibility**: Stories of Black immigrants rarely receive media attention, limiting public awareness and political pressure.

The same systems that oppress U.S.-born Black people (policing, incarceration, and economic marginalization) also target Black immigrants.

By disrupting the myth that immigration is not a Black issue, we can more effectively build community wellness and power that addresses the specific needs of Black migrant communities while strengthening the broader movement for Black liberation. Our shared struggles demand shared solutions.

Organizations Leading the Response

Black-led organizations are at the forefront of protecting immigrant rights. They include:

- **Black Alliance for Just Immigration (BAJI)**: Advocates for racial, social, and economic justice for Black immigrants and Black Americans.
- **UndocuBlack Network**: Provides resources and community for Black undocumented immigrants.
- **Haitian Bridge Alliance**: Supports Haitian and other Black migrants through direct services and advocacy.
- **African Communities Together**: Organizes African immigrants for social and economic justice.
- **Cameroon Advocacy Network**: Focuses on protections for Cameroonian asylum seekers.
- **Black LGBTQIA+ Migrant Project (BLMP)**: Envisions a world without forced migration, where no one is forced to give up their homeland and where all Black LGBTQIA+ people are free and liberated.

Community Wellness and Power Building

Building community power for Black immigrants means creating spaces and systems where they can not only survive but thrive. Black migrant communities face profound needs and resource gaps due to the compounded impacts of anti-Black racism and anti-immigrant legal barriers in the United States. These challenges are often overlooked, leaving our communities to lean on one another to navigate systemic neglect, which includes ensuring access to vital resources such as healthcare, mental health support, educational opportunities, and creating safe spaces for youth.

Community Power Building

Community power building is centered on uplifting, mobilizing, engaging, and educating Black immigrants and Black Americans through outreach, direct action, advocacy, and base building. We work to build community power by organizing on the ground to support Black liberation, recognizing that 1 in 4 Black people in the United States are immigrants or the children of immigrants (Pew Research Center, 2026). Inspired by the legacy of the civil rights movement, we aim to carry this work forward by deepening civic engagement and mobilizing our communities to fight for lasting change.

BAJI's national efforts and partnerships with local organizations fuel efforts to grow a strong base, build political power, and elect leaders who truly represent us, while holding current officials accountable. A key feature of this work is uniting the Black diaspora through campaigns like "Blackness is...," ensuring our communities stay politically engaged and are not divided across party lines.

Our strategies include:

- **Powerbuilding and Community Conversations**: We are engaging in 30,000 conversations with the Black Diaspora community members in the next year alone.
- **Mutual Aid & Resources Sharing**: Posting bonds to release immigrants from detention, coordinating donations (e.g., backpacks for recently arrived migrants), providing legal resources, connecting immigrants to translation services.
- **Policy, research and legal**: BAJI's legal work combats the criminalization and deportation of Black immigrant communities through a powerful three-pronged approach, which includes direct legal representation, impact litigation, and legal training in communities facing removal. BAJI's policy and research work advocates at the local, national and international levels for policy and legislation that effectively address the needs of Black migrants based on their human rights and dignity.

Policy Recommendations

Immediate Actions:

1 **Promote Dignity Not Detention**:

- End the use of county jails and private prisons for immigration detention.
- Divest funds from immigration detention and digital detention alternatives, and use those funds for welcoming and care services.
- Establish binding standards for medical care for detained migrants, with particular attention to Black immigrants' health needs.

2 **Establish Community-Based Alternatives to Detention**:

- Fund community-based case management programs, which have proven 98% court appearance rates. This high compliance rate demonstrates that detention is unnecessary and that migrants, when supported through community-based programs, reliably attend their immigration proceedings. These alternatives are more humane and more cost-effective than detention.
- Eliminate cash bonds, which disproportionately impact Black immigrants.
- Create specialized community-led programs for vulnerable populations, including LGBTQIA+ asylum seekers.

3 **Expedited Processing for Black Asylum Seekers**:

- Establish fast-track humanitarian pathways with streamlined processing specifically for Black asylum seekers who face compounded dangers throughout their migration journeys.

4 **Detention Moratorium**:

- Implement an immediate moratorium on detention for all migrants, prioritizing trans and gender expansive people asylum seekers.
- Emergency healthcare access for Black migrants seeking asylum.

5 **Safe Housing and Community Space Guarantee**:

- Provide immediate access to safe, affirming housing and fund community-based alternatives for Black migrants seeking asylum.
- Create dedicated funding for Black migrant community centers and safe spaces, recognizing that 20% have no access to friends at all.

Medium-Term Solutions:

1 **Pathways to Permanent Status**:

- Create legislation providing permanent residence for long-term TPS holders.
- Establish a streamlined process for asylum seekers from countries in crisis.
- Reform visa quotas to address the historical exclusion of African countries.

2 **Address Racial Disparities in Immigration Enforcement**:

- Mandate data collection on race in all immigration proceedings.
- Create oversight mechanisms to identify and address discriminatory patterns.
- End the police-to-deportation pipeline, 287G agreements, and deputizing law enforcement and military personnel as ICE enforcement agents.

3 **Support for State and Local Inclusion**:

- Provide federal funding for refugee and immigrant support services.
- Support state and local policies that expand access to education, healthcare, and driver's licenses regardless of status.

4 **Transform the Legal Immigration System**:

- Remove asylum and refugee quotas.
- Create new immigration pathways for climate refugees.
- Implement reparative policies that acknowledge historical harms.
- Eliminate the enforcement arm of the immigration system and institute an administrative immigration system that recognizes migration as a human right.

5 **UN Human Rights Council (UNHRC) Protocols**:

- Support the UNHRC in creating concrete pathways for Black migrants fleeing persecution and apply international pressure on the United States and other nations to establish protocols enabling safe passage at borders.
- Establish international standards recognizing the compounded vulnerabilities faced by Black LGBTQIA+ individuals.

6 **Disability Justice Framework**:

- Implement comprehensive immigration system accommodations for disabled migrants, recognizing that 47% of Black trans migrants have disabilities.
- Ensure all immigration proceedings, detention facilities (pending abolition), and integration services are fully accessible, with specialized support for Black LGBTQIA+ migrants living with chronic conditions, mental health disabilities, and mobility limitations.

7 **Philanthropic Long-Term Investment**:

- Philanthropic institutions must make multi-year commitments to organizations centering LGBTQIA+ asylum seekers and refugees, moving beyond short-term grants to address the funding crisis threatening Black migrant justice work.

Long-Term Structural Change:

1 **Address Root Causes**:

- Implement climate finance mechanisms that support adaptation and mitigation in vulnerable nations.

2 **Intersectional Movement Building**:

- Challenge social justice organizations to move beyond "solidarity" rhetoric toward a genuine understanding of interconnected liberation struggles, recognizing how the nonprofit industrial complex has fragmented movements and undermined collective power.

3 **Disaggregated Data Collection**:

- Require collection and public reporting of data disaggregated by race, immigration status, gender identity, and sexuality across all immigration systems.
- Fund research initiatives led by Black migrants themselves to document experiences and guide policy.

4 **Abolitionist Framework Implementation**:

- Abolish immigration detention as part of the broader prison abolition movement, recognizing that abolition must be the solution for immigration, poverty, and mental health crises.
- Invest in community-based alternatives, mutual aid networks, and transformative justice approaches.

Call to Action: What Black Communities Can Do Now

Immediate Response (Next 30 Days)

- **Support Legal Defense**: Contribute to emergency legal funds for immigrants facing deportation through organizations like BAJI.
- **Contact Elected Representatives**: Ask them to support legislation establishing permenant protections for immigrant communities.
- **Create Safe Spaces**: Foster third spaces that are loving and accepting.

Medium-Term Mobilization (Next 6 Months)

- **Build Coalitions**: Form broad-based community coalitions connecting immigrant rights to racial justice, housing, education, and healthcare.
- **Civic Engagement**: Register voters in Black immigrant communities where eligible and educate about candidates' immigration positions.
- **Community Education**: Host "Know-Your-Rights" workshops specifically addressing the needs of Black immigrants.

Sustained Movement Building (1–3 Years)

- **Develop Leadership**: Invest in leadership development for Black immigrants, particularly youth, women, and LGBTQ+/SGL people.
- **Create Alternative Systems**: Build community-based support systems, including housing cooperatives, worker-owned businesses, and mutual aid networks.
- **Shape the Narrative**: Document and share stories of Black immigrants' contributions and resilience to counter harmful stereotypes.

The Global–Local Connection: Diaspora Issues and Local Impact

Understanding the connections between United States foreign policy, immigration policy, and the wellbeing of Black communities is essential for effective advocacy. United States interventions in countries like Haiti, Somalia, and the Democratic Republic of Congo have contributed to conditions that drive migration. Yet, the United States immigration system penalizes those seeking safety from these conditions.

Effective immigration advocacy requires understanding how global policies and local actions intersect. Communities can:

1. **Build coalitions between Black immigrants and U.S.-born Black communities**: Recognizing shared experiences of anti-Black racism can strengthen advocacy efforts.
2. **Connect humanitarian aid and immigration policy**: Advocating for responsible foreign policy alongside immigrant rights creates a more comprehensive approach.

3 **Support local sanctuary policies**: Cities and states can implement policies that protect immigrants regardless of federal enforcement priorities.
4 **Develop community support networks**: Local communities can create systems to provide legal services, healthcare, education, and other resources to immigrant populations.

By thinking globally and acting locally, communities can address the root causes of migration and the immediate needs of immigrant populations.

Conclusion

Immigration policy is racial justice policy. For the 5.6 million Black immigrants in the United States and the communities they are part of, current policies represent an existential threat. The overlapping oppressions of anti-Blackness and anti-immigrant sentiment create a unique burden that demands an intersectional response. Shared experiences of Blackness in America bind together Black migrants and Black Americans. The systems and policies that criminalize, deport, and exclude Black migrants inevitably harm Black American communities through severed relationships, diminished resources, and reinforced racist ideologies.

Our liberation is linked, our struggles interconnected, and our futures inseparable. By understanding Black immigrants' unique challenges, building coalitions between U.S.-born and immigrant Black communities, and taking concrete action at local, national, and international levels, we can forge a movement powerful enough to create lasting change. As we navigate this critical moment, we must remember that the struggle for immigrant rights is inseparable from the broader movement for Black liberation. ***We*** must keep **us** safe.

Key Organizations and Resources

Black-Led Immigration Organizations

- Black Alliance for Just Immigration (BAJI): www.baji.org
- UndocuBlack Network: www.undocublack.org
- Haitian Bridge Alliance: www.haitianbridge.org
- African Communities Together: www.africans.us
- Cameroon Advocacy Network: www.cameroonadvocacynetwork.org
- Black LGBTQIA+ Migrant Project: www.transgenderlawcenter.org/blmp

Legal Resources

- Immigration Law Help: www.immigrationlawhelp.org
- Asylum Seeker Advocacy Project: www.asylumadvocacy.org
- National Immigration Project: www.nipnlg.org

Research and Policy Resources

- Black Alliance for Just Immigration https://baji.org/resources/
- Black Immigrant Research Initiative (Pew Research Center): www.pewresearch.org/topic/race-ethnicity/racial-ethnic-groups/black-americans/
- Migration Policy Institute: www.migrationpolicy.org
- American Immigration Council: www.americanimmigrationcouncil.org

Notes

1 https://immigrationforum.org/article/temporary-protected-status-fact-sheet/
2 https://www.refugeesinternational.org/perspectives-and-commentaries/setting-the-record-straight-on-chnv/

References

Al Jazeera (2025). Which countries are on Trump's travel ban list, and who will be affected? https://www.aljazeera.com/news/2025/6/5/which-countries-are-on-trumps-travel-ban-list-and-who-will-be-affected

All Things Considered. (2025). *Florida is moving ahead with 'Alligator Alcatraz,' despite widespread pushback.* https://www.npr.org/2025/06/24/nx-s1-5443268/alligator-alcatraz-florida-everglades-migrant-detention-center

American Bar Association. (2025). No refuge from hate: Homophobia in Africa and xenophobia in the United States creates perilous conditions for Black LGBTI migrants. *Human Rights Magazine.* https://www.americanbar.org/groups/crsj/resources/human-rights/2025-march/homophobia-africa-xenophobia-us-perilous-conditions-black-lgbti-migrants/

American Civil Liberties Union. (2025). What You Need to Know About Alligator Alcatraz. https://www.aclu.org/news/immigrants-rights/floridas-secretive-immigration-detention-center-explained

American Immigration Council. (2024). *Data Snapshot: The number of Black immigrants in the US continues to rise*. https://immigrationimpact.com/2024/02/09/data-number-of-black-immigrants-in-the-us/

Bailey, Chelsea, Isabel Rosales, and Alaa Elassar. (2025). *'Alligator Alcatraz': What to know about Florida's new controversial migrant detention facility. CNN.* https://www.cnn.com/2025/07/01/us/what-is-alligator-alcatraz-florida

Black Alliance for Just Immigration. (2023). *Criminalizing Blackness: An analysis of the impacts of the 1994 crime bill and 1996 immigration bill on Black people*. https://baji.org

Black LGBTQIA+ Migrant Project. (2025). *Shifting the narrative; Changing the world: Black LGBTQIA+ migrants defining our own experiences*. https://bit.ly/BLMPReport

Human Rights First. (2022). *Black Immigrants Face Unique Challenges*. https://www.humanrightsfirst.org/library/black-immigrants-face-unique-challenges

Human Rights First. (2026). *ICE Air Expands Deportation and Domestic Transfer Flights to Record Levels in First Year of Second Trump Administration*. https://www.humanrightsfirst.org/library/ice-air-expands-deportation-and-domestic-transfer-flights-to-record-levels-in-first-year-of-second-trump-administration

Johnson, K. (2025). *Trump Administration reaffirms and expands travel bans*. Nilan Johnson Lewis.

Montanaro, D. (2025). Trump revokes parole for more than half a million migrants. *NPR*. https://www.npr.org/2025/03/05/nx-s1-5224958/trump-revokes-parole-for-migrants

Morgan-Trostle, J., Zheng, K. (2016). *The state of Black immigrants, part II: Black immigrants in the mass criminalization system*. Black Alliance for Just Immigration; NYU School of Law Immigrant Rights Clinic. https://baji.org/wp-content/uploads/2020/03/sobi-fullreport-jan22.pdf

Mutsaka, Farai. (2025). *Trump's expanded travel ban hits Africa the hardest but reactions are muted. Associated Press / The Washington Post.* https://www.washingtonpost.com/world/2025/12/17/travel-ban-restrictions-africa-muted-responses/4256b4d0-db9b-11f0-b484-4459fa8e79e5_story.html

Pew Research Center. (2026). *Key findings about Black immigrants in the U.S.* https://www.pewresearch.org/short-reads/2026/03/20/key-findings-about-black-immigrants-in-the-us/

The Associated Press. (2025). *From deportation to court, key events in Kilmar Abrego Garcia's fight with the Trump administration*. https://apnews.com/article/kilmar-abrego-garcia-immigration-deportation-trump-timeline-11cbaf1c1fbd2475a49e40d97bc620f2

U.S. Citizenship and Immigration Services. (2025). *Temporary protected status designated country: Haiti*. https://www.uscis.gov/humanitarian/temporary-protected-status/temporary-protected-status-designated-country-haiti

United States Immigration and Customs Enforcement (2026). Delegation of Immigration Authority Section 287(g) Immigration Nationality Act.

Section VI

Infrastructure and Environment

This section examines how infrastructure and environmental systems—from the air we breathe to the internet we access, from the land we steward to the homes we inhabit—have been deliberately designed to extract from Black communities while serving as mechanisms of both material harm and social control. Together, these Black Papers demonstrate that infrastructure is never neutral but always reflects power relations, revealing that achieving Black liberation does not require incremental reforms, but fundamental redesign of systems determining where we live, how we move, what we breathe, and whether we thrive.

"Green Dreams Deferred: Environmental Justice in Black America" documents how environmental racism operates as deliberate policy rather than accident, tracing from redlining that concentrated pollution in Black neighborhoods through highway construction that destroyed thriving communities to contemporary digital redlining of renewable energy investments. Black Americans face 56% more pollution than they generate. In comparison, white Americans encounter 17% less, with Black Americans 75% more likely to reside near industrial sites and 1.5 times more likely to suffer asthma from air pollution. This Black Paper examines flashpoint crises, from Flint's lead-contaminated water serving predominantly Black residents to Hurricane Katrina's devastation, revealing how climate vulnerability maps onto racial segregation, to Cancer Alley's petrochemical corridor, where Black communities experience cancer rates far exceeding national averages. The 47th presidential administration's 2025 dismantling of all environmental justice funding, offices, programs, and advisories represents a systematic erasure of protections. Yet, this Black Paper argues that Black communities have always been ecological justice leaders, from the 1968 Memphis Sanitation Workers Strike through Warren County's 1982 resistance, creating the movement to contemporary organizing in frontline communities. Policy demands include the Environmental Justice Act with community veto power over toxic facilities, establishing a Green Reparations Fund addressing historical harms, a just transition ensuring 50% of renewable energy investments are directed to Black communities, and cumulative impact assessments preventing new pollution in already-burdened areas.

DOI: 10.4324/9781003752646-22

"Rooted Resilience: Black Land Stewardship in the Face of Climate Crisis" reclaims Black agricultural traditions as both wealth-building strategy and climate solution, documenting how systematic land theft reduced Black farm ownership from 14% of all United States farmers in 1920 to less than 2% today—a loss representing trillions in stolen generational wealth. This Black Paper grounds its analysis in Fannie Lou Hamer's wisdom that "they can't starve you or evict you if you own a piece of land and know what to do with it," examining how Black land ownership creates food sovereignty in communities where 39.5 million Americans live in food deserts, with Black neighborhoods having significantly fewer supermarkets than white areas. The analysis traces from West African agricultural knowledge that sustained enslaved communities through Reconstruction-era Black farming prosperity systematically destroyed by violence and discriminatory USDA policies, to contemporary movements like Soul Fire Farm's Farming While Black and National Black Farmers Association's organizing, demonstrating how Black land stewardship offers regenerative practices combating climate change while building community wealth. As climate gentrification displaces Black communities from increasingly valuable land while extreme weather disproportionately devastates Black neighborhoods with inadequate infrastructure, this Black Paper argues land ownership represents both economic security and political power, presenting policies, including USDA reparations for discrimination, protection against their property exploitation, community land trusts preventing displacement, and agricultural education programs restoring Black farming knowledge.

"Housing As A Human Right" exposes how housing policy has functioned as a primary mechanism for creating and maintaining racial wealth gaps, with homeownership rates revealing that while approximately 75% of white families own homes, only 45% of Black families do—a gap actually greater today than in 1960 during Jim Crow. This Black Paper documents the architecture of exclusion from Federal Housing Administration's 1934 redlining explicitly refusing to insure mortgages in Black neighborhoods through urban renewal's "Negro removal" destroying thriving communities, to contemporary manifestations including algorithmic discrimination in mortgage approvals where Black applicants face denial at significantly higher rates even when controlling for income, appraisal bias systematically undervaluing homes in Black neighborhoods by 12.5%, corporate investors purchasing single-family homes at scale and converting them to rentals blocking Black wealth building, and gentrification extracting value Black residents created through decades of community building. The analysis documents how housing instability compounds across systems: Black households comprise 37% of people experiencing homelessness despite being 13% of the population, while short-term rental platforms like Airbnb remove housing stock from Black neighborhoods, driving up rents, and climate change increasingly threatens Black communities living in flood zones and heat islands due to historical redlining. Policy recommendations include strengthening Fair Housing Act (FHA) enforcement with community monitoring power, reforming FHA programs, reducing barriers to Black homeownership, establishing first-time buyer programs with down payment assistance, implementing rent control and "just cause eviction" protections, funding community land trusts and cooperative housing models, and requiring racial equity impact assessments for all housing policy.

"Pathways To Mobility: Transportation Infrastructure and Policy in the United States" demonstrates how transportation systems have been weaponized to destroy Black communities while limiting access to opportunity, beginning with the Interstate Highway System's 1956 launch that displaced 475,000 families with Black neighborhoods bearing disproportionate impact as highways were intentionally built along racial boundary lines or placed to create barriers between Black and white areas. This Black Paper documents ongoing harms: Black Americans are twice as likely to be struck and killed while walking due to underfunded infrastructure in their neighborhoods, Black families spend 33% more than the national average on combined housing and transportation costs, creating structural barriers to wealth-building; and transportation access remains a critical obstacle with rural residents struggling to reach healthcare, employment, and services. Yet transportation also represents a wealth creation pathway, from Hartsfield-Jackson Atlanta Airport employing over 63,000 people, many from Black communities due to Mayor Maynard Jackson's 1970s requirement that Black-owned businesses receive 25% of airport contracts, to unionized transit jobs providing middle-class stability. The analysis presents solutions from Birmingham's on-demand transit increasing job accessibility from 10% to 90%, to complete streets design prioritizing pedestrian safety, to the Justice40 Initiative ensuring 40% of infrastructure investments reach disadvantaged communities. Policy demands include equity-centered planning with racial equity impact assessments, integrated transportation connecting people to healthcare/education/employment, first mile/last mile solutions, public transit expansion in underserved areas, and Vision Zero commitments eliminating traffic deaths, prioritizing Black neighborhoods.

"Digital Equity is a Civil Right" argues that reliable, affordable high-speed internet access represents essential infrastructure for participating in contemporary society, yet deeply entrenched structural barriers limit Black Americans' digital adoption through what researchers call the "three-legged stool" of access, affordability, and digital skills. This Black Paper documents digital redlining mirroring historical housing discrimination, as government and Internet Service Providers prioritize broadband deployment in communities expecting faster return on investment while underinvesting in Black neighborhoods—the same communities that telecommunications infrastructure neglected during the Jim Crow era. With most Americans living in areas with only one broadband provider, thereby creating local monopolies, the average monthly costs of $78 represent a significant burden, resulting in 4 in 10 low-income Americans being "subscription-vulnerable," or unable to afford broadband consistently. The 2024 expiration of the Affordable Connectivity Program (ACP) left 22 million households without financial support, disproportionately impacting Black families. Digital exclusion compounds across systems: students unable to complete homework, seniors unable to access telehealth in rural areas, entrepreneurs unable to launch businesses, workers unable to access job training, and communities unable to organize effectively. Yet this Black Paper celebrates Black digital innovation from early adoption, demonstrating technology's liberatory potential to contemporary tech entrepreneurship, arguing that solutions require treating broadband as a public utility with rate regulation, permanent affordability programs replacing expired ACP, community-owned broadband networks, digital literacy programs in trusted community institutions, and tech industry accountability for algorithmic bias.

"Securing Black America: A Revolutionary Framework for True National Security". This Black Paper documents how the traditional national security apparatus has historically surveilled and suppressed Black freedom movements, from COINTELPRO through contemporary fusion centers, while failing to protect Black communities from actual threats, with inadequate hate crime prosecution, disaster response that abandons Black neighborhoods (as seen post-Katrina), and cybersecurity funding bypassing Black institutions. The analysis demands a complete reimagining centering Black safety through community-led security initiatives, replacing militarized policing, equal disaster response and recovery with pre-positioned resources in vulnerable communities, cybersecurity funding for Black-serving institutions, financial fraud protection and digital literacy programs, and defense against voter suppression through election security, focusing on protecting Black participation. This revolutionary framework recognizes that protecting Black communities from these threats represents a prerequisite for genuine national security rather than a peripheral concern.

Together, these Black Papers demonstrate that infrastructure and environmental systems determine life chances as fundamentally as any explicit policy, shaping where Black communities can live, what air they breathe, what water they drink, how they move through space, whether they can participate digitally, and whether they experience basic safety. They challenge readers to recognize that incremental improvements to unjust systems cannot achieve justice—that we require fundamental redesign starting from the needs of those most harmed. This section articulates infrastructure and environment as sites where oppression operates most materially and where transformation offers most concrete improvements to daily life, calling for investments proportionate to centuries of extraction, community control over resources and decision-making, and recognition that Black environmental leadership, land stewardship, and community organizing have always pointed toward more sustainable and equitable futures for all.

Chapter 16

Green Dreams Deferred

Environmental Justice in Black America

*LaTricea D. Adams**

Executive Summary

Environmental injustice in Black America represents a continuum of systemic oppression stretching from the forced labor of slavery through contemporary climate apartheid. This Black Paper (Paper) examines how Black communities have borne disproportionate environmental burdens throughout American history, from enslaved Africans' forced exposure to toxic swamps to the current communities subjected to the threats of industrial pollution and climate change. Through historical analysis and contemporary case studies, we trace the development of environmental racism from plantation extraction to modern "sacrifice zones," with links to the state of Black people's health. Additionally, we highlight the emergence of a robust environmental justice movement led by Black activists and scholars. As the current administration dismantles federal environmental justice protections, this analysis calls for a renewed commitment to Black-led solutions, which include green reparations, the creation of renewable energy within our communities, and coalition-building rooted in principles of self-determination. The Paper concludes that achieving environmental justice requires policy changes and fundamentally reimagining how Black people and communities relate to their land, health, and power in America.

* Supported by braintrust authors: Brea Baker, Leilah Naila Jones, and Kelcey P. Morrow.

DOI: 10.4324/9781003752646-23

Introduction: An Unjust Environment

Now more than ever, the United States of America has reached an inescapable point of reckoning, grappling with the intersection of race, public health, and our environment. The struggles for civil, human, social, and environmental justice have been inextricably linked, and now it cannot be ignored. Environmental injustice (EI) is not merely an issue of ecological concern. It is the air in our lungs, the water in our taps, and the soil under our feet. EI is a result of violent, systematic neglect, tracing a direct line from the legacies of slavery to the modern realities of environmental sacrifice zones. Both the history and journey of the environmental justice movement serve as a vital thread woven through the Black American experience, stretching from the brutalities of slavery to the present-day struggles against environmental racism. Understanding this history and its ongoing impacts is essential to building a future where our dreams of green spaces, clean air and water, and healthy homes are no longer deferred, but realized.

This Paper argues that environmental racism against Black communities represents a foundational feature of American capitalism that requires policy reform and a fundamental restructuring of how decisions about land, industry, and community health are made. By tracing the evolution of environmental injustice from slavery, Jim Crow, to the present day, and examining historical and contemporary case studies, this Paper positions Black-led environmental justice organizing as a transformative force. It illuminates how these movements confront systemic neglect and reimagine relationships between people, place, and power, calling for a renewed commitment within the Black community to build sustainable and liberated futures.

Historical Foundations: A Toxic Legacy

The base of EI in Black America can be traced back to the slave ships. While these incubators of disease and torture manifested the development of viruses like Zika and yellow fever, the relentless dispossession of enslaved Africans has been linked to ecological disruptions in migration patterns for many aquatic life forms. Enslaved Africans were subjected to strenuous labor on plantations, where their bodies were exploited for agricultural production. Black Americans were environmental engineers, forced to clear swamps, plant cotton, and mine lands that enriched white planters while poisoning Black bodies.

The environmental burdens of slavery fell disproportionately harder on Black women, who endured exploitation as agricultural workers and reproductive laborers. Enslaved women worked in fields while pregnant and exposed to pesticides and extreme weather. This practice, while centuries old, echoes the high maternal and infant mortality rates still seen amongst Black women and children and contemporary environmental health disparities. Black children, forced into labor at younger ages, faced developmental impacts from lead exposure in paint production and other toxic industries that would shape lifelong health outcomes.

Post-Emancipation, "freedmen's" towns were pushed onto floodplains, toxic lowlands, or near railroad hubs, sites deemed unfit for white residents (Berry, 2020). The land they toiled on was often poisoned by the practices that sustained the plantation economy. This exploitation set a precedent for the disregard of Black lives in environmental decision-making.

Following the Civil War, the realities of Jim Crow quickly overshadowed the promise of freedom, and codified systemic racism and environmental injustice. Black communities were systematically marginalized and faced discriminatory practices such as redlining, which restricted access to quality housing and safe neighborhoods. This segregation extended to environmental hazards; neighborhoods predominantly inhabited by Black residents were often located near toxic waste sites and industrial facilities. We see these hazards extend into the future, as a 2019 National Academy of Sciences study found that African Americans face 56% more pollution than they generate, while white Americans encounter 17% less pollution than their own contributions (Tessum et al., 2019). Additionally, African Americans are 75% more likely to reside near industrial sites compared to white Americans, increasing their risk of harmful exposures to fumes from these sites that are linked to serious health issues such as asthma, congenital disabilities, cancer, and cardiovascular diseases (University of Michigan School of Public Health, 2021). Considering these facts, the *innovation* and economic surge of the Industrial Revolution that carried throughout American Slavery and into Post-Emancipation—it gave birth to the act of *dumping* polluting industries into Black communities, deeming them as the *paths of least resistance*, which both the Father of the Environmental Justice Movement, Dr. Robert Bullard, and Dr. Beverly Wright define as "areas [that] are typically politically disempowered, poorer, and disproportionately home to Black people" (Dearing, 2023).

The Emergence of Environmental Justice as a Movement

Before it was formally established as a term, the fight for environmental justice was first seen on plantations. The introduction of composting has been recorded as a practice amongst enslaved Africans and attributed to their preconceived herbalist and agricultural knowledge from home. This fight continued in the 1960s and 1970s, particularly during the 1968 Sanitation Workers Strike in Memphis, Tennessee. The strike, led by African American workers, highlighted the hazardous working conditions and lack of protection for workers in the waste management industry (McGrath, 2011). This event marked a turning point in the Civil Rights and Environmental Justice movements, highlighting the intersection of labor rights and environmental justice. In 1982, the term "environmental racism" was coined by Dr. Benjamin Chavis, a civil rights leader and environmental activist, to describe the disproportionate impact of environmental hazards on communities of color (Commission for Environmental Cooperation, n.d.). The following year, in Warren County, North Carolina, a predominantly Black community resisted the construction of a toxic waste landfill in their backyard, sparking a national movement (Bullard, 1990). Environmental justice has evolved from the humble agricultural practices of our ancestors to acts of resistance by their descendants.

While initially unsuccessful in preventing the landfill, the Warren County protests established crucial organizing models that continue influencing environmental justice advocacy. The campaign demonstrated the power of peaceful, nonviolent direct action that results in coalition-building between civil rights and environmental organizations, and a strategic use of media in exposing environmental racism. Twenty years later, community organizing secured state funding for cleanup and health monitoring, proving that sustained resistance can achieve long-term victories. The Warren County model of combining grassroots organizing, legal advocacy, and policy pressure has been replicated in successful campaigns from Cancer Alley to Chicago's Southeast Side.

This struggle led to the development of the 17 Principles of Environmental Justice, crafted at the First National People of Color Environmental Leadership Summit in October of 1991 in Washington, D.C. (Principles of Environmental Justice, 1991). The creation of the Jemez Principles followed in December 1996 (Southwest Network for Environmental and Economic Justice, 1996), which have become cornerstones of the environmental justice movement. Dr. Robert Bullard, often called the "Father of Environmental Justice," has been a leading voice in the environmental justice movement. His work has exposed the systemic nature of environmental injustices and advocated for policy changes to address these issues (Bullard, 1990). Hazel Johnson, known as the "Mother of Environmental Justice," and who was born in what is now called "Cancer Alley" in Louisiana, also made significant contributions, particularly in her work to address environmental hazards in urban communities like Chicago (People for Community Recovery, n.d.).

Johnson's work in Chicago's Altgeld Gardens public housing development demonstrated how Black women's leadership drives environmental justice organizing. Her organization, People for Community Recovery, successfully documented the health impacts of nearby toxic sites, secured health studies, and created a model for community-controlled research that has been adopted nationwide. Similarly, the work of Dolores Huerta and the United

Farm Workers, while primarily focused on labor rights, established crucial precedents for environmental health protections that benefit Black agricultural workers across the South.

The establishment of the Environmental Protection Agency's (EPA) Office of Environmental Justice in 1992 also marked a significant step toward addressing environmental injustices, as did the historical establishment of the inaugural White House Environmental Justice Advisory Council during the Biden–Harris administration and Justice40 initiative, which aimed to direct 40% of climate investments to disadvantaged communities (White House, 2024).

Through the EPA's efforts, grants were distributed to communities disproportionately affected by environmental pollution, improvements were made to infrastructure across the country, and efforts toward inspections and compliance monitoring were enhanced. In addition, the National Environmental Justice Advisory Council (NEJAC), established in 1993, provided policies and programs that guided the EPA in supporting community redevelopment, strengthening systems to include marginalized communities in decision-making regarding environmental hazards, and incorporating their recommendations.

As of 2025, the 47th presidential administration has dismantled all funding (including federal grants), offices, programs, and advisories associated with environmental justice (White House, 2025; EPA, 2024).

Contemporary Environmental Racism

The consequences of historical discrimination and environmental racism are evident today. Black communities continue to bear a disproportionate burden of environmental harms. Other forms of marginalization exacerbate these impacts. Black women face environmental health risks during pregnancy and childbirth, elderly Black residents in frontline communities that experience the first and most impactful effects of environmental harm experience accelerated health decline, and Black Lesbian, Gay, Bisexual, Transgender, Queer+, and same-gender loving (LGBTQ+/SGL) people often lack access to the healthcare needed to address pollution-related illnesses.

Climate change compounds these injustices and disproportionately impacts already vulnerable communities. Black neighborhoods, often lacking resources and infrastructure, are more vulnerable to extreme weather events like hurricanes and floods. While 2025 marked the 20th anniversary of Hurricane Katrina, the intensity of extreme storms has increased significantly over time. For example, the 2017 devastation of Hurricane Harvey in Houston exposed these disparities—Black and Latinx communities suffered greater losses and faced slower recovery due to systemic neglect and underinvestment, very similarly to what was seen in places like New Orleans and Mississippi post-Katrina (Taylor, 2014). Climate change and extreme heat have also disproportionately impacted Black maternal health and birth outcomes. A study found there was a statistically significant association between heat, ozone, or fine particulate matter and adverse pregnancy outcomes, with Black mothers and birthing people at greater risk than any other racial group (Bekkar et al., 2020).

The Flint Water Crisis, where a predominantly Black community was exposed to lead-contaminated water due to a change in water source and a lack of proper treatment, stands as a stark example (Clark, 2016). Similarly, Benton Harbor, Michigan, a majority-Black city, faced a prolonged water crisis with high lead levels, leading to community outrage and demands for action (PBS News Hour, 2022). Jackson, Mississippi, a city with a majority Black population, has also suffered from failing water infrastructure, resulting in residents being exposed to unsafe water for extended periods (Schrader, 2022). In Newark, New Jersey, elevated lead levels in the water supply prompted extensive lead pipe replacements after community activism and legal action (Marshall, 2022).

Unfortunately, EI has been pervasive, affecting more than the waters in residential areas and neighborhoods. The mass incarceration system has been the face of environmental vulnerabilities, with prisons disproportionately located near toxic sites and Black prisoners facing higher exposure to environmental hazards both inside facilities and in the communities they return to upon release.

Environmental racism bears a new face as the development and deployment of Artificial Intelligence (AI) technologies are creating new avenues for inequitable environmental burdens. In Memphis, the location of Elon Musk's xAI supercomputer facility in the predominantly Black neighborhood of Boxtown has sparked significant controversy. The facility's methane gas turbines, which power the energy-intensive AI operations, release harmful pollutants like formaldehyde and NOx, exacerbating existing health issues and environmental injustices (SELC, 2024). Additionally, legitimate community fears of AI and data centers raise questions surrounding the stability of already weak power grids and water conservation. This situation highlights a pattern in which Black communities are exploited and bear the burdens of environmental hazards fostered for the advancement of technology. The rush to *AI dominance* without considering the consequences on Black, frontline communities demonstrates a long road ahead to achieve environmental justice.

Beyond Memphis, cryptocurrency mining operations are disproportionately located in Black communities due to lower property values and weaker political resistance. In Texas and Kentucky, Bitcoin mining facilities generate massive energy demands and noise pollution in predominantly Black neighborhoods. Meanwhile, "green gentrification" displaces long-term Black residents as cities invest in environmental improvements like parks and bike lanes without anti-displacement protections, as seen in Atlanta's BeltLine development and Washington, D.C.'s Anacostia waterfront. These cases, though current, emphasize the ideas previously stated within this Black Paper. Without deliberate protections through policy and practice, incidents of environmental injustice will continue to expand just as the world expands with new technologies and trends.

Models of Resistance and Victory

Despite ongoing challenges, Black communities have created powerful models of environmental justice organizing that demonstrate the possibility of transformative change. These victories provide tactical blueprints for current and future organizing efforts.

Architects of Environmental Relations: Before our ancestors were subjugated to slavery, they had a profound connection with the natural world and the benefits it provides to its inhabitants. In many African cultures, the land was cultivated to provide food and offer healing, protection, and spiritual connection through plant and herbal knowledge. Agricultural pioneers, such as Dr. George Washington Carver, were instrumental in introducing farming methods such as crop rotation and composting; methods that have led to increasing the productivity of soil and diverting material that would have gone to landfills, which are also disproportionately located near Black communities (Talt, 2020).

Community Land Control and Cooperative Ownership: The Dudley Street Neighborhood Initiative in Boston's predominantly Black and Latino Roxbury neighborhood successfully leveraged eminent domain laws to reclaim vacant lots and build community-controlled affordable housing and urban farms. Their model of resident-led planning and community land trusts has been replicated in Detroit, Oakland, and other cities, demonstrating how communities can gain control over environmental decisions affecting their neighborhoods.

Energy Democracy and Just Transition: The Richmond, California community transformed its relationship with the Chevron refinery through decades of organizing. The Richmond Progressive Alliance, led by Black and Latino residents, elected a city council majority committed to environmental justice and negotiated a $90 million community benefits package focused on renewable energy and health investments. Similarly, Black-led energy cooperatives in Georgia and North Carolina demonstrate how communities can own and control renewable energy development.

Food Justice and Urban Agriculture: Growing Power in Milwaukee, founded by Will Allen, created an urban agriculture model that addresses food apartheid and environmental restoration in Black communities. The organization's approach to turning abandoned lots into productive growing spaces while providing job training and healthy food access has influenced similar efforts nationwide, from Detroit's urban farms to Chicago's Growing Home initiative.

Policy Victories and Legal Strategies: The Cancer Alley Environmental Justice Coalition's campaign to halt planned petrochemical expansions demonstrates how community organizing combined with legal advocacy can achieve concrete wins. Their work documenting cumulative health impacts and demanding that environmental racism be addressed in permitting decisions led to multiple permit denials and established legal precedents for environmental justice claims.

Toward Green Dreams Realized: The Path Forward

Black America must prioritize environmental justice and turn our green dreams and aspirations into actionable change. This transformation requires concrete policy demands, organizing strategies, and a vision for systemic change that addresses the root causes of environmental racism.

To best address climate change, we must prioritize significant investments in clean, renewable energy, incorporating voices from the Black community and demanding access to the economic benefits of this burgeoning industry.

We must also demand robust regulations and laws that not only protect public health but also hold polluters accountable for their actions that, by and large, directly and disproportionately impact Black communities.

We should also unapologetically advocate for "green reparations" that address historical injustices, providing resources and support to communities disproportionately affected by environmental degradation.

Black coalition-building and collaboration are essential to developing inclusive policies that genuinely reflect the needs and values of Black America.

Cultural and Spiritual Dimensions

We must evoke the spirit of Sankofa as well as the Kwanzaa Principles to empower ourselves and our communities through education and awareness so that Black America can reimagine what our communities look and feel like, not the exhausting toils of resisting white supremacy, colonization, and imperialism. This means:

- Reconnecting with African and Indigenous land-based spiritual practices.
- Teaching children about sustainable relationships with the environment.
- Healing trauma from environmental violence through ceremony and community care.
- Visioning abundance rather than scarcity in our environmental relationships.

Environmental justice in Black America is a story of deferred dreams of freedom, land, health, and dignity. It is also a story of unyielding hope and fierce determination. Recognizing the history of environmental injustice is the first step toward reclaiming our green dreams.

In the words of the great ancestor Fannie Lou Hamer, Black folks are "sick and tired of being sick and tired," and we must summon the spirit of the ancestors to fight for environmental justice for all.

Call to Action: Your Role in Realizing Dreams

The path from deferred dreams to realized liberation requires us to act urgently and intentionally. Environmental justice cannot be achieved through wishful thinking or incremental reform—it demands bold action, strategic organizing, and unwavering commitment to Black liberation. The moment is now. The climate crisis intensifies daily, the 47th presidential administration accelerates environmental racism, and Black communities continue to suffer and die from toxic exposure. But we also stand at an unprecedented possibility, with proven organizing models, policy frameworks, and a growing movement ready to transform our relationship with land, health, and power.

If You Are a Community Member

Start Where You Are. Environmental justice begins with knowing your neighborhood: document pollution sources, air quality, and health impacts in your community. Use tools like the EPA's EJSCREEN (while still available) and community science monitoring to gather evidence. Connect with neighbors experiencing similar health issues. Form or join a community environmental health committee.

Demand Accountability. Attend city council and zoning board meetings where environmental decisions are made. Speak during public comment periods. Demand cumulative impact assessments before any new industrial permits are approved. Insist on community benefit agreements that include health monitoring and local hiring requirements.

Build Community Power. Register voters in your neighborhood, especially around environmental issues. Support candidates who reject polluter money and champion environmental justice. Run for local environmental boards, school boards, and city councils yourself. The decisions made at these levels directly impact your family's health.

If You Are an Organizer or Advocate

Center Community Leadership: Ensure that frontline community members lead campaigns affecting their neighborhoods. Provide resources and technical assistance without taking over. Build organizing skills within communities rather than creating dependence on outside organizations.

Connect the Struggles: Link environmental justice to housing, healthcare, education, and criminal justice reform. Environmental racism cannot be defeated in isolation; it requires comprehensive approaches that address the root causes of oppression.

Scale Up Successful Models: We do not need to reinvent the wheel when there are opportunities to be inspired by one another. Study and replicate victories like Richmond, California's refinery campaign, Newark's lead pipe replacement, and Detroit's urban agriculture movement. Adapt these models to local conditions while maintaining community control and environmental justice principles.

If You Are a Policymaker or Elected Official

Lead with Courage: Introduce environmental justice legislation at every level of government. Co-sponsor the Environmental Justice Act of 2026. Establish Green Reparations funds in your jurisdiction. Create community veto power over toxic facility permits.

Reject Polluter Influence: Refuse campaign contributions from fossil fuel companies, chemical manufacturers, and waste management corporations. Establish conflict-of-interest policies that prevent former polluter executives from serving in environmental agencies.

Center Community Voices: Require meaningful community engagement—not just public comment periods—in all environmental decision-making. Establish community environmental health advisory boards with budget authority and veto power over harmful projects.

If You Are a Student or Educator

Transform Environmental Education: Integrate an environmental justice curriculum into all educational levels. Teach the true history of environmental racism alongside solutions and resistance strategies. Connect students with local environmental justice campaigns for hands-on learning.

Support Student Organizing: Facilitate student-led environmental justice clubs and campaigns. Help students research and document environmental issues in their communities. Connect student organizing to broader movement work.

Use Your Institution's Power: Pressure schools and universities to divest from fossil fuels and invest in community-controlled renewable energy. Demand that research institutions partner with frontline communities and share data and resources.

If You Are a Healthcare Worker

Document and Advocate: Screen patients for environmental exposures and document patterns of pollution-related illness. Advocate for environmental health protections as public health necessities to support community health surveillance programs.

Connect Health and Environment: Educate colleagues and patients about the links between environmental racism and health disparities. Support policies that address environmental determinants of health, not just individual behavior change.

If You Are a Legal Advocate or Law Student

Strengthen Legal Tools: Develop test cases that establish environmental racism as a civil rights violation. Support community groups filing environmental justice lawsuits. Advocate for private rights of action in environmental justice legislation.

Provide Community Legal Support: Offer pro bono services to environmental justice organizations. Train community members in legal advocacy skills. Support efforts to establish environmental justice legal clinics.

Immediate Actions Everyone Can Take

This Week:

- Research environmental hazards in your zip code using online mapping tools; start by finding out whether you live in or near a "sacrifice zone."
- Attend one local government meeting where environmental decisions are made.
- Connect with one environmental justice organization in your area.
- Share this Black Paper with five people in your network.

This Month:

- Join or start a community environmental health monitoring effort.
- Contact your representatives about environmental justice legislation.
- Participate in a community action around environmental health.
- Support Black-led environmental justice organizations financially.

This Year:

- Run for local office or support environmental justice candidates.
- Organize a community forum on environmental health in your neighborhood.
- Start or join a campaign for specific environmental improvements.
- Build ongoing relationships with frontline environmental justice communities.

The Vision We Are Fighting For

We are not simply fighting against pollution, toxic facilities, and environmental racism. We are fighting for a transformed relationship between Black communities and the land, air, and water that sustains us. We envision:

- Black children breathe clean air and drink pure water as a birthright, not a privilege.
- Black communities are controlling decisions about what gets built in our neighborhoods.
- Black workers leading the renewable energy economy and benefiting from green jobs.
- Black families living in homes powered by community-owned solar and wind.
- Black elders aging with dignity in environments that support health and healing.
- Black land restored from centuries of extraction and available for community ownership.

This vision is not utopian but achievable through sustained organizing, strategic policy advocacy, and unwavering commitment to liberation. Every successful environmental justice campaign brings us closer to this reality.

The ancestors who survived the Middle Passage, endured slavery, resisted Jim Crow, and built the Civil Rights Movement passed us a legacy of resistance and determination. They cleared the swamps and planted the cotton under coercion, but they also created freedom songs, underground railroads, and liberation movements that changed the world.

Now it is our turn. The climate crisis gives us no choice but to act with revolutionary urgency. Environmental racism gives us clear targets for our organizing. And the success stories documented in this Paper provide us with proof that victory is possible.

The question is not whether we can achieve environmental justice but whether we will act with the courage and commitment required to realize our green dreams.

The time for deferred dreams is over. The time for environmental liberation is now.

Join us. Organize with us. Fight with us. Win with us.

References

Bekkar, B., Pacheco, S., Basu, R., & DeNicola, N. (2020). Association of air pollution and heat exposure with preterm birth, low birth weight, and stillbirth in the US: A Systematic Review. *JAMA Network*, 3(6), e208243.

Berry, Diane. (2020). Floodplain Apartheid: The legacy of segregated ecology. *Journal of Black Environmental History*, 14(2), 45–67.

Bullard, R. D. (1990). *Dumping in Dixie: Race, class, and environmental quality*. Westview Press.

Clark, Kristen. (2016). *The environmental racism flowing in Flint*. Open Society Foundations: Voices.

Commission for Environmental Cooperation. (n.d.). Dr. Benjamin Chavis.

Dearing, Aissa. 2023. *Toward environmental justice: Key concepts*. https://daily.jstor.org/toward-environmental-justice-key-concepts/

Environmental Protection Agency (EPA). (2024). Year in accomplishments: EPA highlights progress on environmental justice and climate protection. *U.S. Environmental Protection Agency*. https://www.epa.gov/newsreleases/year-accomplishments-epa

Marshall, Nyah. (2022). The fight for a better environment continues for Newark residents. *Howard University News Service*. https://hunewsservice.com/environment/the-fight-for-a-better-environment-continues-for-newark-residents/

McGrath, A. (2011). The sanitation workers strike: A fight for justice and dignity. *Labor History*, 52(3), 257–272.

PBS News Hour. (2022). Benton Harbor's Black community fuming over "environmental racism," water crisis. https://www.pbs.org/newshour/show/benton-harbors-black-community-fuming-over-environmental-racism-water-crisis

People for Community Recovery. (n.d.). Hazel M. Johnson's Legacy.

Principles of Environmental Justice. (1991). First national people of color environmental leadership summit.

Schrader, E. (2022). *They let us down: Water crisis in Jackson, Mississippi, flows from systemic racism*. Southern Poverty Law Center.

Southern Environmental Law Center (SELC). (2024). Elon Musk's xAI facility is polluting South Memphis. https://www.selc.org/news/elon-musks-xai-facility-is-polluting-south-memphis/?gad_source=1&gad_campaignid=16633369656&gbraid=0AAAAAD99pXCL_qUFWAcbofARorN9Fwwej&gclid=Cj0KCQjw39zSBhDhARIsANammDvomli-Jx0D1g-d4KDLcgwdgej83O1B3xHYnIZ8GIxRVQxHsHrKsiYaArhSEALw_wcB

Southwest Network for Environmental and Economic Justice. (1996). Jemez Principles for Democratic Organizing. https://ejnet.org/files/ej/jemez.pdf

Talt, Gina. (2020). The ComPOSTer: Juneteenth reflections. *S.C.R.A.P. Lab*. Retrieved October 23, 2025, from scraplab.princeton.edu/2020/06/the-composter-juneteenth-reflections/

Taylor, D. (2014). *Toxic communities: Environmental racism, industrial pollution, and residential mobility*. New York: NYU Press, 150–164.

Tessum, C.W., Apte, J.S., Goodkind, A.L. (2019). *Inequity in consumption of goods and services adds to racial–ethnic disparities in air pollution exposure*. https://www.pnas.org/doi/full/10.1073/pnas.1818859116

University of Michigan School of Public Health. (2021). *The Inequitable Impact of the Environment on Health*. https://sph.umich.edu/podcast/season3/the-inequitable-impact-of-the-environment-on-health.html

White House. (2024). Justice40 Initiative. Washington, DC.

White House. (2025). Initial rescissions of harmful executive orders and actions. Washington, DC.

Chapter 17

Rooted Resilience

Black Land Stewardship in the Face of Climate Crisis

*Bunny McKensie Mack and Brea Baker**

Executive Summary

This Black Paper (Paper) examines the historical and contemporary relationship between Black Americans and land ownership, highlighting the legacy of discrimination, dispossession, and environmental racism that has diminished Black land ownership from approximately 14% in the early 20th century to less than 2% today. Through historical analysis, personal narratives, and case studies, this Paper demonstrates how climate change disproportionately impacts Black communities while presenting asset-based frameworks for land reclamation, environmental justice, and community resilience. The discussion culminates in policy recommendations that address historical injustices while creating pathways toward equitable land access, climate resilience, and environmental justice for Black communities across America.

* Supported by braintrust author: Victoria Kirby York.

DOI: 10.4324/9781003752646-24

Introduction

Black land ownership peaked between 1910 and 1920 when Black Americans controlled approximately 14% of land across the United States, including thriving cities like Tulsa, Oklahoma, and (earlier) Wilmington, North Carolina. Over the next few decades, the entrepreneurship and communities our ancestors built were burned, bombed, and intimidated until Black people owned less than 1% of land. This statistic still stands in 2026. So, remember, every time you see a Black landowner, homeowner, or legacy-keeper, you see a miracle. You are witnessing someone who refused to give up on a birthright that had been bled and toiled for. Knowing their stories helps us to understand the baton we have picked up.

The legacy of Black land stewardship and ownership represents both a painful history of dispossession and a powerful testament to resilience and determination. This Paper examines the historical context of Black land ownership in America, the current challenges facing Black landowners in the context of climate change and environmental racism, and the policy solutions needed to create more equitable pathways to land ownership and ecological justice for Black communities.

This systematic dismantling of Black land ownership represents one of America's most consequential, yet under-acknowledged economic injustices. The land dispossession of Black Americans through both legal and extralegal means has destroyed trillions of dollars in potential intergenerational wealth. Today, as climate change intensifies and environmental injustices multiply, Black communities face heightened vulnerability precisely because of this historical theft of land-based resources and power.

Key Terms

- **Heirs' Property Laws**—a process for land and assets to be passed down to multiple heirs who own a percentage of the land or property shared; most common in the absence of a will or trust. Heirs' property laws are the leading cause of involuntary Black land loss.
- **Eminent Domain**—the power of the government to take any private property for "public use"; eminent domain is disproportionately used against Black land and homeowners.
- **Climate change**—long-term negative changes to Earth and its natural environment, including warming temperatures, melting ice caps, worsening natural disasters, and more.
- **Climate gentrification**—when wealthy people and businesses displace lower-income people of color to shield themselves from the impacts of climate change by moving to areas above sea level or resilient to natural disasters and extreme heat.
- **Greenwashing**—when wealthy people and businesses cover up their contributions to climate change by pretending to be sustainable or environmentally friendly without actually curbing their negative behaviors.
- **Fossil fuels**—coal, oil, and natural gas; energy sources that are toxic and non-renewable, meaning we will eventually run out of these sources.
- **Fracking**—drilling for oil or gas by injecting water, sand, and other chemicals deep into the ground; this process contaminates groundwater, pollutes the air, and increases the chances of earthquakes.
- **Renewable or clean energy**—energy sources that will always be around, like wind, solar (the sun), and hydro (water); these energy sources do not need to be "extracted" and can be harnessed without hurting the planet.
- **Reparations**—truth and reconciliation in the aftermath of immense harms and human rights abuses such as genocide, slavery, mass incarceration,

and more; examples of reparations include public apologies, monuments to survivors and their descendants, financial restitution, the return of stolen goods or property, and systemic incentives like educational investments and affirmative action.

- **Just Transitions**—shifting toward a sustainable or green economy in a way that is equitable for every member of society, especially those most vulnerable to the changes; i.e., ensuring that replaced industries create opportunities for new jobs and that working-class people can affordably take part in new energy sources like electric vehicles, solar panels, and more.
- **Environmental Justice**—the fair treatment and meaningful involvement of all people regardless of race, color, national origin, or income, concerning the development, implementation, and enforcement of environmental laws.

Historical Context and Legacy Stories

Grandma Marj

On February 8, 1973, a Black woman and factory worker from Mississippi named Marj bought a 1,000-square-foot, four-bedroom, two-bath house on 7,000 square feet of property on the Southside of Chicago. Nine months later, the United States would experience one of the worst economic recessions in its history. Inflation was high, the economy was slow, and oil prices rose 400%. The recession would last 16 months, and Marj would keep the house and the family financially afloat for the next 50 years.

Marj was a grandmother, a community defender, and a Libra who kept a revolver with a pristinely pastel-colored painted ceramic handle in a shoebox in her room. She also cared deeply about her family and community. She had a quiet strength about her that neighbors knew not to test. In the backyard, there was an apple tree and another tree, of which most folks did not know the variety, that stood so tall you could not see the top looking up from the ground, and still cannot to this day.

Two years ago, Marj's grandchild, Bunny, begged their aunt to let them take over the land and the house, which the family had been unable to take adequate care of (not for any lack of trying) since Marj passed away in 2019. This year, Bunny began renovating the house and the land to make it as resilient as possible with climate change in mind and the family's future as a first priority. They call the house Magnolia, after the state flower of Mississippi. Friends who have never been there tell Bunny when they visit that they can feel the "grandma energy" in the air, to which they laugh because they feel their grandmother's presence whenever they go.

The installation of solar panels and heat pumps is the beginning of a beautiful journey where Bunny asks themselves daily, "If our family ever found themselves in need of shelter once more, could the house where eight of us once wove our lives together, still open its arms and welcome them home?" Could this be a house they could own and feel safe knowing they were living in a place they had invested in with love, care, and aspirations for the future of a Black family, Marj's Black family?

Baker Family Land

Louis Baker was born enslaved and bought his first piece of land—350 acres in North Carolina—nearly a decade after the Emancipation Proclamation was signed. That land, purchased alongside his first wife, was eventually passed on to his children, including two sons: Albert and Frank. Albert and Frank farmed the land as their father had, buying more land along the way. Before his death, Albert deeded some of this land to the local school district for the creation of one of the county's first schools for Black children.

Frank passed on most of his inheritance to his son, Frank Jr. At its prime, the land grew to be a 600-acre farm, which Frank Jr. operated alongside his wife and 17 children. Unfortunately, over the course of the 20th century, the Baker family lost hundreds of acres of land through predatory debt, heirs' property laws, and manipulative legal "agreements." In the 21st century, this land—and newly purchased land—remains a site of joy and communion for the Baker family, hosting weddings, funerals/repasts, reunions, and more.

The Value of Land Ownership for Black Communities

Land ownership is not only possible but necessary for Black America's economic and environmental viability. This does not mean the journey is easy, but it is worth it. Though this economy is not what we need or deserve, we come from a people who have always made a way. Land has been such a powerful tool and foundation for weathering these storms. We cannot always control the conditions we work under, but we can control our hope, resilience, and perseverance.

Economic Benefits and Wealth Building

Real estate is an investment and wealth-building tool. As our elders say, they are not making more land. It is one of the few constants in this world that appreciates with time and is incredibly useful while you own it.

Land ownership represents one of America's few reliable paths to intergenerational wealth. Land became even more crucial as an economic asset for Black communities, which had historically been denied access to other wealth-building opportunities. According to the Federal Reserve's 2022 Survey of Consumer Finances, the median wealth for Black households is $40,300, compared to $285,000 for white households—a ratio of approximately 1:7 (Federal Reserve, 2023). Land ownership has the potential to narrow this wealth gap significantly.

Food Security and Sovereignty

Land ownership and gardening or farming are also an antidote to poverty and food insecurity. As Fannie Lou Hamer noted, they cannot starve or evict you if you own a piece of land and know what to do with it. Land ownership allows us to grow our food, control its quality, and steward natural resources needed to survive.

The United States Department of Agriculture (USDA) has identified more than 39.5 million Americans living in "food deserts," with Black neighborhoods having significantly fewer supermarkets than white neighborhoods of comparable size and socioeconomic status (USDA, 2023). Black-owned farms and community gardens provide critical access to fresh, culturally appropriate foods while creating green spaces that benefit entire communities.

Political Power and Agency

The power of being a true stakeholder cannot be underestimated. At one point, land ownership was necessary to vote, serve on juries, run for office, and engage politically. Though many of those rules have evolved, owning a deed gives you control of what happens to the land and the people who depend on it.

As Leah Penniman said in her book *Farming While Black*, "Black land matters now and forever."

Climate Change and Environmental Racism

> The idea of freedom is inspiring. But what does it mean? If you are free in a political sense but have no food, what's that? The freedom to starve?
>
> Angela Davis

Land has the power to be a vehicle for building wealth, and our investment in the natural world around us extends beyond profit. The quality of the land, air, and water we have access to matters. Historically, discriminatory practices like redlining and racial zoning pushed Black people to live on land that no one else wanted, including regions that repeatedly flooded, destroying houses, belongings, and farms in its wake.

We come from people who have cared for, bought, sold, and protected land on multiple continents and know the power of reciprocity and giving more than you take or giving about the same that you receive. We need the land to be healthy because we need clean air, water, and soil to feed and nourish ourselves. As the effects of climate change worsen, the value of land across cities and states will skyrocket, as those with the most wealth will seek to migrate to the lands of people whose regions are least impacted by a changing climate. Climate gentrification describes the process of people with the most wealth purchasing and taking over land and neighborhoods (through policies like eminent domain), which become more appealing, as specific areas become uninhabitable due to floods, hurricanes, air pollution, or heat waves. On a planet with increasing climate change disasters each year, Black people often suffer first and hardest. But why?

Disparate Impact Statistics

- Black people in the United States live in the South. As climate change worsens, southern states will see more potent and damaging hurricanes, destroying property and land and increasing flooding (Environmental Defense Fund, 2024).
- It is estimated that by the year 2050, nearly 20% of homes owned by Black people will be at increased risk of some form of storm damage (McKinsey & Company, 2023).
- According to a study by the Congressional Budget Office in 2023, flood insurance coverage is not standard in communities where Black people are the majority, and Black people are less likely to be covered by flood insurance when compared to their white peers.
- Even when we consider air pollution, predominantly Black communities are often referred to as "sacrifice zones" due to their proximity to air pollution across varied levels of class. That means that even Black people with financial wealth are still more likely to live in areas with high rates of air pollution. More than any other racial group in the United States, Black people are exposed to more pollution from every type of pollution source that exists, including factories, agriculture, vehicle emissions, construction sites, residential pollution, and pollution from restaurants.

Climate Impact Visualization

Climate impact data reveals stark patterns of environmental injustice. When mapped against demographic data, flood risk zones, air pollution concentrations, and extreme heat vulnerability show apparent racial disparities. The United States Environmental Protection Agency's (EPA) EJScreen tool demonstrates that the average Black American lives in a census tract with higher particulate matter than 54% of all Americans, while experiencing 38% more exposure to nitrogen dioxide (EPA, 2023). Mapping tools from the First Street Foundation show that properties in majority-Black neighborhoods are 25% more likely to flood than the average American home when controlling for region and property value.

Case Studies in Climate Injustice

Freedom to own land is one thing, but we want more than the right to own land. We want to own land where the water is clean and safe to drink, where the air and tree planting choices will not increase our chances of developing asthma or other life-threatening conditions. We want land fertile enough to grow our food without worrying about what we have worked so hard to build being washed away by floods every year or every decade. Here are some examples of how people-made climate disasters impact our communities across the country.

The LA Wildfires

On January 7, 2025, disastrous wildfires spread rapidly across Los Angeles. The fires burned for nearly a month, burning over 57,000 acres of land, displacing 200,000 people, causing billions of dollars in damage, and leading to the loss of 29 lives. Scientists note that these wildfires happened in part because of climate change. In Los Angeles, wildfires are common; however, as the climate changes, the wildfire season is getting longer and longer, while the rains that usually put out wildfires, when they begin, are getting shorter and shorter. Scientists say that a warming climate makes these wildfires more common and difficult to extinguish when they start.

While many mainstream media outlets focused on damages to the homes of wealthy celebrities, historic Black neighborhoods, and homes that had been in Black families for generations, received less media attention, leading many to assume that the only neighborhoods affected were those of multimillion-dollar mansions. Less than seven days after the fires began spreading, two-thirds of the people who lost their lives were in the city of

Altadena. In this historic Black community, which was reduced to ashes and rubble, Black homeownership was double the national rate.

Insurers have reduced or eliminated coverage for wildfires in the face of worsening climate disasters. In the days following the fires, disaster gentrification set in, with developers contacting families to buy their land at low prices. The goal was to redevelop and make huge profits from the trials of lower-income families who could not afford to rebuild without institutional support.

In an article from Capital B News (2025), Adam Mahoney, an Altadena native and environmental professor at UC Berkeley, was quoted as saying:

> This isn't just a crisis for the wealthy neighborhoods often portrayed in media coverage. The majority of the folks who were displaced, with nowhere to go, were not wealthy millionaires or billionaires, celebrities, or actors or actresses. They were people just like the people in Appalachia, whose homes were floating down rivers, or the folks who have experienced fires along the Northeast coast of the United States. We are all in the heat of the climate crisis right now.

The Story of Freedom Hill

Freedom Hill is a documentary by Resita Cox, which tells the story of the environmental racism washing away the first town incorporated by freed, formerly enslaved African people in America. That town is Princeville, North Carolina, located next to the Tar River. In the 1800s, it was decided that land that white people could not inhabit was to be offered to formerly enslaved African people looking for towns to call their own. Before the town was incorporated, those residing there called it Freedom Hill in 1865, 20 years before it was chartered as Princeville.

The story is told through the lens of Marquetta Dickens, a Princeville native and activist, and a founder of the local community development organization Freedom Org. Marquetta is a former North Carolina State basketball player who moved back home to advocate for her community while also examining why flooding so regularly damages the town of fewer than 1,250 people.

In the last 25 years, Princeville has witnessed two 100-year floods: disastrous flooding from Hurricane Floyd in 1999 and again in 2016. Some residents remember being able to reach up and touch the traffic lights from boats 20 feet above the ground.

In 2024, Princeville received an $11 million grant for a flood reduction infrastructure project intended to help the town build a community outside the high risk of flooding it has endured since the 1800s. The infrastructure planning was initially reported to include stormwater management, wastewater collection, water distribution, and more services to support new housing and services.

Clean Drinking Water and Flint, Michigan

Outside of Flint, Michigan, many may be unaware that the city's water crisis, which disproportionately impacted Black people and communities, stemmed from a decision to save money. In 2014, city managers changed the water source from Detroit's Lake Huron system to the Flint River. Following this, residents began reporting changes in water color, taste, and smell, with skin rashes and hair loss becoming common. Despite this, state and city officials continued to insist on the safety of the water.

When the water source was changed in 2014, it caused corrosion of the city's lead and galvanized pipes, releasing lead and other pollutants into the drinking water. Some tests found that the water in Flint was more than 100 times the legal lead level. The Flint River was naturally high in chloride, leading to metal corrosion, and lacked the chemical compounds needed to reduce or control the corrosion of metal pipes.

Eventually, the water crisis initiated by environmental racism led to tens of thousands of people being exposed to lead poisoning and Legionnaires' disease, a severe pneumonia caused by the bacteria Legionella. This condition, which can lead to long-term fatigue, neurological and neuromuscular challenges, or Post-Traumatic Stress Disorder (PTSD), may also prove fatal if left untreated. Flint reconnected the water source to the original Detroit water system, but the damage to the health and wellbeing of Flint residents had already been done. In 2024, the Centers for Disease Control and Prevention (CDC) reported:

- 66% of households reported one or more adult members experiencing at least one behavioral health issue "more than usual."
- 54% of households reported that at least one child experienced at least one behavioral health issue "more than usual."
- 34% of individuals self-reported symptoms of anxiety, and 29% self-reported symptoms of depression.
- 51% of households felt that the physical health of at least one member had worsened due to the Flint water crisis.

Because Flint refused to act in the best interests and health of its residents in providing clean and safe drinking water, 9,000 children reportedly experienced elevated blood lead levels, leading to learning and behavioral challenges.

There is no such thing as a safe level of lead exposure. Once you are exposed, even low levels can cause developmental delays, learning challenges, and behavioral health issues. The lead water mains (a large, underground pipe that delivers water from a central source to a network of smaller pipes), which exacerbated the water crisis in Flint, are disproportionately found in Black and Brown communities, with Chicago, Illinois, hosting the most lead water mains of any other city in the nation. This disparity arises from racist housing policies, which have led to higher concentrations of lead infrastructure in Black and Brown neighborhoods. Our communities being directly involved in decisions about how water is sourced, provided, and protected is critical to our ability to survive and thrive in the long term.

Cancer Alley, Louisiana

Cancer Alley is an approximately 85-mile stretch of land along the Mississippi River from New Orleans to Baton Rouge. Communities in this region live next to 200 fossil fuel and petrochemical plants and factories. These companies have created a "sacrifice zone" in Louisiana, where high-risk pregnancies, miscarriages, infertility, respiratory disease, and cancer are prevalent.

Sometimes we think of pollution as a magic cloud that floats into the sky and away from all the people who could be detrimentally impacted if they came into contact with it. However, this is not an accurate picture. Chemicals extracted for use by human beings do not easily disappear, become contained, or dissipate. Petrochemicals, for example, are chemicals made from fossil fuels—the remains of plants and animals that lived hundreds of millions of years ago. Primarily, they are coal, oil, or natural gas.

If a person had a barrel of oil and wanted to get rid of it, likely they would not just go to their backyard and pour into the ground, pour it into the rivers they drink from, or burn it in a way that runs the risk of elders, parents, children, and other community members breathing it in and getting sick from it. And yet this is something the largest petrochemical companies in the world attempt to get away with this every day. They continue to dump their waste on the ground, water, and air of neighborhoods they do not live in or ever plan to visit—our communities. Not only that, but a recent study conducted by Tulane University (2024) found that Black people are not only among the most underpaid in the petrochemical industry, but also among those most detrimentally impacted by the pollution these industries create.

In addition, in Louisiana, many of these same companies polluting Black communities are profiting from significant tax breaks in exchange for job creation. It has been reported that the State's Industrial Tax Exemption Program grants up to 100% exemptions in property taxes in exchange for the creation of new jobs. According to a recent report from Fact Company (2024), "for each job created in Cameron Parish, where large natural gas ports have been built in recent years, companies were exempted from $590,000 in local taxes."

But residents are fighting back. In 2022, activists successfully halted the creation of 10 new chemical plants on 2,400 acres along the Mississippi River just one mile from an elementary school. The project would have brought 1200 jobs to a disenfranchised Black community, but it would have also meant over 800 tons of toxic pollution and greenhouse gases emitted annually. Residents knew that what was better than the economic benefit of new jobs was not having increased pollution in a community already challenged by environmental racism and environmental injustice.

The cases discussed in this section—Los Angeles wildfires, Princeville flooding, Flint water poisoning, and Cancer Alley pollution—illustrate a fundamental truth: environmental racism manifests through different mechanisms but produces similar outcomes. Whether through neglect, disinvestment, intentional exploitation, or post-disaster predation, Black communities bear disproportionate climate and environmental burdens while having significantly fewer resources to respond. This pattern emerges not from natural disaster but from constructed vulnerability—a vulnerability engineered through decades of policy choices that have consistently devalued Black lives, health, and property.

Policy Solutions and Recommendations

There are so many urgent issues that the Black community is facing. However, we cannot fix any of them on a dying planet, or when hurricanes, wildfires, and environmental neglect hit our communities. We cannot address police brutality or mass incarceration as we're being poisoned through contaminated water. We cannot access better housing when our people are starving and do not have clean and healthy food to eat. All of these issues are intertwined, and for us to see ourselves in the future, we must have a future worth running towards.

While expanding existing programs is crucial, the unprecedented scale of historical land theft and current climate threats necessitates innovative policy approaches. The following recommendations represent cutting-edge solutions that combine traditional knowledge with modern technological and legal frameworks to create new pathways for Black land sovereignty and climate resilience.

Land Access and Retention

Any framework for Black land justice must acknowledge that all American land discussions occur in the context of Indigenous dispossession. Black and Indigenous communities share histories of land theft through different but interconnected mechanisms of white supremacy. Emerging coalition models like the Black-Indigenous Solidarity Network demonstrate how these communities can work together toward land justice without replicating colonial frameworks. Principles of stewardship rather than ownership, reciprocity rather than extraction, and collective rather than individual benefits inform many Black agricultural traditions and align with Indigenous land ethics. These principles should guide land justice movements and policy development.

Expand Community Land Trusts

Land trusts acquire land and property and then sell that land back to people well below market price, making land and home ownership more accessible to people who may not otherwise be able to afford it.

Federal, state, and local governments should allocate funding to create and expand Black-led community land trusts. Efforts should include:

- Tax incentives for property donations to community land trusts in historically Black neighborhoods.
- Streamlined processes for converting vacant or abandoned properties into land trust holdings.
- Educational programs to help community members understand and participate in land trust governance.
- Scaling successful models like the Macon-Bibb County Community Land Trust in Georgia, which has helped over 100 Black families achieve homeownership since 2021.

Reform Heirs' Property Laws

Heirs' property laws are a process for passing land and assets down to multiple heirs who own a percentage of the land or property shared. They are most common in the absence of a will or trust. Heirs' property laws are the leading cause of involuntary Black land loss.

States should adopt the Uniform Partition of Heirs Property Act[1] (UPHPA), which has been enacted in only 26 states as of 2025. Additional measures should include:

- Providing free or subsidized legal services for heirs' property owners to create clear titles.
- Creating state-level task forces to identify and protect heirs' property from predatory practices.
- Establishing "right of first refusal" laws that give co-owners priority to buy out shares before partition sales.
- Initiating tax relief for families resolving complex heirs' property issues.
- Requiring courts to consider the historical and heritage value of land in partition decisions.

Eminent Domain Reversals and Protections

Eminent domain is the power of the government to take any private property for "public use"; it is disproportionately used against Black land and homeowners. Eminent domain was prominently used against Black land ownership to establish the Tennessee Valley Authority (TVA), federal and state interstate systems, public transit systems (bus and rail lines and stations), landfills, and sewage and utility plants.

In the case of unjust eminent domain seizures, local elected officials may decide to return land or property taken unjustly in eminent domain reversals. Examples include land or property taken but not used for the purposes they initially claimed, or providing just and equitable compensation to those who did not receive it when they should have.

Additional protections should include:

- Creating an independent review board for eminent domain cases involving historically marginalized communities.
- Requiring community benefit agreements when eminent domain is used in Black neighborhoods.
- Implementing stronger "public use" definitions that prevent taking private property primarily for economic development.
- Establishing a national commission to investigate and provide recommendations on historical eminent domain abuses against Black communities.

Agricultural Justice

True Restitution for USDA Discrimination

A 1999 class action lawsuit against the USDA for decades worth of anti-Black discrimination resulted in a historic billion-dollar settlement for Black farmers. Unfortunately, narrow terms on who qualified for restitution meant over 70,000 Black farmers did not receive their due. There can and should be more widespread investments in Black farmers who were bankrupted, disenfranchised, and stripped of their opportunities to participate in the agricultural economy.

- Establish a new USDA Office of Black Farmer Affairs with decision-making authority.
- Create an expedited claims process for previously excluded Black farmers.
- Implement a debt forgiveness program specifically for Black farmers affected by historical discrimination.
- Provide grants rather than loans for new Black farmers to acquire land and equipment.
- Allocate funds for regenerative agriculture training programs specifically targeted at Black farmers.
- Establish a national Black agricultural cooperative development program.

Farmland Acquisition Support

Create federal and state programs to help Black farmers acquire farmland.

- Low-interest or no-interest loans for first-time Black farm purchasers.
- Land matching programs connecting retiring farmers with aspiring Black farmers.
- Geographic Information System (GIS) mapping of available farmland with specific outreach to Black farming organizations.
- Tax incentives for landowners who sell farmland to historically disadvantaged farmers.
- Creation of agricultural development districts in historically Black communities with favorable zoning and tax structures.

Environmental Justice

Climate Resilience Infrastructure Investment

Create targeted climate resilience infrastructure investments in historically Black communities.

- Prioritize flood protection, hurricane mitigation, and wildfire prevention in vulnerable Black communities.
- Require community input and leadership in all resilience planning processes.
- Create local hiring requirements for all climate infrastructure projects.
- Develop specialized disaster insurance programs for historically redlined neighborhoods.
- Establish climate resilience centers in predominantly Black neighborhoods that provide education, emergency services, and planning resources.

Pollution Accountability

Strengthen environmental regulations and enforcement in environmental justice communities.

- Require cumulative impact assessments for new industrial developments in already-polluted areas.
- Create stricter penalties for violations in environmental justice communities.
- Establish community monitoring programs with regulatory enforcement authority.
- Require bond posting for potential environmental cleanup before industrial operations begin.
- Implement "polluter pays" funding mechanisms for community health monitoring.

Removal of Lead and Other Harmful Chemicals From Land, Food, and Water

In 2023, the EPA called for a ten-year deadline to eliminate all lead service lines and pipes connecting a water main to a building or house. These are known as the Lead and Copper Rule Improvements. Lead service lines, which are highly common in predominantly Black and Brown communities, represent the highest numbers of lead exposure through drinking water.

Although the EPA has been gutted under the 47th presidential administration, several states nationwide have already received millions of dollars from the EPA to eliminate these lead exposure risks. Review your state's progress on lead service line removal via the Environmental Defense Fund's Map of Public Lead Service Line Replacement Programs (edf.org). Additionally, we should advocate to:

- Accelerate the timeline for lead service line replacement in Black communities from ten years to five years.
- Create a national database of lead infrastructure with transparent tracking of replacement progress.
- Provide free water testing for all residents in historically redlined neighborhoods.
- Establish mandatory soil testing for urban agriculture projects in formerly industrial areas.
- Implement stricter standards for chemical runoff near Black farming communities.
- Create a national fund for soil remediation in contaminated Black neighborhoods.

Economic Justice

Reparations

Many proposals have been introduced for slavery reparations, including baby bonds and racially specific guaranteed income. Currently, the following legislation is being considered by Congress:

- H.R. 40,[2] a bill introduced decades ago to create a national commission to study reparations. If passed, H.R. 40 would not immediately lead to the implementation of reparations.
- The Truth, Racial Healing, and Transformation Commission, a bill built on successful reparations efforts in South Africa and elsewhere, would create a commission that addresses states and provides a path forward for our nation to heal from one of its original sins.
- The Reparations Now Resolution merges elements from the two earlier bills while including a formal apology from the United States government for Slavery and the anti-Black policies and programs that followed.
- The Federal Government Equity Improvement Act would establish statutory requirements for federal agency equity advisory teams, an Equitable Data Working Group, and an interagency working group to allow agencies, nongovernmental organizations, and stakeholders to share best practices in the collection and use of data for assessing barriers to equity, among other things. The bill would continue the Biden–Harris administration's data collection efforts that provided credible and broad insights into the impacts of government-sanctioned discrimination against historically excluded communities. The data is critical for effective government

solutions, legal restitution and redress for those harmed, and categorical reparations for communities, families, and institutions harmed by centuries of anti-Black federal government programs and policies.
- The Equity in Agency Planning Act would amend various agency performance planning requirements to ensure that agencies prioritize improving the equitable provision of services in their agency goals. The bill would ensure that systemic inequities and disparate impacts are addressed throughout federal government programs and policies, creating a pathway for all to benefit from and access them.

It is also worth noting that at least four statewide reparations commissions (**New York, California, Maryland, and Illinois**) exist, and dozens more are being held in cities and universities around the country to explore the possibilities of reparations.

We can advocate to:

- Pass H.R. 40 to establish the Commission to Study and Develop Reparation Proposals for African Americans, along with the other congressional bills described above.
- Expand state and local reparations commissions with a specific focus on land restoration.
- Implement "land back" pilot programs in counties with documented land theft.
- Create tax credits for descendants of enslaved people purchasing homes or farmland.
- Establish "heritage conservation zones" around historically Black land with special protections.
- Create targeted educational debt forgiveness for descendants of enslaved people pursuing agricultural education.
- Ensure federal protections for Black farmers growing cannabis and building cannabis-related businesses as reparations for the discriminatory War on Drugs.
- Collaborate with the United Nations (U.N.) to address the issue of global reparations, particularly in the context of slavery and colonialism. The U.N.'s Basic Principles and Guidelines on the Right to Remedy and Reparation for Victims of Gross Violations of International Human Rights Law and Serious Violations of International Humanitarian Law held that any full and adequate reparations scheme must include the following five forms of reparations:

    1. Restitution (restoring victims to their original situation).
    2. Compensation (providing financial compensation for economic damages like lost income, property, and opportunities).

3 Rehabilitation (offering medical, psychological, social, and legal support to help victims recover from the harm they suffered).
4 Satisfaction (addressing the psychological and emotional harm caused by violations, including acknowledgement of guilt, apologies, truth-seeking, and memorials).
5 Guarantees of non-repetition (implementing reforms to prevent future violations).

- The United Nations has called on former colonial powers, such as the United Kingdom, France, and Portugal, to consider reparations and debt cancellations for their former and current colonies and territories. We must urge the inclusion of other colonial powers, such as the United States, Denmark, and Spain, in these efforts. Additionally, we must push all affiliated countries to meaningfully invest in the newly established Global Reparations Fund. The plundering and theft of African and majority Black nations' resources and land by other nations must end.

People of African descent across the world impacted by the institution of chattel Slavery must be made whole through as many channels, nations, and institutions as possible.

Just Transitions/Green Economy

To ensure everyone can take part in the sustainable economy we deserve, we must prioritize that working-class people can be retrained and funneled into good-paying careers, ensuring climate solutions are affordable and accessible to the non-wealthy, and adequately evaluating the potential negative outcomes of new technologies.

We can work to:

- Create targeted green jobs training programs in historically Black communities.
- Provide subsidies for solar installation, energy efficiency upgrades, and other climate resilience measures in Black neighborhoods.
- Establish community-owned renewable energy projects with wealth-building mechanisms for residents.
- Create pathways for Black-owned businesses in the renewable energy supply chain.
- Implement stronger labor protections for workers transitioning from fossil fuel industries.
- Require community benefits agreements for renewable energy projects in Black communities.

Demand the Disbursement of Inflation Reduction Act Funds

In August 2022, the Inflation Reduction Act was passed (under the Biden–Harris Administration) to invest billions of dollars into clean energy initiatives, reducing pollution and greenhouse gas emissions, promoting sustainable uses of energy, and funding environmental and climate justice programs and organizations in communities disenfranchised by economic divestment and sacrifice zones. When the 47th President returned to office, he signed an executive order halting the release of grants to address environmental pollution across Black and Brown communities. Now there is a court battle over the disbursement of money guaranteed to nonprofits and other organizations nationwide seeking to make the environments we live, breathe, eat, and drink in better for us all.

We can:

- Create a congressional oversight committee specifically focused on equitable IRA (Individual Retirement Account) fund distribution
- Establish a legal defense fund for environmental justice organizations seeking to challenge funding blockages.
- Implement automatic disbursement mechanisms for future climate legislation that cannot be administratively halted.
- Create state-level bridge funding programs to support environmental justice work during federal funding gaps.
- Develop community monitoring tools to track IRA fund distribution and impact.
- Establish a coalition of state attorneys general to challenge improper withholding of environmental justice funds.

New Policy Recommendations

Black Climate Sovereignty Zones

Establish federally recognized "Black Climate Sovereignty Zones" in historically Black communities with significant environmental challenges:

- Create special tax designations that provide tax benefits and investment incentives for Black-owned climate resilience businesses.
- Implement streamlined permitting for green infrastructure and renewable energy projects.
- Establish community-controlled environmental oversight boards with regulatory authority.
- Provide matching grants for community-led climate adaptation and mitigation projects.

- Create special disaster response protocols with community-determined priorities.
- Fund traditional ecological knowledge repositories and training centers to preserve Black agricultural wisdom.

Black Farmer Cooperative Grant Program

Establish a dedicated program to revitalize Black agricultural cooperatives and consider the following:

- Provide startup capital for new Black agrarian cooperatives with a focus on sustainable practices.
- Fund shared equipment pools, processing facilities, and distribution networks specifically for Black farmers.
- Create marketing assistance programs for Black-grown agricultural products.
- Establish regional Black farmer training centers focusing on both traditional and innovative growing methods.
- Fund intergenerational knowledge transfer programs to connect elder Black farmers with youth.
- Develop farm-to-school programs specifically connecting Black farmers to schools in Black communities.

Digital Land Rights Protection System

Create a blockchain-based land rights registration system to protect Black land ownership and work to accomplish the following:

- Establish a secure, immutable record of Black land ownership to prevent fraudulent transfers.
- Create a simplified interface for recording historical family claims to property.
- Provide automatic notification of any attempted changes to land title or ownership.
- Fund community "digital land rights defenders" to help community members navigate the system.
- Create a legal presumption in favor of blockchain records in cases of contested ownership.
- Establish a special fund to help Black landowners digitize historical ownership documents.

Community Investment Trusts and Land Bonds

Create financial instruments specifically designed for Black community land acquisition and development, and advocate for the following:

- Establish Community Investment Trusts that allow neighborhood residents to purchase shares in local real estate with as little as $10–$100 monthly investments.
- Create Bonds that raise capital specifically for Black land acquisition and improvement projects.
- Develop Climate Resilience Bonds that fund infrastructure improvements in historically Black neighborhoods with high climate vulnerability.
- Create Tax Incentives for private investment in Black-led land projects through Opportunity Zone reforms.
- Establish Revolving Loan Funds specifically for Black land acquisition and climate adaptation projects.
- Develop Insurance Products that pool risk across Black-owned properties to reduce individual premiums while building collective assets.

Call to Action

The policies outlined in this Black Paper require sustained advocacy, community organization, and political pressure. Individual actions, while important, must connect to systemic change. Each person reading this document has unique skills, resources, and positioning that can be leveraged toward land justice. Whether you are a landowner, policymaker, community organizer, or concerned citizen, identify your sphere of influence and deploy it intentionally. Remember that land justice for Black communities is not separate from broader environmental justice—it is foundational to creating a climate-resilient future for everyone.

People and Organizations to Follow

- Black Environmental Leaders Association (BELA) provides a forum for community environmental education, which can serve as the basis for a deeper understanding and commitment to land, water, air, transportation and energy issues.
- Black Girl Environmentalist, led by Wawa Gatheru, is a national organization dedicated to addressing the pathway and retention issue in the climate movement for Black girls, women, and gender-expansive people.
- Intersectional Environmentalist, led by Leah Thomas, envisions a world where the communities and voices most impacted by environmental injustice have the power, resources, and platforms to lead their communities into complete liberation.
- Rural Beacon Initiative, led by William Barber III, partners with those most impacted by the climate crisis today to build the most impactful solutions of tomorrow.
- Where Is My Land (WIML), led by Kavon Ward, helps Black Americans discover connections to stolen land through research, data, and technology.
- Philly Thrive organizes for environmental, racial, and economic justice in the poorest big city in the United States.
- Rise St. James is a faith-based grassroots organization fighting for environmental justice in St. James Parish, Louisiana. It is working to defeat the proliferation of petrochemical industries.

Deeper Reading

- The Case for Reparations—an article by Ta-Nehisi Coates
- Rooted: The American Legacy of Land Theft & The Modern Movement for Black Land Ownership—Brea Baker
- A Terrible Thing to Waste: Environmental Racism and Its Assault on The American Mind—Harriet Washington
- What If We Get it Right? Visions of Climate Futures—Ayana Elizabeth Johnson
- We Refuse: A Forceful History of Black Resistance—Kellie Carter Jackson
- Hammer and Hoe: Alabama Communists During the Great Depression—Robin D.G. Kelley
- The Color of Law: A Forgotten History of How Our Government Segregated America—Richard Rothstein
- Farming While Black: Soul Fire Farm's Practical Guide to Liberation on the Land—Leah Penniman
- Black Faces, Black Spaces: Rethinking African American Underrepresentation in Recreational Fishing—an academic paper by Cassandra Y. Johnson and J.M. Bowker

- Clean and White: A History of Environmental Racism in the United States—Carl A. Zimring

Deeper Watching

- Freedom Hill (documentary)
- Katrina Babies (documentary)
- Homeplace Under Fire (documentary)
- Inhabitants: Indigenous Perspectives on Restoring Our World (documentary)
- The Neutral Ground (documentary)
- Black Land Matters (documentary series)
- Cooked: Survival by Zip Code (documentary)

Immediate Action To Take

- Support Where Is My Land's local petitions for eminent domain reversals
- Call your local congress representatives and tell them that you want them to demand that funds approved by Congress for the Inflation Reduction Act be disbursed to Black-led organizations and communities in alignment with the laws of the United States. Find the number for your local Congress representative here.
- Join or start a community land trust in your neighborhood.
- Support Black-owned farms and food producers in your region, starting with Black Farmers' Market.
- Participate in local environmental justice campaigns.
- Start or join a community garden in your neighborhood.
- Attend your local zoning and planning board meetings to advocate for environmental justice.
- Create family documents and archives detailing land ownership, and create wills to prevent heirs' property complications.
- Organize community know-your-rights workshops about eminent domain.
- Support legal defense funds for environmental justice organizations.

Notes

1 "The **Uniform Partition of Heirs' Property Act** (UPHPA) seeks to address partition action abuses that have led to significant property loss, especially for Black Americans. The act is sponsored by the **Uniform Law Commission**, which provides states with non-partisan, well-conceived and well-drafted legislation that brings clarity and stability to critical areas of state statutory law. Each state decides whether to adopt or not adopt legislation sponsored by the Commission." https://landtrustalliance.org/resources/heirs-property-toolkit/uniform-partition-of-heirs-property-act/

2 "A bill originating in the House of Representatives is designated by the letters "H.R.", signifying "House of Representatives", followed by a number that it retains throughout all its parliamentary stages." (https://www.house.gov/the-house-explained)

Bibliography

Baker, B. (2024). *Rooted: The American legacy of land theft & the modern movement for Black land ownership*. One World.

Barber, W. J., III. (2023). The green new deal and Black: Forging a path to environmental justice. *Harvard Environmental Law Review, 47*(1), 122–148.

Centers for Disease Control and Prevention. (2024). *Community assessment for public health emergency response (CASPER) after the Flint water crisis: May 17–19, 2024*. U.S. Department of Health and Human Services.

Coates, T. (2014). The case for reparations. *The Atlantic*. https://www.theatlantic.com/magazine/archive/2014/06/the-case-for-reparations/361631/

Congressional Budget Office. (2023). *Federal flood insurance for residential properties: Current coverage and alternatives (Publication No. 59493)*. U.S. Government Printing Office.

Cox, R. (Director). (2022). *Freedom Hill* [Film]. Resita Cox Productions.

Davis, A. Y. (2012). *The meaning of freedom*. City Lights Publishers.

Environmental Defense Fund. (2024). *Climate impacts on Black communities in the American South*. https://www.edf.org/climate-impacts-black-communities

EPA (2023). *EJ Screen. Environmental justice mapping and screening tool*. Washington, DC.

Fact Company. (2024). Tax breaks and environmental justice: The Louisiana paradox. *Fact Company Economic Analysis, 12*(4), 34–39.

Federal Reserve. (2023). *Survey of consumer finances, 2022*. Board of Governors of the Federal Reserve System.

Gilio-Whitaker, D. (2019). *As long as grass grows: The indigenous fight for environmental justice*. Beacon Press.

Hamer, F. L. (1971). *Nobody's free until everybody's free* [Speech transcript]. National Women's Political Caucus, Washington, DC.

Jackson, K. C. (2023). *We refuse: A forceful history of Black resistance*. Basic Books.

Johnson, A. E. (2023). *What if we get it right?: Visions of climate futures*. One World Publications.

Johnson, C. Y., & Bowker, J. M. (2022). Black faces, black spaces: Rethinking African American underrepresentation in recreational fishing. *Journal of Environmental Management, 301*, 113940.

Kelley, R. D. G. (2015). *Hammer and hoe: Alabama communists during the Great Depression (25th anniversary ed.)*. University of North Carolina Press.

Mahoney, A. (2025). LA wildfires devastate historic Black communities: The untold story. *Capital B News*. https://capitalbnews.org/la-wildfires-black-communities

McKinsey & Company. (2023). *Climate risk and response: Physical hazards and socioeconomic impacts on Black homeownership*. McKinsey Global Institute.

Penniman, L. (2018). *Farming while Black: Soul Fire Farm's practical guide to liberation on the land*. Chelsea Green Publishing.

Reese, A. M. (2019). *Black food geographies: Race, self-reliance, and food access in Washington, D.C.* University of North Carolina Press.

Rothstein, R. (2017). *The color of law: A forgotten history of how our government segregated America*. Liveright Publishing.

Thomas, L. (2022). *The intersectional environmentalist: How to dismantle systems of oppression to protect people + planet*. Voracious.

Tulane University Environmental Research Center. (2024). Petrochemical industry employment and health outcomes by race in Louisiana. *Environmental Justice, 17*(2), 89–103.

U.S. Department of Agriculture. (2023). *National food access research atlas*. Economic Research Service.

Washington, H. A. (2019). *A terrible thing to waste: Environmental racism and its assault on the American mind*. Little, Brown Spark.

Zimring, C. A. (2016). *Clean and white: A history of environmental racism in the United States*. New York University Press.

Chapter 18

Housing as a Human Right

Marcia L. Fudge, Imani D. Edwards, David J. Johns, Jonathan M. Cox, and Jasmine Esquilin

Executive Summary

The United States of America has not delivered its promise of liberty and justice for all. Housing, which affects every aspect of life, has been one of the areas where this failure has been painfully evident for far too many Black people. To ensure housing justice and close the racial housing and wealth divides, it is critically important to address institutional racism and how it is manifested in discriminatory practices, including redlining, predatory lending, and housing devaluation. This Black Paper (Paper) outlines some of the ways structural racism has put the Black community at a considerable economic disadvantage, resulting from extreme housing instability.

Key Statistics:

- The Black–white homeownership gap today is wider than the gap observed following the passage of the Fair Housing Act in 1968; in 1970, the gap was closer to 23.8 percentage points.
- The Black homeownership rate was approximately 44.1% in 2022, compared to 72% for white Americans, creating a gap of approximately 28 percentage points (National Association of Realtors, 2025).
  - This gap has widened from approximately 27 percentage points in 2012.
- Black homeownership peaked at 49.7% in 2004 before the foreclosure crisis. Current rates remain significantly below that level (Zillow, 2024).
- Between 2013 and 2023, the Black homeownership rate increased by about 2.7 percentage points, representing a slow, but steady recovery and narrowing the overall gap slightly during that decade (NAR, 2025).
- In majority-Black neighborhoods, 12.5% of homes are undervalued compared to only 7.4% in majority-white areas (Freddie Mac, 2021).
- Black Americans represent approximately 12% of the United States population but nearly 32% of people experiencing homelessness (Henry et al., 2024).

DOI: 10.4324/9781003752646-25

Note: This Black Paper primarily uses 'Black people,' 'Black families,' and 'Black communities' while acknowledging the diversity within Black America. We recognize that Black families include single parents, multigenerational households, lesbian, gay, bisexual, transgender, queer/questioning+/same-gender loving (LGBTQ+/SGL) people and families, and additionally diverse family structures. Housing discrimination affects all Black people, including Black transgender and gender expansive people Black people with disabilities, and Black immigrants and refugees who navigate additional challenges in accessing housing and building wealth. Our use of 'Black families' encompasses this beautiful diversity of our experiences and ways of making meaning.

History of Racial Inequity in Housing

Stable, safe, and affordable housing is a foundational determinant of overall wellbeing and success for people and communities. Research tells us that when families have access to quality and affordable housing, children have better school attendance, academic performance, and health outcomes (Taylor, 2018). Throughout history, many Black people have overcome seemingly insurmountable odds and achieved success despite socially engineered challenges. Many achieve this through homeownership. In 2021, the Centers for Disease Control (CDC) reported that children raised in stable housing in opportunity-rich neighborhoods benefit from access to strong social networks and community resources (Centers for Disease Control and Prevention, 2021). Children who receive these benefits are more likely to graduate from high school, attend college, and have higher incomes as adults (Acosta, 2022).

From the formation of what would become known as the United States of America, property rights and land ownership have been closely tied to power, wealth, social status, and political influence. The American system of chattel enslavement was designed to dehumanize Black people and viewed Black bodies as a significant form of currency, designating human beings as legal property. The brutal and barbaric system deemed Black people as the largest single financial asset in the country and formed the foundation of the United States economy. Enslavers amassed generational wealth through forced labor, while enslaved people and their descendants were systematically denied property, education, wages, legal recognition, and the right to vote (Baptist, 2014).

To preserve this racial wealth disparity, many states established a system restricting voting rights to white male property owners ("land owning gentry"). This property requirement effectively excluded large segments of the population, including the poor, women, enslaved people, indentured servants, and Indigenous communities. The legacy of these early oppressive policies not only had long-term consequences in shaping racial and economic disparities in land ownership and wealth, but also continued to shape politics even after the Civil War and the passage of the 13th and 14th Amendments.

Systematic Exclusion and Oppression

Purposefully, white Americans designed community expansion with deeply segregated neighborhoods. Some of the first racial zoning laws explicitly prohibiting Black people from buying or renting homes in white neighborhoods started in Baltimore, Maryland. Although Black civil rights activists fought these zoning laws through the courts, segregation persisted through various mechanisms, including:

- **Racially Restrictive Covenants**: Private legal agreements embedded in property deeds barring the sale of homes to Black people and other disenfranchised groups. Multiple homeowners often sign these covenants on a block to create a legally binding pact among neighbors to preserve the racial purity of the area (Baltimore City Department of Planning, 2018).
- **Redlining**: The Home Owners' Loan Corporation, a federally government-sanctioned corporation, developed color-coded maps of neighborhoods signaling their constructed "risk level." The areas marked in red, predominantly Black neighborhoods, are deemed hazardous and denied access to loans or insurance, which leads to long-term disinvestment. Redlining codified racial segregation into national housing policy and ensured Black

Americans would be excluded from the most significant engine of wealth creation in United States history (Rothstein, 2017).

- **GI Bill and Veteran Loans**: The GI Bill (Servicemen's Readjustment Act of 1944) was designed to help returning World War II veterans by offering benefits like low-interest home loans. The GI Bill has failed to lift as many Black veterans as possible into the middle class because of anti-Black discrimination and differential enforcement. Many local Veterans Affairs (VA) offices and banks deny Black applicants mortgages, and the Federal Housing Administration (FHA) has refused to insure loans in predominantly Black neighborhoods or for Black buyers in white neighborhoods (Almeida, 2021).
- **White Flight and Suburbanization**: Levittown, in Long Island, New York, was one of the first mass-produced suburban housing developments and a symbol of postwar middle-class prosperity for white Americans. The developer explicitly marketed and sold homes only to white families using racially restrictive covenants. As cities become more racially diverse, data show white racial anxiety has fueled white flight to these racially restricted suburban areas. Census data show Levittown remains predominantly white, with Black people only making up 1.9% of its population (U.S. Census Bureau, n.d.).
- **Blockbusting and Steering**: Real estate professionals actively enforce segregation by refusing to show homes to Black buyers in white areas (steering). They also spread fear about the potential for rapid decline in property value that would occur if Black neighbors moved in, encouraging white homeowners to sell quickly and cheaply (blockbusting) and move to new white communities. These actions contribute to the devaluation of Black neighborhoods and the segregation of American communities (Smokler, 2021).
- **Urban Renewal**: Funded federally and implemented by state and local governments, urban renewal projects have labeled numerous Black communities as blighted and destroyed them under the promise of progress. Examples include the construction of the Cross Bronx Expressway that displaced tens of thousands of mostly working-class Black and Puerto Rican residents (Guimond, 2013), and the destruction of nearly all of Southwest Washington, D.C., to create government offices and luxury housing that has displaced thousands of Black people and families (Gillette, 1995).
- **Subprime Lending**: In the early 2000s, banks and mortgage companies disproportionately targeted Black borrowers, marketing subprime loans with high interest rates, labeling them high-risk mortgages, even when Black borrowers qualified for better terms and rates. These predatory lending practices led to massive foreclosures during the 2008 financial crisis, with Black communities suffering the highest rates of home loss (Rugh & Massey, 2010).
- **Appraisal Discrimination**: Unjust housing appraisal practices are persistent forms of racial discrimination. A 2021 report by Freddie Mac found

homes in predominantly Black and Latino neighborhoods were more likely to be appraised significantly below the actual value compared to similar homes in predominantly white neighborhoods. In majority-Black neighborhoods, 12.5% of homes were undervalued, compared to only 7.4% in majority-white areas (Freddie Mac, 2021). According to a 2021 survey by the Appraisal Institute and data from the United States Bureau of Labor Statistics, over 95% of real property appraisers are white, and more than 75% are male, adding to the racial bias and discrimination issues within the industry (Appraisal Institute, 2021; U.S. Bureau of Labor Statistics, 2021).

There's more...

Climate Change and Environmental Racism

The escalating climate crisis disproportionately impacts Black communities through housing, creating a modern iteration of environmental racism that compounds historical discrimination. The flood risk maps of many major cities closely resemble the redlining maps of the 1930s, demonstrating how climate change amplifies the effects of past racist housing practices (Center for American Progress, 2025).

By race, Black homeowners pay more for homeowners' insurance than any other racial/ethnic community. In 2023, the median homeowners' insurance cost was $1,360 for Black homeowners, compared to $1,310 for white, $1,330 for Asian, and $1,300 for Hispanic homeowners (NAR, 2025).

Additionally, insurance companies implement a practice called "bluelining," where they draw metaphorical blue lines around climate-vulnerable communities and either refuse coverage or charge prohibitively high premiums. Research shows that between 2013 and 2022, insurance costs as a percentage of mortgage payments more than doubled, jumping from 7–8% to over 20% (First Street Foundation, 2024). One in 13 homeowners nationwide is now uninsured, leaving at least $1.6 trillion in unprotected market value (Consumer Federation of America, 2024).

Black homeowners face compounded vulnerability because redlining has concentrated Black communities in flood-prone areas with inadequate infrastructure. A 2024 Urban Institute study found that low- and moderate-income neighborhoods of color are the most likely to face a very high risk of riverine flooding when proper risk calculations are used—the opposite of the conclusions drawn from the Federal Emergency Management Agency's (FEMA) original methodology. Without insurance, homeowners cannot maintain mortgages, threatening the stability of entire Black communities.

A 2020 study of 108 American cities found that residents in formerly redlined neighborhoods experience significantly hotter temperatures—up to 13 degrees higher in some cities. Temperature increases result from a lack of green spaces and increased heat-absorbing concrete and asphalt surfaces

(Hoffman et al., 2020). As heat waves become more frequent with climate change, these temperature disparities both create and compound serious health risks and increase cooling costs for Black people who already face higher housing cost burdens.

As climate disasters increase in frequency and severity, Black people and families face displacement pressures from multiple directions. Wealthier residents seeking "climate havens" are driving gentrification in historically Black neighborhoods perceived as safer from climate risks; at the same time, those in high-risk areas cannot afford to relocate or rebuild after disasters. FEMA's own research shows reconstruction funds often fail to reach low-income and minority residents whose homes sustain the most damage (Panfil [New America], 2024).

The Altadena Fires: A Case Study in Climate Injustice

The January 2025 Eaton Fire in Altadena, California, provides a devastating contemporary example of how climate change disproportionately impacts Black communities. The fire, which burned for 24 days, destroyed more than 9,000 buildings and killed at least 19 people, making it the fifth-deadliest and second-most-destructive wildfire in California history (CAL FIRE, 2025).

Altadena, an unincorporated community in Los Angeles County, has been home to a thriving Black middle-class community for generations. The predominantly Black west Altadena neighborhood bore the brunt of the disaster—yet received evacuation orders hours after wealthier, whiter east Altadena residents. All but one of the 19 confirmed deaths occurred in west Altadena, the predominantly Black neighborhood that received delayed emergency warnings (Jeong, 2026). California Congresswoman Sydney Kamlager-Dove called for a "full-scale investigation" into whether Altadena was deliberately "sacrificed" during the emergency response (CNN, 2025).

The disaster exemplifies multiple dimensions of housing injustice converging in a climate emergency: inadequate infrastructure in historically disinvested Black neighborhoods; delayed emergency response reflecting systemic devaluation of Black lives; loss of irreplaceable generational wealth accumulated despite centuries of anti-Black discrimination; and the threat of opportunistic land speculation targeting displaced Black homeowners. Community organizations like "Altadena Not for Sale" and community land trust efforts have mobilized to prevent wealthy outside investors from extracting what remains of Black wealth in the aftermath (Del Cid Lugo 2025).

For many Black families, the fires destroyed not just structures but generations of accumulated memories, heirlooms, and community ties. Dr. Dorothy Ludd-Lloyd, a long-time Altadena resident, lost her family home and keeps repeating, "I don't know if I'm going to make it," according to family members. Her granddaughter emphasized, "There's no words to describe her level of devastation. And it's not about things. She wants people to know that they were there" (CNN, 2025). The Altadena fires demonstrate how climate disasters accelerate existing racial inequities by converting environmental racism from slow-moving structural violence into acute catastrophic loss concentrated in Black communities.

Short-Term Rental Platforms and Affordable Housing

The rise of short-term rental platforms like Airbnb and VRBO (Vacation Rentals by Owner) has fundamentally transformed housing markets in ways that disproportionately harm Black communities seeking affordable housing. Since 2011, the short-term rental industry has grown by 800%, removing significant housing stock from the long-term rental market (Granicus, 2023).

Research consistently demonstrates that short-term rentals reduce affordable housing availability and drive up the cost of rent. A University of Massachusetts study found that in Boston, Massachusetts, a one standard deviation increase in Airbnb listings relative to total housing units in a census tract is associated with rent increases of 0.4%, with the highest-concentration areas seeing increases of 1.3% to 3.1%, or up to $93 per month at citywide mean rents (Horn & Merante, 2017). National research from UCLA and USC found that a 10% increase in Airbnb listings leads to a 0.42% increase in rents and a 0.76% increase in home prices (Barron et al., 2021).

The debate around short-term rental regulations reveals complex dynamics affecting Black communities. While some argue that regulations like New York City's Local Law 18 disproportionately hurt Black and Latino homeowners who rely on hosting income, research shows the broader negative impact on Black renters far exceeds the benefits to the small percentage of hosts. In investor-heavy markets, Black renters face higher costs while institutional investors convert properties to short-term rentals at scale.

Analysis of New York City's rental market shows that while less than 1% of households were Airbnb hosts, the median renter lost $125 annually due to rent increases. Critically, evidence suggests that low-income and Black and Latino renters experienced different impacts: the median Black renter paid $134 more annually, Hispanic renters paid $113 more, while white renters paid $152 more—reflecting different residential patterns and market exposures (Harvard JCHS, 2024).

Short-term rentals accelerate gentrification in historically Black neighborhoods that become desirable to tourists. As property values rise due to short-term rental profitability, long-term Black residents are increasingly unable to afford their homes. This process is particularly severe in cities like New Orleans, where entire historically Black neighborhoods have been transformed into short-term rental zones, displacing multi-generational Black families.

Corporate Ownership of Single-Family Homes

Wall Street's entry into the single-family housing market represents one of the most significant threats to Black homeownership and wealth-building in America. Institutional investors—companies with access to capital enabling them to own large numbers of single-family homes—have fundamentally reshaped housing markets in ways that disproportionately harm Black people.

Prior to 2011, no single investor owned more than 1,000 single-family homes. By 2022, 32 institutional investors collectively owned 450,000 single-family homes, with the five largest investors controlling nearly 300,000 homes (Government Accountability Office, 2024). MetLife Investment Management projects that institutional investors may control 40% of United States single-family rental homes by 2030. In the first quarter of 2024, investors purchased 14.8% of all homes sold nationwide, with some cities, like Springfield, Kansas City, and St. Louis, seeing investors purchase around one in five homes.

Evidence clearly demonstrates that institutional investors specifically target Black neighborhoods. A United States House Financial Services Committee investigation found that the five largest institutional investors tended to acquire homes in neighborhoods with higher concentrations of Black residents" (U.S. House of Representatives, Committee on Financial Services, 2022). In Mecklenburg County, North Carolina, between 2011 and 2021, institutional investors purchased nearly 7% of all single-family homes sold, with concentration rising in neighborhoods with above-average Black populations (Billings & Soliman, 2025).

Research on Atlanta, Georgia's housing market found that large investment firms' concentrated investment in single-family rentals weakened local homeownership, mainly for Black residents. The study concluded that "institutional scale matters in explaining a significantly diminished homeownership during this period," specifically for Black families (An, 2024).

Homes near properties purchased by institutional investors see property values decline by 1–2%, contributing to the erosion of Black wealth. Institutional investors raise rents at 60% higher rates than average increases when first acquiring properties, and a higher investor share in neighborhoods correlates with faster rent increases for all landlords. These companies also file for evictions at higher rates than small landlords, which can permanently harm tenants' ability to find non-corporate housing.

The conversion of owner-occupied homes to rental properties in Black neighborhoods fuels negative social impacts, including reduced voter engagement, lower property maintenance, and increased crime. Research shows that homeownership is strongly linked to civic engagement, and the shift to absentee corporate ownership erodes community stability in Black neighborhoods.

Institutional investors have decisive advantages over individual Black homebuyers: access to cash, ability to make quick offers, lower borrowing costs, and no need for mortgage approval. This puts Black families—who already face higher mortgage denial rates (24% for Black applicants compared to 10% for white applicants)—at a severe competitive disadvantage in markets where investors are active (Zillow, 2024).

Wall Street investment firms are aggressively buying up single-family homes, directly driving up housing costs and blocking Black families from homeownership. In the first quarter of 2024 alone, institutional investors purchased 19% of all homes sold in America—nearly one in five homes went to corporations instead of families (Redfin, 2024). This corporate takeover of family housing represents one of the most urgent threats to Black wealth-building in a generation.

The concentration is even more severe in cities with large Black populations. In Atlanta, 30% of single-family rental homes are owned by Wall Street investors, systematically excluding Black families from homeownership opportunities (Redfin, 2024). These corporations do not buy homes to live in them—they buy homes to extract wealth from communities through inflated rents and property speculation.

By 2022, just 32 institutional investors owned 450,000 single-family homes, with the five largest controlling nearly 300,000 homes (U.S. Government Accountability Office, 2024). Industry projections show these investors could control 40% of all single-family rental homes by 2030 if their expansion continues unchecked—a complete transformation of homeownership into corporate extraction.

Corporate investors deliberately target Black neighborhoods. The United States House Financial Services Committee documented that the five largest institutional investors "tended to acquire homes in neighborhoods with Black populations significantly greater than the national average". This is not a coincidence. It is a strategy. Wall Street firms see Black neighborhoods as opportunities for profit extraction precisely because historical discrimination has made these communities vulnerable.

Research on Atlanta found that corporate investment "weakened local homeownership, mainly for Black residents" (An, 2024). When Wall Street buys up homes in Black neighborhoods, they remove properties from the ownership market permanently, converting homes that could build Black wealth into corporate rental properties that extract wealth instead.

Corporate landlords use computer algorithms to set rents higher than market rates to maximize profits while pricing Black families out of their own neighborhoods (Redfin, 2024). They raise rents at 60% higher rates than average when first acquiring properties, and their presence in neighborhoods correlates with faster rent increases for all landlords (Philadelphia Federal

Reserve, 2024). Corporate landlords also file for evictions at higher rates than small landlords, creating permanent barriers for Black renters trying to access future housing.

The Competitive Disadvantage for Black Families

Black families cannot compete against cash-heavy Wall Street firms. Corporate buyers make immediate all-cash offers, waive inspections, and close in days—advantages individual families simply do not have. For Black families already facing mortgage denial rates of 24% compared to 10% for white applicants (Zillow, 2024), competing against corporations with unlimited access to capital is nearly impossible.

When a Black family views a home they could afford, a Wall Street investor can outbid them with cash before they even complete their mortgage application. This is not a fair market. It is systematic exclusion masquerading as an investment strategy. The result is that Black families who are ready, willing, and financially capable of homeownership are locked out of the housing market by corporate money.

Federal Response and Ongoing Gaps

In January 2026, the 47th occupant of the Oval Office announced restrictions aimed at limiting institutional investor purchases of single-family homes. While any acknowledgment of this crisis is a step forward, significant questions remain about enforcement, scope, and whether these restrictions will meaningfully protect Black communities from ongoing corporate extraction.

More fundamentally, proposed restrictions on future purchases do nothing to address the 450,000 homes corporations already own (U.S. Government Accountability Office, 2024). These existing holdings continue to extract wealth from Black communities every month through inflated rents. Without policies that actively return these properties to community ownership, Wall Street maintains its stranglehold on family housing.

Additionally, any restrictions on corporate investors mean nothing if they come alongside cuts to Federal Housing Administration (FHA) programs, rental assistance, fair housing enforcement, and first-time homebuyer programs that Black families rely on to access homeownership.

Call to Action

Demand aggressive enforcement: Wall Street firms will seek workarounds through subsidiary companies and complex corporate structures. We need robust enforcement with adequate funding and penalties severe enough to deter corporate hoarding of family homes.

Fight for property return policies: Advocate for policies that require corporations to sell properties to owner-occupants, with priority for existing renters and Black first-time homebuyers. Tax incentives for maintaining large rental portfolios should be eliminated, while tax benefits for selling to owner-occupants should be created.

Support "right of first refusal" laws: Demand legislation giving renters and local families the first opportunity to purchase properties before any investor—corporate or individual—can buy them, especially in neighborhoods with high Black populations.

Build community ownership alternatives: Support community land trusts, cooperative housing models, and municipal acquisition programs that can purchase properties from existing investors and maintain permanent affordability for Black families.

Require radical transparency: Demand public accountability to track and report all investor purchases by property location, neighborhood demographics, purchase price, subsequent rent charges, and eviction rates. Communities cannot fight what they cannot see.

Connect to anti-displacement organizing: Wall Street's housing extraction connects directly to gentrification, climate displacement, and the erosion of Black neighborhoods. Housing justice organizations must name corporate ownership as a driver of multiple forms of community harm.

Protect and expand public programs: Fight cuts to every program that helps Black families access homeownership—FHA loans, down payment assistance, fair lending enforcement, housing counseling, and rental assistance. Corporate restrictions are meaningless without robust public investment in Black homeownership pathways.

Wall Street's systematic purchase of family homes is wealth extraction at scale. These corporations are not providing housing—they are blocking homeownership, inflating rents, destabilizing communities, and converting what should be family wealth-building into corporate profit. This is a deliberate business model, and it requires a deliberate, aggressive response that prioritizes Black families' right to own homes in their own communities.

Gentrification and Displacement

Gentrification Pressures in Historically Black Neighborhoods

Gentrification—the influx of capital and wealthier, typically white residents into historically Black urban neighborhoods—represents a profound threat to Black communities, eroding the cultural fabric and displacing long-time residents to extract the wealth and community assets Black people built over generations.

Black residents face displacement through multiple mechanisms: direct displacement when rising rents or property taxes force moves; exclusionary displacement when rising costs prevent Black families from moving into changing neighborhoods; and cultural displacement when the arrival of new amenities and residents fundamentally alters neighborhood character without benefiting Black residents.

The intersection of gentrification with short-term rentals, corporate investment, and climate migration compounds displacement pressures. Neighborhoods once avoided by white residents because of racist perceptions are "discovered" by white people and investors, which leads to rapid increases in property value, benefiting white newcomers who can afford to buy while displacing Black renters who built the community.

Gentrification fuels wealth extraction from Black communities. The schools, parks, infrastructure improvements, and investments that Black residents advocate for—sometimes for decades—are sometimes only funded once white residents occupy communities. Black homeowners may see property values rise, but often sell under pressure from rising property taxes. This process transfers wealth to new, typically white owners. Too often, Black residents receive no compensation despite being forced out of communities they helped build.

Government policies frequently accelerate gentrification through tax incentives for developers, zoning changes favoring luxury development, and public investment that follows white residents rather than serving existing Black residents. Community Development Block Grants (CDBG) and other federal funds intended to improve low-income communities sometimes catalyze gentrification when not paired with strong anti-displacement protections.

Black Agency in Urban Change

While gentrification represents a profound threat to Black communities, it is essential to recognize that Black residents are not merely passive victims of urban change. Sociologist Marcus Anthony Hunter's groundbreaking work *Black Citymakers: How the Philadelphia Negro Changed Urban America* (2013) documents how Black Philadelphians actively shaped urban space and political power across more than a century of dramatic transformation. Hunter demonstrates that Black residents were "by no means mere casualties of the large-scale social and political changes that altered urban dynamics across the nation after World War II," but instead were strategic actors who "framed their own understandings of urban social change, forging dynamic inter- and intra-racial alliances" (Hunter, 2013).

Hunter's research reveals that Black communities engaged in housing activism and led anti-urban renewal mobilization efforts. They strategically shaped their own migration patterns to create and sustain Black urban enclaves. Even in the face of systematic displacement from neighborhoods like Philadelphia's historic Black Seventh Ward, Black residents exercised agency—not as victims forced from their homes, but as citymakers who made calculated decisions about when to leave, where to go, and how to build new communities. This framework of Black urban agency is critical for contemporary housing justice movements. This framework reminds us that Black communities possess deep wells of strategic knowledge, organizational capacity, and political sophistication developed through generations of navigating housing discrimination. Successful anti-gentrification organizing must build on this tradition of Black citymaking, centering Black residents not as problems to be solved but as primary architects of solutions that preserve community, build power, and resist displacement while creating pathways to opportunity.

Student Loan Debt Impact on Black Homeownership

Student loan debt represents a particularly severe barrier to Black homeownership, reflecting both the necessity of education for economic mobility and the racial wealth gap that forces Black families to rely more heavily on loans. In an effort to address this inequity, in 2021, the Federal Housing Administration (FHA) made a rule change on how student loan debt impacts the debt-to-income ratio when seeking an FHA-insured mortgage. If payments are being made, lenders can now use the actual monthly repayment amount. If payments are not being made, lenders now calculate 0.5% of the outstanding student loan balance. Before the rule change, lenders calculated 1% of the outstanding student loan balance. (Lane, 2021).

In 2023, nearly half (42%) of Black homebuyers reported having student loan debt with an average balance of $46,000—the highest among all racial groups (NAR, 2025). This debt compares to significantly lower rates and balances for other groups.

In spite of this rule change, black borrowers still carry student debt longer and in higher amounts due to several factors, including less family wealth. Black students are more likely to attend for-profit institutions with higher costs and lower completion rates. Additionally, employment discrimination means Black graduates earn less on average, making repayments and overall mortgage qualification more difficult.

Technology and the Digital Divide in Housing Access

Access to technology and reliable internet connectivity has become essential for housing access, yet the engineered digital divide disproportionately affects Black communities, and this divide is ever-expanding. Finding rental listings, applying for mortgages, accessing homebuyer education, and even paying rent online all require reliable internet access and digital literacy—resources that remain unequally distributed.

According to Federal Communications Commission data, Black households are less likely to have home broadband access. There are significant broadband divide in both urban and rural Black communities. This digital divide creates concrete barriers to housing opportunities, resulting from online-only rental applications that exclude non-connected households. Frequently, the best deals and listings appear online first. Additionally, mortgage pre-approval and homebuyer education increasingly occur via digital platforms.

The shift to algorithm-driven rental and mortgage applications also raises concerns about embedded bias. Automated decision-making systems can perpetuate historical discrimination, with Black applicants facing rejections based on factors that correlate with race, even when race is not explicitly considered. Advocacy for algorithmic transparency and accountability in housing is essential to prevent technology from becoming another mechanism of discrimination.

Preserving Progress and Current Challenges

For the majority of the country's existence, housing discrimination was legal. Black people have consistently faced discrimination in the sale, rental, and financing processes that determine the type, location, and quality of our homes. Through increased Black representation in lawmaking bodies at every level of government, coupled with community activism, policy shifts have focused on righting historical wrongs, improving housing quality for renters, and addressing barriers to homeownership. As communities brace for devastating cuts in funding and services, it is essential to understand existing policies and support systems.

Fair Housing Act

The Fair Housing Act of 1968 prohibits discrimination in housing based on race, color, national origin, religion, sex, familial status, and disability. The Act entitles everyone to equal opportunity and access to housing. It makes it illegal for a landlord to refuse to rent to you because of your race, ethnicity, disability, or because you have children; a real estate agent to only rent or sell you a home in specific areas; and financial institutions to deny you a loan or charge you higher fees because of your race, ethnicity, disability status, or the community you buy in.

Federal Housing Administration (FHA) Loans and Mortgage Insurance

Federal Housing Administration (FHA) mortgage insurance is a critical vehicle for increasing the Black homeownership rate. The FHA provides mortgage insurance to approved lenders, increasing the loan products available to borrowers. FHA-approved lenders are the primary sources of mortgages for low-to-moderate-income households seeking to purchase a single-family home, duplex, condominium, or multifamily property. Some 80% of FHA loan borrowers are first-time homeowners (Urban Institute, 2025). Because of this mortgage insurance, FHA lenders offer a lower down payment minimum, averaging 3.5% compared to 20% for a conventional mortgage.

FHA loans and mortgage insurance have a lower credit score requirement of 580, compared to 620 to 680 for conventional loans. Without FHA mortgage insurance, borrowers with credit scores below 620 would likely be ineligible, and those between 620 and 680 would have to make a 20% down payment to access these vehicles.

If you are buying a home or refinancing, explore the options available to you through an approved FHA lender. Know the types of loan options available. Ask questions about down payment requirements. Understand how student loan debt may affect your approval limits and how your relationship status may provide you with additional advantages or burdens in the mortgage loan and insurance process.

When considering FHA Loans, it is also important to acknowledge that 80% of FHA borrowers are first-time homebuyers. Black homebuyers are more likely than any other racial/ethnic group to be first-time purchasers, with 49% of Black buyers purchasing their first home, compared to just 20% of white buyers (NAR, 2025). This disparity reflects the persistent racial wealth gap and limited intergenerational wealth transfer in Black families. Because Black buyers disproportionately lack inherited down payment assistance, access to family homes, generational housing wealth, or other privileges associated with whiteness, FHA loans and down payment assistance programs are particularly critical for Black homeownership.

Rental Assistance Programs

Established in 1974, Section 8 (officially known as the Housing Choice Voucher Program [HCV]) requires tenants to pay 30% of their income toward fair market rents, with the remaining 70% paid to the landlord by the local housing authority with funds from the United States Department of Housing and Urban Development (HUD) (Center on Budget and Policy Priorities, 2009). These vouchers often provide low-income households with stable housing and facilitate mobility out of areas of concentrated poverty to safer communities with quality schools, healthcare, and employment opportunities.

HUD rental assistance is insufficiently funded, with only 1 in 4 eligible households receiving assistance. It is worth noting that these rental assistance programs primarily serve heads of households aged 62 years or older and people with disabilities.

Homelessness Programs

Black households have historically been overrepresented among those experiencing homelessness or housing insecurity. Per the *2022 Annual Homeless Assessment Report* to Congress, despite constituting approximately 12% of all households in the United States, Black people accounted for 37% of the population without permanent housing—including people who may be doubled up or couch surfing (Henry et al., 2024).

Continuums of Care coordinate homeless services at the local level, working to address the disproportionate representation of Black people among those experiencing homelessness.

The McKinney–Vento Homeless Assistance Act plays a critical role in ensuring educational stability for children and youth experiencing housing insecurity. Subtitle VII-B of the Act, which authorizes the Education for Homeless Children and Youth (EHCY) Program, is the primary federal legislation protecting the educational rights of students experiencing housing instability (National Center for Homeless Education, 2025).

Under McKinney–Vento, children and youth who lack a fixed, regular, and adequate nighttime residence are considered homeless and entitled to specific protections and services. McKinney–Vento supports students sharing housing with others due to loss of housing or economic hardship, living in motels or shelters, or residing in cars, parks, or other locations not designed for regular sleeping (U.S. Department of Education, 2025). Given that Black children represent 32% of those experiencing homelessness despite being only 12% of the child population, McKinney–Vento provisions are particularly critical for Black students.

Key protections under McKinney–Vento include:

- Immediate enrollment in school, even without the typically required documents like proof of residency, medical records, or previous academic records
- The right to remain in the school they attended when permanently housed
- Transportation assistance
- Access to the programs and services available to other students, including free and reduced lunch, Title I services, summer-, after-, and out-of-school programs
- College and career counseling, including assistance with the Free Application for Federal Student Aid (FAFSA) and verification of homelessness status for independent student designation
- Protection of privacy, with living arrangements protected under the Family Educational Rights and Privacy Act (FERPA) and not considered directory information

Every public school district is required to designate a local homeless education liaison who serves as the primary contact for students and families experiencing homelessness. Know who your designee is before you need to engage them. However, as is the case with other housing support programs, McKinney–Vento is chronically underfunded, and many eligible students never receive the services and protections to which they are legally entitled. Advocates emphasize the need for increased federal funding, better coordination between education and housing agencies, and strengthened enforcement to ensure Black students experiencing housing instability can access the educational stability that is their legal right.

Community Development Block Grants (CDBG)

The Community Development Block Grant (CDBG) is a federal program providing flexible funding to local governments to support affordable housing, economic development, public services, and neighborhood revitalization, especially for low-income communities.

Grants are awarded based on a formula and disbursed to cities and counties that collaborate with residents to address community development activities aimed at combating neighborhood blight through revitalization and economic development projects (HUD Exchange, 2025). By law, 75% of CDBG-funded activities must benefit low- and moderate-income people. The

CDBG program is one of the most effective funding sources for addressing local housing and community development needs, including preventing community deterioration from disinvestment.

Housing Discrimination Against Black LGBTQ+/and Same-Gender Loving (SGL) People

Black LGBTQ+/SGL people and families face intersectional discrimination in housing, experiencing bias based on a range of factors: race/ethnicity, sexual orientation, gender identity, and expression. Black transgender, gender-expansive, and intersex people face particularly severe barriers, including:

- Higher rates of housing instability and housing insecurity, with Black transgender people experiencing homelessness at rates significantly higher than the general population.
- Discrimination by landlords who refuse to rent to transgender tenants or harass them.
- Barriers to shelter access, particularly for Black transgender women who are often excluded from women's shelters.
- Difficulty accessing mortgages due to name/gender marker mismatches on identification documents and credit reports.
- Unique vulnerability during housing searches when gender presentation may differ from legal documents.

While the Fair Housing Act prohibits discrimination based on sex, and recent court decisions have interpreted sex to include sexual orientation and gender identity, discrimination prohibition enforcement remains inconsistent. Many Black LGBTQ+/SGL people experience discrimination that is difficult to prove. Advocates emphasize the need for explicit inclusion of sexual orientation and gender identity in fair housing protections and stronger enforcement mechanisms.

Housing Challenges for Black Immigrants and Refugees

Black immigrants and refugees face unique housing barriers that compound racial discrimination, including:

- Language barriers make it challenging to navigate rental applications, execute lease agreements, and find success in the homebuying process.
- Lack of credit history makes mortgage and rental approval difficult, even with a stable income.
- Immigration status concerns may make people reluctant to report housing discrimination or unsafe conditions, and may result in exclusion from federal housing programs.

- Unfamiliarity with housing systems, tenant rights, and available resources can serve as roadblocks.
- Discrimination based on national origin, accent, or immigration status, in addition to race.
- Predatory lending and rental scams target immigrant communities.

Black immigrants contribute significantly to their communities, but often cannot access the same homeownership pathways enabling previous generations of immigrants to build wealth. Ensuring housing access for Black immigrants and refugees requires linguistically accessible services, credit-building alternatives, immigration status-blind housing policies, and explicit prohibitions on national origin discrimination.

State-Level Housing Policy

Housing policy varies dramatically across states, creating unequal protection and opportunity for Black Americans depending on location. Consider the following regional disparities in home ownership:

Black homeownership rates vary dramatically across states, ranging from as low as 9–15% in North Dakota to 57% in Mississippi—a nearly 50 percentage point spread (NAR, 2025). States with the highest Black homeownership rates include Mississippi (57%), South Carolina (55%), and Delaware (54%). The lowest rates appear in North Dakota (9–15%), South Dakota (22%), and Hawaii (24.2%).

These variations reflect different historical patterns, state policies, economic conditions, and demographic compositions. The Black–white homeownership gap exceeds 30 percentage points in 37 states. It exceeds 40 percentage points in 10 states, demonstrating that housing inequity is a national crisis requiring both federal and state-level action.

While processing these regional differences, consider the following:

Fair Housing Enforcement: Some states have stronger fair housing laws than federal protections, explicitly including source of income, sexual orientation, and gender identity as protected classes. States including California, Connecticut, Delaware, District of Columbia, Maine, Massachusetts, Minnesota, New Jersey, New York, Oregon, Rhode Island, Vermont, and Wisconsin provide these expanded protections. Black residents in states without these protections face greater exposure to discrimination.

Eviction Protections: State eviction processes vary significantly. Some states require just cause for eviction, provide right-to-counsel in eviction proceedings, or mandate longer notice periods. Others allow rapid eviction with minimal tenant protections. States like California, Maryland, New Jersey, and Washington have implemented stronger tenant protections, while many Southern states, where the majority of Black people in the United States reside, offer minimal protections.

Public Housing Caps: Several states, including Illinois and Texas, maintain statutory caps restricting the number of public housing units. Caps directly limit affordable housing options in states with significant Black populations. Advocates are working to repeal these arbitrary limits.

Short-Term Rental Regulations: Cities and states have taken varied approaches to regulating short-term rentals. New York City implemented strict regulations requiring hosts to register and be present during rentals. Other jurisdictions have imposed caps on the number of days properties can be rented or the number of properties hosts can list. Some states have preempted local regulation, preventing cities from limiting short-term rentals even when they harm local housing markets.

Corporate Investor Restrictions: States are beginning to respond to institutional investor purchases of single-family homes. As of 2024, lawmakers in eight states have introduced bills to limit or penalize corporate investors who purchase single-family homes, though most face opposition from the single-family rental lobby.

Down Payment Assistance Programs: Many states and municipalities offer down payment assistance specifically for first-time or first-generation homebuyers. These programs vary widely in availability, eligibility criteria, and funding levels. Black potential homebuyers should research programs available in their state and locality.

Call To Action: Demand Housing Justice

Consider the following as you effectively advocate for your community, civically engage with government officials, and empower the people!

Housing as a Human Right

- Contact your Congressional representatives and ask that they revise the Housing Act to codify housing as a fundamental right by introducing a framework that is similar to education and healthcare entitlements that include enforceable remedies.

Housing Discrimination

- Locate the Fair Housing Initiative Program (FHIP) organization nearest you and learn about your rights under the Fair Housing Act.
- Advocate for the following:
    - Ensure fair housing and lending laws are fully enforced.
    - Increase funding to support fair lending enforcement.
    - Require technology, including Artificial Intelligence, to comply with civil rights and consumer protection laws.
    - Renovating and developing homes in communities where homes are (see the Neighborhood Homes Investment Act).

  - Create Redlining Reparations Zones.
  - Establish a Restorative Housing Fund to fuel reparative investments for historically excluded Black neighborhoods.

- Contact the National Fair Housing Alliance to report any concerns about fair housing violations and to learn how you might support efforts to combat housing discrimination.
- If you believe you are a victim of housing discrimination, contact your local nonprofit fair housing organization and your state and local government agencies.

Affordable Homeownership

- Advocate for municipal down payment assistance programs specifically addressing the racial homeownership gap. These programs must be designed to support Black first-generation/first-time homebuyers, include Equality Act civil rights protections for all members of our beautifully diverse community, prevent steering into specific neighborhoods, and be connected to existing programs such as the Home Investment Partnership Program (HOME) and Community Development Block Grants (CDBG). Assistance programs should include counseling.
- Participate in community-based financial literacy and homebuyer education initiatives.
- Find and work with a HUD-certified Housing Counselor. Services are often free if you are a first-time home buyer, facing foreclosure, eviction, or homelessness. If you come across specific workshops with a fee, those fees can be waived through certain housing counseling agencies if you cannot afford them.
- Encourage local credit unions and community development financial institutions (CDFIs) to develop specialized mortgage products for Black potential homeowners.
- Appeal to local officials for permanent inclusion of on-time rent payments in the loan underwriting process. Rental payments are often not reported to credit bureaus, which, if done, could boost credit scores. Including rent payments could help many potential homebuyers improve their credit scores, making them eligible for loans with lower down payments, better interest rates, and lower fees.
- Contact HUD and lawmakers to support policies that minimize the impact of student debt on mortgage qualification.

Affordable Rental Programs

- Support inclusionary zoning laws requiring new developments to include affordable housing units and expand zoning reform to eliminate single-family-only zoning, allowing for more duplexes, triplexes, and apartments.

Incentives can be provided to developers to encourage building, such as providing density bonuses and streamlining permitting processes.

- Legalize and streamline the approval process for accessory dwelling units, including basement apartments, backyards, and garage spaces. These units can increase the overall supply of affordable housing without requiring major new large-scale development, support multigenerational living, and help older adults age in place with the support of their communities.
- Lift state and federal limits on the number of public housing units that local housing authorities can develop or manage. Several states, including Illinois and Texas, maintain statutory caps restricting the number of public housing units. Repealing these state-level limits and amending the Housing Act to authorize expansion beyond current caps can empower housing authorities to respond to the nation's affordable housing shortage more effectively. To operationalize this expansion, legislators should:
- Remove public housing unit caps.
- Amend the Housing Act to remove implicit or explicit constraints on new public housing development and to authorize dedicated appropriations for new construction.
- Pair repeal efforts with financing innovations. For example, combine the Rental Assistance Demonstration (RAD) program with green bonds, infrastructure funds, and public–private investment models that support both affordability and sustainability.
- Ensure RAD protections remain in place to prevent displacement and maintain long-term affordability.
- Increase funding available through the Low-Income Housing Tax Credit (LIHTC) to produce more affordable housing units.

Housing Insecurity/Homelessness

- Identify your local Continuum of Care (CoC) to learn about the services they provide and how you can support them in petitioning for ongoing funding and additional resources.
- Advocate for CoCs' equity measures, including impact assessments, and racial equity goals (e.g., proportional representation for assistees).
- Fund eviction prevention legal aid, especially in states without right-to-counsel.
- Establish national shelter standards for privacy, safety, and anti-discrimination.
- Participate in the community planning process for your local Community Development Block Grant.

If you believe you are being discriminated against, seek shelter, contact the closest Fair Housing Initiative Program (FHIP) and Fair Housing Assistance Program (FHAP).

Community Development Block Grants (CDBG)

Each jurisdiction receiving Community Development Block Grants (CDBG) funding must have a plan outlining how the money will be used. Your representatives should naturally defend ongoing CDBG funding to local and county governments. AND, they will need your support. When you contact their offices, ask, "What can I do to be helpful in the fight to preserve CDBG funding?"

Make sure your community is prioritized by doing the following:

- Get a copy of the *Consolidated Plan* and/or *Annual Action Plan* for your jurisdiction and share it with community members.
- Participate in the community meetings, hearings, and other public forums focused on how funding is used.
- Express support for and/or raise concerns about the priorities in your district's plan. Consistent engagement will capture their attention and stress the importance of including you and your community in the planning process.

An informed people are best positioned to fight against injustice and for liberation. To live in a just society where quality affordable housing is truly a human right, we must actively engage in creating it. While some are focused on stripping away protections provided under the Fair Housing Act, we must strategically prepare our path forward to ensure safe and stable housing and close racial wealth gaps. The State of the People, in part, is determined by people realizing they have power, owning that power, and using it to advance their collective position!

Personal Financial Preparation for Homeownership

While systemic change is essential, individuals and families can take steps to prepare for homeownership by:

Building and Monitoring Your Credit:

- Request free credit reports annually from all three credit bureaus (annual creditreport.com).
- Challenge errors on credit reports that may be suppressing scores.
- Make all payments on time, including utilities and rent.
- Keep credit utilization below 30% of available credit.
- Avoid opening new credit accounts in the 6–12 months before applying for a mortgage.

Establish Savings:

- Open a dedicated homebuying savings account, even if starting small.
- Investigate Individual Development Account (IDA) programs that match savings for first-time homebuyers.
- Explore whether your employer offers homebuyer assistance programs.
- Consider setting up automatic transfers to savings accounts.
- Research state and local first-time homebuyer programs that may offer down payment assistance.

Seek Homeownership Education:

- Complete HUD-approved homebuyer education courses (often required for down payment assistance programs).
- Connect with local HUD-certified housing counseling agencies for one-on-one guidance—counseling is often free.
- Attend first-time homebuyer workshops offered by banks, credit unions, and community organizations.
- Learn about different loan types, including FHA, VA (for veterans), USDA (for rural areas), and conventional mortgages.
- Understand the total costs of homeownership beyond the mortgage payment (property taxes, insurance, maintenance).

Address Student Loan Debt Strategically:

- Explore income-driven repayment plans that lower monthly payments.
- Investigate public service loan forgiveness if you work for qualifying employers.
- When applying for mortgages, document your actual monthly student loan payment rather than accepting the lender's calculations based on total debt.
- Understand how student loan debt affects debt-to-income ratios and plan accordingly.

Research Housing Target Market:

- Study neighborhoods where you want to buy, including school quality, amenities, and future development plans.
- Attend open houses to understand market prices and what your budget can afford.
- Research property tax rates and trends in target areas.
- Consider total commute costs when evaluating affordability.

- Look for areas with strong tenant protection laws if you plan to purchase a multi-family property and rent units.

Digital Organizing Strategies for Housing Justice

Leverage technology to organize for housing justice in your community:

Build Digital Networks:

- Create or join Facebook groups, WhatsApp chats, or Slack channels focused on housing justice in your community.
- Use social media to document housing conditions, share resources, and coordinate advocacy.
- Start neighborhood-specific groups to track displacement, rent increases, and landlord practices.
- Connect with national housing justice organizations through their social media channels and email lists.

Utilize Mapping and Data Tools:

- Use eviction tracking tools to identify buildings and landlords with high eviction rates.
- Access property ownership databases to identify corporate landlords in your community.
- Utilize displacement risk-mapping tools to understand gentrification pressures.
- Share data visualizations to make housing injustice visible to broader audiences.

Coordinate Advocacy Campaigns:

- Manage online petition campaigns for specific policy changes.
- Organize virtual town halls to educate community members on housing issues.
- Use scheduling tools to coordinate meeting attendance and testimony at city council meetings.
- Create phone and email banking campaigns to pressure elected officials.
- Document and share stories of housing discrimination and displacement to humanize the crisis.

Access Digital Resources:

- Bookmark and share digital housing rights resources in multiple languages.
- Create shared Google Docs or Notion pages with community-specific housing resources.
- Use video tutorials to help community members navigate online rental applications, credit monitoring, and homebuyer education.
- Connect to virtual legal aid and housing counseling services.
- Subscribe to housing justice newsletters and policy updates.

References

Acosta, S. (2022). *Stable housing is foundational to children's well-being*. Center on Budget and Policy Priorities: Off the Charts. https://www.cbpp.org/blog/stable-housing-is-foundational-to-childrens-well-being

Almeida, L. (2021). *A history of racist federal housing policies*. Massachusetts Budget and Policy Center. https://massbudget.org/2021/08/06/a-history-of-racist-federal-housing-policies/

An, B. Y. (2024). The influence of institutional single-family rental investors on homeownership: Who gets targeted and pushed out of the local market? *Journal of Planning Education and Research, 44*(4), 2231–2250. https://doi.org/10.1177/0739456X231176072

Appraisal Institute. (2021). *Appraiser diversity initiative*. https://www.appraisalinstitute.org

Baltimore City Department of Planning. (2018). *History of inequity in Baltimore*. https://planning.baltimorecity.gov/sites/default/files/History%20of%20Inequity%20in%20Baltimore%209-12-18.pdf

Baptist, E. E. (2014). *The half has never been told: Slavery and the making of American capitalism*. Basic Books.

Barron, K., Kung, E., & Proserpio, D. (2021). The effect of home-sharing on house prices and rents: Evidence from Airbnb. *Marketing Science, 40(1)*, 23–47.

Billings, S., & Soliman, A. (2025). Institutional investors and neighborhood change in single-family housing markets. *Real Estate Economics*, advance online publication.

CAL FIRE. (2025). *Eaton Fire*. California Department of Forestry and Fire Protection. https://www.fire.ca.gov/incidents/2025/1/7/eaton-fire

Center for American Progress. (2025). *Managing the climate change-fueled property insurance crisis*. Center for American Progress.

Center on Budget and Policy Priorities. (2009). *Section 8 rental assistance*. CBPP Policy Basi2020cs.

Centers for Disease Control and Prevention. (2021, March 10). *Healthy people 2030: Social determinants of health*. U.S. Department of Health and Human Services.

CNN. (2025). *The Black community in Altadena is reeling from what they've lost to the Eaton Fire*. https://www.cnn.com/2025/01/19/us/altadena-california-wildfire-black-community

Consumer Federation of America. (2024). *Homeowners insurance crisis: Millions uninsured*. CFA.

Del Cid Lugo, A. (2025). Altadena residents sift through calls to sell – but the soul is not for sale. LA Public Press https://lapublicpress.org/2025/02/altadena-real-estate-not-for-sale-eaton-property/

First Street Foundation. (2024). *The growing cost of climate risk in U.S. housing markets*. First Street Foundation.

Freddie Mac. (2021). *Racial and ethnic valuation gaps in home purchase appraisals*. https://www.freddiemac.com/research/insight/20210920_home_appraisals

Gillette, H., Jr. (1995). *Between justice and beauty: Race, planning, and the failure of urban policy in Washington, D.C.* Johns Hopkins University Press.

Granicus. (2023). *Are short-term vacation rentals contributing to the housing crisis?* Granicus Government Blog. https://granicus.com/blog/are-short-term-vacation-rentals-contributing-to-the-housing-crisis

Guimond, C. C. (2013). *Battle for the Bronx: Neighborhood revitalization in a gentrifying city*. [Doctoral dissertation, University of California, Berkeley].

Henry, M., Watt, R., Mahathey, A., Ouellette, J., & Sitler, A. (2024). *The 2022 Annual Homeless Assessment Report (AHAR) to Congress*. U.S. Department of Housing and Urban Development.

Hoffman, J. S., Shandas, V., & Pendleton, N. (2020). *The effects of historical housing policies on resident exposure to intra-urban heat: A study of 108 US urban areas. Climate*, 8(1), 12.

Horn, K., & Merante, M. (2017). Is home sharing driving up rents? Evidence from Airbnb in Boston. *Journal of Housing Economics*, 38, 14–24.

HUD Exchange. (2025). *Community Development Block Grant program*. U.S. Department of Housing and Urban Development.

Hunter, M. A. (2013). *Black Citymakers: How the Philadelphia Negro changed urban America*. Oxford University Press.

Joint Center for Housing Studies (JCHS) of Harvard University. (2024, January). *America's rental housing 2024*. harvard.edu

Lane, B. (2021). *FHA Changes Student Loan Rules to Make It Easier to Qualify*. New American Funding. https://www.newamericanfunding.com/learning-center/housing-news/fha-changes-student-loan-rules-to-make-it-easier-to-qualify/

National Association of Realtors. (2025). *2025 Snapshot of Race and Home Buying in America*. NAR Research Division.

National Center for Homeless Education. (2025). *McKinney–Vento Homeless Assistance Act*. U.S. Department of Education. https://nche.ed.gov/legislation/mckinney-vento/

Panfil, Y. (2024). *Why housing justice is key to climate justice*. New America. https://www.newamerica.org/insights/why-housing-justice-is-key-to-climate-justice/

Redfin. (2024). Investor home purchases in Q1 2024.

Rothstein, R. (2017). *The color of law: A forgotten history of how our government segregated America*. Liveright.

Rugh, J. S., & Massey, D. S. (2010). Racial segregation and the American foreclosure crisis. *American Sociological Review, 75(5)*, 629–651.

Smokler, A. (2021, March 3). *Repairers of the breach*. National Association of REALTORS®. https://www.nar.realtor/newsroom/op-eds-and-letters-to-the-editor/repairers-of-the-breach

Taylor, L. (2018). *Housing and health: An overview of the literature*. Health Affairs Health Policy Brief. https://www.healthaffairs.org/do/10.1377/hpb20180313.396577

U.S. Bureau of Labor Statistics. (2021). *Occupational Employment and Wage Statistics: Appraisers and Assessors of Real Estate*. https://www.bls.gov

U.S. Census Bureau. (n.d.). *QuickFacts: Levittown CDP, New York*. Retrieved April 16, 2025, from https://www.census.gov/quickfacts/fact/table/levittowncdpnewyork

U.S. Department of Education. (2025). *Identifying and supporting students experiencing homelessness from pre-school to post-secondary ages*. https://www.ed.gov/teaching-and-administration/supporting-students/identifying-and-supporting-students-experiencing-homelessness-from-pre-school-to-post-secondary-ages-us-department-of-education

U.S. Government Accountability Office. (2024). *Rental housing: Information on institutional investment in single-family homes (GAO-24-106643)*. GAO.

U.S. House of Representatives, Committee on Financial Services. (2022, June 28). *Where have all the houses gone? Private equity, single family rentals, and America's neighborhoods* [Staff Memorandum]. https://www.congress.gov/event/117th-congress/house-event/114969

Urban Institute. (2025). *Federal Housing Administration and first-time homebuyers*. UI Housing Finance Policy Center.

Zillow. (2024). *Black homeownership rate rises, but hasn't returned to 2004 level*. Zillow News. https://www.zillow.com/news/black-homeownership-rate-rises-but-hasnt-returned-to-2004-level/

Chapter 19

Pathways to Mobility

A Black Paper on Transportation Infrastructure and Policy in the United States

*David J. Johns**

MYTH: Transportation policy is "race-neutral."
REALITY: From highway construction through neighborhoods to public transit funding decisions, transportation policy has historically been shaped by and reinforced racial disparities.
MYTH: Rural Black communities do not need transportation investments as much as urban areas
REALITY: Rural Black communities face some of the most severe transportation barriers, with limited transit options and longer distances to essential services.
MYTH: Transportation choices are individual decisions, not structural issues
REALITY: Historical policies and investment patterns have systematically limited transportation options in Black communities, making individual "choices" constrained by structural barriers.

* Supported by braintrust authors: Christopher Coes, Cyntasia Palmer, Jada Capri Ward, and Nadia French-Graham.

DOI: 10.4324/9781003752646-26

Key Terms

Reliable transportation means a consistent, dependable, safe, and affordable way for people to get where they need to go. It allows access to essential services, employment, education, healthcare, and social connections without excessive time burdens, unpredictable delays, or financial hardship. Reliability encompasses:

Temporal consistency: Transportation that arrives and departs on predictable schedules with minimal unexpected delays or cancellations

Geographic accessibility: Transportation that serves communities equitably, without significant gaps in coverage for specific neighborhoods or regions

Financial sustainability: Transportation that remains affordable relative to household income, without imposing disproportionate cost burdens

Physical accessibility: Transportation that accommodates individuals of all physical abilities and health conditions

Operational resilience: Transportation that maintains functionality during varying conditions, including weather events, peak demand periods, and other stresses

Safety and security: Transportation that protects users from physical harm, harassment, or other safety concerns

These definitions recognize that reliability is multidimensional and that a transportation system can only be considered truly reliable when it meets all these criteria. For Black communities that have historically experienced transportation injustice, ensuring comprehensive reliability, rather than focusing on just one dimension, is essential for creating equitable transportation systems.

Executive Summary

Transportation infrastructure is foundational to opportunity in America. When done right, it connects people to jobs, raises property values, strengthens local economies, and creates wealth-building conditions.

For Black Americans, particularly in the South, in small, rural, and isolated communities, transportation has always played a profound and complex role. From the forced crossings of the Middle Passage, to the movement of the Underground Railroad, from *Plessy* v. *Ferguson* to the Montgomery Bus Boycott, and from the legacy of the Pullman Porters to today's unionizing Amazon truck drivers—transportation has been both a site of oppression and a powerful engine for liberation and economic advancement.

This Black Paper (Paper) examines how transportation and infrastructure policy decisions have affected and continue to affect life opportunities for Black Americans, focusing on historical context, current disparities, promising solutions, and actionable recommendations.

Black Americans disproportionately bear the deadly consequences of our transportation systems. Every year, more than 39,000 people are killed on America's roads—and far too often, it is Black and brown communities who bear the greatest burden. Black Americans are more than twice as likely to be struck and killed while walking, primarily because they live in neighborhoods with underfunded infrastructure, poor lighting, and fast-moving traffic (Smart Growth America, 2024a).

Transportation costs create significant economic barriers for Black families. Black families spend up to 33% more than the national average on combined housing and transportation costs (Smart Growth America, 2024b). That's not just an economic hardship. It is a structural barrier to building wealth and stability across generations.

Environmental injustice is pervasive in transportation planning. Environmental justice is no different. Black Americans are 1.5 times more likely to suffer from asthma caused by air pollution—often because their communities were intentionally placed near highways, rail yards, and freight corridors (American Lung Association, 2025). These are not random outcomes. They are the legacy of infrastructure decisions that have long devalued Black life and health.

The Interstate Highway System, begun with the Federal Aid Highway Act of 1956, had devastating consequences for Black communities nationwide. The timing of significant highway development was not coincidental; courts were striking down traditional tools of racial segregation, such as racial zoning. In some cases, highways were intentionally built along formal racial boundary lines or placed to create barriers between Black communities and white areas at the request of white community members. Between the 1950s and 1970s, the initial construction of the federal interstate highway system resulted in massive displacement. The United States Department of Transportation estimates suggest that more than 475,000 households and more than one million people were uprooted nationwide (U.S. Department of Transportation, 2022 a,b). The impact of this construction was not random; highways were frequently and deliberately routed through low-income and Black neighborhoods, which were often labeled blighted by policymakers and urban planners. This intentional displacement used infrastructure as a tool of segregation, physically isolating Black and other communities of color and causing disproportionate harm through the destruction of homes, businesses, and community institutions (Archer, 2021; Mohl, 2004).

Encouragingly, innovative solutions are emerging. From Birmingham, Alabama, a collaboration between the city and private industry launched an on-demand microtransit service to cover areas where fixed-route transit was insufficient. This service dramatically reduces commute times—a trip that once took 90 minutes by bus can now take about 15 minutes by microtransit. Columbia's cable car system is another powerful model. The system connects marginalized hillside communities to main metro lines, integrating residents who were once physically and socially isolated from the rest of the city. This innovative cut to commute times provides improved access to jobs, education and social opportunities, proving that equitable transportation is possible (Brand & Davila, 2011. Research found that job accessibility for working-age people more than doubled in areas with the cable car line (Bocarejo, 2014).

Wealth Creation Through Transportation Infrastructure

The transportation sector has long been a cornerstone of economic opportunity for Black Americans. From bus operators to airport logistics professionals, public transit and transportation hubs have provided stable, unionized jobs with real pathways to the middle class. These are not just jobs—they are ladders of mobility, rooted in our communities.

Take Hartsfield-Jackson Atlanta International Airport, for example. It is consistently recognized as the largest job center in Georgia, employing over 63,000 people, many from neighboring Black communities in Fulton, DeKalb, and Clayton counties (Invest Clayton, n.d.; Georgia Trend, 2024). The airport's full economic footprint is substantial, stretching across the Southeast. It supports more than 448,000 jobs and generates $82 billion in total economic impact. Its air cargo operations alone support over 103,600 jobs, providing vital roles in logistics and freight, generating steady incomes for families who have historically been locked out of other sectors (AJC.com, 2020).

But none of this happened by accident. In the 1970s, Mayor Maynard Jackson—Atlanta's first Black mayor, who served from 1974 to 1982—insisted on a radical shift in city contracting. Before his administration, Black firms received less than 1% of the city contracts. Jackson implemented a pioneering Minority Business Enterprise program and halted the $500 million airport expansion project until a compromise was reached. His leadership resulted in a mandate that minority- and women-owned businesses receive at least 25% of all airport construction contracts (Capital B News, 2024; *Black Enterprise*, 2023). This policy faced fierce resistance from the white business establishment class, but ultimately succeeded in creating Black millionaires and building generational wealth while establishing a new, inclusive standard for public procurement that became known as "the Atlanta Way" (Next City, 2019). To be sure, Mayor Jackson's leadership not only reshaped the skyline but also built a legacy of Black entrepreneurship and community wealth that continues today.

Mayor Jackson's model lives on through the United States Department of Transportation's Disadvantaged Business Enterprise (DBE) and Airport Concessions Disadvantaged Business Enterprise (ACDBE) programs. These programs are among the most effective tools for wealth creation in Black and Brown communities (USDOT, n.d.-a). While cumulative national totals are difficult to derive from publicly reported data, state-level data provides a clear picture of the program's impact. The California Department of Transportation (Caltrans) reported awarding over $114 million in DBE-certified commitments in 2023–2024. This Caltrans program aims to provide fair opportunity in federally-assisted contracts and drives investment into communities that have long been excluded from the economic upside of infrastructure development (USDOT, n.d.-b).

Employment and Economic Impact

The transportation sector is one of Black Americans' most significant sources of quality employment. Public transit agencies have historically been major employers of Black workers, offering unionized positions with benefits that provide pathways to the middle class. Transportation hubs like airports create many jobs for people with various skills and education levels.

Air cargo operations at airports like Hartsfield-Jackson are major economic drivers, supporting approximately 103,600 jobs in the Atlanta region alone (AJC.com, 2020). These logistics and freight handling positions provide essential income streams to communities that might otherwise face limited economic opportunities.

Land Use, Community Development, and Property Values

Across the country, Americans—predominantly Black, rural, and working-class communities—are expressing an apparent and growing demand for access to safe, walkable neighborhoods. According to the National Association of Realtors' 2023 Community & Transportation Preferences Survey, nearly 80% of Americans value walkability, and a majority say they would pay more to live in a community where jobs, shops, parks, and transit are accessible without a car (National Association of Realtors, 2023). This preference is even stronger among millennials and communities of color.

But while demand surges, the supply of walkable neighborhoods remains deeply constrained by outdated zoning laws. The Smart Growth America's Foot Traffic Ahead 2023 report found that walkable urban places—known as WalkUPs—make up just 1.2% of land in the 35 largest United States metro areas. Yet, they account for nearly 20% of the National Gross Domestic Product (GDP) (Smart Growth America, 2023). These places are economic engines: they generate more economic output per acre, create more jobs, and command higher real estate premiums compared to car-dependent areas. And yet, walkable development is still the exception rather than the norm. Zoning regulations in the vast majority of metropolitan regions make it illegal to build mixed-use, walkable places, which disproportionately impacts affordability and access to opportunity for communities of color and low-income households (World Economic Forum, 2023).

The walkability gap is especially stark in Black neighborhoods, where systemic barriers have long suppressed property values and access to economic development. A 2018 report by the Brookings Institution, titled "The Devaluation of Assets in Black Neighborhoods," found that owner-occupied homes in majority-Black neighborhoods are undervalued by $48,000 per home. This persistent gap in valuation amounts to a staggering $156 billion in lost equity nationwide for Black homeowners (Perry et al., 2018). Importantly, this devaluation persists even after controlling for neighborhood factors like education, crime rates, household income, and walkability. The same report found that commercial property in Black neighborhoods is also systematically undervalued relative to comparable assets in white neighborhoods, limiting access to capital and stifling local entrepreneurship, and reinforcing cycles of disinvestment (Perry et al., 2018).

Business Growth and Entrepreneurship

Transportation services and infrastructure projects create opportunities for business ownership and entrepreneurship (USDOT & SBA, 2022). The Small Business Administration (SBA) actively supports minority-owned businesses through programs like the 8(a) Business Development Program, which provides access to contracting opportunities that help many small businesses grow. During the 2023 fiscal year, the federal government exceeded its annual goal by allocating 12.1% (or a record-breaking $76.2 billion) in eligible federal contracting dollars to small disadvantaged businesses, with transportation contracts forming a significant portion of these opportunities (SBA, 2024).

In Atlanta, the ongoing Beltline project—transforming former railway corridors into multi-use trails—demonstrates how transportation infrastructure can be reimagined to foster economic development in previously disconnected communities (Atlanta Beltline, Inc., n.d.). With the United States Department of Transportation awarding a $25 million federal contract via the Raise grant, this project is connecting communities intentionally segregated for generations by large infrastructure projects by linking affordable housing and job centers across previously insurmountable transportation barriers (U.S. Department of Transportation, 2023).

Airports as Economic Engines

Airports are some of the transportation system's most powerful engines of wealth creation. Beyond direct employment, airports generate economic ripple effects across regions by supporting business travel, attracting investment, and facilitating the movement of goods.

Data from the Transportation Research Board indicates that United States airports facilitate the movement of more than 1.9 million passengers and more than 38,000 tons of cargo daily (Transportation Research Board, 2021). The industry generates approximately $507 billion yearly in economic activity nationwide (Airports Council International-North America, 2023).

The airline industry is a major employer, supplying 11.5 million United States jobs, including 1.2 million jobs at airports and more than 10 million jobs created indirectly in the communities surrounding airports and related industries across the country (Airports Council International-North America, 2023).

Internationally, airports are increasingly recognized as potential economic development and poverty reduction tools, especially for disadvantaged communities. The concept of "airport cities" or "aerotropolises"—planned urban developments that integrate airports into the economic and social fabric of communities—represents an opportunity to maximize the wealth-building potential of aviation infrastructure and connect residents to global supply chains (Klaus, 2022).

Challenges and Future Opportunities

Despite the transportation infrastructure's economic potential, historical and ongoing disparities in investment have limited the wealth-building opportunities for Black communities. Moving forward, the opportunity is to ensure that transportation investments are deployed equitably and that employment and business opportunities generated by them reach communities that have been historically excluded.

Federal programs like the Justice40 Initiative are trying to fix historical inequities by ensuring a significant portion of federal investment benefits reach marginalized communities. Established by Executive Order 14008, Justice40 sets a 40% government-wide goal that benefits from named federal investments, including in clean transportation, affordable housing, and workforce development, reaching communities historically marginalized by underinvestment and overburdened by pollution (The White House, n.d.).

By prioritizing both access to transportation services and access to transportation-related economic opportunities, policymakers can leverage infrastructure investments to build wealth in Black and Brown communities that have historically carried the environmental, economic, and social burdens of transportation decisions without receiving corresponding benefits (USDOT, n.d.-c; Equitable & Just National Climate Platform, n.d.).

New Technologies Reshaping Transportation

Emerging technologies are rapidly transforming transportation systems, creating opportunities and challenges for Black communities. From autonomous vehicles to advanced air mobility, these innovations can increase accessibility, create new job categories, and address historical inequities—but only if equity considerations are deliberately integrated into their development and deployment.

Autonomous Vehicles: Promise and Peril

Autonomous vehicles (AVs) represent one of the most significant technological shifts poised to reshape transportation in the coming decades. These self-driving vehicles could substantially benefit Black communities, particularly by addressing transportation gaps in areas underserved by traditional transit.

Research shows the potential benefits of AV technology for underserved communities. AVs could improve road safety, increase accessibility for people with disabilities and older adults, reduce emissions through electrification, and provide reliable transportation options in areas with limited transit service (Bipartisan Policy Center, 2024). These benefits could be especially significant for Black communities that have historically experienced disproportionate transportation barriers.

Serious equity concerns regarding autonomous vehicles must be addressed. A 2019 study led by researchers at the Georgia Institute of Technology found that existing object detection systems used in some AVs were less likely to recognize people with darker skin tones (Morgan Magazine, 2024; Samuel, 2019). The study reveals that some systems had a 39% failure rate for people with dark skin compared to a 9% failure rate for people with light skin, revealing a significant performance discrepancy. Other studies confirm this trend, with research reflecting how poor lighting conditions can exacerbate the problem, making darker-skinned people more susceptible to misdetection

(Li, et al., as cited in Pires de Brandao et al., 2024; Samuel, 2019). Without addressing these algorithmic biases, these technologies can perpetuate and exacerbate existing racial disparities in transportation safety.

Additionally, the economic implications of AV deployment for Black workers must be considered. Black workers rely upon driving occupations, including bus and long-haul truck driving and taxi and ride-share services, more than any other racial group. In fact, Black workers are more than three times as likely to be employed as bus drivers, taxi drivers, or chauffeurs compared to other racial/ethnic communities. Employed Black men are also more likely to work in transportation and utilities industries compared to white, Hispanic and Asian men.

Widespread automation could threaten these otherwise stable, middle-class transportation jobs without thoughtful transition planning and workforce development programs (Congressional Black Caucus Foundation, 2021; Economic Policy Institute, 2019). Losing transportation jobs could be particularly harmful because driving occupations often provide a wage premium for Black workers, paying more than available non-driving alternatives.

Policy considerations for equitable AV deployment must include specific, proactive measures to mitigate these risks, including:

1 Ensuring the affordability and accessibility of AV services for low-income communities.
2 Addressing algorithmic biases in vehicle detection systems.
3 Creating workforce transition programs for drivers and other transportation workers.
4 Developing shared AV models that complement rather than replace public transit.

Advanced Air Mobility: New Dimensions of Transportation

Advanced Air Mobility (AAM) represents another transformative technology with significant implications for Black communities. This emerging transportation sector includes electric vertical takeoff and landing (eVTOL) aircraft that can transport people and goods in urban, suburban, and rural environments (think the robots delivering everything in mid-town Atlanta, for example).

AAM has significant economic potential, with projections suggesting it could create tens of thousands of new jobs, contribute billions in wages and benefits, and generate substantial tax revenue by 2035. These economic opportunities could benefit Black communities if deliberate efforts are made to ensure equitable access to jobs, training, and business opportunities in this growing sector.

From an access perspective, AAM could address transportation challenges in both urban and rural Black communities. In urban settings, AAM could reduce commute times and increase job accessibility. Rural areas could improve access to healthcare, education, and economic opportunities by overcoming geographic barriers that have historically isolated rural Black communities.

However, without intentional equity-focused planning, AAM could become an exclusive transportation mode available only to wealthy people. Experts have emphasized that integrating equity into transportation projects enhances overall societal wellbeing by breaking down barriers and promoting economic development in historically marginalized areas. This principle must guide AAM development.

Some promising approaches for equitable AAM implementation include:

1 Integrating AAM with existing public transportation systems to increase accessibility.
2 Developing AAM services focused on connecting affordable housing with job centers.
3 Creating inclusive workforce development programs to ensure diverse representation in AAM jobs.
4 Using AAM to address specific transportation challenges in underserved communities, such as medical transportation in rural areas.

Artificial Intelligence and Mobility Data

Artificial Intelligence (AI) is increasingly shaping transportation planning and operations through applications like "Mobility AI." These technologies analyze vast amounts of transportation data to optimize routing, manage congestion, and improve system efficiency.

When developed with equity considerations, AI tools could help identify and address transportation disparities affecting Black communities. For example, AI analysis could identify patterns of unequal service, helping transportation agencies target improvements to underserved areas.

However, significant concerns exist about AI's potential to perpetuate or amplify biases. Research has shown that bias can be embedded in computer algorithms that drive transportation technologies, with some systems less able to detect people with darker skin than those with lighter skin. AI blind spots underscore the critical importance of diverse representation in technology development and rigorous equity testing of AI systems.

Micro Mobility and Last-Mile Solutions

Electric scooters, bike share programs, and other micro-mobility options represent important innovations for addressing "last-mile" transportation challenges. These services could be particularly valuable in Black communities that have historically experienced limited public transit access.

However, early deployment patterns of micro-mobility services have often failed to prioritize equity, concentrating services in wealthier, predominantly white neighborhoods. More promising models have emerged recently, with some cities requiring micro-mobility providers to ensure equitable vehicle distribution and affordable payment options for unbanked individuals.

Building an Equitable Technological Future

As transportation technologies evolve, centering equity in their development and deployment will be critical. Centering equity requires:

1 **Inclusive decision-making processes** that meaningfully involve Black communities in planning and implementation.
2 **Diverse representation** in technology development, from engineering to testing to deployment.
3 **Intentional equity assessments** to identify and address potential disparate impacts.
4 **Collaborative approaches** that integrate new technologies with existing community assets and needs.
5 **Workforce and Business development initiatives** that prepare Black workers for new transportation careers.

By taking these approaches, emerging transportation technologies can help address rather than reinforce historical inequities, creating more accessible, safe, and economically beneficial transportation systems for Black communities.

This Paper documents these historical injustices while highlighting emerging solutions. From Birmingham, Alabama, where on-demand transit has increased job accessibility, to Detroit's SMART Flex program, which has significantly expanded transit network coverage, innovative approaches demonstrate that equitable transportation is possible. This Paper offers concrete recommendations for policymakers, community leaders, and advocates seeking to create more equitable transportation systems that serve the needs of all Americans, with particular attention to addressing the unique challenges faced by Black communities in rural and Southern regions.

Historical Context: How We Got Here

The Segregation of Transportation Infrastructure

The racial inequities that characterize America's transportation infrastructure are not accidental. In a 2021 interview with TheGrio, Transportation Secretary Pete Buttigieg acknowledged that "there is racism physically built into some of our highways" (TheGrio, 2021). As President Biden's $2.3 trillion infrastructure plan took shape, it included $20 billion specifically to 'reconnect neighborhoods cut off by historic investments'—an acknowledgment of this troubling legacy.

The construction of interstate highways in the 1950s and 1960s demolished many thriving Black neighborhoods and displaced thousands of residents (National Academies of Sciences, Engineering, and Medicine, 2022a,b; Archer, 2021; Rothstein, 2017). In a 2016 speech in Overtown, Miami, then-Transportation Secretary Anthony Foxx noted that the first two decades of the federal interstate system displaced 475,000 families and more than one million people. The devastation of Overtown—a vibrant Black community in Miami—exemplifies this pattern; approximately 10,000 residents were displaced by the construction of Interstate 95 (PBS NewsHour, 2021; ThinkProgress, 2016).

The impact of transportation decisions extends beyond physical displacement. Highway construction from the 1950s and 1960s served as a tool to cement racial segregation. In many cities, these highways acted as physical and psychological barriers dividing Black communities from the rest of the town, contributing to pockets of intense racial segregation and concentrated poverty.

Transportation Policy as Racial Policy

The history of public transportation in the United States has been shaped significantly by the Federal Aid Highway Act of 1956, which prioritized building national highway networks over public transit. This legislation and rising car ownership contributed to diminished public transportation infrastructure by moving homes and jobs from urban centers to suburbs by the early 1960s. Critically, the interstate highway system disproportionately cut through Black and other communities of color, contributing to racial and economic segregation of cities and concentrated poverty that continues today.

This legacy is not merely historical—it remains embedded in today's communities and continues to shape lives. Research shows that people living, working, and learning within 300 meters of interstates are exposed to significantly higher levels of hazardous air and noise pollution than the general population, creating ongoing health burdens for those communities.

Current Disparities and Challenges

Access to Transportation and Mobility

Every year, more than 39,000 people are killed on America's roads (NHTSA, 2025)—and far too often, it is Black and Brown communities who bear the greatest burden. Black Americans are more than twice as likely to be struck and killed while walking (Governors Highway Safety Association, 2021; Smart Growth America, 2022), mainly because they live in neighborhoods with underfunded infrastructure, poor lighting, and fast-moving traffic. The Centers for Disease Control and Prevention (CDC) also provides extensive information on these racial disparities in pedestrian death rates.

At the same time, Black families are spending up to 33% more than the national average on combined housing and transportation costs. That is not just an economic hardship—it is a structural barrier to building wealth and stability across generations.

In addition, a recent study revealed that nearly 6% of United States adults lack reliable transportation for daily activities, a problem that directly impacts health outcomes (Hardy, 2024a,b). This transportation insecurity disproportionately affects communities of color, exacerbating racial and economic disparities by limiting mobility and forcing dependence on car ownership (McLauren, 2020).

During the COVID-19 pandemic, these disparities became even more apparent. Black Americans were disproportionately represented in essential fields such as transportation, healthcare, law enforcement, and food preparation—making them more susceptible to the virus (Tai et al., 2020). Many relied on public transportation, lived in crowded or multigenerational homes, or worked in environments that increased their exposure risk.

Limited transportation options pose significant barriers to healthcare access in rural areas. A 2019 policy brief from the National Conference of State Legislatures (2019) found that 64% of surveyed Rural Health Clinic staff members reported difficulties finding specialists for patient referrals. For many rural residents, reliable transportation—defined as consistent, dependable, safe, and affordable—remains a critical barrier to accessing healthcare and public health services.

According to the United States Department of Transportation (USDOT) Advisory Committee on Transportation Equity's 2024 report, these disparities are deeply systemic and require comprehensive policy reforms at multiple levels of government. The report highlights how historical patterns of disinvestment created a "transportation opportunity gap," particularly impacting Black Americans in both urban and rural settings by contributing to longer commutes, higher transportation costs, and diminished access to essential services (U.S. Department of Transportation, 2024).

Infrastructure Inequities

The infrastructure in rural areas, where many Black communities are located, remains inadequate. The United States Department of Transportation's Federal Highway Administration estimates that 40% of public roads in rural areas are "inadequate for current travel" (Purdue University, 2025; Rural Health Information Hub, 2025). In comparison, nearly 50% of bridges over 20 feet long are currently considered "structurally deficient" (Rural Health Information Hub, 2025).

Low-income and minority communities often face a double burden: inadequate or substandard infrastructure that prevents safe active transportation and proximity to highways and transportation facilities that produce poor air quality, leading to higher rates of conditions like asthma (PBS NewsHour, 2021). These disproportionate environmental exposures are caused by historical inequities, like redlining and race-driven zoning that shape neighborhood environments as well as housing options and quality (Enterprise Community partners, 2025; McLauren, 2020; Mohl, 2004; Tai et al., 2020). As a result of policy conditions, these communities are also less likely to have convenient access to parks, healthcare facilities, and healthy food options.

Data analysis reveals that 87% of the 200 least-productive bus networks in the country are located in rural counties with fewer than 50,000 residents. More troublingly, over 80% of these inefficient transportation systems are located in counties where annual household income is less than the United States median, demonstrating how transportation inequity compounds economic disadvantage (Institute for Transportation and Development Policy, 2024; United Way of York County, n.d.; Urban Institute, 2020).

Economic and Healthcare Impacts

Transportation inequity has significant economic consequences. Living near health hazards like waste sites leads to higher healthcare expenses, while poor infrastructure limits economic opportunity. Conversely, access to public transportation can significantly raise property values and enable people from underserved communities to travel to better-paying jobs and access different services.

A geographic information systems analysis demonstrated significant racial disparities in access to healthcare facilities, with Black residents in many counties having longer driving distances to the closest healthcare facility than white residents. These disparities showed considerable geographic variation, with significant racial gaps concentrated in the Southeast region.

In rural areas, approximately 29% of residents who reported healthcare access problems could not find transportation for health-related needs (Rural Health Information Hub, 2025). In a more recent survey, 4.6% of rural respondents said they missed or delayed routine health checkups because they lacked transportation, while 4.1% missed chronic health appointments for the same reason (Ballard Brief, 2025).

Having access to a vehicle enables people to reach health facilities. Vehicle access may be critical in rural areas, where missed or delayed nonemergency medical treatment is often attributable to a lack of access to a vehicle (Ballard Brief, 2025; Rural Health Information Hub, 2025).

Recent Policy Developments and Promising Solutions

Biden Administration Infrastructure Initiatives

The Biden–Harris Administration began reversing decades of infrastructure disinvestment, allocating $4 billion to reconnect communities previously cut off from economic opportunities by building needed transportation infrastructure in underserved communities, including Black communities.

The Bipartisan Infrastructure Law represents an unprecedented investment in modernizing America's infrastructure, with provisions specifically addressing historical inequities. The law includes $66 billion for rail improvements, representing the most significant investment in passenger rail since Amtrak's inception and a significant investment in rail safety.

In March 2024, President Biden announced $3.3 billion in funding to reconnect and rebuild communities in more than 40 states, divided by transportation infrastructure, recognizing the historical harm caused by these divisions (The White House, 2024a; USDOT, 2024c). These funds were distributed through the Reconnecting Communities Pilot and the Neighborhood Access and Equity programs to address these historical harms. The Biden Administration emphasized how these programs are crucial for facilitating equitable development and restoring community trust and connectivity (USDOT, 2024a).

For example, the Reconnecting Atlanta's Southside Communities: Atlanta Beltline to Flint River Trail project received this funding. This project is a multi-jurisdictional regional solution employing multi-use trails to address challenges caused by major interstate construction near Hartsfield-Jackson Atlanta International Airport, which cuts through residential neighborhoods (USDOT, 2024b).

Rural Infrastructure Investments

In February 2024, the United States Department of Agriculture (USDA) announced funding for 216 projects in 45 states, Puerto Rico, and the Northern Mariana Islands to bring high-speed internet, clean water, state-of-the-art infrastructure, and economic growth to rural communities (USDA, 2024b). These $772.6 million in investments are intended to benefit over 1 million residents in remote areas by providing reliable high-speed internet access, clean water, and support for rural families, agricultural producers, and small businesses (USDA, 2024a).

The Biden–Harris Administration invested significantly in expanding clean energy, transforming rural power production, creating jobs, and spurring economic growth in rural areas (The White House, 2024b). Through programs like the Powering Affordable Clean Energy (PACE) and the Electric Infrastructure Loan and Loan Guarantee Program, these investments aim to reduce electricity costs for rural families and small businesses while preventing power outages due to extreme weather exacerbated by climate change (USDA, 2023).

Successful On-Demand Transit Models

Innovative on-demand transit solutions are emerging as effective means to address transportation gaps in Black communities (United Way of York County, n.d.).

Birmingham, Alabama—a majority-Black city—implemented an on-demand transit service in 2019 that has dramatically increased job accessibility. Before the launch of Birmingham On-Demand, only 10% of the city's jobs were accessible by public transportation. That number has increased to 90%, demonstrating the transformative impact of targeted transit investments on job accessibility (Jaros et al., 2021).

In Detroit, America's largest majority-Black city, the Suburban Mobility Authority for Regional Transportation (SMART) introduced SMART Flex in 2021, an on-demand microtransit service to supplement fixed routes. The service has significantly expanded the transit network's reach, with over 70% of riders starting or ending trips in commercial districts or buildings not covered by existing fixed routes. The service addresses the significant gap between car ownership (only 11% of residents are car-free) and transit use (only 2% take transit to work) (TransitCenter, 2023; Urban Institute, 2020).

In Memphis, the Downtown Memphis Commission, Memphis Area Transit Authority, and the Memphis Medical District Collaborative, launched Groove On-Demand, a service specifically designed to help residents of North Memphis neighborhoods access jobs downtown, connect visitors using distant parking to destinations, and also to provide healthcare workers with reliable transit options (TransitCenter, 2023; Urban Institute, 2020). This service exemplifies how targeted transit investments can support economic development while addressing equity concerns.

On-demand transit has also shown promise in rural communities with high demand density, where transit agencies can cost-effectively operate such services as alternatives to fixed routes (Beyer et al., 2021; Rural Health Information Hub, 2025). This approach is particularly effective when implemented in partnership with Transportation Network Companies (TNCs) and taxis that offer supplemental services. The success of these models is heavily dependent on community engagement and diverse funding strategies, as demonstrated by successful implementations on the Blackfeet Indian Reservation in northwest Montana and the City of Wilson's RIDE service (Beyer et al., 2021).

Equity-Focused Transportation Planning Frameworks

Transportation agencies are increasingly adopting formal frameworks to evaluate the equity impacts of their decisions.

Chicago uses an Equity Transit-Oriented Development (eTOD) Scorecard to evaluate potential transportation projects based on their impacts on vulnerable neighborhoods, helping decision-makers mitigate adverse effects or choose alternative solutions (Chicago Metropolitan Agency for Planning, 2021; Smart Growth America, 2024a).

The California Department of Transportation (Caltrans) is developing a transportation equity index to identify equity-based priority populations and is establishing related metrics to evaluate transportation impacts (Caltrans, n.d., 2024). By seeking community and stakeholder input on environmental, accessibility, and socioeconomic indicators, Caltrans aims to create a more rigorous approach to assessing project proposals from an equity perspective.

Racial equity impact studies are emerging as a powerful tool to systematically analyze how racial groups will be affected by proposed transportation projects (Archer, 2020; Smart Growth America, 2024b). These studies allow jurisdictions to anticipate potential damage that infrastructure development projects could have on impacted communities and identify various interventions to move forward equitably. Notably, advocates in Syracuse, New York, are using this approach as they engage with the planned removal of an elevated portion of Interstate 81, which historically decimated the predominantly Black 15th Ward when it was constructed in the 1950s (Archer, 2020; Bloomberg City Lab, 2021).

Local and Municipal Challenges

Public Transit in Black Communities

While it is widely recognized that rural communities often lack access to reliable and efficient public transportation, the scale of this problem is substantial. According to 2019 American Community Survey data, more than one million households in primarily rural counties lack access to a private vehicle (TRIP, 2022; United Way York County, n.d.). This transportation gap disproportionately affects Black rural residents (Ballard Brief, 2025).

Transportation options in rural communities are limited; only 36% offer access to airline, rail, and bus services (Rural Health Information Hub, 2025). However, demand for regionally focused, connected, and accessible public transit solutions is rising in these areas.

Even in urban areas where healthcare facilities may be closer, low-income neighborhoods often rely on aging transportation infrastructure, unreliable service, or fixed routes with service areas that do not align with medical facility destinations. These issues compound existing disparities in healthcare access.

Road Safety and Infrastructure Quality

Rural roadways have a disproportionately high number of fatalities compared to urban areas (Governors Highway Safety Association, 2021). While only 19% of Americans live in rural areas, 47% of motor vehicle fatalities occur on rural roads (National Highway Safety Administration, 2022; Smart Growth America, 2024b). The Department of Transportation has adopted a Safe System Approach through the National Roadway Safety Strategy to address these disparities.

The terrain and environmental constraints in many rural areas result in roads built from gravel or dirt, which pose potential safety hazards (Purdue University, 2025; Rural Health Information Hub, 2025). Additionally, the frequency of travel on rural roads has increased as tourism to national parks, predominantly in rural regions, continues to grow (TRIP, 2022).

Coordination and Fragmentation Issues

Rural communities often experience fragmentation and duplication of services among programs—such as Medicaid and Veterans Affairs—serving the same geographic areas. This lack of coordination among local and state agencies leads to inefficient use of limited resources.

Anticipating Critique and Challenges

While this Paper advocates for significant changes to transportation policy and infrastructure, we recognize several legitimate concerns that might be raised.

Resource Constraints and Fiscal Responsibility

Critics may argue that the scale of investment required to address historical inequities is financially unsustainable, particularly in rural areas with lower population density and smaller tax bases. While these concerns are valid, we contend that intelligent, targeted investments—particularly in flexible mobility solutions like on-demand transit—can provide cost-effective alternatives to traditional infrastructure projects. Any cost–benefit analysis must include the economic benefits of connecting people to opportunities, healthcare, and education.

Technology Gaps and the Digital Divide

The increasing reliance on digital technologies for transportation solutions (app-based ride services, real-time transit information) risks further excluding those without reliable internet access or digital literacy (Center for Digital Democracy, 2023; Rural Health Information Hub, 2025). Approximately 15% of Americans lack bank accounts or have limited access to banking services, disproportionately affecting Indigenous and low-income communities, which could limit their ability to use digital payment systems for transportation services (FDIC, 2023; United Way of York County, n.d.). Any technological solution must be accessible to all residents, with non-digital alternatives available for those who lack digital access (Governors Highway Safety Association, 2021).

Unintended Consequences of Investment

New investments in historically underserved communities could accelerate gentrification and displacement if not paired with affordable housing policies and community ownership models. Transportation agencies and municipalities must proactively adopt measures to protect existing residents to ensure they can benefit from improved connectivity without being priced out of their neighborhoods.

Implementation Challenges

The coordination required across multiple agencies, jurisdictions, and funding sources creates significant implementation hurdles. Many rural and small urban jurisdictions lack the technical expertise and staffing capacity to design and manage complex transportation systems or compete effectively for federal funding. Investment in capacity building and technical assistance must accompany financial support.

Climate Considerations

Climate-related risks disproportionately impact Black Americans. We are 34% more likely to live in areas with the highest projected increases in childhood asthma diagnoses due to climate-driven air pollution (Ballard Brief, 2025), 40% more likely to live in areas with the highest projected increases in extreme temperature-related death (Urban Institute, 2020) and more likely to depend on public transportation systems, which are vulnerable to climate disruptions (Center for Digital Democracy, 2023; Enterprise Community Partners, 2025).

Equitable transportation solutions can simultaneously address racial justice and climate concerns by:

- Expanding electric transit options in neighborhoods with high pollution burdens.
- Developing climate-resilient transportation infrastructure in vulnerable communities.
- Creating green jobs in the transportation sector for residents of environmental justice communities.
- Implementing anti-displacement measures alongside sustainable transportation investments.

What Works: Case Study

Local Perspective

In 2018, Richmond, Virginia, implemented a Transit Network Redesign that serves as a case study for equity-centered transportation planning (TransitCenter, 2022). The redesign increased the number of residents with access to frequent transit services from 30,000 to over 120,000. Most importantly, the improvements addressed historical infrastructure disparities. As a result of this redesign, the percentage of Black residents within walking distance of frequent service increased from 35% to 72%.

Key elements of this redesign included a data-driven approach, extensive community engagement centering Black voices, connecting previously isolated neighborhoods to job centers, and a governance structure that ensured continued accountability to equity goals.

This redesign significantly increased access to frequent transit services for residents, particularly Black residents, leading to improved job access, reduced commute times, and economic benefits.

International Perspective

Drawing on international examples would provide valuable insights and inspiration. **Highlighted recommendations include**:

1. **Medellín, Colombia's Integrated Transportation System**. Their cable car system connecting informal settlements in hillside neighborhoods to the metro system has transformed mobility for low-income residents while addressing multiple equity dimensions (Blanco et al., 2020; Urban Institute, 2020).
2. **Paris, France's "15-Minute City" Concept**. This approach ensures all residents can access essential services within a 15-minute walk or bike ride, demonstrating how planning can reduce car dependency while improving quality of life (Urban Institute, 2020).
3. **Seoul, South Korea's Public Space Transformation**. The Cheonggyecheon Stream restoration project converted an elevated highway into a public greenway, demonstrating how transportation infrastructure can be reimagined to serve environmental and community needs (Wired, 2021; Urban Institute, 2020).

Call to Action: Toward Equitable Transportation Systems

Based on the evidence, research, and successful models presented in this Paper, we call for coordinated action on multiple fronts to address transportation and infrastructure inequities affecting Black communities:

For Federal Policymakers

- **Implement Targeted Infrastructure Investment**: Expand funding programs specifically designed to address historical transportation inequities in Black communities, with particular attention being paid to rural and Southern regions where disparities are often greatest. The Justice40 initiative should ensure that 40% of federal infrastructure investments reach disadvantaged communities.

- **Strengthen Environmental Justice Protections**: Require robust environmental and equity impact assessments that explicitly account for racial equity when evaluating new transportation projects, including retroactive reviews of existing infrastructure.
- **Support Public Transit Innovation**: Increase federal support for innovative public transit solutions in rural areas, including demand-responsive services and microtransit options that have proven successful in communities like Birmingham and Detroit.
- **Address Digital Equity**: Invest in broadband infrastructure while ensuring transportation systems remain accessible to those without digital access through alternative payment methods and booking systems.

For State and Local Governments

- **Adopt Equity-Centered Planning Processes**: Implement racial equity impact assessments for all transportation planning and ensure meaningful participation of Black community members in decision-making processes. Follow Chicago's example of using an Equity Transit-Oriented Development (eTOD) Scorecard to evaluate project impacts.
- **Coordinate Across Agencies**: Develop integrated transportation plans for healthcare, education, employment, and social services, recognizing that mobility solutions must connect people to essential services.
- **Implement First-Mile/Last-Mile Solutions**: Invest in solutions that connect people from their homes to public transit and from transit to their final destinations, following Detroit's SMART Flex model, which has successfully expanded the transit network's reach.
- **Prioritize Safety Improvements**: Target road safety improvements in Black communities through the Safe System Approach, particularly in rural areas with disproportionately high fatality rates.

For Community Organizations and Advocates

- **Document Local Transportation Needs**: Conduct community-based participatory research to document specific transportation needs and challenges, providing evidence for targeted interventions.
- **Build Advocacy Coalitions**: Form coalitions with environmental justice, public health, education, and economic development organizations, following the example of Syracuse, where advocates are ensuring racial equity in the anticipated removal of Interstate 81.
- **Pursue System Change**: Advocate for fundamental reforms to transportation planning processes that have historically excluded Black perspectives, aiming for structural change rather than incremental improvements.
- **Develop Community-Led Solutions**: Explore community-owned and operated transportation options, particularly in rural areas with limited commercial providers. Look to successful models like the Blackfeet Indian Reservation's microtransit service in northwest Montana.

For Private Sector and Technology Providers

- **Extend Service to Underserved Areas**: Transportation Network Companies and micro-mobility providers should develop equitable service models for rural and low-income areas, potentially through partnerships with public agencies.
- **Design Inclusive Technologies**: Ensure mobility technologies are accessible to those with disabilities, limited English proficiency, or limited technological literacy.
- **Support Integrated Payment Systems**: Develop systems that allow seamless payment across transportation modes while accommodating those without bank accounts or smartphones.

Conclusion

Transportation is not merely about moving from one place to another—it is about access to opportunity, health, education, and economic mobility. The historical and ongoing inequities in transportation infrastructure and policy have had profound impacts on the lives and opportunities of Black Americans, particularly in rural and Southern regions.

While recent federal initiatives and innovative local solutions represent significant strides in addressing these disparities, real, transformative change requires a comprehensive approach that treats transportation as a vital pillar of racial justice. Creating truly equitable transportation systems will require sustained commitment, significant investment, and a fundamental transformation in planning, funding, and implementing transportation infrastructure.

By taking action on the recommendations outlined in this Black Paper, policymakers, community leaders, advocates, and private sector partners can help build transportation systems that connect instead of divide, provide pathways to opportunity rather than barriers, and serve all communities equitably. The future prosperity of Black communities—and of the nation as a whole—depends on our collective ability to build transportation systems that work for everyone.

Bibliography

Airports Council International - North America. (2023). *U.S. Airports generate $1.2 trillion in economic activity and support 11.5 million U.S. jobs*. [Press release]. https://airportscouncil.org/

American Lung Association. (2025). The unequal burden of asthma on the Black community. https://www.lung.org/blog/asthma-burden-on-black-community

American Public Transportation Association. (2020). *Moving the nation through crisis: Mobility recovery & restoration task force report*. https://www.apta.com/research-technical-resources/research-reports/mobility-recovery-restoration-task-force-report/

American Society of Civil Engineers. (2021a). *2021 Infrastructure report card: Bridges*. https://2021.infrastructurereportcard.org/cat-item/bridges-infrastructure/

American Society of Civil Engineers. (2021b). *2021 infrastructure report card: Roads and Infrastructure*. https://2021.infrastructurereportcard.org/cat-item/roads-infrastructure/

Archer, D. (2020). White men's roads through Black men's homes: Advancing racial equity through highway reconstruction. *Vanderbilt Law Review, 73(5)*, 1259–1342.

Archer, D. (2021). Transportation policy and systemic inequity in American cities: How highway planning affected black communities. *Iowa Law Review*.

Atlanta Beltline, Inc. (n.d.). *Our commitment to fostering healthy communities*. https://beltline.org/about-us/peoplesproject/

Avila, E. (2021). *Urban cultural history and the development of American highways*. UCLA Department of History.

Ballard Brief. (2025). *Rural communities face unique barriers to healthcare access*.

Beyer, J., Goldhammer, A., Callow, M. (2021). *Mobility solutions for rural communities*. AASHTo, NCHRP.

Biden–Harris Administration. (2024a). *The Biden–Harris Administration advances equity and opportunity for Black Americans and communities across the country.* [Factsheet]. The White House. https://www.whitehouse.gov/briefing-room/statements-releases/2024/02/06/fact-sheet-the-biden-%E2%81%A0harris-administration-advances-equity-and-opportunity-for-black-americans-and-communities-across-the-country-2/

Biden–Harris Administration. (2024b). *Biden–Harris Administration announces over $770 million for rural infrastructure projects during Investing in America Tour*. USDA. https://www.usda.gov/media/press-releases/2024/02/21/biden-harris-administration-announces-over-770-million-rural

Biden–Harris Administration. (2024c). *President Biden announces over $3 billion to reconnect communities that have been left behind and divided by transportation infrastructure* [Fact sheet]. The White House. https://www.whitehouse.gov/briefing-room/statements-releases/2024/03/13/fact-sheet-president-biden-announces-over-3-billion-to-reconnect-communities-that-have-been-left-behind-and-divided-by-transportation-infrastructure/

Bipartisan Policy Center. (2024) *Driving equity: The benefits and impact of autonomous vehicles on underserved communities.*

Black Enterprise. (2023). *Maynard Jackson: The ultimate champion of Black business.* https://www.blackenterprise.com/maynard-jackson-the-ultimate-champion-for-black-business/

Blanco, H., Flores, L. & Franco, V. (2020). Urban development and social equity: The case of Medellín, Colombia. In sustainable cities and communities. IntechOpen.

Bloomberg City Lab. (A. Sisson). (2021). *The case for racial equity impact studies in urban planning.*

Bocarejo, J. (2014). *An innovative transit system and its impact on low-income users.* (Publication No. 5354). World Transit Research. End Press. https://www.worldtransitresearch.info/research/5354/

Brand, P., & Davila, J.D. (2011). Transport and social inclusion: Utopian or pragmatic project? The case for Medellin's Metrocables. *Journal of Latin American Urban Studies.*

Bullard, R.D., Johnson, G.S., & Torres, A.O. (Eds.). (2004). *Highway robbery: Transportation racism & new routes to equity*. South End Press.

California Department of Transportation (Caltrans). (2024, May). *Racial equity action plan 2023-2025.*

California Department of Transportation (Caltrans). (n.d.). *Transportation equity index: Project overview*. dot.ca.gov

Caltrans. (2023). *Executive management dashboard, November 2023.* California Department of Transportation. https://dot.ca.gov/-/media/dot-media/programs/civil-rights/documents/dass-reports/november-2023/executive-mgmt-dashboard-nov-2023-a11y.pdf

Capital B News. (2024). *Maynard Jackson left lasting imprint on Atlanta airport.* https://atlanta.capitalbnews.org/maynard-jackson-legacy-airport/

Center for Black Health & Equity. (2023). *Roads built by injustice: Historical impacts of highway construction on Black communities.* https://centerforblackhealth.org/issues/equity-centered-policies/roads-built-by-injustice/

Center for Digital Democracy. (2023). *Rural America's digital dilemma: Bridging the broadband gap for inclusive growth.*

Centers for Disease Control and Prevention. (2019). *Mobility challenges for rural communities*. Rural Health Information Hub.
Centers for Disease Control and Prevention. (2024). *Pedestrian safety*. U.S. Department of Health & Human Services.
Chicago Metropolitan Agency for Planning. (2021). *CMAP Board approves new criteria for evaluating transportation projects on equity and climate*.
City of Birmingham & Va Transportation (n.d.). *Birmingham On-Demand*. https://www.birminghamal.gov/government/city-departments/department-transportation/department-transportation-key-initiatives/birmingham-on-demand
Civil Rights Project & Center for Community Change. (2003). *Moving to equity: Addressing inequitable effects of transportation policies on minorities*. Harvard University.
Clyburn, J. E., & Moore, G. L. (2020). *The future of transportation in the Black community*. Congressional Black Caucus Foundation. https://www.cbcfinc.org/publications/
Congressional Black Caucus Foundation. (2021). *Driverless jobs: Autonomous vehicles & a just transition for Black drivers*. https://www.cbcfinc.org/publications/transportation/driverless-jobs-autonomous-vehicles-a-just-transition-for-black-drivers/
Department of Housing and Urban Development. (2023). *Housing and Transportation Affordability Index*.
Department of Transportation. (2021). *The critical role of rural communities in the U.S. transportation system*. https://www.transportation.gov/rural/grant-toolkit/critical-role-rural-communities
Department of Transportation. (2023). *Health and equity in transportation planning*. https://www.transportation.gov/mission/health/health-equity
Economic Policy Institute. (2019). *Black and Hispanic men could face disproportionate job loss due to transportation automation*. https://www.epi.org/blog/transportation-automation-job-loss/
Eisenberg, Y., Heider, A., Sutor, R., McDonald, A., & King, A. (2022). Hostile vehicle architecture and its impacts on community mobility. *Journal of Urban Planning and Development*.
Enterprise Community Partners. (2025). *Air quality: A silent stressor in vulnerable communities*.
Equitable & Just National Climate Platform. (n.d.) *Justice40 Initiative*. https://ajustclimate.org/justice40_guide.html
Federal Deposit Insurance Corporation (FDIC). (2023). *How America banks: Household use of banking and financial services* (2021 FDIC National Survey).
Federal Highway Administration. (2022). *Rural road safety and infrastructure condition report*.
Foxx, A. (2016). *Transportation's role in building equitable communities*. Center for American Progress.
Georgia Trend. (2024). *Still soaring: Hartsfield-Jackson Atlanta International Airport*. https://www.georgiatrend.com/2024/08/30/still-soaring-hartsfield-jackson-atlanta-international-airport/
Governors Highway Safety Association. (2021). *An analysis of traffic fatalities by race and ethnicity*. GHSA.

Hardy, L. (2024a). Transportation insecurity in the United States: Prevalence and implications for health equity. *Journal of Transport & Health*.

Hardy, S. (2024b, January 11). Millions of Americans lack reliable transportation. *U.S. News & World Report*. https://www.usnews.com/news/health-news/articles/2024-01-11/millions-of-americans-lack-reliable-transportation

Heaps, W., Abramsohn, E., & Skillen, E. (2021). *Public transportation in the US: A driver of health and equity*. Health Affairs. https://www.healthaffairs.org/do/10.1377/hpb20210630.810356/

Howell, K., Mueller, E., & Wilson, B. (2018). *One way or another: Evidence on the disruption of transportation in a low-income, predominantly Black community in Chicago*. Urban Affairs Review.

Hughes, B., Grose, T., Steinmetz, K., & Kodjak, D. (2022). *Road safety and injury outcomes by race and ethnicity: A spatial analysis of us counties*. Traffic Injury Prevention.

Institute for Transportation and Development Policy. (2024). *The high cost of transportation in the United States*. https://itdp.org/2024/01/24/high-cost-transportation-united-states/

Invest Clayton. (n.d.). *Hartsfield-Jackson Atlanta International Airport*. Retrieved December 8, 2025. https://www.investclayton.com/atlanta-international-airport.php

Jaros, S., Offen, K., & Silverman, E. (2021). *Ride-hailing, transit, and equity: Evidence from the Birmingham On-Demand service*. TransitCenter.

Johnson, A. & Patterson, K. (2022). Disparities in police enforcement in urban transit systems. *Journal of Urban Affairs*.

Joint Center. (2017). *The impact of automation on Black jobs*. https://jointcenter.org/the-impact-of-automation-on-black-jobs/

Klaus, K. (2022). *From airports to aerotropolises: The evolution of modern aviation centers*. International Airport Review.

Li, J., Wang, S., Wang, H., & Zhou, B. (as cited in Pires de Brandao et al., 2024). *Towards understanding confounding factors in object detection under challenging weather*. arXiv. https://arxiv.org/html/2406.00219v1

Litman, T. (2022). *Evaluating Transportation Equity*. Victoria Transport Policy Institute. https://www.vtpi.org/equity.pdf

McLauren, S. (2020). Health disparities, transportation equity and complete streets. *International Journal of Environmental Research and Public Health, 17(5)*, 5585.

Mohl, R.A. (2004). Stop the road: Freeway revolts in American cities. *Journal of Urban History, 30(5)*, 674–706.

Morgan, G. (1923). *Traffic signal*. U.S. Patent No. 1,475,024. Washington, DC: U.S. Patent and Trademark Office.

Morgan Magazine. (2024). *Uprooting bias in artificial intelligence*. https://magazine.morgan.edu/artificial-intelligence/

National Academies of Sciences, Engineering, and Medicine. (2021). *Resource guide for improving diversity and inclusion programs for the public transportation industry*. The National Academies Press. https://nap.nationalacademies.org/read/26230/chapter/4

National Academies of Sciences, Engineering, and Medicine. (2022a). *Racial equity, Black America, and public transportation: A review of economic, health, and social impacts*. The National Academies Press. https://nap.nationalacademies.org/catalog/26710/racial-equity-black-america-and-public-transportation-volume-1-a-review-of-economic-health-and-social-impacts

National Academies of Sciences, Engineering, and Medicine. (2022b). *Racial equity, Black America, and public transportation, Volume 1: A review of economic, health, and social impacts*. The National Academies Press.

National Association of Realtors. (2023). *2023 Community & transportation preferences survey*. https://www.nar.realtor/reports/nar-community-and-transportation-preferences-surveys

National Conference of State Legislatures. (2019). *Transportation barriers to health care access* (Policy Brief).

National Highway Traffic Safety Administration. (2022) *Rural and urban traffic fatalities 2020* (Data Note DOT HS 813 361). U.S. Department of Transportation. https://crashstats.nhtsa.dot.gov/#!/

National Highway Traffic Safety Administration. (2025) *Pedestrian and overall road traffic crash deaths* (Traffic Safety Facts). U.S. Department of Transportation.

National Recreation and Park Association. (2012). *Parks and recreation in underserved areas: A public health perspective*.

National Rural Health Association. (2022). *Rural public health: Improving the health and well-being of rural populations*. Rural Health Information Hub. https://www.ruralhealthinfo.org/topics/rural-health-disparities

Next City. (2019). *Why public procurement is a civil rights issue*. https://nextcity.org/urbanist-news/why-public-procurement-is-a-civil-rights-issue

Ng, A.E., Adjaye-Gbewonyo, D., & Dahlhamer, J. (2024). *Lack of reliable transportation for daily living among adults*. Centers for Disease Control and Prevention. National Center for Health Statistics. www.cdc.gov

NYU School of Law. (2024). *Fighting for equity in transportation policy and infrastructure*. https://www.law.nyu.edu/centers/race-inequality-law/our-work/race-and-community-equity/transportation-policy

Pal, A., & Zhang, Y. (2017). *Free-floating bike sharing: Solving real-life large-scale static rebalancing problems*. Transportation Research Part C: Emerging Technologies.

PBS News. (2021). *How infrastructure has historically promoted inequality*. https://www.pbs.org/newshour/politics/how-infrastructure-has-historically-promoted-inequality

Perry, A.M., Rothwell, J., & Harshbarger, D. (2018). *The devaluation of assets in Black neighborhoods: The case of residential property*. Brookings Institution.

Poole, S. & Paul, P. C. (2023). A champion for Atlanta: Maynard Jackson: 'Black mecca' burgeoned under leader. *The Atlanta Journal-Constitution*. https://www.ajc.com/news/atlanta-news/a-champion-for-atlanta-maynard-jackson-black-mecca-burgeoned-under-leader/E7QREDVYH5AKXFDZOVK7ZO2XZA/

Purdue University (K.R. Beard). (2025). Accessibility challenges encountered by people with physical and sensory disabilities in rural communities.

Robert Wood Johnson Foundation. (2023). *More than one in five adults with limited public transit access forgo healthcare because of transportation barriers*.

Rosenbaum, A., Hartley, S., & Holder, C. (2011). Analysis of diesel particulate matter health risk disparities in selected US harbor areas. *American Journal of Public Health, 101(S1)*, S217–S223.

Rothstein, R. (2017). *The color of law: A forgotten history of how our government segregated America* (First ed.). Liveright Publishing Corporation, a division of W.W. Norton & Company.
Rowangould, G. (2013). A census of the US near-roadway population: Public health and environmental justice considerations. *Transportation Research Part D: Transport and Environment, 25*, 59–67.
Rural Health Information Hub. (2024). *Barriers to transportation programs in rural areas*. https://www.ruralhealthinfo.org/toolkits/transportation/1/barriers
Rural Health Information Hub. (2025). *Transportation to support rural healthcare overview*. https://www.ruralhealthinfo.org/
Samuel, A. (2019). *Self-driving cars may be more likely to hit you if you have dark skin*. MT Technology Review. https://www.technologyreview.com/2019/03/01/136808/self-driving-cars-are-coming-but-accidents-may-not-be-evenly-distributed/
Sanchez, T. W., Stolz, R., & Ma, J. S. (2003). *Moving to equity: Addressing inequitable effects of transportation policies on minorities*. The Civil Rights Project at Harvard University.
Sayyadi, R., & Awashti, A. (2018). *A simulation-based optimization approach for identifying critical air pollution sources in urban areas*. Environmental Pollution.
SBA. (2024). *Biden–Harris Administration awards record-breaking $179 billion in federal procurement opportunities*. U.S. Small Business Administration. https://www.sba.gov/article/2024/04/29/biden-harris-administration-awards-record-breaking-178-billion-federal-procurement-opportunities
Smart Growth America. (2023). *Foot traffic ahead 2023: Ranking walkable urbanism in America's largest metros*. https://www.smartgrowthamerica.org/knowledge-center/foot-traffic-ahead-2023/
Smart Growth America. (2024a). *Equitable development strategies: A guidebook for transportation practitioners*.
Smart Growth America. (2024b). *Dangerous by design 2024*. https://www.smartgrowthamerica.org/signature-reports/dangerous-by-design/
Smart Growth America and the National Complete Streets Coalition. (2022). *Dangerous by Design 2022*. smartgrowthamerica.org
Tai, D. B. G., Shah, A., Doubeni, C.A., Sia, I. G., & Wieland, M. L. (2020). The disproportionate impact of COVID-19 on racial and ethnic minorities in the United States. *Clinical Infectious Diseases, 71(15)*, 2463–2470.
The White House. (2024a). *Biden–Harris Administration announces new investments to cut costs and expand access to clean energy in rural America* [Fact sheet]. bidenwhitehouse.archives.gov
The White House. (2024b). *President Biden announces over $3 billion to reconnect communities that have been left behind and divided by transportation infrastructure*. [Fact sheet]. https://bidenwhitehouse.archives.gov/briefing-room/statements-releases/2024/03/13/fact-sheet-president-biden-announces-over-3-billion-to-reconnect-communities-that-have-been-left-behind-and-divided-by-transportation-infrastructure/
The White House. (n.d.) *Justice40 Initiative*. https://ajustclimate.org/justice40_guide.html
TheGrio. (2021). *Buttigieg says racism built into US infrastructure was "conscious choice."* https://thegrio.com/2021/04/06/pete-buttigieg-racism-us-infrastructure/

ThinkProgress (J. Leigngang). (2016). *Top infrastructure official explains how America used highways to destroy Black neighborhoods.* https://archive.thinkprogress.org/top-infrastructure-official-explains-how-america-used-highways-to-destroy-black-neighborhoods-96c1460d1962/

Transportation for America. (2025). *Transit equity day highlights the need for transit in rural communities.* https://t4america.org/2025/01/31/transit-equity-day-highlights-the-need-for-transit-in-rural-communities/

Transportation Research Board. (2021). *ACRP Research Report 235: The impact of air cargo on regional economic development and jobs.* National Academies Press.

Transportation Research Board. (2022). *Synthesis of information related to transit practices: Microtransit solutions in rural communities.* https://rip.trb.org/View/2190462

Treuhaft, S., & Karpyn, A. (2010). *The grocery gap: Who has access to healthy food and why it matters.* PolicyLink and the Food Trust.

TRIP, Inc. (National Transportation Research Group). (2022, October 13). *U.S. rural roads & bridges have significant deficiencies as the nation addresses supply chain challenges and high traffic fatality rates.*

U.S. Bureau of Labor Statistics (2022). *Labor force characteristics by race and ethnicity, 2022.* https://www.bls.gov/opub/reports/race-and-ethnicity/2022/

U.S. Department of Agriculture (USDA). (2023, December 12). *Biden–Harris Administration announces $156 million to bring reliable clean energy to rural communities across the nation* [Press release]. www.usda.gov

U.S. Department of Agriculture (USDA). (2024a). *Biden–Harris Administration invests $772 million in 45 states to strengthen essential rural services and create economic opportunity* [Press release]. www.usda.gov

U.S. Department of Agriculture (USDA). (2024b). *Rural infrastructure investments announced by USDA in February 2024.* [Fact Sheet]. www.rd.usda.gov

U.S. Department of Transportation. (2022a). *U.S. Department of Transportation releases national roadway safety strategy to address crisis of increasing roadway fatalities and serious injuries.* [Press Release].

U.S. Department of Transportation. (2022b). Beyond traffic 2045: Trends and choices.

U.S. Department of Transportation. (2023). *U.S. Department of Transportation awards $25 million RAISE grant for 2.2. Miles of Atlanta Beltline multi-use trail.* Atlanta Beltline. [Press Release]. https://beltline.org/press-release/u-s-department-of-transportation-awards-25-million-raise-grant-for-2-2-miles-of-atlanta-beltline-multi-use-trail/

U.S. Department of Transportation. (2024). *U.S. Department of Transportation's commitment to investing in and protecting Black communities.* https://www.transportation.gov/briefing-room/us-department-transportations-commitment-investing-and-protecting-black-communities

U.S. Department of Transportation. (n.d.-a). *Disadvantaged business enterprise (DBE) program.* https://www.transportation.gov/civil-rights/disadvantaged-business-enterprise

U.S. Department of Transportation. (n.d.-b). *What is disadvantaged business enterprise (DBE)?* https://www.transportation.gov/osdbu/disadvantaged-business-enterprise/what-disadvantaged-business-enterprise-dbe

U.S. Department of Transportation (n.d.-c). *Justice40 fact sheet.* https://www.transportation.gov/sites/dot.gov/files/2023-05/Justice40%20Fact%20Sheetupdated.pdf

U.S. Department of Transportation & SBA. (2022). *Biden–Harris Administration announces groundbreaking partnership to connect small and disadvantaged businesses to historic infrastructure investments.* U.S. Department of Transportation. [Press release]. https://www.transportation.gov/briefing-room/biden-harris-administration-announces-groundbreaking-partnerships-connect-small-and

U.S. Department of Transportation (USDOT). (2024a). *Biden–Harris Administration announces history making $3.3 billion for locally led projects* [Press release]. https://www.transportation.gov/briefing-room/biden-harris-administration-announces-history-making-33-billion-locally-led-projects

U.S. Department of Transportation (USDOT). (2024b). *Reconnecting Communities & Neighborhoods (RCN) Grant Program FY 2023 Awards Factsheets.* https://www.transportation.gov/sites/dot.gov/files/2024-03/RCN%20FY23%20Awardees%20Factsheet.pdf

U.S. Department of Transportation (USDOT). (2024c). *Reconnecting Communities projects are under threat. Here is what's at stake and where.* Transportation for America. https://t4america.org/2025/04/29/reconnecting-communities-projects-are-under-threat-here-is-whats-at-stake-and-where/

United Health Foundation. (2021). *Health Disparities Report.*

United Way of York County. (n.d.) *Trapped by geography: How transportation inequality hurts low-income families.* https://www.unitedway-york.org/news/trapped-geography-how-transportation-inequity-hurts-low-income-families#:~:text=A%20transportation%20study%20by%20United,%2C%20education%2C%20and%20health%20care

Urban Institute. (2020). *The unequal commute.* https://www.urban.org/features/unequal-commute

Via. (2023). *4 Black communities are building equity-focused transit with new technology.* https://ridewithvia.com/resources/4-black-communities-are-building-equity-focused-transit-with-new-technology

Wells, I. B. (1885). *Challenging railroad segregation.* Digital Public Library of America.

World Economic Forum. (2023, March 1). *Why walkable urban areas are America's efficient economic engines.* https://www.weforum.org/stories/2023/03/why-walkable-urban-areas-are-america-s-efficient-economic-engines/

Yamanouchi, K. (2020). Hartsfield-Jackson generates billions in economic activity in region. *The Atlanta Journal-Constitution.* https://www.ajc.com/business/hartsfield-jackson-generates-billions-economic-activity-region/1yb862FcDLyUjmLkoa1gjP/

Zhang, W., & Wang, F. (2024). Measuring transit equity of an on-demand multimodal transit system. *Journal of the American Planning Association.* https://www.tandfonline.com/doi/full/10.1080/01944363.2024.2323470

Chapter 20

Digital Equity is a Civil Right

*Nicol Turner Lee and Alisa Valentin**

Executive Summary

> There is never time in the future in which we will work out our salvation. The challenge is in the moment. The time is always now.
>
> —James Baldwin, *Nobody Knows My Name*, 1961

Digital equity is a civil right. As education, healthcare, employment, financial services, and civic participation move online, millions of Black Americans remain locked out—not by choice, but by design.

The Crisis

- **68% of Black adults** have home broadband compared to 83% of white adults.
- **Black founders received just 1.3%** of $288 billion in venture capital between 2020 and 2021.
- **Despite comprising 13% of the workforce**, Black talent represents just 4.4% of board roles and 3.7% of technical positions in information technology.
- **Average monthly broadband costs** ($78) continue to force impossible choices for individuals and families between connectivity and basic needs like food and housing.

These disparities stem from three interconnected barriers—the "three-legged stool" of digital exclusion: access, affordability, and digital skills. These factors are worsened by digital redlining, where internet service providers deprioritize Black neighborhoods and also by persistent underinvestment in in Black talent.

* Supported by braintrust authors: David J. Johns, Ebonie C. Riley, Dee C. Marshall, Courtney R. Snowden, Chris Lewis, DeShuna Elisa Spencer, and A. Prince Albert III

DOI: 10.4324/9781003752646-27

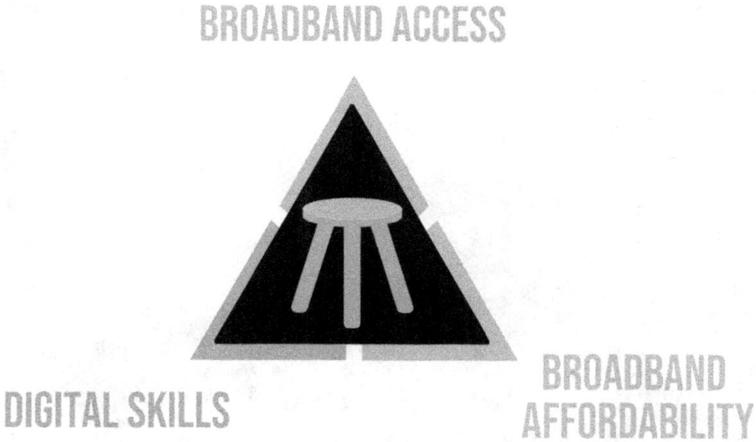

The Elimination Crisis: The 47th presidential administration, alongside a Republican-controlled Congress, has significantly disrupted the federal digital equity infrastructure. This includes terminating the Digital Equity Act's Competitive Grant Program; the failure to restore funding for the Affordable Connectivity Program (ACP), which ended in 2024 after serving more than 23 million households; and changes to federal research and higher-education funding impacting programs serving Historically Black Colleges and Universities (HBCUs), which serve as the bellwether for Black technological innovation and community digital access.

Our Legacy, Our Future: Black Americans have been instrumental in technological innovation throughout history—from Lewis Latimer's telecommunications breakthroughs to contemporary leaders like Timnit Gebru and Joy Buolamwini fighting for ethical Artificial Intelligence (AI). Yet Black communities remain disproportionately excluded from the digital economy as workers, entrepreneurs, and decision-makers.

This Black Paper (Paper) calls for comprehensive policy reform, targeted investments, and concrete action to ensure equitable access to high-speed internet, support HBCUs as anchor institutions for digital innovation, and guarantee that technology serves Black liberation rather than deepening inequality. Digital equity must be approached with the same urgency as voting rights, education access, and economic justice—because in 2026, they are inseparable.

Pursuing Digital Equity

Technology can empower the path toward economic and social liberation for Black Americans—or deepen systemic inequalities. The choice is ours to make.

The internet has become inescapable. Consumers depend on it for essential tasks, Black entrepreneurs need it to find capital and build networks. Elementary to college students require it for education. Reliable, affordable high-speed internet creates the infrastructure necessary for engagement in entrepreneurial ecosystems and facilitates economic opportunities that could help close the racial wealth divide. Research shows that broadband access is a key driver of entrepreneurship, lowering barriers to starting and scaling businesses and ensuring that individuals are connected to vital services (Whitcare & Ki, 2023; Zook et al., 2017).

Yet deeply entrenched structural barriers limit Black Americans' full adoption of digital technologies. These are not individual choices but systemic failures. Cost remains the primary barrier: with average monthly broadband hovering near $80, low-income households face impossible choices between connectivity and basic needs. According to 2025 research, around 4 in 10 low-income Americans are "subscription vulnerable"—unable to afford broadband consistently (Horrigan, 2025). For households earning less than $30,000 annually, monthly broadband expenses can consume a significant portion of disposable income, leading to service disconnection and reconnection cycles that can destabilize economic security.

Geographic barriers compound the problem. Rural Black communities lack digital infrastructure entirely, creating economic exclusion zones where residents cannot participate in the digital economy regardless of talent, ambition, or effort. While urban areas often have infrastructure, they may only have unaffordable services due to monopolistic pricing. Both scenarios have devastating consequences for healthcare access (especially telehealth for chronic conditions like hypertension and diabetes that disproportionately affect Black communities), business development, education, and wealth creation.

The rapid deployment of artificial intelligence (AI) exacerbates these inequities. When systems are designed without input from Black people who care about Black people and fail to reflect Black experiences, systems reinforce existing discrimination in credit, housing, healthcare, education, employment, and even access to voting. Without urgent policy action, Black Americans, who already face significant disparities in internet access, will experience greater exclusion from participating in and contesting decisions that determine access to opportunity.

Access to affordable, reliable internet—and the skills to use, design, and govern the technologies built on it—are essential to full participation in modern life. Thus, Black communities face a defining choice: build a future where technology opens opportunity, or allow it to entrench disparities by benefiting a few while leaving everyone else vulnerable to exclusion and exploitation. These are the reasons why policy decisions must be grounded in the principle that digital equity is a civil right. This charge to Black communities is also not new; Black innovators have and continue to shape technological innovation.

The Legacy of Black Innovation

The marginalization of Black communities in today's digital ecosystem stands in contrast to their historic and ongoing contributions to technological progress. Black Americans have long been instrumental in shaping and advancing the systems that define modern life.

Lewis H. Latimer, born in 1848, became an inventor and patent holder who helped engineer the early lightbulb in Thomas Edison's lab and later invented the early telephone with Alexander Graham Bell. His innovations helped lay the foundation for the nation's electrical and communications infrastructure.

The legacy continued throughout the twentieth century through innovators like **Dr. Shirley Jackson**, a pioneering physicist and former head of the United States Nuclear Regulatory Commission. Her work was pivotal in creating touch-tone telephones, fiber-optic cables, call waiting, and caller ID, transforming telecommunications before mobile devices. She was inducted into the Women in Technology International Hall of Fame in 2016.

Dr. Mark Dean, born in Jefferson, Tennessee, in 1962, made groundbreaking contributions to computer science, establishing the Industry Standard Architecture bus, the color printer, and the first-ever gigahertz chip.

In the internet era, **Dr. Marian Croak**, a pioneering computer scientist and engineer, holds over 200 patents and is widely recognized as a key architect of Voice over Internet Protocol (VoIP) technology, which revolutionized global communication. Her innovations at AT&T and Google fundamentally shaped modern telecommunications and internet infrastructure, making real-time voice and video communication accessible to billions.

Today, Black innovators continue to shape the future of artificial intelligence while challenging the inequities that have been embedded in these systems. **Timnit Gebru** has emerged as a leading authority on algorithmic bias after exposing high margins of error in AI models at Google, which led to her termination (Hana &Whitaker, 2020; Simonite, 2021). Gebru worked closely with Dr. **Joy Buolamwini**, a digital activist formerly associated as a research with MIT, whose *Gender Shades* project exposed the misidentification of Black people by facial recognition technologies that continue to be used by law enforcement despite such inaccuracies (Buolamwini & Gebru, 2018).

These and other technology innovators are not anomalies, but part of a continuous tradition of Black leadership from technical and non-technical backgrounds that has consistently advanced society despite persistent exclusion from resources, recognition, and decision-making power. The question before us is not whether Black communities possess the genius to lead technological innovation—history has proven this beyond doubt. The question is whether society will actively create the conditions for Black genius to flourish and ensure its benefits reach all communities, particularly those from which it originates. The premise of Black genius also starts with a call for digital equity and justice.

Digital Equity is a Civil Rights Obligation

Black Americans led the Civil Rights Movement in the 1960s, championing equal access to voting, education, employment, transportation, and housing for all Americans. Today, that fight extends to the digital realm, where limited access to affordable, high-quality internet and digital services blocks Black Americans from thoroughly enjoying their civil rights.

As digital systems increasingly determine eligibility, opportunity, and participation, the stakes are higher. What has become clear is that technology cannot hold itself accountable, particularly when built on biased data, without transparency, and is centered on profit over people. The burden of algorithmic failures falls heaviest on those with the least power to challenge them: Black communities, communities of color, low-income communities, people with disabilities, and rural residents. These communities face a double-edged sword: disproportionately monitored and tracked by algorithms, and simultaneously undercounted in broadband access, digital skills resources, and among those who design the systems.

Algorithmic systems now function as gatekeepers to essential public benefits, healthcare, education, employment, financial services, voting, and housing. Black communities face a double-edged sword: disproportionately targeted and monitored through predictive policing and risk scores, yet simultaneously undercounted in broadband access, digital skills resources, and representation among those who design the systems.

This means Black communities are subject to systems of control and exploitation while invisible when it comes to investment, protection, and profit. This reality demands that policy leaders treat digital equity with urgency.

The Origins of the Digital Divide

The term "digital divide" was first coined by Larry Irving, the former Administrator of the National Telecommunications and Information Administration (NTIA) under the Clinton Administration. In the mid-1990s, Irving and his team issued the report series, *Falling through the net: Defining the Digital Divide*, which examined the "divide between those with access to new technologies and those without. They described this divide as "one of America's leading economic and civil rights issues" (Irving et al., 1995).

Nearly thirty years later, this problem persists as the internet has become an imperative. This transformation is not merely cultural or economic—it is technical and reversible. Communications networks are currently finalizing their transition from copper wire, TDM (Time-Division Multiplexing) protocol-based systems to all Internet Protocol (IP) networks using fiber and wireless infrastructure. This "IP transition" means that even 20th-century communication tools (landline phones, fax machines, alarm systems, and credit card processing) now depend entirely on broadband networks to function. The internet is no longer one option among many for communication and commerce; it is the foundational infrastructure upon which all modern communication systems operate. To lack broadband access today is to be excluded from the world's entire communications ecosystem.

This reality became unmistakably clear during the 2020 COVID-19 pandemic, when more than 50 million K-12 students were sent home from school and were required to transition to remote learning. At the time, approximately 30% of all public K-12 students lived in households either without an internet connection or lacking a device adequate for distance learning (Chandra et al., [Common Sense Media], 2020).

The Pandemic Revealed the Divide

- 30% of K-12 students lacked adequate broadband for distance learning.
- New York: 27% without an adequate broadband connection.
- California: 25% without adequate connection.
- Mississippi: 50% without adequate connection.
- Arkansas: 46% without adequate connection.

However, years after the end of the pandemic, the digital access inequities persist 2024 data from the Pew Research Center found that 68% of Black adults subscribe to home broadband as compared to 83% of white adults (Pew Research Center, 2025). Income also remains a key factor, with only 57% of households with incomes under $30,000 have a home broadband subscription compared to 76% of households making $70,000 and 88% of households making $100,000 or less (Pew Research Center, 2025).

Digital inclusion practitioners and policy leaders often describe this challenge as the "three-legged" stool encompassing: 1) broadband access, 2) broadband affordability, and 3) digital skills. Each "leg" enables people to engage consistently and effectively online, building digital proficiency and agency to navigate both current and future digital environments. Persistent barriers demonstrate systemic underinvestment in communities not regarded as "economically profitable." Black Americans have been disproportionately impacted, facing the compounded effects of limited access, high costs, and gaps in digital skills—leaving communities without the stable foundation necessary for digital participation.

Policy responses to these issues must be deliberate and coordinated. The National Urban League's (2021) Lewis Latimer Plan for Digital Equity and Inclusion has long been recognized as a comprehensive framework for addressing these systemic barriers because it recognizes that digital equity requires coordinated investment across multiple sectors in digital infrastructure, service affordability, and individual skills development.

Digital Redlining

Where one lives matters. For decades, since the 1930s, public and private entities redlined neighborhoods, denying Black people equitable access to competitive housing markets and necessary loans to achieve homeownership, despite being qualified. The neighborhoods where they were allowed to purchase homes had lower appraisals and were starved of resources. Housing redlining not only obstructs home ownership and wealth creation—it also provides an outline for which neighborhoods would be the last to receive broadband investments. Housing discrimination contributed to segregation and poverty, now manifesting in the lack of digital access in marginalized communities. Beyond structural biases, the consequences of disconnection contribute to worse health outcomes, educational distress, and limited connections to employment opportunities, information, and networks (Turner Lee, 2024).

Digital redlining happens when the government or Internet Service Providers (ISP)s, prioritize the deployment of high-speed internet in communities where they expect a faster return on the investment (Ballard Brief, 2022; Smart Growth America, 2024). The Lawyers' Committee for Civil Rights Under Law (2023) summarized digital redlining as having deep roots in American history, beginning with segregation and redlining in the housing market. The Federal Housing Administration furthered segregation efforts by refusing to insure mortgages in and near Black neighborhoods while subsidizing builders mass-producing subdivisions for white citizens. This Jim Crow era infrastructure underinvestment in Black communities also included underinvestment in telecommunications infrastructure (Lawyers Committee for Civil Rights Under Law, 2023).

Policy reforms, intentional investments, and concrete actions will ultimately drive digital equity for Black communities, especially when strengthened by a permanent, future-proof approach that ensures equitable access to high-speed internet wherever one lives. No community, institution, or individual should be left offline.

The Affordability Crisis and Market Failure

Most people in the United States live in areas with only one broadband provider, subjecting consumers to whatever prices that provider charges, with nowhere else to go for alternatives. Even though most Americans experience local monopolies in the broadband market (or, for a fortunate few, duopolies), there has never been a serious push to regulate broadband rates as we have for other essential utilities.

State Public Utility Commissions routinely regulate market prices for electricity and water—essential utilities with similar monopoly characteristics—ensuring that consumers are not subjected to exploitative pricing. Yet broadband remains exempt from such regulatory frameworks at both the state and federal levels. Instead, policymakers of both parties accept monopoly pricing capitulation to industry, and have instead debated potential subsidies to assist low-income Americans. This represents a fundamental policy failure: rather than regulating supply-side pricing as we do for other utilities, we subsidize demand while allowing providers to maintain monopolistic pricing structures. The result is a wealth transfer from taxpayers to telecommunications corporations while failing to address the root cause of unaffordability and lack of access.

For low-income or even middle-income households, price, regardless of choices, remains a significant barrier to broadband adoption. The average monthly broadband cost is $78 a month (Pew Research Center, 2024). According to 2025 research, 4 in 10 low-income Americans are subscription-vulnerable, creating "uncertainty and churn in broadband at the low-income end of the market" (Horrigan, 2025). For households earning less than $30,000 annually, this represents a significant portion of disposable income, leading to chronic affordability stress and disconnection/reconnection cycles that destabilize economic security.

The Lifeline program, created in 1985 under the Reagan administration to help low-income households obtain vital voice service, still only offers a $9.25 subsidy, despite the ever-increasing service cost (FCC, n.d.). The COVID-19 public health crisis led to the creation of the Emergency Broadband Benefit, offering a $50 monthly discount, which transitioned to the Affordable Connectivity Program (ACP) under the Biden–Harris administration's Infrastructure Investment and Jobs Act. The ACP provided a $30 monthly discount. The ACP expired in mid-2024 without bipartisan renewal, leaving more than 22 million households without financial support (Pew Research Center, 2025).

Without access to affordable, reliable broadband, Black communities cannot experience the full benefits of technology, which impacts access to economic opportunities, healthcare, education, and civic life. We did not get here by accident. Our policymakers can and must make equity-centered choices so that everyone can thrive in this digital ecosystem.

Geographic and Healthcare Barriers

Rural residents struggle to maintain connectivity as small business owners, workers needing upskilling, people seeking healthcare services, or students seeking educational resources (Harrison, 2021). The absence of consistent broadband in rural Black communities creates economic exclusion zones where residents cannot participate in the digital economy, limiting employment opportunities, business development, and wealth creation regardless of talent, ambition, or effort.

Urban areas where broadband is available often face unaffordable service due to a lack of competition. Where options exist, infrastructure is often inadequate or unreliable.

The healthcare consequences are life-threatening. Seniors and people from low-income families in small, rural, and isolated communities lack adequate means to connect to medical providers concentrated in larger towns and cities. For Black elders managing chronic conditions like hypertension, diabetes, and heart disease—conditions that disproportionately affect Black communities—the inability to access telehealth services can result in delayed diagnoses, missed medication adjustments, and preventable health complications. This digital healthcare divide becomes a literal life-and-death issue, exacerbating existing health disparities and contributing to higher mortality rates.

Black Elders and Digital Consent, Risks, and Barriers

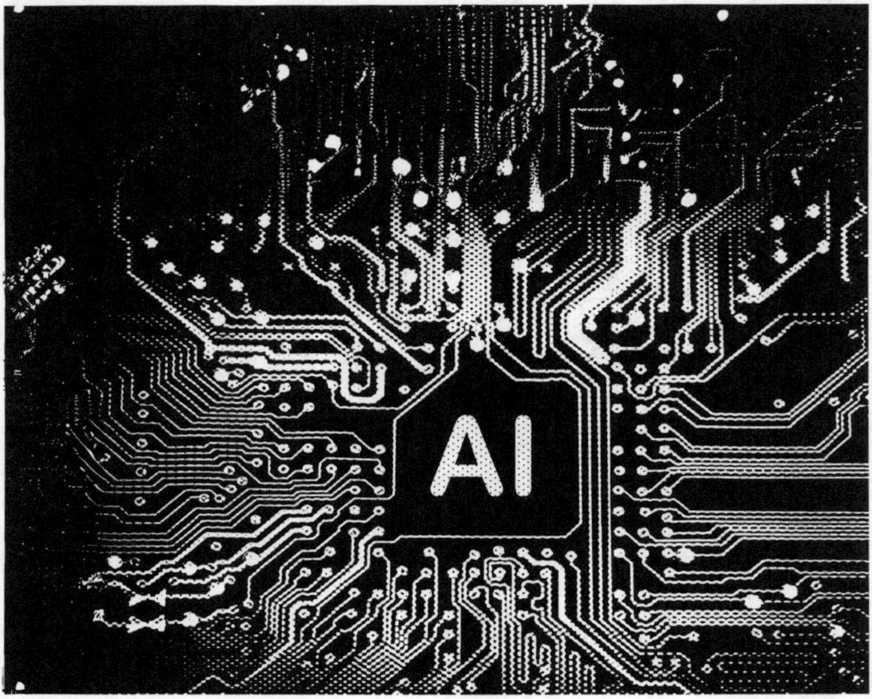

Black elders face immediate risk from AI-integrated systems. Consent to tracking, data collection, biometric identification, and automated decision-making is often hidden in digital processes that too many cannot understand. Without targeted education and trusted navigation support, elders are vulnerable to fraud, identity theft, denial of services, and digital surveillance.

Telehealth platforms, which became essential during COVID-19, present particular challenges. Many systems require multi-step authentication, app downloads, and navigation of complex interfaces—barriers that prevent elders from accessing healthcare. Additionally, automated prescription systems, Medicare portals, and benefit eligibility platforms increasingly use AI-driven decision-making without clear explanation or appeal processes.

Digital equity requires culturally grounded education for elders in every digital system that now affects daily life. This includes support with recognizing phishing attempts, understanding privacy settings, navigating telehealth platforms, and protecting against financial scams that disproportionately target older adults through digital channels.

Administrative and procedural barriers in digital systems facilitate structural exclusion. Confusing portals, multi-step authentication, inaccessible interfaces, and unclear documentation disproportionately deny or delay access to essential services. For digital neophytes, having to share personal and sensitive information on digital platforms is more than an inconvenience. It invites risks and exacerbates digital inclusion through:

- Public benefits portals requiring extensive documentation uploads without clear guidance.
- Healthcare systems mandating app-based appointment scheduling without phone alternatives.
- Employment applications that auto-reject candidates based on incomplete digital profiles.
- Financial services requiring smartphone-based two-factor authentication.
- Rental applications processed entirely through algorithms without human review.

Digital equity demands user-centered design, clear support pathways, and accessible alternatives. Every digital system administering essential services must provide non-digital pathways and human assistance for those who need it.

The Challenges of Now

The 47th presidential administration's so-called "efficiency" compounds digital accessibility, privacy, and equity issues. One clear example of how digital inequities impact our communities is the widespread closures of government agencies and their associated field offices, such as the Social Security Administration field offices, the United States Department of Education, and the phasing out of phone support across agencies. As a result of these closures, aging people, low-income people, people with limited abilities, and rural Black residents are left with fewer options to engage with governmental services. Barriers to engagement include driving hours to reach a field office, which requires transportation, time, and money, or accessing government offices through online services, which further elevates the need for broadband policy reforms on the federal, state, and local levels (Pew Research Center, 2024; Rural Health Information Hub, 2025; Urban Institute, 2023).

The Department of Government Efficiency (DOGE), established via executive order on January 20, 2025, reportedly deployed AI to identify waste, fraud, and abuse. The "move fast and break things" approach with the use of AI has, and will continue to have, harmful impacts on the country's most marginalized communities, especially the digitally invisible (Civil Discourse with Joyce Vance, 2025). Resulting harms from these intentional policies to disarm Black consumers of their agency will require significant time, resources, expertise, and advocacy to undo because they are rooted in the longstanding, systematic exclusion.

Black Exclusion from the Tech Economy

Even as enthusiastic and influential consumers of technology products and services, Black communities have not reaped the same economic or policy-driven benefits of technological innovation. Black representation in tech entrepreneurship and business ownership remains particularly dismal.

The Tech Exclusion Gap

- Black talent: 13% of the labor force, 4.4% of board roles, and 3.7% of technical positions.
- Black founders: 1.3% of $288B venture capital (2020–2021).
- First venture fund: Black investors ($30.5M) vs. peers ($57M).
- Of 11,790 VC-funded companies, only 222 were Black-founded.

A 2022 study from the National Association for the Advancement of Colored People (NAACP) and Kapor Center found (Kapor Center, 2023; NAACP and Kapor Center, 2022):

- Black workers are paid 4% less than their peers and are often hired in lower-level roles than their qualifications justify.
- Almost half of Black technologists experienced racial inequality in hiring, promotion, leadership opportunities, and salaries.
- Beyond capital gaps, Black tech entrepreneurs face critical infrastructure constraints: limited access to cloud computing and high-performance computing resources, inadequate cybersecurity infrastructure, insufficient data governance frameworks, and exclusion from procurement pathways connecting startups to corporate and government customers.

This study also found that power drives the technology ecosystem and influences wealth creation, and that "public displays of commitments to Black lives have not yielded widespread systemic changes in the policies, structures, and practices excluding Black people" (NAACP, 2022). These disparities are reflected in the lack of representation of Black policy influencers and policymakers, contributing to major blind spots when developing and implementing technology and telecommunications policies.

For years, federal investments prioritized the connectivity needs of white, rural communities, even as Black and low-income communities faced the same circumstances and experienced similar outcomes from living in digital deserts (Center for Digital Democracy, 2023; Pew Research Center, 2025). For digital equity to be prioritized as a civil rights concern, the fullness of Black participation in—and contributions to—our digital ecosystem must be represented.

Systematic Dismantling and the Imperative to Rebuild

The 47th presidential administration's systematic dismantling of digital equity infrastructure has been swift and devastating. That includes the elimination of:

- The Affordable Connectivity Program (leaving 23+ million households without broadband subsidies);
- Digital Equity Act grant programs at the national, state, and local levels;
- Federal research funding for HBCUs limiting their ability to function as anchor institutions for digital equity in Black communities. HBCUs have historically served dual roles as both research centers investigating technology policy and bias, and as community hubs providing digital access, skills training, and advocacy. Research funding supports the faculty, infrastructure, graduate students, and community partnerships that enable this work. Without it, HBCUs cannot maintain the computing resources, broadband infrastructure, or technical expertise needed to study digital inequity while simultaneously addressing it through community programs. This elimination represents a strategic attack on institutions uniquely positioned to center black experiences in technology development and hold algorithmic systems accountable; and
- Diversity, equity, and inclusion initiatives across federal agencies.

Combined, this represents more than a policy reversal. It is the intentional erasure of infrastructure that, while limited, provided essential support to Black communities.

Rebuilding requires more than restoration—it demands structural transformation that future administrations cannot easily dismantle. This includes:

- **Statutory Protection**: Digital equity programs must be enshrined in legislation, not executive orders or annual appropriations that can be eliminated with an administration change.
- **Multi-Sector Funding**: Reliance on federal funding alone creates vulnerability. Community-led organizations, philanthropic partnerships, and public-private collaborations must create redundant support systems.
- **Institutional Anchors**: HBCUs, Black-led research institutions, and community partners must be positioned as permanent stewards with sustained funding mechanisms that transcend political cycles. Such mechanisms must include: multi-year operating support rather than annual appropriations subject to political volatility; dedicated funding for technology infrastructure including high-speed broadband networks, computing resources, and data centers; cybersecurity investments to protect research data and institutional systems; endowed faculty research positions focused on digital equity, AI ethics, and technology policy; and sustained support for community-facing programs including digital literacy training, broadband adoption initiatives, and tech entrepreneurship development. These funding structures should be established through a combination of federal legislation, state-level commitments, philanthropic endowments, and public–private partnerships that create redundancy and resilience against single-point political interference.

Fintech and Algorithmic Financial Systems

Financial technology ("fintech") systems now mediate access to loans, rental approval, payroll, insurance, and benefits. When these systems use biased data inputs such as zip codes, payment histories from low-income neighborhoods, phone type, mobility patterns, or social network connections, they create digital proxies for race and poverty. Even though the system never explicitly "sees" race, these systems enable discrimination at scale.

Algorithmic underwriting affects:

- Credit scoring and loan approvals
- Rental housing applications
- Insurance premiums and coverage
- Small business financing and microloans
- Payroll access and earned wage advances
- Public benefits eligibility and distribution

Civil rights protections must extend to fintech because these systems are critical inputs for economic mobility. They determine access to capital, housing stability, business formation, and countless wealth-building opportunities. Without oversight and enforcement, algorithmic discrimination perpetuates historical redlining through digital means.

Energy, Data Centers, and Community Impact

As AI development accelerates, energy consumption and data center infrastructure have emerged as critical policy concerns. Data centers now consume approximately 2–3% of United States. electricity, with AI-driven centers projected to triple consumption by 2030. The race to build data centers creates both opportunity and risk for Black communities.

Data centers are increasingly placed in Black and low-income communities due to:

- Lower land costs.
- Fewer organized and resourced political obstacles.
- Proximity to existing industrial infrastructure.
- Less political capital to resist environmental burdens.

Yet these facilities often bring

- Significant energy consumption is straining local grids.
- Environmental burdens including: noise, heat emissions, and water usage.
- Minimal local employment (highly automated operations).

- Property tax breaks that reduce community revenue.
- No guarantee of broadband access despite proximity to infrastructure.

Historical patterns of extractive infrastructure used to plot locations for highways, waste facilities, and industrial zones are being replicated with data centers. The environmental burdens are imposed on Black communities while benefits flow elsewhere.

The NAACP's Data Center Blueprint provides essential guidance for ensuring data center development benefits host communities. Minimum community benefits must include:

- **Local hiring commitments**: Data centers represent long-term infrastructure investments that should create sustainable career pathways for community residents rather than importing external workforces. Local hiring commitments must include pre-apprenticeship programs, technical training partnerships with local community colleges and HBCUs, and clear advancement pathways from entry-level positions to skilled technical roles.
- **Community broadband access**: Community networks nationwide have demonstrated ways to make free or subsidized high-speed internet a component of digital infrastructure that supports all residents. Data centers should be required to extend fiber connections and provide community broadband access as a condition of approval.
- **Energy infrastructure investment**: Low-income and hard-to-reach areas, especially those plagued by blight and disinvestment, require grid improvements and renewable energy deployment strategies. Data center developers should be required to invest in upgrading local electrical grid infrastructure, deploying on-site renewable energy generation, and contributing to community-wide renewable energy projects that reduce energy costs for all residents.
- **Environmental protections**: Strict emissions standards, water conservation requirements, and noise mitigation measures enforced through partnerships with state environmental agencies, local health departments, and community environmental justice organizations. These protections must include regular air quality monitoring, limits on water consumption that compete with residential needs, and acoustic standards that prevent noise pollution in residential areas. Communities must have enforcement authority and resources to hold data center operators accountable for violations.
- **Revenue sharing**: Fair tax contributions without breaks that deplete community resources. For example, Virginia's data center tax exemption program has cost localities hundreds of millions in foregone revenue while providing minimal community benefit. In contrast, jurisdictions like Montgomery County, Maryland, have negotiated community benefit agreements that include direct revenue sharing, infrastructure investments, and

workforce development funding. Data centers should contribute property tax, sales tax, and energy consumption taxes commensurate with their infrastructure impact and market profitability.

- **Community governance**: Local oversight boards with binding authority over siting decisions, operational permits, and compliance monitoring. Binding authority matters because advisory roles without enforcement power allow companies to ignore community concerns while claiming "community engagement." Binding authority ensures that communities can reject projects that fail to meet benefit standards, require operational changes when environmental or employment commitments are violated, and participate meaningfully in decisions that affect their health, environment, and economic future.
- **Transparency**: Public reporting on energy use, environmental impact, and community benefit delivery is a critical component of good governance because it enables community accountability and prevents "greenwashing" or benefit-washing, which happens when companies claim community investment without delivering measurable outcomes. Transparent reporting allows residents, journalists, researchers, and advocates to verify compliance, identify disparities, and demand corrective action when commitments are not met. This includes quarterly public reports on: local hiring numbers and wage levels, energy consumption and sources, water usage, environmental emissions, tax contributions, and community investment fulfillment. Without transparency, community benefit agreements become meaningless promises rather than enforceable commitments.

Without these protections, data centers represent digital colonization—extracting community resources while providing minimal benefit.

AI's energy demands intersect with climate justice. Black communities disproportionately bear environmental burdens while receiving fewer benefits from technological advancement. Any data center development must:

- Prioritize renewable energy sources
- Minimize water consumption in water-stressed communities
- Offset carbon emissions
- Contribute to community climate resilience infrastructure

This Paper acknowledges, but does not comprehensively address the energy and environmental dimensions of digital equity. Further research should examine:

- Energy justice frameworks for AI infrastructure;
- Community ownership models for data centers;
- Climate resilience and digital infrastructure; and
- Environmental impact assessments for algorithmic systems.

Digital Wellbeing as Public Health

Digital wellbeing must be treated as a public health, rather than a lifestyle, issue. Black communities face disproportionate harassment, trauma, media disinformation, and algorithmic targeting online. These exposures impact mental health, community stability, and civic trust.

Platform algorithms amplify content that generates engagement, often prioritizing sensational or emotionally charged material. For Black users, this means increased exposure to videos of police violence, racist commentary, conspiracy theories, and coordinated harassment campaigns. The psychological toll of this constant exposure—particularly for young people—adds to a public health crisis related to isolation, depression, and violence.

Digital equity requires

- Accountability mechanisms from platforms for algorithmic harm;
- Safety support for communities targeted by coordinated harassment;
- Mental health resources addressing digital trauma; and
- Equitable access to supportive AI tools, such as health navigation chatbots, tutoring systems, legal aid models, business plan generators, market research tools, and financial planning assistants.

Civil Rights Enforcement for Automated Decisions

Enforceable civil rights protections must govern automated decisions. The opacity of algorithmic systems makes discrimination harder to detect and challenge, requiring proactive oversight rather than reactive complaint-based enforcement.

Essential enforcement mechanisms include

- Mandatory civil rights audits of decision-making systems;
- Public reporting of disparities by race and geography;
- Notification when automated tools are used in decisions;
- Guaranteed right to appeal automated determinations; and
- Enforcement through equity-centered civil rights infrastructure.

Black Data Equity and Governance

Data from Black communities powers AI models, policy decisions, and digital services, yet Black communities still lack ownership, consent and receive no benefit. Oftentimes, our data is extracted, analyzed, and monetized without our governance or fair compensation. Digital equity requires Black-governed data spaces—including those anchored in HBCUs with targeted research initiatives—to protect, store, and ethically analyze data. As AI evolves, we will need:

- Community-governed training curricula and praxis that accurately represent Black experiences;
- Black-led language models grounded in our lived realities;
- Data protection frameworks that prevent misrepresentation;
- Benefit-sharing mechanisms when our data generates profit; and
- Safeguards against political targeting through data analysis.

HBCUs and Black-led research institutions are highly capable and well-positioned to serve as anchors for this data stewardship, building capacity to analyze, protect, and govern data in ways that serve community interests rather than extract value.

Naming the Risk: Digital Apartheid

We must name the threat clearly—a society where one group enjoys digital access, opportunity, safety, and profit while another is excluded, surveilled, or harmed constitutes digital apartheid.

Digital apartheid manifests when

- Infrastructure investment systematically bypasses Black neighborhoods;
- Algorithms encode historical discrimination into automated decisions;
- Surveillance technology disproportionately monitors Black communities;
- Digital systems create barriers to essential services;
- AI-powered tools serve some communities while harming others; and/or
- Economic opportunities concentrate among those with digital access and literacy.

Protecting our communities from digital apartheid is the unfinished work of the Civil Rights Movement. It requires the same moral clarity, strategic organization, and sustained commitment that characterized previous struggles for justice.

Beyond Productivity: Technology for Human Flourishing

The dominant narrative around AI emphasizes worker productivity—making workers more efficient, automating tasks, and reducing labor costs. This framing has never served Black communities. Increased productivity has historically meant job displacement without safety nets, wage suppression despite output increases, concentration of wealth among owners, and elimination of pathways to economic security. We must demand more. Technology should serve human flourishing, not merely corporate efficiency.

Measuring Success Differently

Corporate efficiency gains, labor cost reductions, or shareholder returns should not measure success. Success should be measured by lives saved and improved, inequities reduced, opportunities created, communities strengthened, and knowledge preserved and expanded. This is the standard. Anything less is unacceptable.

The Star Trek Vision: Technology for Liberation

Science fiction has long imagined technology that eliminates scarcity, disease, and inequality—freeing humanity to pursue knowledge, creativity, and exploration. This is not fantasy; it is the standard we should demand from AI development. What would it mean for AI to actually serve Black communities?

Health Equity and Disease Eradication

AI should be deployed to:

- Cure diseases that disproportionately impact Black communities: Sickle cell disease, maternal mortality, hypertension, diabetes;
- Eliminate diagnostic bias: AI systems that accurately diagnose across skin tones and recognize symptoms in diverse populations;
- Predict and prevent: Early detection systems for conditions with high Black mortality rates; and
- Democratize care: Telemedicine and AI-assisted diagnosis in healthcare deserts. For example, researchers at MIT developed an AI system to improve sickle cell disease management. The work should center on technology designed to address health inequities, not exacerbate them.

Solving Structural Discrimination

AI could identify and eliminate discrimination if designed with this intention. Consider the following:

- Hiring bias detection: Systems that flag discriminatory patterns in recruitment.
- Housing discrimination identification: AI that detects redlining and predatory lending.

- Criminal justice reform: Algorithms that identify sentencing disparities and wrongful convictions.
- Educational equity: Adaptive learning systems that close achievement gaps.

Consider, for example, that New York City high school students, Derrick Webster Jr. and Beckett Zahedi, developed an AI tool (Realer Estater) to help people find affordable housing by identifying landlords willing to accept housing vouchers. Real Estater uses AI and custom algorithms to combine publicly available data with real estate listings, allowing users to easily identify undervalued and rent-stabilized apartments (sometimes listed 30-50% below market value). Realer Estater is a shining example of technology solving real community problems.

Economic Democratization

Technology should democratize wealth, not concentrate it. Here is what we envision:

- Business formation tools: AI assistants that guide entrepreneurs through licensing, tax compliance, and market research.
- Capital access: Algorithms that identify creditworthy borrowers excluded by traditional metrics and facilitate access to support.
- Market expansion: Platforms connecting Black businesses to customers and supply chains.
- Financial planning: AI that provides sophisticated wealth management previously available only to the wealthy and well-resourced.

Cultural Preservation and Environmental Justice

- Language preservation: AI systems that teach, preserve, and reclaim African American Vernacular English as well as African and Diasporic languages.
- Historical recovery: Digitization and AI-assisted analysis of Black historical records.
- Cultural production: Tools that amplify Black creativity without extractive exploitation.
- Pollution detection: AI monitoring of air and water quality in Black neighborhoods.
- Climate adaptation: Predictive systems for extreme weather impacts on vulnerable communities.
- Resource allocation: Algorithms ensuring equitable distribution of climate resilience infrastructure.

If communities are asked to bear the risks of AI (e.g., job displacement, surveillance, algorithmic discrimination, energy consumption, environmental burdens), they must receive commensurate benefits.

Required Actions for Public and Private Entities

To move from potential to reality, specific institutional commitments are required.

Federal Government

- Establish dedicated funding for AI health equity research focused on diseases disproportionately affecting Black communities.
- Mandate diversity requirements for all federally funded AI health research teams and datasets.
- Create regulatory frameworks requiring FDA-approved medical AI systems to demonstrate equity across demographic groups before market approval.
- Fund the development of representative health datasets that include adequate Black patient data with proper consent and governance.

State and Local Governments

- Require algorithmic impact assessments for all AI systems used in public benefits administration, criminal justice, housing, and education.
- Establish independent algorithmic auditing offices with subpoena power and enforcement authority.
- Create public procurement standards prioritizing AI tools that demonstrate bias mitigation and equity outcomes.
- Invest in public AI infrastructure (computing resources, datasets, technical expertise) available to community organizations and researchers investigating discrimination.

Private Sector

- Technology companies developing health AI must commit to representative data collection, regular bias audits, and transparent performance reporting across demographic groups.
- Venture capital firms should establish dedicated funds for AI applications addressing health and social equity.
- Healthcare systems must establish AI ethics boards with community representation and binding authority over deployment decisions.
- Companies deploying AI in hiring, lending, housing, or criminal justice must provide public reporting on disparate outcomes and demonstrate continuous improvement toward equity.

Academic and Research Institutions

- HBCUs and minority-serving institutions must receive dedicated funding to build AI research capacity focused on equity applications.
- All AI research using human subjects or data must include equity analysis as a standard component of methodology and peer review.
- Establish open-access repositories of equity-focused AI tools and datasets available to researchers and practitioners.

Accountability Mechanisms: Without enforcement, these commitments become aspirational rather than operational. Required accountability mechanisms include: public reporting on equity metrics; independent audits with public results; community oversight boards with decision-making authority; and legal liability for discriminatory AI systems with clear remedies for harmed individuals and communities.

Advancing Digital Equity by Mobilizing Black Communities

Writer James Baldwin wrote: "*There is never time in the future in which we will work out our salvation. The challenge is in the moment. The time is always now*" (Baldwin, 1961). Achieving digital equity in the Black community requires advocacy and action that honors its urgency and interconnectedness with other social movements. This effort must be created by us and for us, with roots in the lived experiences of people who understand that the repetition of history can hide behind the veils of new technological systems.

The digital disenfranchisement of Black communities carries the same weight as other forms of racism and discrimination because it forecloses our progress in an information-driven economy. Such disenfranchisement can also show up in the spread of misinformation and disinformation about Black, Latino, Indigenous, and otherwise Queer communities that dissuade our communities from taking advantage of their inalienable rights of freedoms, particularly voting.

In keeping with the legacies of Black inventors and innovators in the global digital economy, Black Americans should not have to feel a lack of belonging in the field. Instead, the memories of past and present ancestors should inform the future, and historic institutions should drive current and future narratives of empowerment.

In addition to people, HBCUs exist within Black communities as institutional anchors with "best-in-class" access to research and programs that can drive greater participation of Black students and communities in Science, Technology, Engineering, and Math (STEM). These institutions must also prepare students for entrepreneurship and business ownership in the digital economy, connecting technical skills with business acumen and access to capital. For instance, Howard University's Institute for Intellectual Property and Social Justice, led by Professor Lateef Mtima, exemplifies how HBCUs can lead in ensuring technological innovation serves social justice. The Institute's work on intellectual property rights, cultural expression, and equitable innovation frameworks provides essential scholarship for protecting Black creativity and knowledge production in the digital age.

The professional accreditation of HBCUs matters in accomplishing these goals, especially by promoting faculty engagement and student research opportunities. Howard University is the only HBCU with R1 status (typically reserved for institutions with very high research capability and success), which comes with a track record of acquiring research grants (more than $50 million), generating a set number of doctoral students (more than 70 research doctorates), and offering students opportunities in lucrative and needed careers, especially those in the sciences (Carnegie Classification of Institutions of Higher Education, n.d.). Benefits of R1 status are measurable and include access to large-scale federal and private research grants, a tool for attracting and retaining world-class faculty and top-tier graduate students innovating within their fields, increased visibility, and invitations to partner with other elite institutions and major corporations on interdisciplinary projects. R1 universities often serve as economic engines, creating jobs and supporting entrepreneurs, companies, and industries within the university community. With the increasing attacks on federal research funding, alumni and general supporters of these institutions will need to help avert any downgrades in educational offerings and faculty support through increased contributions.

Black communities must advocate for access to relevant digital upskilling, especially in areas like AI, to ensure our presence in employment and entrepreneurship sectors. Digital skilling is not about preparing Black communities to participate in an economy designed by others. It is about positioning Black innovators to lead the design of technologies that serve humanity. From Lewis Latimer's telecommunications breakthroughs to Dr. Marian Croak's revolutionizing of global communication, Black technical leadership has consistently prioritized broad societal benefit over narrow commercial gain.

The AI-driven Latimer Project, which Black innovators lead, is a new venture working to develop the first Large Language Model that will be culturally responsive to our language and behavioral attributes (Latimer Project, n.d.-a). Referred to as the Black version of Chat-GPT, the Latimer Project is currently curating with AI Black artifacts in language, culture, history, and other nuances for future generations (Latimer Project, n.d.-b; NBC News, 2024). In light of the current attacks on Diversity, Equity, and Inclusion (DEI), and attempts by the current administration to weaponize and erase Black experiences using advanced technologies, the next generations of computer and data scientists, anthropologists, sociologists, educators, historians, photojournalists, and other experts must work diligently to counter such removal and extinction.

History has already demonstrated that Black communities have positioned themselves as exemplary figures in this space. We must take action to close the digital divide, demand accountability from AI systems, and account for the force of innovation. It must be driven by us and for us, with special privilege given to those institutions that have historically served in our best interest.

Policy Recommendations: Advancing Digital Equity

To translate the principles outlined in this Paper into concrete action, we propose the following policy recommendations for federal and state leaders, as well as the private sector.

Federal Level

Advance a comprehensive Digital Civil Rights framework that guarantees nondiscriminatory access to essential digital services. This framework must explicitly address algorithmic discrimination in fintech, employment platforms, and public benefits administration.

Representative Yvette Clarke, Chair of the Congressional Black Caucus (CBC), has reintroduced the AI Civil Rights Act, which provides essential protections against algorithmic discrimination. This Paper endorses this legislation and calls for its immediate passage to establish enforceable civil rights protections for automated decision-making systems.

Develop a permanent broadband subsidy. Congress must establish a permanent, adequately funded successor to the Affordable Connectivity Program, with a subsidy of at least $30/month to match current market rates for reliable service. This should also increase with inflation.

Create a Community Broadband Infrastructure Grant Program. Establish a dedicated federal grant program (minimum $5 billion over 5 years) to fund the development, deployment, and operation of community-owned broadband networks in underserved Black communities, with priority given to projects that demonstrate community governance and equitable pricing structures.

Codify a Digital Civil Rights Act. Develop comprehensive legislation addressing digital redlining by government and private sector actors, and safeguards that prevent algorithmic bias and online harassment.

Invest in HBCU Research Initiatives. Stop the elimination of funding for STEM and other science programs at HBCUs that limit innovation and research focused on the development of ethical AI, digital inclusion, and culturally responsive technology.

Reinstitute the Americorps Program and Digital Equity Grants. Congress must re-establish national volunteer programs like Americorps that have supported Black communities, advancing digital literacy and training. Congress must also reinstate the recently eliminated Digital Equity Grant program to allow state and local governments to design and deploy connectivity programs that work for their constituents.

Support K-12 AI Literacy education core curriculum integration, ensuring that all students, particularly those in underserved communities, develop critical skills to navigate, question, and shape AI systems. Similar to the financial literacy requirements adopted by several states, AI literacy should be recognized as essential preparation for civic and economic participation.

Congress members Espaillat, Clarke, and Lieu have introduced legislation mandating AI literacy education. This Paper endorses this legislation and urges its passage as essential infrastructure for democratic participation in an AI-mediated society.

State and Local Level

1 **Broadband Infrastructure Expansion**: States must have access to funding and other resources from the government and public/private sector partnerships that advance widespread connectivity in all cities, communities, and rural areas where people are in the most need of high-speed broadband service.

2 **Community Broadband**: Remove legislative barriers to community-owned broadband networks and establish dedicated grant programs to fund their development and operation, particularly in underserved urban and rural areas with significant Black populations. Community-owned networks offer local control, competitive pricing, and responsiveness to community needs that corporate ISPs often fail to provide.

3 **Digital Skills Programs**: Fund community-based digital skills training through schools, libraries, community centers, and faith-based organizations in Black communities, and allow states and cities to access underutilized grants to advance digital equity, e.g., summer youth programming, community development block grants, etc.

4 **Public Access**: Create and maintain technology hubs with high-speed internet, computing devices, and technical support in underserved communities.
5 **Responsible AI Policies**: Develop and implement responsible AI policies at the state level, drawing on emerging frameworks while centering civil rights and community protection. States should not wait for federal action but should establish ethical AI standards, impact assessment requirements, and enforcement mechanisms.

Private Sector

1 **Inclusive Hiring and Retention**: Implement transparent diversity metrics and accountability measures to hire, retain, and advance Black talent in technology roles. This must extend to entrepreneurial support programs, venture capital investment committees, and accelerator leadership.
2 **Community Data Stewardship**: Fund community data stewardship initiatives housed at HBCUs or Black-led research institutions to ensure ethical protection, governance, and benefit-sharing of data derived from Black communities. These institutions should develop the capacity to create and maintain Black-governed AI training datasets.
3 **Investment in Black Innovation**: Establish dedicated venture funds and incubators that intentionally support Black tech entrepreneurs, emphasizing solutions and addressing community needs. Critically, Black founders are often over-indexed on mentorship programs and under-indexed on actual capital deployment. Too many lack access to early-stage checks that are large enough to support meaningful product development, team building, and market validation—the foundation necessary to attract follow-on funding and achieve scale. Create pathways for Black founders to access not only capital but also networks, technical infrastructure (cloud computing credits, AI/ML computing resources, cybersecurity tools), procurement opportunities with corporate and government customers, and strategic partnerships. These ecosystem supports must complement, not substitute for, substantial capital deployment. The venture capital industry must acknowledge that its historical exclusion of Black founders represents both a moral failure and a market inefficiency, and commit to structural change in investment patterns, not merely symbolic programs or performative gestures.
4 **Ethical Technology Design**: Prioritize AI that reflects the lived experiences of all people, and ensure that these systems are designed in accordance with civil and human rights laws. Adopt mandatory impact assessments for new technologies to evaluate potential harms to Black communities before deployment.

5 Develop responsible AI policies that include regular algorithmic audits, transparent decision-making processes, and clear accountability structures.
6 Establish dedicated venture funds and incubators that specifically support Black tech entrepreneurs, emphasizing solutions that address community needs. Create pathways for Black founders to access not only capital but also networks, technical infrastructure, and strategic partnerships.

These proposed recommendations provide the beginning of a roadmap to address the immediate connectivity challenges of Black communities, while emboldening a bolder future for technology innovation. Implementation will require coordinated action across government, industry, and civil society, with Black communities centered in decision-making processes at every level.

Conclusion: A Call to Digital Justice

The fight for civil rights has always been for equitable access and inclusion—whether at the ballot box, in education, in business ownership, or in economic opportunities. As these fundamental rights increasingly intersect with the digital ecosystem, this struggle must be approached with the same historical urgency and moral clarity that defined previous civil rights movements.

The systemic invisibility of Black communities—manifested through underrepresentation in the tech sector, limited access to affordable broadband, exclusion from entrepreneurial capital and support, and the erasure of our lived experiences in automated systems—demands intervention through a framework of digital justice. In closing, Black people must demand more, starting with a series of actions to ensure we are more visible in an accelerated technological environment.

1 **Policy Reform**: Black people must hold their elected and appointed officials accountable to ensure more permanent broadband subsidies, competitive markets, support for Black-owned businesses and entrepreneurs, and anti-discrimination related to internet access and AI.
2 **Institutional Investment**: HBCUs must continue to be centers of technological innovation and research, cultivating the next generation of Black innovators and entrepreneurs.
3 **Community Empowerment**: Black communities must have access to contemporary and future-proof digital skills that will ensure their competitiveness in the existing and emerging fields as workers, business owners, and innovators— some of which will not be specifically targeted to the tech sector.
4 **Representation**: Black leadership must be present, visible, and hold power in technology companies, policy bodies, venture capital firms, entrepreneurial ecosystems, and regulatory agencies to secure greater representation.
5 **Technological Sovereignty**: Black-led initiatives, like the Latimer Project, and their founders must be supported and elevated to center Black experiences in technological development. This includes data governance, algorithmic auditing capacity, and independent technical infrastructure.

The unfinished work of civil rights in the digital age is before us. The future of Black liberation is inextricably linked to digital equity, not merely as consumers of technology, but as creators, regulators, business owners, and beneficiaries.

Bibliography

Baldwin, J. (1961). *Nobody knows my name: more notes of a native son*. Dial Press.

Ballard Brief. (2022). *Disproportionate exposure to air pollution for low-income communities in the United States*. ballardbrief.byu.edu

Buolamwini, J., & Gebru, T. (2018). Gender shades: Intersectional phenotypic darker skin study. In *Proceedings of the 1st Conference on Fairness, Accountability and Transparency* (pp. 77–91). ACM.

Carnegie Classification of Institutions of Higher Education. (n.d.). *Standard Classifications*. https://carnegieclassification.acenet.edu

Center for Digital Democracy. (2023). *Rural America's digital dilemma. Bridging the broadband gap for inclusive growth*.

Chandra, S., Chang, A., Day, L., Fazlullah, A., Liu, J., McBride, L., Mudalige, T., and Weiss, D. (2020). *Closing the K-12 digital divide in the age of distance learning*. Common Sense Media. https://www.commonsensemedia.org/sites/default/files/

featured-content/files/final_-_what_it_will_take_to_permanently_close_the_k-12_digital_divide_vfeb3.pdf
Civil Discourse with Joyce Vance. (2025). *The week ahead.* Substack. https://joycevance.substack.com/p/the-week-ahead-e49
Deloitte (2023). *Racial and ethnic diversity in the U.S. technology: Examining where the industry stands.* Deloitte Insights.
Diallo, R. (2026). Aisha: An AI Chatbot That Centers Blackness. *The Washington Informer.* https://www.washingtoninformer.com/aisha-ai-black-sources/
Federal Communications Commission. (2021). Affordable connectivity program. https://www.fcc.gov/acp
Federal Communications Commission. (n.d.). *Lifeline programs for low-income consumers.* FCC
Federal Reserve Bank of St. Louis. (n.d.) *The impact of the digital divide on economic opportunity.* Federal Reserve Bank of St Louis.
Gebru, T., Morgenstern, J., Vecchione, B., Vaughan, J. W., Wallach, H., Daumé III, H., & Crawford, K. (2021). Datasheets for datasets. *Communications of the ACM,* 64(12), 86–92.
Ghaffary, S., & Gopal, P. (2021). *Timnit Gebru's new research center is a rebuke to Google.* Vox.
Harrison, D. (2021). *Affordability & Availability: Expanding Broadband in the Black Rural South.* Joint Center for Political and Economic Studies. https://jointcenter.org/wp-content/uploads/2021/10/Affordability-Availability-Expanding-Broadband-in-the-Black-Rural-South.pdf
Horrigan, J.B. (2025). Making progress, targeting gaps. *Lessons from broadband adoption trends.* Benton Institute for Broadband & Society. https://www.benton.org/publications/broadband-adoption-trends
Irving, L., Levy, J., & McConnaughey, J. (1995). *Falling through the net: Defining the Digital Divide.* National Telecommunications and Information Administration. https://www.ntia.doc.gov/legacy/ntiahome/fallingthru.html
Kapor Center. (2023). Diversity in tech: Key facts and figures. Kapor Center
Kapor Center & VC Include. (2022). State of tech diversity: The Black tech ecosystem data pack (KC22001). https://www.kaporcenter.org/wp-content/uploads/2022/03/KC22001_black-tech-report.final_.pdf
Latimer Project. (2024). *Building culturally responsive AI for Black communities.* https://latimerproject.org
Latimer Project. (n.d.-a). *About Us.* https://latimerproject.org
Latimer Project. (n.d.-b). *Our vision: building an ethical and culturally relevant AI future.* https://latimerproject.org
Lawyers' Committee for Civil Rights Under Law. (2023). *Digital redlining: Addressing roots of discriminatory practices in telecommunications.* https://www.lawyerscommittee.org/digitalrights
Lin II, R.-G., Money, L., & Greene, S. (2023). A coronavirus mystery: Why New York was hit so much harder than L.A. County. *Los Angeles Times.* www.latimes.com
McKinsey & Company. (2021). *Diverse teams win: Why inclusion matters.* McKinsey & Company.
NAACP & Kapor Center. (2022). *Black representation in the technology sector technology report.* https://www.kaporcenter.org/blackreptech

National Digital Inclusion Alliance. (2023). *Digital equity and inclusion best practices.* https://www.digitalinclusion.org/best-practices

National Science Foundation. (2022). *HBCU research status and federal funding.* https://www.nsf.gov/statistics/hbcu-research

National Urban League (2021). The Lewis Latimer Plan for Digital Equity and Inclusion, https://nul.org/program/lewis-latimer-plan

NBC News. (2024). The Latimer Project: A Black version of ChatGPT is on the horizon.

Pew Research Center. (2024). *Americans' Use of Mobile Technology and Home Broadband.* https://www.pewresearch.org/wp-content/uploads/sites/20/2024/01/PI_2024.01.31_Home-Broadband-Mobile-Use_FINAL.pdf

Purdue Center for Regional Development. (n.d.). Broadband's impact on rural America. Purdue Center

Raji, I. D., Gebru, T., Redberg, E. M., & Zevenbergen, B. (2019). Gender shades: An analysis of adversarial attacks on commercial facial recognition systems. *Proceedings of the ACM Conference on Fairness, Accountability, and Transparency (FAT* '19)* (pp. 241–250).

Rural Health Information Hub. (2025). Barriers to transportation programs in real areas. Rural Health Information Hub

Simonite, M. (2021). Google's AI ethics row shows just how messy the field is. *Wired.* www.wired.com

Smart Growth America. (2024). *Equitable development strategies: A guidebook for transportation practitioners.* smartgrowthamerica.org

Stancati, M., Brody, L., & Fontdegloriam, X. (2020). The pandemic sent 1.5 billion children home from school. Many might not return. *Wall Street Journal.* www.wsj.com

The White House. (2021). *Infrastructure Investment and Jobs Act Summary: Broadband Provisions.* https://www.whitehouse.gov/briefing-room/statements-releases/2021/11/06/fact-sheet-the-bipartisan-infrastructure-deal/

The White House. (2024). *FACT SHEET: Biden–Harris Administration announces new investments to cut costs and expand access to clean energy in rural America.* [Press release] bidenwhitehouse.archives.gov

The White House. (2025a). *Establishing and implementing the President's "Department of Government Efficiency."* https://www.whitehouse.gov/presidential-actions/2025/01/establishing-and-implementing-the-presidents-department-of-government-efficiency/

The White House. (2025b). *Implementing the President's "Department of Government Efficiency" cost effective initiative.* https://www.whitehouse.gov/presidential-actions/2025/02/implementing-the-presidents-department-of-government-efficiency-cost-efficiency-initiative/

Turner Lee, N. (2023). *Digitally Invisible: How the Internet Is Creating the New Underclass.* Harvard University Press.

Valentin, A. (2018). *Why Rural Communities of Color are Left Behind: A Call for Intersectional Demographic Broadband Data.* Public Knowledge. https://publicknowledge.org/why-rural-communities-of-color-are-left-behind-a-call-for-intersectional-demographic-broadband-data/

Valentin, A. (2025). Countering the Politics of Deservingness in the Fight for Digital Equity. https://www.techpolicy.press/countering-the-politics-of-deservingness-in-the-fight-for-digital-equity/

Valentin, A. & Ruiz, C. (2026). *The Blueprint for Equitable Digital Participation*. Public Knowledge, UnidosUS, and National Digital Inclusion Alliance. https://publicknowledge.org/policy/the-blueprint-for-equitable-digital-participation/

Chapter 21

Securing Black America

A Revolutionary Framework for True National Security

*Nicole Tisdale**

Executive Summary

Black Americans face five critical security threats that our government's narrow definition of "national security" ignores. This Black Paper (Paper) reveals how hate crimes, extreme weather, cyberattacks, online scams, and foreign misinformation campaigns create a security crisis in Black communities—and provides concrete solutions to help us keep us safe.

* Supported by braintrust authors: Kayla Jones and Kelcey P. Morrow.

DOI: 10.4324/9781003752646-28

The Five Threats:

1 **Hate-Driven Violence**: White supremacist attacks remain the most lethal domestic threat.
2 Extreme Weather: Black communities face higher heat-related health risks (U.S. Environmental Protection Agency, 2021a, 2021b) and slower disaster recovery (McKinsey Institute for Economic Mobility, 2024).
3 **Digital Attacks**: Cyberattacks on under-resourced hospitals and schools—including many that serve Black communities—can cause longer, more damaging service disruptions.
4 **Online Scams**: Black Americans are twice as likely to lose money to digital fraud (Truecaller, 2024).
5 **Foreign Influence**: Coordinated campaigns specifically target Black voters to suppress civic participation.

The Solution: A complete reimagining of national security that centers Black safety through:

- Community-led security initiatives.
- Equal disaster response and recovery.
- Cybersecurity funding and aid for Black-serving institutions.
- Financial fraud protection.
- Defense against digital voter suppression.

We hope this Paper will help you understand and fight security threats in our communities. Share it at church, community meetings, and with local officials. Use it to start conversations, demand change, and hold leaders accountable.

Introduction: A Revolutionary Approach to National Security for Black Communities

For generations, the concept of national security has been narrowly defined by the United States government's primary focus on military power, foreign threats, and the protection of economic interests. This limited definition has failed Black communities across America, leaving us vulnerable to persistent threats that endanger our lives, homes, communities, and democratic participation.

The promise of real national security ensures justice and equal protection for everyone in their everyday lives. Yet Black communities still face serious safety gaps that impede that promise of equal protection and justice. It should be noted that these gaps did not appear by accident. They result from systemic injustice, historical oppression, and ongoing policy failures. These gaps have created a national security crisis that requires immediate attention and action from policymakers, community leaders, and advocates nationwide.

The State of the People movement recognizes five critical national security threats that disproportionately hurt Black Americans:

1 **Hate-Driven Violence in Our Communities**: Domestic terrorism[1] and racially motivated attacks threatening our physical safety.
2 **Extreme Weather Threatening Our Neighborhoods**: Environmental disasters are hitting Black communities harder, with fewer resources for recovery.
3 **Digital Attacks on Our Hospitals, Schools, and Water Systems**: Cyber threats disrupting essential services with greater impacts in our communities.
4 **Online Scams Targeting Our Families**: Financial predators extracting money from Black households.
5 **Foreign Influence and False Information Undermining Our Civic Power**: Coordinated campaigns designed to suppress our political voice.

Each of these threats causes disproportionate harm to Black Americans and represents a failure of our national security infrastructure to fulfill its most basic purpose: **protecting all citizens equally**.

As communities across the country mobilize for policy changes that affect multiple areas of our lives, the State of the People movement calls for a complete revision and a new mode of thinking about national security priorities. We seek to educate, organize, and build collective power to implement policy solutions that address these building inequities that are impacting our communities. This Paper offers a roadmap for that urgent work as we rally, rebuild, and reimagine what is possible for Black communities.

Our vision of national security centers on Black safety, wellbeing, and full democratic participation as essential components of true national security—not as special interests that can be argued down or dismissed. By understanding these threats and advocating for specific policy changes, we can build a national security framework that truly protects all Americans and fulfills the promise of equal protection under law.

National Security and the Black Community: A History

American national security has primarily focused on increasing the strength of the nation's military presence and power, as well as police forces and resources across the country. Yet it should be noted that, in conjunction with the known history of national security, there is also the long, complicated history between the Black community and national security measures. This history is rooted in issues of exclusion, excessive surveillance, and unrequited civil rights.

Some examples of issues between the Black community and national security include, but are not limited to:

- The segregation of the military during World War I and World War II: Segregationist beliefs pushed the idea that Black servicemen and women were inferior, preventing them from attaining leadership positions, adequate living conditions, and equal pay. Yet these ideas were disproved by the example set by the Tuskegee Airmen, the 6888th Postal Battalion, and every brave serviceman and woman who made the ultimate sacrifice in the name of freedom for a country that did not offer it to them. Their service contributed to the momentum that ultimately led to the desegregation of the United States military (Moye, 2010).
- The enactment of Operation COINTELPRO during the Civil Rights Movement: COINTELPRO secretly monitored the actions of civil rights leaders such as Dr. Martin Luther King Jr., Malcolm X, and the Black Panther Party. While they operated under the guise of preventing communism, their

efforts were made to weaken leaders they were afraid could strengthen the fight for Black freedom (U.S. Senate, 1976). Not only was the operation a blatant disregard for personal privacy; it also led to massive distrust between the Black community and the people who promised their actions were meant to protect.

- The disproportionately large number of Black Americans who were drafted during the Vietnam War: Many Black draftees were placed in combat positions, and more Black casualties came out of the Vietnam War than the number of Black Americans who were recruited into the armed forces (Moskos & Butler, 1996). Many citizens and prominent figures, like Muhammad Ali, publicly disapproved of the war and questioned the purpose of fighting a war abroad while being denied civil rights at home, which increased public criticism and distrust of national security measures.
- The expansion of homeland and counterterrorism measures after the terrorist attacks on September 11th: Similar to Operation COINTELPRO, monitoring and surveillance efforts were increased for Black Muslim and African immigrant communities (Cainkar, 2009). Meanwhile, Black American communities were also being disproportionately impacted by the increase in militarized policing systems funded by federal homeland security programs (Kraska, 2007).
- The current monitoring of Black leaders and Black Lives Matter activists: These recent efforts have been concerted by the Federal Bureau of Investigation (FBI), which has occasionally labeled these individuals as "extremists" like Cold War-era practices (Theoharis, 2018).

This history has created a hostile and widely distrustful relationship between our communities and the system that promises to protect all citizens in this country. Yet we do not write this to say that American national security is too broken to be repaired. We have the hope and belief that through education, change, and collaboration, the dream and promise of national security can be met and felt. It cannot be, though, if we do not know what is working well and what needs to be fixed.

Hate-Driven Violence: A Growing Threat to Our Lives

What is Hate-Driven Violence?

Hate-driven violence refers to attacks against Black Americans based on racism, which includes, but is not limited to: mass shootings, attacks on homes and businesses, threats against schools and churches, and online harassment that leads to real-world harm. While these attacks have deep historical roots, today's threats use modern technology and are fueled by conspiracy theories that spread quickly online.

Why It Matters to Black Communities

Black Americans face an unequal and disproportionate risk from domestic terrorism, particularly from white supremacist extremists. According to the Department of Homeland Security (DHS), racist violence against Black communities remains one of the most persistent and deadly threats in the United States. From 2017 to 2022, white supremacist attacks were responsible for the majority of deaths in domestic terrorist incidents (Anti-Defamation League, 2023; Center for Strategic and International Studies, 2020).

Daily Impact

The impact of hate-driven violence goes beyond physical harm. Many Black Americans experience:

- Fear of gathering in public spaces at religious and faith institutions, grocery stores, or community events.
- Anxiety and stress that lead to physical and mental health problems.
- Children with developmental impacts from living with constant fear.
- Decreased participation in civic activities due to safety concerns.

These effects can fundamentally change how we live our lives, limiting our freedom and community connections. The constant threat of violence creates a form of chronic stress that affects health, education, and economic opportunity.

Voices From Our Communities

Policy Actions Needed

To address hate-driven violence against Black communities, our government must take the following actions:

Federal Policy Changes:

- Increase funding for the Department of Justice's Civil Rights Division to prioritize the prosecution of hate crimes.
- Mandate that the FBI report on white nationalist groups' activities and require quarterly congressional briefings and public notifications of threat reports.
- Create a national task force on eliminating racially motivated violence with direct input from affected communities.
- Require impact assessments that measure how anti-extremism policies affect Black communities.
- Develop standardized metrics to evaluate the effectiveness of hate crime prevention programs.

State and Local Policy Changes:

- Establish independent community oversight boards for hate crime investigations.
- Implement mandatory hate crime training for all law enforcement personnel.
- Develop rapid response protocols for threats against Black houses of worship, including churches, mosques, synagogues, and community centers.
- Fund community-based violence prevention and intervention programs in vulnerable neighborhoods.

Extreme Weather: Growing Threats to Our Neighborhoods

Understanding The Threat

Due to climate change, extreme weather events are becoming more frequent and severe. These events include hurricanes, floods, heat waves, wildfires, and winter storms. While these extreme weather events affect everyone, they hit Black neighborhoods harder and longer, creating disproportionate suffering and slower recovery. Prime examples of extreme weather affecting Black communities include Hurricane Katrina, the Texas winter storms in the early 2020s, and the wildfires in Altadena, California (McKinsey Institute for Economic Mobility, 2024).

Why Extreme Weather Matters to Black Communities

Historical housing discrimination has forced many Black people and families into areas more vulnerable to extreme weather. Several Black neighborhoods are located in areas that are prone to high-rise flooding and urban heat islands. Black neighborhoods are also known to have much older infrastructure and systems that are not built to withstand the extreme consequences of these weather events. In addition, these neighborhoods are also known to receive a limited amount of resources (if they receive any), which results in not being prepared before or receiving help to recover after an event.

Direct Impact

When extreme weather hits, the impacts ripple through every aspect of life in Black communities. These combined effects can permanently change neighborhoods and disrupt generations of community building.

Health Impacts:

- Higher rates of heat-related illnesses and deaths.
- More exposure to mold, contaminated water, and other health hazards after floods.
- Increased mental health challenges from trauma and displacement.

Economic Impacts:

- Repeated home damage that insurance may not fully cover.
- Loss of work days and income during recovery.
- Declining property values in repeatedly affected areas.

Community Impacts:

- Damage to churches, community centers, and gathering places.
- Displacement of families and breakdown of neighborhood networks.
- Interruption of community services and support systems.

What Can Be Done

By demanding better systems, we can reduce the devastating impacts of extreme weather on our neighborhoods. To better protect our communities from extreme weather threats, our government must implement these policies:

Federal, State, and Local Policy Changes:

- Develop neighborhood emergency response networks.
- Create cooling centers and shelter options within Black communities.
- Distribute disaster aid and faster assistance equitably.
- Investment in climate-resistant structures and systems in Black neighborhoods.
- Support programs to help homeowners make their homes more disaster-resistant.
- Reform insurance practices that discriminate against Black communities.

Digital Attacks: Threats to Our Essential Services

What is This Threat?

Digital attacks, or cyberattacks, are attempts to damage, disrupt, or gain unauthorized access to computer systems that run essential services. These attacks on hospitals, schools, water systems, and other basic services can cut off critical resources and expose sensitive personal information.

Why Digital Attacks Matter to Black Communities

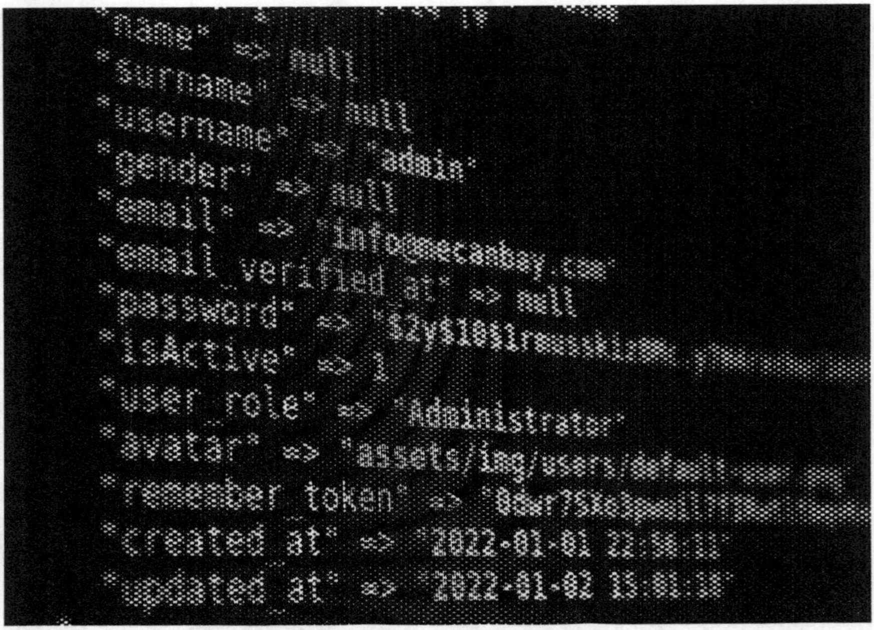

When digital attacks hit essential services, Black communities often face more extended outages and slower recovery (U.S. Department of Health and Human Services, 2023):

- Hospitals and clinics serving predominantly Black communities often have less funding for cybersecurity.
- Schools in Black neighborhoods may lack the resources to recover from attacks quickly.
- Water and power systems in many Black communities already struggle with aging systems.

Recent attacks show how these threats disproportionately harm our communities:

- In 2023, ransomware attacks on healthcare systems increased by 128%, with some targeting safety-net and community hospitals that disproportionately serve Black and low-income patients (Office of the Director of National Intelligence [ODNI], 2024).

- School districts and areas with large Black populations and Historically Black Colleges and Universities (HBCUs) have faced weeks-long outages after attacks.
- Water system attacks in under-resourced areas have left communities with safety concerns and disruptions to safe water.

How Digital Attacks Affect Daily Life

Digital attacks on essential services create severe disruptions that can have lasting consequences. For families already facing economic challenges, these disruptions can create crises that take months or years to overcome.

In Healthcare:

- Delayed medical care for chronic conditions and emergencies.
- Exposure of sensitive health information.
- Increased costs that may be passed on to patients.
- More profound mistrust of healthcare systems from past harms to Black communities.

In Schools:

- Disruption to classes, learning, food, and other critical services.
- Exposure of sensitive student records, related to mental health, physical abuse, and parental financial records.
- Limited access to free meal programs and other support services.

In Utilities:

- Water safety concerns.
- Billing problems that lead to service shutoffs.
- Delayed repairs to critical systems.

Policy Actions Needed

To protect Black communities from the disproportionate harm of digital attacks on essential services, our government must implement these policies:

Federal Policy Changes:

- Establish a Digital Equity Program that provides cybersecurity funding to hospitals, schools, and utilities serving predominantly Black and low-income areas.

- Create a Digital Safety Net requirement for essential services to maintain backup systems that function during cyberattacks.
- Develop a Cyber Equity Division within the Department of Homeland Security focused on protecting vulnerable communities.

State and Local Policy Changes:

- Mandate equity impact assessments for all cybersecurity funding allocation decisions.
- Create cyber strengthening grants specifically for organizations serving historically underinvested communities.
- Establish community technology centers that provide education on digital security and emergency preparedness.

Online Scams: Financial Predators Targeting Our Families

Understanding The Threat?

Online scams are schemes designed to steal money or personal information through deception. While anyone can be targeted, scammers increasingly create tactics specifically aimed at Black Americans, exploiting trust in community organizations and taking advantage of financial pressures.

Why Online Scams Matter to Black Communities

Black families face disproportionate harm from online scams (Consumer Reports, 2024):

- Black Americans are twice as likely to lose money to digital scams compared to white Americans (Consumer Reports, 2024).
- Nearly half (47%) of Black Americans report losing money to phone scams at least once (Truecaller & The Harris Poll, 2024).

- Across all racial groups, more than half of scam victims have been victimized more than once (AARP, 2021).

Several factors make our communities more vulnerable to certain types of scams:

- Scammers often impersonate trusted community organizations like churches, Black-owned businesses, or government agencies.
- Black consumers are more likely to use payment methods with limited fraud protection, like Cash App (Federal Trade Commission, 2021).
- Economic pressures can make "too good to be true" offers more tempting during financial hardship.

Direct Impact

The money lost to scams represents resources that could have been used for education, homeownership, healthcare, and other investments in our families and communities. The impact of scams goes beyond just immediate financial losses:

Financial Harm:

- Money lost to scams is rarely recovered, creating lasting financial setbacks.
- Stolen personal information can lead to ongoing identity theft and damaged credit.
- For families already facing economic challenges, these losses can be devastating.

Community Impact:

- Erosion of trust in legitimate organizations and services.
- Reduced participation in online banking and digital services out of fear.
- Communities are becoming more isolated as people avoid online interaction.

Policy Actions Needed

To combat the targeted exploitation of Black communities through online scams, our government must implement these policies:

Federal Policy Changes:

- Launch federal efforts to investigate and dismantle international scam networks that target Black communities.
- Strengthen protections for users of payment apps and mobile banking services.
- Create specific regulations addressing predatory practices targeting Black consumers.
- Fund a nationwide initiative to research and address racial disparities in digital financial fraud.
- Require payment platforms to implement enhanced verification systems and fraud reimbursement programs for all consumers.

State and Local Policy Changes:

- Mandate financial awareness education in schools with specific information on recognizing and avoiding digital scams.
- Create dedicated units within state attorneys general's offices focused on prosecuting fraudsters who target Black communities, including extreme weather victims and aging communities.
- Establish community-based recovery funds to help scam victims recover losses when traditional methods fail.
- Develop public awareness campaigns in partnership with trusted community organizations and Black-owned media.

Foreign Influence and False Information: Undermining Our Civic Power

Understanding the Threat?

Foreign influence operations are coordinated campaigns by other countries to spread false or misleading information in the United States. Law enforcement and intelligence agencies have confirmed that these operations specifically target Black Americans with sophisticated tactics designed to suppress voting, create division within our communities, and weaken our collective political power. These digital attacks represent a direct national security threat to democratic participation in Black communities.

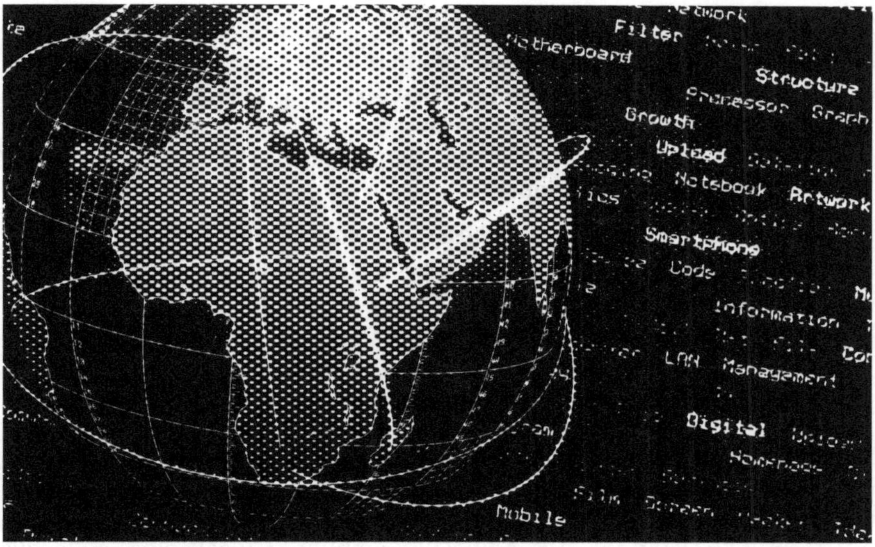

Why Foreign Influence and False Information Matter to Black Communities

Evidence shows that these operations deliberately target Black Americans:

- Senate investigations found that "no single group of Americans was targeted by Russian information operatives more than African Americans" (U.S. Senate Select Committee on Intelligence, 2019).
- More than 66% of Facebook ads from Russian operations contained race-related terms (Howard et al., 2018).
- Foreign actors create fake accounts pretending to be Black activists or organizations
- These highly sophisticated campaigns use cultural references and language that resonate specifically with Black communities.

How Foreign Influence Impacts Daily Life

These operations represent a modern form of voter suppression, using digital tools to restrict Black political power. These foreign influence operations harm Black civic power in several critical ways:

Reduced Political Participation:

- Confusion about voting procedures directly decreases voter turnout.
- Discouragement messaging makes some potential voters feel their vote doesn't matter.
- Division within communities makes it harder to organize for common goals.

Erosion of Trust:

- Persistent exposure to misleading content damages trust in legitimate news and information.
- Lower trust in democratic institutions leads to reduced civic participation.
- Community divisions are artificially amplified, weakening collective action.

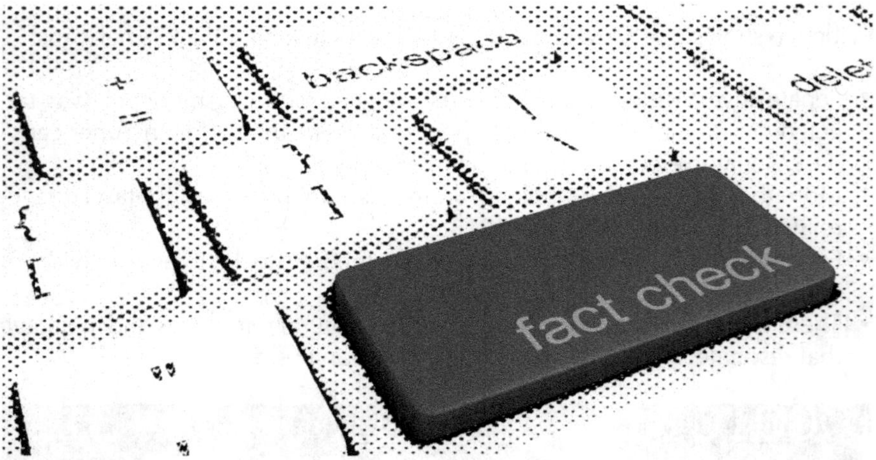

Policy Actions Needed

To protect Black communities from foreign influence operations that undermine our civic power, our government must implement these policies:

Federal Policy Changes:

- Require social media platforms to identify and remove foreign influence campaigns targeting Black voters rapidly.
- Implement mandatory reporting requirements for technology companies when they detect coordinated influence operations.
- Require the United States intelligence agencies to provide quarterly reports to Congress on foreign influence operations targeting Black communities.
- Create a Congressional Commission on Digital Democracy and Racial Equity to monitor government protection efforts.
- Establish civil penalties for platforms that fail to take reasonable measures against foreign influence campaigns targeting protected groups.

State and Local Policy Changes:

- Create rapid response teams to counter false election information in real time across multiple platforms and languages.
- Fund partnerships between local election officials and trusted community organizations to disseminate accurate voting information.
- Develop media awareness campaigns with an emphasis on identifying disinformation targeting racial communities.

Conclusion: A New Vision for National Security That Protects Black Communities

The threats documented in this Paper represent an urgent national security crisis for Black Americans. From targeted domestic terrorism to digital warfare on essential services and financial services, to coordinated foreign attacks on our democratic participation, these dangers demand immediate action from our national security apparatus.

For too long, America's national security framework has primarily focused on external threats and military responses while overlooking the devastating security gaps experienced in Black communities. This narrow vision of national security has left our neighborhoods vulnerable to terrorism, climate disasters, digital attacks, financial predators, and information wars. When national security policies fail to protect Black Americans equally, they fail to fulfill their most fundamental purpose.

The State of the People movement calls for a comprehensive restructuring of national security priorities and investments. We demand a national security system that:

1 Proactively protects Black Americans from domestic terrorism and racially motivated violence.
2 Ensures equal protection from, and response to, environmental security threats.
3 Guarantees technological security and digital rights for vulnerable communities.
4 Safeguards Black financial security from targeted misuse and fraud.
5 Defends our democratic participation from foreign interference.

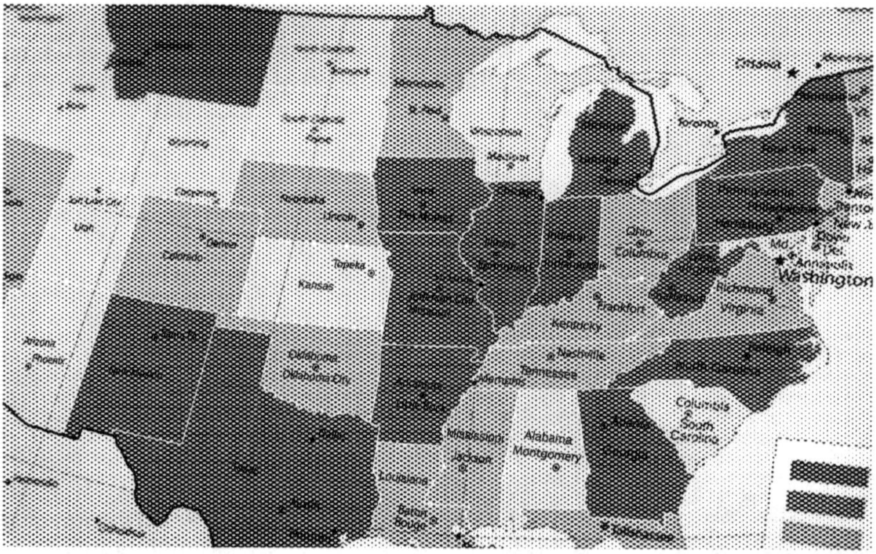

Note: A current map of the U.S. showing states and state capitals can be found at https://commons.wikimedia.org/wiki/File:US_map_-_states_and_capitals.png (accessed September 2026).

We are building a national coalition to advance these security priorities as we mobilize across Atlanta, Durham, Montgomery, Birmingham, New Orleans, Newark, Richmond, Detroit, Jackson, Louisville, Los Angeles, and more. Our movement asserts that true national security must address Black communities' specific threats, not as a secondary concern but as a central national mandate.

The national security issues outlined in this Paper are a matter of civil rights and national importance. A nation cannot claim to be secure when millions of its citizens face disproportionate, preventable threats to their safety, homes, essential services, economic stability, and political voice. By implementing the policy solutions outlined in this Paper, we can build a stronger, more comprehensive national security framework that truly protects all Americans.

The State of the People movement stands ready to partner with government agencies, elected officials, and institutions willing to reimagine national security through this more inclusive lens. At the same time, we will continue to organize, advocate, and demand accountability when these systems fail our communities. Our security is non-negotiable—and it is fundamental to America's security as a whole.

From Paper to Progress: A Call to Action

The security threats documented in this Paper represent an urgent crisis demanding immediate, sustained action at multiple levels. We call on all stakeholders—community members, organizations, elected officials, and government agencies—to implement this comprehensive security framework.

Community-Level Actions:

- Join local State of the People efforts and learn more at www.stateoftheppl.com.
- Participate in Community Security Mapping sessions to identify vulnerabilities in your neighborhood.
- Form Community Emergency Response Teams trained to address all five threat areas.

- Document and report security threats through our secured community reporting system.
- Advocate with local officials for the policy changes outlined in this Black paper.

Organizational Partnerships:

We invite partnerships with organizations across sectors to implement this framework:

- Civil Rights Organizations: the National Black Justice Collective (NBJC), National Association for the Advancement of Colored People, National Urban League, Color of Change.
- Faith Communities: Black church networks, interfaith coalitions, religious leadership councils.
- Academic Institutions: HBCUs, research centers, policy institutes.
- Technology Sector: Cybersecurity firms, social media platforms, digital rights organizations.
- Healthcare Providers: Hospital systems, community health centers, mental health organizations.

- Financial Institutions: Banks, credit unions, and consumer protection organizations.
- Legal Advocacy Groups: American Civil Liberties Union (ACLU), Lawyers' Committee for Civil Rights, legal aid societies.
- Emergency Management: Disaster response organizations, climate resilience networks.

Accountability Framework:

Progress can be tracked and reported through:

- Annual State of Black Security Report assessing improvements in all five threat areas.
- Quarterly Community Security Scorecards for each State of the People Power Tour host city.
- Public Security Equity Dashboard tracking implementation of policy recommendations.

- Community Feedback Forums and Listening Sessions with elected leaders, collecting ongoing input on security challenges and solutions.
- Independent evaluation of program effectiveness conducted by research partners.

This is a defining moment for our movement and our nation. By mobilizing collectively around this comprehensive security framework, we can build communities where Black Americans are truly protected from the full spectrum of contemporary threats. Join us in making America's promise of equal protection a reality for all communities.

Notes

1 Christopher Wray, former Director of the Federal Bureau of Investigation (FBI) from 2017 to 2025, testified before the Senate on March 2, 2021 on the January 6 riot at the U.S. Capitol—"We need to be abundantly clear that the white supremacists and other extremists are the most significant domestic terrorism threat facing the United States today." Wray was nominated by the 47th President and took office on August 2, 2017 to serve a 10-year term as specified by federal law. After his reelection, on November 30, 2024, the 47th President nominated Kash Patel, current Director of the FBI, to replace Christopher Wray. On December 11, 2024, Wray announced he would resign in January 2025, leaving office with the Biden–Harris administration. https://www.rev.com/transcripts/fbi-director-christopher-wray-testifies-on-capitol-attack-domestic-terrorism-full-hearing-transcript-march-2

Bibliography

AARP. (2021). *Consumer Fraud in America: The Black Experience*. AARP Research. https://www.aarp.org/pri/topics/work-finances-retirement/fraud-consumer-protection/scam-experiences-african-american-black/

Anti-Defamation League. (2023). Right-wing extremist terrorism in the United States. https://www.adl.org/resources/report/right-wing-extremist-terrorism-united-states

Bai, N. (2024). *More Black Americans die from the effects of air pollution*. Stanford Medicine News. https://med.stanford.edu/news/all-news/2024/07/more-black-americans-die-from-effects-of-air-pollution.html

Berberian, A. G., Makkar, M., Campos, G. O., Kim, B. J., & Corlette, S. (2022). Racial disparities in climate change-related health effects in the United States. *Current Environmental Health Reports, 9*(3), 451–464. https://www.ncbi.nlm.nih.gov/pmc/articles/PMC9363288/

Cainkar, L. (2009). *Homeland insecurity: The Arab American and Muslim American experience after 9/11*. Russell Sage Foundation.

Consumer Reports. (2024). *Consumer Reports study reveals nearly half of consumers have experienced cyberattacks or digital scams*. https://www.consumerreports.org/media-room/press-releases/2024/10/consumer-reports-study-reveals-nearly-half-of-consumers-have-experienced-cyberattacks-or-digital-scams/

Dahl, K. (2024). *African Americans are disproportionately exposed to extreme heat*. Harvard Primary Care. https://info.primarycare.hms.harvard.edu/perspectives/articles/african-americans-extreme-heat

Dudziak, M. L. (2000). *Cold War civil rights: Race and the image of American democracy*. Princeton University Press.

Federal Trade Commission. (2021). *Serving communities of color: A staff report on the Federal Trade Commission's consumer protection and antitrust initiatives.* https://www.ftc.gov/system/files/documents/reports/serving-communities-color-staff-report-federal-trade-commissions-efforts-address-fraud-consumer/ftc-communities-color-report_oct_2021-508-v2.pdf

Greenblatt, J. (2019). *Russian disinformation trolls targeted Black American voters at an alarming rate.* GQ. https://www.gq.com/story/russian-trolls-targetting-black-voters

Hansen, V. (2022). His mom was killed in a racist attack in Charleston. Now he's helping Buffalo. *NPR*. https://www.npr.org/2022/05/22/1100587931/his-mom-was-killed-in-a-racist-attack-in-charleston-now-hes-helping-buffalo

Howard, P. N., Ganesh, B., Liotsiou, D., Kelly, J., & Francois, C. (2018). *The IRA, social media and political polarization in the United States, 2012–2018*. Computational Propaganda Research Project, University of Oxford.

Human Rights Watch. (2024). Disinformation about US elections targets communities of color. https://www.hrw.org/news/2024/08/15/disinformation-about-us-elections-targets-communities-color

Intelligence Committee of the U.S. Senate. (2019). Report volume 2: Russia's use of social media with additional views (116th Congress, first session). https://intelligence.senate.gov/sites/default/files/documents/Report_Volume2.pdf

Jones, S. G. (2020). The escalating terrorism problem in the United States. *Center for Strategic and International Studies*. https://www.csis.org/analysis/escalating-terrorism-problem-united-states

Julien, J. P., Smith, K. L., Washington, D. C., & Thompson, M. R. (2024). Impacts of climate change on black populations in the United States. *McKinsey Institute for Economic Mobility*. https://www.mckinsey.com/institute-for-economic-mobility/our-insights/impacts-of-climate-change-on-black-populations-in-the-united-states

Kraska, P. B. (2007). Militarization and policing—Its relevance to 21st century police. *Policing: A Journal of Policy and Practice, 1*(4), 501–513. https://doi.org/10.1093/police/pam065

Medical Xpress. (2014). *Extreme Weather Kills 2,000 in U.S. Each Year: CDC*. https://medicalxpress.com/news/2014-07-extreme-weather-year-cdc.html

Medintz, S. (2024). *Digital scams more likely to hurt Black and Latino consumers*. Consumer Reports. https://www.consumerreports.org/money/scams-fraud/black-latino-consumers-more-likely-to-lose-money-in-scams-a7652153980/

Moskos, C. C., & Butler, J. S. (1996). *All that we can be: Black leadership and racial integration the Army way*. Basic Books.

Moye, J. T. (2010). *Freedom flyers: The Tuskegee Airmen of World War II*. Oxford University Press.

Office of the Director of National Intelligence. (2024). Ransomware attacks surge in 2023. https://www.dni.gov/files/CTIIC/documents/products/Ransomware_Attacks_Surge_in_2023.pdf

Petrie, M. (2021). *Consumer fraud in America: The Black experience*. AARP Research. https://www.aarp.org/pri/topics/work-finances-retirement/fraud-consumer-protection/scam-experiences-african-american-black/

Sinnar, S. (2022). *Stanford's Shirin Sinnar on the Buffalo shooting, hate crimes, and domestic terrorism*. Stanford Law School. https://law.stanford.edu/2022/05/16/stanfords-shirin-sinnar-on-the-buffalo-shooting-hate-crimes-and-domestic-terrorism/

Thakur, D., & Hankerson, D. L. (2021). *A research agenda for online disinformation, race, and gender*. Center for Democracy & Technology. https://cdt.org/wp-content/uploads/2021/02/2021-02-10-CDT-Research-Report-on-Disinfo-Race-and-Gender-FINAL.pdf

Theoharis, A. (2018). *A culture of secrecy: The government versus the people's right to know*. University Press of Kansas.

Tisdale, N. (2024). The hidden injustice of cyberattacks. *Wired*. https://www.wired.com/story/cybersecurity-marginalized-communities-problem/

Truecaller. (2024). America under attack: The true cost of spam & scam calls in America. 2024 U.S. spam and scam report. https://publicinterestnetwork.org/wp-content/uploads/2024/10/US-SpamScam-Report_2024_0307.pdf

U.S. Department of Health and Human Services. (2023). 2022 healthcare cybersecurity year in review, and a 2023 look ahead. https://www.hhs.gov/sites/default/files/2022-retrospective-and-2023-look-ahead.pdf

U.S. Department of Homeland Security. (2024). Homeland threat assessment 2025. https://www.dhs.gov/sites/default/files/2024-10/24_0930_ia_24-320-ia-publication-2025-hta-final-30sep24-508.pdf

U.S. Environmental Protection Agency. (2021a). Black and African American communities and climate change. https://www.epa.gov/system/files/documents/2021-11/factsheet_black-and-african-american.pdf

U.S. Environmental Protection Agency. (2021b). *Climate change and social vulnerability in the United States: A focus on six impacts (EPA 430-R-21-003)*. https://www.epa.gov/system/files/documents/2021-09/climate-vulnerability_september-2021_508.pdf

U.S. Office of the Director of National Intelligence. (2024). Ransomware attacks surge in 2023. https://www.dni.gov/files/CTIIC/documents/products/Ransomware_Attacks_Surge_in_2023.pdf

U.S. Senate, Select Committee on Intelligence. (2019). *Report on the Select Committee on Intelligence, United States Senate, on Russian active measures campaigns and interference in the 2012 U.S. election, Volume 2: Russia's use of social media with additional views (S. Rep. No. 116-290)*. U.S. Government Publishing Office.

U.S. Senate, Select Committee to Study Governmental Operations with Respect to Intelligence Activities. (1976). *Final report: Book II, intelligence activities and the rights of Americans*. Washington, DC: U.S. Government Printing Office.

Section VII

Public Safety & Justice

This section confronts the fundamental truth that policing and criminal justice systems in America were never designed to keep Black people safe but rather to control, contain, and extract from Black communities—from slave patrols through convict leasing to contemporary mass incarceration. Together, these Black Papers demonstrate that achieving genuine public safety requires not reforming systems working precisely as designed but abolishing carceral logics while building community-led alternatives rooted in prevention, healing, accountability, and collective care.

"Policing in America: Reimagining Public Safety in Black Communities" establishes that punitively policing Black people and Black bodies is as American as apple pie, tracing modern policing's roots in slave patrols that treated Black people as property requiring control and surveillance. This Black Paper documents how criminal statutes expanded to criminalize normal behaviors from "willful defiance" in classrooms to "loitering" in neighborhoods, increasing the probability of police interactions disproportionately enforced in Black communities. While brutality at the hands of violent officers disproportionately affects Black people, fewer than 2% of police officers face accountability—with current national leadership seeking to diminish oversight further. The analysis presents data revealing that Black Americans are killed by police at 2.5 times the rate of white Americans, that use-of-force incidents concentrate in Black neighborhoods regardless of crime rates, and that traffic stops function as pretextual mechanisms for surveillance, generating billions in fines and fees extracted from Black communities. This Black Paper argues transformation requires a paradigm shift from seeing police as warriors to recognizing communities as worthy of genuine safety, presenting alternatives, including community-based crisis response teams like CAHOOTS in Eugene showing 5–8% decrease in arrests while saving $8.5 million annually, violence interrupters addressing conflicts before escalation, and investments in economic security, mental health services, and youth programs addressing root causes rather than punishing symptoms.

"Unshackling Our People: Ending Mass Incarceration Through Community Power and Policy Transformation" documents how nearly 2 million people

DOI: 10.4324/9781003752646-29

remain incarcerated in America today—a 900% increase since 1925—with Black Americans comprising 33% of the prison population despite being only 13% of the United States population. This Black Paper traces the throughline from slavery's legal codification of Black subjugation through Black Codes criminalizing poverty and autonomy after emancipation, Jim Crow's legalized segregation, the War on Drugs' targeted criminalization despite similar drug use rates across races, to contemporary mass incarceration functioning as a mechanism of racial and economic control. The analysis reveals how mandatory minimums and three-strikes laws created permanent punishment for nonviolent offenses, how cash bail keeps 450,000 unconvicted people caged daily because they cannot afford freedom, how private prison corporations profit billions while extracting wealth from Black families through commissary charges and phone rates, and how formerly incarcerated people face lifetime barriers to employment, housing, voting, and public benefits creating permanent underclass. This Black Paper presents a comprehensive framework for decarceration through prevention, investing in housing and education, diversion, expanding community alternatives, elimination of mandatory minimums and cash bail, restoration centering directly impacted leadership in reentry, and abolition building power through coalition strategy—providing an eight-year implementation roadmap from 2025 through 2033, achieving a 75% reduction in incarceration.

"How We Keep Us Safe: A Guide on Gun Safety for Black Communities" addresses gun violence as the leading cause of death for Black youth while acknowledging the complex relationship between Black communities and firearms rooted in histories of both racist disarmament and armed self-defense during the civil rights struggle. This Black Paper documents that Black Americans experience gun homicide at rates eight times higher than white Americans, that Black women face intimate partner gun violence at disproportionate rates, and that Black trans women are murdered at alarming rates, often with firearms—yet also recognizes that some Black communities view gun ownership as protection given the state's failure to ensure safety. The analysis presents comprehensive prevention strategies, including community violence interruption programs like Cure Violence, showing 40–70% reductions in shootings, hospital-based violence intervention programs providing wraparound services to shooting survivors, reducing reinjury, economic opportunity initiatives addressing root causes, trauma-informed mental health services, and extreme risk protection orders allowing temporary firearm removal during crisis. For gun owners, this Black Paper provides secure storage guidance, emphasizes child access prevention, and highlights Black-led organizations like BlackGunsLivesMatter offering culturally competent safety training. This framework refuses both dismissing legitimate safety concerns and accepting gun violence as inevitable, instead demanding investments in prevention, intervention, and healing that actually keep Black people safe.

Together, these Black Papers refuse the premise that safety requires cages, that justice demands punishment, or that Black communities need control rather than care. They challenge readers to recognize that every dollar spent on policing and incarceration represents resources stolen from education, housing, healthcare, and community programs that actually create conditions for thriving. This section articulates public safety not as the absence of Black people from public space but as the presence of resources supporting life, not as a threat of violence from armed enforcers but as community capacity to address harm through accountability and healing, not as systems extracting from Black communities but as collective power-building alternatives. From reimagining policing through community-based crisis response to abolishing cash bail and ending mass incarceration, from community violence interruption to comprehensive gun safety strategies that honor Black communities' complex relationship with firearms, these Black Papers present both immediate harm reduction strategies and long-term abolitionist vision—honoring the truth that we need both the radical and the right now, that binary thinking serves oppression while expansive solutions build liberation.

Chapter 22

Policing in America

Reimagining Public Safety in Black Communities

Brittany Packnett Cunningham

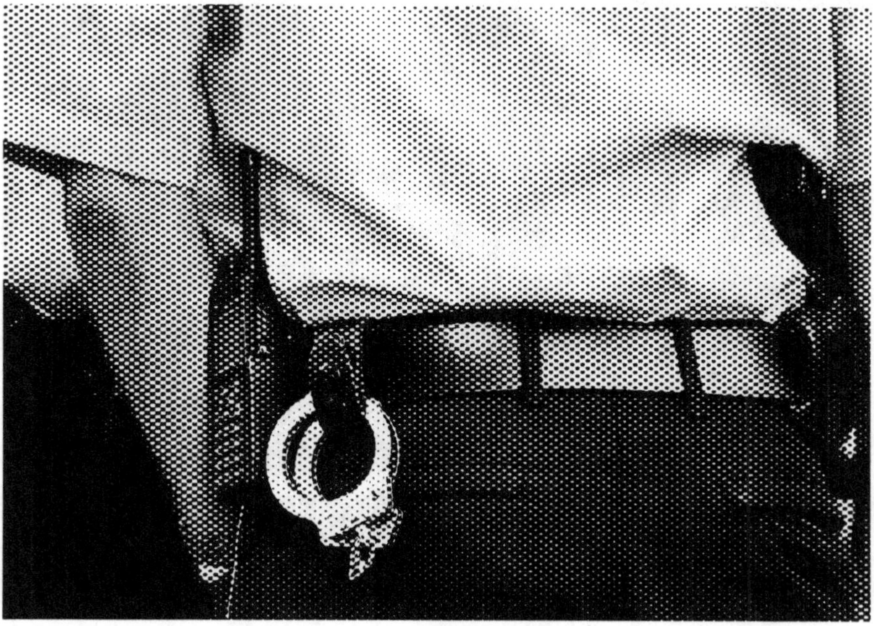

Policing has never been—and will never be—a neutral proposition for Black people in America. The concept of "public safety" too often excludes keeping us, our neighbors, or our communities safe. Policing has historically protected the rest of America—and her property—from us (Alexander, 2020). As scholars of carceral studies note, "Public safety as conceived and implemented in the United States has prioritized the protection of white property and social order over the bodily autonomy of Black communities" (Ritchie & Ritchie, 2021). As we examine the real, unadulterated State of the People, one must begin here: punitively policing Black people and Black bodies is as American as apple pie.

DOI: 10.4324/9781003752646-30

This systemic truth extends far beyond individual actors. While police departments have often lacked diversity and harbored avowed white supremacists in their ranks, the entire system itself demands scrutiny (Bell, 2023). Recent data from the Washington Post's Fatal Force database shows that police kill Black Americans at more than twice the rate of white Americans, a disparity that has persisted despite years of protests and calls for reform (Washington Post, 2023). Modern policing's roots in "slave patrols" have created institutions that too often replicate the treatment of Black people as property and our bodies as sources of free—or cheap—labor to be controlled, collected, and conditioned to create American capital (Hadden, 2001; Roberts, 2022).

When we examine the African American protest tradition, the role of police in managing the boundaries of the state is clear. Police punish protesters as soldiers would an insurrection, but only when that resistance is Black (Kelley, 2016). The disparate response to racial justice protests following George Floyd's murder compared to its response during the January 6, 2021 insurrection on Capitol Hill terrifyingly exemplify this continuing double standard in the policing of public assembly (Glawe, 2023). From "willful defiance" in classrooms to "loitering" in neighborhoods, criminal statutes have expanded to include normal child and adult behaviors, increasing the probability of police interactions, with enforcement disproportionately targeting Black communities (Kaba, 2020; Butler, 2021). Research from the Sentencing Project (2023) documents that Black youth are over four times more likely than their white peers to be detained or committed to juvenile facilities, with school discipline policies serving as primary drivers of this "school-to-prison pipeline." (Sentencing Project, 2023).

While brutality at the hands of the most violent police officers disproportionately affects Black people, fewer than 2% of police officers ever face accountability. What is worse is that the current national leadership seeks to diminish this already minimal oversight (Mapping Police Violence, 2023). The Police Crime Database reveals that between 2005 and 2022, only 165 officers were charged with murder or manslaughter for on-duty killings, despite thousands of fatal police shootings during this period (Stinson & Wentzlof, 2023).

What America needs—and Black America requires—is a fundamental paradigm shift from seeing police as warriors to recognizing our communities as worthy of genuine safety. True public safety emerges not from increased surveillance and punishment, but from investment in community resources, mental health services, education, housing stability, and economic opportunity (McDowell & Fernandez, 2022). These Papers, including the Paper on Policing and Police Violence, constitute a complete and revolutionary reimagining of public safety, thoughtfully examining each step toward transformation.

Though the strategies, tactics, and approaches throughout this section may appear varied, collectively they acknowledge the complexity of Black America's relationship with a system fragmented among 18,000 local departments and confusingly divided between municipal, state, and federal jurisdictions (Edwards et al., 2019). Together, these Black Papers honor two concurrent truths:

1. **The Necessity of Radical Reconstitution**: Nothing less than a radical reconstitution of public safety will suffice to ensure the future safety of Black America, her children, and her children's children. This reimagining must include abolition of jails, prisons, and policing as we know it—not to destroy what exists, but to make room to fund and create what we need (Ritchie & Ritchie, 2021; Wang, 2022).
2. **Addressing Immediate Needs**: On the path to the radical, the ***right now*** still exists. We cannot build the ideal without addressing the material needs of our communities in the present, reducing harm, risk, and the opportunity for violence to occur (Taylor, 2016; Gilmore, 2022).

Some may argue that immediate reforms lack a radical orientation. Others may say radical visions disregard pressing needs. To this, we respond: just like the expansiveness of our promise as a people, our solutions must live in the both/and. Binary outlooks and either/or thinking are tools of white supremacy designed to deepen disagreement rather than foster repair. We ask that you consider the totality of these chapters—and The Black Papers in their entirety—as you use them to inform your work. For it is together—with all our best ideas and most communal engagement—that we will get free.

References

Alexander, M. (2020). *The new Jim Crow: Mass incarceration in the age of colorblindness* (10th anniversary ed.). The New Press.

Bell, M. C. (2023). Anti-Blackness as official policy: How municipal governance produces and legitimizes patterns of Black exclusion. *Georgetown Law Journal, 112*(1), 1–58.

Butler, P. (2021). *Chokehold: Policing Black men*. The New Press.

Edwards, F., Lee, H., & Esposito, M. (2019). Risk of being killed by police use of force in the United States by age, race-ethnicity, and sex. *Proceedings of the National Academy of Sciences, 116*(34), 16793–16798.

Gilmore, R. W. (2022). *Abolition geography: Essays towards liberation*. Verso Books.

Glawe, J. (2023). *Unequal force: Measuring disparities in police response to protests*. Urban Institute.

Hadden, S. E. (2001). *Slave patrols: Law and violence in Virginia and the Carolinas*. Harvard University Press.

Kaba, M. (2020). Yes, we mean literally abolish the police. *The New York Times*. https://www.nytimes.com/2020/06/12/opinion/sunday/floyd-abolish-defund-police.html

Kelley, R. D. G. (2016). *Freedom dreams: The Black radical imagination*. Beacon Press.

Mapping Police Violence. (2023). Police accountability in the United States: Annual report 2023.

McDowell, M. G., & Fernandez, L. A. (2022). Alternative forms of safety and security: Community-based approaches as resistance. *Social Justice, 49*(1–2), 1–15.

Ritchie, A. J., & Ritchie, B. E. (2021). *The crisis of criminalization: A call for a comprehensive philanthropic response*. Barnard Center for Research on Women.

Roberts, D. (2022). *Torn apart: How the child welfare system destroys Black families—and how abolition can build a safer world*. Basic Books.

Sentencing Project. (2023). Racial disparities in youth incarceration persist. https://www.sentencingproject.org/publications/racial-disparities-in-youth-incarceration-persist/

Stinson, P. M., & Wentzlof, C. A. (2023). On-duty shootings: Police officers charged with murder or manslaughter, 2005–2022. *Criminal Justice Faculty Publications, 116*(1), 1–15.

Taylor, K-Y. (2016). *From #BlackLivesMatter to Black liberation*. Haymarket Books.

Wang, J. (2022). *Against innocence: Race, gender, and the politics of safety*. Haymarket Books.

Washington Post. (2023). Fatal Force: Police shootings database. https://www.washingtonpost.com/graphics/investigations/police-shootings-database/

Chapter 23

Unshackling Our People

Ending Mass Incarceration through Community Power and Policy Transformation

Caitlin Radigan, Kirsten F. Wilder, Jada Capri Ward, Jasmine Esquilin, Roshana Agarrat, Kelcey P. Morrow, and Nadia French-Graham

Executive Summary

Nearly two million people are incarcerated in America today, representing a 900% increase since 1925. Black Americans comprise 33% of the prison population despite being only 13% of the United States population. This is not coincidental; it is the direct result of policies designed to replace slavery and Jim Crow with a new system of racialized control.

DOI: 10.4324/9781003752646-31

This Black Paper (Paper) presents a comprehensive framework for ending mass incarceration through:

- **Prevention**: Investing in housing, education, and healing-centered programs.
- **Diversion**: Expanding community-based alternatives and decriminalizing survival behaviors.
- **Decarceration**: Repealing mandatory minimums, eliminating cash bail, and closing detention centers.
- **Restoration**: Centering directly impacted leadership in reentry and policy design.
- **Abolition**: Building power through coalition strategy and popular education.

Addressing the impact of mass incarceration on Black people requires federal, state, and local action—from repealing the 1994 Crime Bill to funding restorative justice hubs. Most importantly, our work requires that we reject the narrative that incarcerated people are beyond redemption. Our people are brilliant, resilient, and deserve liberation.

An Urgent Call to Action

The effects of mass incarceration on our communities and society can no longer be ignored. Nearly two million people—many of whom identify as

Black or Latino—wake up every day in jails and prisons across the United States (Vera Institute of Justice, 2024). Every day, incarceration separates families, destabilizes communities, and wastes human potential. Each day we delay dismantling mass incarceration is another day we remain trapped in a vicious cycle that has persisted for nearly two centuries in this country. This Paper is not just a policy paper—it is an urgent call to action for anyone who believes in justice, dignity, and liberation. It is a call to all who believe in restoration and rehabilitation over punishment and destruction.

Introduction: The Incarceration Nation

Mass incarceration in the United States is not simply a failure of the criminal justice system—it is a continuation of racialized control of Black and Brown communities that's rooted in the legacy of slavery and segregation. The United States incarcerates more people than any other country in the world. Yet the racialized foundation of this carceral state is often overlooked or entirely ignored in public discourse. This Paper affirms what generations of scholars, organizers, and community leaders have long asserted: that the struggle against mass incarceration is a struggle for Black liberation rooted in unbiased and unobscured truth.

The framing of mass incarceration as a racial justice issue requires more than a shift in language. It calls for a radical reimagining of our societal values. As Michelle Alexander (2020) argues in *The New Jim Crow,* mass incarceration represents a new replication of racial caste in America. A system designed not to manage crime, but to criminalize Blackness. Blackness, as articulated by Khalil Gibran Muhammad in *The Condemnation of Blackness,* refers to a constructed concept used to justify discriminatory practices against Black Americans through associations with criminality. Through racially discriminatory laws, policing practices, and public policies, the system has manufactured a permanent underclass, labeling people "felons" and stripping them of rights, dignity, and a sense of belonging within society. Mass incarceration has shifted from a means of controlling crime to a means of controlling Black and other minoritized communities and our way of life.

The scope of this phenomenon is evident in the data. In 1925, fewer than 200,000 people were incarcerated in the United States. Today, nearly two million people are incarcerated—an increase of almost 900% over the past century (Vera Institute of Justice, 2024). Black Americans, who comprise only 13% of the United States population, make up 33% of the sentenced prison population (Alexander, 2020). These disparities are not coincidental. They result from deliberate policy decisions that disproportionately target and incarcerate Black communities.

In *The Condemnation of Blackness*, Khalil Gibran Muhammad (2010) illustrates how the criminalization of Black communities was constructed through distorted data and public discourse in the early 20th century, laying the groundwork for today's racialized punishment system. Muhammad notes that in the late 20th century, white sociologists, scholars, and researchers used data collected from cities and areas with large Black populations to justify claims of intellectual inferiority and alleged increased crime. Although subsequent research and analysis have exposed the inaccuracies of these conclusions, these harmful narratives continue to shape policies that surveil and punish, rather than invest in healing and restoration.

Mass incarceration has perpetuated a narrative that people who are incarcerated are unproductive, harmful, and undeserving of the same respect afforded to those who have never been imprisoned.

We reject that narrative.

We reject the myth that people who have been incarcerated are broken or dangerous. We reject the notion that people who are (or were) formerly incarcerated are beyond redemption. We know they are brilliant, creative, and resourceful. They are deserving of dignity and second chances. Our communities have always turned pain into power, resistance into resilience, and survival into vision. It is time for our policies to reflect that truth, and for our society to see that potential in us.

This Paper aims to uplift that truth by advancing a liberatory framework that challenges mass incarceration at its roots. This is not a call for incremental reform but a radical reining of justice. We write with urgency and conviction, recognizing that each day we delay restructuring this system is another day someone's potential remains locked away.

It should be noted that the system is not broken, but rather intentionally built the way it operates today. Yet those committed to liberation and restoration intend to dismantle this system and replace it with one rooted in healing, accountability, and meaningful reintegration.

What We Mean by Abolition

Abolition is both a long-term goal and a strategic framework. It calls for completely rethinking how safety and accountability work in our society. Rather than relying on prisons, jails, detention centers, and traditional policing, abolition focuses on building systems of care, healing, and community support. At its core, abolition means addressing the real causes of harm—poverty, trauma, and lack of resources—rather than punishing people for the symptoms of those problems. It also recognizes that the current system cannot simply be reformed because it is working as it was designed—to control and harm Black communities.

Abolition does not mean immediately closing all prisons or abandoning accountability. It is not unrealistic or disconnected from other struggles. Abolition is deeply tied to the movements for housing, healthcare, education, and economic justice. As scholar and activist Ruth Wilson Gilmore explains, abolition is "presence, not absence." Abolition is about creating life-affirming institutions while simultaneously dismantling systems that produce harm. Abolition poses a simple, yet powerful question: What must be built to render prisons obsolete? The answer is clear—communities where everyone has housing, healthcare, education, meaningful work, and belonging, and where harm is addressed through healing and transformation rather than punishment. While these forms of community already exist in limited ways, abolition calls for their expansion until they become the norm rather than the exception.

Historical Context: From Chains to Cells

Mass incarceration in the United States cannot be understood in isolation; it must be seen as the latest chapter in a long history of racialized social control. From slavery to the modern prison system, racial oppression has consistently adapted to the legal and cultural norms of each era.

Following emancipation, Reconstruction began to rehabilitate the nation after the Civil War and extend civil rights and opportunities for the newly freed enslaved population. However, to maintain control over the Black people and keep them disenfranchised, Southern states enacted the Black Codes. The Black Codes imposed severe limitations on Black people's freedom, criminalizing everyday activities under vague charges such as "vagrancy"[1] and "loitering," while reinforcing white political and economic dominance in the South. These laws facilitated mass arrests and allowed the state to lease Black labor to private industries through convict leasing—a system that re-enslaved people under the guise of punishment (Davis, 2003). It is estimated that by the 1870s, 95% of the people arrested in Southern states were Black (Vera Institute of Justice, 2024).

During the Reconstruction and Progressive eras, a series of developments intensified the disenfranchisement and criminalization of Black people. First, as documented by Muhammad (2010), Progressive Era researchers misinterpreted health, crime, and mortality data comparing Black and white populations to justify claims of Black inferiority and to rationalize higher crime rates in predominantly Black communities. Second, court decisions in cases such as *Plessy* v. *Ferguson*[2] validated the "separate but equal" doctrine, ushering in the Jim Crow era. The rise of Jim Crow laws entrenched racial segregation and disenfranchisement, permitting separate and unequal treatment while further criminalizing Black life. Simultaneously, the continued emergence of "scientific racism" framed Blackness as inherently criminal, embedding racist assumptions into criminology and public policy (Muhammad, 2010).

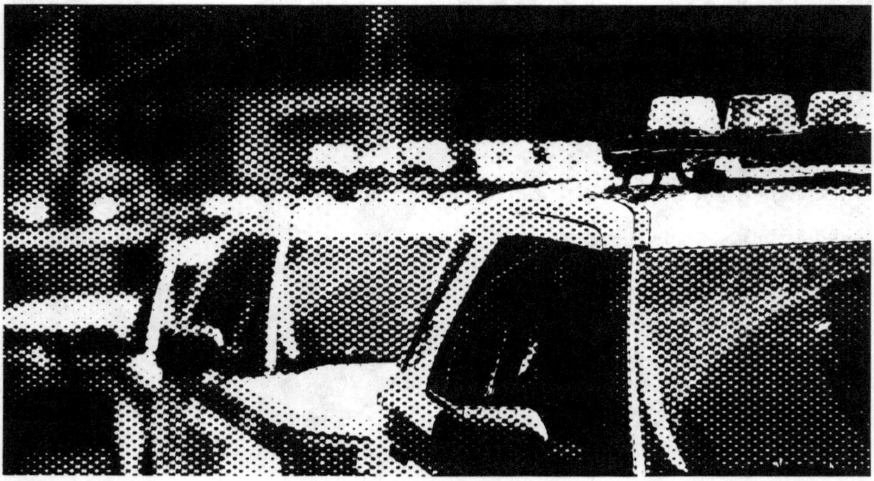

By the late 20th century, the Civil Rights era ushered in laws and policies that demolished Jim Crow. However, practices designed to maintain Black disenfranchisement and incarceration were swiftly modernized rather than eliminated. The War on Drugs, launched under President Richard Nixon and escalated under Ronald Reagan, George H.W. Bush Sr., and Bill Clinton, was set in motion as a way to combat illegal drug use, distribution, and exchange. Through racially coded language, legislation, financial incentives, and even the distribution of military-grade weapons, incarceration rates expanded massively across nearly two and a half decades. As noted by Alexander (2020), from 1985 to 2000, offenses connected to drugs led to two-thirds of the increase in the population of federal prisons, and over half of the state prison population increase. By 1991, one in four Black men was under the supervision of the criminal justice system (Alexander, 2020). There were significant increases in traffic stops, sweeps, and raids in an attempt to find "suspected" illegal drug activity, though many of these actions barely yielded any significant drug finds (Alexander, 2020). Despite similar rates of drug use across racial groups, Black people were disproportionately arrested and sentenced through mandatory minimums, "three strikes" laws,[3] lack of access to quality legal representation, and pressure to take plea deals to avoid heftier sentencing (Alexander, 2020; Forman, 2017).

Modern policing has continued this legacy. Strategies such as broken-windows policing, stop-and-frisk, and surveillance technologies have kept Black communities under constant scrutiny and state violence (Vitale, 2017). Contemporary policing increasingly relies on surveillance technologies that amplify racial bias and expand carceral control. These technologies include facial recognition, predictive policing algorithms, electronic monitoring, and social media tracking. Often developed for military applications, these technologies treat Black neighborhoods and communities as territories requiring constant surveillance rather than deserving investment and care. As noted in a report by Ghandnoosh (2023), Black Americans experience higher police encounters through traffic stops, pedestrian stops, and school policing. Police officers tend to engage in investigatory traffic stops with Black Americans over infractions such as failures to signal, malfunctioning car lights, or expired licenses. These patterns have resulted in higher rates of police stops involving Black drivers, increased investigatory stops among Black drivers under the age of 40, and elevated levels of distrust toward law enforcement.

The criminalization of Blackness is not limited to legal punishment—it is a cultural and psychological project. It marks Black people as dangerous, shaping social stigma that extends into housing, education, employment, healthcare, and civic life. Once labeled a "felon," Black Americans face legalized discrimination and exclusion from public benefits, voting rights, and economic opportunity (Alexander, 2020).

The consequences of incarceration are multigenerational. Children of incarcerated parents experience trauma, instability, and often incarceration themselves. Entire communities are left devastated by cycles of surveillance and imprisonment. These harms are not isolated events but manifestations of systemic racial trauma (Kaba & Ritchie, 2022).

Mass incarceration did not emerge in response to rising crime rates. It arose to fill the void left by the legal end of slavery, Jim Crow, and segregation. As Angela Davis (2003) explains, the prison system was never about public safety—it was about suppressing Black resistance and containing the consequences of inequality.

The highest incarceration rates occur in communities most devastated by economic divestment and historical neglect. These communities are areas with higher poverty rates, lower opportunities, and people of specific demographics. High incarceration rates also persist in regions that economically depend on incarceration for profit. However, places that venture into building bigger or more jails do not always consider the costs of building and maintaining a jail, especially when the profit does not equal the price.

Incarceration is not a malfunction of the justice system. It is *the* function of a system designed to manage and control Black life. It is a system that must be dismantled and replaced with one that genuinely protects communities and promotes collective wellbeing.

Legacy of Slavery → Black Codes → JimCrow → WaronDrugs →
Modern Policing

The throughline from slavery to present-day mass incarceration reveals a consistent structure of racial control:

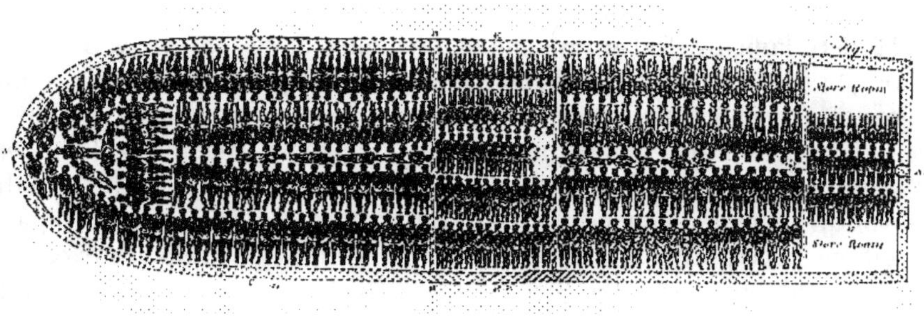

1. **Legacy of Slavery**: During the Trans-Atlantic Slave Trade, approximately 12.5 million Africans were forcibly taken from their land to the Americas. The system of slavery built a racial caste system that dehumanized Black people and embedded racialized economic and social hierarchies. Even after abolition, institutions, including universities, profited from its legacy (Council of Independent Colleges). Furthermore, it was common during this era that captured runaway enslaved people and people who dared to aid them were thrown into local prisons before they were returned to their white slaveholders or faced the cruel penalties of the law.
2. **Black Codes**: During the Civil War, President Abraham Lincoln signed the Emancipation Proclamation, effectively ending the legal practice of slavery in the United States. After Emancipation and during the period of Reconstruction, Southern states enacted laws called Black Codes to constrain Black mobility and labor. These codes criminalized poverty and autonomy, continued forced labor under the guise of legal order, and essentially kept Black Americans at the mercy of White Americans. (History.com Editors, 2022). It comes as no surprise that with practices like these, the population of incarcerated individuals at this time was primarily Black Americans.
3. **Jim Crow Laws**: Post-Black Code era, Jim Crow laws were designed between the late 19th century and early 20th century. These laws were created in response to legal decisions that upheld the idea of separate but equal institutions, as well as ideas of Black people's inferiority made from biased and misconstrued research. These laws legalized segregation and enforced racial hierarchies across all aspects of life, embedding white supremacy into law and culture (Encyclopedia Britannica, n.d.).
4. **The War on Drugs**: Enacted in the 1970s under President Richard Nixon, the War on Drugs was formed to combat the use of illegal drugs that was becoming standard practice across the United States. However, it should be noted that this campaign disproportionately criminalized Black and

Brown communities, despite similar drug use rates across races. Policies like mandatory minimums and three-strikes laws deepened racial disparities in incarceration (Drug Policy Alliance, 2015). They led to a massive increase in the country's incarcerated population within two and a half decades (Alexander, 2020).

5 **Modern Policing**: Today, policing in the United States has evolved from its origins in slave patrols,[4] and continues to use practices steeped in systemic racism. Black communities face disproportionate surveillance, violence, and incarceration, reinforcing longstanding racial inequities. In recent years, thanks to the actions of the Black Lives Matter Movement and the worldwide media attention given to the murder of George Floyd,[5] organizations have pushed for policies that call for the dissolution of excessive force and targeting of the Black community. However, now that the 47th presidential administration has pushed for an increase in police monitoring and militarization of our communities, the fight against racist policing practices is back to the same hurdle it has fought for over a century and a half (American Civil Liberties Union, 2018).

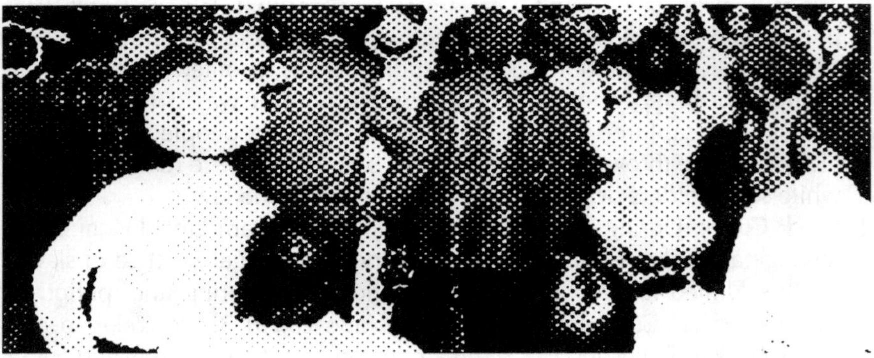

The Digital Carceral State: Technology as Control

Modern policing increasingly relies on surveillance technologies that extend state control beyond prison walls and deepen racial bias. Facial recognition systems, for example, misidentify Black faces at far higher rates than white faces, leading to wrongful arrests and privacy violations. Clearview AI and similar companies have built databases of billions of faces without consent, disproportionately targeting Black communities. Predictive policing tools such as PredPol claim to prevent crime but instead recycle historical arrest data, repeatedly directing police to the same over-policed Black neighborhoods. Similarly, risk-assessment algorithms such as COMPAS have been shown to label Black defendants as higher-risk than white defendants, even when their criminal histories are comparable.

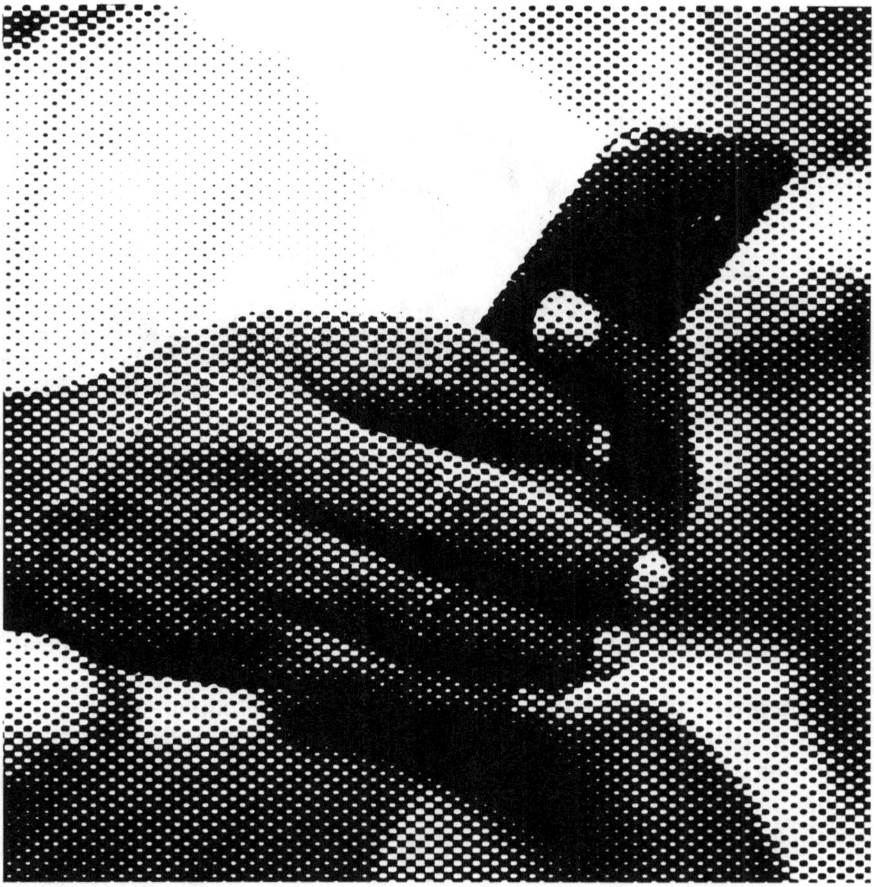

Electronic monitoring and social media surveillance expand this digital web. People subject to electronic monitoring face extensive restrictions, high fees, and punishment for minor technical issues. At the same time, law enforcement increasingly monitors online speech and associations—particularly among Black and Brown youth. Together, these technologies turn entire communities into sites of constant surveillance rather than places for investment and care, creating a digital extension of the same system that drives mass incarceration.

The Mass Incarceration Price Tag

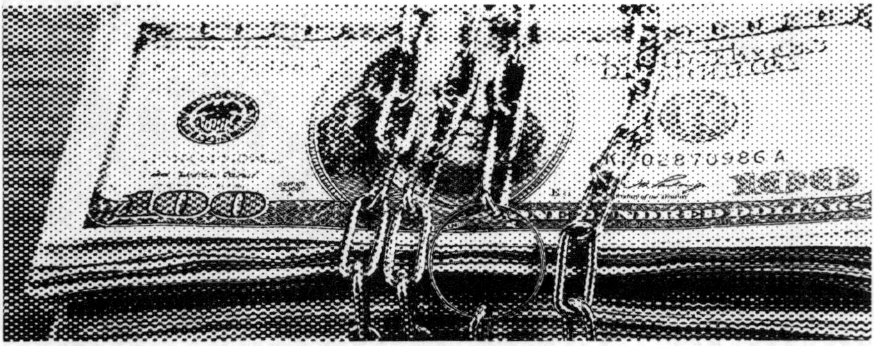

Mass incarceration is a form of economic control. It extracts wealth from Black and Brown communities through fines, fees, bail, commissary profits, and unpaid prison labor.

The prison industrial complex generates billions in profit while impoverishing the communities it claims to serve. People and families who support incarcerated people too often struggle to make their own basic needs while managing the financial needs of their family members or loved ones locked away.

Furthermore, prisons built on the idea that they will provide for the community actually drive the community into deeper poverty (Seligman & Nam-Sonenstein, 2024). Economic justice requires not just ending mass incarceration but dismantling the extractive economic relationships that sustain it.

The financial burden of incarceration extends beyond prison walls. Families spend a total of $5.6 billion annually on commissary deposits, prison accounts, and other direct support for necessities and other items their family members might need (Elderbroom et al., 2025). These costs disproportionately impact Black families, who have significantly lower median wealth than white families. Meanwhile, corporations capitalize on this suffering, charging families up to $25 for a 15-minute phone call and inflating commissary prices by as much as 600% (Weill-Greenberg & Corey, 2024). These exploitative practices show that mass incarceration has become a means of social control—keeping people locked away while imposing a crushing financial burden on those who support them.

Criminalization, Control, and Generational Trauma

Mass incarceration is not simply a consequence of crime—it is a calculated system of racialized social control that criminalizes Black identity and perpetuates generational harm. Maxine Dennis, in "The Criminalization of Blackness," reveals how the systemic devaluation of Black life fosters internalized oppression, leading individuals to internalize blame and shape a collective experience of trauma. She argues that the justice system not only targets Black bodies but constructs Blackness itself as inherently criminal, creating psychological and social wounds that are passed down through generations (Dennis, 2020).

This criminalization is not accidental. As Learning for Justice explains, in "Mass Incarceration as a Form of Racialized Social Control," the United States justice system continues the legacy of slavery and Jim Crow by reinforcing racial hierarchies through incarceration. Mass incarceration serves as a modern tool for managing marginalized populations under the guise of law and order through:

- **Disenfranchisement**: Felony convictions strip voting rights, diminishing Black political power.
- **Legal Discrimination**: Criminal records legitimize discrimination in employment, housing, education, and public benefits.
- **Over-Policing**: Black neighborhoods experience disproportionate policing, arrests, and surveillance.
- **Media & Political Narratives**: Racialized depictions of criminality fuel public support for harmful policies.

Current Landscape: The Data Behind the Crisis

Pretrial detention has increased by 433% from 1970 to 2015, primarily driven by the expansion of monetary bail systems that disproportionately impact marginalized communities. Black men, women, and LGBTQ+ youth are disproportionately detained pretrial due to an inability to afford bail, which contributes to poorer case outcomes and destabilizing consequences, including job loss, housing insecurity, and an increased risk of future incarceration (Woods & Khan, 2023).

Black Americans represent 13.7% of the United States population, yet they account for over 38% of the total incarcerated population and 46% of people serving sentences of at least ten years (Ghandnoosh et al., 2022). In 2022, among every 100,000 people, 1,826 were Black men, and 64 were Black women, compared to 337 white men and 40 white women (Korhonen, 2024).

Disparities among youth are similarly staggering. Although Black youth comprise only 15% of the total United States population, they account for 46% of the youth incarcerated nationally. Today, the youth incarceration rate was 87 per 100,000, but for Black youth, the rate soared to 293 per 100,000, compared to 49 for white youth (Rovner, 2025).

Intersectional Impact: LGBTQ+, Women, and People with Disabilities

Mass incarceration disproportionately harms people who exist at the intersections of multiple marginalized identities. LGBTQ+ people, particularly Black trans women, are an example of one of those marginalized communities. According to The Sentencing Project (2022), members of the LGBTQ+ community are incarcerated at rates three times higher than the overall adult population. Recent national data suggests that over 90,000 people who identify as gay, lesbian, or bisexual were in prisons, with an additional 34,000 more individuals in jail (The Sentencing Project, 2022). LGBTQ+ people face heightened criminalization through laws targeting sex work, homelessness, and gender expression. Once incarcerated, LGBTQ+ people—especially transgender people—are at heightened risk of daily humiliation, physical and sexual abuse, and prolonged solitary confinement, often denied gender-affirming care and protection, with non-heterosexual prisoners three times more likely to report sexual abuse than others (Marksamer & Tobin, 2013).

Women represent the fastest-growing incarcerated population, with rates increasing by 700% since 1980 (The Sentencing Project, 2018). According to a 2024 report from the Prison Policy Initiative, approximately 196,000 women and girls are currently incarcerated in the United States. An additional 93,000 women are held in local jails, and 9,000 women are held in federal agencies, such as United States Immigration and Customs Enforcement (ICE) centers and United States Marshall Services (Kajstura & Sawyer, 2024). Black women are incarcerated at twice the rate of white women, often for survival-related offenses linked to poverty, domestic violence, homelessness, and substance use. LGBTQ+ women face severe overrepresentation in the United States carceral system. While only about 3.4% of the general female population identifies as lesbian or bisexual, over 33% to 42% of women in state prisons identify as lesbian, bisexual, or queer, (Jones, 2021) a disproportionate amount of them identifying as Black. The statistics are similar for queer girls in the juvenile justice system. Furthermore, data on the incarceration rates of women in the United States are limited. These limitations are linked to disruptions from the COVID-19 pandemic, the increased attention given to data of incarcerated men, and the limited sources not regularly updated by researchers and data scientists (Kajstura & Sawyer, 2024).

While in prison, women are subjected to mistreatment, abuse, and sometimes inhumane treatment. Examples of this mistreatment include lack of access to menstrual products, increased health issues due to being in unhygienic facilities, and even physical and sexual assault from corrections officers and inmates (Abasguliyeva et al., 2024). Even vulnerable medical conditions, like pregnancy, do not protect incarcerated women from abuse in prisons. Pregnant women in prison may be shackled during labor and separated from their newborns, perpetuating cycles of family separation and exacerbating psychological trauma.

Another highly vulnerable population within the incarcerated system includes people living with disabilities and mental health challenges, with an estimated 32% of incarcerated people reporting at least one disability (Legal Center for Youth Justice and Education, 2020). Over half of the population in prisons and jails struggles with a mental illness, and they often receive solitary confinement and punishment through physical force instead of the appropriate treatment that they need. When mental illness is criminalized rather than treated, jails become one of the largest mental health institutions in the country. This tragic reality reflects a fundamental failure to provide community-based care and support.

Juvenile Justice and Foster Care Pipelines

An example of one of those systems is foster care. The foster care-to-prison pipeline remains a significant pathway through which youth, especially Black youth, are criminalized early. It is estimated that approximately 90% of foster youth will have contact with the juvenile justice system before exiting the child welfare system (Juvenile Law Center, 2018). Many foster youth experience trauma, instability, and behavioral challenges that frequently result in law enforcement involvement. Historical patterns of Black family disruption through systems like Child Protective Services contribute to overrepresentation in both foster care and juvenile justice systems (Arredondo et al., 2014).

When systems default to probation rather than providing systems of care, probation fuels the foster care to prison pipeline. When a young person is placed on probation, they must meet requirements established by the judge. Probation requirements can include curfews, check-ins, mandatory community service, and restitution (The Annie E. Casey Foundation, 2021). Though intended as an alternative to incarceration, probation often extends surveillance, particularly for Black and Brown youth. Many are punished not for new crimes but for technical violations like missing appointments, transportation struggles, or unstable housing.

According to the "End Endless Probation" report, youth of color are disproportionately placed on probation, and, once placed, they remain under supervision longer than their white peers. These extended supervision periods delay critical developmental milestones like graduation, employment, or housing stability, and instead increase the risk of re-involvement with the justice system. For foster youth—who already lack consistent adult support—this approach exacerbates trauma, reinforces institutionalization, and delays self-sufficiency.

Unfortunately, probation, oftentimes, becomes a trap within the system of mass incarceration instead of a path toward rehabilitation. In addition, research has shown that being in a supervised probation program has little impact on stopping delinquent behavior or the potential of reoffending (The Annie E. Casey Foundation, 2021). Probation penalizes the symptoms of poverty and systemic neglect instead of addressing root causes. Ceasing endless probation and replacing it with healing-centered, developmentally appropriate alternatives is essential to disrupting the cycles of harm experienced by foster youth and youth involved in the juvenile justice system.

The School-to-Prison Pipeline: Criminalizing Childhood

Black students are nearly four times more likely than white students to be suspended for the same behavior (U.S. Department of Education, 2023). This disparity begins as early as preschool, where Black children make up 19% of enrollment but 47% of out-of-school suspensions. The rise of zero-tolerance policies in the 1990s turned ordinary childhood behaviors—like talking back, dress code violations, or being late—into punishable offenses, pushing students toward law enforcement instead of counseling or support. The increased presence of school resource officers has led to higher arrest rates without improving safety (NAACP LDF, 2013; U.S. Government Accountability Office, 2024). Black students are arrested at school at rates five times higher than their white peers (U.S. Department of Education Office for Civil Rights, 2018).

The criminalization of normal adolescent development is especially damaging. During adolescence, the brain—particularly the prefrontal cortex responsible for impulse control and decision-making—is still developing. Yet, instead of responding to mistakes with guidance and care, the system often treats them as crimes, creating lifelong consequences for developmentally typical behavior.

Black girls are frequently punished for "defiance" or "attitude," reflecting adultification bias and the policing of Black femininity. LGBTQ+ youth, especially Black trans students, face higher levels of school discipline and criminalization. Students with disabilities are suspended twice as often as their peers, with Black disabled students facing the highest rates overall.

The path forward requires removing police from schools and investing in counselors, social workers, and restorative justice programs. Schools must end zero-tolerance policies and stop suspensions or expulsions for nonviolent behavior. Discipline should be trauma-informed and culturally responsive, and data-sharing between schools and law enforcement should cease. Finally, adopting community school models that provide wraparound services can help ensure every student learns in an environment of safety, care, and belonging.

Intersection with Poverty, Education, Housing Instability, and Mental Health

Since 1980, the number of people under probation and parole has multiplied dramatically, intensifying pressure on community supervision systems. While some progress has been made toward rehabilitation through substance use counseling, mental health services, and diversion programs, systemic issues—such as poverty, lack of education, housing instability, and untreated trauma—continue to impede long-term success (The Sentencing Project, 2024).

For many Black people, early involvement with the justice system results from deeply rooted systemic inequities. Educational systems that devalue Black contributions and reinforce narrow definitions of success push many youth out of academic spaces and into carceral ones. Black students are often subject to discretionary discipline, face tokenization, and internalize stigmatizing narratives about their worth and potential (Henderson et al., 2021). These harmful experiences can erode mental health, increase substance use, and perpetuate cycles of incarceration.

Upon release, formerly incarcerated individuals frequently find themselves ill-equipped to navigate a society that offers little support for reintegration. Structural barriers like education gaps, limited access to employment, fractured family networks, and stigma surrounding mental health create significant challenges. The carceral system not only conditions people for confinement but also systematically denies them the tools needed to rebuild their lives post-release.

Trends in Sentencing, Pretrial Detention, Bail, Probation, and Parole

Although crime rates have declined since the 1970s, incarceration rates have continued to rise, with sentencing lengths increasing significantly. People of color, particularly Black and Latinx people, remain overrepresented in both federal and state prison populations. According to a March 2025 report created by the United States Sentencing Commission, there are currently 154,155 people serving sentences in federal prisons, with 34.9% of those identifying as Black, and 30.7% identifying as Hispanic. At the federal level, drug offenses dominate, while violent offenses account for the majority of state incarcerations (The Sentencing Project, 2024). The average guideline minimum for people in federal prison was 173 months, while the average actual imprisonment period was 152 months (United States Sentencing Commission, 2025).

The privatization of prisons and probation systems exacerbates these problems.[6] The profit-driven nature of private prisons and probation companies often leads to poor conditions, limited staffing, and excessive fees, disproportionately affecting low-income individuals and communities of color. The broader Prison Industrial Complex (PIC), encompassing private industry and government partnerships, thrives on mass incarceration and sustains systems of racial and economic control. Despite comprising less than 5% of the global population, the United States incarcerates nearly 20% of the world's prison population, with Black men imprisoned for drug offenses at rates 13 times higher than white men (Tufts Prison Divestment, 2025).

Learning from Global Success: Evidence-Based Alternatives

Mass incarceration in the United States evolved through decades of punitive policy decisions that prioritized punishment over rehabilitation, often without evidence that such approaches improved public safety. In contrast, countries such as Norway, Germany, and the Netherlands have shown that accountability and community safety can be maintained with far lower incarceration rates, demonstrating viable alternatives to the United States model.

In Norway, maximum sentences rarely exceed 21 years, and prisons emphasize education, therapy, and job training. Correctional officers must have college degrees and receive extensive conflict resolution and counseling training. Cells resemble dormitory rooms rather than cages, and incarcerated individuals maintain connections to family and community. Norway's recidivism rate of 20%, compared to the United States rate of 68%, proves that rehabilitation-focused systems work. These models prioritize human dignity, education, and reintegration over punishment and isolation.

Germany's system focuses on resocialization, with the constitutional mandate that imprisonment's primary purpose is rehabilitation. Incarcerated individuals work regular jobs, attend university classes, and gradually reintegrate into society through supervised release programs.

It is estimated that the United States spends more than $40,000 to incarcerate Federal inmates while State incarceration costs vary by state and is roughly around $60,000, on average, according to the Federal Bureau of Prisons, while the costs of rehabilitation programs would range from $10,000 to $15,000 annually (Elevations Health, 2025). Rehabilitation models cost significantly less than United States mass incarceration while achieving better outcomes for public safety, victim satisfaction, and individual rehabilitation. They prove our current system represents a policy choice, not an inevitable response to crime. Surely, if developed countries such as these can find ways to restore their incarcerated individuals, our country can follow their example.

Community Impact: What It Costs Us

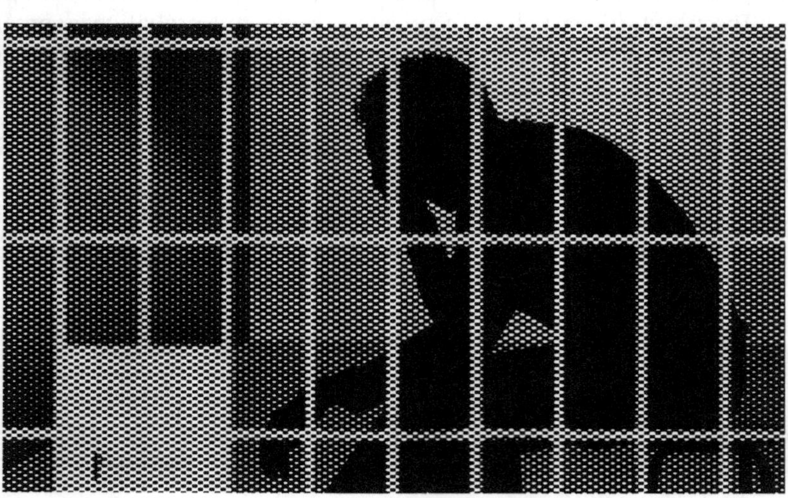

Mass incarceration inflicts immeasurable harm on people and communities, particularly Black and Brown communities, which punitive policies have long targeted. The consequences extend beyond prison walls—fracturing families, eroding trust in institutions, and undermining opportunities for generational advancement.

Children with incarcerated parents lose emotional support, financial stability, and consistent caregiving. One in nine Black children has had a parent incarcerated, compared to one in 57 white children (The Sentencing Project, 2021). Such disruptions frequently result in developmental challenges, mental health concerns, and declines in academic performance.

Incarceration frequently functions as a modern-day form of state-sanctioned family separation, echoing the historical trauma experienced by enslaved and Indigenous communities. Families are left to navigate grief, stigma, and survival with little institutional support. Upon release, returning citizens encounter thousands of legal restrictions that limit access to housing, employment, education, and civic participation (Council of State Governments, 2023).

Formerly incarcerated individuals often face de facto second sentences. They are barred from voting, denied professional licenses, and frequently rejected by employers, regardless of skill or rehabilitation. These compounding barriers entrench cycles of poverty and destabilization (Alexander, 2020).

The school-to-prison pipeline further perpetuates harm by criminalizing minor misbehavior and disproportionately targeting Black, Brown, and disabled students. Zero-tolerance policies, discretionary discipline, and school policing disrupt education and condition students to expect punishment rather than support. Black students are nearly four times more likely to be suspended and more frequently referred to law enforcement than their white peers (U.S. Department of Education, 2023).

United States jails and prisons are sites of trauma—not rehabilitation. Incarcerated individuals face elevated rates of mental illness, worsened by isolation, overcrowding, and violence. Over 40% of incarcerated people report mental health conditions, yet access to care remains insufficient (Bureau of Justice Statistics, 2021). Women, LGBTQ+ people, and those with prior trauma histories are especially vulnerable (Kaba & Ritchie, 2022).

The Economic Case for Decarceration

The United States spends approximately $80 billion annually on incarceration—more than the federal education budget (Prison Policy Initiative, 2023). The annual cost of incarcerating one person is nearly 68% of formerly incarcerated individuals return to prison within three years of their release. (American Civil Liberties Union, 2018). In contrast, effective community-based programs cost $3,000–$15,000 per person annually and achieve recidivism rates below 30%.

The economic multiplier effect of community investment far exceeds the costs of incarceration. Every dollar invested in education returns $7 to the economy. Every dollar invested in substance abuse treatment saves $4–12 in reduced crime and healthcare costs (National Institute on Drug Abuse, as cited in NIH, 2017). Violence intervention programs cost $45,000 per participant but save $87,000 in criminal justice costs alone (RAND Corporation, 2016).

Mass incarceration imposes costs on communities that far exceed the direct expenditures associated with prisons and jails. When a primary wage earner is incarcerated, families lose an average of $35,000 in annual income. Children with incarcerated parents are 70% more likely to drop out of school, perpetuating cycles of poverty. These costs compound across generations, representing trillions in lost economic potential.

Conversely, states that have reduced incarceration have seen economic benefits. Since 2007, Texas has averted roughly $2 billion in prison-construction costs by expanding treatment and community-based options, while overall crime fell by about 40% through 2019 (Council of State government,

2010). California's early release programs saved $2.8 billion in three years. These examples demonstrate that decarceration is not only a moral imperative but also an economically advantageous strategy.

Policy Gaps & Structural Failures

Despite decades of advocacy, effective diversion programs remain underutilized, particularly for people with mental illnesses or those charged with nonviolent offenses. In over-policed communities, diversion programs are often inaccessible or structurally inadequate. Underfunded public defense remains a serious equity issue. Many defenders manage caseloads far above national standards, reducing their ability to advocate effectively (National Legal Aid & Defender Association, 2022). Meanwhile, over-policing and discriminatory enforcement practices continue to drive racial disparities (Alexander, 2020; Hinton et al., 2018). Reentry services are fragmented, underfunded, and often inaccessible. Without adequate housing, mental healthcare, or employment support, many individuals struggle to reintegrate and face high risks of recidivism (Urban Institute, 2020). The United States spends billions of dollars on incarceration, yet only a fraction is directed toward reentry programs. Deep-rooted financial and political incentives—like arrest quotas, immigration detention contracts, and private prison lobbying—sustain the status quo (Eisen, 2017). These structural mechanisms prioritize incarceration over rehabilitative care.

Community-led initiatives like restorative justice programs, credible messenger models, and participatory defense networks demonstrate that safety and accountability are achievable without relying on punitive measures. To end mass incarceration effectively, it is necessary to divest from systems of harm and reinvest in the communities most impacted. Ending mass incarceration requires confronting structural failures, closing policy gaps, and building a future defined not by punishment but by dignity, equity, and collective freedom. Achieving that goal also requires replacing the for-profit models that dominate federal prisons with evidence-based rehabilitation and reentry programs.

True Victim-Centered Justice

True victim-centered justice recognizes that the current system fails victims by prioritizing punishment over healing and accountability. Thus, the practice of restorative justice processes should be introduced. Restorative justice practices place the victim's needs at the center of their treatment. Such an approach opens pathways to services such as getting answers to questions, acknowledgment of their pain, and opportunities to repair broken relationships, which the current carceral system rarely provides. Most advocates of the restorative justice process want offenders to get help, make amends, and change their behavior rather than serve a sentence locked in a cage. Community-based accountability processes focused on restoring and bringing offenders back to society provide the healing and transformation that punishment cannot.

Research consistently shows that victims prefer restorative approaches to traditional prosecution. In cases of serious harm, 89% of victims who participated in restorative justice reported satisfaction with the process, compared to 34% satisfaction with traditional court proceedings (Park University, 2024). Victims in restorative processes report reduced fear, increased understanding of the offense, and greater confidence that the harm will not recur.

The current system's focus on punishment often retraumatizes victims through adversarial court proceedings, lengthy delays, and a lack of meaningful involvement in case resolution. Restorative justice centers victim agency, allowing them to ask questions, express impact, and participate in determining appropriate responses to harm. The data from these studies show the benefits as clear as day. Restorative justice is a better method than the traditional prosecution practices that feed the Prison Industrial Complex.

Vision for Liberation: Prescriptive Solutions

The path toward ending mass incarceration is not just about deconstructing what exists but also concerns imagining and building what could be. A liberatory vision requires more than incremental policy adjustments; it demands a comprehensive transformation of societal approaches to safety, justice, and care. This vision is grounded in prevention, community-centered alternatives, dismantling punitive laws, and rebuilding systems rooted in dignity and collective wellbeing.

To begin, we must focus on **prevention**. This means investing in the root causes of harm: lack of housing, inequitable education, and the absence of healing-centered, youth-driven programs. Safety is not created by surveillance or punishment; it is cultivated through opportunity, stability, and care. Accordingly, school-based policing and surveillance that disproportionately target Black and Brown youth must be eliminated, with funding redirected toward Black-led violence interruption initiatives and restorative justice programs that provide support proactively.

It is also essential to **divert** people from the criminal legal system entirely. Community-based diversion models should be expanded, especially those implemented before charges are filed or court processes begin. Poverty, substance use, and acts of survival must be decriminalized—behaviors frequently penalized rather than addressed through supportive care. Rather than involving police in mental health crises, youth conflicts, or homelessness, we must fund and deploy trained crisis responders who center on de-escalation and trauma-informed care.

Legal frameworks that uphold mass incarceration must be dismantled, including the repeal of mandatory minimum sentencing laws and three-strikes policies that limit judicial discretion and disproportionately impact communities of color. We must abolish cash bail, close youth detention centers, and eliminate laws that criminalize youth behavior and reproductive choices. These policies have long served as tools of social control rather than justice.

Finally, we must **rebuild** community-fueled safety and care systems through the leadership, insight, and expertise of those who have survived incarceration. People with incarceration experience possess unique insight into structural barriers to reentry, and their perspectives should inform all aspects of reintegration policy. Reentry programs must be adequately funded, designed, and led by those directly impacted. These reforms are the infrastructure of abolition that make prisons obsolete. Achieving this includes dismantling barriers to housing, education, and employment, and restoring full civic participation, especially voting rights. Affirming the leadership of directly impacted people is essential to any just and sustainable future.

As co-author Caitlin Radigan shared during public testimony:

> I've been incarcerated as a foster child. I've been incarcerated as a pregnant teenager. I've been incarcerated as an adult while navigating homelessness and addiction. Many of the crimes I committed were acts of survival—securing food, shelter, or safety. Institutionalized from a young age, I reached a point where I saw no future outside of death or a prison cell.
>
> But systems change when we do. Today, I speak out not just as a survivor, but as a graduate, a parent, an author, and an advocate. My journey reveals how deeply this system fails to meet basic human needs and how it entrenches people—especially Black and Brown youth—into a cycle of incarceration. Yet it also shows what's possible when we invest in healing, education, and community-led pathways forward. This is not just my story—it's one of thousands. And every one of them deserves to be heard.
>
> (Radigan, 2024)

Liberation requires more than the absence of incarceration; it demands the presence of care, opportunity, and justice. By acting on these prescriptive solutions—investing in prevention, expanding diversion, dismantling punitive structures, and rebuilding systems around lived expertise—we move from punishment to possibility and from systemic harm to collective healing. This is how we build a future where everyone has what they need, not only to survive, but to thrive.

Beyond Punishment: What Victims Actually Want

Recent research shows many crime victims prefer interventions that prevent future harm and promote healing, rather than solely imposing longer sentences. National surveys of crime survivors find strong support for rehabilitation, treatment, and community-based alternatives over incarceration, often by two-to-one margins. Many survivors desire that people who caused harm take responsibility, receive appropriate support, and demonstrate behavioral change. Survivors report greater satisfaction and improved emotional outcomes when they can participate in restorative justice processes (Alliance, 2022). Restorative programs commonly report high survivor satisfaction and lower reoffending compared with traditional prosecution, and recent reviews note positive psychological impacts for victims, including reduced fear and a greater sense of closure.

Simultaneously, the current criminal legal system frequently fails to provide survivors with what they identify as essential: clear explanations of why the harm occurred, meaningful participation in accountability processes, evidence of behavioral change, practical restitution for losses, and ongoing support for their own healing. Surveyed survivors consistently favor redirecting resources from prisons and jails to mental healthcare, substance-use treatment, employment, education, and violence-prevention services.

Restorative Justice in Practice

For The People works nationally to transform the justice system by partnering with prosecutors, lawmakers, and communities to reduce incarceration and reunite families. The organization pioneered prosecutor-initiated resentencing (PIR). This reform enables prosecutors to review previous cases and request sentence reductions for people who have demonstrated rehabilitation or no longer present a threat to public safety. Since facilitating the passage of the nation's first PRI law in California in 2018, For The People has expanded this model to six additional states, resulting in the safe release of hundreds of people from incarceration.

Founded in 2001, The Community Justice Center (CJC) is a Black-founded and Black-led peer organization in Nebraska that seeks to repair harm and restore relationships within the community. The organization accomplishes this by addressing harm experienced by survivors, holding offenders accountable, and attending to the collective consequences of criminal behavior. The organization implements an intensive program designed to reduce recidivism by educating people who have caused harm on strategies to reduce violent behaviors and understand the victim's impact. To date, the organization has serviced over 16,000 justice-involved individuals.

Common Justice (Brooklyn & Oakland) operates as an alternative to incarceration for violent felonies. Young people aged 16–26 who cause serious harm, participate in intensive accountability processes, including victim dialogue, community service, education, and employment support. Since 2013, the program has maintained recidivism rates below 20% while achieving high victim satisfaction.

Ahimsa Collective (Oakland): Provides transformative justice responses to gender-based violence without relying on police or prisons. The organization uses community accountability processes that center on survivor healing while supporting people who caused harm in changing their behavior. The data is precise: restorative approaches serve victims better than punishment—yet our system prioritizes cages over healing.

Co-founded by Dr. David Ragland, The Truth Telling Project (TTP) operates the Grassroots Reparations Campaign (Chicago), which centers reparative and restorative processes within Black communities. Through truth-telling, reparations frameworks, and community healing practices, TTP works to address historical and ongoing harm while promoting collective accountability and justice.

Restorative Justice Hubs (Chicago) form a community-led collective that establishes local restorative justice "hubs" in neighborhoods most impacted by violence and systemic inequities. Their work includes community accompaniment, accountability circles, and comprehensive wraparound support to foster safety, repair, and belonging.

The Solutions Not Punishment Collaborative (SNaP Co.) (Atlanta) is a Black, trans, and queer-led organization building community-based safety alternatives and leadership. Their initiatives include training programs, mutual aid through the "Taking Care of Our Own" fund, and local restorative and transformative justice practices rooted in Black trans feminist frameworks.

Project South: Institute for the Elimination of Poverty & Genocide (Atlanta) is a Black-led movement institution advancing transformative and healing justice initiatives throughout the South. It co-convenes regional collaborations, including transformative justice collectives, and supports the development of community-based safety alternatives that center equity and self-determination.

Based in New Orleans, the Promise of Justice Initiative (PJI) (New Orleans) centers abolition, decarceration, and community-led alternatives to punishment. Alongside impact litigation and community support, PJI integrates restorative frameworks for survivors and communities affected by systemic harm, emphasizing repair and transformation.

The Restorative Justice Initiative (RJI) (New York City) is a multi-sector network in New York City that connects and supports restorative justice programs, practitioners, and community partners across the five boroughs. It serves as a key resource for East Coast referrals, partnerships, and program development.

Restorative Justice for Oakland Youth (RJOY) (West Coast) is a nationally recognized organization whose healing-centered youth diversion model has influenced restorative justice practices across the United States. While based in Oakland, RJOY's training resources and model offer valuable frameworks for adaptation in other regions.

Several Black-led funds and collaborative grant makers, such as the Black-Led Movement Fund, provide essential financial and strategic support to restorative and transformative justice initiatives. These funding bodies often support groups like SNaP Co. and Project South, making them valuable partners for scaling community-based justice work nationwide.

Call to Action: Abolition Is a Strategy, Not a Slogan

Building Power for Liberation: Coalition Strategy and Movement Building

Ending mass incarceration requires building a multiracial, intergenerational movement that centers the leadership of directly impacted people. That means forming coalitions between formerly incarcerated people, families of incarcerated people, faith communities, labor unions, students, and abolitionist organizations. Power is built through voter registration, candidate recruitment, direct action, mutual aid, and community education.

Core Coalition Partners

- **Directly Impacted Leaders**: Formerly incarcerated people and their families must lead strategy and messaging.
- **Faith Communities**: Religious leaders provide moral authority and can mobilize congregations for justice.
- **Labor Unions**: Workers understand exploitation and can connect economic justice to criminal justice reform.
- **Youth Organizations**: Students can disrupt the school-to-prison pipeline and build generational change.
- **Racial Justice Groups**: Organizations fighting white supremacy across issues provide strategic alignment.

Power-Building Strategies

- **Electoral**: Recruiting formerly incarcerated candidates, voter registration in impacted communities.
- **Direct Action**: Mass mobilizations, civil disobedience, and disruptive protests to create urgency.
- **Mutual Aid**: Providing immediate support while building relationships and political consciousness.
- **Popular Education**: Teaching communities about connections between issues and strategies for change.
- **Cultural Strategy**: Shifting narratives about crime, punishment, and safety through art, media, and storytelling.

Coalition Principles

- **Nothing About Us Without Us**: Directly impacted people must hold decision-making power.
- **Intersectional Analysis**: Understanding how systems of oppression reinforce each other.
- **Community Care**: Providing healing and support while fighting for systemic change.
- **Shared Leadership**: Distributing power across racial, gender, class, and geographic lines.

Coalition Building in Practice

Building effective coalitions requires more than shared values—it demands a commitment to distributing power, sharing resources, and taking collective action. Successful examples show how movements across sectors can align their strengths while maintaining autonomy. The Movement for Black Lives (M4BL), a coalition of more than 150 Black-led organizations, developed the BREATHE Act to shift resources from policing toward community care, modeling how unified demands can drive bold national policy. The Jobs Not Jails Coalition brings together labor unions, formerly incarcerated workers, and community groups to oppose prison construction and create living-wage jobs, proving that economic justice and decarceration are deeply connected. Faith communities and Black churches have also played a crucial role, offering bail funds, reentry housing, and moral guidance. Networks like the Samuel DeWitt Proctor Conference continue to challenge punitive narratives and uplift a vision of restoration and healing.

Critical Alliance-Building Practices

- Partner with disability justice organizers challenging the criminalization of mental illness.
- Collaborate with immigrant rights groups opposing ICE detention.
- Connect with housing justice movements addressing the criminalization of homelessness.
- Join education advocates working to dismantle the school-to-prison pipeline.
- Build with Indigenous movements resisting carceral approaches to justice.

The strongest coalitions understand that mass incarceration cannot be dismantled in isolation—it must be addressed alongside struggles for housing, healthcare, education, and economic equity.

Mass incarceration is one of the most urgent challenges of modern times. It relies on a biased system (particularly toward low-income and/or Black people) and economic exploitation.

Local Policy Demands: To advance justice and equity, we must eliminate cash bail systems[7] that disproportionately impact low-income and Black communities, replacing them with pretrial services rooted in care rather than oppression. This includes divesting from policing and incarceration and investing in critical areas such as housing, public health, education, and employment. A moratorium on jail construction should be enforced, alongside a phased closure of existing carceral infrastructure. Additionally, we must decriminalize poverty by rolling back legislation that targets homelessness, mental illness, and substance use, while funding non-police crisis response teams that prioritize community-based solutions over punishment.

State Policy Demands: We must repeal punitive sentencing laws such as mandatory minimums and three-strikes statutes that entrench racial disparities and contribute to mass incarceration. In their place, we should reinvest in reentry and rehabilitation by funding transitional housing, trauma-informed care, job placement, and educational support for returning citizens. Expanding access to justice also requires the creation of automatic, no-cost expungement processes for non-violent convictions. Furthermore, we must reform supervision systems by eliminating technical parole and probation violations that unjustly funnel individuals back into prison, prioritizing support over surveillance.

Federal Policy Demands: We must dismantle harmful federal laws like the Prison Litigation Reform Act and the 1994 Crime Bill, which incentivize incarceration and restrict the rights of incarcerated individuals. This includes abolishing United States Immigration and Customs Enforcement (ICE) detention by closing immigration detention centers and investing in community-based services that support migrants with dignity and care. Enacting the People's Justice Guarantee is essential to advancing legislation rooted in decarceration, restorative justice, and community reinvestment. Additionally, federal incentives for incarceration should be eliminated by redirecting grant funding away from carceral expansion and toward housing, mental health services, and violence prevention initiatives.

Digital Policy Demands: To advance justice in the digital age, we must ban facial recognition technology in policing and criminal legal proceedings, prohibit predictive policing algorithms and risk assessment tools, and end electronic monitoring except as a voluntary alternative chosen by the individual. Governments should be required to conduct algorithmic impact assessments before adopting any technology that influences criminal legal outcomes, while also enacting strong data privacy protections and a legally enforceable right to algorithmic transparency. Finally, digital surveillance infrastructure must be defunded, with those resources redirected to community-led safety programs that prioritize care, accountability, and human dignity over control.

Legislation and Campaign Blueprint: Legislation and strategic campaigns must center community empowerment, decarceration, and systemic transformation. At the local level, the Community Reinvestment Act mandates that cities reallocate 25% of police budgets to essential services like housing, education, and mental health. On the state level, the Restorative Justice and Alternatives to Incarceration Act establishes restorative justice hubs and funds community-based alternatives to incarceration. Nationally, the Federal Dignity and Liberation Act proposes enforceable decarceration targets, a ban on solitary confinement, and investment in post-release support.

To advance these goals, campaigns should begin with community mapping and listening sessions that engage directly impacted individuals in shaping priorities. Policy design and legal drafting should be grounded in collaboration with movement lawyers and scholars. Coalition building and public education efforts can strengthen multi-sector alliances and amplify awareness through digital platforms. Legislative advocacy and power-building strategies must equip communities to testify, organize, and run for office to influence change from within.

Accountability Metrics: To measure progress and ensure accountability, key metrics include the number of people released due to policy reforms, the percentage of municipal budgets redirected from policing to public services, reductions in recidivism through restorative justice interventions, improved outcomes in employment, education, and housing for formerly incarcerated individuals, and increased community participation in governance and budgeting processes.

A Vision for What Real Safety Looks Like: Community Care, not Cages

Community safety begins with meeting people's basic needs, like stable housing, education, healthcare, mentorship, food, and career connections. When people have what they need to survive and thrive, they are less likely to experience or perpetuate harm. True safety is collective, not carceral. It is created by providing housing, education, economic dignity, and care over cages, surveillance, and armed forces.

A powerful example of this model is Project Pinnacle in Georgia, founded by The Honorable Judge Asha Jackson in 2012. Through her visionary leadership, Project Pinnacle has become a critical model for community-driven alternatives to incarceration, emphasizing restorative justice, support for those impacted by the criminal legal system, and decarceration. Judge Jackson's work exemplifies how transformative leadership rooted in lived experience and community care can challenge systemic injustice and build pathways toward true liberation and safety. This court-based initiative targets first-time, nonviolent felony offenders between 17 and 25 years of age, offering a one-year intensive mentorship program that includes life skills development, legal education, and community engagement. Participants meet regularly in court, receive tailored support, and, upon successful completion, can have their records sealed, which helps them access employment, education, and housing (Project Pinnacle, 2025). With a recidivism rate of 3% (Project Pinnacle, 2025), Project Pinnacle demonstrates that community-rooted alternatives to incarceration can effectively disrupt cycles of criminalization and lay the foundation for transformative justice.

Organizations like For The People are paving the way for decarceration through models grounded in healing, justice, and community. Founded in 2019 by Hillary Blout, a former prosecutor turned visionary reformer, For The People is transforming how the legal system views accountability. Blout authored and led the passage of AB 2942,[8] the first law in the country to empower prosecutors to revisit and reduce excessive sentences, offering a powerful alternative to punishment. Through Prosecutor-Initiated Resentencing (PIR), her organization has trained District Attorneys in multiple states, leading to the safe release and reunification of individuals and families impacted by mass incarceration. Blout's work reimagines prosecutorial discretion as a tool for liberation, redemption, and systemic change, restoring dignity to those the system once discarded.

These models prove that justice rooted in care and community is not only possible, but is already happening. Across courtrooms and community organizations, leaders reshape lives, restore hope, and illuminate a future where safety is built rather than imposed. By centering healing, accountability, and support over punishment, these initiatives demonstrate that community safety does not require incarceration and surveillance. Instead, we can invest in people, nurture potential, and build a justice system that reflects dignity, equity, and collective wellbeing values.

A Final Call to Action

We must unshackle our people. We must end mass incarceration, divest from punitive systems, and invest in Black liberation and community healing. Mass incarceration was constructed to replace chattel slavery and segregation as tools of control. Its functions, derived from Black Codes, Jim Crow laws, and redlining, are highlighted through racially targeted policing, surveillance, and systemic legal discrimination. Nearly two million people are currently incarcerated in the United States, which is the highest rate in the world, with Black and Latino people vastly overrepresented behind bars (Vera Institute of Justice, 2024). Black Americans make up only 13% of the United States population but comprise 33% of the sentenced prison population. These disparities are not coincidental; they are the direct result of policies that criminalize Blackness and manufacture a racial underclass labeled "felons," stripped of their rights, dignity, and opportunities. We reject the myth that incarcerated people are broken, dangerous, or beyond redemption. We know our people are brilliant, resilient, and deserving of a future filled with hope and opportunity.

Mass incarceration is not inevitable; it is a political and policy choice. And just as it was built, it can be dismantled. We can choose a different path rooted in truth, dignity, and collective care. Such a transformation requires a radical reimagining of justice, based not on punishment, but on restoration, healing, and accountability. It requires us to see incarceration not as a solution, but as a barrier to safety, health, and liberation. We write with the urgency of knowing that someone's potential remains locked away every day, and it is too long. This is not just a policy critique but a moral call to action. A call to those who believe in freedom, recognize our communities' brilliance, are ready to build a future where cages are replaced with care, and where justice truly means belonging and a possibility for all.

Take Action Today

This Black Paper means nothing without action. Here is what you can do right now:

For Individuals:

- Join or donate to organizations led by formerly incarcerated people.
- Attend a court-watching program to observe how the system functions.
- Write letters to imprisoned people through Black & Pink, Write A Prisoner, or other programs.
- Contribute to bail funds supporting pretrial release in your community.
- Sign up for political education workshops on prison abolition.
- Vote for prosecutors, judges, and legislators committed to decarceration.
- Hire formerly incarcerated people if you are in a position to do so.
- Challenge criminalization narratives when you hear them.

For Organizations:

- Adopt "ban the box" policies, removing criminal history questions from applications.
- Provide paid internships and employment to formerly incarcerated people.
- Fund community-based alternatives to police and prosecution.
- Divest from companies profiting from mass incarceration.
- Use your institutional voice to advocate for decarceration policies.
- Partner with directly impacted organizations, following their leadership.

For Policymakers:

- Co-sponsor H.R. 619 (Reversing the Youth Prison Population Act).
- Introduce prosecutor-initiated resentencing legislation in your state.
- Eliminate money bail in your jurisdiction.
- Close youth detention centers and redirect funding to community programs.
- End contracts with private prison companies.
- Expunge criminal records automatically and without fees.
- Restore voting rights to all people with convictions.

For Communities:

- Start a participatory defense hub in your area.
- Launch a community bail fund—Create a welcome home reentry program.
- Organize court watching to monitor prosecutorial and judicial conduct.
- Build relationships with incarcerated people through visitation programs.
- Host political education sessions on abolition and transformative justice.
- Support families navigating the system. The time for liberation is now. No matter how small, every action moves us closer to a world where our people are free.

Notes

1 Vagrancy laws were statutes that criminalized "idleness," unemployment, homelessness, or simply being in public without proof of work or residence—tools widely embedded in the post-Civil War Black Codes to arrest Black people and funnel them into coerced labor. https://www.britannica.com/topic/Black-Codes

2 *Plessy* v. *Ferguson* (1896) was the U.S. Supreme Court decision that upheld a Louisiana segregation law and announced the "separate but equal" doctrine, holding that state-mandated racial segregation did not violate the Fourteenth Amendment. The ruling supplied the constitutional basis for Jim Crow laws, legitimizing racially segregated public life until it was repudiated by *Brown v. Board of Education* (1954). https://www.britannica.com/event/Plessy-v-Ferguson-1896

3 "Three Strikes and You're Out" laws, which require judges to impose life sentences for third convictions for certain offenses (Loehr, 2025). First enacted in Washington in 1993 and adopted in California in 1994, these laws significantly increased incarceration rates, with a disproportionate impact on Black and Latino communities (NAACP, n.d.-b; Sentencing Project, n.d.).

4 Slave patrols were organized groups of white men in the 18th and 19th centuries tasked with enforcing discipline on enslaved people—catching runaways, monitoring gatherings, and suppressing resistance. Historians widely view them as a direct precursor to modern American policing.

5 George Floyd, a 46-year-old Black man, was murdered on May 25, 2020, in Minneapolis, Minnesota, when a police officer knelt on his neck for more than nine minutes. His death, captured on video, sparked global protests against police brutality and systemic racism.

6 On January 26, 2021, President Joe Biden signed an executive order (EO) on "Reforming Our Incarceration System to Eliminate the Use of Privately Operated Criminal Detention Facilities." Its purpose was to ensure that incarceration and correctional facilities were prioritizing rehabilitation and redemption. "To decrease incarceration levels, we must reduce profit-based incentives to incarcerate by phasing out the Federal Government's reliance on privately operated criminal detention facilities. The EO also required the Attorney General now to renew the Department of Justice contracts with privately operated criminal detention facilities, as consistent with applicable law. https://bidenwhitehouse.archives.gov/briefing-room/presidential-actions/2021/01/26/executive-order-reforming-our-incarceration-system-to-eliminate-the-use-of-privately-operated-criminal-detention-facilities/

7 Cash bail is used as a guarantee that a defendant will return for a trial or hearings. The money is returned after they make all necessary court appearances, otherwise

the bail is forfeited to the government. Cash bail is used as a guarantee that a defendant will return for a trial or hearings. The money is returned after they make all necessary court appearances, otherwise the bail is forfeited to the government. https://www.brennancenter.org/our-work/research-reports/how-cash-bail-works

8 "Assembly Bill No. 2942 (AB 2942) was a bill passed by the California State Legislature in 2019 that gives prosecutors the discretion to reevaluate past cases. The prosecuting agency will evaluate the case and has discretion to then recommend a modified sentence if appropriate." https://sjcda.org/special-programs/ab-2942

Bibliography

Abasguliyeva, K., Misenheimer, A., Ram, S., Tromboo, H., & Tsoi, K. W. (2024). Prison in pink: The struggles of female incarceration. *The Cambridge Journal of Human Rights and Social Transformation*.

Alexander, M. (2020). *The New Jim Crow: Mass Incarceration in the age of colorblindness* (10th anniversary ed.). The New Press.

Alliance for Safety and Justice. (2022). Crime survivors speak 2022: National survey of victims' views on safety and justice. https://allianceforsafetyandjustice.org/wp-content/uploads/2022/09/Alliance-for-Safety-and-Justice-Crime-Survivors-Speak-September-2022.pdf

American Civil Liberties Union. (2018). Mass incarceration. https://www.aclu.org/issues/smart-justice/mass-incarceration

Annie E. Casey Foundation. (2021). *Frequently asked questions about juvenile probation*. https://www.aecf.org/blog/frequently-asked-questions-about-juvenile-probation

Arnold, H. & Liebling, A. (2012). *The prison officer* (2nd ed.). Routledge.

Arredondo, M. I., Kiba, R. J., & Williams, N. T. (2014). More than a metaphor: The contribution of exclusionary discipline to a school-to-prison pipeline. *Equity & Excellence in Education, 47*(4), 546–564.

Borealis Philanthropy. (n.d.). *Black-led movement fund*. Borealis Philanthropy. https://borealisphilanthropy.org/black-led-movement-fund

Bureau of Justice Statistics. (2021). Indicators of mental health problems reported by prisoners. https://bjs.ojp.gov/library/publications/indicators-mental-health-problems-reported-prisoners-survey-prison-inmates

Council of Independent Colleges. (n.d.). Legacies of American slavery: Reckoning with the past. https://cic.edu/opportunity/legacies-of-american-slavery/

Council of State Governments. (2023). National inventory of collateral consequences of conviction. https://csgjusticecenter.org/publications/the-national-inventory-of-collateral-consequences-of-conviction/

Council of State Governments Justice Center. (2010). Justice reinvestment in Texas: Assessing the impact of the 2007 Justice Reinvestment Legislation. https://csgjusticecenter.org/publications/justice-reinvestment-in-texas-assessing-the-impact-of-the-2007-justice-reinvestment-legislation/

Davis, A. Y. (2003). *Are prisons obsolete?* Seven Stories Press.

Dennis, M. (2020). The criminalisation of Blackness. In A. Motz, M. Dennis, & A. Aiyegbusi (Eds.), *Invisible trauma: Women, difference and the criminal justice system* (p. 21). Routledge.

Dholakia, N. (2024). *Jailing for profit: When budgets depend on locking people up.* Vera Institute of Justice. www.vera.org/news/jailing-for-profit-when-budgets-depend-on-locking-people-up

Drug Policy Alliance. (2015). *The Drug War, Mass Incarceration and Race.* https://www.unodc.org/documents/ungass2016/Contributions/Civil/DrugPolicyAlliance/DPA_Fact_Sheet_Drug_War_Mass_Incarceration_and_Race_June2015.pdf

Dwue, G. (2007). The impact of "three strikes" laws on crime rates: A review of the literature. *Justice Research and Policy, 9*(1), 1–25.

Eisen, L.-B. (2017). *Inside private prisons: An American dilemma in the age of mass incarceration*. Columbia University Press.

Elderbroom, B., Mayer, P., & Rose, F. (2025). *We can't afford it: Mass incarceration and the family tax.* Fines and Fees Justice Center. https://finesandfeesjusticecenter.org/articles/we-cant-afford-it-mass-incarceration-and-the-family-tax/?utm_source

Elevations Health. (2025). *Cost of rehabilitation vs. incarceration: A comparative analysis.* https://elevationshealth.com/cost-of-rehabilitation-vs-incarceration/

Encyclopaedia Britannica. (n.d.). *Plessy v. Ferguson.* https://www.britannica.com/event/Plessy-v-Ferguson-1896

Encyclopedia Britannica. (n.d.). Jim Crow Laws. https://www.britannica.com/event/Jim-Crow-law

Equal Justice Under Law. (n.d.). The private prison industrial complex. https://equaljusticeunderlaw.org/thejusticereport/privateprisonindustrialcomplex

For The People. (n.d.-a). Hillary Blout. https://www.fortheppl.org/team/hillary-blout

For The People. (n.d.-b). Our work. https://www.fortheppl.org/work

Forman, J., Jr. (2017). *Locking up our own: Crime and punishment in Black America.* Farrar, Straus and Giroux.

Ghandnoosh, N. (2023). *One in five: Disparities in crime and policing.* The Sentencing Project. https://www.sentencingproject.org/reports/one-in-five-disparities-in-crime-and-policing/

Ghandnoosh, N., & Nellis, A. (2022). *How many people are spending over a decade in prison?* The Sentencing Project.

Ghandnoosh, N., & Stammen, E. (2022). *Incarcerated LGBTQ+ adults and youth.* The Sentencing Project. https://www.sentencingproject.org/policy-brief/incarcerated-lgbtq-adults-and-youth/

Henderson, H., & Wyatt Bourgeois, J. (2021). Penalizing Black hair in the name of academic success is undeniably racist, unfounded, and against the law. *Brookings.* https://www.brookings.edu/articles/penalizing-black-hair-in-the-name-of-academic-success-is-undeniably-racist-unfounded-and-against-the-law/

Hinton, E., Henderson, L., & Reed, C. (2018). *An unjust burden: The disparate treatment of Black Americans in the criminal justice system.* Vera Institute of Justice. https://www.vera.org/publications/for-the-record-unjust-burden-racial-disparities

History.com Editors. (2022). *Black codes.* History. https://www.history.com/articles/black-codes

Jones, A. (2021). *Visualizing the unequal treatment of LGBTQ people in the criminal justice system.* Prison Policy Initiative. https://www.prisonpolicy.org/blog/2021/03/02/lgbtq/

Juvenile Law Center. (2018). What is the foster care-to-prison pipeline? https://jlc.org/news/what-foster-care-prisonpipeline

Kaba, M., & Ritchie, A. J. (2022). *No more police: A case for abolition*. The New Press.

Kajstura, A., & Sawyer, W. (2024). *Women's mass incarceration: The Whole Pie 2024*. Prison Policy Initiative. https://www.prisonpolicy.org/reports/pie2024women.html

Korhonen, V. (2024). Rate of imprisonment in the United States in 2022, by Race and Gender. *Statista*. https://www.statista.com/statistics/818001/rate-of-imprisonment-in-the-us-by-race-and-gender/

Learning for Justice. (n.d.). *Mass incarceration is a form of racialized social control*. Southern Poverty Law Center. https://www.learningforjustice.org/sites/default/files/general/Mass%20Incarceration%20as%20a%20Form%20of%20Racialized%20Social%20Control.pdf

Legal Center for Youth Justice and Education. (2020). *Information on the prevalence of learning disabilities in the prison population*. JJ Education Blueprint. https://www.jjeducationblueprint.org/examples/information-prevalence-learning-disabilities-prison-population-regional-education/

Loehr, D. (2025). *The eugenic origins of three strikes laws: How "habitual offender" sentencing laws were used as a means of sterilization*. The Sentencing Project. https://www.sentencingproject.org/reports/the-eugenic-origins-of-three-strikes-laws-how-habitual-offender-sentencing-laws-were-used-as-a-means-of-sterilization/

Marksamer, J., & Tobin, H. (2013). *Standing with LGBT prisoners: An Advocate's guide to ending abuse and combating imprisonment*. National Center for Transgender Equality.

Muhammad, K. G. (2010). *The condemnation of Blackness: Race, crime, and the making of modern urban America*. Harvard University Press.

NAACP. (n.d.-a). Criminal justice fact sheet.

NAACP. (n.d.-b). Origins of modern-day policing. https://naacp.org/find-resources/history-explained/origins-modern-day-policing

NAACP LDF. (2013). *Police in schools*. NAACP Legal Defense and Education Fund.

National Institute on Drug Abuse (as cited in National Institutes of Health). (2017). *Spend a dollar on drug treatment, and save more on crime, health care costs*. The New York Times. https://www.nytimes.com/2017/04/24/upshot/spend-a-dollar-on-drug-treatment-and-save-more-on-crime-reduction.html

National Legal Aid & Defender Association. (2022). *2022 impact report*. https://www.nlada.org/nlada-impact-report-2022

Network of Care. (n.d.). Trends in probation and parole in the United States. *Tarrant County Probation*. https://probation.networkofcare.org/tarrant-tx/HealthLibrary/Article?docType=noc&articleId=2362

Park University. (2024). The role of restorative justice in modern criminal justice administration. www.park.edu/blog/the-role-of-restorative-justice-in-modern-criminal-justice-administration/

Pratt, J. (2008). Scandinavian exceptionalism in an era of penal excess. *British Journal of Criminology, 48*(2), 119–137. https://academic.oup.com/bjc/article-abstract/48/2/119/422635

Prison Policy Initiative. (2023). Economics of incarceration. https://www.prisonpolicy.org/research/economics_of_incarceration/

Project Pinnacle. (2025). *Second chances. Lasting change*. https://projectpinnacle.org/

Project South. (n.d.). Project South: Institute for the elimination of poverty & genocide. https://projectsouth.org

Promise of Justice Initiative. (n.d.). Promise of Justice Initiative. https://promiseofjustice.org

Radigan, C. (2024). *National Best Practices Prosecution Conference*, Salt Lake City, Utah.
RAND Corporation. (2016). The benefits and costs of social programs (Research Report RR-1629-RC). www.rand.org
RAND Corporation, National Center for State Courts, American Bar Association Standing Committee on Legal Aid and Indigent Defense, & Law Office of Stephen F. Hanlon. (2023). *National public defense workload study*. RAND Corporation. https://www.rand.org/pubs/research_reports/RRA2559-1.html
Restorative Justice for Oakland Youth (RJOY). (n.d.). The truth telling project. https://thetruthtellingproject.org/programs
Restorative Justice Hubs. (n.d.). Restorative justice hubs. https://rjhubs.org
Restorative Justice Initiative (RJI). (n.d.). Restorative justice initiative. https://restorativejustice.nyc
Rovner, J. (2025). *Black disparities in youth incarceration*. The Sentencing Project. https://www.sentencingproject.org/fact-sheet/black-disparities-in-youth-incarceration/
Rovnet, J. (2025). *Black disparities in youth incarceration*. The Sentencing Project. https://www.sentencingproject.org/fact-sheet/black-disparities-in-youth-incarceration/
Seligman, E., & Nam-Sonenstein, B. (2024). *10 ways that mass incarceration is an engine of economic injustice*. Prison Policy Initiative. https://www.prisonpolicy.org/blog/2024/08/27/economic_justice/
SnapCo. (n.d.). Solutions, not punishment collaborative. https://www.snap4freedom.org/about
The Sentencing Project. (2018). Incarcerated women and girls, 1980–2016 [Fact sheet]. https://www.prisonpolicy.org/scans/sentencingproject/incarcerated_women_and_girls_1980_2016.pdf
The Sentencing Project. (2021). Parents in prison. https://www.sentencingproject.org/publications/parents-in-prison/
The Sentencing Project. (2024). Mass incarceration trends. https://www.sentencingproject.org/reports/mass-incarceration-trends/
The Truth Telling Project. (n.d.). *Grassroots reparations campaign*. The Truth Telling Project. https://thetruthtellingproject.org/grc
Tufts Prison Divestment. (n.d.). (2025). *The PIC and mass incarceration*. Tufts University. https://sites.tufts.edu/prisondivestment/the-pic-and-mass-incarceration/
U.S. Department of Education Office for Civil Rights. (2018). *2015–2016 Civil Rights Data Collection: School climate and safety*. U.S. Department of Education.
U.S. Department of Education Office for Civil Rights. (2023). Civil rights data collection: School climate and safety. https://www.ed.gov/sites/ed/files/about/offices/list/ocr/docs/crdc-discipline-school-climate-report.pdf
U.S. Government Accountability Office. (2024). *K-12 Education. Differences in student arrest rates widen when race, gender, and disability are considered*. U.S. Government Publishing Office.
United States Sentencing Commission. (2025). *Quick facts on individuals in the federal bureau of prisons*. U.S. Sentencing Commission. https://www.ussc.gov/sites/default/files/pdf/research-and-publications/quick-facts/BOP_2025.pdf
Urban Institute. (2020). Returning home: Understanding the challenges of prisoner reentry. https://www.urban.org/policy-centers/justice-policy-center/projects/returning-home-study-understanding-challenges-prisoner-reentry

Vera Institute of Justice. (2019). Justice denied: The harmful and lasting effects of pretrial detention. https://www.vera.org/publications/for-the-record-justice-denied-pretrial-detention

Vera Institute of Justice. (2022). *Diversion programs, explained*. https://www.vera.org/diversion-programs-explained

Vera Institute of Justice. (2024). Ending mass incarceration: The causes of mass incarceration. https://www.vera.org/ending-mass-incarceration/causes-of-mass-incarceration

Vitale, A. S. (2017). *The end of policing*. Verso Books.

Weill-Greenberg, E., & Corey, E. (2024). *Locked in, priced out: How prison commissary price-gouging preys on the incarcerated*. The Appeal. https://theappeal.org/locked-in-priced-out-how-much-prison-commissary-prices

Woods, A., & Khan, Q. (2023). *Pride has always been about ending mass incarceration*. American Civil Liberties Union. https://www.aclu.org/news/lgbtq-rights/pride-has-always-been-about-ending-mass-incarceration

Chapter 24

How We Keep Us Safe

A Guide on Gun Safety for Black Communities

*Joshua Miller**

Lead Author's Introductory Note

Born and raised in Alabama, I was a young Same-Gender Loving/gay boy reared in Black church tradition. By the time I was 10 years old, my father had taught me how to drive his truck and shoot a gun. Early on, I was exposed to the need for firearms as well as the harm they could pose. This experience informs my position on the issue of gun violence prevention. When drafting this Black Paper (Paper), I did not just want to discuss it strictly from a legislative and policy perspective. I wanted to speak about it with the understanding that the readers of these Papers are often beacons within the Black community. Black gun owners, Black Queer folks, and all other kinds of Black folks who share similar backgrounds and unique perspectives but may not be exposed to the Gun Violence Prevention Movement—this Paper is for you.

Thank you to those leading the State of the People Black Papers Project and Power Tour Initiative.

Thank you to our community—our Black trans sisters in particular—for continuing the tradition of joyful resilience in the face of oppression.

Gun Safety Laws DO Save Black Lives

Gun Violence is a Public Health Crisis

In this country, with Black lives constantly hanging in the balance, Black folks are affected by gun violence the most. Gun violence is the leading cause of death for Black children. Recent data shows that gun violence—whether by homicide, suicide, or accident—is the leading cause of death for Black men ages 15 to 44 (Giffords Law Center, 2025; Williams et al., 2019). Despite making up about 6% of the United States population, Black males account for more than half of the gun homicide victims (Giffords Law Center, 2025; NAACP, 2022).

* Supported by braintrust authors: Jada Capri Ward, Nadia French-Graham, Leilah Naila Jones, and Quenton Johnson.

DOI: 10.4324/9781003752646-32

Additionally, Black people are nearly 3 times more likely than white people to be killed by the police (Alang et al., 2017; Edwards et al., 2019). As a result, Black communities with exposure to heightened levels of gun violence experience trauma and mental health issues like depression and thoughts about suicide (Bor et al., 2018; Smart Growth America, 2024; Williams et al., 2019). This public health crisis must be confronted.

DID YOU KNOW? If you filled a room with 100 Americans, only six would be Black men. But if you looked to fill that same room with 100 gun homicide victims, more than 50 would be?[1] Black women are three to five times more likely to be fatally shot than white women (Violence Policy Center, 2025). Black women also experience the highest rates of intimate partner firearm homicide in the United States (Violence Policy Center, 2025). Black transgender women account for between 63% and 65% of all transgender gun homicide victims, despite representing an infinitesimal fraction of the total United States population (Advocates for Trans Equality, 2025; Everytown for Gun Safety Support Fund, 2024). In the first half of 2025, 10 out of 11 recorded transgender homicide victims were Black trans women, all of whom were killed with a firearm (Human Rights Campaign, 2025). This illustrates how gun violence disproportionately impacts our community.

Gun Laws Save Black Lives

Here's the deal: it will take the collaborative efforts of all kinds of Black folks—Black gun owners, community leaders and advocates, policymakers, and more, to keep communities safe. Our work must include legislative change in gun safety laws at the local, state, and federal levels of government to reduce the mortality rate caused by gun violence. For example, states that require permits to carry concealed guns in public saw an 11% drop in gun homicide rates compared with a 13–15% increase in homicide rates in states that weakened their gun permitting system (Everytown for Gun Safety, 2022c). Despite what others say, gun safety laws *are* effective in saving lives, especially Black lives.

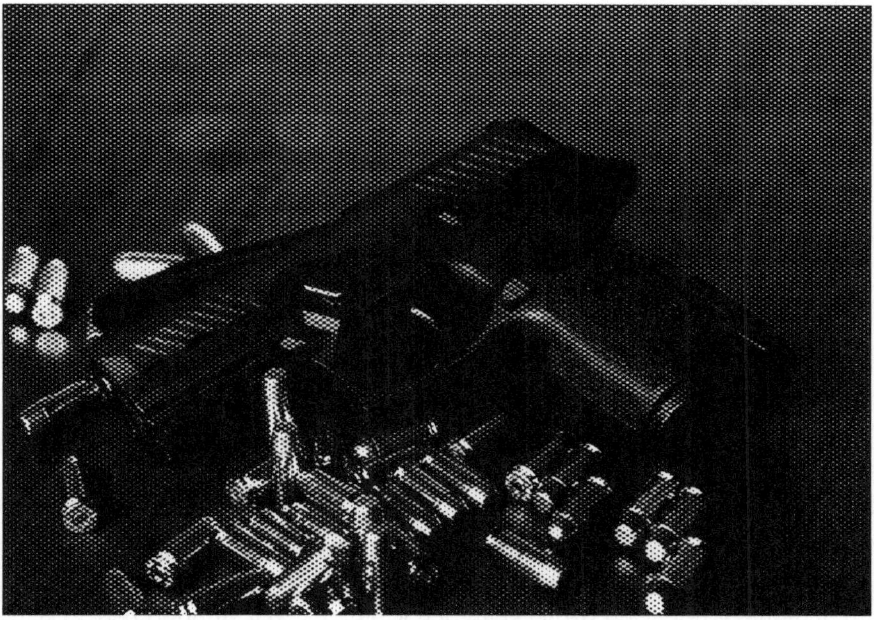

The Lie About Chicago and Inner City Gun Violence

Let's debunk this myth: "Strong gun safety laws in cities like Chicago do not work." False. Guns used in crimes committed in Chicago and other cities are often traced back to states with weaker gun safety laws, which emphasizes the importance of passing and implementing strong gun safety laws in all states. According to federal trace data, a significant portion of guns recovered in Chicago originates from outside Illinois, particularly from states with less restrictive gun laws, including Indiana, Wisconsin, Mississippi, and Kentucky. Approximately 60% of firearms recovered in Chicago come from out-of-state dealers, with Indiana alone accounting for more than 20% of these weapons (Chicago Police Department, 2017). This pattern is known as *interstate gun trafficking*, with guns purchased legally in states with weak regulations flow into cities with stronger laws (Chicago Police Department, 2017).

A 2023 study by the Department of Justice found that Chicago's "time-to-crime"—that is, the period between a gun being purchased and its recovery in a crime—was only 2.8 years compared to 6.3 years in New York and 4.2 years in Los Angeles (Bureau of Alcohol, Tobacco, Firearms and Explosives, 2023). This shorter "time-to-crime" period is a strong indicator of illegal trafficking. The evidence is clear: Chicago's gun violence problem is due not to the failure of strong gun laws but rather to the exploitation of weak laws in neighboring jurisdictions (Chicago Police Department, 2017).

Background Checks for All Gun Sales

One action that can be taken at the Congressional level to address these problems is a requirement for universal background checks on all gun sales. Universal background checks would ensure that folks with a long history of domestic abuse, restraining orders, and/or mental illness (who could be harmful if armed) are prohibited from obtaining a gun.

There are, however, dangerous loopholes in current gun laws. While federally licensed firearm dealers are required to conduct background checks, in many states private sales, including those at gun shows, online marketplaces, or in-person transactions, may transfer firearms without any background check. This loophole is not a minor technicality. An estimated 22% of all gun owners acquired their most recent firearm without a background check between 2013 and 2015 (Miller et al., 2017).

Background checks are critical for keeping guns out of dangerous hands. The checks have stopped over 4 million prohibited purchases since 1994, including over 3,600 purchases in 2014 alone that were blocked due to adverse mental health findings (Everytown for Gun Safety, 2021b). When implemented alongside strong state licensing laws, background checks have been linked to significant reductions in homicides, suicides, shootings of law enforcement officers, and mass shootings. Closing the private sale universal background checks loophole would significantly strengthen our ability to prevent gun violence in Black communities.

Stopping the Sale of Ghost Guns

Ghost guns are homemade firearms, meaning they are not federally licensed and are therefore untraceable. Research has shown that gun traffickers and far-right extremists prefer ghost guns. Under the Biden Administration in 2022, the Bureau of Alcohol, Tobacco, Firearms and Explosives (ATF) updated and administered a rule to outlaw ghost guns (ATF, 2022; U.S. Department of Justice, 2022). When the rule was challenged in front of the Supreme Court of the United States (SCOTUS) in 2025, the challenge was defeated (see: United States Supreme Court Case *Bondi* v. *VanDerStok* for more).

Stopping Concealed Carry Reciprocity (CCR)

In 2025, far-right Republican Congressional lawmakers attempted to turn the United States into the wild, wild west (even more) by introducing a law called Concealed Carry Reciprocity (CCR). CCR would eliminate any gun safety laws at the state level and force all states to allow anyone—licensed or not, trained or not, with a history of violent crime or not—to buy a gun (Everytown for Gun Safety, 2025b). Imagine if every person involved in the January 6th insurrection[2] had been legally armed.

The evidence is clear: when states weaken their concealed carry permitting systems, violence increases. Research from Johns Hopkins University found that states that weakened their concealed carry permitting systems experienced a 13–15% increase in gun homicide rates (Siegel et al., 2019). In contrast, states maintaining strong permitting requirements saw an 11% decrease in gun homicides. In Missouri, after repealing its permit-to-purchase law in 2007, the state experienced a 47% increase in its gun homicide rate within the first decade (Everytown for Gun Safety, 2025a).

A particularly alarming case occurred in 2022 when a person with an out-of-state concealed carry permit, which would not have qualified under the state's new standards, killed three people at a community gathering (Everytown for Gun Safety, 2025a). If CCR becomes law, this type of tragedy could become more common, as the weakest permitting standards would become the national standard. Black communities, already disproportionately impacted by gun violence, would bear the heaviest burden of these dangerous policies.

Addressing Gun Violence by Police and Police Brutality

Police violence is gun violence. In 2025, 93% of civilian deaths caused by police were because of a firearm (Campaign Zero, 2025). The situation becomes more detrimental for Black folks when we analyze police brutality statistics. Black people are still about 3 times more likely than White people to be killed by police (Campaign Zero, 2025; Harvard T. H. Chan School of Public Health, 2020). Meaningful gun prevention requires confronting this country's enduring foundations in white supremacy, its influence and development of current law enforcement systems, and pursuing promising and proven effective reduction reform policies and practices. Some of those policy solutions could include:

- Banning the use of deadly and unnecessary force and requiring officers to intervene when another officer is using lethal force.
- Supporting police in honoring a commitment to community engagement and relationship building.

- Developing advanced bias detection systems and addressing harmful behaviors exhibited in early officer recruitment and training.
- Creating an independent and transparent process to investigate police shootings and other deadly uses of force.
- Having a clear, honest, and timely reporting system for use-of-force and police misconduct investigations.

Visual Storytelling: Understanding Gun Violence Through Data Visualization

Complex statistics and data become more impactful and accessible when presented visually. These visual representations help communities understand patterns of gun violence and effective interventions.

Racial Disparities in Gun Violence

While Black Americans make up approximately 13% of the United States population, they experience:

- 58% of gun homicide victimizations.
- 56% of non-fatal shooting injuries.
- Black men specifically represent 6% of the population, but are over 50% of gun homicide victims.

(Everytown for Gun Safety, 2025c)

Sources of Crime Guns in Cities with Strong Gun Laws

Guns move from states with weak gun laws to cities with stronger regulations:

- Chicago: 60% of crime guns come from out of state, primarily from Indiana (21%), Mississippi (8%), and Wisconsin (4%) (City of Chicago, 2017).
- New York City: 85% of crime guns come from out of state, primarily Georgia, Virginia, and the Carolinas (New York State Office of the Attorney General, 2016).
- Baltimore: 65% of crime guns come from outside Maryland (Everytown for Gun Safety, 2021c)

Community Violence Intervention (CVI) Works

Outcomes in neighborhoods with community violence intervention programs compared to similar neighborhoods without:

- Oakland: 31% reduction in gun homicides over 6 years in CVI areas (Webster et al., 2012).
- Baltimore: 56% reduction in non-fatal shootings in Safe Streets zones (Webster et al., 2012).
- Chicago: 43% decrease in violent arrests for youth summer employment participants (Heller, 2014).

Economic Impact of Gun Violence in Black Communities

The financial burden of gun violence:

- $280 billion annual cost to the United States economy from gun violence (Everytown for Gun Safety, Crowding out Funding for Vital Public Services Report, 2021a).
- $40,000 average decrease in home values after a shooting (Irvin-Erickson et al., 2017).
- 20% reduction in business growth in high gun violence neighborhoods (Irvin-Erickson et al., 2017).
- $2.2 million lifetime cost per gun homicide (Miller et al., 2020).

These visualizations make complex data accessible, allowing community members, policymakers, and advocates understand both the scope of gun violence and proven solutions to reduce it. Presenting information visually allows us to communicate more effectively and mobilize action for change.

Our History, Our Context: Black Americans and Firearms

The relationship between Black Americans and firearms is a complex one, and shaped by history. From the post-Civil War Black Codes prohibiting Black gun ownership to the armed self-defense groups like the Deacons for Defense who protected civil rights workers in the 1960s, American history informs today's conversations. The Mulford Act of 1967,[3] passed in California specifically to disarm the Black Panthers' community patrols, demonstrates how gun control has sometimes targeted Black self-defense. Understanding our history helps contextualize both the desire for gun ownership among some Black Americans and the push for stronger gun safety laws to protect Black lives.

Social Media Toolkit: Amplifying Our Message

Social media provides powerful platforms for educating our communities, organizing for change, and holding elected officials accountable. This toolkit offers strategies to advocate for gun safety.

Key Messaging for Impact

Effective social media advocacy relies on clear, compelling messaging:

Core Messages to Amplify:

- Black communities deserve safety without sacrificing civil liberties.
- Gun violence is preventable, not inevitable.
- Community-led solutions are most effective.
- Gun safety laws do save Black lives.
- We must address the root causes of violence and implement common-sense gun laws.

Crafting Shareable Content

Create content that's easily shared and understood:

Digestible Statistics:

- Black men are 14x more likely to be shot than white men. This is not about culture—it is about policy and systemic racism. #BlackLivesMatter #GunSafety #StateofthePPL.
- Did you know? States with universal background checks have 15% fewer gun homicides. Our communities deserve this protection. #Background ChecksNow.
- In 2023, guns became the leading cause of death for Black children. We can change this. #ProtectOurKids #EndGunViolence.

(Everytown for Gun Safety: Black History Month Key Research Stats, 2025c)

Digestible Statistics:

- Share stories to humanize statistics.
- Highlight community heroes working to prevent violence.
- Create content and facilitate ways for survivors to share their experiences and compensate them for their labor.
- Use "A day in the life" content to show the reality of living with gun violence.

Visual Content:

- Infographics comparing gun laws and outcomes.
- Maps showing gun trafficking routes into communities.
- Before/after visuals of community transformation.
- Quote cards featuring Black gun violence prevention leaders.
- Explainer graphics on how specific gun laws work.

Effective Hashtags

Use and follow hashtags that amplify your message:

- #BlackGunSafety
- #CommunityOverGuns
- #EndGunViolence
- #HonorWithAction
- #ProtectOurCommunities
- #SafetyIsJustice
- #WeDeserveSafety
- #StateofthePPL
- #SayHerName

#SayHerName is a social movement and digital media campaign launched to bring awareness to Black women, girls, and femmes who are victims of state-sanctioned violence, frequently gun violence.

Create location-specific hashtags for local organizing:

- #SafeChicago
- #AtlantaAgainstGunViolence
- #PhillyPeacemakers

Digital Organizing Strategies

Move beyond awareness to action:

BlueSky, Threads, Twitter/X Campaigns:

- Organize tweet storms directed at specific legislators.
- Live-tweet during legislative hearings on gun bills.
- Create Twitter spaces to discuss community safety strategies.
- Use thread formats to explain complex policy issues.

Instagram Activism:

- Share infographics on statistics relevant to Black communities.
- Host Instagram Lives with gun violence prevention experts.
- Create highlight collections of local safety resources.
- Use location tags to organize neighborhood initiatives.

Facebook Community Building:

- Create private groups for survivor support.
- Organize community safety events through the Events feature.

- Share longer-form analyses of gun policies.
- Utilize Facebook fundraising for local intervention programs.

TikTok Education:

- Create short explainer videos on gun safety topics.
- Use trending sounds to spread awareness.
- Share quick safety tips for gun owners.
- Highlight youth-led prevention initiatives.

Leverage YouTube to share long-form content and shorts.

Countering Misinformation

Be prepared to address common myths and misinformation:

Effective Responses to Common Arguments:

- More guns = more safety" → "Research consistently shows that more guns lead to more gun deaths. States with higher gun ownership have more gun homicides.
- Gun laws only affect law-abiding citizens." → "Background checks have stopped over 4 million prohibited purchases since 1994.
- "Chicago proves gun laws do not work" → "60% of guns recovered in Chicago come from states with weaker gun laws, showing we need uniform national standards.

Online Safety Reminder: When advocating online, protect yourself:

- Consider creating advocacy-specific accounts separate from personal profiles.
- Be cautious about sharing identifying information.
- Document and report threatening responses.
- Connect with established organizations for support.

Remember that online advocacy is most effective when connected to offline action. Use digital platforms to organize community meetings, contact elected officials, and build coalitions for real-world change.

Trauma-Informed Approaches: Healing Our Communities

Gun violence inflicts deep trauma not only on victims but on entire communities. Understanding and addressing this trauma is essential for interrupting cycles of violence and building community resilience.

Understanding Community Trauma

Gun violence creates complex trauma that affects entire neighborhoods:

- Direct trauma for victims and their families.
- Secondary trauma for witnesses and first responders.
- Vicarious trauma for community members who hear about incidents.
- Collective trauma that affects community identity and cohesion.
- Intergenerational trauma which is passed from parents to children.

Research shows that children living in neighborhoods with high rates of gun violence experience symptoms similar to those of combat veterans with Post Traumatic Stress Disorder (PTSD). These trauma responses manifest as:

- Hypervigilance and difficulty concentrating.
- Emotional numbing and detachment.
- Sleep disturbances and nightmares.
- Physical health problems.
- Substance use as self-medication.
- Higher rates of anxiety and depression.

Culturally Responsive Healing Practices

Black communities have developed culturally affirming approaches to trauma healing that build on community strengths:

Community Healing Circles: Based on traditional African and Indigenous practices, healing circles provide:

- Safe spaces to process grief and trauma collectively.
- Recognition of cultural and spiritual dimensions of healing.
- Connection to ancestral wisdom and resilience.
- Peer support that reduces isolation.
- Collective storytelling that reframes community narratives.

Faith-Based Healing Models: Black churches and other faith communities offer:

- Spiritual frameworks for understanding and transcending trauma.
- Rituals that honor losses and facilitate mourning.
- Community support networks for practical and emotional needs.
- Meaning-making processes that foster post-traumatic growth.
- Integration of traditional mental health support with spiritual practice.

Arts-Based Healing: Creative expression provides powerful healing pathways:

- Murals that transform sites of violence into memorial spaces.
- Music and dance as embodied forms of trauma release.
- Theater programs that allow youth to express and transform trauma.
- Digital storytelling that amplifies community voices and experiences.
- Visual arts that process grief and envision healing.

Building Trauma-Informed Systems

Beyond individual and community healing, systems that interact with gun violence, survivors must become trauma-informed:

Trauma-Informed Policing

- Training officers to recognize trauma responses rather than misinterpreting them.
- Creating victim advocacy units with community members.
- Implementing notification protocols that minimize additional trauma.
- Partnering with community mental health providers.

Trauma-Informed Healthcare

- Training emergency department staff on cultural humility.
- Incorporating violence intervention specialists in trauma units.
- Providing long-term follow-up support beyond physical recovery.
- Creating healing-centered physical environments.

Trauma-Informed Schools

- Training teachers to recognize and respond to trauma symptoms.
- Creating safe spaces for processing community violence.
- Implementing restorative rather than punitive discipline.
- Offering high-quality and culturally competent school- and community-based mental health services.

By integrating trauma-informed approaches across systems, we can break cycles of violence and build pathways to collective healing and resilience in Black communities affected by gun violence.

Healing Our Community: Mental Health and Gun Violence

Trauma from gun violence creates lasting mental health impacts in Black communities. Organizations like Therapy for Black Men and Black Mental Health Alliance provide culturally responsive care that acknowledges both historical and ongoing trauma. Community healing circles, like those organized by Healing Justice, create spaces for collective processing of grief and trauma. These approaches emphasize that effective mental health support must be accessible and culturally affirming. For Black gun owners, understanding the connection between mental health and responsible ownership is crucial for preventing suicide, which accounts for more than 60 of 100 gun deaths nationally (Everytown for Gun Safety, Gun Safety Report 2024e).

Mental health stigma in Black communities often appears in unique forms, with many turning to faith communities or family networks instead of formal services. Culturally responsive approaches include:

- Faith-based mental health initiatives like The Confess Project's barber shop mental health program.[4]
- Community-led healing circles that incorporate cultural traditions.
- Peer support networks specifically for Black gun violence survivors.
- Trauma-informed approaches that acknowledge historical context.

Discussion Questions:

- How might mental health stigma in your community prevent people from seeking help after experiencing gun violence?
- What culturally affirming mental health resources exist in your community?
- How can we better support the mental health of both survivors and witnesses of gun violence?

International Perspectives: What We Can Learn from Global Gun Violence Prevention

The United States is not alone in facing gun violence, but our rates of gun deaths far exceed those of other wealthy nations. Looking at international approaches can provide valuable insights for preventing gun violence in Black communities.

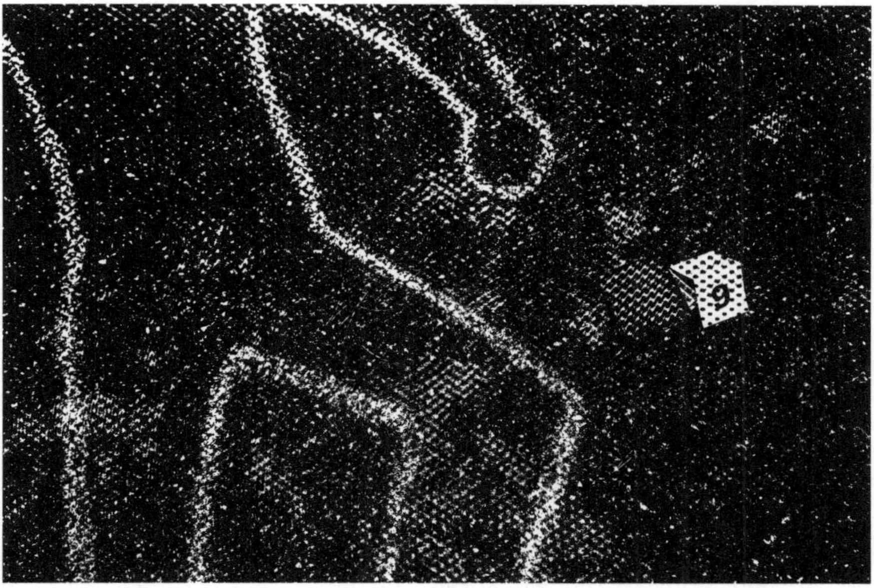

Global Context: Understanding the Scale

When it comes to gun violence, the United States is an outlier among high-income countries (Institute for Health Metrics and Evaluation, 2023). The United States gun homicide rate is 25 times higher than the average of other high-income countries.

This disparity is even more pronounced in Black communities, where the gun homicide rate is approximately 10 times higher than the overall United States rate (Giffords Law Center, 2025).

Successful International Approaches

Australia's Rapid Response. After a mass shooting in 1996, Australia implemented comprehensive gun reform:

- Banned semi-automatic rifles and shotguns.
- Instituted a mandatory buyback program that removed 650,000 firearms.
- Created unified gun registration and licensing.
- Required a "genuine reason" to own a firearm.

Results: Gun homicides dropped by 60% over the next decade, with no subsequent mass shootings for 22 years. Suicide by firearm decreased by 65% (Giffords Law Center, 2025; Everytown for Gun Safety, 2025d).

Canada's Targeted Approach. Canada maintains a hunting culture while implementing:

- Comprehensive background checks, including interviews with references.
- 28-day waiting periods.
- Required safety training.
- Bans on assault-style weapons.
- Safe storage requirements.

Results: Canada's gun homicide rate is roughly one-third of the United States rate despite significant levels of gun ownership (Global News, 2023; Institute for Health Metrics and Evaluation, 2023).

The United Kingdom's Public Health Framework. The UK approaches gun violence as a public health issue by:

- Banning handguns and semi-automatic weapons.
- Requiring police home visits before gun licenses are granted.
- Requiring medical disclosure for mental health conditions.
- Implementing early intervention programs for at-risk youth.

Results: The UK has one of the lowest gun homicide rates in the world, at 0.04 per 100,000 people (Aizenman, 2021).

Lessons for Black Communities

While the United States has a unique gun culture and constitutional framework, several international approaches could be researched for adaptation:

Community-Based Adaptations of Global Models

- Scotland's Violence Reduction Unit model has been successfully adapted in American cities with large Black populations.
- Brazilian Ceasefire initiatives have been effectively modified for United States urban settings.
- Jamaica's Peace Management Initiative provides relevant strategies for community mediation.

Culturally Responsive International Approaches

- New Zealand's engagement with Indigenous communities during gun reform provides a model for inclusive policy development.
- South Africa's focus on addressing the historical context of violence offers relevant lessons for the United States

Transferable Policy Elements

- Universal background checks (implemented in nearly all high-income countries).
- Waiting periods (shown to reduce suicide and impulsive violence globally).
- Safe storage requirements (effective at reducing accidents and theft internationally).
- Red flag laws[5] (variations exist in several countries with positive outcomes).

State-by-State Guide: Gun Laws Affecting Black Communities

Gun laws vary dramatically across states, creating a patchwork of protections and vulnerabilities. This guide helps you understand how gun laws in different states affect Black communities, focusing on states with large Black populations.

States with Stronger Gun Safety Protections

California

- Universal background checks ✓
- Assault weapons ban ✓
- Significant capacity magazine restrictions ✓
- Waiting periods for purchases ✓
- Ghost gun regulations ✓
- Domestic violence restrictions ✓
- Red flag laws ✓
- Safe storage requirements ✓

New York

- Universal background checks ✓
- Assault weapons ban ✓
- Large capacity magazine restrictions ✓

- Permit required to purchase handguns ✓
- Ghost gun regulations ✓
- Domestic violence restrictions ✓
- Red flag laws ✓
- Safe storage requirements ✓

Illinois

- Universal background checks ✓
- Assault weapons ban ✓ (in some localities)
- Permit required to purchase firearms—Firearm Owner's Identification (FOID) card ✓
- Waiting periods for purchases ✓
- Ghost gun regulations ✓
- Domestic violence restrictions ✓
- Red flag laws ✓

Maryland

- Universal background checks for handguns ✓
- Assault weapons ban ✓
- Large capacity magazine restrictions ✓
- Permit required to purchase handguns ✓
- Waiting periods for handgun purchases ✓
- Ghost gun regulations ✓
- Domestic violence restrictions ✓
- Red flag laws ✓

States with Weaker Gun Safety Protections

Georgia

- Universal background checks ✗
- Assault weapons ban ✗
- Large capacity magazine restrictions ✗
- Permit-less carry allowed ✓
- Stand your ground law ✓
- Preemption of local gun laws ✓
- No waiting periods ✗

Texas

- Universal background checks ✗
- Assault weapons ban ✗
- Large capacity magazine restrictions ✗

- Permit-less carry allowed ✓
- Stand your ground law ✓
- Preemption of local gun laws ✓
- No waiting periods ✗

Florida

- Universal background checks ✗ (except at gun shows in some counties)
- Assault weapons ban ✗
- Large capacity magazine restrictions ✗
- Stand your ground law ✓
- Preemption of local gun laws ✓
- Red flag laws ✓

Louisiana

- Universal background checks ✗
- Assault weapons ban ✗
- Large capacity magazine restrictions ✗
- Permit-less carry allowed ✓
- Stand your ground law ✓
- Preemption of local gun laws ✓
- No waiting periods ✗

The Impact of State Laws on Black Communities

States with stronger gun laws have lower rates of gun deaths, including both homicides and suicides. Black communities in states with weaker gun laws face higher risks:

- States without universal background checks have 15% higher gun homicide rates (Everytown for Gun Safety, 2025a).
- States with permitless carry laws saw a 13–15% increase in violent crime after implementation (Everytown for Gun Safety, 2025a).
- States with strong domestic violence firearm restrictions saw intimate partner homicides decrease by 14% (Everytown for Gun Safety, 2025a).
- States with red flag laws have seen reductions in firearm suicides between 7% and 13% (Everytown for Gun Safety, 2025a).

Interstate Trafficking Impact

Weak laws in one state affect safety in neighboring states:

- Nearly 60% of crime guns recovered in Chicago come from outside Illinois, primarily from states with weaker gun laws (Everytown for Gun Safety, 2025d; U.S. Department of Justice, 2023c).
- 85% of crime guns recovered in New York City come from out of state (Everytown for Gun Safety, 2025d).
- Interstate trafficking routes (known as "iron pipelines") funnel guns from states with weak laws to cities with stronger regulations (Everytown for Gun Safety, 2025d).

Understanding your state's laws can help you:

- Know your rights and responsibilities as a gun owner.
- Identify priorities for advocacy in your state.
- Recognize when traveling across state lines with a firearm might create legal issues.
- Better understand how guns move into your community.

ACTION STEP: Research your specific state's laws at gifford.org/lawcenter or everytown.org/state.

Legislative Advocacy Guide: Making Your Voice Heard

Creating change requires both community action and policy reform. This guide will help you effectively advocate for stronger gun laws and policies that protect Black communities.

Understanding the Legislative Process

Before advocating, understand how laws get made:

1. Bills are introduced in the state legislature or Congress.
2. Committees review and revise bills.
3. If approved in committee, the full chamber votes.
4. If passed, the bill goes to the other chamber (House or Senate).
5. If both chambers approve, it goes to the executive (Governor or President) to sign or veto

Most gun safety bills die in committee before ever getting a vote. Focusing advocacy on committee members can be particularly effective.

Tracking Gun Legislation

Stay informed about pending gun legislation:

- Sign up for alerts from gun safety organizations like Everytown, Giffords, or March for Our Lives.
- Use LegiScan (www.legiscan.com) to track bills in your state and that otherwise impact you and those you love.
- Follow your representatives on social media for updates on their positions.
- Attend town halls and public hearings when gun-related bills are being discussed.

Effective Contact Methods

When contacting elected officials:

Phone Calls:

- Identify yourself as a constituent (give your address/zip code).
- Be specific about the bill number or issue.
- Share a brief personal connection to the issue.
- Make a clear ask (vote yes/no, co-sponsor, etc.).
- Be polite but firm.
- Follow up.

Sample Phone Script: "Hello, my name is [YOUR NAME], and I'm a constituent from [YOUR ADDRESS]. I'm calling to urge Representative [NAME] to vote YES on House Bill XXX, which would require background checks on all gun sales. This issue matters to me because [PERSONAL CONNECTION]. Will the Representative commit to supporting or sponsoring this bill?"

If yes: "I'm glad my representative supports the bill. Is the representative willing to help recruit additional members to support the bill?"

If no: "Please share any important information or insights for the representative to learn more about supporting the bill. Please share any communities they need to hear from to be moved to 'yes.'" (*Write down the responses and follow up with a meeting request to share the information needed or invite the constituencies the representative needs to hear from.)*

"Thank you for your time. I look forward to staying in touch."

Letters and Emails:

- Keep communications brief (1-page maximum).
- Personalize your message with your own experiences.
- Focus on 1–2 key points.
- Include relevant local statistics.
- Incorporate points connecting the legislation outcomes to the personal experiences. or self-interest of the lawmaker.
- End with a specific request.
- Follow up.

In-Person Meetings:

- Schedule in advance through the official's office.
- Bring 1–2 other constituents if possible.
- Prepare a concise (2-minute) personal story.
- Share key data points relevant to the district they represent, or connections to their personal experiences and self-interest.
- Leave behind a one-page fact sheet.
- End with a specific request.
- Follow up with a thank-you note.

Building Collective Power

Your voice is amplified when joined with others:

- Form a local advocacy group focused on gun safety.
- Partner with existing community organizations.
- Coordinate "call-in days" where many constituents contact officials on the same day.
- Organize delegations to lobby days at your state capitol.
- Use social media to rally support and share legislator responses publicly.

Holding Officials Accountable

Track how officials vote and hold them accountable:

- Attend town halls and ask public questions about gun safety positions.
- Write letters to the editor mentioning officials by name.
- Use election seasons to highlight candidates' gun safety records.
- Thank officials who support gun safety and respectfully but firmly challenge those who don't.
- Support candidates who prioritize gun violence prevention.
- Follow up.

What You Can Do Today:

- Find your representatives at usa.gov/elected-officials.
- Save their contact information in your phone.
- Sign up for action alerts from a gun safety organization.
- Schedule a calendar reminder to call your representatives monthly about gun safety.

Consistent, persistent advocacy creates change. Your voice matters, especially when combined with others in your community committed to ending gun violence.

We Keep Us Safe

Community Violence Intervention Programs

What are Community Violence Intervention Programs?

Community Violence Intervention Programs (CVI or CVIP) are organizations and programs designed to provide support to folks in communities most affected by gun violence. The goal of CVI is to address the reasons that gun violence occurs—joblessness, community disinvestment, and systemic racism. CVI programs can come in different forms.

Hospital-based Violence Intervention Programs (HVIP)

Usually taking place in trauma centers, emergency rooms, and health clinics, hospital-based CVI programs usually happen right after a traumatic violent event has occurred. Engaging the patient right after a violent event has happened is meant to reduce the likelihood of retaliation or some kind of repeat of violent actions. Services like mental health counseling, financial and educational support are provided.

Crime Prevention Through Environmental Design (CPTED)

This type of CVI programming involves taking abandoned buildings, empty car lots, and underdeveloped parks and turning them into livable green spaces to help make folks in these communities feel safe.

Street Outreach

Community leaders or violence interventionists/interrupters usually lead this kind of CVI programming. These efforts focus on building relationships with survivors, community members, and individuals at risk of committing violence. Bringing these groups together, violence interrupters seek to resolve conflict.

Benefits of CVI Programs

Cities that started CVI programs in their communities saw the effects of gun violence decrease. For example, participants in Chicago's summer youth employment program experienced a 43% decrease in violent arrests. In Baltimore, HVIP participants were six times less likely than nonparticipants to be hospitalized for a violent injury. These programs are proven to work. Funding and support for CVI programs should continue.

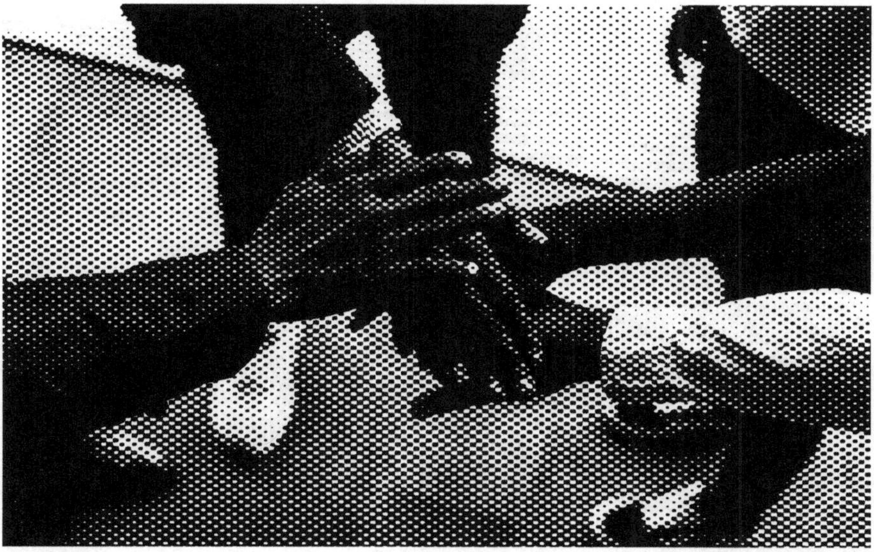

Breaking the Cycle: Economic Opportunity and Gun Violence Prevention

When economic opportunity increases, gun violence often decreases. In cities where targeted economic development programs like the Cure Violence model have been implemented, gun violence has decreased by up to 30% in participating neighborhoods (Cure Violence Global, 2021). Organizations like the Brotherhood Sister Sol in Harlem, New York, combine economic education with violence prevention, providing pathways to employment while addressing the root causes of violence. These programs recognize that economic justice and gun violence prevention are interconnected struggles.

Economic interventions that have proven effective include:

- Targeted workforce development in high-violence neighborhoods.
- Community-owned businesses that reinvest profits locally.
- Affordable housing initiatives that stabilize communities.
- Financial literacy programs that create pathways to economic mobility.

Success Stories: Black Communities Leading the Way on Gun Violence Prevention

While gun violence continues to devastate our country, there are powerful success stories of Black-led initiatives creating real change. These examples prove that with the right approaches, resources, and community leadership, we can reduce gun violence, build safer neighborhoods, and strengthen the country.

Oakland Ceasefire: Community Partnership Model

In Oakland, California, gun homicides decreased by 31% between 2012 and 2019 through the implementation of the Ceasefire strategy, a partnership between community leaders, law enforcement, and social service providers (Braga et al., 2019a, 2019b). This model:

- Identified people at the highest risk for gun violence.
- Connected them with supportive services, including job training and mental healthcare.
- Engaged respected community elders as violence interrupters.
- Created accountability through focused law enforcement on the most violent offenders.

The program's success came from centering Black community leadership and expertise throughout every phase (Northeastern University, 2019).

Advance Peace: Transforming Lives Through Fellowship

The Advance Peace Fellowship in Richmond, California, reduced firearm assaults by 55% over five years by taking an innovative approach that included (Coburn et al., 2022):

- Identifying young men at the highest risk for gun violence involvement.
- Offering them 18-month fellowships with daily mentorship and life coaching.
- Providing stipends for meeting life goals and remaining uninvolved in violence.
- Connecting them with trauma recovery services.

LIFE Camp: Community-Centered Healing

In South Jamaica, Queens, New York, LIFE Camp reduced shootings by 40% from 2010 to 2019 in its target area through several community-led initiatives, including (Reuters, 2021):

- Trauma-informed conflict mediation.
- Employment opportunities for at-risk youth.
- Therapeutic support through their Peace Cafes.
- Community events that reclaimed public spaces.

Their "Peace is a Lifestyle" approach demonstrates how cultural change within communities can transform patterns of violence (Reuters, 2021).

Scaling What Works

These success stories share common elements:

- Centering the voices and leadership of directly impacted communities.
- Addressing root causes through economic opportunity and healing.
- Using data-driven approaches to direct resources.
- Building trust between institutions and communities.
- Investing adequate financial resources over multiple years.

When these programs receive consistent funding and community support, they demonstrate that gun violence is not inevitable. Black communities are leading the way in developing holistic, evidence-based approaches that save lives.

Faith in Action: The Black Church's Role in Gun Safety

Many Black churches across America are taking an active role in addressing gun violence. Programs like "Guns Down, Lives Up," organized by faith communities in Chicago, have facilitated gun buyback programs. Rev. Michael

McBride's LIVE FREE Campaign has trained clergy nationwide to approach gun violence as both a spiritual and public health crisis. These faith-based approaches combine the church's traditional role as a sanctuary with practical community intervention.

Faith communities can contribute to gun violence prevention through:

- Hosting gun buyback programs with no questions asked.
- Providing space for conflict mediation and resolution.
- Offering trauma support and counseling.
- Facilitating intergenerational dialogues about community safety.
- Partnering with secular organizations to provide comprehensive support.

Young, Black, and Leading: Youth-Led Gun Safety Movement

Black youth are not just victims of gun violence—they are leading the movement to end it.

Youth-led initiatives making an impact include:

- Peace Warriors programs in schools that train peer mediators.
- Youth-led community policing alternatives.
- Student-designed gun violence awareness campaigns.
- Teen-led advocacy at state legislatures.
- Youth-guided research on effective intervention strategies.

Digital Safety and Online Threats: Protecting Black Communities in Virtual Spaces

The weaponization of online spaces presents new threats to Black communities. Extremist groups use social media to organize, recruit, and target communities of color with both online harassment and real-world violence. Understanding this digital dimension of gun violence is essential for comprehensive community safety.

Online Radicalization and Targeted Threats

White supremacist and extremist groups actively recruit and organize online. Recent studies show:

- More than half of the Black people surveyed said they were harassed because of race/ethnicity (compared to 17% of white people) (Pew Research, 2021).

- Over 75% of mass shooters targeting Black communities shared their intentions or racist ideologies online before committing violence (Peterson et al., 2023).
- Algorithms on social media platforms can accelerate radicalization by exposing users to increasingly extreme content (Regehr et al., 2025).

The Buffalo supermarket shooting in 2022, where 10 Black people were murdered, demonstrated the deadly connection between online radicalization and real-world violence. The shooter was radicalized online and specifically targeted a Black neighborhood.

Digital Self-Defense Strategies

Black communities can employ several strategies to protect themselves from online threats:

Recognize warning signs: Learn to identify concerning online content that may indicate real-world threats

- Direct threats of violence.
- Sharing weapons with threatening messages.
- References to previous mass shootings or white supremacist attacks.
- Detailed plans targeting specific locations.

Report harmful content: Most major platforms have tools to report threats, harassment, and violent content.

- Document threats with screenshots before reporting.
- Follow up if no action is taken.
- Report serious threats to local law enforcement and the FBI.

Protect Personal Information:

- Regularly audit your digital footprint and remove sensitive personal information.
- Change your passwords frequently.
- Use privacy settings on social media accounts.
- Be cautious about sharing location information.
- Consider using a Virtual Private Network (VPN) for additional online privacy.

Community Monitoring and Support:

- Create neighborhood watch groups that include online monitoring.
- Share information about potential threats with community members.
- Develop response plans for online threats that may become real-world dangers.

The Economic Impact of Gun Violence on Black Communities

Gun violence is not only a public health crisis—it's also an economic crisis. The financial burden of gun violence falls disproportionately on Black communities, creating cycles of disinvestment and poverty that compound the trauma of violence itself.

Community Economic Impact

Gun violence depresses property values, drives out businesses, and reduces economic opportunity. Research shows that:

- Each homicide in a census tract is associated with a 1.5% reduction in housing values (Irvin-Erickson et al., 2017).
- Neighborhoods with high rates of gun violence experience 35% fewer new retail and service establishments (Irvin-Erickson et al., 2017).
- After a surge in gun violence, home values in Black neighborhoods drop by an average of 4%, compared to 1% in predominantly white neighborhoods (Irvin-Erickson et al., 2017).

Our Land, Our Lives: Gun Safety in Rural Black Communities

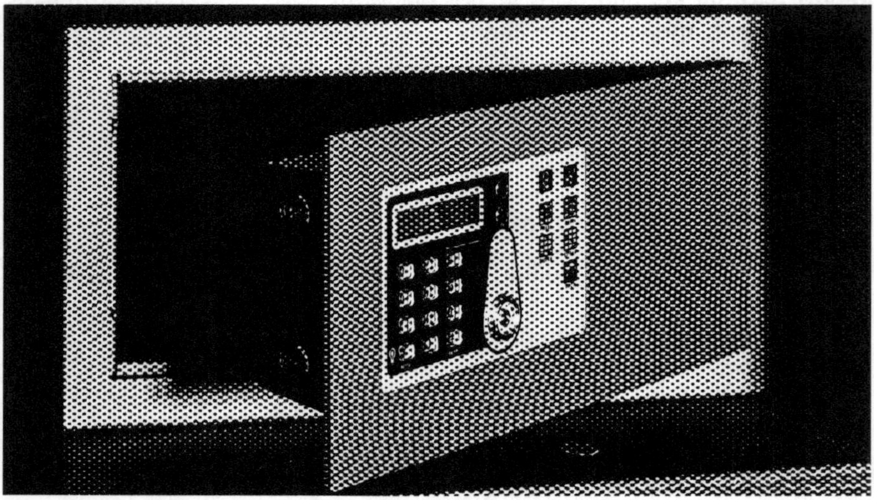

Many Black communities have unique relationships with firearms. In many rural areas, guns are tools for hunting, protecting crops from predators, and family protection. Organizations like the National African American Gun

Association report that rural Black gun owners often emphasize heritage and self-reliance alongside safety concerns. Community-based approaches in rural settings might look different, from church-based gun safety classes to intergenerational hunting groups that teach responsible firearm practices.

Rural gun safety challenges include:

- Limited access to secure storage options.
- Fewer resources for gun safety education.
- Longer emergency response times.
- Different cultural contexts around firearms.

Rural Black gun owners often navigate complex tensions between traditional values, practical concerns, and safety considerations. Organizations like the Rural Black Gun Owners Association provide specialized training to address these unique needs while emphasizing safety education.

If You are Gonna Strap Up, Here's What You Need to Know

Responsible Black Gun Ownership

Black Gun Owners

Here is the cold, hard fact: the presence of a firearm makes the environment more dangerous. Several studies and reports support that. However, many Black folks are obtaining a gun license, buying a gun, and completing firearm training. Black women, in particular, represent the fastest-growing demographic of new gun owners in the United States. While Black gun owners are not the same everywhere, protection is the main reason Black people are choosing to arm themselves. If this applies to you, please review all state and local laws, requirements for licensing, and get training from vetted instructors. The most important things you can do as a Black gun owner are to know your rights and store your firearm securely.

Multiple peer-reviewed research studies demonstrate that access to firearms in a home significantly increases the risk of homicide, suicide, and accidental injury. Research from the Johns Hopkins University School of Public Health shows that having a gun in the home increases the risk of homicide by about 300%, with risks particularly high in households experiencing domestic violence (Johns Hopkins Bloomberg School of Public Health, 2024; Mayors Against Illegal Guns, 2025). Studies published in the *New England Journal of Medicine* have consistently found that access to firearms is a significant risk factor for suicide completion, with gun-related suicide attempts being fatal approximately 90% of the time compared to less than 5% for other standard methods (Anglemyer et al., 2014; Conwell et al., 2002).

Secure Storage

Accidental shootings are one of the most common forms of gun violence, occurring daily. Additionally, hundreds of thousands of guns are stolen. Many of those stolen firearms surface on the underground market, where they are made available to people who might have violent histories. Gun owners must securely store their firearms.

Different Secure Storage Devices

Luckily, different types of devices allow gun owners to store their firearms according to individual needs. Consider the following:

- Full-sized gun safe—can store multiple firearms and lock with biometric, key, or passcode.
- Lockbox—smaller than a full-sized safe; can be locked by biometric, key, or passcode.
- Console/vehicle gun safe storage in a car, and can be locked by biometric, key, or passcode.
- Gun case—can hold one firearm; meant for transit or storing at home; external lock.
- Trigger lock—this locks the trigger of a single gun.
- Cable lock—this is a cable that runs through the action of a single weapon to prevent firing.

BeSMART

Launched in 2015, BeSMART is a resource designed to promote responsible gun ownership and stop child gun deaths. The goal of BeSMART is to encourage honest conversations around gun ownership.

- S—Secure all guns in your home.
- M—Model responsible gun ownership.
- Ask about unsecured guns in other homes.
- R—Recognize the role of guns in suicide.
- T—Talk to your friends and family about BeSMART.

No, They're Not Like Us

Holding Gun Companies Accountable

Gun Companies Marketing to Black Folks

As more Black Americans choose to purchase firearms, gun companies are expanding their marketing campaigns and strategies beyond the traditional target demographic of middle-aged white men. However, Black people thinking about buying a firearm and new Black gun owners should not be fooled. Gun companies have no interest in meaningfully engaging Black communities. They've proven this to be true over time.

Connections to Extremists

Gun companies are often connected to extremist groups. For example, a new online firearms company, GrabAGun, reportedly considered Blake Masters as part of its board of directors. Masters is a poster child for far-right and pro-2nd Amendment (2A) groups. One of his most notable quotes is "We do have a gun violence problem in this country, and it's gang violence. It is people in Chicago and St. Louis shooting each other. Very often, you know, Black people, frankly" (Roberts, 2022).

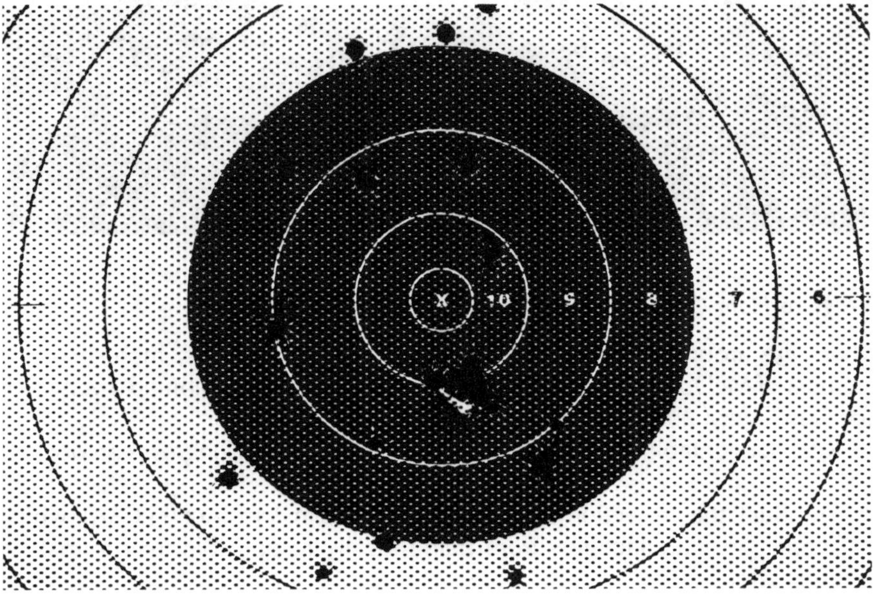

Gun Companies Enjoy Legal Protections as Black Lives Are Stolen

Firearm companies have one overriding interest: protecting their bottom line. Every year in the United States, over 100,000 people are shot and killed, or wounded, the majority being Black (Everytown for Gun Safety, 2024b). And gun companies have taken much care so that they are not legally responsible. Guns are not regulated in the same way as other products. Firearm regulations are out of date, and the gun industry is actively investing in rolling back any regulatory powers granted to the ATF and other related government agencies. Gun companies and manufacturers are protected from legal actions against them, despite frequent violations.

Ways to Hold Gun Companies Accountable

There are around 78,000 gun dealers in the United States, more than the number of McDonald's, Subway, and Wendy's locations combined (Everytown for Gun Safety, 2023).

Real accountability needs to be taken. Here is what Congress can do:

- Roll Back the Protection of Lawful Commerce in Arms Act (PLCAA), which keeps gun manufacturers from being legally responsible for not making guns safer.
- Propose up-to-date legislation on how gun dealers conduct their business.

Support the implementation of smart safety features, like thumb scan or passcode, which would help keep firearms from children or criminals

She's One of Us, and She Deserves to Live Too

Gun Violence Against Black Trans Women

Hate-motivated Speech, Anti-trans Laws, and Gun Violence Against the Trans Community

All Black lives matter, and all Black people deserve to thrive, including Black trans women, who are particularly targeted by gun violence at an alarming rate. But this is no coincidence. As anti-trans talk and attitudes spread, anti-trans laws and bad gun laws are passing in several state assemblies. Folks with extremist views have easy access to firearms, creating an environment that is not safe for Black trans women.

The statistics on Black trans women are especially stark. Black transwomen account for the majority of victims of fatal anti-transgender violence. Since 2013, Black trans women have accounted for more than six in 10 (60.8%) of all known victims of fatal violence against transgender people. In the 12 months leading up to November 2024, half of all victims of fatal violence in the transgender community were Black trans women (HRC, 2025).

One study that analyzed data from 2013 to 2021 found that Black transgender women were significantly more likely to be fatally shot by a gun than non-Black transgender women (Halliwell et al., 2024).

Homicide Rates of Black Trans Women

In 2023, there were 35 reported homicides of transgender people. Of those homicides, 80% were committed with a gun. And Black trans women are unfortunately the majority of all these homicides. From 2017 to 2023, there were 263 homicides of transgender people. 73% of these people were killed with a gun. From 2017 to 2023, more than 6 in 10 gun homicides of transgender people (63%) were of Black trans women (Everytown for Gun Safety, 2024c).

Community Voice: Black Trans Perspective

"In Atlanta, T.K. Hill, Ashley Burton, KoKo Williams, Tee Tee Dangerfield, and many others have tragically succumbed to the harsh realities of gun violence. Their stories are often overlooked by mainstream media, which frequently fails to address the core issues or offer real solutions. Instead, we are presented with a narrative that skews identity rather than disrupts the falsehoods that enable the violence to begin with.

As an organization, the Solutions Not Punishment Collaborative (SnapCo.) envisions a safer Atlanta where gun violence is not addressed through punishment, but through community-based initiatives that promote collaboration, understanding, and support for Black and Trans people in our community. SnapCo.'s Trans Safety Initiative focuses on empowering the Trans community by providing essential resources aimed at reducing gun violence and minimizing police interactions. This initiative emphasizes practical solutions, ensuring that Trans individuals have access to the necessary documentation, like passports, technology, and skills needed to navigate hostile environments safely.

Investing in Trans leadership and empowering them, both locally and statewide, is a vital tool in reclaiming our autonomy, preventing, and navigating the impacts of gun violence."—Toni-Michelle Williams, Executive Director, Solutions Not Punishment Collaborative.

Gender-Affirming Healthcare Saves Lives

As anti-trans legislation and dangerous gun laws proliferate, trans people are forced to live in fear, frequently compounding trauma, mental health crises, and suicidality. In this context, access to healthcare becomes a crucial, lifesaving resource. Gender-affirming healthcare provides various types of social and medical services for trans folks, which is especially important in stopping Lesbian, Gay, Bisexual, Transgender, Queer and Same-Gender Loving (LGBTQ+/SGL) suicide. For example, suicide attempts are significantly lower (31%) among LGBTQ+ young adults from highly accepting families, compared to 57% among those from less accepting families (Be SMART Fact Sheet: Protecting LGBTQ+ Youth from Firearm Suicide, 2024). Gender-affirming healthcare helps create an accepting environment and leads to trans folks thriving.

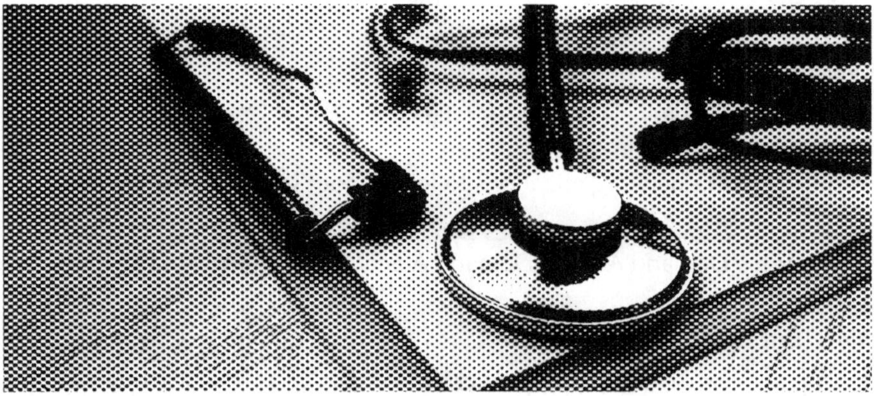

It is essential to understand that gender-affirming healthcare is based on established medical consensus, not political ideology. Consider for a moment how often cisgender people pursue gender-affirming care without discussion (see: Viagra, breast augmentation, and rhinoplasty, for example). Leading medical organizations—such as the American Medical Association, the American Academy of Pediatrics, the American Psychological Association, and the World Professional Association for Transgender Health—recognize gender-affirming care as medically necessary and evidence-based. Peer-reviewed research consistently shows that access to gender-affirming care significantly reduces depression, anxiety, and suicidal ideation among transgender people. Multiple long-term studies show that denying this care increases suicide risk, whereas providing it saves lives. Politicians who attempt to override medical experts, families, and patients by restricting this healthcare are placing vulnerable people at higher risk of violence, including gun violence. In communities where both gun access is high and healthcare access is limited, the risks multiply, with particularly devastating consequences for Black trans women.

Us Helping Us

Time to Lock In

Do You Want to Get Involved? Act Locally

- Join and volunteer at a local gun violence prevention organization in your communities:
  - Everytown for Gun Safety Survivor Network Sign-up.
  - Moms Demand Action Volunteer Sign-up.
  - Giffords Gun Owners for Safety Sign-up.

Wanna Change Policy? Act Electorally

- Vote for gun safety-minded candidates.
- Consider running for elected office.
- Engage gun safety organizations to learn about safety-minded candidates:
  - Brady Campaign Candidates Directory.
  - Moms Demand Action: Demand A Seat Training Program.

Black-Led Gun Safety Resources

- Community Justice (nationwide)—Policy and advocacy led by communities of color.
- LIVE FREE Campaign (nationwide)Faith-based approach to ending gun violence.
- GoodKids MadCity (Chicago)—Youth-led violence prevention.
- The TraRon Center (Washington, D.C.)—Healing and advocacy for gun violence survivors.
- Mothers/Men Against Senseless Killings (Chicago)—Community-based violence prevention.
- Life Camp, Inc. (New York)—Youth development and violence intervention.
- Armed And Educated, Inc. (Louisville, Ky) Community safety organization promoting a safe & responsible firearm culture.

Free Safety Resources

- Project ChildSafe—Free gun locks available nationwide.
- Local police departments—Many offer free gun locks to community members.
- Operation LIPSTICK—Resources for addressing women's roles in gun trafficking.

- Black Mental Health Alliance—Trauma support for communities affected by gun violence.
- Everytown Community Safety Fund—Grants for local violence prevention initiatives.

What You Can Do This Week

- Check if your local police department offers free gun locks.
- Have a conversation with one family member about gun safety.
- Follow one Black-led gun safety organization on social media.
- Research your local representatives' positions on gun safety.
- Attend a community meeting about public safety in your neighborhood.

Discussion Questions

- How do historical contexts shape different perspectives on gun ownership in Black communities?
- What role can faith communities play in gun violence prevention?
- How might economic opportunity initiatives contribute to reduced gun violence?
- What culturally specific approaches to mental health support would be most effective in your community?

- How can we better protect Black trans women from gun violence?
- What strategies have been most effective for youth-led gun violence prevention?
- How do rural and urban Black communities face different challenges regarding gun safety?
- What policy changes would make the most significant difference in your community?

Notes

1 This statistic describes the sad and stark racial disparity in gun violence by comparing population representation to victimization rates. Organizations like Everytown for Gun Safety, Giffords Law Center, and Brady United frequently use this analogy to contextualize Centers for Disease Control and Prevention (CDC) data.

2 "On the afternoon of Jan. 6, 2021, as Congress was meeting to certify the results of the 2020 presidential election, a violent and *heavily armed mob* of supporters of the 45th President stormed the U.S. Capitol. While lawmakers and staff were shepherded to secure locations or barricaded behind doors, the rioters pushed past severely outnumbered Capitol Police officers, breaking windows and Republican Congressional vandalizing offices, many with disturbingly violent intentions toward members of Congress and Vice President Mike Pence for their having refused to succumb to the 45th president's attempts to overturn the election in his favor. Five people were killed, including one Capitol Police officer who was beaten by rioters." https://americanoversight.org/investigation/the-january-6-attack-on-the-u-s-capitol/

3 The Mulford Act was signed into law by California's Republican governor Ronald Reagan with the support of the National Rifle Association to outlaw the open carrying of loaded firearms, in response to members of the Black Panther Party who openly carried loaded firearms while conducting patrols in Oakland neighborhoods to protect Black residents from police brutality (American Psychological Association, 2023).

4 "The Confess Project of America is a national organization that fosters mental health advocacy in marginal and underrepresented communities."

5 "Extreme Risk Protection Orders or 'Red Flag' laws allow family members or law enforcement to petition a judge to remove a firearm from the environment of a person deemed at risk of harming themselves or others" (American Academy of Pediatrics, 2025).

Bibliography

Advocates for Trans Equality. (2025). A4TE releases 2025 trans day of remembrance report. https://transequality.org/news/a4te-releases-2025-trans-day-remembrance-report

Aizenman, N. (2021). *Gun violence deaths: How the U.S. compares with the rest of the world.* NPR. https://www.npr.org/sections/goatsandsoda/2021/03/24/980838151/gun-violence-deaths-how-the-u-s-compares-to-the-rest-of-the-world

Alang, S., McAlpine, D., Mouzon, D., & Lewis, T. (2017). Police brutality and black suicidal ideation: Moderating effects of perceived stress and religiosity. *Journal of Urban Health, 94*(1), 101–111.

Alcohol, Tobacco, Firearms and Explosives (ATF). (2022). *Final rule: Definition of "frame or receiver" and identification of firearms*. U.S. Department of Justice. www.atf.gov

Anglemyer, A., Horvath, T., & Rutherford, G. (2014). The accessibility of firearms and risk for suicide and homicide victimization among individuals in high-income countries: A systematic review and meta-analysis. *Annals of Internal Medicine, 160*(2), 108–117.

BeSMART. (2024). Protecting LGBTQ+ youth from firearm suicide.

Bor, J., Venkataramani, A. S., Williams, D. R., & Tsai, A. C. (2018). Police killings and their spillover effects on the mental health of Black Americans: A population-based, quasi-experimental study. *The Lancet, 392*(10144), 302–310.

Brady United. (2025). Smoking gun: U.S. Supreme Court upholds lifesaving AFT ghost gun rule.

Braga, A. A., Barao, L. M., Zimmerman, G., Brunson, R., Papachristos, A.V., Wood, G., & Farrell, C. (2019a). *Oakland Ceasefire Evaluation Report*. Northeastern University. Page 2.

Braga, A. A., Barao, L. M., Zimmerman, G., Brunson, R. K., Papachristos, A. V., Wood, G., & Farrell, C. (2019b). *Oakland Ceasefire evaluation: Final report to the City of Oakland*. Northeastern University. https://cao-94612.s3.amazonaws.com/documents/Oakland-Ceasefire-Evaluation-Final-Report-May-2019.pdf

Bureau of Alcohol, Tobacco, Firearms and Explosives. (2023). *National firearms commerce and trafficking assessment (NFCTA), Volume II: Crime guns*. U.S. Department of Justice. https://www.atf.gov/firearms/docs/report/nfcta-volume-ii-part-iii-crime-guns-recovered-and-traced-us/download

Campaign Zero. (2025). Mapping police violence report.

Chicago Police Department. (2017). Gun trace report. Page 10.

City of Chicago. (2017). *Gun trace report*. Chicago Police Department & Mayor's Office. https://www.chicago.gov/content/dam/city/depts/mayor/Press%20Room/Press%20Releases/2017/October/GTR2017.pdf

Conwell, Y., Paterniti, D. A., Lyness, J. M., Seidl, T. L., Bassney, J., Li, G., & Caine, E. D. (2002). Risk factors for suicide in older adults: Results from the MacArthur Foundation study of successful aging. *The New England Journal of Medicine, 347*(23), 1743–1750.

Corburn, J., Nidam, Y., Fukutome-Lopez, A. (2022). Urban Institute. The art and science of urban gun violence reduction: Evidence from the advance peace program in Sacramento, California. *Urban Science*. 6(1), 6. https://www.mdpi.com/2413-8851/6/1/6

Cure Violence Global. (2021). The evidence of effectiveness. Pages 6, 8, and 12.

Donohue, J. J., Aneja, A., & Weber, K. D. (2019). Right-to-carry laws and violent crime: A comprehensive assessment using panel data and a state-level synthetic control analysis. *Journal of Empirical Legal Studies, 16*(2), 198–247.

Drane, K., & Nguyen, A. (2025). *Gun violence in black communities*. Giffords Law Center.

Edwards, F., Esposito, M., & Lee, H. (2019). Risk of being killed by police use of force in the United States by age, gender, and race/ethnicity. *Proceedings of the National Academy of Sciences, 116*(34), 16793–16798.

Edwards, F., Esposito, M., & Lee, H. (2021). Fatal police violence by race and state in the USA, 1980–2019: A network meta-regression. *The Lancet, 398*(10307), 1239–1255.

Everytown for Gun Safety. (2021a). New Everytown Report: Aftermath of gun violence costs $280 billion each year, crowding out funding for vital public services.

Everytown for Gun Safety. (2021b). 2020 FBI data obtained by Everytown shows background checks stopped over 300,000 illegal gun sales, a record high, nearly double 2019 numbers. https://www.everytown.org/press/2020-fbi-data-obtained-by-everytown-shows-background-checks-stopped-over-300000-illegal-gun-sales-a-record-high-nearly-double-2019-numbers/#:~:text=NEW%20YORK%20%E2%80%93%20According%20to%20FBI,to%20people%20with%20felony%20convictions
Everytown for Gun Safety. (2021c). *Everytown and the City of Baltimore announce partnership on innovative platform to identify gun trafficking patterns*. https://www.everytown.org/press/everytown-and-the-city-of-baltimore-announce-partnership-on-innovative-platform-to-identify-gun-trafficking-patterns/
Everytown for Gun Safety. (2022a). Community-led public safety strategies fact sheet.
Everytown for Gun Safety. (2022b). Five things to know about crime guns, gun trafficking, and background checks.
Everytown for Gun Safety. (2022c). Permitless carry fact sheet. https://everytownresearch.org/report/permitless-carry-carrying-a-concealed-gun-in-public-with-no-permit-and-no-training/
Everytown for Gun Safety. (2022d). Violence intervention programs fact sheet.
Everytown for Gun Safety. (2023). Inside the gun shop report.
Everytown for Gun Safety. (2024a). Firearm suicide in the United States: fact sheet.
Everytown for Gun Safety. (2024b). Gun violence in America report.
Everytown for Gun Safety. (2024c). New Everytown data on transgender homicides reveals concentration in the South.
Everytown for Gun Safety (2024d). Update background check laws fact sheet.
Everytown for Gun Safety. (2024e). *Gun suicide*. https://www.everytown.org/issues/gun-suicide/
Everytown for Gun Safety. (2025a, February 3). Require permits to carry concealed guns in public.
Everytown for Gun Safety. (2025b, March 12). Chaos and uncertainty: A concealed carry mandate is dangerous and unpopular.
Everytown for Gun Safety. (2025c). Black history month: Key research stats.
Everytown for Gun Safety. (2025d). Gun safety policies save lives. https://everytownresearch.org/rankings
Everytown for Gun Safety Support Fund. (2024). How guns fuel violence against transgender people in America.
Giffords Law Center. (2025). Gun violence in Black communities report
Halliwell, P., Fletcher, R., Lee, L., & Smith, L. R. (2024). Characterizing the prevalence and perpetrators of documented fatal violence against Black transgender women in the United States (2013–2021). *Violence Against Women*. Sage Journals. https://journals.sagepub.com/doi/10.1177/10778012241289425
Harvard University: T. H. Chan School of Public Health. (2020). Black people are more than three times as likely as white people to be killed during a police encounter.
Heller, S. B. (2014). Summer jobs reduce violence among disadvantaged youth. *Science*, *346*(6214), 1219–1223. https://pubmed.ncbi.nlm.nih.gov/25477459/
Human Rights Campaign. (2025). Fatal violence against transgender and gender non-conforming people I 2025 statistics. https://hrc-prod-requests.s3-us-west-2.amazonaws.com/Research/Trans-Violence-2025.pdf
Irvin-Erickson, Y., Lynch, M. Gurvis, A. Mohr, E, & Bai, B. (2017) *Research Report: A neighborhood-level analysis of the economic impact of gun violence*. Urban Institute.

Johns Hopkins Bloomberg School of Public Health. (2024). *The evidence base for gun violence prevention laws*. Johns Hopkins Center for Gun Violence Solutions.
Lickenbrock, G. (2025). U. S. Supreme Court upholds lifesaving ATF ghost gun rule. *Smoking Gun*. https://smokinggun.org/us-supreme-court-upholds-atf-ghost-gun-rule/
Mayors Against Illegal Guns. (2025). Domestic violence and firearms fact sheet.
McPhedran, S., & Baker, J. (2006). Australia's 1996 gun law reforms: Faster falls in firearm deaths, firearm suicides, and total suicides. *Injury Prevention, 12*(6), 365–370.
Miller, G. F., Barnett, S., Florence, C., Harrison, K. M., Dahlberg, L., & Mercy, J. (2020). National Institutes of Health. Costs of fatal and nonfatal firearm injuries in the United States. *National Library of Medicine*. doi:10.1016/j.amepre.2023.09.026
Miller, M., Hepburn, L., & Azrael, D. (2017). Firearm acquisition without background checks: Results of a national survey. *Annals of Internal Medicine, 166*(4), 233–239. https://pubmed.ncbi.nlm.nih.gov/28055050/
NAACP. (2022). NAACP & Kapor Center technology report.
New York State Office of the Attorney General. (2016). *Target on trafficking: New York crime gun analysis*. https://ag.ny.gov/sites/default/files/reports/target-on-trafficking-2016.pdf
Peterson, J., Densley, J., and Higgins, S. (2023). How Mass Public Shooters Use Social Media: Exploring Themes and Future Directions. *Sage Journals*. https://journals.sagepub.com/doi/10.1177/20563051231155101
Pew Research Center. (2021). *The state of online harassment*. https://www.pewresearch.org/internet/2021/01/13/the-state-of-online-harassment/
Regehr, K., Shaughnessy, C., Zhao, M., Cambazoglu, I., Turner, A., & Shaughnessy, N. (2025). Normalizing toxicity: The role of recommender algorithms for young people's mental health and social wellbeing. *Frontiers in Psychology, 16*, Article 1523649. https://pubmed.ncbi.nlm.nih.gov/41280165/
Reuters. (2021). The 'Peace Mobile' - New York City's anti-crime project on wheels.
Roberts, L. (2022). Blake Masters blames Black people for gun violence. But guns? No problem. *The Arizona Republic*. https://www.azcentral.com/story/opinion/op-ed/laurieroberts/2022/06/07/blake-masters-blames-gun-violence-not-guns-but-black-people/7545707001/
SCOTUSblog. (2025). Supreme Court allows ghost gun regulation to remain in effect. www.scotusblog.com
Siegel, M., Boine, C., Xuan, Z., Ross, C.S., Galea, S., & Fleeger, E.W. (2019). The relationship between state firearm laws and homicide in the United States, 1991-2016. *The Journal of General Internal Medicine, 34*(10), 2026–2033.
Smart Growth America. (2024). Equitable development strategies: A guidebook for transportation practitioners.
Tiry, E., Jackson, A., & Thompson, P. (2022). *Economic costs of gun violence in Washington, DC*. Urban Institute.
U.S. Department of Justice. (2022). Justice Department announces new rule to combat ghost guns [Press release]. www.justice.gov
U.S. Department of Justice. (2023a). Chicago gun trafficking study [Study on Time-to-Crime Statistics].
U.S. Department of Justice. (2023b). Justice Department releases data on firearms recovered in ATF's Chicago field division in 2021.
U.S. Department of Justice. (2023c). *National firearms commerce and tracking assessment (NFCTA): Crime gun intelligence and trafficking (Volume II)*. Bureau of Alcohol, Tobacco, Firearms and Explosives. https://www.atf.gov/media/15471/download

Violence Policy Center. (2025). *Nine out of 10 women murdered by men are killed by someone they know and nearly two-thirds die by gunfire*. VPC Release. https://vpc.org/press/nine-out-of-10-women-murdered-by-men-are-killed-by-someone-they-know-and-nearly-two-thirds-die-by-gunfire-new-violencepolicy-center-study-finds/

Vogel, E. A. (2021). The State of Online Harassment. Pew Research Center. https://www.pewresearch.org/internet/2021/01/13/the-state-of-online-harassment/

Webster, D. W., Whitehill, J. M., Vernick, J. S., & Parker, E. M. (2012). *Evaluation of Baltimore's Safe Streets program: Effects on gun violence*. Johns Hopkins Bloomberg School of Public Health.

Williams, D.R., Lawrence, J.A., & David, B.A. (2019). Racism and health. Evidence and needed research. *Annual Review of Public Health, 40*, 105–125. https://www.annualreviews.org/content/journals/10.1146/annurev-publhealth-040218-043750

Section VIII

Reparations & Repair

This section examines how genuine repair for centuries of anti-Black violence requires not incremental reforms but transformative interventions addressing stolen labor, denied citizenship, and extracted wealth. Together, these Black Papers demonstrate that reparations encompass far more than financial compensation—they demand constitutional recognition, political enfranchisement, and economic reconstruction, creating conditions for Black communities to thrive rather than merely survive.

"Reparations: Healing Our People's Hearts and Our Nation's Soul" establishes that reparations represent justice as opposed to charity, documenting how 246 years of slavery extracted an estimated $97 trillion in unpaid labor at 2009 values while creating a wealth divide growing today, with Black median household wealth at $44,900 compared to white households' $285,000. This Black Paper traces the throughline from Reconstruction's broken promise of "40 acres and a mule" through Jim Crow's systematic theft of Black-owned land to contemporary manifestations, including redlining, mass incarceration's extraction through fines and fees, and discriminatory lending costing Black families billions. Drawing on international precedents from Germany's Holocaust reparations to South Africa's Truth and Reconciliation Commission, the analysis presents reparations as a customary remedy for crimes against humanity recognized globally. Darity and Mullen estimate $10.7 trillion required to close the racial wealth divide, while research shows Northern financial institutions like Citibank, Bank of New York, and Bank of America profited immensely from slavery financing—demonstrating corporate accountability extends beyond Southern plantations. This Black Paper argues reparations must include direct cash payments to descendants, land redistribution, debt cancellation, guaranteed income programs, educational investments, healthcare equity initiatives, and criminal justice reform—presenting a comprehensive framework addressing multiple dimensions of harm while creating conditions for intergenerational wealth building.

"From Capitol to Commonwealth: The Historical Imperative and Contemporary Case for Washington, D.C. Statehood" documents how more than 700,000 Americans in the nation's capital—a population exceeding

DOI: 10.4324/9781003752646-33

Wyoming and Vermont—remain denied voting representation in Congress despite fulfilling all citizenship obligations, including military service and federal taxation. This Black Paper traces D.C.'s founding in a compromise that embedded slavery into the capital's foundation, with enslaved people comprising 25% of the population by 1800 and their unpaid labor constructing the Capitol and White House while wages enriched owners rather than workers. The Organic Act of 1801 marked the beginning of systematic disenfranchisement as residents lost congressional representation previously enjoyed as Maryland and Virginia citizens, with a pattern of granting then withdrawing democratic rights recurring throughout history until 1878's complete disenfranchisement following the Compromise of 1877, ending Reconstruction—particularly targeting the District's growing Black American population comprising over 50% of voters. Congressional control enabled systematic segregation enforced by Mississippi Senator Theodore Bilbo, a Ku Klux Klan member, using his Senate Committee chairmanship in the 1940s. This Black Paper argues that H.R. 51's proposed "Douglass Commonwealth" provides a straightforward path to maintain a smaller federal district around core government buildings while granting statehood to the remaining District, following the precedent of 1846 congressional retrocession returning Alexandria and Arlington to Virginia. The analysis presents D.C. statehood as a democratic imperative and a civil rights issue, noting that more than 8,000 District residents currently serve in the armed forces. District residents pay more federal taxes per capita than any state, yet Frederick Douglass's 1877 observation persists: D.C. residents remain among the only people denied the elective franchise.

Together, these Black Papers demonstrate that repair requires more than acknowledgment of past harms—it demands material transformation, creating conditions Black communities have been systematically denied for centuries. They challenge readers to recognize that every dimension of Black life has been shaped by theft and exclusion: stolen labor built national wealth while excluding Black people from benefits, and denied citizenship keeps D.C. residents disenfranchised in the capital they helped create. This section articulates reparations not as favor or charity but as justice owed, not as a single payment but as comprehensive reconstruction, not as looking backward but as creating futures where Black people finally experience the freedom, prosperity, and self-determination that centuries of resistance have demanded. From $10.7 trillion wealth gap closure to D.C. statehood, these Black Papers present a vision of repair as a radical reimagining of what becomes possible when we center Black liberation not as aspiration but as an actionable demand with concrete timelines, measurable outcomes, and unapologetic insistence that the time for transformation is now.

Chapter 25

From Capital to Commonwealth

The Historical Imperative and Contemporary Case for Washington, D.C. Statehood

*Rev. Mark A. Thompson**

Executive Summary

This Black Paper (Paper) examines the historical foundations and contemporary arguments for statehood in Washington, D.C. by tracing the systematic disenfranchisement of the District's residents from the nation's founding through the present day. Built on the labor of enslaved people and established through political compromise, the federal capital has denied its residents full democratic participation for over two centuries. Today, more than 700,000 Americans in the District of Columbia—a population larger than two states—remain without voting representation in Congress despite fulfilling all obligations of citizenship, including military service and federal taxation. The fight for D.C. statehood is not merely a political issue; it is a fundamental question of democratic principles and civil rights that demands immediate affirmative congressional action.

* Supported by braintrust authors: Jada Capri Ward, Nadia French-Graham, and Jonathan M. Cox

DOI: 10.4324/9781003752646-34

Introduction

"The seat of government ought never to have been planted there," declared Frederick Douglass in 1877, speaking about the nation's capital (Douglass, 1877). His words capture a fundamental contradiction that persists today: the United States, founded on principles of democratic representation, maintains a capital city whose residents are denied full participation in the democracy they help sustain.

Washington, D.C.'s ongoing colonization reflects the broader tensions of American democracy, from slavery and civil rights to federalism and representation. More than 700,000 Americans live in the District today, contributing billions in federal taxes, serving in the military, and participating in all aspects of American civic life except the most fundamental—electing voting representatives to Congress.

This Black Paper (Paper) traces the historical development of D.C.'s unique political status, from its establishment through political compromise, rooted in slavery, to the modern Civil Rights Movement's embrace of statehood as a democratic imperative. The evidence shows that making D.C. a state is not just a political choice but a constitutional and moral need. It would help fix a glaringly hypocritical example of unfair treatment in American democracy.

Historical Foundations: Compromise, Slavery, and Systematic Disenfranchisement

The Original Compromise

The establishment of Washington, D.C. as the nation's capital resulted from political expediency rather than democratic principle. In 1783, Philadelphia served as the Continental Congress's[1] seat when unpaid Continental Army soldiers staged an insurrection, blocking congressional doors and demanding wages (Hamilton, 1783). This event pushed Congress to look for a capital city that the federal government could fully control. The desire for control led to the "District Clause[2]" being added to the Constitutional Convention.

Foundationally, D.C. became the location of the nation's capital through the Compromise of 1790. The Broadway musical *Hamilton* immortalized the political horse-trading that would define the District's future through the "The Room Where It Happens" number. Alexander Hamilton, Thomas Jefferson, and James Madison negotiated a deal whereby Hamilton secured southern votes for federal assumption of state debts in exchange for locating the new capital between the slave states of Maryland and Virginia (Chernow, 2004).

Built by Enslaved Labor

> *Slavery was [the city's] idol, and, like all idol worshippers, its people howled with rage when this ugly idol was called in question.*
>
> —*Frederick Douglass*

In 1790, President George Washington signed the Residence Act, officially establishing the capital between Maryland and Virginia, two states that allowed slavery. The federal government's decision to exploit enslaved labor rather than pay wages fundamentally shaped the District's development. By 1800, when Congress and the President moved to Washington, more than 8,000 people lived in the city, and about 25% of them were enslaved (Berlin, 1998).

The wages that should have compensated the enslaved workers who constructed the United States Capitol and White House instead enriched their owners, who leased their human property to the federal government. Slave pens operated within sight of both the Capitol and Executive Mansion, creating what Douglass described as a city where "slavery was [the city's] idol, and, like all idol worshippers, its people howled with rage, when this ugly idol was called in question" (Douglass, 1877).

The Systematic Removal of Democratic Rights

Since the establishment of Washington, D.C., as the nation's capital, the federal government has not only exploited its Black population, but also kept D.C. the only national capital in the world without representation in its respective national legislature. The Organic Act of 1801 marked the beginning of systematic disenfranchisement. When Congress assumed control of the District of Columbia, residents lost the congressional representation they had previously enjoyed as citizens of Maryland and Virginia. This loss of voting rights has lasted for more than 200 years.

Equal
All Children
WE WANT
Schools
First Class
Pupils

The pattern of granting and then withdrawing democratic rights has become a recurring theme in D.C. history:

- **1802**: Congress granted Washington City its first municipal charter, allowing white male taxpayers to elect a 12-member council while the president appointed the mayor.
- **1820**: Residents gained the right to elect their mayor.
- While the Compromise of **1850** did not altogether abolish slavery in the District of Columbia, the District's number of enslaved African Americans was less than a quarter of the capital's more than 13,000 African Americans (Mann, 2019). D.C. was on its way to becoming Chocolate City.
- Following Congress's **1861** Emancipation Act enabling the Union Army to seize any enslaved person in service to the Confederacy, Lincoln emancipated the District's enslaved population on April 16, 1862. He then promptly paid enslavers $300 reparations for each person freed.
- **1867**: African American men won the franchise in municipal elections, preceding the 15th Amendment.
- **1871**: Congress created a territorial government with limited local representation.
- **1878**: The Organic Act of 1878 completely disenfranchised District voters following the Compromise of 1877, which ended Reconstruction. This final disenfranchisement particularly targeted the District's growing African American population, which comprised over 50% of voters by 1878 (Green, 1967).

For the next 95 years, Congress, particularly senators and representatives from southern states, exercised absolute authority over a city whose residents had no voice in their governance.

Civil Rights and the Modern Movement for Democracy

Segregation and Legal Challenges

Congressional control enabled systematic racial segregation in the nation's capital. In the 1940s, Mississippi Senator Theodore Bilbo, who was a known Ku Klux Klan member, used his power in Congress to support strict segregation laws in D.C. (Lewis, 2009). As a result of anti-Black legislated segregation, D.C. schools became so overcrowded that students attended in shifts, while residents organized protests and legal challenges.

The District's unique federal status created additional legal complexities in civil rights litigation. In *Bolling* v. *Sharpe*, one of five cases that formed the 1954 *Brown* v. *Board of Education* case, lawyers James Nabrit and George E.C. Hayes used the Fifth Amendment to make their argument because the Fourteenth Amendment only applies to states, not D.C. (Kluger, 1975).

The Civil Rights Movement Embraces D.C. Democracy

The modern Civil Rights Movement recognized D.C. voting rights as integral to the broader struggle for democratic participation. On August 6, 1965, after the Voting Rights Act was signed, Dr. Martin Luther King Jr. led a march for Home Rule in D.C. (Fenston, 2024). The juxtaposition was deliberate: while the Voting Rights Act extended democratic participation to previously disenfranchised populations across the South, the residents of the nation's capital remained without representation.

Key civil rights organizations have actively supported D.C. democracy:

- **1966**: The Student Nonviolent Coordinating Committee (SNCC), led by Marion Barry and James Forman, launched the Free D.C. Campaign, implementing business boycotts to pressure for local self-governance.
- **1967**: Under pressure from the Civil Rights Movement, President Lyndon B. Johnson replaced the D.C. Board of Commissioners, appointed a nine-member council and appointed D.C.'s first Mayor, Walter E. Washington.
- **1968**: Congress established an 11-member school board for the District of Columbia. Julius Hobson, a member of the Congress of Racial Equality and founder of the D.C. Statehood Party, was among the first elected.
- **1971**: Rev. Walter Fauntroy, appointed by Dr. Martin Luther King, Jr. to coordinate the 1963 March on Washington, became the District's first elected congressional delegate, albeit without voting power.
- **1973**: With the help of the newly formed Congressional Black Caucus, Congress passed the Home Rule Act, allowing residents to elect a mayor and city council while retaining congressional oversight of local laws and budgets.
- **1980**: Nearly 60% of D.C. voters support a local ballot referendum supporting Statehood, implementing the Tennessee Plan for admission into the Union as a state.
- **1990**: D.C. voters elect SNCC veteran Eleanor Holmes Norton as a non-voting Delegate to Congress and the first shadow congressional delegation under the Tennessee Plan, including Rev. Jesse Jackson as a United States Senator.
- **1993**: A summer of civil disobedience led by D.C. residents, including Mayor Sharon Pratt, led to the first-ever vote for D.C. Statehood in Congress.

Contemporary Challenges and Progress

Despite Home Rule, Congress has repeatedly intervened in District affairs, most notably through the 1995 imposition of a Financial Control Board that further eroded local democracy. Legal challenges have consistently affirmed congressional authority while acknowledging that only Congress can remedy the situation.

In *Adams* v. *Clinton* (2000), three judges—including future Attorney General Merrick Garland—ruled that D.C. residents are not guaranteed a vote in Congress under the Constitution. They also said Congress could make D.C. a state without changing the Constitution (*Adams* v. *Clinton*, 2000). This ruling undermined longstanding conservative arguments that D.C. statehood requires a constitutional amendment.

The Contemporary Case for Statehood

Democratic Principles and Representation

The United States remains the only democratic nation that denies citizens of its capital voting representation in the national legislature. This anomaly violates fundamental democratic principles that the United States promotes globally while denying them to its citizens.

D.C. residents fulfill all obligations of citizenship:

- **Military Service**: More than 8,000 District residents currently serve in the armed forces (Norton, 2024).
- Since World War I, nearly 200,000 District residents have served in the military (District of Columbia, 2025).
- Approximately 2,000 of these residents lost their lives while serving in conflicts abroad in defense of American democracy (District of Columbia, 2025).
- **Federal Taxation**: District residents pay more federal taxes per capita than any state in the nation (Norton, 2024). In 2004 and 2025, the District's per-person contribution was nearly triple that of the highest-paying state (USAFacts, 2025).
- The District contributes more in total federal income taxes than 19 states (Norton, 2022). When considering total federal taxes from all sources, the District's contribution has historically surpassed that of up to 23 individual states (Norton, 2022).

Population and Economic Justification

With approximately 700,000 residents, Washington, D.C., exceeds the population of Wyoming and Vermont. The District maintains a robust economy with a $21 billion local budget funded primarily through locally raised revenues and has passed 29 consecutive balanced budgets (D.C. Office of the Chief Financial Officer, 2023).

Congressional Precedent

Historical precedent affirms that D.C. statehood can be facilitated by regular congressional action. In 1846, Congress voted to retrocede Alexandria and

Arlington counties to Virginia, demonstrating its authority to alter the District's boundaries through majority vote. The same constitutional authority that enabled this territorial reduction can enable statehood for the remaining District while preserving a smaller federal capital area around core government buildings.

H.R. 51: The Washington, D.C. Admission Act

H.R. 51 passed the House of Representatives in 2020 and 2021. It offers a straightforward way for D.C. to become a state.

The bill addresses constitutional concerns by:

- Maintaining federal control over core government facilities
- Preserving the 23rd Amendment's electoral college provision for the reduced federal district
- Following established precedent for congressional boundary modifications
- Ensuring continuity of federal operations

Call to Action

The time for D.C. statehood has arrived. For too long, political expedience has trumped democratic principle in treating the nation's capital. The systematic disenfranchisement that began with slavery and continued through segregation cannot persist in the 21st century. Nor can the parallel injustice persist in the United States territories, where millions of American citizens—from Puerto Rico to Guam to the United States Virgin Islands—remain excluded from full participation in the democracy they defend and sustain through service in the armed forces, paying federal taxes, and more.

Citizens across all 50 states must recognize that D.C. statehood strengthens rather than weakens American democracy. When 700,000 Americans lack voting representation in Congress, the entire democratic system suffers diminished legitimacy—even more so when millions of American citizens live under federal authority without having a meaningful way to shape it. To correct these entwined injustices, Congress must act. **The solution requires**:

1 **Immediate Congressional Action**: Senators and Representatives must pass H.R. 51 without delay, recognizing that democratic principles outweigh partisan considerations, and they must also advance legislation or constitutional measures that grant full representation and voting rights to all American citizens, regardless of geography.
2 **Public Education and Advocacy**: Citizens must contact their representatives to support D.C. statehood and educate their communities about this civil rights issue.
3 **Historical Recognition**: Americans must acknowledge that D.C.'s disenfranchisement represents an ongoing injustice rooted in slavery and perpetuated through systematic exclusion.

As Frederick Douglass observed in 1877, Washington, D.C. residents were "the only people of the Republic denied the exercise of the elective franchise," alongside American women (Douglass, 1877). Women technically won the right to vote in 1920; however, Black people did not win the right to vote until the 1965 Voting Rights Act. And still, people in D.C. wait for full voting rights more than 240 years after the Declaration of Independence said governments get "their just powers from the consent of the governed."

The Douglass Commonwealth awaits congressional recognition. American democracy demands nothing less than the complete enfranchisement of all its citizens.

Notes

1 "The Continental Congress served as the government of the 13 American colonies, and later the United States, from 1774 to 1789. The First Continental Congress, comprised of delegates from the colonies, met in 1774 in reaction to the Intolerable Acts, a series of measures imposed by the British government after the colonies resisted new taxes." https://www.history.com/articles/the-continental-congress
2 "Article I, in Section 8, Clause 17 of the Constitution, grants Congress the following enumerated power: To exercise exclusive Legislation in all Cases whatsoever, over such District (not exceeding ten Miles square) as may, by Cession of particular States, and the Acceptance of Congress, become the Seat of Government of the United States, and to exercise like Authority over all Places purchased by the Consent of the Legislature of the State in which the Same shall be, for the Erection of Forts, Magazines, Arsenals, dock-Yards, and other needful Buildings;–And" https://constitution.congress.gov/browse/article-1/section-8/clause-17/

References

Adams v. *Clinton*, 90 F. Supp. 2d 35 (D.D.C. 2000).

Berlin, I. (1998). *Many thousands gone: The first two centuries of slavery in North America*. Harvard University Press.

Chernow, R. (2004). *Alexander Hamilton*. Penguin Books.

D.C. Office of the Chief Financial Officer. (2023). *District of Columbia comprehensive annual financial report, fiscal year 2023*. Government of the District of Columbia.

District of Columbia. (2025). About DC Statehood. statehood.dc.gov

Douglass, F. (1877). *Our national capital [Speech]*. Hillsdale College. Retrieved from https://douglassarchives.org

Fenston, J. (2024). *50 Years of Home Rule: A history of D.C.'s struggle for (semi-) self governance*. WAMU. https://wamu.org/story/2/?4/01/2/?9/history-district-self-government-home-rule-2/??ref=51st.news

Green, C. M. (1967). *The secret city: A history of race relations in the nation's capital*. Princeton University Press.

Hamilton, A. (1783). [Letter to George Washington regarding the mutiny of soldiers]. *The papers of Alexander Hamilton*, Vol. 3. Columbia University Press.

Kluger, R. (1975). *Simple justice: The history of Brown v. Board of Education and Black America's struggle for equality*. Knopf.

Lewis, D. L. (2009). *The race to Fashoda: European colonialism and African resistance in the scramble for Africa*. Weidenfeld & Nicolson.

Mann, L. (2019). *The complexities of slavery in the nation's capital*. The White House Historical Association.

Norton, E.H. (2022). *Norton introduces new IRS data show D.C. pays more federal taxes than 23 states and more federal taxes per capita than any state*. Office of Congresswoman Eleanor Holmes Norton.

Norton, E.H. (2024). *Norton introduces resolution recognizing D.C. servicemembers and veterans*. Office of Congresswoman Eleanor Holmes Norton.

USAFacts. (2025). Which states contribute the most and least to federal revenue? https://usafacts.org/articles/which-states-contribute-the-most-and-least-to-federal-revenue/

Chapter 26

Reparations

Healing Our People's Hearts and Our Nation's Soul

*Marcus Anthony Hunter, Dreisen Heath, and David J. Johns**

Executive Summary

This Black Paper (Paper) examines the historical context, principles, and practical recommendations justifying reparations for Black Americans. Drawing on international precedents, legal frameworks, and recent initiatives, we articulate a comprehensive approach to reparations that extends beyond financial compensation to address psychological, cultural, spiritual, and structural harms. Our multidimensional framework offers actionable recommendations for policymakers, community leaders, and institutions seeking to implement meaningful reparative justice initiatives. This Paper synthesizes findings from historical research, legal analysis, economic studies, and contemporary case studies of reparations initiatives. This Black Paper serves as both an educational resource and an advocacy tool for advancing the cause of reparations at the federal, state, local, institutional, and communal levels.

Introduction

The conversation about reparations for Black Americans has evolved significantly over time, yet many still associate it solely with the unfulfilled promise of "40 acres and a mule." This historic view fails to capture the breadth of what reparations can and should entail. As advocates and scholars dedicated to advancing racial justice, we aim to expand understanding of the many forms reparations can take and highlight existing examples where Black communities have received some form of redress. By highlighting these real examples of repair, we honor the progress made and build upon what meaningful reparations look like for Black Americans moving forward.

* Supported by braintrust authors: Leilah Naila Jones, Raymond A. Winbush

DOI: 10.4324/9781003752646-35

Historical Context

Slavery and Racial Capitalism

The founding and building of the United States relied upon the 400+ years of the lives and labor of Africans who were enslaved. Considered legally as chattel or property, Africans were used to increase the wealth and power of the dominant (white) majority. At the time of the Civil War, the Africans who were enslaved were the nation's most significant financial resource.

Post-Emancipation through the Jim Crow Era

Sharecropping, convict-leasing, lynching, and other forms of racial terror were imposed upon newly freed Black Americans to intentionally prevent people, families, and communities from thriving. Black Americans were systematically denied representation, access, land, capital, and civil rights. The federal government failed to deliver on reparative policies and promises, such as maintaining the Freedmen's Bureau Bill and resourcing "40 acres and a mule."

20th-Century Systemic and Structural Racism

Black Americans were intentionally excluded and blocked from New Deal-era benefits, G.I. Bill[1] provisions, and federal housing programs. Restrictive covenants, redlining, urban removal, and predatory lending worsened and perpetuated the Black–white wealth and achievement divides. Underfunded public education and labor discrimination reinforced patterns of inequality seeded by American slavery.

Contemporary Harms

Racial disparities persist in health, wealth, incarceration, police brutality, and an excessive portion of political offices. The racial wealth divide remains substantial as white families have 8–10 times more wealth than the average Black family. Additionally, there have been circumstantial veils over these disparities and accompanying censorship that silences their presence, vibrancy, and undeniability within the primary political systems of America.

The Case for Reparations

Legal and International Framework

Survivors of Japanese American incarceration, the Holocaust, South African Apartheid, Argentinian State terror, the Kenyan Mau Mau uprising, and forced sterilization have fought for and received some form of reparations. These atrocities have been recognized for the harm caused to particular groups of people, and all have been survivor-led achievements. As Ta-Nehisi Coates (2014) powerfully argued in his landmark essay "The Case for Reparations," reparations represent not just compensation for past wrongs but "America's maturation out of the childhood myth of its innocence into a wisdom worthy of its founders" (Coates, 2014).

Although these historical atrocities have been recognized on national and international fronts, the residual effects of the trauma remain for survivors and their descendants. The same remains true for Black Americans. The United Nations (UN) has publicly recommended and advocated for reparations in response to the egregious centuries-long atrocities associated with the enslavement of African people in America and its enduring impacts. Part of the reparative process for the history of American slavery involves recognizing the need and right to redress for crimes against humanity, systemic rights violations, and racial discrimination under its conventions. As of the date, we're authoring this Black Paper, no monetary resolution or any form of material reparations has been made on behalf of the United States to Black American people.

Economic Justification

Compensation would dramatically increase and improve the United States economy. Monies would help to close the racial disparities in life expectancy, provide debt relief, supply immediate accessibility to new capital, and support new entrepreneurial endeavors. This would include the development of small businesses, educational attainment, and eliminating the wealth divide.

Darity and Mullen (2020) estimate that a compensation package of $10.7 trillion would be required to close the racial wealth gap, while Craemer (2015) calculated that reparations based on unpaid labor with compound interest could range from $5.9 trillion to $14.2 trillion.

Montero (2024) provides compelling evidence of how Northern financial institutions—not just Southern plantation owners—profited immensely from slavery. His research demonstrates that major banks still operating today, including Citibank, Bank of New York, and Bank of America, were deeply complicit in financing the institution of slavery and saw their fortunes rise dramatically through these investments. American history challenges the notion that slavery's economic benefits were primarily a Southern phenomenon and strengthens the case for corporate accountability in the reparation's movement.

Moral, Ethical, and Spiritual Imperative

A lack of accountability and redress at federal, state, and local levels perpetuates systemic harm and communal decay. Reparations are a customary remedy, nationally and internationally renowned for their effectiveness. **Reparations are a form of justice, not charity**. Reparations are the actionable repairs that can provide equity and opportunity to the Black community for crimes perpetrated against our community by the United States government.

Reparations must be directly connected to the harms caused, as the remedy must be aligned with the injury or injuries. Coates emphasizes that reparations require a "national reckoning" involving more than just financial payment but a transformation in how America understands its history and identity (Coates, 2014). The multifaceted nature of the harms requires numerous forms of repair.

Reparations primarily address institutional, systemic, and governmental accountability. However, in some instances, they also necessitate addressing individual accountability, particularly when people and their egregious actions directly enforce structural systems of violence against Black Americans. Contemporary reparations models and frameworks offer valuable guidance, and reparations processes are never one-size-fits-all. Reparations must be explicitly shaped by survivor and descendant communities, reflecting their unique experiences and the particular harms endured.

Radical Reparations: A Multidimensional Framework

In "Radical Reparations: Healing the Soul of a Nation" (2024), Dr. Marcus Anthony Hunter challenges the prevailing approach to reparations in the interest of economic solutions. While financial compensation is essential, the damages of enslavement on the African American community far exceed what monetary compensation alone could repair, and relying solely on economics would continue a pathology of neglect for African American needs.

Dr. Hunter's in-depth research brings scholarly expertise and practical advocacy to this topic. He has worked closely with Oakland Mayor and former Congresswoman Barbara Lee to develop the Truth, Racial Healing, and Transformation (TRHT) initiative to establish the first-ever United States Truth, Racial Healing, & Transformation Commission.

The Seven Dimensions of Radical Reparations

Our innovative approach to this work defines seven types of reparations that together create a holistic framework for addressing historical injustices.

Political Reparations: Implementation Examples

Political reparations ensure representation, protect voting rights, and eliminate barriers to political participation. Examples include:

- Establishing dedicated seats or proportionate Black American representation in legislative bodies.
- Creating independent Black political commissions with oversight authority on policies impacting Black communities.

- Implementing automatic voter registration and expanded voting access in historically disenfranchised communities.
- Providing dedicated funding for Black political organizing and civic engagement programs.
- Creating permanent advisory councils at all levels of government to review legislation for racial equity impacts.

Intellectual Reparations: Implementation Examples

Intellectual reparations recognize and celebrate Black intellectual contributions, reform educational systems, and address knowledge gaps. Examples include:

- Mandating comprehensive Black history in K-12 curricula nationwide.
- Funding Black research institutes at universities and independent think tanks.
- Creating endowed positions for Black scholars in academic institutions.
- Establishing grant programs specifically for Black intellectual property development.
- Promoting Black authorship and publication through dedicated publishing funds.
- Digitizing and preserving Black intellectual archives and making them freely accessible.

Legal Reparations: Implementation Examples

Legal reparations seek restorative justice, reform the criminal legal justice system, and create lasting legal protections against discrimination. Examples include:

- Comprehensive expungement of records for non-violent drug offenses.
- Compensation for those wrongfully convicted or imprisoned.
- Legal clinics dedicated to addressing racial discrimination and historical harms.
- Reforms to qualified immunity and police accountability measures.
- Creation of specialized courts focused on restorative rather than punitive justice.
- Reform of legal education to include critical race perspectives.

Economic Reparations: Implementation Examples

Economic reparations provide financial compensation, business development opportunities, and address the racial wealth gap. Examples include:

- Direct cash payments to descendants of enslaved persons.
- Baby bonds and trust accounts for Black children.
- 800+ credit score adjustments.
- Interest-free business loans and grants for Black entrepreneurs.
- Tax credits and exemptions for Black homeowners in previously redlined areas.
- Debt forgiveness programs targeting student loans and predatory lending victims.
- Community investment funds controlled by Black-led organizations.

Spatial Reparations: Implementation Examples

Spatial reparations address housing discrimination, land ownership, community development, and environmental justice. Examples include:

- Land trusts and land return initiatives.
- Subsidized homeownership programs in areas of previous discrimination.
- Environmental remediation in historically neglected neighborhoods.
- Infrastructure investment prioritizing Black communities.
- Community-controlled development zones with tax benefits.
- Historical preservation of Black cultural landmarks and neighborhoods.

Social Reparations: Implementation Examples

Social reparations repair the social fabric, rebuild community institutions, and support cultural development. Examples include:

- Community centers and gathering spaces in Black neighborhoods.
- Funding for Black arts, culture, and community celebrations.
- Mental health and healing services specializing in racial trauma.
- Support for Black family reunification and genealogical research.
- Investment in Black media, journalism, and communications infrastructure.
- Programs connecting diaspora communities across national boundaries.

Spiritual Reparations: Implementation Examples

Spiritual reparations heal collective trauma, support cultural heritage, and reclaim ancestral connections. This dimension acknowledges the deep spiritual and cultural damage inflicted by disconnection from African religious practices, languages, and cultural traditions. Examples include:

- Funding for research, preservation, and teaching of traditional African spiritual practices.

- Supporting pilgrimages to ancestral sites in Africa for healing and connection.
- Establishing healing centers that incorporate traditional African healing methodologies.
- Creating memorials and sacred spaces to honor ancestors lost to slavery and racial violence.
- Supporting intergenerational trauma healing through culturally grounded therapeutic practices.
- Protecting and preserving sacred sites and burial grounds of enslaved ancestors.
- Funding translations of spiritual texts from African languages and traditions.
- Educational programs reconnecting Black Americans with ancestral languages and practices.
- Ritual development addressing collective grief and historical trauma.
- Supporting the revitalization of African naming ceremonies and practices.

Spiritual reparations recognize that the harms of slavery and its aftermath extend beyond the material realm into the domain of spirit, identity, and ancestral connection. By addressing these spiritual dimensions, we acknowledge that true healing must nurture the soul alongside the body and mind.

Creative Storytelling as a Tool for Understanding

What makes our approach particularly innovative is the use of creative storytelling as a vehicle for exploring these ideas. Inspired by civil rights attorney and scholar Derrick Bell, Dr. Hunter employs three "parables" based on historical events to illustrate the comprehensive reparations' meaning and potential impact.

1. Imagine if 40 Acres and a Mule happened? What would America look and sound like? What would be the challenges and obstacles for the Black Community? *The Parable of Jubilee, South Carolina*, takes these questions as a starting point to explore an imagined Black territory on the verge of gaining independence after fulfilling Sherman's promise of "40 acres." Through this parable, we get to see reparations in action, and also visit with some of the internal conflicts, politics, and debates of the Black Community.
2. Did you know that in 1903, the Zionist Congress unanimously endorsed placing Israel in Uganda? What would the world look like if Israel were in Africa rather than Palestine? One of the most prominent examples of reparations is for Holocaust survivors and descendants. *The Parable of New Jerusalem Uganda* explores what might have happened if Zionist plans for a Jewish settlement in Uganda had come to fruition, examining the impact on local African communities, the role of anti-African sentiment in constructing reparative justice, and global solutions.

3 How do you pay people back for multigenerational losses, state-sanctioned interference, and systemic racism and incarceration? Despite the British slave trade formally ending in 1827, enslaving Black Africans persists, most notably through the Arab slave trade. Consider a Nigerian village that has survived the European slave trade only to have the Arab slave trade and colonization endanger its lives and livelihoods. *The Parable of the People's Republic of South Africa* is a multigenerational family history tracing the descendants of Nigerians kidnapped into slavery. The parable follows their journey through escape and business success. The parable culminates in the legacy of loss and struggle following Apartheid and its legal end.

Through these imaginative scenarios, we offer readers an accessible way to make sense of and further explore the deep historical wounds that require healing and the multidimensional approach needed to achieve true reconciliation and equity.

Reparations in Practice: Insights from Advocacy

Dreisen Heath, a respected reparatory justice expert who founded the Why We Can't Wait Reparations Network and is a former Human Rights Watch researcher, emphasizes that reparations must be community-driven and multifaceted. Heath's Tulsa-born perspective and advocacy for H.R.[2] 40/S. 40 (the bill to study reparations and develop proposals) highlights that reparations represent a fundamental pillar of racial justice, not just a one-time economic transaction. Heath worked closely with former Congresswoman Cori Bush to create the Reparations Now Resolution, which provides the most comprehensive framework for pursuing reparations for Black Americans in the United States Congress.

Heath notes that reparative justice is an important pillar of racial justice; you cannot achieve racial justice unless there is a repair for these past and ongoing harms. The push for reparations must happen simultaneously at international (across the African diaspora), national (the federal government), local (state and municipal governments), institutional (colleges, religious organizations, corporations, media), and communal (families taking up their own fights) levels, creating a comprehensive approach to addressing historical injustices and their continued effects.

Dr. David J. Johns, CEO and Executive Director of the National Black Justice Collective (NBJC), brings a crucial perspective on how intersectional identities must be considered in reparations frameworks. His continued work emphasizes that there must be a form of repair to address the unique experiences of all Black Americans, including Lesbian, Gay, Bisexual, Transgender, Queer+ and Same-Gender including Black LGBTQ+/SGL people who often face compounded discrimination and erasure.

Dr. Johns' education policy and civil rights advocacy background enable him to facilitate the holistic healing process that informs the well-diagnosed framework for reparations. This healing-based framework requires transformative dialogue and recognition of the diversity within Black communities. His work reminds us that adequate reparations must account for how various forms of oppression intersect and affect different members of the Black community in unique ways.

Core Reparations' Principles

There are five internationally recognized reparations forms (as outlined by the United Nations and adopted by the UN General Assembly in 2005 as the "Basic Principles and Guidelines on the Right to a Remedy and Reparation for Victims of Gross Violations of International Human Rights Law"). Before the creation of the UN Principles, Black Americans had self-emancipated, petitioned successfully for reparations, and organized in multiple ways to seek meaningful reparations. These principles build on that undeniable legacy:

1 **Restitution**: to restore the victim to their original situation before the harm occurred.
2 **Compensation**: monetary payment for assessable economic harm and damage caused by the violation.
3 **Rehabilitation**: services and other supports to assist victims in recovering from harm and the ensuing trauma.

4 **Satisfaction**: harm acknowledgment and the symbolic and formal gestures that affirm victims' dignity.
5 **Guarantees of Non-Repetition**: preventing harm recurrence through systemic change, reform, and transformational policy.

Reparations for Non-Black Communities: Historical Precedents

The United States has a history of providing reparations, creating important precedents for Black reparations claims. These examples demonstrate that reparations are not a foreign concept in American politics but are a routine practice and have been implemented in various forms for different groups.

Redress and Reparations for the Incarceration of Japanese Americans

In 1988, the Civil Liberties Act granted reparations to Japanese Americans who were forcibly removed from their homes and incarcerated in concentration camps during World War II. This comprehensive program included:

- A formal government apology acknowledging the wrongdoing.
- $20,000 payments to each survivor of incarceration and forced removal (approximately $40,000 in today's dollars).
- Public education funding for Japanese incarceration and forced removal
- Community healing initiatives.

The movement for Japanese American redress and reparations involved decades of organizing, education, and advocacy. Key factors in its success included:

- Well-documented historical evidence of the internment.
- The relatively recent timeframe (many victims were still alive).
- Identifiable victims.
- Tireless grassroots organizing from organizations like The National Coalition for Redress/Reparations (NCRR) (presently known as Nikkei for Civil Rights & Redress).
- Simultaneous legal battles, including *Korematsu* v. *United States*.
- Solidarity between prominent Black American and Japanese American advocates in Congress, including Congressman Mervyn Dymally and Senators Daniel Inouye and Spark Matsunaga.

These successful reparations program demonstrates that the United States government can acknowledge historical wrongs, issue formal apologies, and provide monetary compensation when sufficient political will exists.

Native American Reparations Efforts

The United States government has made various attempts to provide reparations to Native Americans for land seizures and other injustices, though these efforts have been more complex and often less successful:

- The Indian Claims Commission (1978) set aside $1.3 billion as compensation for 176 tribes.
- Land returns and recognition of sovereignty in some cases.
- Educational benefits and healthcare programs.

These efforts have been widely criticized as insufficient compared to the scale of harm inflicted, with implementation problems resulting in many receiving minimal direct benefits. The Native American reparations experience highlights the challenges of designing effective programs when:

- The harms occurred over centuries rather than a discrete period, and documentation may be incomplete or previously destroyed.
- The scale of loss (land, culture, population) is immense.
- The political power of the affected group is limited.

Additional Reparations Examples

Other significant reparations precedents include:

- **German Holocaust Reparations**: Germany has paid billions in reparations to Israel, individual Holocaust survivors, and German refugees. Reparations payments are largely tax-exempt in most countries and most U.S. states.
- **Rosewood Massacre**: Florida paid $2.1 million to survivors of the 1923 Rosewood Massacre, where racist mobs destroyed a majority-Black town. Descendants of the massacre were awarded educational scholarships.
- **Chicago Police Torture**: Chicago created a $5.5 million reparations fund for Black men who were tortured by police during the 1970s and 1980s. In addition, within their reparations package, they developed an 8th- and 10th-grade curriculum on police torture and reparations. The tortured men were granted free counseling services and free tuition at Chicago's city colleges.
- **North Carolina Eugenics Program**: In 2013, North Carolina became the first state to compensate victims of a state-sponsored forced sterilization program. The reparations program was limited and only provided payments of up to $50,000 per person to victims with records in the official Eugenics Board files, excluding hundreds who judges and county-level social workers sterilized. **Timber Creek**: The High Court of Australia awarded $2.5 million to the Ngailwurru and Nungali Peoples for economic and cultural loss resulting from the violation of their title rights.

- **Canadian Military "LGBT Purge"**: The Canadian government officially apologized, ended its discriminatory policies, and paid $145 million in a legal settlement after targeting and discriminating against LGBTQ+ people who served in the Canadian Armed Forces before the late 1990s.

Recent Examples of Black Reparations in the United States

While comprehensive federal reparations for slavery and its continuing harms have not yet been enacted, there are growing examples of local and institutional reparations efforts specifically for Black Americans. As we acknowledge historic progress across dozens of initiatives, we must also hold these processes accountable for delivering complete repair for Black Americans:

- **California Reparations Task Force**: In 2020, California became the first state to establish a reparations task force, with the intention of studying its role in perpetuating the legacy of slavery and propose recommendations. The task force released its final report in 2023, recommending financial compensation for housing discrimination, mass incarceration, over-policing, and health disparities. In 2025, California established a state-controlled Bureau of Descendants of American Slavery dedicated to providing genealogy services and verifying eligibility for reparations programs. California's progress inspired the States of Illinois and New York to explore their own reparations processes.
- **Evanston, Illinois**: In 2021, Evanston became the first city to implement a reparation housing program, allocating the first $10 million in tax revenue from recreational marijuana sales and real estate transfer taxes to fund housing grants for Black residents affected by local discriminatory housing policies between 1919 and 1969. The program provides up to $25,000 per eligible household for home down payments, mortgage payments, or home repairs.
- **Asheville, North Carolina**: In 2020, the city council unanimously approved a reparations plan that includes investments in areas where Black residents face disparities. In 2025, the Community Reparations Commission recommended specific programs and resources to address generational wealth disparities, health, housing, and criminal justice. Buncombe County set aside $2.9 million toward implementing recommendations.
- **Greenbelt, Maryland**: In 2023, the city established a $340,000 reparations fund to support community organizations serving Black residents, focusing on education, mental health services, and housing assistance.
- **Baltimore, Maryland**: In 2024, Baltimore voters approved the Community Reinvestment and Reparations fund (Question G), creating a Community Reinvestment and Reparations fund through a charter amendment. 35% of the state's cannabis tax revenue is distributed to local jurisdictions, including Baltimore City, for reparative programs.

- **Washington, D.C.**: In 2025, the Insurance Database Amendment Act took effect after clearing the mandatory month-long congressional review period. In addition to setting up a 12-member commission to recommend reparations for D.C.'s Black residents, it also requires the Department of Insurance, Securities, and Banking to establish a slavery-era database of records, including insurance policies on enslaved persons.
- **Detroit, Michigan**: The Detroit Justice Center's "Land Back" initiative focuses on reclaiming and repurposing vacant land in historically Black neighborhoods, converting former sites of industrial environmental harm into community-owned assets.

Institutional Reparations

- **Georgetown University**: Georgetown has established a reparations fund to benefit descendants of the 272 enslaved people who were sold by the university in 1838 to pay off debts. Students voted to create a semesterly fee to support educational and healthcare programs for descendants.
- **Princeton Theological Seminary**: The seminary has committed $27.6 million to reparations initiatives, including scholarships and fellowships for descendants of enslaved people. Their program includes historical research initiatives, curriculum changes, and dedicated facilities for studying the legacy of slavery.
- **Virginia Theological Seminary**: In 2019, the seminary established a $1.7 million reparations fund to provide direct payments to descendants of enslaved laborers who built the institution. It has also implemented a rigorous genealogical research program to identify eligible recipients.
- **Harvard University**: In 2023, Harvard pledged $100 million to address its legacy of slavery through research, memorialization, and educational programs. The university is establishing partnerships with Historically Black Colleges and Universities (HBCUs) and creating scholarship programs for descendants.
- **Churches and Religious Institutions**: The Episcopal Diocese of Maryland established a $1 million reparations fund in 2020 and began distributing grants in 2022, while the Virginia Theological Seminary created a $1.7 million fund to pay descendants of enslaved persons who worked at the institution. The United Methodist Church has developed a comprehensive denominational reparations framework that includes financial and non-financial elements.

The Path Forward: A Comprehensive Approach to Reparations

Based on our collective research and advocacy work, we propose a comprehensive approach to reparations that includes:

1 **Acknowledgment**: Official recognition of historical wrongs and their continuing impacts through formal apologies, memorials, permanent markers, and education initiatives.
2 **Community-Led Process**: Ensuring that reparations processes are guided by affected communities rather than imposed from above.
3 **Multidimensional Redress**: Moving beyond cash payments to address all seven dimensions of reparations identified in Dr. Hunter's framework.
4 **Institutional Reform**: Creating structures to prevent the recurrence of discrimination and ensure equal protection and opportunity.
5 **Intergenerational Healing**: Addressing the psychological and cultural trauma that has affected multiple generations of Black Americans.
6 **Societal Transformation**: Eliminating systems and views that exploit Black communities and replacing them with ones rooted in dignity, understanding, and equity.

Policy Recommendations

Federal Action

- Pass H.R. 40 and S. 40 to establish a national reparations commission.
- Pass the Reparations Now legislation to provide direct payments and debt relief.
- Pass Truth, Racial Healing, and Transformation legislation to create a national Truth Commission.
- Pass the Third Reconstruction legislation to eliminate American poverty.
- Pass the G.I. Repair Bill to provide direct payments and benefits to Black veterans.
- Redirect corporate subsidies and wealth taxes to a reparative fund for descendants.
- Mandate repatriation and reclamation of stolen Black cultural artefacts and human remains from federal institutions, museums, and military holdings.
- Preserve and repatriate ownership of Black cultural institutions.
- Permanently preserve and protect Black burial grounds.
- Repair historic underinvestment in HBCUs.
- Eliminate all medical debt held by Black Americans.
- Launch targeted Black wealth initiatives (land and property grants, business support, cooperative economics).
- Establish a federal "Right to Return" program prioritizing housing in neighborhoods where Black families were displaced.
- Establish federal preemption, overriding local zoning laws that prevent Black families from returning to areas they were displaced from.
- Establish eminent domain protections preventing displacement in historically Black neighborhoods.

- Enact federal protections for Black intellectual, cultural, and creative works.
- End economic, political, legal, and social exploitation practices against Black Americans.

State and Local Governments

- Fund housing reparations (Evanston, IL model).
- Provide subsidies for or abatement of property taxes for descendants.
- Invest in HBCUs, public health, and educational access.
- Invest in culturally grounded community health initiatives for descendants.
- Create dedicated tax revenue and annual tax credit streams for reparations funds.
- Alleviate barriers to end-of-life care and burial services for descendants.
- Permanently document and memorialize Black Americans' societal impact and contributions.
- Establish permanent tax exemption zones in historically Black communities.
- Transfer public property and facilities to Black-led entities for community governance.
- Fund cultural corridor recreation, rebuilding the Black institutions, businesses, and communal gathering places destroyed.
- Establish truth commissions to document local histories of harm.
- Implement policies to address environmental racism.
- Reform zoning laws that perpetuate segregation.

Private Sector & Institutions

- Acknowledge and document institutional complicity.
- Create and fund reparative justice endowments and equity initiatives.
- Establish corporate, academic, and/or media atonement funds proportional to historical and ongoing complicity.
- Implement preferential contracting and procurement for Black-owned businesses.
- Develop executive leadership, ownership, and governance pipelines for Black employees.
- Audit and transform discriminatory institutional practices.
- Fund and facilitate the return of cultural items and oral histories to Black communities.
- Establish a fund for reparative restitution for past intellectual property theft of Black thinkers and creatives.
- Partner with community-based and Black-led reparative justice organizations for implementation.

Models in Motion: Recommended Organizations and Coalitions

The following organizations and coalitions represent leading models for reparations advocacy and implementation:

National Coalition of Blacks for Reparations in America (N'COBRA): Founded in 1987, N'COBRA has been at the forefront of the reparations movement for decades, developing comprehensive frameworks for implementation.

Movement for Black Lives (M4BL) Reparations Policy Table: Their comprehensive policy platform addresses multiple dimensions of reparations through both legislative and community-based approaches.

Black Farmers Justice Coalition: Working to address the systematic dispossession of Black farmers through direct land return, legal support, and policy advocacy.

William Darity and Kirsten Mullen's "From Here to Equality" Project: Their research provides detailed economic analysis and implementation frameworks for federal reparations programs.

Samuel DeWitt Proctor Conference: This faith-based coalition is mobilizing religious institutions to address their historical complicity in slavery and implement reparative practices.

Reparation Generation: A multi-racial initiative providing direct reparative transfers for housing to Black Americans while advocating for broader systemic change.

ZEAL: A Black arts cooperative providing emerging strategies for cultural equity and educating Black communities about reparations through creative interventions such as their multimedia anthology on global Black reparations entitled *The Remedy is Solidarity*.

Black-Led Community Initiatives: Organizations like the Chicago Torture Justice Center, the Linnentown Project, East Oakland Collective, Equity and Transformation Chicago, and the Greensboro Reparations Commission demonstrate effective local implementation.

Academic Research Centers: The Center for the Study of Slavery and Justice at Brown University, the William Monroe Trotter Collaborative For Social Justice at the Harvard Kennedy School, the Loyola Law School Anti-Racism Center, the Thurgood Marshall Civil Rights Center at Howard University School of Law, the Institute for the Study of Human Rights at Columbia University, and UCLA's Bunche Center provide critical research support.

International Partnerships: The CARICOM Reparations Commission, the Africa World Reparations and Repatriation Truth Commission, and the United Nations Working Group of Experts on People of African Descent offer models for international coordination.

The Path Forward: A Comprehensive Approach to Reparations

Based on our collective research and advocacy work, we propose a comprehensive approach to reparations that includes:

Acknowledgment: Official recognition of historical wrongs and their continuing impacts through formal apologies, memorials, permanent markers, and education initiatives.
Community-Led Process: Ensuring that reparations processes are guided by affected communities rather than imposed from above.
Multidimensional Redress: Moving beyond cash payments to address all seven dimensions of reparations identified in Dr. Hunter's framework.
Institutional Reform: Creating structures to prevent the recurrence of discrimination and ensure equal protection and opportunity.
Intergenerational Healing: Addressing the psychological and cultural trauma that has affected multiple generations of Black Americans.
Societal Transformation: Eliminating systems and views that exploit Black communities and replacing them with ones rooted in dignity, understanding, and equity.

Conclusion

Reparations for Black Americans represent a moral imperative and practical necessity for creating a more just and equitable society. The enactment of deserved compensation to African Americans provides much-needed clarity to all Americans on the committed wrongdoings and violations perpetrated through the practice of enslavement. By expanding our understanding of what reparations can entail beyond direct monetary payments, we can create more comprehensive and effective approaches to addressing historical injustices and their ongoing impacts.

The examples of successful reparations programs for other communities demonstrate that the United States is capable of acknowledging past, present, and future atrocities that occurred on American soil and taking meaningful steps toward repair. The growing momentum for Black reparations at local, institutional, and communal levels provides a foundation for broader efforts at the federal level.

As we continue expanding this framework, we must remember that reparations are not simply about compensating for past harms, but additionally curating possibilities that exceed any current cultural and systemic limitations for Black Americans. This implementation invites all Americans to thrive regardless of race, gender, sexual orientation, gender identity and expression, or other aspects of identity. True reparations must be radical—going to the root of systemic injustice—and comprehensive, addressing all dimensions of harm that have affected Black communities.

The time is now. Reparations are a feasible and ambitious pathway toward a more inclusive and healthier society and democracy. The United States has the legal foundation, precedent, and resources to repair and heal the damage. With a net worth of at least $124 trillion, the United States has the opportunity to be a bold example and testimony of the mutually beneficial impacts of reparative justice. We call on leaders at every level to move from reluctant acknowledgment to direct action. Justice delayed is justice denied.

Notes

1 Originally established to provide services and benefits to World War II veterans, the Servicemen's Readjustment Act of 1944, also known as the G.I. Bill of Rights, was signed by President Franklin D. Roosevelt on June 22, 1944, after it had passed the House and the Senate unanimously (National Archives Foundation, 2025).

2 "A bill is the form used for most legislation, whether permanent or temporary, general or special, public or private. A bill originating in the House of Representatives is designated by the letters 'H.R.', signifying 'House of Representatives', followed by a number that it retains throughout all its parliamentary stages. Bills are presented to the President for action when approved in identical form by both the House of Representatives and the Senate" (United States House of Representatives, 2026).

References

Coates, T. (2014). The case for reparations. *The Atlantic, 313*(5), 54–71.

Craemer, T. (2015). Estimating slavery reparations: Present value comparisons of historical multigenerational reparations policies. *Social Science Quarterly, 96*(2), 639–655.

Darity, W., & Mullen, A. K. (2020). *From here to equality: Reparations for Black Americans in the twenty-first century*. University of North Carolina Press.

Hunter, M. A. (2024). *Radical reparations: Healing the soul of a nation*. Random House.

Montero, D. (2024). *The stolen wealth of slavery: A case for reparations*. Legacy Lit.

Conclusion

The Work Continues: A Love Letter to Those Who Will Carry It Forward

When Angela Rye called me that early morning with her "crazy idea," neither of us could have fully imagined what we were setting in motion. We knew we were answering a call that echoed across generations—from the Niagara Movement of 1905 to the Gary Political Convention of 1972, from the March on Washington to the Movement for Black Lives. But we didn't know that this project would become what you now hold: the most comprehensive Black policy agenda produced in a generation, a blueprint for liberation crafted by over 100 of our brightest minds, and yes, a love letter to our community.

As I write these final words, I am humbled and encouraged by what we have built together. Twenty-six chapters. Eight critical policy domains. Hundreds of specific recommendations. Thousands of hours of research, writing, debate, and revision. But more than that: a living testament to the power of collective Black genius, the resilience of our organizing traditions, and the audacity of our hope.

Where We Stand

We benefit ourselves by being clear-eyed about this moment. As this book goes to print in 2026, we face formidable challenges. Many of the gains we have fought hard for—in voting rights, in reproductive justice, in environmental protection, in criminal justice reform—face coordinated assault. The institutions we have built face unprecedented threats. The very democracy many have bled to perfect now exists at a crossroads.

Overcoming seemingly insurmountable odds is not new to us. Our ancestors built freedom dreams while enslaved. They organized for voting rights while being attacked with fire hoses and police dogs. They imagined economic justice while redlining confined them to the margins, and white racial mobs stole property and suppressed prosperity. They demanded educational equity while bombs exploded in their children's schools and places of worship. Our ancestors have always done the impossible because they understood that impossibility is simply the limit of someone else's imagination.

DOI: 10.4324/9781003752646-36

We stand in that lineage. We inherit their courage, their strategic brilliance, and their refusal to accept the world as it is when they could envision the world as it should be. And we understand what they understood: that policy is not abstract, that governance is not distant, that power is not given but taken and should be wielded with equity-centered precision and purpose.

What Makes This Moment Different

The Black Papers represent something our predecessors called for but could not fully realize: sustained infrastructure for collective liberation. This is not a moment. This is a movement with mechanisms—a foundation built upon freedom dreams.

The teams that came together to power the State of the People tour—organizers, policy experts, artists, educators, faith leaders, business owners—are still meeting. Still organizing. Still demanding power. In 13 cities across this nation, we activated networks that remain activated. We created infrastructure that persists beyond any single event or election cycle.

Power building matters because our history shows us that moments of mobilization alone are necessary but insufficient. The Gary Convention produced a powerful agenda, but it lacked the institutional staying power to translate vision into sustained policy change. The limitations were not in the quality of the ideas—many of their demands remain unfulfilled today—but in the absence of infrastructure to carry the work forward across administrations, across generations, across the inevitable setbacks and victories that characterize any long-term struggle.

We learned from those gaps. The Black Papers exist not as a static document but as a living framework supported by ongoing organizing, digital resources at stateoftheppl.com, policy toolkits, community education initiatives, and a growing network of individuals and organizations committed to implementation. Every chapter in this volume connects to action. Every policy recommendation links to an organizing strategy. Every vision is grounded in the practical work of building power.

The Power of Collective Genius

One of the most profound revelations of this project has been witnessing what happens when we create space for Black people to think together, to strategize together, to dream in Afrofuturistic technicolor together without apology or compromise. The contributors to this volume—educators, scholars and activists, former White House officials, policy wonks at every level of government, and grassroots organizers, attorneys, and artists—brought their full selves to this work. They brought their expertise, yes, but also their lived experience, their ancestral knowledge, their righteous anger, and their required hope.

In these pages, we hope you have found sophisticated policy analysis that never loses sight of the people policies are meant to serve; data and statistics animated by stories of real families, real communities, real lives; and technical precision married to moral clarity. This is what Black intellectual tradition looks like when it is unleashed—rigorous and accessible, strategic and visionary, grounded and soaring.

The process of creating this work has itself been transformative. Contributors who began as colleagues became comrades. Policy examination fueled conversations about purpose-driven pursuits. The work of writing became the work of building community, of strengthening networks, of modeling the collaborative governance we seek to create at scale.

From Analysis to Action: The Path Forward

While reading this book is important, using this book is essential. The Black Papers were designed as tools for change, and tools only have value when wielded. Here is what we ask—our beseechment of those who have journeyed with us to these final pages:

First, find your political home(s). Whether you are a seasoned organizer or taking your first steps into civic engagement, or an experienced advocate, you need community. You need places where you can grow in your understanding of power and your capacity to build it. That might be a local grassroots organization. It might be a national network like State of the People, the National Women's Law Center, the National Center for LGBTQ Rights, or the National Black Justice Collective. It might be a union, a faith or spiritual community, a professional association, or a mutual aid collective. What matters is that you root yourself somewhere, that you commit to showing up, that you build the relationships that sustain long-term struggle.

Second, tithe politically. Our movements need resources—not just our labor and our passion, but our financial investment. Consider contributing regularly to organizations like State of the People, the National Black Justice Collective, and the many organizations whose leaders contributed their expertise to this volume. Political tithing is not charity; it is investment in our collective liberation. It is recognition that the infrastructure of freedom requires sustained funding, that the organizations doing this work cannot survive on good intentions alone.

Third, visit stateoftheppl.com and engage with the resources we have cultivated. The website extends what these pages begin—offering digital tools, data visualizations, advocacy guides, and ongoing analysis. Download the policy briefs. Share them with your networks. Use them in your organizing, your teaching, your advocacy. Our collective work is living scholarship, meant to inform and inspire action.

Fourth, do work where you are. Bring these ideas into your spheres of influence. If you are an educator, teach from this framework. If you are a policymaker, let these recommendations shape your agenda. If you are a community organizer, use these chapters to ground your campaigns. If you are a student, let this work inform your research and activism. If you are a parent, let it guide your advocacy for yourself, your children, and your community. If you are a faith leader, let it inspire your prophetic witness. We all have platforms, however modest. Use them. As the saints say, "Let Him Use You". Yes, YOU, beloved.

Fifth, hold power accountable. The recommendations in this book are not suggestions for consideration; they are demands for implementation. Every elected and appointed official who claims to serve Black communities should be measured against these standards. This includes self-appointed leaders. Every candidate should be asked where they stand on these policies (and others impacting Black people and those who claim to love us and collective freedom). Every administration on every level of government (local, state and federal) should be evaluated by how much of this agenda it advances. We must be strategic in our support and ruthless in our accountability.

For Those Who Will Carry This Forward

I want to speak directly to the young people (our beloved babies) who inherit this work, who are building on what we have started, who will push beyond what we have imagined. You are why we engage in this labor with love. You are the future we are fighting for. And I need you to know: you are not starting from scratch.

You inherit a powerful tradition. You have frameworks to build upon, networks to plug into, and organizations that have poured into fortifying the foundation. Not that you need it, but should you find yourself desiring permission, you've got it. You have permission to do it differently, to question what we have built, to imagine what we cannot yet see. Your job is not to replicate our strategies but to adapt them, to innovate, to meet the moment you are in with the tools it requires.

Some of you will take these policy recommendations and push for their implementation. Some will take the methodology we have modeled and apply it to emerging issues we have not yet addressed. Some will use this framework to hold us—and the next generation of leaders—accountable. Some will build on our analysis to create new forms of organizing, new technologies for mobilization, and new strategies for wielding power. All of this is necessary. All of this is welcome.

Remember that change is not linear. You will experience setbacks. You will face opposition that is better funded, better organized, and more ruthless than you can imagine. It's easy to organize around hate. You will be tired. You will be discouraged. You will wonder if it is worth it. You will be tempted to become a grifter. In those moments, come back to this: you are part of a continuum of struggle that has never broken. Every generation has faced its own version of impossible, and every generation has found a way forward. You will too. We need you too. Yes, YOU!

Ancestral Wisdom, Future Vision

Our ancestors understood something we must never forget: the work of liberation is not completed in a single lifetime. They planted trees under whose shade they would never sit. They built institutions they would never see fully realized. They fought for rights they would never personally enjoy. They did this because they understood that freedom is a relay race, not a solo sprint. Each generation runs their leg, then passes the baton.

This book is our baton pass. We have run this leg—gathering the research, synthesizing the analysis, building the coalitions, and creating the infrastructure. Now we extend it to you: to the organizers who will mobilize around these recommendations, to the policymakers who will champion them, to the educators who will teach from them, to the students who will build upon them, to the young people who will inherit the world we are fighting to create.

But even as we honor our ancestors, we must also envision our descendants. What world are we building for children not yet born? What institutions are we creating that will outlast us? What norms are we establishing that will become the floor, not the ceiling, of what future generations demand? The Black Papers are our answer to these questions—not complete, not perfect, but earnest and comprehensive and rooted in both the wisdom of those who came before and the dreams of those yet to come.

This Is Love

I return, in these final paragraphs, to where I began: with Angela's call, with the big idea; that became this comprehensive agenda, with the recognition that all of this—the research, the writing, the organizing, the vision—is an act of love.

Love for our community, in all its beautiful diversity. Love for the single mother working three jobs who deserves economic policies that value her labor. Love for the child in an under-resourced school who deserves educational equity. Love for the elder facing health disparities who deserves quality care. Love for the organizer fighting for voting rights who deserves the infrastructure to sustain that fight. Love for the entrepreneur building generational wealth who deserves policies that support, not hinder, Black business. Love for the incarcerated person who deserves justice, not punishment. Love for the transgender youth who deserves to live fully and freely. Love for the immigrant who deserves to belong. Love for all of us, in our full humanity.

This is what love looks like in policy form: comprehensive, detailed, strategic, and unapologetic. Love that refuses to accept incrementalism when transformation is required. Love that believes our people deserve not just survival but thriving. Love that understands that Black liberation is not a niche issue but a prerequisite for collective freedom. Love that refuses what my mentor, Dr. Freeman Hrabowsky, refers to as the "tyranny of either/or" and celebrates the beauty of "both/and"—both immediate relief and structural change, both local action and national policy, both electoral engagement and grassroots organizing, both holding power accountable and building our own.

Every contributor to this volume brought that love. Every organization that partnered with State of the People brought that love. Every person who showed up at a tour stop, who shared our content, who engaged with our vision—you brought that love. It is that love that will sustain us through the difficult work ahead.

The Work Continues

I began this journey with how Angela began our early morning call with the disclaimer: "You can't say no."

I end this iteration of this freedom project with my own call to you: Don't say no. Not to the difficulty of this work. Not to the length of the struggle. Not to the audacity of imagining a world where Black people are fully free. Not to your own capacity to contribute to that vision.

Say yes.
Say yes to organizing.
Say yes to learning.
Say yes to building.
Say yes to accountability.
Say yes to solidarity.
Say yes to the long haul, to completing your leg of the race.
Say yes to each other.
Say yes to the belief that another world is not only possible but inevitable if we do the work to build it.

The Black Papers are not an ending. They are a beginning. They are an invitation. They are a challenge. They are a roadmap for the journey we must take together. The destination—a world where Black people are free to live, to love, to create, to thrive without the constraints of systemic oppression and stochastic terrorism—has been clear since our ancestors first resisted bondage. What The Black Papers offer is clarity about the path: specific, strategic, and grounded in both our historical wisdom and our contemporary analysis.

The work continues. It continues in policy chambers and in the streets. It continues in classrooms and in boardrooms. It continues in faith spaces and in community centers. It continues in electoral organizing and in mutual aid networks. It continues in the creative work of artists and in the analytical work of researchers. It continues in the daily acts of resistance and in the long-term strategic planning. It continues through you.

We have identified tools and proven strategies. We have mapped the terrain. We have identified the opportunities and the obstacles. We have contributed to the infrastructure and modeled collaboration. Now it is your turn. Add your voice to the chorus. Bring your gifts to the struggle. Find your place in the movement. And when you do, know that you exist in a long line of freedom fighters who believed, despite all evidence to the contrary, that we could build a better world.

They were right. We can. We will. Together.

With love and in solidarity,

Dr. David J. Johns
Editor in Chief, The Black Papers
CEO & Executive Director, National Black Justice Collective

Take Action:

Visit stateoftheppl.com to access digital resources, policy toolkits, and ongoing analysis.

Find your political home—join an organization where you can grow in organizing and power.

Tithe politically—invest in State of the People, the National Black Justice Collective, and organizations led and fueled by contributors to this volume.

Share this agenda—use these policy recommendations in your advocacy, teaching, and organizing.

Hold power accountable—demand that elected officials commit to implementing these recommendations.

The work continues. Will you join us?

Let's all get free!

Index

Pages in *italics* refer to figures and pages in **bold** refer to tables.

For Product Safety Concerns and Information please contact our EU
representative GPSR@taylorandfrancis.com
Taylor & Francis Verlag GmbH, Kaufingerstraße 24, 80331 München, Germany

www.ingramcontent.com/pod-product-compliance
Lightning Source LLC
LaVergne TN
LVHW020756241026
850861LV00034B/416
9781041270904